Govt. - CE - '16-'17

32 chapters

beg. 8-8-16

4.5 pages per school day including work - not just reading to finish by day 180

AMERICAN GOVERNMENT

AMERICAN GOVERNMENT

Allan O. Kownslar
Terry L. Smart

CONSULTANTS

Charles A. Fleischman
Chairperson, Social Studies Department, Cherry Hill High School East, Cherry Hill, New Jersey

L. Tucker Gibson
Associate Professor of Political Science, Trinity University, San Antonio, Texas

J. J. Landman
Chairperson, Social Studies Department, Roosevelt Senior High School, Los Angeles, California

Amy Loewen
Curriculum Specialist, Portland Public Schools, Portland, Oregon

David H. Lynn
Chairperson, Social Studies Department, Swissvale Area High School, Pittsburgh, Pennsylvania

William Marks
Director of Social Studies, Dallas Independent School District, Dallas, Texas

Guy H. Raner, Jr.
Social Studies Department, Canoga Park High School, Los Angeles Unified School District, California

Ann E. Turney
Social Studies Department, Arlington High School, Arlington, Texas

Webster Division
McGraw-Hill Book Company

New York • St. Louis • Dallas • San Francisco
Auckland • Bogotá • Düsseldorf • Johannesburg
London • Madrid • Mexico • Montreal • New Delhi
Panama • Paris • São Paulo • Singapore
Sydney • Tokyo • Toronto

ALLAN O. KOWNSLAR and TERRY L. SMART are nationally known social studies curriculum specialists. Allan O. Kownslar received his undergraduate degree from Trinity University, San Antonio, Texas and his doctorate from Carnegie-Mellon University, Pittsburgh, Pennsylvania. Dr. Kownslar taught social studies for fifteen years in public schools in San Antonio, Amherst, Massachusetts, and Pittsburgh. Since that time Dr. Kownslar has become a nationally known social studies curriculum consultant. He is the author or coauthor of eleven social studies programs and author of numerous articles on the teaching of social studies. He is currently on the faculty of Trinity University. Terry L. Smart received his undergraduate degree from Indiana University and his doctorate degree from the University of Kansas. Dr. Smart began his teaching career in the Houston, Texas public schools. Dr. Smart has served as a social studies curriculum specialist and consultant. He is the author of *Fundamentals of the American Free Enterprise System,* a text for secondary schools, and has written and produced several educational television programs. He is currently on the faculty of Trinity University.

Credits for pictures used in this book appear on pages 639–640. Acknowledgments to the sources of copyrighted excerpts appear immediately after the excerpts.

Editorial Development: Don E. Neal, Elizabeth Blackert
Design Supervisor: Bennie Arrington
Photo Editor: Rosemary O'Connell
Production Supervisor: Angela Kardovich

Additional Editing: Norman Lunger
Photo Research: Suzanne Volkman, C. Buff Rosenthal
Design: Aspen Hollow Artservice
Charts, Graphs, and Maps: J. & R. Services, Inc.
Cover: Ben Kann

Library of Congress Cataloging in Publication Data

Kownslar, Allan O
    American government.

    Bibliography: p.
    Includes index.
    1. United States—Politics and government—Handbooks, manuals, etc. I. Smart, Terry L., joint author.
II. Title.
JK274.K69   320.9'73'092   78-25819
ISBN 0-07-035406-5

Copyright © 1980 by McGraw-Hill, Inc. All Rights Reserved. Printed in the United States of America. No part of this publication may be reproduced, stored in a retrieval system, or transmitted, in any form or by any means, electronic, mechanical, photocopying, recording, or otherwise, without the prior written permission of the publisher.

How to Use This Book

American Government has been written to help students understand their country's government and feel that they are part of it. This nation began as an experiment in government by the people, and from the beginning, its success has depended on the willingness of the people to take part in their government.

The subject of government is a vast one that embraces many large ideas and countless pieces of information, large and small. There are thirty-three chapters in this book, organized into twelve units. Students need help in finding their way through that much information, weighing it, and relating it to themselves as individuals. One way to proceed is to ask yourself a series of questions.

What is this unit about, and how does it touch my life? Each unit begins with a short introduction that tells what the unit is about and recounts an anecdote that puts the subject in human and concrete terms. In this way, the subject of the unit is brought out of the realm of abstraction and related to the world of reality.

What is the chapter about, and what guides are provided? Each chapter opens with a keynote picture spread. For example, the picture that opens Chapter 1, on pages 16–17, strikes the note of political heritage. A sailing ship, symbolizing the past and the timeless seas, moves toward the Statue of Liberty, symbol of the United States. To the right of each keynote picture is a brief summary of the chapter. The students' goals are then set down in a short list. Turning the pages of the chapter, students can quickly spot the major subjects, represented by headings printed in color. Illustrations—including not only pictures but also charts, graphs, and maps (listed on page 13)—give immediacy and concreteness to the subject matter.

Within each main section, key sentences are printed in italics. For review purposes, students can quickly look back over the section and pick out these key sentences. New terms are also printed in italics at their first occurrence, and definitions are provided. Pronunciation aids are given for difficult words at their first use. A glossary is printed in the back of the book as a ready reference list of the more important terms.

What aids are given in understanding and applying the chapter subject matter? At the end of each main section of a chapter is a set of questions to help students check their knowledge and understanding. The last question in the set, marked with a special symbol (○), gives students a chance to apply what they have read. By giving thought to these questions, students begin to explore their own attitudes toward government and to discover what kinds of attitudes others may hold. The last main section of each chapter poses a Problem that challenges students to deal with a concrete situation. These problems, which are varied in nature and scope, expose students to a broad range of issues.

At the chapter end is a full-page Chapter Review that provides further ways for students to check what they have learned and to extend their knowledge. Each Chapter Review includes vocabulary development—not simply a list of terms but an exercise that calls for putting new terms to use. Another exercise gives practice in recalling and comparing information. Finally, the Chapter Review offers special activities—individual or group projects, to be used as class work or field work, in order to extend and deepen the students' knowledge and understanding.

What help is given in organizing and applying the information within the unit? Each unit ends with a two-page Unit Review. It begins with a reading that summarizes the important ideas in the unit. Following this reading are questions that build comprehension and classification skills. All of the Unit Reviews include writing exercises that not only help develop writing skill but also help students to organize and evaluate their own attitudes toward government. Each Unit Review ends with a list of books for further reading.

What help is given in locating information? A reference map on the next two pages provides geographic orientation and also includes some basic historical facts for quick location. The Table of Contents on pages 8–13 leads students to the major subject areas of the book. In addition, the contents list includes references to the Problems, the Chapter Reviews, and the Unit Reviews. The reading list for each unit can be located easily by turning to the Unit Review. At the back of the book are the Declaration of Independence and the Constitution of the United States. Detailed headings in the Constitution can be used as a guide to its contents. The glossary, to which many students will want to refer often, is followed by an extensive index, carefully prepared with the students' needs in mind.

American Government looks both toward the past and toward the future. As an experiment, this nation was built on past knowledge and ideas; but through the years, it has applied new knowledge and new ideas to make its government work. Students living in an age of exploration are better able than earlier students to imagine what a giant step was taken by the British colonies when they declared that they had a right to a government based on the consent of the governed. If the students are able to recapture the hope and sense of possibility with which that declaration was made, they will have taken their own giant step.

The key that unlocks hope and a sense of possibility is awareness that we *are* our government—that government is not something that happens to us but something we *cause* to happen. This book encourages students to achieve that awareness.

Table of Contents

How to Use This Book   5
Reference Map   6

UNIT I: OUR POLITICAL HERITAGE   14

Chapter 1:   **Political Ideas from the Ancient World**   16
    Problem: Why Are Laws Necessary?   22
    Chapter Review   25

Chapter 2:   **Political Ideas from Western Europe**   26
    Problem: How Would You Start from Scratch?   39
    Chapter Review   41

Chapter 3:   **Political Ideas from the Thirteen Colonies**   42
    Problem: What Does the Declaration of Independence Mean?   56
    Chapter Review   61

Chapter 4:   **Formation of Our Federal Government**   62
    Problem: What Does the Constitution Mean by "the People"?   75
    Chapter Review   78

   Unit Review   79

UNIT II: THE LEGISLATIVE BRANCH OF THE NATIONAL GOVERNMENT   81

Chapter 5:   **The Congress of the United States**   82
    Problem: How Secret Should a Lawmaker's Personal Finances Be?   100
    Chapter Review   103

Chapter 6:   **How Congress Works**   104
    Problem: Should Our Lawmaking Process Be Less Complicated?   120
    Problem: Do Our Federal Lawmakers Use Their Time Wisely?   125
    Chapter Review   128

   Unit Review   129

UNIT III: THE EXECUTIVE BRANCH OF THE NATIONAL GOVERNMENT   131

Chapter 7: **The Presidency**   132
Problem: How Public Should a President Be?   150
Problem: When Should a President Be Declared Disabled?   152
Chapter Review   153

Chapter 8: **The Executive Departments**   154
Problem: Who Would Make the Best Head of Each Cabinet-Level Department?   167
Chapter Review   171

Chapter 9: **Independent Agencies**   172
Problem: How Do Independent Regulatory Agencies Affect Individuals?   185
Chapter Review   186

Unit Review   187

UNIT IV: THE JUDICIAL BRANCH OF THE NATIONAL GOVERNMENT   189

Chapter 10: **The Federal Court System and the High Court**   190
Problem: Should There Be a Means of Declaring a Supreme Court Justice Disabled?   203
Chapter Review   205

Chapter 11: **Some Historic Supreme Court Decisions**   206
Problem: What Would Your Decision Be?   217
Chapter Review   219

Chapter 12: **The Lower Federal Courts**   220
Problem: Should We Have a Mini-Supreme Court?   228
Chapter Review   230

Unit Review   231

UNIT V: OUR LIVING CONSTITUTION   233

Chapter 13: **Our Bill of Rights**   234
Problem: What Does Our Bill of Rights Mean?   241
Chapter Review   249

Chapter 14: **Our Growing Constitution**   250
    Problem: How Should "Due Process"
       Apply to Native Americans?   262
    Problem: Should Young People Have to
       Pay Taxes?   264
    Chapter Review   265

Chapter 15: **Rights and Legislation**   266
    Problem: Should Workers Be Forced
       to Retire Because of Age?   279
    Problem: How Much Should the Public
       Have a Right to Know?   281
    Chapter Review   283

Chapter 16: **Rights and Court Decisions**   284
    Problem: To What Extent Should
       Reporters Be Allowed to
       Protect Their News Sources?   297
    Problem: Should Lie Detector Tests Be
       Allowed?   299
    Chapter Review   302

    Unit Review   303

UNIT VI: GROWTH OF OUR NATIONAL GOVERNMENT   305

Chapter 17: **The Size of Our National Government**   306
    Problem: Have We Too Many Federal Rules?   320
    Problem: When Should a Federal
       Agency Be Abolished?   321
    Chapter Review   323

Chapter 18: **Financing Our National Government**   324
    Problem: How Much Is Enough for
       National Defense?   337
    Problem: What Should We Do about
       Welfare Programs?   338
    Chapter Review   342

    Unit Review   343

UNIT VII: STATE GOVERNMENT   345

Chapter 19: **Formation and Goals of State Government**   346
    Problem: Can State Governments Show the
       Way?   359
    Chapter Review   361

Chapter 20: The Operation of State Governments   362
    Problem: What Are Some Problems in Getting a Bill through a State Legislature?   376
    Chapter Review   380

    Unit Review   381

UNIT VIII: LOCAL GOVERNMENT   383

Chapter 21: Functions and Types of Local Government   384
    Problem: How Can Police Relations with Communities Be Improved?   399
    Chapter Review   401

Chapter 22: The Special Problems of Big Cities   402
    Problem: Who Should Pay for Public Schools?   410
    Problem: What Special Problems Do Mayors of Big Cities Face?   411
    Chapter Review   414

    Unit Review   415

UNIT IX: POLITICAL PARTIES AND CAMPAIGNS   417

Chapter 23: The Role of Political Parties   418
    Problem: How Do Our Political Parties Operate at the Grass Roots?   427
    Chapter Review   429

Chapter 24: Primaries and Conventions   430
    Problem: Should We Have a National Presidential Primary?   443
    Chapter Review   445

Chapter 25: The Candidate in the Race   446
    Problem: What Are the Campaign Demands upon a Presidential Candidate?   459
    Chapter Review   462

    Unit Review   463

UNIT X: THE VOICE OF THE PEOPLE   465

Chapter 26: The Voting Process   466
    Problem: Should We Try to Get Out the Vote?   480
    Chapter Review   483

Chapter 27: **Pressure Groups and Direct Actions**   484
  Problem: Should There Be a National
     Initiative and Recall?   495
  Problem: What Causes Pressure Groups
     to Form?   496
  Problem: How Does Lobbying Work?   500
  Chapter Review   503

Chapter 28: **Measuring and Shaping Public
     Opinion**   504
  Problem: How Is Propaganda Used
     in Political Campaigns?   515
  Chapter Review   518

  Unit Review   519

**UNIT XI: FORMS OF GOVERNMENT IN
     OTHER COUNTRIES**   521

Chapter 29: **Other Forms of Democratic
     Government**   522
  Problem: What Were the Weaknesses of
     the Fourth French Republic?   537
  Chapter Review   539

Chapter 30: **Communist Government**   540
  Problem: Can Human Rights Be Protected
     under a Communist Government?   554
  Chapter Review   558

  Unit Review   559

UNIT XII: COMPARATIVE ECONOMIC SYSTEMS   561

Chapter 31: **The Free Enterprise System in the
     United States**   562
  Problem: What Are Some Advantages of
     Different Forms of Business Organization?   574
  Chapter Review   577

Chapter 32: **Socialism**   578
  Problem: What Did the Socialist Party
     Stand for in the 1930s?   588
  Chapter Review   591

Chapter 33: Communism as an Economic System 592
Problem: How Does Communism Operate Outside the Soviet Union? 601
Chapter Review 605

Unit Review 606

The Declaration of Independence 608
The Constitution of the United States 610
Glossary 620
Index 626

Lists of Charts, Graphs, and Maps

Reference Map of the United States 5–6
Sources of Our Political Heritage in the Ancient World (map) 18
Direct Democracy in Ancient Athens 20
Representative Democracy in the Roman Republic 21
The English Parliament by 1400 32
Four Main Elements of Our Political Heritage 39
The Thirteen Colonies (map) 51
North America in 1763 (map) 52
Legislative Branch 84
Inside the United States Capitol Building 85
Congressional Districting in a Two-District State 94
Major Steps by Which a Bill Becomes a Law 113
The Process of Electing a President and a Vice President 134
Popular and Electoral Votes for President in 1968 (map) 137
Order of Succession to the Presidency 138
Executive Office of the President (organization chart) 148
Inside the White House Office Wing 149
The Department of State (organization chart) 164
The Judicial Branch 192
Two Main Paths to the United States Supreme Court 199
The Schedule of the Supreme Court 200
United States Judicial Districts and Circuits (map) 222
Routes of Appeal within the Federal Court System 224
How the United States Constitution Can Be Amended 236
Civilian Employees of the Federal Government (graph) 316
Federal Civilian Payrolls (graph) 317
Federal Land in Each State (graph) 319
The Budget Time Line 328
Trend in Federal Expenditures (graph) 329
Where Each Federal Dollar Goes (graph) 331
Where Each Federal Dollar Comes From (graph) 331
Trend in Federal Budget Surplus and Deficit (graph) 334
The Federal Debt (graph) 336
Formation of the States (map) 353
The State Government Dollar (graph) 356
A Typical State Executive Branch 372
Typical Route of Appeal in a State Court System 375
The Local Government Dollar (graph) 388
Growth of Urban Population (graph) 392
Main Types of City Government (graph) 393
Mayor-Council Type of City Government 394
Commission Type of City Government 394
Council-Manager Type of City Government 395
National Political Parties 421
Typical Organization of a Major Political Party 427
Typical Congressional Campaign Organization 449
Bilingual Election Requirements (map) 473
Voting Registration in Eleven Southern States, 1960 and 1976 (graph) 474
Voter Turnout in National Elections (graph) 479
Percent of Popular and Electoral Vote Received by Winning Presidential Candidates (graph) 480
Western Europe (map) 525
Inside the British House of Commons 530
Inside the Chamber of the French Assembly 536
The Soviet Union (map) 542

Our Political Heritage

UNIT 1

Not long ago, two California taxpayers decided that the counties and cities in their state were spending too much money. Both believed that the way to reduce spending was "not to give them the money in the first place." So the two, Howard Jarvis and Paul Gann, drew up a proposal to reduce taxes.

Little interest was shown in the proposal at first. Then Jarvis and Gann began to circulate a petition to have their proposal placed before the California voters for action. To draw attention to their proposal, Jarvis and Gann spoke about it to voters throughout the state and advertised it on the radio.

Many people began to favor the plan. Many others raised objections to it. Some said that it went too far. Some others said that it would not achieve its purpose of cutting back taxes and spending. Still others said that the tax savings would go to the rich and the losses in services would be suffered by the poor.

In a few weeks, Jarvis and Gann had more than 1,264,000 signatures on their petition, more than twice as many as they needed. The proposal went on the ballot as Proposition 13.

Meanwhile the state legislature took action to fend off the sweeping tax reduction that was being proposed. The legislature's milder proposal to cut taxes was placed on the ballot as Proposition 8. (The numbers were assigned according to the order in which the proposals went on the ballot.)

When California voters made their choice, 65 percent of them voted for Proposition 13. For good or bad, the Jarvis-Gann proposal went into effect one month later.

Jarvis and Gann, the people who opposed their plan, the voters who favored it, and the lawmakers were all taking political action. *Politics* has been defined as the struggle over who gets what, when, and how. Viewed in this way, politics is a question of power. *Political action,* then, is doing something about the sharing of power. It is sometimes called *political participation.*

The people of this country have long believed in the kinds of political action taken by Jarvis and Gann. Would they have taken the same action in China? Very likely not. In Chile? Probably not. Why the difference? Clearly, there are differences between countries in the kinds of political action one may take.

Every country has some machinery for deciding how its people shall behave toward one another and how the country shall act in relation to other countries. This machinery is the *government* of the country.

As long as people have lived in groups, they have had government of some kind, whether they were aware of it or not. A tribe, a club, even the student body in a school, has some form of government. It may be very simple, and it may change over time. Not every member need take part in it. But a means of political decision-making exists.

A club might have a very simple type of government. A country, depending on its size, its history, and the life its people lead, might have a rather simple or a very complex type of government. Any study of the government of the United States must deal with government of a very complex type.

The people of the United States know, in general, what behavior is expected of them and what they can expect of others in their country. So do the people of mainland China and the Chinese on Taiwan. So do the people of Chile. This suggests that some learning takes place. In fact, it does. This learning process is called *political socialization*.

When did you first learn something about our system of government? Perhaps it was when you saw a flag and asked what it meant, or when someone mentioned the President and you asked who that was. Political socialization begins at a very early age, and it goes on all our lives.

As we begin to learn about our system of government, we also form opinions about it. As we learn more, we either reinforce or revise our opinions. They, too, are part of our political socialization.

Abraham Lincoln once summed up the government of the United States as a government "of the people, by the people, and for the people." These words expressed Lincoln's belief not only about what the government was but also about what it should be. The words were Lincoln's, but the beliefs they summed up were not new with him. These beliefs, with changes in shades of meaning, had been passed on from person to person over time. When political beliefs—ideas and attitudes about the nature of government—are passed on over time, they form a *political heritage*. The political heritage of the people of the United States is the subject of this unit.

The first chapter deals with our heritage of political ideas from the ancient world. Chapter 2 discusses the political ideas that the people of the thirteen colonies derived from Western Europe. Chapter 3 takes up colonial contributions to our political heritage. Chapter 4 examines the ideas upon which our federal government was founded.

Political rallies are an important part of our political heritage. This painting of a rally was made in 1838.

Chapter 1

Political Ideas from the Ancient World

Our political ideas have a history that goes back far before the American Revolution. Some of them, in fact, can be traced to civilizations that flourished many thousands of years ago. We have borrowed some of these ancient ideas, shaping them to our own needs and ways of life. This chapter will explore how those ideas began and what they mean to us today.

Goals

- To learn what some peoples of the ancient Middle East contributed to our political heritage.
- To learn how the ancient Greeks and Romans affected our present thinking about government.
- To consider why laws are necessary.

IDEAS FROM THE ANCIENT MIDDLE EAST

What does it mean to you when somebody says, "The judge threw the book at him"? You know at once that *laws*—rules of behavior—are involved. You also know that these laws are set down in writing. Laws that are written down in exact, ordered form are said to be *codified*. The "book," in other words, is the *code* of laws.

Laws are made in several ways: by the actions of people in positions of authority, by

Chapter 1: Political Ideas from the Ancient World

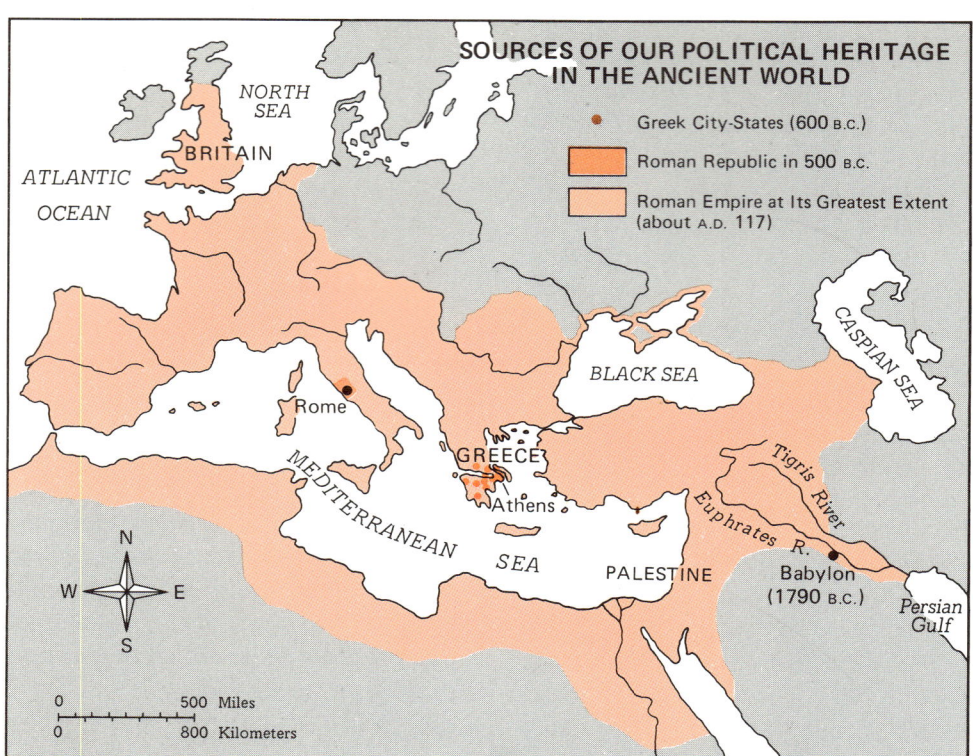

the decisions of all members of a society, or by the customs of a people. Laws in the United States today are always written and always codified. This is not so in every country, even now. In ancient times, it was rarely so.

The first known written code of laws is nearly four thousand years old. It is the Code of Hammurabi, named for an Amorite (AM-uh-rite) king who ruled in the city of Babylon about 1790 B.C. (See the map above.) If the judges at Babylon at that time "threw the book" at anybody, the "book" would have knocked that person dead. For the Code of Hammurabi was chiseled on stone columns taller than the king himself. You can see one of these columns to this day if you visit Paris, France, where it is kept in the Louvre museum. Another copy of Hammurabi's laws is preserved in the area where they first applied, in a museum in Teheran, Iran (Persia).

To people today, some parts of the Code of Hammurabi seem strict indeed. One law said that a person who destroys another's eyesight shall have an eye put out. That idea lives on in our saying, "An eye for an eye and a tooth for a tooth." Other laws fixed the rules of business life or of agriculture, which was the main occupation of the Amorites. For example, farmers were responsible for keeping their dikes repaired. If a farmer neglected a dike and it broke and flooded a neighbor's field of grain, the farmer had to pay for the grain.

By having the laws written down and codified, Hammurabi let people know what they could and could not do. Before that, there was no sure way of knowing what was permitted and what was forbidden. One judge might apply one set of rules to a case while another judge might apply completely different rules to a similar case. It all depended on the arbitrary judgment of one person.

Today, we follow the same custom of recording our laws. Rules passed by our lawmakers are printed and available for anyone to see. Unless laws are publicly available, we do not regard them as binding.

Each of us is subject to many different sets of laws. Some laws say what is permitted, such as how fast you may drive. Some other laws say what is required, such as paying a federal income tax. Still other laws say what is prohibited, such as smoking in elevators. Federal laws apply to everyone in the United States. State laws apply to activities within each state. Then there are rules that apply only to local cities and counties. At each level, the rules are written down and codified.

Like the Amorites, the early Hebrews of Israel had a set of laws that they put in writing. The Hebrews, or Jews, were another people who lived in the ancient Middle East. Their laws have come down to us in what is called the Old Testament.

Unlike the Code of Hammurabi, the laws of the Hebrews were closely based on religious beliefs. This can be seen in the Ten Commandments. According to the Old Testament, Moses passed on the Ten Commandments from God to the Jews. These rules told the Hebrews how they must live in order to honor the one god in whom they believed.

The Ten Commandments amounted to a strict moral code that distinguished right from wrong. For example, one commandment stressed that stealing was wrong. Another commandment required all Hebrews to honor their parents. Still another warned against telling lies about a neighbor.

These rules, and many similar ones, were written down and passed along from one generation to the next. They eventually became part of the religious beliefs of Christians and Moslems. They have influenced many of our own ideas of right and wrong, and thus form the basis of many of our laws today.

Questions

1 What is a law?

2 What was the Code of Hammurabi? In what ways is it part of our political heritage?

3 What was one contribution the Hebrews made to our political heritage?

◻ Would you prefer to have rule by law or rule by the person who happened to be in charge at the time? Explain.

IDEAS FROM ANCIENT GREECE AND ROME

The next set of ideas in our political heritage comes from the ancient world of Greece and Rome.

Democratic Government

It was in ancient Greece that the idea of democracy first came into being. The word itself comes from the Greek word *demos,* meaning "people," and *kratia,* meaning "rule." Thus *democracy* means "rule by the people."

Democracy arose in Greece more than twenty-five hundred years ago. At that time—about 600 B.C.—Greece was made up of *city-states.* Each city and the land around it was a *state,* or nation—in other words, an independent country. Before democracy developed,

This sculpture shows Hammurabi with part of his laws. The sculpture is kept in the British Museum in London.

Chapter 1: Political Ideas from the Ancient World

DIRECT DEMOCRACY IN ANCIENT ATHENS

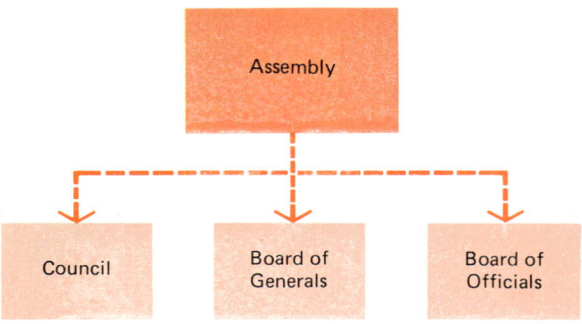

In this simplified chart, the broken lines indicate election or appointment. The Assembly selected a Council to preside over its meetings, a Board of Generals to lead the army and navy, and a Board of Officials to carry out certain limited duties. For example, though this board directed the courts of justice, groups of citizens took turns in judging court cases.

these city-states had other forms of government. Most were at first ruled by kings and later by small groups of people from the upper classes, often rich landowners. Some city-states then moved again to government by a single ruler, but this time a dictator. *Dictators* govern as they please, without regard for what most of the people desire. About 600 B.C., middle-class merchants and farmers led revolts against some of these dictators and helped set up democracies in certain city-states.

Rule by the people in these city-states did not mean that *all* of the people had a voice. Indeed, there has probably never been a government in which everybody had a voice. In Athens, for example, three large groups were shut out—women, slaves, and males who were not yet of adult age.

Democracy in the city-states was direct democracy. This is a form of government in which the people take a direct part. In those city-states that had a democratic government, all free male adults were members of the Assembly and took turns in holding office. The people's Assembly had the main task of running the government. The chart above shows the government of ancient Athens, the city-state where direct democracy reached its fullest form.

Direct government by the people works best in small groups. It was possible in the Greek city-states because each of them was small. In our time, direct democracy is still practiced in New England towns. It is rarely found elsewhere, except in private groups.

Repeated wars weakened the Greek city-states. Finally they were taken over by Rome, a rising power to the west. That city was already larger than any of the Greek city-states, and its government differed from theirs.

Ancient Rome had developed a representative democracy. Power rested with the people, but instead of ruling directly, they elected individuals to speak and act for them. Because of Rome's large population, direct rule by the people would have been difficult, or impossible. A representative democracy is also called a *republic*. Rome was a republic from 509 B.C. to 31 B.C. The United States, too, is a republic. Representative democracy is the form of government in our national, state, and most of our local political units. That is why, when we pledge allegiance to the flag, we use the words, "The republic for which it stands." Representative democracy can also be found in some clubs and private groups.

Like ancient Greece, the Roman Republic did not give all of the people a voice in government. Again, slaves, women, and young males had no say. In Rome, moreover, those who participated did not all have an equal voice.

Roman society had two main classes, and power was divided on class lines. At the top were the *patricians* (puh-TRISH-unz), or wealthy aristocrats. These high-born rich numbered about three hundred families. Below the patrician class were the *plebeians* (pli-BE-unz), or common people. This class included farmers, workers, and merchants. Some were rich, but most were poor. All free adult male patricians and plebeians belonged to the assemblies that were the basis of Roman government in the time of the Republic. But the voting system gave greater power to the patricians.

The assemblies did not govern Rome directly. Instead, they elected representatives

This mural shows the Roman Senate in 64 B.C. What can be learned about the Senate by studying this picture?

Broken lines indicate election or appointment. The solid line indicates the power to affect decisions without the power to elect or appoint. The organization of government in the Roman Republic varied over the years, and this chart is a simplified version of one form of organization.

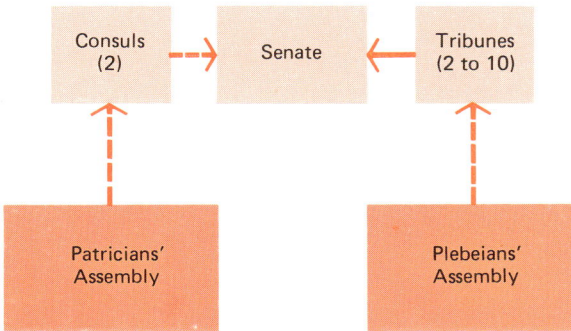

REPRESENTATIVE DEMOCRACY IN THE ROMAN REPUBLIC

to act for them. (See the chart above.) The most important elected officials were two consuls, who shared the position of head of state. Each had a veto power over the other so that neither could become a dictator. The two consuls were elected annually by the Patricians' Assembly. The consuls, in turn, appointed senators from among the patrician class. Once appointed, a senator served for life. The Senate made policy and was the most powerful part of the government. The Plebeians' Assembly elected two or more tribunes to speak for them. The tribunes could *veto,* or reject, Senate actions. (*Veto* means "I forbid" in Latin.) Power struggles brought changes in this system of government, but Rome remained a republic for nearly five hundred years. By the end of that time, Romans were on the march through Europe and North Africa, conquering as they went. Success abroad and troubles at home at last combined to replace representative government with government by dictators and, later, emperors.

Roman Laws

As Rome's size and power grew, its system of laws became highly refined. Two distinct sets of laws came into being. One, called *civil law,* applied only to citizens. The

Emperor Justinian I, here giving a blessing, is noted not only for his code of laws but also for his religious activities.

other, called *common law,* applied to all people under Roman rule. Common law applied to slaves, people who lived in conquered areas, and certain others.

For nearly five hundred years after the end of the Republic, Rome was the center of a vast empire. Its extent is shown on the map on page 18. Thus, the effect of Roman law was felt over great distances. Among other things, Rome laid down rules concerning sales and contracts anywhere in the empire. Roman law also provided for private ownership of property.

Roman ideas of law remained even after the Western Roman Empire collapsed in A.D. 476. By that time, however, the Roman laws themselves had become confusing. This problem bothered Justinian, an emperor of the Eastern Roman Empire, and he decided to bring Roman law up to date. His lawyers spent five years making a systematic collection of what they thought were the best Roman laws. By the year 533, they had put them together in the Code of Justinian. This set of laws became so popular that it was later used by most countries in Europe.

A modified form of Roman law is still in effect in many places today. The French emperor Napoleon Bonaparte ordered a revision of the Code of Justinian in 1804. This revision, called the Napoleonic Code, remains the basis of French law and has influenced the laws of other European nations. French settlers brought their ideas of law to Louisiana. There, parts of the Napoleonic Code are still in effect. Elements of Spanish law, closely influenced by the Napoleonic Code, can still be found in Texas and other Southern states that were once under Spanish rule.

Questions

1 What is democracy? Where did the idea arise?

2 How was democracy practiced in ancient Greece? In ancient Rome?

3 Who was Justinian? Why was Justinian's Code important?

◇ Which would you prefer to be a part of—a direct democracy or a representative democracy? Explain.

PROBLEM: WHY ARE LAWS NECESSARY?

Among the political ideas we inherited from the ancient world was a belief in rule by law. Let us now examine this idea more closely.

In the following selections, you will find some laws from Hammurabi's Code, from the writings of the early Hebrews, and from ancient

Rome. Standard English is used in these samples. As you read them, ask yourself:

- *What human behavior are these laws meant to regulate or control?*
- *Why might these laws have been needed?*

Hammurabi's Code

The following laws of the ancient Amorites are samples from Hammurabi's Code. These sample laws applied only to free men and free women—that is, nobles and common people. The code also contains some laws that applied to slaves.

If a free man accuses another free man and brings a charge of murder against him, but does not prove it, the accuser shall be put to death.

If a woman wine seller gives one flask of drink on credit, she shall receive fifty measures of grain at harvest-time.

If a free man, upon presenting a field, orchard, house, or goods to his wife, leaves a sealed document with her, her children may not enter a claim against her after the death of her husband. She may give her inheritance to a son but not to an outsider.

Adapted from Theophile J. Meek's translation in James B. Pritchard (ed.), *Ancient Near Eastern Texts Relating to the Old Testament,* Princeton University Press, Princeton, 1950, pp. 166, 170, 172. Reprinted by permission of Princeton University Press.

Hebrew Laws

Some Hebrew laws from the Old Testament follow.

When you march up to attack a city, first offer it terms of peace. If it agrees to your terms of peace and opens its gates to you, all the people to be found in it shall serve you in forced labor. But if it refuses to make peace with you and instead offers you battle, lay seige to it. And when the Lord, your God, delivers it into your hand, put

According to the Bible, God gave Moses the Ten Commandments on Mount Sinai. They are, perhaps, the most famous Hebrew laws.

every male in it to the sword. But the women and children and livestock and all else in it that is worth plundering you may take as your booty, and you may use this plunder of your enemies which the Lord, your God, has given you.

—Deuteronomy 20:10-14

Whenever someone kills another, the evidence of witnesses is required for the execution of the murderer. The evidence of a single witness is not sufficient for putting a person to death. —Numbers 35:30

New American Bible, copyright © 1970 by the Confraternity of Christian Doctrine, Washington, D.C. Used by permission of copyright owner. All rights reserved.

The last law, about witnesses, is a common requirement in modern times. See the United States Constitution in the appendix to this book for a similar clause relating to treason (Article III, Section 3).

Chapter 1: Political Ideas from the Ancient World

Roman Civil Laws

Following are samples of Roman civil laws.

Each person is responsible for mending the road in front of his land. If the paving stones are not kept in place, then anyone may drive beasts across the person's land.

If the wind bends your neighbor's tree across your boundary, you may remove that tree.

If a person maims another's arm or leg, that person shall pay for the injury or lose an arm or leg.

For breaking a free man's bone with hand or club, the fine shall be 300 pieces of silver. For similarly injuring a slave, the fine shall be 150 pieces of silver.

If an animal causes damage, its owner shall either surrender the animal or pay for the damage.

A person who secretly cuts another's crop by night, or who pastures an animal on it, shall be hanged. If the guilty person is under 14, that person shall be whipped, or else pay double damages.

Any person who intentionally burns down any building, or a heap of grain beside a house, shall be bound, whipped, and put to death by burning at the stake. If a person commits such an act by negligence, that person shall pay for the damage. If the person is too poor to pay, a lighter punishment shall be given.

Adapted from the Loeb Classical Library, translated by E. H. Warmington, *Remains of Old Latin,* Vol. III, Cambridge, Mass.: Harvard University Press, 1938, pp. 425–505 *passim*.

Questions

1 What kind of human behavior does each of these laws regulate?

2 Do you think that these laws are fair? What makes a law fair?

3 Why do you think those societies codified their laws? Why might any society wish to do so?

⬠ What do you suppose could happen to any society without laws? Do you think that laws are necessary? Explain.

Chapter 1: Political Ideas from the Ancient World

Chapter 1 Review

Developing Your Political Vocabulary

1 How do the terms in each pair below differ in meaning? Give one example of each.
  a law/code
  b representative democracy/direct democracy
  c Roman civil law/Roman common law

2 Which of the terms listed in question 1 could be applied to your student council? To a club?

Recalling and Comparing

1 Briefly compare what the ancient Amorites and Hebrews contributed to our political heritage.

2 What political ideas did the ancient Greeks leave us? Give examples.

3 How did the ancient Romans help provide us with a political heritage? Cite some examples.

4 What part of our heritage can be traced back to Napoleon Bonaparte?

5 What does it mean to say, "We have rule by law, not by individuals"?

6 Of all the political ideas we inherited from the ancient world, which *three* do you think are the most important today? Tell why you chose those three.

Special Activities

1 Prepare a bulletin-board display showing how people and ideas from the ancient world contributed to our political heritage.

2 With the help of library books, write a biographical sketch about Hammurabi, giving special attention to the history of his code of laws.

3 Prepare a chart comparing direct democracy in Athens and representative democracy in the Roman Republic.

4 Prepare a chart showing the organization of two clubs or other private organizations, one based on a system of direct democracy and the other on a system of representative democracy.

5 Read a selection from the *Republic* by Plato, the Greek political thinker. He wrote in the form of conversations among friends. Write a summary of the political views in the selection.

6 The Greek city-states of Athens and Sparta were very different. Make a study of the political contrasts between the two city-states and report your findings to the class.

7 Make a study of the beginnings of the Roman Republic and the conditions that brought about a change from monarchy to democracy. Report your findings to the class, including your opinions about the reasons for the change.

8 Make a study of the power struggles during the Roman Republic that brought shifts in the role of the Plebeians' Assembly, the Senate, and the consuls. Write a report of your findings and your opinions on the reasons for the shifts of power. See if you can make any comparisons to government in modern times.

9 Consider what might be arguments for and against the following statement: "The main reason for having laws that regulate human behavior is to protect weaker people from stronger people." Do you agree or disagree with that statement? What are your reasons?

Chapter 2

Political Ideas from Western Europe

Beginning with the Native Americans, many different peoples settled the area that is now the United States. However, the settlers whose ideas about government left the deepest stamp on this country were mainly English or of English stock. This is because the thirteen colonies that were the origin of the United States were English colonies. How the political ideas of the people in the thirteen colonies were shaped is the subject of this chapter. The "Great Charter" of England, and the nobles forcing the king to sign it, are fitting keynote pictures.

---- Goals ----

- *To learn how some events in English history contributed to our political heritage.*
- *To see how some European political thinkers influenced our present way of life.*
- *To consider why early political ideas are a valuable part of our heritage.*

THE ENGLISH POLITICAL BACKGROUND

Like the United States, England was settled by many peoples—Angles, Romans, Norse, French, and others. And all of these were mixtures of various other peoples going back beyond the dawn of written history. Thus, English life and thought were molded by many different traditions.

Chapter 2: Political Ideas from Western Europe

Popular Sovereignty: Rule by the People

Over the years, the English experienced various types of government. We can divide government into two main types—*authoritarian* and *democratic*. Both form part of the English experience. Let's look at these two main types and some subtypes.

Authoritarian government places power in the hands of one or a few strong individuals. There is little if any check on the ruler or rulers in authoritarian government. They may rule justly, or they may rule by whim. They may allow individual rights, or they may ignore them. It all depends on the rulers in power.

There are many kinds of authoritarian government. The main subtypes are:

Monarchy. In a monarchy, the right to rule is passed down from one generation of a family to the next. When a ruler dies, another member of the ruling family—usually the oldest son or daughter—takes over. An hereditary ruler is called a *monarch*. Monarchs are known by such titles as king, queen, empress, or emperor. England was a monarchy when it first sent settlers to North America. Some present-day governments are monarchies. For instance, Saudi Arabia is ruled by a king with wide powers. Some countries of Western Europe are monarchies but are no longer authoritarian because the monarch is now a figurehead.

Dictatorship. A *dictator*, as you may recall, is someone who governs without regard for what most of the people desire. Rule by such a person is called a *dictatorship*. The basic difference between monarchy and dictatorship is that dictatorship is not hereditary. Parts of ancient Greece were ruled by dictators in the seventh century B.C. In modern times, dictators have arisen in many countries, particularly in times of strife. England had a dictator for a short time in the seventeenth century. Hitler ruled Germany as a dictator from 1934 to 1945.

One early dictator was Julius Caesar, who ruled Rome during the period after the end of the Roman Republic.

Oligarchy (OLL-i-gar-kee). While dictatorship is rule by one person, *oligarchy* is rule by a few. The term comes from the Greek words *oligos,* meaning "few," and *archia,* meaning "rule." Except in the number of persons holding power, oligarchy closely resembles dictatorship. Oligarchy itself can be divided into two separate categories.

1. *Aristocracy.* When a select group of individuals runs the government, we call it an *aristocracy* (ar-is-TOK-ruh-see). The term comes from the Greek words *aristos,* meaning "best," and *kratia,* meaning "rule." Some thinkers have argued that the ideal government would be one run by people who devoted their entire lives to developing their ability to rule. The Greek philosopher Plato, for example, drew up a plan for a government that would be run by individuals who were given special training and education so that their rule would be just and good. Such a government would perhaps be in keeping with the Greek meaning of the term *aristocracy*. But in real life, "the

Chapter 2: Political Ideas from Western Europe

best" has usually meant "the rich." That was the case at certain periods in ancient Greece and Rome when aristocracies of rich landowners were in control. Their rule served their own interests, but not always the interests of the common people.

2. *Military Oligarchy.* In some countries, an aristocracy of rich people rules in collaboration with a small military group. Such a government is called a *military oligarchy*. Several Latin American countries have known this type of rule in modern times. In Nicaragua, for example, a single family of wealthy civilians and generals dominated the country for more than forty years, beginning in the 1930s.

In contrast to these authoritarian types of government, *democratic government places power in the hands of the citizens as a whole.* As we have seen in Chapter 1, a democratic government does not necessarily give a voice to *all* of the people in a country. That is, some people may not be considered full citizens. Even the most democratic countries give voting rights only to those who have reached a certain age, for example. Nevertheless, a significant number of people share in making government policies in a democracy.

We have already discussed the two main types of democracy. They are:

1. *Direct Democracy.* We noted earlier that *direct democracy* is a form of government in which the people take a direct part, as in the ancient Greek city-states. Some present-day New England towns hold town meetings at which voters decide on policy. Important questions are decided by a vote of the whole membership, not by elected or appointed officials. A limited form of direct democracy is practiced in some states. They give all voters the right to decide certain political issues or to demand a law or a state constitutional amendment. We saw an example in the introduction to Unit I. Some political thinkers question the value of even limited forms of direct democracy when very large numbers of people are involved.

2. *Representative Democracy or Republic.* In a representative democracy, the people elect individuals to represent them and make the major decisions. The Roman Republic was a representative democracy, and so is the government of the United States today.

Our political heritage involves many events that took place as England slowly moved from an authoritarian to a democratic government. The changes began in the struggle for power between kings and local nobles—lords and barons.

William the Conqueror invaded England in 1066. He made himself monarch and proceeded to spread his control over all England.

Rule of Law under a Constitution

After the Roman troops had gone, the struggle for power in England seesawed back and forth. First the king, then the nobles gained control. The seesaw stopped in 1066 when William, Duke of Normandy in France, conquered England. William the Conqueror, as he was known, placed power firmly in his own hands as king of all of England. William strengthened the English monarchy by reducing the power of the nobles. His control of the entire kingdom laid the foundation for a strong central government. Another English king, Henry II, brought further change to English government. This great-grandson of William the Conqueror became king in 1154.

The system of law in the English colonies can be traced back to Henry II in the twelfth century. He appointed judges who traveled about England and held court in many different places on their circuits. In the past, the leaders of each community had determined what punishment would fit a certain crime. Punishments were harsh in some places, and mild in others. Gradually, the decisions made by Henry's judges, and by later judges, came to apply all over England. The rules were intended to be uniform—the same for all districts. This growing body of rules came to be known as *English common law.*

English common law was different from Roman common law. In the first chapter, we saw that Roman common law applied to non-Romans, and Roman civil law applied only to Roman citizens. There was no such distinction in English law. When we speak of English common law, we mean the entire system of laws in England and countries it colonized. English common law has also been called "judge-made law" because it relies heavily on the decisions of judges in earlier cases. These decisions are *precedents* (PRESS-i-dents).

English common law can be divided into public law and private law. *Public law* regulates the relations of individuals and their government. *Criminal law* is part of public law. Criminal law includes rules that everybody must obey. For example, there are rules against murder. Murder is not considered to be a dispute between individuals but a crime against the authority of government. The government has forbidden murder, and thus anyone who murders is committing a wrong against society, as well as against the individual victim.

In contrast to public law, *private law* deals with disputes between individuals or organizations over their legal rights and duties. For example, if you borrow money and fail to pay it back on time, you may face legal action. The lender can go to court with a lawsuit, or case, against you. That suit would be a private suit, between individuals. The legal term is *civil suit,* or *civil case.* In such a suit, the person doing the accusing—in this case, the lender—is called a *plaintiff.* The person accused—that's you—is known as the *defendant.*

Our jury system also has its roots in the time of Henry II. In each district, Henry appointed small groups of people to advise the judges who came around to hold court. These local people were required to report, under oath, every crime they knew to have taken place since the judge's last visit.

This was the origin of the *grand jury system* that we use today. Under the grand jury system, groups of from twelve to twenty-three persons, called *jurors,* are still used to advise officials on whether there is sufficient evidence to bring an accused person to trial.

Henry II, building on earlier customs, also helped lay the basis for *trial by jury.* Henry II made it possible for either the plaintiff or the defendant in a civil case to request a hearing. Together, the plaintiff and defendant then went before a judge and were heard in the presence of twelve local citizens. The judge asked the twelve to state, under oath, if they thought the plaintiff's statements were true. The judge would decide the case in accordance with the citizens' answers. Out of this practice grew the

Chapter 2: Political Ideas from Western Europe

Before jury trials were common, legal disputes were often settled by trials by combat or trials by ordeal. In the picture above, a man and a woman are deciding a marital dispute by combat. Whoever wins the contest will be declared legally in the right. Below, a woman runs across white-hot plowshares in a trial by ordeal. If her feet are not deeply burned, she will be declared innocent of the charges against her.

idea of trial by jury, which is a fundamental part of our legal system today.

Henry's son John was responsible—against his will—for another major advance in English government. John became king in 1199, while England was at war with France. He tried to collect new taxes from the nobles, saying he needed more money to pay for the war. Some of the nobles resisted, replying that John was spending too much on luxuries. In 1215, the nobles forced John to sign a document called the Magna Charta (MAG-nuh KAR-tuh). The term is a Latin one meaning "Great Charter." Copies of this "Great Charter" were made and sent to various places in England so that its terms would be known throughout the land. Some copies are now preserved in the British Museum in London.

In time, the Magna Charta became the basis on which English constitutional government was built and civil liberties for all were guaranteed.

Just what did the Magna Charta say? One provision was that the king could not tax the nobles without their consent. A similar idea appeared in the thirteen colonies before the Revolution, when the colonists protested that there should be "no taxation without representation." The Magna Charta also provided for the continuance of trial by jury. Here, in

A seal like the one below was placed on the Magna Charta to make it official. This was the seal of King John.

Chapter 2: Political Ideas from Western Europe

modern language, are some other parts of the Magna Charta:

> No free man shall be imprisoned except by the lawful judgment of his peers [equals] or by the law of the land.
>
> To no one will we [that is, the monarch] deny or delay right or justice.
>
> We will appoint as judges, constables, and sheriffs only such persons as know the law of the kingdom and desire to observe it.
>
> If anyone, without the lawful judgment of his peers, has been deprived by us of lands, castles, liberties, or rights, we will at once restore them. And if a dispute arises about this, the matter will be decided by twenty-five nobles.
>
> No scutage [shield money, paid by nobles who did not wish to serve in the king's army] or aid [grant to the king] shall be taken in our kingdom except by the advice of our kingdom.
>
> To obtain this advice, we will summon the bishops and nobles to meet on a certain day and place.

John gave in to the nobles for two reasons—he needed money and he needed soldiers. The money and the soldiers could be supplied only by the nobles. At first, the Magna Charta's provisions applied only to the upper classes—the nobles. The Magna Charta was important to the nobles because it codified their existing rights. By signing it, King John bound himself to respect those rights. Later, though, King John took a different view. He maintained that the Magna Charta had no value because he had been forced to sign it. Several centuries passed before the promises in the Magna Charta were fully put into effect even for the nobles. More centuries passed before similar rights were assured to the common people.

Despite a shaky beginning, the Magna Charta established the principle that the power of the king was not absolute.

The Rise of Representative Democracy

In the centuries that followed John's signing of the Magna Charta, other English kings bargained from time to time in order to get what they wanted or needed. Gradually, these bargains gave more rights to the English people. Out of this slow process came many of the rights that Americans hold dear today. One of the most important outcomes was the rise of representative democracy.

A first step toward representative democracy was the broadening of the group from which members of the king's council were chosen. In the time of King John, only the upper classes of English society had any voice—and a small voice, at that—in government. The two leading forces were the nobility and the Roman Catholic Church, which was then England's official church. As provided in the Magna Charta, a group of important church leaders, or bishops, met with the king, from time to time, to give advice. This group was the king's council.

In 1265, some of the nobles revolted against Henry III, John's son. For a while, they virtually ran the country. Their leader, Simon de Montfort (MONT-furt), tried to win support from other classes by calling together an assembly, or *parliament* (a word from old French and Latin meaning "speaking conference"). Besides nobles and bishops, de Montfort invited two knights from each district and two commoners—usually successful merchants—from each town. The nobles' revolt failed, but a precedent had been set. After that,

THE ENGLISH PARLIAMENT BY 1400

Parliament	
House of Lords (upper house)	House of Commons (lower house)
Nobles, other members of the upper class, and church leaders	Knights and commoners, or property owners

Chapter 2: Political Ideas from Western Europe

knights and commoners met with the king's council, now officially called Parliament. But for a long time, Parliament's role remained merely to give advice, not to make laws.

By 1400, Parliament had two branches, as it has today (see chart opposite). An upper branch, the House of Lords, included nobles and church leaders. The lower branch, the House of Commons, included the knights and commoners. These commoners were members of the middle class—merchants or other property owners—who were elected by that class to represent them in the House of Commons. Parliament was to this extent a representative assembly. It became more fully so in 1832 when members from the lower classes were added.

Parliament's position was still a shaky one in 1400 and it remained so for more than two hundred years. Sometimes it was ignored altogether—until there was need for money. Then the monarch would turn to Parliament for help and Parliament would often bargain for greater power in return for helping to raise the money. In this way, Parliament gradually gained control over the king's power of taxation and the right to approve all important decisions before they became law.

Finally, after much struggle, Parliament acquired the right to pass laws on its own. From this step toward representative democracy came our own practice of having laws passed by an elected assembly. The practice was brought to North America by English colonists. It accounts for our state assemblies and legislatures and our federal Congress.

Another step in the rise of representative democracy was Parliament's passage of the Petition of Right in 1628. Like the Magna Charta, this document put restrictions on the king and stated some important principles that would later be recognized as basic rights of English citizens. But the king at the time, Charles I, simply ignored the Petition of Right. He dissolved Parliament and ruled without it for 11 years.

The Petition of Right was a reaction to the claim of monarchs that they were above the law because God had granted them the right to rule over others. This idea of the *divine right of kings* had a long history. But in 1628, many members of Parliament felt that it had been carried too far. In the Petition of Right, Parliament insisted on its own right to criticize the king. In particular, it condemned:

1. The forcing of rich people to make loans to the crown.
2. The imprisonment of political critics without a trial by jury.
3. The lodging of troops in private homes without the homeowner's consent.
4. The practice of declaring martial law in peacetime and thereby suspending many rights. (Normally, martial law is declared in time of war or unrest. It puts military leaders in control in place of civilian leaders.)

Two giant steps for mankind!

This committee of the House of Commons is investigating prison conditions. By seeing conditions in the prisons and talking with prisoners, the committee was able to advise the House on needs for new laws to improve treatment.

Though the Petition of Right had no immediate practical effect, it foreshadowed a revolution that further reduced the powers of the king. When Charles I finally called Parliament back, its mood was angry and resentful. As king, Charles I headed the official Church of England. This is a Protestant church set up in 1534 by King Henry VIII when he broke with the Roman Catholic Church. Many members of Parliament were Puritans—a term used at the time for Protestants who wanted to simplify, or purify, the ritual of the Church of England. The Puritans also wanted to cut down the king's power. Puritans in the House of Commons managed to pass a law that created a court to try Charles I for treason against the rights of the English. The result was a civil war, known as the Puritan Revolution, in which the king's forces were defeated. In 1649, Charles was tried, found guilty, and beheaded.

For a time, England had no monarch. A Puritan named Oliver Cromwell became head of the government. Before long, Cromwell ignored Parliament and ruled as a dictator.

Many English people were as unhappy with Cromwell's dictatorship as they had been with Charles's monarchy. They had an opportunity to make a change when Cromwell's son Richard took over after Cromwell's death. Richard proved unable to rule, and he resigned. Leaders from the old Parliament then decided to seek a middle ground—a monarchy that was answerable to the people. They invited back the son of the former king, who became Charles II. The new king had to promise to accept the acts passed by the Puritan Parliament before the revolution.

The love affair between Parliament and the king soon soured. When Charles's brother and successor, James II, tried to establish

Chapter 2: Political Ideas from Western Europe

greater royal power, Parliament made a move to replace him. They invited Mary, a daughter of James II, and her husband, William of Orange, to come to England from the Netherlands. William landed in England with a large army, and James II fled. This nearly bloodless event is known as the Glorious Revolution. William and Mary became the monarchs of England, but Parliament was now clearly in charge. This became apparent the next year, 1689, when Parliament wrote—and the monarchs approved—a Bill of Rights.

The English Bill of Rights was a major landmark in the development of democratic government. It set clear limits on what any king or queen of England could do, and, at the same time, it protected the rights of the English people. Here are some of the provisions of the English Bill of Rights:

Monarchs have no divine right to rule. They do so at the will of Parliament. Their decisions may not infringe on the established rights of the English people.
Accused persons have a right to a trial by jury.
English people have a right to petition the government when they feel it has done something that wrongs them.
Punishment for a crime should not be cruel or unusual, nor fines excessive.
The monarch may not suspend Parliament or its laws, or put any taxes into effect without the express approval of Parliament.

Colonists who came to North America from England brought with them the ideas of both the Petition of Right and the English Bill of Rights. The ideas took root and grew. The fear of losing those rights was to be a major cause of the American Revolution in 1776.

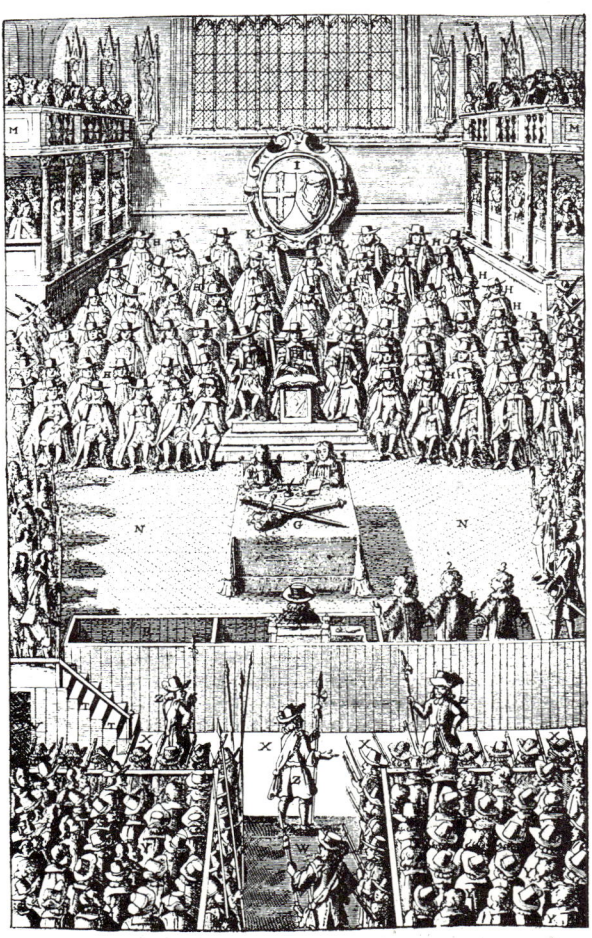

Charles I was tried by a "Rump Parliament." It is so called because it had driven out members who favored the king.

Questions

1 Who was Henry II? How did his actions contribute to our political heritage?

2 What is English common law? How does it differ from Roman common law?

3 What was the Magna Charta? In what way is it a part of our political heritage?

4 What is a "parliament"? What institutions in our government grew out of the English Parliament?

5 Briefly describe some basic provisions in the Petition of Right (1628) and the English Bill of Rights (1689).

◯ Which *one* of the following do you think was the most important: the Magna Charta, the Petition of Right, or the English Bill of Rights? Why?

Chapter 2: Political Ideas from Western Europe

SOME EUROPEAN POLITICAL THINKERS

The people in the thirteen colonies were influenced in their ideas about government not only by English experience but also by what they read. Most educated people in the colonies were familiar with Greek and Roman history. Many had read the writings of Greeks and Romans on how governments worked and how they ought to work. Political turmoil in Europe in the seventeenth and eighteenth centuries inspired further thought about government.

The writings of a series of great European political thinkers profoundly influenced the colonists. These thinkers sought to apply reason to the study of government.

They began at the beginning. What was the origin of government? Was there ever a time when people had no government? For argument's sake—since it was impossible to prove or disprove—they decided to assume that there had indeed been such a time. They called it a *state of nature*. This, they said, was a condition in which people lived without any rules and without any government to make rules.

At this point, let us add to our previous list of types of government one other term, which is related to the ideas of these political thinkers.

Anarchy. This is a condition where, in theory, everyone is free and equal and there is no government. The term comes from Greek words meaning "no leader." So far as we know, anarchy has never existed in the real world for any length of time. Yet some seventeenth-century thinkers believed that people once lived in that way. Life in a condition of anarchy, or a state of nature, was not necessarily a life of bliss.

Social Contract Theory

The theory that people sought to escape from the state of nature, or anarchy, by making

Beginning with William and Mary (above), English monarchs felt the effect of ideas advanced by political theorists.

an agreement among themselves is called the social contract theory. This theory was much in fashion around the time of the American Revolution, though it was not without rivals. We will examine three major thinkers whose ideas contributed to the social contract theory.

Thomas Hobbes (1588–1679) defended monarchies on the ground that they originated in a social contract. Hobbes was a supporter of Charles I and fled to France during the Puritan Revolution. In 1651, he wrote a book with the title *Leviathan* (luh-VIGH-uh-thun). A leviathan is a sea monster, and Hobbes was comparing government to a huge beast created by human hands.

Hobbes declared that every person had a right to live without a government. This right was a *natural right*, one that was part of human nature. But, he said, such a life of anarchy was

Chapter 2: Political Ideas from Western Europe

Thomas Hobbes believed that without a king who was all-powerful, people's lives would be "poor, nasty, and brutish."

John Locke was a court favorite during the reign of William and Mary. Their friendship helped to make his ideas known.

so unpleasant that at some point people would decide to give up that right. They would enter into a social contract, surrendering power to one or more persons, and thus form a government or a state.

Hobbes did not recognize the right of the people to revolt once they had entered into a social contract. This was because, in his view, dissent would lead to civil war and, finally, a return to anarchy. Nor did Hobbes believe that a monarch should have to answer to the will of the people. The state had to have absolute power. Nevertheless, Hobbes's ideas about the social contract were to be given a different twist later on.

John Locke (1632–1704) insisted that when people enter a social contract, they keep the right to change their government. This idea was central to Locke's thinking. His views, published in *Two Treatises on Civil Government* in 1690, had a wide influence. Some scholars believe that, of all European writings, these essays of Locke's had the greatest effect on our nation's political history. Thomas Jefferson, author of the Declaration of Independence, had read Locke's essays. So had most of the educated people in the thirteen colonies by 1776.

Locke differed sharply with Hobbes. In the first place, Locke painted a much brighter picture of the state of nature. Second, he argued that people do not sign away their rights when they enter a social contract. On the contrary, Locke said, people enter such a contract in order to hold their rights more securely. Locke was on the side of those in England who believed that the power of a monarch should be limited. Third, Locke believed that a monarch had a contractual arrangement with the people, and that a monarch who broke that contract lost the right to rule.

This last idea of Locke's found an echo in the thirteen colonies' Declaration of Independence. In it, and later in the United States Constitution, we find many of Locke's ideas.

Chapter 2: Political Ideas from Western Europe

Among other things, Locke argued that people in any society should:

1. Have the right to hold and own property.
2. Have freedom of speech.
3. Have the right to worship as they please.
4. Give to the government only those powers necessary to keep the peace and to judge lawbreakers and punish them.
5. Have the right to break the social contract and, if necessary, change the government when it failed to serve the public interest.

When writing about "the people," Locke had in mind the propertied classes of England. His stress on property rights made him a great favorite of middle-class people, who were still struggling to protect their property rights against interference by the government. Later political thinkers were to stress the rights of a broader group of people: rich, middle class, and poor together.

Jean-Jacques Rousseau (roo-SO) (1712–1778) carried forward and broadened the idea of a social contract. Rousseau, a Swiss citizen who lived much of his life in France, published a book entitled *The Social Contract* in 1762. Rousseau minced no words. He insisted on the right of *all* people to have a voice in government. All were "citizens," regardless of property ownership, religion, or sex. "Liberty," said Rousseau, "cannot exist without equality." Much of what he said angered the middle and upper classes.

Rousseau argued that the only law or government that people have to obey is the law or government they make for themselves. We can see the ideas of Rousseau and Locke in the second paragraph of the Declaration of Independence, which states that governments derive "their just powers from the consent of the governed." This is a clear statement of the social contract theory.

Rousseau was a perfect example of an outsider in society. He opposed almost everything about the society of his time.

Balancing the Powers of Government

The colonial leaders also derived from European thought the idea that there should be a separation of powers within government. This idea was put forward in a book by a French nobleman, the Baron de Montesquieu (mon-tess-KYOO) (1689–1755). Montesquieu's *The Spirit of Laws* was translated into English in 1750 and was well-known to the Americans who wrote the United States Constitution.

In his book, Montesquieu argued that the powers of government—legislative, executive, and judicial—should be separated. Montesquieu had studied history and observed the governments of his day. He concluded that it was dangerous to give too much power to one person, or to any group of persons. They were too likely to abuse that power. So Montesquieu advocated breaking up any government into three separate parts. That way, each part could check or balance the others.

Montesquieu's idea of dividing government into three branches was adopted by the

Chapter 2: Political Ideas from Western Europe

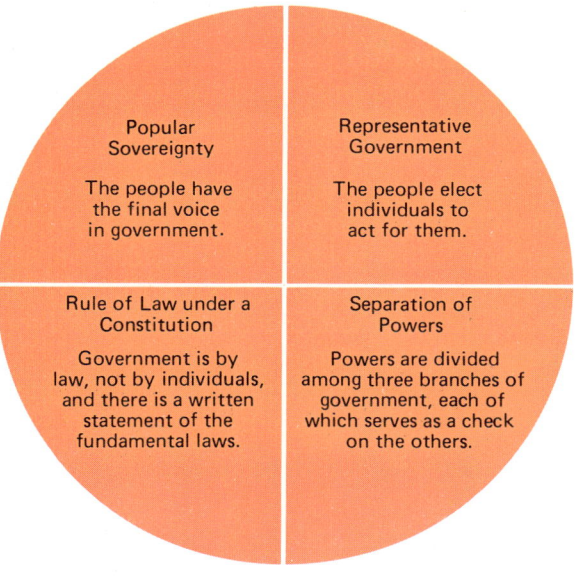

FOUR MAIN ELEMENTS OF OUR POLITICAL HERITAGE

- **Popular Sovereignty** — The people have the final voice in government.
- **Representative Government** — The people elect individuals to act for them.
- **Rule of Law under a Constitution** — Government is by law, not by individuals, and there is a written statement of the fundamental laws.
- **Separation of Powers** — Powers are divided among three branches of government, each of which serves as a check on the others.

PROBLEM: HOW WOULD YOU START FROM SCRATCH?

In Chapter 2, you have been studying the political heritage of the English colonists in America. The following imaginary situation helps to show how basic the political ideas they inherited are to our own thinking. The tale takes place in the distant future. One can only hope that the kind of disaster it involves will never occur. As you read the tale, think about these questions:

- *What happened to the people on the spaceship?*
- *What political problems might they face?*

A Tale of the Future

Earth time: A.D. 2189. Tensions are building to a danger point. The nations of the world are engaged in a desperate struggle for military supremacy. The arms race has exposed the people of Earth to a growing threat of total nuclear war. Scientists warn that this could destroy the planet Earth.

As world leaders try to prevent war, a group of scientists decides to act. With the aid of a computer, Think-Vac 300D, the scientists select and assemble 500 people. These people have been carefully selected to represent the skills necessary to reconstruct our civilization. The scientists' goal: to send these 500 people to start a colony on a new planet.

The scientists have already chosen a planet that is very similar to Earth. It has air, water, and food resources. Most important, it is uninhabited. But it is far away, in another solar system.

As rapidly as possible, the scientists build a rocket to carry the colonists to their new planet. It is a race against time. Will the rocket lift off before the outbreak of war?

It does. The rocket is deep in space when its occupants hear that the people of Earth are at war. Throughout their long trip,

framers of the United States Constitution in 1787. The framers also wrote a system of checks and balances into the Constitution. This plan of government went beyond Montesquieu, but it was a logical extension of his ideas.

The chart above shows the four main elements of our political heritage. The type of government shown on the chart is the kind we have in our nation and in each of our fifty states.

--- **Questions** ---

1 Identify each of the following and tell how each contributed to our political heritage: Thomas Hobbes, John Locke, Jean-Jacques Rousseau, the Baron de Montesquieu.

2 Of these four, which *one* do you think had the most important ideas? Why did you select that one?

⌂ Which would you prefer—a condition of anarchy or membership in a social contract? Explain.

Chapter 2: Political Ideas from Western Europe

the colonists listen to the increasingly grim news from home. In the final stages of descent to the Earth-like planet that will be their new home, the colonists watch their televiewer in horror. The Earth crumbles into dust and is no more.

In landing, the rocket passes through a high-energy force field. All memory of the past is erased from the minds of the colonists. The memory banks of the rocket's computers are also wiped clean. Somehow, the rocket lands safely.

The colonists are puzzled. Who are they? Why are they here? They are still able to eat, drink, breathe, speak. Food and shelter are at hand. The group feels an instinctive need to survive. But then what?

Adapted and used by permission of Morgan Jack Cronin, Olive Paschal, and Robert Stein, Jr.

Questions

1 What *political* problems might the 500 people face on their new planet?

2 How do you think they would deal with these problems? Would you expect anarchy? Monarchy? Some other solutions? Explain.

3 Suppose that you are the only one of the 500 with any memory of our early political heritage. What political ideas would you suggest these people use from the ancient Middle East? From ancient Greece and Rome? From early modern Europe?

⌂ What do you now think is important about our early political heritage? Why?

Chapter 2 Review

Developing Your Political Vocabulary

How do the terms in *a-e* differ in meaning? Give one example for each term.
- **a** authoritarian/democractic
- **b** monarchy/dictatorship
- **c** oligarchy/anarchy
- **d** public law/private law
- **e** plaintiff/defendant

Recalling and Comparing

1 Give *six* examples of events in English history that contributed to the political heritage of the United States.

2 What were *two* ideas of Western European writers that contributed to our political heritage? Cite at least one person's name with each idea.

3 How can you explain why the rich political and cultural traditions of China, India, and other parts of Asia had relatively little effect on the formation of our nation in the eighteenth century?

4 Why do you think the Spanish settlers in North America did not directly influence the political thinking in the thirteen colonies?

5 What, if any, influence do you think the Native Americans had on our political heritage from colonial times? Explain.

6 Do you think that political ideas are an important part of any people's heritage? Explain.

Special Activities

1 Prepare a bulletin-board display illustrating people and ideas from Western Europe that contributed to our political heritage.

2 Select *one* of the English rulers mentioned in Chapter 2 and, with the help of library books, write a biographical sketch about that ruler. Note how the person felt about democracy and individual freedoms.

3 Prepare a poster in which you illustrate or diagram the basic political ideas of Thomas Hobbes, John Locke, Jean-Jacques Rousseau, and the Baron de Montesquieu.

4 Prepare a chart of the various systems of government reviewed at the beginning of this chapter. Find present-day countries with each kind of government and list the names of these countries in the proper categories on your chart.

5 Make a study of the English jury system as it developed under Henry II and compare it with our present jury system.

6 Make a study of the Puritan Revolution in England and write a report of your findings.

7 Consider what might be arguments for and against the following statement: "Social contracts are necessary for the survival of a people." Do you agree or disagree? What are your reasons?

Chapter 3

Political Ideas from the Thirteen Colonies

European settlers in the Americas had a splendid opportunity. They were embarking on a new adventure, in mostly uncharted territory. Here was a chance to use the human power of reason to create new forms of government for a new land. The settlers on the Atlantic Coast of North America who were English and started with English political ideas changed those ideas to fit their own needs and dreams. In this chapter, we will look at the new political life they created. We will also examine the growing rift between the colonists and their home country that resulted in the American Revolution.

Goals

- To learn the contributions made by our political heritage from the thirteen colonies.
- To learn the main causes of the American Revolution of 1776.
- To take a new look at the meaning of the Declaration of Independence.

LANDMARK IDEAS FROM THE THIRTEEN COLONIES

Have you ever helped to create a government? The idea is not so far-fetched as it sounds. Not all governments are on such a large scale as those of nations, states, and cities. For example, a club needs certain rules by which to operate, and these rules can be considered a form of government.

Chapter 3: Political Ideas from the Thirteen Colonies

Student councils and clubs give students an opportunity to gain political understanding.

Chapter 3: Political Ideas from the Thirteen Colonies

The Mayflower Compact signed aboard the Pilgrims' ship was a social contract that established a basis for self-government.

Imagine for a moment that you are starting a club. How will you organize it? Who will be eligible for membership? What rules will govern your meetings? What goals will you set for yourselves? Questions as basic as these had to be considered by early settlers in the New World. Let's take a look at the Pilgrims who came to New England on the *Mayflower* in 1620. What did they decide about a government for their colony?

Government by the People

The Pilgrims were a small group of Puritans who did not want to belong to the Church of England or pay taxes for its support. The Pilgrims were also called Separatists, because they wanted to break away, or separate, from the Church of England. They tried moving to the Netherlands, where they could have their own church. Most of the Pilgrims remained in that country, and many of their descendants live there today.

To some of the Pilgrims, however, it was important to live as English people. So they decided to go to America to create a "New England." They obtained a grant allowing them to settle in the London Company's territory—called Virginia—south of the Hudson River. The company counted on making profits on trade with the English colonies. The Pilgrims set out for Virginia, but their ship was blown north to Cape Cod by gale winds.

The Pilgrims had no rules for governing themselves in the new land. What should their first step be? According to Locke, Hobbes, and Rousseau, people in such situations make a social contract. The Pilgrims did just that. While still on their ship, they drew up a contract by which everyone agreed to be bound. This document is called the Mayflower Compact, after the name of the Pilgrims' ship. Here is a modernized version of the Mayflower Compact:

In the name of God, Amen. We, whose names are written below, are loyal subjects of King James.

We have undertaken a voyage to plant the first colony in the northern parts of Virginia. [They were in fact off what is now Massachusetts.] This we have done for the glory of God and the advancement of the Christian faith and for the honor of our king and country.

For these purposes and for the sake of order and survival, we agree to combine ourselves into a civil body politic. We will, from time to time, enact such just and equal laws and choose such officers as shall be for the general good of the colony. And we promise all due obedience to these.

In witness of the above, we have here written our names at Cape Cod on the eleventh of November in the year 1620.

By means of the Mayflower Compact, the Pilgrims created a government by the people. Though they remained subjects of the king, the settlers would make their own laws and choose

Chapter 3: Political Ideas from the Thirteen Colonies

their leaders. Thus did the Pilgrims sow the seeds of democracy in America.

The Pilgrims settled at Plymouth. As more of their group arrived from Europe and the Plymouth colony grew, each church became a meetinghouse with its own leader and other officers. Each member of the church had a vote. Each community was a direct democracy, as some New England communities still are today. The Pilgrims' direct democracy, though, was limited to church members alone.

Far to the south, in the true Virginia territory, a different system was taking shape.

Representative Government

The first representative assembly, or congress, in the English colonies was formed a year before the Mayflower *landed. It was the Virginia House of Burgesses in the Jamestown Colony.* The Jamestown government was not formed from the ground up as the Pilgrims' government was. Instead, a governor appointed by the London Company set up the House of Burgesses. The settlers in Jamestown had been unhappy under arbitrary rule and had not been producing enough tobacco for export to England. As a result, the London Company's profits had been low. The company decided that if the settlers had a representative assembly they would be more content, produce more, and so raise the company's profits. The House of Burgesses, which met for the first time in July 1619, was elected by the adult male settlers. As an elected body, it became a model for representative assemblies in other colonies.

A Written Constitution

Another part of our colonial heritage was the writing of the first constitution in Connecticut in 1639. A constitution *is a set of basic principles upon which a government is organized.* Usually, a constitution defines the powers of the government and tells what rights the people will exercise. In short, it is a plan of government.

The Fundamental Orders of 1639 remained the constitution of Connecticut until 1818—nearly 200 years. The 1818 constitution remained in effect until it was replaced in 1965.

Just as the Pilgrims had left England because they did not like the rules there, the people who settled in Connecticut were fleeing the rules set up by Puritans in Massachusetts. These Puritans had settled at Massachusetts Bay near the Pilgrims at Plymouth. The rules of the Massachusetts Bay Puritans were very strict. Their leaders insisted on complete control without regard for people who had other ideas on how to run the colony.

In 1635 and 1636, small groups left the Massachusetts Bay Colony and migrated down the Connecticut River Valley. One group was led by Thomas Hooker, a Puritan minister who believed that the authority of any government should rest upon the free consent of the people. Hooker and his followers intended to create a more democratic society.

Hooker's group and others settled the towns of Windsor, Wethersfield, and Hartford in what is today Connecticut. In 1639, these Puritan settlers drew up a constitution which they called the Fundamental Orders of Connecticut. In it, they agreed to the following practices, all of which are familiar to present-day Americans:

1. Creation of a representative assembly (then called a general court).
2. Popular election of lawmakers (called deputies) from each town to serve in the assembly.
3. Popular election of officers of the assembly.
4. Popular election of a governor.
5. Popular election of judges.

Soon after 1639, other English colonies began writing their own constitutions. They, like Connecticut, set out rules for local government. And they began setting up other institutions as well.

Public Education

In 1647, Massachusetts established the first system of public education in the English colonies. This schooling, which was paid for by

Early schools were often no more than one-room buildings in which one teacher taught all grade levels together.

tax money, had as its goal the teaching of religion even more than reading and writing. The Puritans of Massachusetts believed that people should not rely on ministers to interpret the Bible but should rely on their own understanding of the words. Therefore, each person should be taught to read.

The Puritans also believed that the Devil, or Satan, wanted to keep people ignorant of the Bible and of education in general. They called the Devil "the Old Deluder," and they were not about to let him delude the young people of Massachusetts. The public education law of 1647 was known as the Old Deluder Law because it was meant to foil the Devil.

The Old Deluder Law was the first step toward our present system of using public taxes to make education available to all. The law provided for the education of children in any town of fifty families or more. Each town of that size was required to appoint a part-time teacher, and all of the adults in the town had to contribute to the teacher's wages. All children of the town were to be taught to read and write. Taxes were imposed on adults in the town to build and maintain the school and to pay the salary of a full-time teacher.

Chapter 3: Political Ideas from the Thirteen Colonies

The royal governor ordered that copies of John Peter Zenger's newspaper be burned. With ceremony, they were.

Chapter 3: Political Ideas from the Thirteen Colonies

Freedom of the Press

Another colonial contribution to our political heritage was freedom of the press. English law prohibited publication of a statement—even if true—that would injure someone's reputation. Such a statement was called *libel*. The law also prohibited any writing that encouraged discontent against the government or resistance to authority. Such a publication was considered *sedition*—as it still is in some nations today. Any writing that excited discontent by exposing government officials to public ridicule was banned as *seditious libel*.

John Peter Zenger was tried for seditious libel in 1735. In his newspaper, the *New York Weekly Journal*, Zenger had sharply criticized the royal governor of New York. Even if what Zenger had written was true, it seemed clear that he had broken the law. But the royal governor was not popular, and Zenger had been held in prison for 10 months before his trial. The jury went against legal tradition and found Zenger not guilty.

The Zenger trial set an important precedent that eventually led to the free press as we know it today. It is no longer a crime for the press to expose the government to ridicule. In fact, we have come to consider the press as a watchdog against abuses by public officials.

Religious Freedom

Another outgrowth of early colonial times was religious freedom. The Puritans themselves did not grant religious freedom to others though they had sought this freedom for themselves. For example, when a certain Obadiah Holmes refused to have his child baptized, he was fined; and when he refused to pay, he was whipped. At times, people were sent out of the colony for such obstinacy.

One who was sent away was a Puritan minister named Roger Williams. He held that the government had no right to punish someone for religious views that were different. In

---

New World, New Rights for Women

Women had legal rights in the New World that they did not have in England. This was largely because of the conditions of life in the colonies.

Under English common law, for example, a married woman could not own property. After a woman married, her property belonged to her husband. In the colonies, however, married women had the legal right to own property. They could also enter into contracts, though they could not do so in England.

These legal rights had important economic meaning for some colonial women. Husbands might grant women legal power to act for them in business matters when they were away. Before marrying, a woman might make a contract guaranteeing her the use of her property and its income after marriage, divorce, or widowhood. It is not suprising, then, that some women were tailors, millers, merchants, printers, or innkeepers. In the Southern colonies, a few women even operated large plantations.

Adapted from an unpublished report by Jacqueline A. Case.

1635, the government ordered him out. At the spot where Williams finally settled, he founded a new colony and called it Providence. Today, Providence is the capital of Rhode Island. Williams advocated religious freedom even for people of the most "anti-Christian conscience or worships," and he wanted his colony to be a center of religious freedom.

Soon after, another Puritan challenged the leaders of Massachusetts. She was Anne Hutchinson, a witty woman with a bold spirit. She was so bold as to argue that some ministers were superior to others. She, like Williams, was banished. And like him, she went to Rhode Island, taking some followers with her. In 1638,

Anne Hutchinson spoke out against what she believed to be the empty forms of religious service preached by church leaders.

this group established the town of Portsmouth.

By daring to criticize the religion imposed by government leaders, Williams and Hutchinson were contributing something new to the colonial heritage. Theirs were the first moves against religious intolerance in the English colonies.

Another step toward religious freedom occurred a few years later in Maryland. That southern colony had been started as a haven for Roman Catholics, but many non-Catholics also settled there. In 1649, when Maryland was only 15 years old, its assembly passed a law known as the Maryland Toleration Act. This law stated that all Christians were to be allowed the free exercise of their religion and that no one was to molest them.

While Maryland's act allowed Protestants and Catholics religious freedom, it provided punishment by death to others. William Penn's Pennsylvania went further toward religious freedom. Penn offered religious freedom to Jews as well as Christians in 1701. As early as 1676, Penn had granted religious freedom to settlers in the province of West New Jersey.

Thus, the movement begun by Williams and Hutchinson was spreading. It led finally to our present system of religious freedom, which guarantees that all people in our nation may worship or not worship as they please.

Questions

1 Who were the Pilgrims? How did they contribute to our political heritage?

Chapter 3: Political Ideas from the Thirteen Colonies

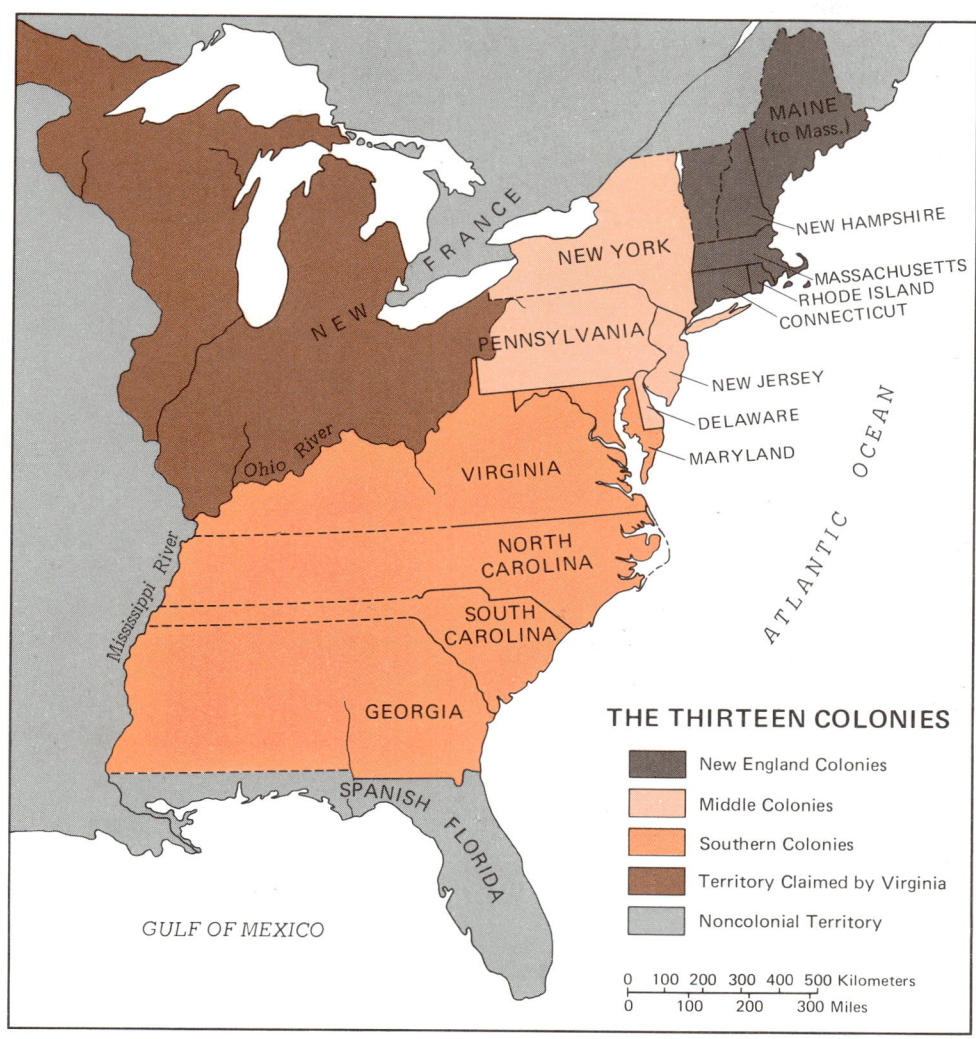

2 How was the Virginia House of Burgesses an example of representative government? Who elected it?

3 What is a constitution?

4 How did Roger Williams and Anne Hutchinson contribute to our political heritage?

⬠ Of all the contributions discussed in this section, which *one* do you think most influences your life today? Explain.

THE BREAK WITH GREAT BRITAIN

Along their broad river valleys and in their forest clearings, the people in the thirteen colonies were beginning to think and live in ways of their own. As generations passed, the colonists seemed less like "transplanted Englishpeople" and more like "Americans." They governed themselves at the local level. New Englanders, for example, elected their local officials at town meetings. Both local and county officials were elected in the Middle Colonies. The Virginia colonists chose delegates to their colony's lawmaking body, the House of Burgesses. Having no representatives in Parliament, the colonists had few ties to the English political system.

For a century and more, England left its American colonies pretty much alone. By the early 1700s, however, the colonists were aware that the home country was tightening its control. They began to feel that they had fewer rights than people living in Great Britain. (England and Wales joined with Scotland in 1707 to form the country of Great Britain.)

Colonial Resentment Starts

One of the first causes of colonial resentment was the Molasses Act of 1733. This act put high duties, or taxes, on molasses imported from non-British islands in the Caribbean. Molasses was imported to New England to make rum. Most of the molasses was bought from sugarcane growers on French, Spanish, and Dutch islands in the Caribbean. Parliament passed the Molasses Act to help British colonists in the Caribbean sell their own sugar and molasses. But to colonists in New England, the act appeared to be aimed at hurting *them* instead.

If it had been enforced, the Molasses Act might have destroyed the growing New England rum industry. But the act was not enforced. Smugglers managed to sneak molasses into New England without paying the tax. The rum industry stayed strong, but colonial resentment was stirred.

A series of acts growing out of the French and Indian War (1754–1763) set the stage for the American Revolution. The war began as a struggle over rival French and British claims to lands in western Pennsylvania and Ohio. In 1756, it became part of a larger war, called the Seven Years' War, between France, Great Britain, and other European countries. When

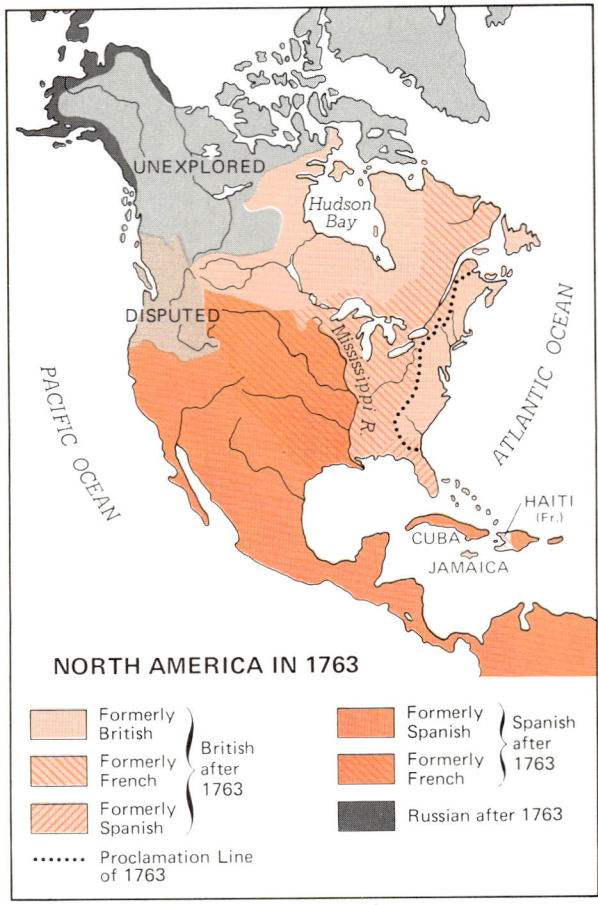

the war was over, the British had control of most of what is now Eastern United States. American colonists cheered the British victory. But the good feelings did not last long, for seeds of discord had been sown by the war.

The French and Indian War had increased troubles between the settlers and the Native Americans, had led to the stationing of large numbers of British troops in America, and had been costly. All of these effects of the war were sources of discord.

The Proclamation of 1763 at the end of the war angered the colonists by banning settlements west of the Appalachian Mountains. This order by King George III was meant to give the British government time to develop a new policy on the western lands. But to Amer-

The stationing of British troops in the colonies often led to resentment and hard feelings among the people.

This cartoon from a British newspaper of 1766 shows a reaction to the end of the Stamp Act in March 1766.

Chapter 3: Political Ideas from the Thirteen Colonies

ican settlers, the Proclamation of 1763 was an outrage. The western lands were begging to be settled, they thought. Why wait?

Revenue-raising acts passed by Parliament led to further troubles with the colonists. The British had spent heavily to finance the war, and they thought it only fair that the colonists help to pay for the war, too. After all, the colonists had benefited from it.

The Sugar Act of 1764 set new duties on molasses and sugar. Unlike the Molasses Act, this one was enforced. Angry colonial merchants saw their profits dip.

The Stamp Act of 1765 placed the first direct tax (as opposed to customs duty) on the thirteen colonies. It raised an uproar. The act required a wide range of printed matter to be marked with a special stamp, for which payment had to be made. The cost of the stamp depended on what it was for. A school or college degree would bear a stamp costing two pounds (480 pence). A stamp for a land deed cost from six pence to five shillings (60 pence). Each sheet of each copy of a newspaper had to have a stamp costing one halfpenny. To the colonists, these were big sums.

There were also new taxes on glass, paper, paint, and tea purchased from abroad. Further changes in the laws on tea in 1773 led to the Boston Tea Party, in which a group of colonists took a protest action by dumping tea from a ship into Boston Harbor. Parliament struck back by passing the Coercive Acts. These acts of 1774, which were aimed at punishing the colonies for the Tea Party, were called the Intolerable Acts by the colonists. One act closed the port of Boston. Another cancelled the charter of the Massachusetts colony. Another gave officials the authority to send a person to Great Britain for trial.

Still another act of Parliament that angered the colonists was the Quebec Act of 1774. It was intended, not to punish the colonists, but merely to update the Proclamation of 1763. The act placed the country north of the Ohio River under control of the Province of Quebec, in present-day Canada. It also put French civil law back into effect there in order to assure Roman Catholics of their religious freedom. Despite the intentions of Parliament, the colonists saw the Quebec Act as another punishment. In addition, the colonists felt threatened because the Province of Quebec was to be governed by an appointed council rather than an elected assembly.

Boston Harbor Closed

Each month in 1976, the magazine of the Smithsonian Institution published a column called "200 Years Ago This Month." The selection below takes the reader back to May 1774 and the Boston Port Act.

The terms of the act read like the tolling of a bell: Beginning June 1, no vessel may enter Boston Harbor. That includes the ferries that link the town proper with its neighbors around the peninsula. Vessels already in port must leave no later than June 14. From the 15th on, the city will cease to exist as a seaport. Its customhouse will move to Plymouth; Salem will become the capital.

After the first sickening shock, Boston reacts most typically—with mass meetings. The militants run through the actions that could be taken to force Parliament to repeal the Boston Port Bill. Most effective might be an embargo, an end to all trade with Great Britain from every port in America. How would the British like to get along without tobacco, for example?

In London, meanwhile, Parliament is still at work on other "Coercive Acts" designed to put Boston in its place. The Americans haven't learned the half of it, yet.

Adapted from a column by Edwards Park in *Smithsonian* magazine, May 1976. Copyright © 1976 Smithsonian Institution.

The First Continental Congress opened in Carpenter's Hall, Philadelphia, with a prayer by the delegates.

The Colonies Draw Together

As their troubles with Great Britain grew, the thirteen colonies began to draw together. At first, each colony had kept pretty much to itself. The colonies had many differences in style of government and often in economic interests. But resentment of Britain slowly brought the colonies closer.

In 1765, twenty-seven people representing nine of the colonies gathered in New York to protest against the Stamp Act. This gathering, known as the Stamp Act Congress, was the first meeting organized by the colonies to voice their grievances against the British. The delegates drew up a declaration to be presented to the king and Parliament. It charged that the Stamp Act undermined the "rights and liberties of the colonists" because only the colonial legislatures could legally impose such taxes. The act was soon repealed.

A further step towards unity was the organizing of *committees of correspondence*. These were groups started by persons who wanted to keep in touch with each other as troubles with Britain brewed. The first committee of correspondence was organized in Boston in 1772. Within three months, there were eighty such committees across Massachusetts. As they spread to other colonies, committees of correspondence became a powerful force for organizing public opinion against the British.

In response to the Intolerable Acts, the colonies decided to meet again. Fifty-six representatives, from every colony except Georgia, gathered at Philadelphia in the late summer and fall of 1774. The gathering is known as the First Continental Congress. Its purpose was to consider action to recover what the colonists felt were their rights. The delegates to the First Continental Congress drafted a Declaration of Rights and sent it off to the king. They also voted to start a boycott against British goods, including tea.

Some delegates had hoped these actions would make the British come to their senses. But the British did not back down. Instead, tensions increased to the breaking point. On April 19, 1775, British redcoats and colonial minutemen clashed at Lexington and Concord.

The gunfire on April 19, 1775 has been called "the shot heard round the world." It was certainly heard in Philadelphia, where the Second Continental Congress met three weeks

Chapter 3: Political Ideas from the Thirteen Colonies

later. This time the delegates were ready to fight. They organized the Continental Army and appointed George Washington its commander in chief.

From that time on, the Second Continental Congress served as the acting government of the colonies. It was not really a legislature. It was a gathering of "ambassadors" from the thirteen colonies and it had no legal basis. But it worked. It organized the fight against the British and rallied support for the colonists' cause.

The Declaration of Independence

By the summer of 1776, all hope of a peaceful end to the conflict with Great Britain had been lost. Delegates to the Second Continental Congress realized this. On July 4, 1776, they adopted the Declaration of Independence, which Thomas Jefferson had drafted at their request.

The Declaration of Independence told why Britain's colonies were rebelling. Their goal was, first, to overthrow an oppressive government. Second, the colonists wanted to replace British rule with a government that did not engage in oppression. But how best to create it? In the writings of Locke, Rousseau, and others, the colonists found their answer.

The Declaration of Independence insisted that a just government must rest on the consent of the people. This was indeed a revolutionary idea. Never before had "government by the the people" been tried on any large scale. Never before had there been such a sweeping effort to put into practice the theories of democracy. The Declaration won the praise of democratic-minded people all over the world—especially in France, where it served as a beacon for the French Revolution in 1789. But many people, even if they liked the ideas in the Declaration, were skeptical. Would it work, they wanted to know. No one could say for certain.

Questions

1 In what ways did the French and Indian War set the stage for the American Revolution?

2 Name *three* revenue-raising acts by Parliament that angered the colonists. What was the colonists' chief complaint?

⌂ Based on the evidence up to this point, do you think that the colonists were justified in declaring their independence? Explain.

PROBLEM: WHAT DOES THE DECLARATION OF INDEPENDENCE MEAN?

The colonial period contributed many ideas to out political heritage, but its greatest single contribution was the Declaration of Independence. On the following pages, you will have a chance to read the Declaration. As you do, ask yourself these questions:

- *What meaning did the Declaration of Independence have for the colonists?*
- *What meaning does it have for us today?*

The Basic Rights of People

The first two paragraphs of the Declaration deal with the basic rights of people. As you read them, ask yourself:

- *What are the basic rights of people?*
- *Why are all people entitled to those rights?*

When in the Course of human events, it becomes necessary for one people to dissolve the political bands which have connected them with another, and to assume among the Powers of the earth, the separate and equal station to which the Laws of Nature and of Nature's God entitle them, a decent respect to the opinions of mankind requires that they should declare the causes which impel them to the separation.

Chapter 3: Political Ideas from the Thirteen Colonies

In CONGRESS, July 4, 1776.

The unanimous Declaration of the thirteen united States of America.

Several copies of the Declaration of Independence were made. This one is in the National Archives.

We hold these truths to be self-evident, that all men are created equal, that they are endowed by the Creator with certain unalienable Rights, that among these are Life, Liberty and the pursuit of Happiness. That to secure these rights, Governments are instituted among Men, deriving their just powers from the consent of the governed, That whenever any Form of Government becomes destructive of these ends, it is the Right of the People to alter or abolish it, and to institute a new Government, laying its foundation on such principles and organizing its powers in such form, as to them shall seem most likely to effect [bring about] their Safety and Happiness. Prudence, indeed, will dictate that Governments long established should not be changed for light and transient [short-lived] causes; and accordingly all experience hath shown, that mankind are more disposed to suffer, while evils are sufferable, than to right themselves by abolishing the forms to which they are accustomed. But when a long train of abuses and usurpations [illegal seizures of power] pursuing invariably the same Object, evinces [reveals] a design to reduce them under absolute Despotism [tyranny], it is their right, it is their duty, to throw off such Government, and to provide new guards for their future security.—Such has been the patient sufferance of these Colonies; and such is now the necessity which constrains [forces] them to alter their former Systems of Government.

Questions

1 What basic human rights are mentioned in this part of the Declaration?

2 Why, according to the Declaration, are all people entitled to these rights?

3 In what way did Jefferson in the Declaration alter the emphasis given by Locke (pages 37–38) to basic rights?

⌂ What does the phrase *life, liberty, and the pursuit of happiness* mean to *you*? Do you think it meant the same thing to the colonists? Explain.

The List of Grievances

The middle section of the Declaration of Independence lists the grievances the colonists had against the British government. These complaints were leveled against King George III though Parliament, as Britain's lawmaking body, was the real author of the acts listed in the Declaration.

As you read, consider:

- *What were the colonists' grievances?*
- *Did they seem to have anything to do with the basic rights of people?*

The History of the present King of Great Britain [King George III] is a history of repeated injuries and usurpations, all having in direct object the establishment of an absolute Tyranny over these States. To prove this, let Facts be submitted to a candid world.

He has refused his Assent to Laws, the most wholesome and necessary for the public good.

He has forbidden his Governors to pass Laws of immediate and pressing importance, unless suspended in their operation till his Assent should be obtained; and when so suspended, he has utterly neglected to attend to them.

He has refused to pass other Laws for the accommodation of large districts of people, unless those people would relinquish [give up] the right of Representation in the Legislature, a right inestimable [priceless] to them and formidable [threatening] to tyrants only.

He has called together legislative bodies at places unusual, uncomfortable, and distant from the depository of their Public Records, for the sole purpose of fatiguing them into compliance with his measures.

He has dissolved Representative Houses repeatedly, for opposing with manly firmness his invasions on the rights of people.

He has refused for a long time, after such dissolutions, to cause others to be elected; whereby the Legislative Powers, incapable of Annihilation [total destruction], have returned to the People at large for their exercise; the State remaining in the mean time exposed to all the dangers of invasion from without, and convulsions within.

He has endeavoured to prevent the population of these States; for that purpose obstructing the Laws for Naturalization of Foreigners; refusing to pass others to encourage their migration hither, and raising the conditions of new Appropriations of Lands. [To appropriate land is to take possession of it.]

He has obstructed the Administration of Justice by refusing his Assent to Laws for establishing Judiciary Powers.

He has made Judges dependent on his Will alone, for the tenure of their offices, and the amount and payment of their salaries.

He has erected a multitude of New Offices, and sent hither swarms of Officers to harass our People, and eat out their substance.

He has kept among us, in times of peace, Standing Armies without the consent of our Legislatures.

This engraving of the time shows some of the colonial leaders who gathered to approve the Declaration of Independence.

He has affected to render the Military Independent of and superior to the Civil Power.

He has combined with others [Parliament] to subject us to a jurisdiction foreign to our constitutions, and unacknowledged by our laws; giving his Assent to their acts of pretended [so-called] legislation:

For quartering large bodies of armed troops among us:

For protecting them, by a mock Trial, from Punishment for any Murders which they should commit on the Inhabitants of these states:

For cutting off our Trade with all parts of the world:

For imposing taxes on us without our consent:

For depriving us in many cases, of the benefits of Trial by Jury:

For transporting us beyond Seas to be tried for pretended offences:

For abolishing the free System of English Laws in a neighbouring Province [Quebec], establishing therein an Arbitrary government, and enlarging its Boundaries so as to render it at once an example and fit instrument for introducing the same absolute rule into these Colonies:

For taking away our Charters, abolishing our most valuable Laws, and altering fundamentally the Forms of our Governments:

For suspending [abolishing] our own Legislatures, and declaring themselves invested with Power to legislate for us in all cases whatsoever.

He has abdicated Government here, by declaring us out of his Protection and waging War against us.

He has plundered our seas, ravaged our Coasts, burnt our towns, and destroyed the lives of our people.

He is at this time transporting large armies of foreign mercenaries to complete the works of death, desolation and tyranny, already begun with circumstances of Cruelty and perfidy [treachery] scarcely paralleled in the most barbarous ages, and totally unworthy of the Head of a civilized nation.

He has constrained our fellow Citizens taken Captive on the high Seas to bear Arms against their Country, to become the executioners of their friends and Brethren, or to fall themselves by their Hands.

He has excited domestic insurrections amongst us, and has endeavoured to bring on the inhabitants of our frontiers, the merciless Indian Savages, whose known rule of warfare, is an undistinguished destruction of all ages, sexes and conditions.

Questions

1 Which of these grievances do you think might have to do with the basic rights of people? Explain.

◌ Of all these grievances, which *one* do you think was the most important for the colonists in 1776? Which *one* is most important for you today? Explain.

Statement of Separation

The closing paragraphs of the Declaration give a justification for the colonists' break with Britain. The colonists explain what they have done to reach a peaceful solution. Then they give their reasons for fighting to escape British rule. As you read, ask yourself:

- *What audience did the colonists have in mind when they wrote this section?*
- *What were the colonists trying to get across to that audience?*

In every stage of these Oppressions We have petitioned for Redress [remedies] in the most humble terms: Our repeated Petitions have been answered only by repeated injury. A Prince [ruler] whose character is thus marked by every act which may define a Tyrant, is unfit to be the ruler of a free People.

Nor have We been wanting in attentions to our British brethren. We have warned them from time to time of attempts by their legislature to extend an unwarrantable jurisdiction over us. We have reminded them of the circumstances of our emigration and settlement here. We have appealed to their native justice and magnanimity [generosity], and we have conjured [begged] them by the ties of our common kindred to disavow [refuse to recognize] these usurpations, which would inevitably interrupt our connections and correspondence. They too have been deaf to the voice of justice and of consanguinity [common ancestry]. We must, therefore, acquiesce in [give in to] the necessity which denounces our Separation, and hold them, as we hold the rest of mankind, Enemies in War, in Peace Friends.

We, therefore, the Representatives of the United States of America, in General Congress Assembled, appealing to the Supreme Judge of the world for the rectitude [rightness] of our intentions, do, in the Name and by Authority of the good People of these Colonies, solemnly publish and declare, That these United Colonies are, and of Right ought to be Free and Independent States; that they are Absolved from all Allegiance to the British Crown, and that all political connection between then and the State of Great Britain is and ought to be totally dissolved; and that, as Free and Independent States, they have full Power to levy War, conclude Peace, contract Alliances, establish Commerce, and to do all other Acts and Things which Independent States may of right do. And for the support of this Declaration, with a firm reliance on the Protection of Divine Providence, we mutually pledge to each other our Lives, our Fortunes and our sacred Honor.

Questions

1 What had the colonists tried to do before declaring their independence?

2 Why was it important for the colonists to show that they had tried to settle their grievances peacefully?

◌ Do you think the people of the present-day United States would support a revolution in another country if the rebels had *not* first tried to reach a peaceful solution? Explain.

Chapter 3: Political Ideas from the Thirteen Colonies

Chapter 3 Review

Developing Your Political Vocabulary

Use each of the following terms in a sentence about our early American political heritage:
- **a** constitution
- **b** representative assembly
- **c** public education
- **d** religious freedom
- **e** seditious libel

Recalling and Comparing

1 What were some differences between the Mayflower Compact and the Fundamental Orders of Connecticut?

2 What was *one* similarity between the Virginia House of Burgesses and the British Parliament?

3 What steps toward religious freedom were taken in colonial times.

4 Did the thirteen colonies have any experience in acting together before the outbreak of the American Revolution? Explain.

5 Did the American Revolution of 1776 have one cause or many causes? Explain your answer.

6 Of all the ideas we inherited from the British colonists in America, which *four* do you think are the most important to us today? Tell why you chose those four.

Special Activities

1 Select *one* of the colonists mentioned in Chapter 3 and write a biographical sketch about that person with the help of library books. Explain how he or she contributed to our political heritage.

2 Obtain information about the reconstructed Plimoth Plantation in Plymouth, Massachusetts, and the Colonial National Historical Park at the site of the Jamestown settlement in Virginia. Report to the class on what a visitor to these restorations might look for as evidence of differences between the two colonies.

3 As a group project, enact a town meeting in Plymouth Colony and a town meeting in present-day New England. Show differences in the kinds of people attending and the problems that concern them.

4 Prepare a skit in which Roger Williams and Anne Hutchinson defend their beliefs about religious freedom against a group who challenge their ideas.

5 Make a study of the kind of government William Penn established in Pennsylvania and report your findings to the class.

6 Make a study of the trial of John Peter Zenger and the tactics used by his lawyer, Alexander Hamilton. Write a skit describing a scene in the courtroom.

7 Make a study of the Proclamation of 1763 and the problems it was intended to solve. Write a report of your findings.

8 Imagine you are an English colonist living in America in the spring of 1776. Write a letter to a friend in Great Britain in which you describe your complaints about British rule in America.

9 Consider what might be arguments for and against the following statement: "Written constitutions are too restrictive on a people." Do you agree or disagree with the statement? Why?

Chapter 4

Formation of Our Federal Government

The Declaration of Independence in 1776 dissolved the ties that linked the colonies to Great Britain, but it forged no new ties. The colonies were now independent not only from Britain but also from each other. In the words of the Declaration, the colonies were "free and independent states"—states meaning nations. There was no government to hold them together in war or in peace. But planning for a federal government had already begun. The formation of that federal government is the subject of this chapter.

--- Goals ---

- To learn the main weaknesses of the Articles of Confederation.
- To see how and why our federal Constitution came into being.
- To examine the structure and organization of our federal government.
- To consider the meaning of the term *the people* as used in the Constitution.

THE ARTICLES OF CONFEDERATION (1781–1789)

Even before the Continental Congress adopted the Declaration of Independence, it appointed a committee to draft a constitution. This committee began work in June 1776 to create a "league of friendship and perpetual

Chapter 4: Formation of Our Federal Government

Union." Within a year, it had drawn up a plan for such a league. The plan, which was called the Articles of Confederation, was quickly approved by the Continental Congress. The next step was for each of the thirteen states to approve, or *ratify*, the Articles. This step took much longer. It was 1781 before the Articles went into effect.

The Articles of Confederation were the first national constitution of the former colonies. The Articles had at least two strong points. First, they gave the people a sense of national identification. Instead of being just residents of Massachusetts or Pennsylvania or Virginia, they were now also residents of the United States of America. Pride in their new nation helped to unify the people during the Revolution. Second, the idea of a national government had been born and was winning increasing support.

Yet, the Articles of Confederation provided for a very weak central government. That was what the people wanted. Having seen the dangers of centralized rule from London, they were wary of the dangers of centralized rule from Philadelphia or New York as well.

Few of the nation's leaders were satisfied with the Articles. As time passed, the following weaknesses became evident:

1. Congress was controlled by the state legislatures. The states chose the delegates to Congress annually, paid them, and could recall them at any time.
2. Congress consisted of only one house, in which each state, no matter what its population, had one vote, as each country has in the United Nations today.
3. There was no independent executive or president to carry out the acts of Congress. When Congress was in recess, a Committee of the States made up of one delegate from each state carried on the government.
4. There was no national court system. Enforcement of any laws passed by Congress was up to state courts.
5. Congress had no power to levy or collect taxes.
6. Congress could not regulate trade among the states or with foreign nations.
7. Congress needed the approval of nine of the thirteen states to enter into treaties, borrow or coin money, or decide the size of the armed forces.
8. Congress could not force obedience to its laws or to the Articles of Confederation.
9. The Articles of Confederation could be changed only with the consent of all thirteen states.

Problems Facing the Nation

The young United States had other problems to overcome. True, it had won the War of Independence. Great Britain finally recognized this fact in a treaty of peace signed on February 3, 1783. But how long could the United States keep its independence? Its military forces were limited, and the new nation was deeply in debt.

The debt was a serious problem. The United States had spent $135 million on the war and still owed $40 million to foreign governments and unpaid soldiers in 1787. Congress was not even able to pay interest on the debt. Many states refused to pay their share of the debt, and the Articles of Confederation gave Congress no power to force payment. The financial troubles of the United States threatened its future. It was clear to all that the national government was weak, and growing weaker.

Not only the national government, but many individuals as well, were in debt. Business was in a depression. Many businesses closed. In western Massachusetts, an uprising of farmers threatened to become open rebel-

Chapter 4: Formation of Our Federal Government

Private individuals as well as governments loaned money to help finance the American Revolution. The picture at the left shows Haym Salomon giving funds to Robert Morris, Superintendent of Finance for the war.

Shays's Rebellion in western Massachusetts led to open conflict when farmers tried to storm the arsenal in Springfield.

One way the Americans paid for the Revolution was by printing paper money. Congress issued this bill in 1778.

lion. In a letter to Thomas Jefferson in 1787, Abigail Adams reported that these farmers and others who had land but no money were being "pressed for taxes." At the same time, she said, "those who possessed money were fearful of lending" because they might be paid back in paper money of little value. There were solid reasons for such fears. Some of the states were printing paper money with little to back it. Paper money that Congress had issued during the war was by then worth only one-thousandth of its face value—the amount printed on it. "Not worth a continental" was a common remark for at least a hundred years.

Revising the Articles

Something had to be done, and the legislature of Virginia took the initiative. In 1786, it called for a convention of delegates from each state to discuss ways of making trade rules uniform. Delegates from only five states showed up for the meeting held that September in Annapolis, Maryland. The delegates decided that there ought to be a general meeting of all the states in order to discuss the whole range of problems facing the nation. The Annapolis meeting recommended that Congress call a general convention, and Congress did. In May 1787, delegates began to gather in Philadelphia, Pennsylvania, for a meeting that became known as the Constitutional Convention. Rhode Island boycotted the convention, but the twelve other states were represented.

The Constitutional Convention was intended only to revise the Articles of Confederation. But the revision was so extensive that the delegates produced a new constitution. Like many others, the delegates feared that either anarchy or tyranny lay in store if the Articles of Confederation were not strengthened. The delegates in Philadelphia, however, decided that the Articles could not be strengthened enough. A new framework of government would be necessary.

Abigail Adams spoke out strongly for things she believed in, including the right of women to take part in politics.

Who were these delegates? All were men. As was to be expected in a society where only white people had rights, all were white. Most were from cities, at a time when 90 percent of the people were farmers. Most were well-to-do. And most were well educated. In a nation of mostly rural people with moderate incomes and limited schooling, the delegates were not representative of "the people." They were the elite (uh-LEET)—community leaders such as landowners and lawyers. As a practical matter, who else could afford to take two or three months off for a convention?

As members of the elite, the delegates shared the same basic ideas about government and had a common interest in maintaining order and stability. Most had served in at least one branch of colonial government. For such an important group, they were relatively young. Five were less that 30 years of age and only four had reached the age of 60. The youngest delegate, Jonathan Dayton of New

Jersey, was only 26. The oldest, Benjamin Franklin, was 81.

George Washington presided over the Constitutional Convention. Thomas Jefferson and John Adams were on diplomatic missions in Europe and could not attend. Patrick Henry did not like the idea of a convention and stayed home in Virginia. Samuel Adams and John Hancock were not selected as delegates. Another patriot of the Revolution, Thomas Paine, was away on business in Europe. Among the distinguished patriots who did attend were James Madison, George Mason, and Edmund Randolph of Virginia; William Paterson of New Jersey; Charles Pinckney of South Carolina; and Alexander Hamilton of New York.

On May 25, 1787, delegates appointed by the state legislatures or governors assembled in Independence Hall in Philadelphia. For the next three and a half months, they worked slowly and carefully to put together a new framework of government for the United States.

> **At the Constitutional Convention**
>
> On an average day, thirty or thirty-five delegates would show up at Independence Hall for a session of the Constitutional Convention. In all, fifty-five delegates came to Philadelphia out of seventy-four originally chosen by the state legislatures.
>
> Some delegates left the convention during the summer because they felt that it was exceeding its authority. In their eyes, the only valid purpose of the gathering had been to revise the Articles of Confederation. They did not want to help draft a brand new constitution.
>
> Adapted from Wright Patman, *Our American Government* (1974), p. 11, by permission of Harper & Row.

Questions

1 What were the Articles of Confederation?

2 Of all the weaknesses in the Articles of Confederation, which *three* do you think were the most important?

3 What types of delegates attended the Constitutional Convention of 1787?

◇ Many Americans in 1776 thought it was a good idea to keep the central government weak. Do you agree or disagree with that idea? Explain.

A NEW CONSTITUTION FOR A NEW NATION

The Constitutional Convention got down to work at once. It immediately agreed to keep its proceedings secret. Though the delegates shared the same basic values, they often differed on details, and they did not want to air their disagreements in public. Thus sheltered, the debate was frank and often heated.

The delegates agreed to create a national government that was federal in form. A *federal government* is one in which states join together to form a union and give up some of their power to the central, or national, government. All states, however, remain equal to each other.

Several plans for organizing a federal government were submitted for consideration. Two of them came to be the center of debate. One, proposed by Edmund Randolph of Virginia, is known as the Virginia Plan. The other, sponsored by William Paterson of New Jersey, is known as the New Jersey Plan.

A Process of Compromise

The Virginia and New Jersey plans differed widely on some key points. This was only natural, since they represented the ideas of two opposing interests. The Virginia Plan expressed the desires of the large states with many

Chapter 4: Formation of Our Federal Government

people, and these states tended to be nationalist—that is, in favor of a strong national government. In such a government, they hoped, their large populations would give them a decisive say. The New Jersey Plan, on the other hand, expressed the desires of the smaller states, which wanted to keep most powers in the hands of the states.

Here is what the Virginia Plan called for:

1. A strong national legislature with two houses. The larger house was to be elected by the people. The smaller house—called a Senate after the ancient Roman Senate—was to be elected by the lower house from persons nominated by state legislatures. The number of seats in each house was to be based chiefly on population.
2. A strong national executive and a strong national judiciary, both to be appointed by the national legislature.
3. More power for the national legislature. This would include the power to bar any state laws that conflicted with national law.

Here is what the New Jersey Plan called for:

1. Maintaining the essential feature of the Articles of Confederation—a single-house legislature with one vote for each state.
2. A national executive with little power and a weak national judiciary.
3. Somewhat more power for Congress, including a limited power to tax.

The chart opposite illustrates the main provisions of the two plans.

The debate grew hot. The convention was deadlocked for weeks as both sides refused to budge. *The key point at issue was how to determine representation in Congress.* Supporters of the Virginia Plan argued that the new federal government should get its authority mainly from the people. The more people a state had, the greater should be its strength in the national government. The trouble with the Articles of Confederation, the large states argued, was that small states and large states had equal voices. The small states, in contrast, liked that feature of the Articles. They feared that they would have little say in a new national government based on the Virginia Plan. On major issues such as tax laws, the large states would be able to outvote the small states.

A constitution was finally agreed upon after a series of compromises, mainly between large and small states. The two sides settled their differences by *compromising*—a process of give and take. Each side made some concessions in order to get part of what it wanted.

The key compromise, called the Connecticut Compromise, was worked out by a committee on which the Connecticut delegates played a major role. On the question of the legislature, the Connecticut Compromise leaned toward the larger states and a strong national government. It proposed a *bicameral legislature*—a lawmaking body with two houses. Representation in the lower house would be based on population. All revenue laws—those dealing with money and taxes—would begin in the lower house. But the plan also had something to please the small states. The upper house, or Senate, would not be based on population. Instead, it would have two members from each state. Moreover, that feature was to be "locked in." The constitution would specify that no change could ever be made in that feature unless all of the states consented.

A second compromise settled another controversy over representation. This disagreement had to do with the counting of slaves. Were they to be counted the same as free persons in determining how many representatives each state should have in the lower house? The Southern states said yes, because that would give them a greater voice. But what about taxes? If the federal government should

Chapter 4: Formation of Our Federal Government

The Virginia Plan and the New Jersey Plan Compared

THE LEGISLATIVE BRANCH

A two-house legislature with one house larger than the other.	A one-house legislature.
Number of members for each state in each house to be based on the population of the state.	Each state to have one vote.
Members of the larger house to be elected by the voters. Members of the smaller house to be nominated by the state legislatures and elected by the larger house.	All members to be chosen by state legislatures.

THE EXECUTIVE BRANCH

One executive—a President—to carry out laws passed by the federal legislature.	Two or more executives to carry out the laws passed by the federal legislature.
President to be chosen by the federal legislature.	Executives to be chosen by the federal legislature.
President to serve one term.	Executives to serve one term.

THE JUDICIAL BRANCH

A supreme court and lesser courts.	A supreme court only.
Judges to be appointed by the federal legislature.	Judges to be appointed by the executive branch.
Judges to serve for life.	Judges to serve for life.

THE STATES

Federal government to admit new states.	Federal government to admit new states.
Federal government to have power to declare illegal any state laws that might conflict with federal laws.	Federal government to have power to declare illegal any state laws that might conflict with federal laws.

impose a tax based on population, would the slaves be counted the same as free persons? Clearly, that would mean higher taxes for the Southern states. So on this question, the Southern states said no. Northern states, meanwhile, took the opposite position since there were not many slaves in the North. The Northern states wanted the slaves counted for tax purposes but not for representation.

The solution was the Three-Fifths Compromise. A slave would count as three-fifths of a free person—both for tax purposes and for representation. That way, the North and the South each got part of what it wanted.

Chapter 4: Formation of Our Federal Government

The Constitutional Convention in session, George Washington presiding. The delegates met in Independence Hall, where the Declaration of Independence had been signed. The building is now part of a National Historical Park in Philadelphia.

A third major compromise balanced various sectional interests on commerce and the slave trade. Commerce—which is another word for trade—can take place either within a single state *(intrastate commerce)* or between two or more states *(interstate commerce)*. It can also take place between one country and another country *(foreign trade)*. Everyone agreed that the states should retain control over *intrastate* commerce. The question was how to deal with interstate commerce and foreign trade.

Northern delegates wanted the new federal government to have full power over interstate commerce and foreign trade. Southern delegates did not. The Southerners feared, for one thing, that the federal government might decide to end the slave trade. They also feared that business interests in the North might have enough votes to enter into treaties or agreements with other countries that would hurt the South's farmers.

A compromise was worked out. The federal government got the power to regulate interstate commerce and foreign trade. But Congress would not be allowed to abolish the slave trade for at least 20 years, until 1807. And any treaty with a foreign country would need the approval of at least two-thirds of the Senate before it could go into effect.

Finally the delegates completed their "bundle of compromises." By September 15, 1787, they had agreed on both the general principles and the details of the new constitution. They signed the new document, and after a farewell dinner together at Philadelphia's City Tavern, they headed home. They had earned the title of Founders of the nation.

Basic Principles of the Constitution

The new Constitution of the United States included certain principles that are basic to our system of government. The Founders had drawn these principles from many sources in their political heritage. Following are the most important.

No person is ever to be above the law. The Founders sought to create a government of laws, not of individuals. For that reason, they tried to make certain that no government official could ever obtain unchecked power.

The federal government is to be based on the separation of powers. The government is divided into three branches—legislative, executive, and judicial. (See the chart on page 72.) The legislative branch has the power to make laws and to oversee the activities of the other branches. The executive branch has the power to carry out the laws and to direct the nation's relations with other countries. The judicial branch has the power to see that the laws and the manner of their enforcement conform to the Constitution.

A system of checks and balances is to prevent the concentration of power in one branch or one individual. This was a direct application of the ideas of Montesquieu. Each branch of government was to have the power to either block or overturn certain actions of other branches.

Ratification of the Constitution

The delegates to the Constitutional Convention had completed only part of their work. The other part was to see that the Constitution was ratified by the states. Since most of the delegates had signed their names to the Constitution, they led the fight for approval. Those few delegates who opposed the Constitution tried to rally opinion against it.

At first, it appeared that those supporting the Constitution had the tougher job. Probably, most people had been expecting merely a revision of the old Articles of Confederation and were opposed to the new plan of government. But a far-ranging national debate changed many minds. Besides, it was not really necessary to convince a majority of the people

Chapter 4: Formation of Our Federal Government

The Three Branches of Our Federal Government as Provided for in the United States Constitution

LEGISLATIVE BRANCH

Congress.

Made up of two houses, one larger than the other.

Number of members from each state in larger house (House of Representatives) to depend on the state's population. In the smaller house (Senate), each state to have two members.

How Chosen
Voters to elect members of larger house. State legislatures to elect members of smaller house (but changed in 1913, to election by voters).

Main Role
To make laws.

Checks and Balances
To see that executive branch carries out laws.

To have power to override a President's veto.

To have power of impeachment of officials in all three branches for wrongdoing. House to impeach (indict) an official, and Senate to try the official.

Senate to approve major officials appointed by President.

Senate to approve treaties made by President.

EXECUTIVE BRANCH

President to be chief executive.

Executive branch also to include Vice President and appointed officials.

How Chosen
President and Vice President to be elected indirectly by the voters.

Main Role
To enforce laws passed by legislative branch.

President also to appoint major officials; to make treaties with foreign countries; and to command armed forces.

Checks and Balances
To have power to veto laws passed by legislative branch.

To appoint judges in the judicial branch.

JUDICIAL BRANCH

A supreme court and lower federal courts.

How Chosen
President appoints judges.

Main Role
To try to all cases arising under the Constitution, under laws of the United States, and under treaties.

Checks and Balances
The power to try cases as noted above conveys power to decide if either legislative or executive branch has exceeded its authority.

The mural above shows James Madison, one of the leaders of the Constitutional Convention, presenting the Constitution to George Washington. The drawing below makes the point that other states will ratify now that nine have done so.

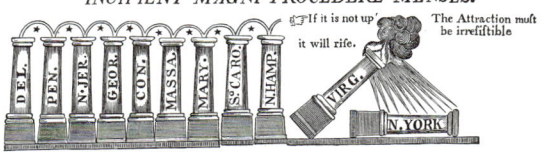

to support the new pact, since there was no public vote on the matter. Instead, as the Constitution itself provided, each state held a convention to consider the new document. The approval of only nine of the thirteen state conventions was required by the Constitution before it could go into effect. You will recall that the Articles of Confederation required approval of any amendment by *all* states. It is not suprising that some people questioned the legality of actions taken at the Constitutional Convention.

People had thought long and hard about how a central government should be run. It had been more than 10 years since the Declaration of Independence. Now, all of the arguments began to come into focus as the nation divided into two camps. Those who favored the new Constitution were called Federalists. Those who opposed it were called Anti-Federalists. Few seemed to be neutral.

The Federalists drew their greatest strength from seaboard and city regions because their arguments appealed strongly to business people and the wealthy. The Anti-Federalists voiced the fears of farmers and inland settlers. But the lines were not rigid. Many city and business people shared the doubts of the Anti-Federalists.

Opponents of the Constitution feared the power of a strong central government. They believed that their own state governments could best protect their interests. For this reason, they wanted to keep the main powers in the hands of the states. The opponents also argued that the federal government might take away the rights they had won in the Revolution. They pointed out that nowhere in the Constitution were those rights spelled out. Ratification of this document, some said, would lead to the "destruction of freedom."

The Federalists believed that the Anti-Federalists were mistaken. The greatest danger, they maintained, was not tyranny but "the dismemberment of the Union." Only a strong national government could defend the nation's interests abroad and protect it from division at home, they argued.

How the States Voted on the Constitution

	State	Date of Vote	For	Against
1	Delaware	December 7, 1787	30	0
2	Pennsylvania	December 12, 1787	46	23
3	New Jersey	December 18, 1787	38	0
4	Georgia	January 2, 1788	26	0
5	Connecticut	January 9, 1788	128	40
6	Massachusetts	February 6, 1788	187	168
7	Maryland	April 28, 1788	63	11
8	South Carolina	May 23, 1788	149	73
9	New Hampshire	June 21, 1788	57	47
10	Virginia	June 25, 1788	89	79
11	New York	July 26, 1788	30	27
12	North Carolina	November 21, 1789	194	77
13	Rhode Island	May 29, 1790	34	32

The Federalist arguments were forcefully made in a series of essays written by Alexander Hamilton, James Madison, and John Jay. The essays first appeared in a New York newspaper and were later published with the title *The Federalist*. Today they are regarded as the key to the ideas of the framers of the Constitution.

Much bargaining went on as the two sides sought to win converts from each other. One strategy used by some Federalists was to propose that a Bill of Rights be added to the Constitution after ratification. Hamilton argued against this idea in *The Federalist,* but the proposal caught on. It answered one of the arguments of the Anti-Federalists and helped sway some votes.

All through the winter of 1787–1788, the battle raged. One state after another held its ratification convention. By June 1788, nine states had ratified—enough to put the new constitution into effect. Three more states ratified the pact that summer, but it was 1790 before the last state, Rhode Island, agreed to the Constitution. (See the chart above.)

In the meantime, Congress set to work to prepare for the new system of government and selected New York as a temporary capital. Later, the seat of government would move to Philadelphia. Only in 1800 would Washington, D.C., become the nation's permanent capital.

Congress also made plans for the nation's first elections. George Washington, well known and widely popular, was the clear choice as the first President. John Adams was elected Vice President. The only real races for office were for the seats in Congress. Those races were mostly over local issues. Twenty-two Senators and fifty-nine Representatives were elected. On March 4, 1789, they met for the first time in Federal Hall on Wall Street in New York.

The great experiment had begun. Here was a representative democracy covering a large area and based on a written constitution. And this constitution would be the highest law in the land. Would the great experiment work? That is the subject of the rest of this book.

Questions

1 Generally speaking, what did the following wish to put into a new constitution?
    a the large states
    b the small states
    c the Southern states
    d the Northern states

Chapter 4: Formation of Our Federal Government

2 How were the wishes of each of these kinds of states settled? Explain your answer with examples.

3 How did the Constitution provide for a system of checks and balances? Cite *two* examples for each branch of government.

4 What single argument seemed to be most important in persuading the states to ratify the Constitution?

⬠ The Constitution would not have been possible without compromise. Do you think there are any political principles that could *never* be compromised? Explain.

PROBLEM: WHAT DOES THE CONSTITUTION MEAN BY "THE PEOPLE"?

The Constitution of 1787 remains the basis of our system of federal government today. But many of the words or terms used in the Constitution now have new shades of meaning. In the following section, we will examine one of those terms: *the people*. As you read, ask yourself:

- *What did* the people *mean to the framers of the Constitution?*
- *What do we mean today when we speak of* the people?

"We, the People"

The preamble, or opening, to the United States Constitution is very brief. Here is what it says:

We, the people of the United States, in Order to form a more perfect Union,

Barbara Jordan gained national attention for her role in the 1970s hearings on the impeachment of President Nixon.

In Praise of the Constitution

One public figure who has often expressed a strong belief in the United States Constitution is Barbara Jordan. In 1977, when she was a member of Congress from Texas, she was interviewed by *Senior Scholastic*. One question was:

What makes you think the Constitution, a 200-year-old document, is workable today?

Her answer:

We know that in 1787, when the Constitution was approved, the drafters did not contemplate that it would take care of the rights of every citizen of this country. But that Constitution was elastic enough to meet demands as they occurred in the country's life and development. And so I praise the Constitution as a document which is flexible enough to adjust to the times we're in. It's been workable for 200 years. There's no reason it won't be workable for another 50 or 100.

From an interview with Barbara Jordan, *Senior Scholastic*, October 6, 1977. Reprinted by permission of Scholastic Magazines, Inc. from *Senior Scholastic*. Copyright © 1977 by Scholastic Magazines, Inc.

George Washington, shown at his second inauguration as President, formed the powers and traditions of the office.

establish Justice, insure domestic Tranquility [peace], provide for the common defense, promote the general Welfare, and secure the Blessings of Liberty to ourselves and our posterity [future generations] do ordain and establish this Constitution for the United States of America.

The writers of the Constitution felt that "the people" should establish the new federal government. There had been no similar preamble to the Articles of Confederation. It was the thirteen states—not the people—that had established that first plan for a central government. But just what did those words "the people" mean?

At the first census, in 1790, the United States had fewer than 4 million inhabitants. A majority of them could neither vote nor hold office for two main reasons.

First, whole classes of people were excluded altogether from the political process because of their age, sex, or race. They could not vote, nor could they hold office. Those completely excluded were Native Americans, males under the age of 21, slaves, and indentured servants. (*Indentured servants* were persons—usually European immigrants—who had signed a contract to work for a period of years in return for their passage to the New World.) Women could vote in New Jersey. Elsewhere, voting and office holding were limited to adult males. In the South, only adult white males could vote. In some Northern states, free black men could also vote.

Second, in addition to age, sex, and race, all states imposed another test. Voters and office-holders had to either own a certain amount of property or pay a certain amount in state or local taxes. Thus, the poor could not vote.

As a result, only 5 or 6 percent of the new nation's population took part in voting for the delegates to the ratifying conventions. In fact, even many of those who were eligible to vote did not do so.

Moreover, the people had had no direct say in choosing the framers of the Constitution. Delegates to the Constitutional Convention were chosen by state legislatures or state governors.

Some observers have seen this as a serious fault. They argue that the government set up by the Constitution was not democratic because it did not represent "the people." It represented only wealthy, influential, white men, the argument goes. If all citizens of the new nation had been allowed to vote on the Constitution, some have said, it would never have passed.

Others, however, defend the Constitution as the cornerstone of United States democracy. They say it is wrong to judge eighteenth-century politics by today's standards. For its day, the Constitution was a democratic document, according to this argument. Limitations on the right to vote were part of the American heritage with its roots in the governments of ancient Greece and Rome and the colonial legislatures. The true strength of the Constitution, say the supporters of this argument, is that it has been able to accommodate change.

Today, there are no longer any property qualifications for voting in national elections. Native Americans and blacks can vote. So can women. The legal age for voting has been lowered to 18. All of these changes were made by legal and constitutional processes. At each stage, the qualified voters and their representatives decided to expand the right to participate in our political system.

Questions

1 How were delegates selected for the Constitutional Convention?

2 Generally, which groups could not vote or hold public office in 1790?

3 What did "we, the people" mean in the United States in 1787 as compared with ancient Greece and Rome? As compared with England under King John?

⌂ What do you think should be the meaning of the term *the people?*

Chapter 4 Review

Developing Your Political Vocabulary

Use each of the following in a sentence about the formation of the United States Constitution.

- **a** confederation
- **b** convention
- **c** delegates
- **d** federal
- **e** compromises
- **f** amendment
- **g** intrastate
- **h** interstate
- **i** checks and balances
- **j** ratification

Recalling and Comparing

1 Name *two* important ideas in the Constitution that were not parts of the Articles of Confederation.

2 What was the most important objection by Anti-Federalists to the Constitution? Do you think it would be a valid objection to the Constitution today? Explain.

3 Refer to the table of state votes on the Constitution (page 74). How could you account for the overwhelming approval of the Constitution in some states and the close vote in others?

4 Do you think it would have made any difference if a few votes had shifted in Virginia, New York, and Rhode Island so that a majority in those states opposed the Constitution? Why or why not?

Special Activities

1 Prepare a skit in which advocates of the Virginia Plan and the New Jersey Plan argue their positions with one another.

2 Make a special bulletin-board display that shows illustrations of the people who took part in the Constitutional Convention of 1787.

3 Compare and contrast the government systems set up in the Articles of Confederation and the United Nations. Summarize your findings in a chart.

4 Make a study of Shays's Rebellion—the rebellion of farmers in Massachusetts in 1786–1787—and the steps taken to restore order. Give your opinions of the actions taken by the farmers and the authorities.

5 Study the problems created by the printing of paper money in the states after the Revolution. Report your findings to the class.

6 Write a biographical sketch about one of the delegates to the Constitutional Convention. In your biography, include information on how the delegate felt about forming a new national government.

7 Make a study of the political ideas of Abigail Adams including her opinions about women's rights. Report your findings to the class.

8 Read selections from *The Federalist* and find examples of arguments that appeal to reason.

9 Prepare a chart listing arguments of Federalists and Anti-Federalists for and against ratification of the Constitution. Do library research in order to find as many arguments as possible.

10 Consider what might be arguments for and against the following statement: "Political compromises may often be necessary to avoid serious problems." Then decide whether you agree or disagree with the statement. What are your reasons?

Unit I Review

Improving Your Reading

Read the selection below and then answer the questions that follow it.

Our earliest political heritage comes from the ancient Middle East. The Amorites, for example, with the Code of Hammurabi, provided us with the idea of a code of specific laws. The Hebrews, in the Old Testament, left us a code of strict laws for moral conduct.

The ancient Greeks gave us the idea of democracy. Some Greek city-states practiced a form of direct democracy. Under it, all eligible voters assembled each year to choose leaders and decide what they wanted their leaders to do for them.

The Romans provided us with the idea of a republic, a system in which the people elect representatives to carry on the work of government. The Roman system led to today's forms of representative governments. The Romans also developed law systems.

Many ideas about government from the ancient world were taken over by the peoples of Western Europe. By 1400, for example, the English Parliament was using some of the earlier ideas of representative democracy. Similarly, codes of civil and criminal law had appeared in some European countries.

A number of Europeans carried on the Greek and Roman practice of writing about how governments ought to work. They studied actual governments, past and present, and tried to imagine the best government possible. Political thinkers like Thomas Hobbes, John Locke, Jean-Jacques Rousseau, and the Baron de Montesquieu had a great influence on the formation of the United States.

Many ideas from Europe were put into practice in the English colonies in America. The Pilgrims, for example, made an agreement for self-government in their Mayflower Compact. The Virginia House of Burgesses introduced representative democracy to this country. A system of representative democracy and separation of powers eventually became part of our federal government.

But the colonists began to find fault with British rule. They thought they were being deprived of their rights and they accused King George III of becoming a tyrant.

With the clash between colonists and British soldiers at Lexington and Concord in 1775, a War for Independence began. The thirteen colonies soon joined together to fight the British. They organized the Continental Army and made George Washington its commander in chief.

The Declaration of Independence in 1776 set forth the colonists' ideas about self-rule. The Declaration vowed to create "government by the people." It borrowed this and other ideas from earlier political thinkers. Such ideas were no longer to be just theory, but actual practice.

The early years of the United States were a time of debate and experiment. The Articles of Confederation were tried and found too weak to be a workable plan of national government. A new constitution was written in 1787 to replace the Articles. This Constitution of the United States went into effect in 1789. It has proved remarkably sturdy and, as amended,

Unit 1 Review: Our Political Heritage

remains the basis of our federal government today.

1 In your own words, summarize this reading in *no more than five* sentences. Your summary should consist of what you regard as the most important points made in the reading.

2 Which *two* of the following types of government are best described as self-government?
- **a** the government of ancient Amorites
- **b** the government of ancient Hebrews
- **c** the government of some ancient Greek city-states
- **d** our federal government

3 Which *one* of the following records is best described as the first written contract for government in the colonies?
- **a** Constitution
- **b** Articles of Confederation
- **c** Mayflower Compact
- **d** Declaration of Independence

Developing Your Writing Skills: What Are Your Attitudes toward Government?

By now you are aware that studying government is one means of political socialization. In your government classroom, you have been learning about this country's political life. At the same time, you have been forming your own attitudes toward it.

At the end of each unit of this book, you will be given an opportunity to express your attitudes as you have formed them up to that point. In Chapters 1–4, you studied some of the main political ideas we inherited from the past. Think back over those ideas and try to decide what your life might be like if our system of government lacked those ideas as its underpinning.

Now decide whether or not our political heritage has any meaning for *you*, and why. Prepare to write your thoughts down in a paragraph on a separate sheet of paper. This paragraph should begin with a *topic sentence* telling what the paragraph is about. Copy the topic sentence below, using either *does* or *does not*, according to your own opinion. The rest of your paragraph should be made up of sentences that give evidence or arguments to support your topic sentence.

My political heritage (does/does not) have meaning for me.

Recommended Reading

Edward S. Corwin and J. W. Peltason: *Understanding the Constitution,* Holt, New York, 1973.

Steward C. Easton: *The Heritage of the Ancient World,* Holt, New York, 1970.

Jeanette Eaton: *Lone Journey: The Life of Roger Williams,* Harcourt Brace Jovanovich, New York, 1944.

Greece and Rome: Builders of Our World, National Geographic Society, Washington, D.C., 1968.

Earl Latham (ed.).: *The Declaration of Independence and the Constitution,* Heath, Lexington, Mass., 1976 (paperback).

Richard B. Morris: *Seven Who Shaped Our Destiny: The Founding Fathers as Revolutionaries,* Harper & Row, New York, 1973.

Katherine E. Wilkie: *Father of the Constitution: James Madison,* Messner, New York, 1963.

René A. Wormser: *The Story of the Law,* Simon & Schuster, New York, 1962.

The Legislative Branch of the National Government

UNIT II

The arrival of a new President in Washington is a major public event. The arrival of a new member of the legislative branch of the federal government is hardly noticed by the public. Yet for the new senator or representative, the step from home to Congress marks a turning point in life. It was as true in 1969 as it is today.

On April 1, 1969, there was a special election in Wisconsin to fill a seat vacated in the United States House of Representatives. That seat had been vacated by Republican Melvin R. Laird, who had resigned in January to become President Richard Nixon's Secretary of Defense. The race to succeed him fell to Walter J. Chilsen, a 45-year-old Republican, and David R. Obey, a 30-year-old Democrat. Obey polled 63,567 votes to Chilsen's 59,512.

Two days later, on April 3, the Obeys—David and Joan—flew to Washington, D.C. They were met at National Airport by former Vice President Hubert Humphrey. "This is the greatest thing since Coca-Cola," said Humphrey, hustling Obey over to the Capitol to be sworn in as the youngest member of the House of Representatives.

Adapted from *To Be a Congressman,* copyright © 1973 by Sven Groenings and Jonathan P. Hawley, Acropolis Books, Washington, D. C., pp. 24–26.

At 30 years of age, David Obey was beginning a new and very demanding job. He would have to speak and act for thousands of people. He would be representing those who voted for him, those who voted for his opponent, and those who did not vote at all.

As a member of Congress, Obey would be called on to take a stand on many of the nation's needs and problems. He would have to work with hundreds of other members, many of whom had ideas different from his own. He would be heaped with advice and flooded with demands from his district. But, first of all, Obey would have to begin finding his way around.

In this unit, you will begin to find your way around Congress. The first chapter deals with the structure and powers of Congress. Then, in the next chapter, you will see how Congress uses its powers.

Chapter 5

The Congress of the United States

There have been other Congresses. The First Continental Congress met in 1774. The Second Continental Congress began its meetings in 1775. But the Congress that now meets in Washington, D.C., is the Congress of the United States. It was created by the framers of the Constitution.

"All legislative powers shall be vested in a Congress of the United States." Those are the words of Article I. Thus, in establishing separation of powers, the Founders gave the lawmaking power to Congress. Article I goes on to say that Congress "shall consist of a Senate and a House of Representatives." Together, the 535 citizens who serve in the two houses of Congress make all the federal laws for the nation's 220,000,000 people. The regulations of federal agencies are not called laws, though they have the force of law.

This chapter will focus on the form and powers of Congress. It will then turn to some related problems.

Goals

- To learn the basic structure of Congress.
- To learn the powers of Congress and the special powers of the House and the Senate.
- To consider the necessity for requiring members of Congress to report their incomes and financial holdings.

Chapter 5: The Congress of the United States

AN OVERVIEW OF CONGRESS

At noon on January 3 of every odd-numbered year, a new Congress meets in Washington, D.C. The First Congress of the United States met in 1789. The Second Congress of the United States met in 1791. Since the life of every Congress is 2 years, the 97th Congress meets in 1981, the 98th in 1983, and so forth.

Each Congress has two sittings, or *sessions,* in its 2-year life. All meetings of the First Congress in 1789 were part of its first session, and all of its meetings in 1790 were part of its second session. During each session, there are recesses for holidays and vacations.

Our federal Congress has two houses. This division into two parts resulted from a struggle among the framers of the Constitution.

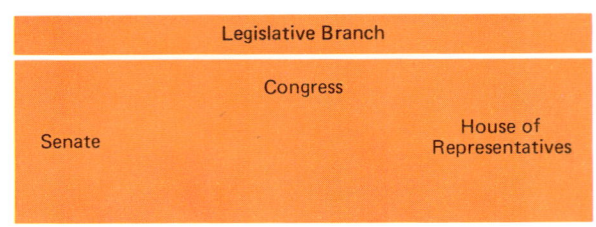

Early in each session, the members of Congress hear the President's State of the Union Message.

Chapter 5: The Congress of the United States

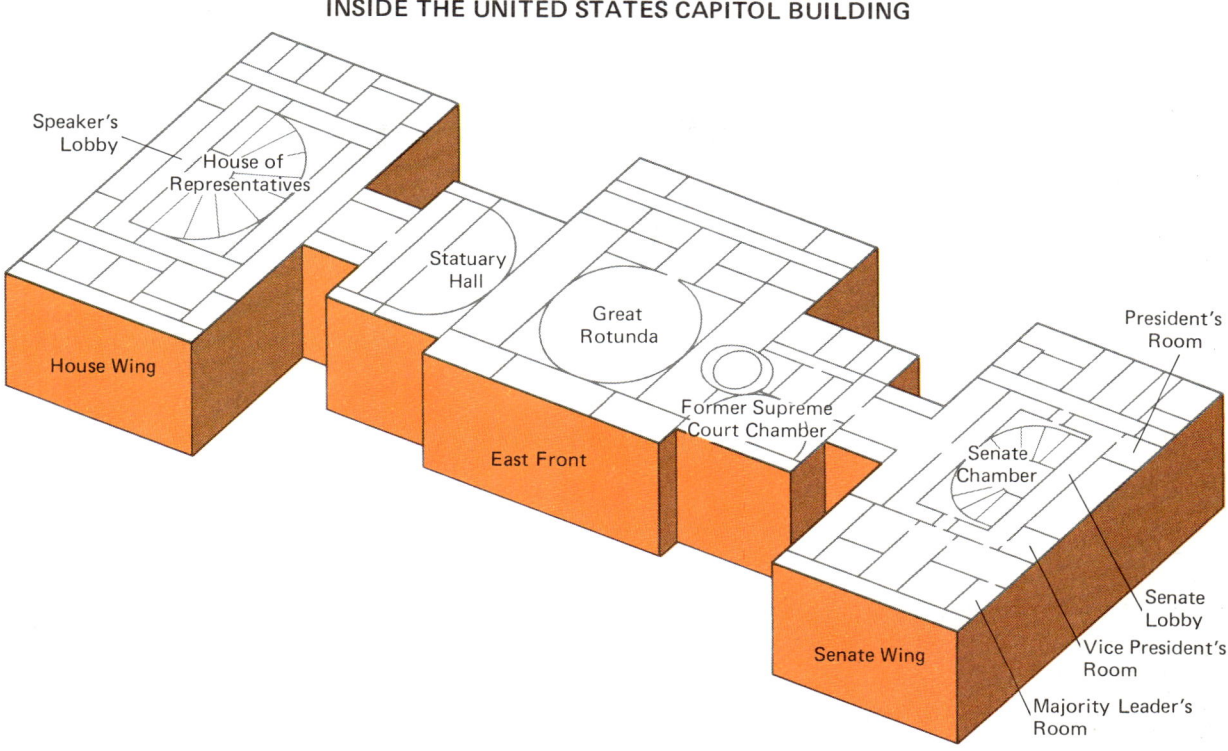

INSIDE THE UNITED STATES CAPITOL BUILDING

The states that had many people wanted each state's number of members in Congress to be decided on the basis of population. The states with fewer people felt they would be swallowed up if that were done. As a compromise, two houses were formed. In this way, it was possible to give all states an equal voice in one house—the Senate—and to give states with larger populations a greater voice in the other house—the House of Representatives. Each house could also serve as a check on the other.

Each house remains in session until its members vote to *adjourn*, to stop business for a time. The Constitution forbids either house to adjourn for more than 3 days without the consent of the other. Once Congress has adjourned, only the President can call a special session.

The Capitol Building in Washington is the meeting place of Congress. The location of the House and Senate chambers, or meeting rooms can be seen on the diagram above, where you will find the House chamber at the left and the Senate chamber at right.

Representatives and senators often work away from the Capitol. They spend much time in their nearby office buildings. They may leave Washington for meetings with informed people. Fact-finding trips may be necessary, as part of the lawmaking process. Members also must keep in touch with their *constituents*—the people who live in their district or state—and try to help them in various ways. Finally, the members of Congress who want to run for re-

Population of the United States:	220,000,000
Congress of the United States:	535
Representatives	435
Senators	100

Chapter 5: The Congress of the United States

election—as most do—must take steps to make this possible.

Powers of Congress

How much power should Congress have? The framers of the Constitution wanted to increase the power of the central government. But they felt that the main power should stay with the state and local governments. Experience under Great Britain had taught the colonists the dangers of being governed from a distance.

Directly or indirectly, much of this book will be about the powers of Congress. This is because Congress makes the laws of the land. Here we will examine the powers that the Founders gave Congress in 1787. Those powers have been added to and subtracted from by *amendments,* or changes, to the Constitution. We will take up amendments in a later unit (Unit V).

The first article of the Constitution spells out what kinds of laws Congress may and may not make. The powers granted and denied to Congress in Article I are summarized in the chart below. Article I refers to both houses. As we shall see later, the Constitution also grants certain powers to each house alone.

Powers of Congress under Article I of the Constitution

Powers Granted (Section 8)

1. To fix and collect taxes, to pay the nation's debts, and to provide for its defense and general welfare	These taxes include *customs duties* and *tariffs,* both of which are taxes on imports, and *excises,* which are taxes on goods and services made, sold, or used within a country.
2. To borrow money	
3. To regulate commerce with other countries, among the states, and with "the Indian Tribes"	*Commerce,* in a general sense, is trade.
4. To make laws dealing with naturalization and bankruptcy	*Naturalization* is the admitting of a foreigner to citizenship. *Bankruptcy* is inability to pay one's debts.
5. To coin money and fix its value, and to fix the standard of weights and measures	To *coin money* is to make coins. The Supreme Court has held, however, that this clause also includes the printing of paper money.
6. To provide for the punishment of counterfeiters	*Counterfeiters* are people who unlawfully make coins, print money, or print federal bonds or notes.
7. To establish post offices and post roads	
8. To grant authors and inventors exclusive rights to their works for a limited time	The grant of an exclusive right to an author is a *copyright.* The grant of such a right to an inventor is a *patent.*
9. To create courts having less power than the United States Supreme Court	*Continued on next page*

Chapter 5: The Congress of the United States

10. To define and punish crimes committed at sea or against international law
11. To declare war, to grant letters of marque and reprisal, and to make laws concerning captures at sea

    Letters of marque and reprisal are papers permitting ships to attack enemy ships.

12. To raise and support armies
13. To provide and maintain a navy
14. To make laws regulating land and naval forces
15. To provide for calling out the militia in order to enforce federal laws, put down insurrections, and drive back foreign invasions

    Militia are state units of the National Guard. *Insurrections* are rebellions.

16. To provide for organizing, arming, and disciplining the militia and for controlling its members when they are on federal duty
17. To govern and administer the District of Columbia and all federal property
18. To make all laws necessary and proper for carrying out the foregoing powers

Powers Denied (Section 9)

1. To suspend the writ of *habeas corpus* except for public safety during a rebellion or a foreign invasion

    A writ of *habeas corpus* (HAY-be-us KOR-pus) is a court order requiring a prisoner to be brought before a court so that the judge may decide whether the prisoner is being held lawfully.

2. To pass any bill of attainder

    A *bill of attainder* is a law punishing a person without trial or improperly stripping someone of personal property.

3. To pass any *ex post facto* law

    An *ex post facto law* is one that makes something a crime *after* it has been done.

4. To pass any direct tax unless it is related to the size of each state's population

    A *direct tax* is one that is paid directly to the government by the person taxed.

5. To place any tax on exports from any state
6. To pass any trade law that favors one state over another
7. To take any money from the federal treasury without appropriations made by law

    An *appropriation* is a sum of money set apart for some special use.

8. To grant any title of nobility

Chapter 5: The Congress of the United States

The Constitution expressly gives Congress the power to "raise and support Armies" and to "provide and maintain a Navy." Congress used its implied powers to establish the Air Force. President Jimmy Carter is shown visiting the Nebraska headquarters of the Strategic Air Command, one arm of the United States Air Force.

As the chart shows, the lawmaking powers of Congress are set out in two sections of Article I. Section 8 sets out the powers granted. Section 9 sets out the powers denied. There are eighteen clauses in Section 8. The first seventeen name specific kinds of laws that Congress can make. These clauses contain the stated powers, or *expressed powers,* of Congress.

In studying the chart, you will see that Congress has a variety of powers, some more general than others. One important group of powers relates to money. Congress may levy taxes (Clause 1*), borrow money (Clause 2), and coin money (Clause 5). Another important group of powers relates to war and national defense. Congress may declare war (Clause 11) and maintain armed forces (Clauses 12, 13, 14). In the words of the Constitution, Congress may also "provide for the common defense" of the United States (Clause 1).

Clause 1 gives Congress the broad power to provide for "the general welfare" of the United States. Another broad power is expressed in Clause 3. This power to "regulate commerce" has proved to be broader than it might seem. As industry grew, so did the meaning of *commerce*—and, in turn, the powers of Congress under Clause 3.

Broad as some of the expressed powers may be, none is as broad as the power granted Congress in Clause 18 of Section I. Clause 18 gives Congress the right to make all laws needed to carry out the powers set down in the other seventeen clauses. As we shall see, the Supreme Court later based an important decision on this clause. The Court held that Clause 18 gave Congress *implied powers*. The powers in Clause 18 are *implied powers* because they are indicated rather than stated. From time to time in the history of our country, Congress has decided that it was "necessary and proper" to act under Clause 18 in order to meet new needs. This is how it was possible to create the United States Air Force in 1947, for example, though the Constitution does not mention an air force. Because its meaning can be stretched, Clause 18 is known as the *elastic clause.*

Through its power to make laws, Congress has gained other important powers. Two are central to its effective functioning. One is the power to carry on investigations. The need to find out whether or not laws are required explains this *investigative power*. The second central power is the power to see that laws are put into effect. This means that Congress can check on the executive branch to see that laws are properly executed. This is called the *legislative oversight power*. Both of these powers are carried out largely by congressional committees in hearings on proposed legislation.

Several powers are denied Congress by Article I, as the chart shows. This is mainly because the framers of the Constitution wanted to avoid abuses of power. That explains why Congress cannot suspend the writ of *habeas corpus* or pass any bill of attainder or any *ex post facto* law. The people in this country felt that the British colonial government had abused its power in these ways.

Article I also forbids any direct tax unless it is related to the size of a state's population. For example, Congress could not levy a tax on property unless the tax was shared among the states according to their population. Whether an income tax is a direct tax is open to question. Because the Supreme Court had decided earlier that it is, Congress proposed an amendment to the Constitution early in the twentieth century to make an income tax possible. The income-tax amendment is Amendment XVI, which became effective in 1913.

Article V gives Congress the power to propose amendments to the Constitution. At least two-thirds of the members of both houses must vote to propose an amendment. State legislatures may also request amendments. (See Chapter 13.)

---

* For convenience, the clauses are numbered in discussing them. They are not numbered in the Constitution itself.

Privileges of members of Congress include eating in the congressional dining room, where prices are generally lower than in other restaurants. Senator Inouye's frank, or printed signature, on the envelope below is an example of the franking privilege, available for members' letters about official business.

Chapter 5: The Congress of the United States

This review of the powers of Congress leaves much to be discussed in later pages. As noted, individual amendments remain to be discussed. Supreme Court rulings will be discussed further in Chapters 11 and 16.

Allowances and Privileges of Members

Besides their salaries, members of Congress receive a number of benefits (see chart). These include office space and money for legislative assistants, or *aides,* and other office staff. Because they have to maintain contact with their home districts or states, members of Congress maintain two offices and two homes. A tax deduction is allowed for the second home. Travel allowances are given for trips between the two places. Money is also available for trips in order to study needs for legislation. Members of Congress have to file reports of their expenditures.

The Constitution states that members of Congress may not be sued for what they say in either house. This freedom of speech and writing holds only for statements made in Congress. It does not mean that the members may say what they please in public without fear of censure or lawsuit. The Constitution also gives representatives and senators limited protection from arrest while attending sessions of Congress.

Records of Congressional Actions

What happens in Congress is on public record. Each house publishes minutes of its proceedings in a *Journal.* Votes together with speeches—often in revised form and with additions—are printed daily in the *Congressional Record* for the public to see. Committees publish their findings and hearings. Many large libraries have committee reports. Some libraries have files of the *Congressional Record* going back to the Continental Congress.

Allowances and Privileges of Members of Congress

Allowances and Benefits

1. Salary of $57,500 a year
2. Pension (to which members contribute) and insurance
3. Free medical service in military hospitals
4. $3,000 tax deduction for maintaining a home in Washington
5. Free office space in Washington and in home state or district
6. Salaries of office staff (varying according to the size of state or district)
7. Free use of the mails for official letters (the "franking privilege")
8. Sums for office supplies, telephone calls, and telegrams
9. Travel allowances for trips between home and Washington (twelve trips per session for representatives, six for senators)
10. Free use of armed forces transportation and free foreign travel

Privileges

1. Freedom from arrest—except for breach of the peace, major crime, or treason—while attending or traveling to or from a session of Congress
2. Freedom from lawsuit for statements made in Congress

Questions

1 How long is the term of a Congress?

2 How many sessions are there in a term of Congress?

3 What are some important powers granted to Congress in Article I of the Constitution?

4 What does the "elastic clause" provide?

Chapter 5: The Congress of the United States

5 What are the laws that Congress *cannot* make according to Article I?

6 Which of these laws would weaken personal freedoms?

7 What privileges are granted to members of Congress? Should there be more? Or should there be fewer?

⌂ Which one of the provisions of Section I do you think is the most important? Why?

THE HOUSE OF REPRESENTATIVES

Of the two houses of Congress, the House of Representatives was designed to be closer to the people. For that reason, representatives have shorter terms than senators. The people have a chance to choose representatives every 2 years. Elections are held in November of even-numbered years (1980, 1982, 1984, and so on). The terms of all representatives expire at the same time. If any member cannot complete the 2-year term for any reason, the governor of her or his state calls a special election to fill that seat.

Since each new term of the House and the Congress begins in the same year (1981, 1983, 1985, and so on), there could be a new House of Representatives with each new Congress. However, usually only about 20 percent of the representatives are new. The other 80 percent are returning through reelection.

A representative's salary is now $57,500 a year. To serve in the House, you must be at least 25 years of age and must have been a citizen of the United States for at least 7 years. You must also be living in the state from which you are elected. These requirements appear in Article I of the Constitution. In addition, members of the House may decide whether or not fellow members are fit to serve. Each house may expel a member by a two-thirds vote (Article I, Section 5).

Members of the House of Representatives and their staffs can watch Congress in session from their offices by the use of closed-circuit television.

Chapter 5: The Congress of the United States

> **Qualifications of Representatives (Constitution, Article I)**
> *Age:* at least 25 years
> *Residency:* inhabitant of the state from which elected, when elected
> *Citizenship:* citizen of the United States for at least 7 years

The Speaker of the House

The presiding officer of the House of Representatives is the Speaker of the House. The Speaker receives a salary of $75,600 a year, plus allowances for expenses.

The Speaker is elected by majority vote of the members. Though the Constitution does not state that the Speaker must be a member of the House, thus far, every Speaker has been a House member.

As the presiding officer, the Speaker rules on all points of order. House members can overrule the Speaker, but that does not often happen. It is important, for example, that the Speaker decides who shall have the floor first, if more than one member wishes to speak. Under the Presidential Succession Act of 1947, the Speaker becomes President of the United States if *both* the President and the Vice President should become unable to serve. This law will be discussed further in Chapter 7.

Size of the House

When the First Congress met in 1789, the House of Representatives had sixty-five members. It now has 435. How did this happen?

The Constitution does not fix the number of representatives. Congress does. The Constitution says that each state *must* have at least one representative. Beyond that, it provides that each state may *not* have more than one representative for every 30,000 or more people and that a count, or *census*, must be taken every 10 years to determine the population. As the country grew, the number of representatives gradually increased until 1913, when the House had 435 members. Because the House seemed large enough, Congress later passed a

Number of Representatives by State (apportionment after the 1970 census[a])

State	#	State	#	State	#
−Alabama	7	Louisiana	8	−Ohio	23
Alaska	1	Maine	2	Oklahoma	6
+Arizona	4	Maryland	8	Oregon	4
Arkansas	4	Massachusetts	12	−Pennsylvania	25
+California	43	Michigan	19	Rhode Island	2
+Colorado	5	Minnesota	8	South Carolina	6
Connecticut	6	Mississippi	5	South Dakota	2
Delaware	1	Missouri	10	−Tennessee	8
+Florida	15	Montana	2	+Texas	24
Georgia	10	Nebraska	3	Utah	2
Hawaii	2	Nevada	1	Vermont	1
Idaho	2	New Hampshire	2	Virginia	10
Illinois	24	New Jersey	15	Washington	7
Indiana	11	New Mexico	2	−West Virginia	4
−Iowa	6	−New York	39	−Wisconsin	9
Kansas	5	North Carolina	11	Wyoming	1
Kentucky	7	−North Dakota	1	Total	435

a. In this apportionment, states marked with a plus sign (+) gained and those marked with a minus sign (−) lost representatives. The number in other states was unchanged.

law establishing 435 as the maximum number of representatives. If we now had one for every 30,000 persons, there would be more than 7,000 representatives in the House. With 435, we have about one representative for every 500,000 people.

The 435 seats in the House are divided among the states according to state population. After each 10-year census, every state is assigned one representative. The remaining House seats are then *apportioned*—divided in fair shares—among the states on the basis of state population. Even after the 1970 census, which showed a total population of more than 200,000,000, six states had only one representative each (see table, page 93). The District of Columbia, Guam, Puerto Rico, and the Virgin Islands do not have members in Congress because they are not states. Each sends a nonvoting delegate to the House. A proposed constitutional amendment, if ratified, will give the District voting membership in the House and two senators.

Congressional Districting

Members of the House are elected from congressional districts. Each district in a state sends one person to the House. If a state has only one representative, then it has only one congressional district. This member is elected "at large"—that is, by all voters in the state.

Who decides how big congressional districts should be? Who decides where their boundary lines should be drawn? State legislatures—with some prodding by the courts—make these important decisions. The power of districting has often been abused in two ways. Both result in bad apportionment, called *malapportionment.*

In the past, districts of very unequal population were common. In a state with two districts, for example, the lines might be drawn to divide the state in half (see A in the chart). Districts 1 and 2 would then be the same size, but the number of people in each could be very

CONGRESSIONAL DISTRICTING IN A TWO-DISTRICT STATE

A. Districts of Different Population Size

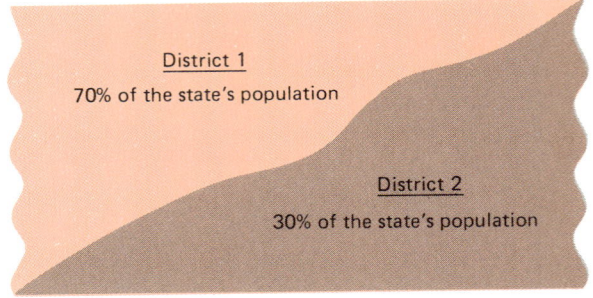

B. Districts about Equal in Population

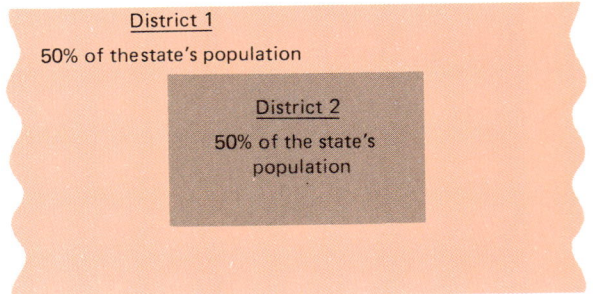

C. Districts about Equal in Population but Very Irregular in Shape

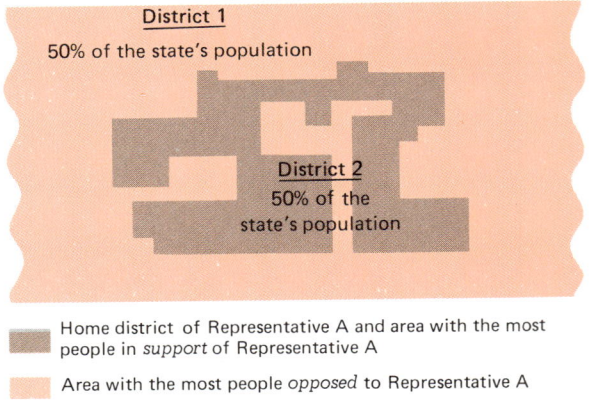

Home district of Representative A and area with the most people in *support* of Representative A

Area with the most people *opposed* to Representative A

different. Inequality of population is a form of malapportionment. It often gave people in the less settled rural areas a greater voice in Congress than urban areas had. As more people moved to cities, city people came to feel that this was unfair to them. So changes have been made in recent years, especially after

Chapter 5: The Congress of the United States

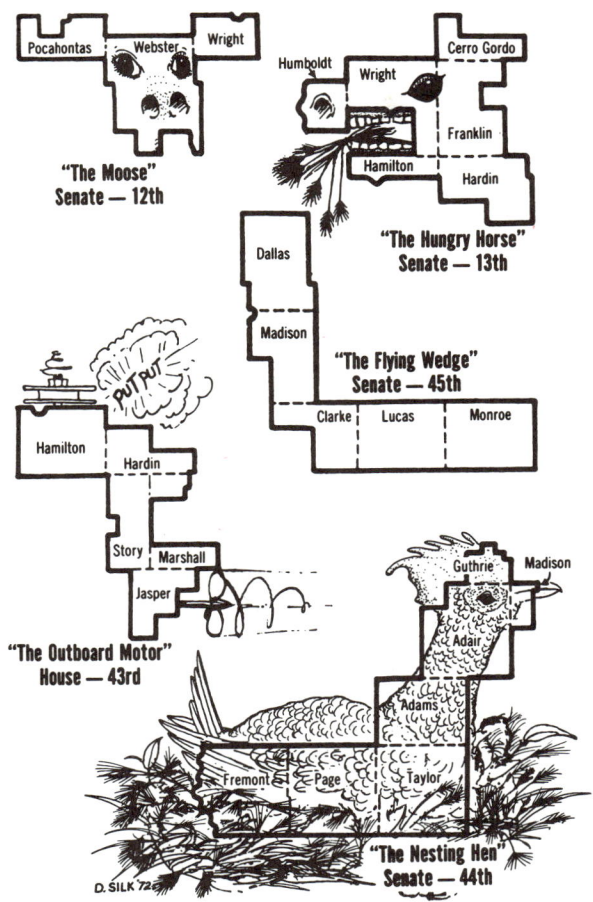

Gerrymandering has often attracted the attention of political cartoonists. This cartoon is a modern example from Iowa.

Supreme Court decisions in the 1960s (discussed in Chapter 26). Many states have redrawn their congressional districts in order to make them as nearly equal as possible in population. The result of such *reapportionment* might look like B in the chart.

State legislatures sometimes draw congressional districts in odd shapes for political reasons. This form of malapportionment is known as *gerrymandering* (JER-ee-man-during). The districts in C on the chart are gerrymandered. Pockets of opposition to a present member of the House have been excluded from that member's district. The areas may have been left out for either of two reasons. The voters may simply have been against this candidate or the areas may have contained particular racial or ethnic groups. Racial gerrymandering was declared unconstitutional by the Supreme Court in 1960. Gerrymandering of any kind is less common now than it was in the past. Yet it can exist even when districts are equal in population.

The Composition of Congress

The makeup of Congress has been changing over the years. In the table on page 96, you will see a comparison of Congress over a span of 25 years. The changes are more marked in the House than in the Senate. Members are younger than in the past. There is a greater representation of minorities and women. Members are drawn from a greater variety of professions and businesses.

Reapportionment is partly responsible for the changes, since it has brought more members from the growing cities and suburbs. Another cause of the changes has been an increase in political participation by minorities and women. With these political shifts, some members of Congress have been unseated. Some others have chosen not to seek reelection, for a variety of reasons. The vacancies thus created have helped to open the way for newcomers from different backgrounds.

As the chart makes clear, minorities and women are still underrepresented in Congress, despite the gains.

Exclusive Powers of the House

The Constitution gives the House certain powers that the Senate does not have. These exclusive powers of the House are listed in the chart on the next page.

Note that *revenue bills*—proposed laws to raise money for the government—must

Chapter 5: The Congress of the United States

Composition of Congress in 1953 and 1978

	House		Senate	
	1953	1978	1953	1978
Total membership	435	435	96	100
Vacancies at time of study	0	2	0	2
Average age, in years	52	50	58	54
Women	12	18	1	0[a]
Minorities:				
Blacks	2	16	0	1
Hispanics	1	4	1	0
Orientals	0	2	0	3
Profession or business:[b]				
Law	249	213	59	64
Business, banking	131	82	28	13
Farming, ranching	51	14	21	6
Education	49	45	17	5
Communications	35	24	10	4
Medicine	5	2	0	0
Workers, craftsworkers	0	6	0	0
Others	6	47	6	6

a. Muriel Humphrey was later appointed to fill a vacancy in the Senate.
b. In 1953, some members of Congress listed more than one profession or business.
U.S. News & World Report, January 30, 1978, p. 32. Copyright © 1978 by U.S. News & World Report, Inc.

Special Powers of the House of Representatives (Constitution, Articles I and II)

1. To originate revenue bills (Article I, Section 7)
2. To elect a President from among the top three candidates when no candidate has received a majority of votes in the electoral college (Article II, Section 1)
3. To bring charges of impeachment (Article I, Section 2)

---

begin in the House. Only after the House has approved them can the Senate act on them.

Note also that the House alone has the power to choose a President under certain circumstances. If no candidate has received a majority of votes in the electoral college, the House may choose among the top three candidates. However, all of the representatives from each state can then cast only one vote. Choice of the President has fallen to the House twice, in 1801 and 1825. The House chose Thomas Jefferson in 1801 and John Quincy Adams in 1825.

Another exclusive power of the House is the power to bring charges of impeachment. To *impeach* is to charge a person with misconduct or wrongdoing in public office. If the House impeaches a government official, the case goes to the Senate for trial. The operation of the checks and balances principle is shown by the House's power to impeach officials of the executive and judicial branches.

In all, the House has impeached thirteen officials—one President, one Cabinet officer, one senator, and ten federal judges. Of these thirteen cases, twelve reached the Senate. Only four ended in convictions. Six impeached persons were found not guilty and the other two cases were dismissed. President Andrew Johnson, impeached in 1868, was one of those

Harvard University runs a special program for newly elected members of Congress. The three new representatives at the left are taking part in the program. Here they are exchanging ideas with a member of a student political club.

found not guilty. The House was preparing to bring charges of impeachment against President Richard Nixon when he resigned in 1974.

Questions
---

1 How many years are there in the term of each member of the House of Representatives?

2 What qualifications are required for election to the House?

3 Who is the chief officer of the House? What are some powers of that officer?

4 How many members does the House of Representatives have? Why is the House limited to that number?

5 Which state has the largest number of representatives? How is the number in each state decided?

6 What are two forms of malapportionment? What purpose does gerrymandering serve?

7 What are three powers granted *only* to the House of Representatives?

⌂ Do you think that the membership of the House should be (a) smaller, (b) larger, or (c) the same as it is now? Explain.

THE SENATE

The framers of the Constitution felt that the Senate should be the more experienced and more conservative of the two houses of

The United States Senate has been called the world's most exclusive club—it has, after all, only 100 members.

Congress. While representatives have 2-year terms, senators serve for 6 years. Unlike the terms of representatives, which expire all in the same year, senators' terms overlap. Every 2 years, the terms of only one-third of the senators expire. Thus the Senate is a continuous body whose rules and procedures are carried over from Congress to Congress. The House reorganizes itself every 2 years.

Each state has two senators, no matter what its size or population. Rhode Island has the same number of senators as Alaska, which has nearly five hundred times its area. And Alaska, with fewer than 400,000 people, has the same number of senators as California, with 22,000,000 people. This is because the Constitution provides that each state can send two persons, and only two, to the Senate. That decision was part of the compromise reached by the framers of the Constitution to gain the support of the small states.

Until 1913, senators were chosen by the state legislatures. Since then, all have been elected by the people in general elections. These elections are held in November of even-numbered years. The two senators from a state are never up for election at the same time unless retirement, resignation, or death creates an unexpected vacancy.

A senator's annual salary is the same as a representative's—$57,500. To serve in the Senate, you must be at least 30 years old and must have been a citizen of the United States for at least 9 years. You must also live in the state in which you are elected. Like the House, the Senate may decide whether or not a member is fit to serve and may expel a member by a two-thirds vote of the membership.

Chapter 5: The Congress of the United States

When a senator dies, someone is usually appointed to that office until the next election. Muriel Humphrey was chosen by the governor of Minnesota to take the place of her husband, Hubert H. Humphrey, on his death.

Qualifications of Senators (Constitution, Article I)

Age: at least 30 years
Residency: inhabitant of the state from which elected, when elected
Citizenship: citizen of the United States for at least 9 years

Officers of the Senate

The Senate is presided over by the President of the Senate, an office held by the Vice President of the United States. As President of the Senate, the Vice President can vote only in case of a tie. To serve when the Vice President is absent, the Senate elects a temporary presiding officer. This officer, called the President pro tempore (pro TEM-puh-ree) or President pro tem, is a member of the Senate. In practice, the majority party member who has the longest service is elected President pro tem. The office of Deputy President pro tempore was created in 1977 for Senator Hubert Humphrey of Minnesota as an award for his outstanding service to the Senate.

Exclusive Powers of the Senate

Like the House, the Senate has some powers that belong to it alone. These exclusive powers are listed in the chart on the following page.

As you can see from the chart, two of these powers enable the Senate to serve as a check on the President. The President appoints major government officials, but the Senate must vote for or against these appointments. It can reject the President's choices, but it seldom does so. The President can make treaties, but only with the Senate's "advice and consent." The Senate can reject a treaty by a two-thirds vote of the members present.

The power to try impeachment cases is a check on the House as well as on executive and judicial officials. Conviction by the Senate requires a two-thirds vote of the members present.

Note that the Senate chooses among the top candidates for Vice President if there is a tie in the votes of the electoral college. This power was used when the Senate chose Richard M. Johnson as Martin Van Buren's Vice President in 1837.

Special Powers of the Senate (Constitution, Articles I and II)

1. To approve or reject major appointments made by the President (Article II, Section 2)
2. To ratify treaties (Article II, Section 2)
3. To elect a Vice President from among the top candidates if there is a tie in the votes of the electoral college (Article II, Section 1)
4. To try cases of impeachment (Article I, Section 3)

Questions

1 How many years are there in a senator's term?

2 During any even-numbered year, what portion of the Senate membership is elected? How does this differ from the House?

3 What qualifications are required for election to the Senate?

4 Who are the main officers of the Senate?

5 What are four powers granted *only* to the Senate?

◇ Do you think it is fair for Alaska to have as many senators as California? Explain.

PROBLEM: HOW SECRET SHOULD A LAWMAKER'S PERSONAL FINANCES BE?

As legislators, members of Congress are supposed to act in the public interest rather than in their own interests or in the interests of particular groups. Yet people who take public office have usually had some other work experience. Most members of Congress were once in law, business, banking, agriculture, or education. Such ties, if continued, could lead to conflicts of interest. For example, a representative might belong to a law firm that does work for the steel industry. That tie might influence the representative's action on a bill having to do with the steel industry.

Some senators and representatives continue their outside business activities. Many more continue to hold investments in stocks, bonds, and real estate that might influence their legislative decisions. The extent to which outside business activities or investments might lead to conflicts of interest has long been a matter of debate.

Both the House and the Senate passed rules in 1977 requiring members to make public reports on their finances each year. Members must report their assets, or financial holdings, and the amount and source of their income. Some members have since urged changes in these rules.

In the following selections, you will find arguments for and against a requirement of public financial disclosure. Similar arguments continue to be advanced. As you read, consider these questions:

- *What arguments are offered for and against requiring public financial disclosure?*
- *Do you favor such required disclosure?*

Arguments for Disclosure

Senator Floyd K. Haskell, Democrat from Colorado:

The financial holdings of members of Congress cannot help but be affected by almost all of our day-to-day decisions. We are consumers, we own property, we pay taxes and have occupations or professions which came before and will probably follow our terms of office. Our decisions affect our private lives just as they do the lives of all private citizens.

But I believe we can guard against conflicts of interest—and appearances of conflicts—through full and public disclosure by all high-level officials, including members of Congress. We must give the electorate the information that will enable it to enforce minimum standards of conduct.

Representative Edward G. Biester, Jr., Republican from Pennsylvania:

Members of Congress should have the same kinds of investment opportunities available to other citizens. A member's actions obviously must be more carefully considered because of his or her involvement with legislation which may affect those particular financial holdings. It is vital to remove any hint of conflict of interest *before* it can be raised, by requiring members to make known the sources and amounts of their finances. The citizen who envisions his elected representative making it rich as a public servant should have the relevant and factual information in hand before arriving at such a conclusion.

Representative Elliott H. Levitas, Democrat from Georgia:

It is clear to me that where a member of Congress has a significant financial stake in the outcome of a particular legislative act, it is difficult for him to be totally objective. For that reason, I think it is important for the voters to assess a member's action and votes in light of his financial interests. Therefore, I would favor full disclosure of all significant financial interests by members of Congress.

Former Representative Alphonzo Bell, Republican from California:

There is always the potential for conflict of interest in politics. Most members of Congress have private interests that may conflict with the public interest. For this reason, I support full disclosure of financial interests by public servants.

Senator Richard S. Schweiker, Republican from Pennsylvania:

I have made it a practice to publicly disclose my financial holdings. I make this disclosure because I believe the people have a right to know the financial holdings of their elected representatives. I do not believe such holdings necessarily lead to a conflict of interest, but the people should have the chance to decide for themselves.

Adapted from "What You Should Expect of Congress: 28 Members Speak Out," *U.S. News and World Report,* November 10, 1975, pp. 36–37. Copyright © 1975 by U.S. News & World Report, Inc.

Tom Braden, a writer on government:

John Gardner [then head] of Common Cause, a citizen's group, is an outspoken advocate for full disclosure. Each member of Congress would be required to list annually her or his assets and liabilities, sources of income, expenses, and connections with any outside businesses.

Gardner's argument—and many members of Congress agree with him—is that if the people know the sources of their representatives' incomes, they will be able to judge whether their representatives are serving public or private interests. Would the people take the trouble to study the record? Maybe not. But an opponent of a lawmaker would certainly study it and could be counted on to mention any flaws at election time. On the other hand, no honest lawmaker has anything to fear from disclosure.

Adapted from Tom Braden, "Government," *Saturday Review,* November 1, 1975, pp. 14–15.

Arguments against Disclosure

Representative James Abdnor, Republican from South Dakota:

I have difficulty in expressing my point of view without fear of misinterpretation.

For example, I do not think members of Congress ought to be "second class" citizens, which I think is the end result when they are subjected to a stronger test of honesty than is the average citizen. By the same token, I do not feel someone who is a crook ought to be given a green light by a form of secrecy that protects him from investigation and disclosure of wrongdoing.

Efforts at achieving disclosure, well meaning as they may be, have a tendency, I believe, to expose individuals who are successful in our system of private enterprise to an undue and unfavorable glare of publicity. It is necessary not to forget that every member of Congress had to be involved in some form of livelihood prior to his or her election to Congress.

Members should not be requested to divest [strip] themselves of their holdings. Just about every member has to, at some point in time, cast a vote that is a direct conflict of interest. In my case, it would be a vote pertaining to agriculture. For others it might be banking, medicine, and so on.

Representative J. Edward Roush, Democrat from Indiana:

The financial holdings of certain members of Congress do represent a potential conflict of interest. It does seem that disclosure in and of itself may not solve the problem, for it does not prevent the continuance of the conflict of interest. The problem is there for a relatively few members.

Adapted from "What You Should Expect of Congress: 28 Members Speak Out," *U.S. News and World Report,* November 10, 1975, pp. 36–37. Copyright © 1975 by U.S. News & World Report, Inc.

Questions

1 What is meant by public financial disclosure?

2 What do you consider to be the most important arguments *in favor of* requiring public financial disclosure for all members of Congress? Explain.

3 What do you consider to be the most important arguments *against* requiring such disclosure? Explain.

4 What arguments for or against such disclosure can you add to those in the selections?

⬠ Do you favor requiring public financial disclosure for members of Congress? Why or why not?

Chapter 5 Review

Recalling and Comparing

1. Briefly describe *two* ways in which qualifications for membership in the House of Representatives and the Senate *differ*.

2. Briefly describe *three* ways in which the powers of the House of Representatives and the Senate *differ*.

3. Briefly describe *four* ways in which the functions of the House of Representatives and the Senate are *similar*.

4. Of the two houses of Congress, do you think one has more power than the other? Explain.

5. Of the two houses of Congress, do you think one *should* have more power than the other? Why or why not?

Special Activities

1. With some other students, prepare short skits in which you illustrate what could happen to some of our basic freedoms if Congress could suspend the writ of *habeas corpus* in time of peace, pass bills of attainder, or pass *ex post facto* laws.

2. Prepare a biographical sketch of your representative. Consult your local library or your representative's office for information.

3. Prepare biographical sketches of your two senators. Consult your local library or the offices of your senators for information.

4. Invite a member of the local staff of your United States representative or of one your senators to discuss the powers of Congress with your class.

5. Choose any state and find out the length of service of each member of Congress from that state. Make a chart showing how many of the members have served one term, two terms, or more.

6. Consider what might be arguments for and against the following statement: "The House of Representatives has too many members." Then decide whether you agree or disagree with that statement and your reasons for doing so.

Developing Your Political Vocabulary

Match each word or phrase in *a-f* with the best definition in *1-6*.

gerrymandering **a**
writ of *habeas corpus* **b**
ex post facto **c**
impeach **d**
constituent **e**
amendment **f**

1. an order requiring that an imprisoned person be brought before a court of law
2. to bring charges of wrongdoing against a public official
3. a change in a constitution
4. the drawing of district lines for political advantage
5. after a deed has been done
6. a voter in the district or state of a member of Congress

Chapter 6

How Congress Works

The Founders, as we have seen, gave Congress a wide range of powers. Congress not only makes laws but can also propose amendments to the Constitution. Congress has the power to declare war. The Senate must rule on presidential appointments and on treaties. It is Congress that selects a President or Vice President when the electoral college cannot reach a decision. Congress also has the power to impeach. It helps prepare the budget. It watches to see that its laws are carried out.

Of all these powers, the power to make laws is the most far-reaching. This is because Congress must constantly gather facts and opinions in order to carry out its lawmaking power. For one thing, members must know the wants and needs of the people in their home districts and states. In addition, members must know the needs and problems seen by experts in particular fields.

How Congress goes about its day-to-day business of making laws is the subject of this chapter. The first section describes how Congress organizes itself on political lines to carry out the lawmaking process. The subject of the next section is the lawmaking process itself. The final part of the chapter will turn to some problems associated with the work of Congress.

Goals

- To learn how Congress is organized politically.

Chapter 6: How Congress Works

- *To learn the role of congressional committees.*
- *To learn how a bill becomes a law.*
- *To consider whether the process of making laws is too complicated.*
- *To consider whether members of Congress use their time wisely.*

CONGRESS AS A POLITICAL BODY

Congress is not only our national legislature but also a political body. Most representatives and senators try to carry out the programs of the political parties to which they belong.

The Constitution does not mention political parties. This is because they did not exist in this country until the 1790s. A *political party* is a group of people who band together to put their ideas about government into action by nominating and electing their own candidates for public office. For nearly two centuries now, most of the members of Congress have been candidates of political parties. So have our Presidents and Vice Presidents.

Today, the Democrats and the Republicans are our two largest political parties. Whichever party wins the largest number of seats in the House is the *majority party* of the House. The other party is the *minority party* of the House. The same is true in the Senate.

Each house of Congress has two party committees, one set up by the majority party and the other by the minority party. A *committee* is a group of people appointed or elected to do certain things. The Democrats in the House call their party committee a *caucus* (KAW-kus). Each of the other party committees is called a *conference*. The four political party committees—the Democratic caucus in the House, the Republican conference in the House, and the Democratic and Republican conferences in the Senate—operate in much the same way.

Members of the Black Caucus are shown here talking with Alex Haley, author of *Roots,* who is second from the right.

The Hispanic Caucus

The Congressional Hispanic Caucus began operation in June 1977. This special caucus in the House is described in the following selection from a news report.

The new body was approved by Speaker Thomas P. O'Neill at the beginning of the session but was unable to find office space until now. Its five members represent four states.

Representative Edward R. Roybal of California will head the new organization. Roybal is California's only Hispanic representative. Besides Roybal, members of the caucus are Representatives Herman Badillo of New York, E. "Kika" de la Garza of Texas, Henry B. Gonzalez of Texas, and Manuel Lujan, Jr., of New Mexico. Lujan is a Republican. All the others are Democrats.

Roybal said the new caucus will lead a national effort to win a bigger place in government for the Hispanic minority. In doing so, the Hispanic Caucus will work with the National Association of Elected Democratic Officials.

Roybal said, in an interview, that he had been trying since 1971 to build a national organization for the Spanish-speaking community. He had decided that a national office and staff were essential to provide a unified Hispanic voice.

"When Eisenhower was President, around 2.4 or 2.5 percent of federal employees were Spanish surnamed," Roybal said. "It's only 3.3 percent today, and that's a national disgrace." One of the results of ineffective political organization is that Latins are underrepresented in Congress, he added.

Adapted from "Hispanic Caucus of 5 Opens Its Doors," by Bob Shannon, June 2, 1977. Copyright © 1977, Los Angeles Times, Reprinted by permission.

The purpose of party committees is to influence the lawmaking process. In each house of Congress, the majority party selects a *majority floor leader* and the minority party selects a *minority floor leader.* The floor leader is the chief spokesperson and legislative strategist for the party. Floor leaders receive $65,000 a year, or $7,500 more than regular members of Congress, to compensate them for their additional responsibilities. Assistant floor leaders, or *whips,* are also selected by the party committees in each house. Party whips help to line up support for the party's position on a bill. At the same time, the political party committees attempt to influence the legislative process through the legislative committees, the subject of the next section.

Members of Congress are organized on special-interest lines as well as political party lines. The caucus form of organization is used by special-interest groups as it is used by political parties. The purpose is the same: to plan legislative strategy. Two dozen or more special caucuses operate in the House of Representatives.

Minorities and women led the way. The first special caucus was the Congressional Black Caucus, formed in the House in 1971. The second group was the Congresswoman's Caucus. Both groups actively promote legislation in their special areas of interest. The Congressional Hispanic Caucus sees its role differently. It seeks to increase the number of Americans of Spanish origin in government. Two other groups concerned with special legislation are the Blue Collar Caucus and the Suburban Caucus. A similar caucus, using the name Northeast-Midwest Coalition, was formed by House members from neighboring states. The members of such groups felt that banding together provided a way for them to act together on their common problems.

Some people have felt that political parties have too much power in Congress. The rise of special-interest caucuses may weaken that power, since these caucuses cross party lines.

Chapter 6: How Congress Works

One important function of a standing committee is to conduct hearings on a proposed law. In the photograph above, the House Judiciary Committee is hearing testimony in the proceedings to impeach President Richard Nixon.

For the present, however, the special caucuses have small memberships. The members may act as a group on certain issues but are likely to be available to their own political parties on other issues. Congress-watchers disagree as to whether such caucuses are here to stay.

Questions

1 What is a political party? What is a majority party in a lawmaking body?

2 How do political parties operate to influence legislation in Congress.

3 What is the role of special-interest caucuses?

⌂ Do you think that political parties should have less influence in Congress? Explain.

LEGISLATIVE COMMITTEES OF CONGRESS

Much, if not most, of the work of the House and the Senate is done in committees. Some of the committees of Congress are permanent ones. Others are temporary. Any committee can set up *subcommittees*—which are smaller committees responsible to the parent committee itself.

The permanent legislative committees of Congress are known as standing committees. Each studies legislative needs in one or a few fields (see chart, pages 110–111). It would be impossible for every member of Congress to be an expert in every field. For this reason, Congress divides its work among standing committees. Most of these committees, in turn, set up subcommittees that are even more specialized.

From time to time, Congress has tried to reduce the number of standing committees. Such reforms have usually led to an increase in the number of subcommittees, since the total amount of work to be done has not decreased. By 1978, the House had twenty-two standing committees and the Senate had fifteen. As you can see from the chart, these committees vary greatly in their areas of concern and in their number of members.

Every member of Congress is assigned to a standing committee. Usually, representatives and senators are permitted to serve on no more than two or three such committees. In this way, members of Congress need not try to become experts in every field.

Long ago, the political parties took to themselves the right to appoint members to the standing committees. It is no suprise, then, that the majority of the members of *every* standing committee in each house are members of the majority party in that house. For example, if in a certain election the Democrats win three-fourths of the seats in the Senate, three-fourths of the members of all the Senate's standing committees will be Democrats. What if a member of Congress does not belong to either the Democratic or Republican party? In that case, the member usually receives an assignment through one of these two political parties. But such a member is not likely to get a place on a very desirable committee.

Whoever occupies the chair of a standing committee is in a powerful position. The chairperson can decide the fate of a bill. The majority party selects the committee chairperson because it has the largest share of the committee membership.

In the past, the chairperson was always chosen by the *seniority rule.* The person with the greatest length of service (seniority) automatically became chairperson. This seniority rule caused problems. One problem was that the senior members were not always the best qualified members. Another problem was that, having served so long, senior members might not represent the views of newer members of the House or Senate. Because of the chairperson's solid grip on power, legislation favored by the majority could easily be blocked.

In the mid 1970s, some Democrats in the House objected to the seniority rule. They complained that the chair of the House Ways and Means Committee had been occupied too long by one person. Besides, the chairperson of that powerful committee was able to decide who could serve on *other* standing committees. In the mid 1970s, the Democratic caucus of the House undermined the seniority rule by holding separate and secret votes on selection of chairpersons of each of the standing committees. The caucus also took away the Ways and Means Committee's power to choose members of other committees.

Chapter 6: How Congress Works

Standing Committees of Congress and Their Fields of Concern (as of 1978)

Agriculture—House
Agriculture, Nutrition, and *Forestry*—Senate
Matters relating to farming and forestry in general, farm credit, farm price controls, crop insurance, livestock inspection, soil conservation, and rural electrification. Senate also deals with nutrition.

Appropriations—House
Appropriations—Senate
Matters relating to the allotment of money for the support of the federal government and examination of the departments and operations of the executive branch. Senate also deals with postal service.

Armed Services—House
Armed Services—Senate
Matters relating to operations of the military establishment, naval oil reserves, and strategic materials.

Banking, Housing, and Urban Affairs—House
Banking, Finance, and Urban Affairs—Senate
Matters relating to the Federal Reserve System, the value of the dollar, price or rent controls, federal deposit insurance, and public and private housing.

Budget—House
Budget—Senate
Matters relating to budget outlays required by existing and new legislation, and study of budgets proposed by the President.

District of Columbia—House only
Matters relating to governing the District of Columbia.

Education and Labor—House
Human Resources—Senate
Matters relating to education and labor, such as child labor, minimum wages and hours, settlement of labor disputes, and the federal school lunch program.

Energy and Natural Resources—Senate only
Matters relating to the use of energy sources and the protection of natural resources and public lands.

International Relations—House
Foreign Relations—Senate
Matters relating to relations with other governments, the United Nations, and international money organizations; the diplomatic service; federal loans to foreign countries; protection of United States citizens in other countries; supervision of the American Red Cross; and declaration of war.

Government Operations—House
Government Affairs—Senate
Budget and accounting measures other than appropriations, including dealings of the federal government with states and towns or cities. Senate also concerns itself with international organizations of which the United States is a member, with matters relating to the District of Columbia, and with the civil service.

House Administration—House only
Matters relating to the operation of the House of Representatives, the holding of federal elections, the settling of contested elections, and the management of the Library of Congress.

Interior and Insular Affairs—House only
Matters relating to the maintenance of public lands, public mineral resources, and foreign possessions; also, the rights and lands of Native Americans.

Interstate and Foreign Commerce—House
Commerce, Science, and Transportation—Senate

Continued on next page

Most matters relating to commerce, communication, and transportation. Senate concerns itself, in addition, with the operation of the Merchant Marine, Coast Guard, and Weather Bureau, the operation of inland waterways, conservation of fish and wildlife, supervision of the Bureau of Standards, and matters relating to science.

Judiciary—House
Judiciary—Senate
Matters relating to federal courts, impeachments, proposed constitutional amendments, civil rights, interstate contracts, immigration and naturalization services, apportionment of representatives, meetings of Congress and attendance of its members, the Patent Office, claims against the federal government, bankruptcy, mutiny, spying, counterfeiting, and protection of trade and commerce.

Merchant Marine and Fisheries—House only
Most matters relating to the merchant marine, navigation laws, the Coast Guard, the Panama Canal, federal fisheries, and federal wildlife organizations.

Post Office and Civil Service—House only
Matters relating to postal service, the civil service, the federal census, and the National Archives.

Public Works and Transportation—House
Environment and Public Works—Senate
Matters relating to construction and maintenance of federal buildings, bridges, dams, and roads; flood control; improvement of rivers and harbors; and pollution of waterways.

Rules—House
Rules and Administration—Senate
House concerns itself with rules governing the order of business for the House of Representatives and with the creation of new standing committees. Senate deals with the operation of the Senate, the holding of federal elections, the settling of contested elections, the management of the Library of Congress, and the creation of new standing committees.

Science and Technology—House only
General matters relating to scientific and astronautical research, the National Aeronautics and Space Administration, the National Science Foundation, the Bureau of Standards, science scholarships, and outer space.

Small Business—House only
Matters related to the funding and regulation of small business.

Standards of Official Conduct—House only
Matters relating to the regulations and standards of conduct for members, officers, and employees of the House.

Veterans' Affairs—House
Veterans' Affairs—Senate
Matters relating to laws that deal with military veterans.

Ways and Means—House
Finance—Senate
Matters relating to proposed revenue and tax measures, customs duties, transportation of taxable goods, the Social Security program, trade agreements with other countries, the federal debt, and the deposit of federal money.

Joint Committees (House and Senate)

Atomic Energy	Library
Congressional Operations	Printing
Defense Production	Taxation
Economic	

Most standing committees have special permission to meet during the morning hours when Congress is in session. The Senate Appropriations Committee meets only on the call of its chairperson, but the other committees have regular meeting times.

Most standing committees are composed of members of only one house of Congress. But there is another type of standing committee that is made up of members of both houses. It is called a *joint committee* (see chart, p. 111). On such committees, the two houses have an equal number of members.

Joint committees make it possible for the two houses of Congress to work together on problems that concern them both. However, only the Joint Committee on Atomic Energy has legislative functions. The others carry on investigations.

As the chart shows, there are very few joint committees. Why aren't there more of them? Some people say there should be, and that they should have full powers. These people feel that having separate standing committees for the House and the Senate is a waste of time. In their view, joint committees would bring quicker action by fewer people. They point out, too, that anyone who wanted to speak for or against a bill would then have to appear only before one committee, instead of two. Other people, however, believe that the checks and balances principle works better between the two houses if there are separate House and Senate standing committees.

From time to time, both houses create temporary committees to serve particular needs. These committees are set up for two main purposes. *A temporary committee is sometimes set up to study the need for new laws in a particular field.* It is then called a *select committee* or a *special committee*. Select committees in the House include the Select Committee on Aging and the Select Committee on Ethics. Among those in the Senate are the Select Committee on Small Business and the Select Committee on Indian Affairs. Select committees and special committees often continue to work after Congress adjourns.

Temporary committees are also set up when the two houses cannot agree on the wording of a bill. In that case, the presiding officer of each house appoints a few of its members to a *conference committee*. A *conference committee* is a temporary joint committee. Its purpose is to produce a compromise bill, as we shall see in the next section.

If a committee of Congress wants to, it can meet in secret. It is then said to be in *executive session*. More often, the committees hold public meetings.

All this committee work can create problems for members of Congress. Some members have to sit on many committees. These might include two or three standing committees, subcommittees, a joint committee, and select committees. Keeping well informed about the work of so many committees is impossible. Another problem is the amount of time required to read documents and attend meetings. In some cases, a member is expected to be at two or more committee meetings at the same time.

Questions

1 What is a congressional committee? A subcommittee?

2 What is a congressional standing committee? A joint committee?

3 What are some kinds of temporary committees in Congress? What purposes do they serve?

4 If your representative or one of your senators introduced the following bills, to which standing committees in the House and the Senate might the bills be referred?

    a a bill to allow more money for the purchase of books for school libraries

    b a bill to halt the sale of publicly owned lands

c a bill to provide for the building of new waterways

d a bill to increase the federal minimum wage

◇ Do you think that the present committee system of Congress is a good one? Why or why not?

HOW A BILL BECOMES A LAW

The making of laws is a complicated process. It is not the same in every case, but its general pattern can be described.

A broken line in the chart below means that the bill may die before the next step.

Major Steps by Which a Bill Becomes a Law

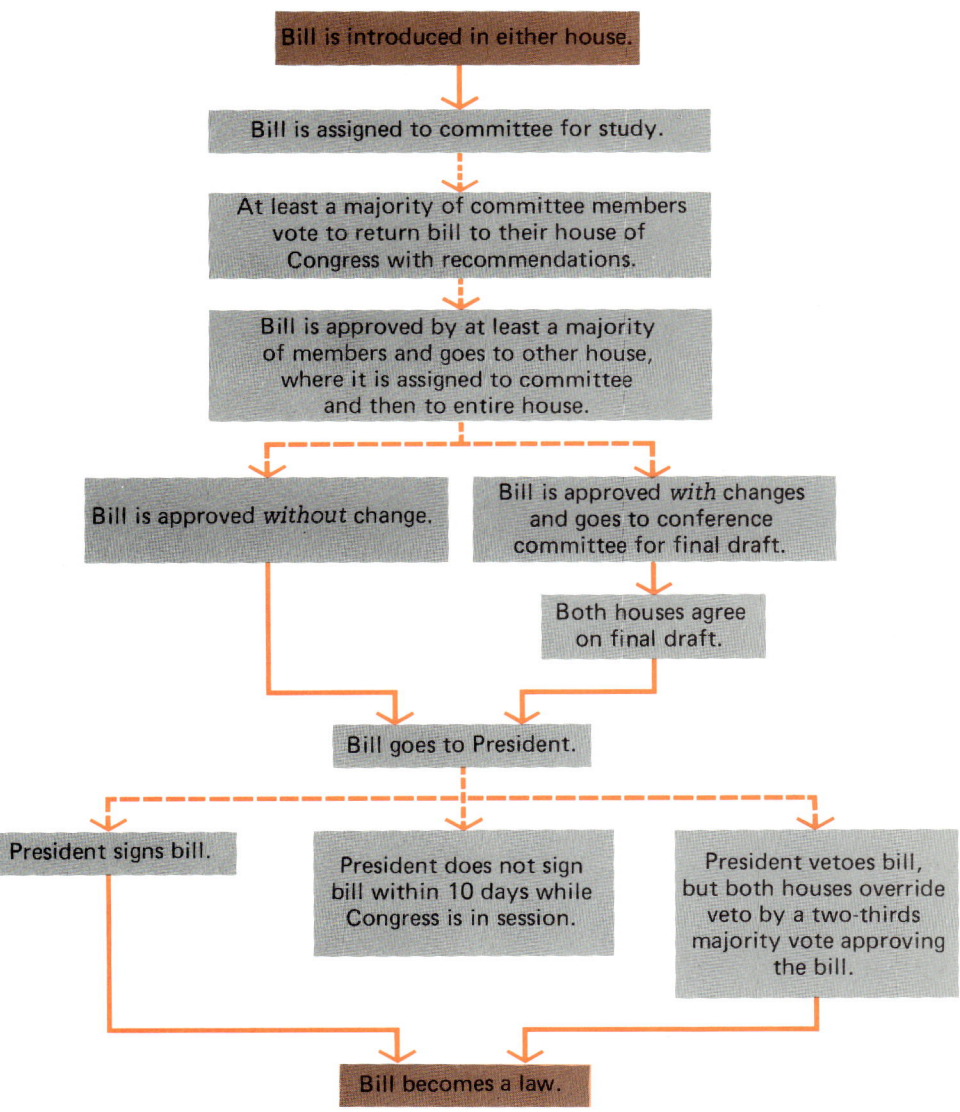

Chapter 6: How Congress Works

First Steps

Laws first appear as bills. A proposed piece of legislation is known as a *bill*, until it is signed into law. If the bill has not been made into law by the end of that term of Congress, it ceases to exist—it "dies." Its supporters have to introduce it again during the next Congress if they want it to have further consideration.

Only members of Congress can introduce bills. The member or members who introduce a bill are the bill's *sponsors.* In writing a bill, members can get help from the Legislative Reference Service, a part of the Library of Congress. Many bills introduced in Congress are drafted by the executive branch. Many others are drafted or suggested by congressional committees, private organizations, or individual citizens.

When introduced, a bill receives a number. These numbers are consecutive throughout that term of Congress. In the 96th Congress, for example, the first bill introduced in the House was numbered HR1; the second, HR2; and so forth. In the Senate, the numbers were S1, S2, and so forth. Bills numbered, say, HR106 and S158 could be on the same subject. They could even be identical, since the same bill is sometimes introduced in both houses. More often, several different bills are filed on the same subject.

A bill must have three "readings" in each house before it can be voted on. "Readings" came into practice before it was possible to reproduce written materials rapidly. A bill has its *first reading* when the Clerk of the House or the Senate reads the bill's title to the members. The Clerk then sends the bill to whichever committee of that house is concerned with that field of legislation. In the Senate, receipt of a bill by a committee is called the bill's *second reading.* The House, as we shall see, uses this term in a different way.

Bills in Committee

When a committee receives a bill, it can do one of three things:

1. Ignore the bill and so let it die in committee.
2. Consider the bill and send it back in much the same form in which it was received.
3. Consider the bill and send it back with minor or major changes.

Perhaps surprisingly, the first option is the one most often used. As a matter of fact, members of Congress often do not expect that the bills they introduce will be passed. In any term of Congress, about 20,000 bills are introduced but only about 1,000 are passed. Most bills die in committee. There is a way of

A few of the many bundles of printed bills that pass through the House documents room on their way to Congress.

Chapter 6: How Congress Works

When a bill is presented in Congress, it is common for private supporters of the bill to attempt to influence the vote.

Chapter 6: How Congress Works

preventing this, but is is not easy. A bill can be taken from a committee and put before a house of Congress, but only if a majority of the members of that house vote for this action.

Committees seldom send bills back unchanged. If they consider a bill at all, they generally make changes.

If a committee regards a bill as important or controversial, the committee will hold public hearings. Hearings are sessions in which a committee hears the testimony of experts and interested persons or groups. People who favor or oppose the bill can make their views known at these hearings. Sometimes the hearings are staged to support the views of key members of the committee. A chairperson, for example, may use the testimony to kill a bill or to move it along with what appears to be general support.

A committee hearing is often the point at which a bill can be most influenced. Amendments can be recommended by individuals or groups. Letters can be sent to committee members, or other means can be used to change, speed, or defeat a bill.

Advance notice of any hearing is published in the *Congressional Record.* As many people as seating arrangements will allow can attend the hearings.

Hearings begin with a brief statement by the committee chairperson and the ranking, or senior, member of the minority party. Then the first witness is called to give testimony for or against the bill. If any members of Congress wish to speak about the bill, they are called first. An official reporter must be present to take down the testimony. Most witnesses, however, read from written statements that are later printed in the committee's record. After giving their testimony, witnesses can answer questions or respond to comments made by committee members.

Among those who speak at hearings are lobbyists. A *lobbyist* is a person, usually acting for an organization, who tries to influence legislation. A lobbyist may be acting for an entire industry, a labor union, a professional association, a group of environmentalists, or any group of people who are interested in obtaining congressional action of some type.

The work of lobbyists consists in trying to get bills passed or defeated and trying to help shape the content of bills. Some lobbyists are experts who, while serving their clients, bring important facts to the attention of members of Congress and congressional committees. You will learn more about lobbyists in Chapter 27.

When all hearings have ended, the committee decides what changes, if any, should be made in the bill. This "marking up" is usually done in closed sessions. The bill is then either dropped or *reported*—that is, sent back to the House or the Senate with the committee's recommendations. If a bill is reported, copies of it are made for all members of that house of Congress. In the House of Representatives, this is known as the bill's *second reading.*

Bills on the Floor

Action on bills on the floor of the House and the Senate is controlled by a complicated set of rules and customs.

Before a bill can be debated, it must be placed on a schedule called a *calendar.* Nor-

---

Principal Calendars of the House of Representatives

Union Calendar
Bills dealing with revenue, appropriations, or federal property
House Calendar
All other public bills (such as bills involving civil rights, new government agencies, or impeachment)
Private Calendar
Private bills (proposed legislation dealing with individuals, such as a bill concerning someone's immigration or naturalization, or a bill intended to correct a wrong done to someone by the government)

This artist's sketch shows Senators Howard Baker and Robert C. Byrd during the Senate floor debate on the Panama Canal treaty.

mally, bills are listed on the calendar in the order in which they are reported. To move a bill on the calendar, the Rules Committee of the House or the Senate must make a special rule enabling the bill to be taken up out of order. Thus, the Rules Committee has significant control over which bills will be considered by the members during each term of Congress. Since the Rules Committee can also make special rules to limit debate and amendments, its role is a powerful one. The heads of other standing committees often seek special rules in order to move bills more quickly through Congress. The ability to get special rules is one source of a chairperson's power.

The Senate has a single calendar, but the House has different calendars for different types of bills. The main House calendars are the Union Calendar, the House Calendar, and the Private Calendar (see chart opposite).

Bills are either private or public. A *private bill* deals with one person. The House receives many such bills and has a special calendar for them. All other bills are *public bills.*

In considering bills on the Private Calendar and those on the Union Calendar, the House may sit as a "Committee of the Whole." This speeds action on the many private bills and on revenue and appropriation bills. Attendance of 100 members is then enough for a *quorum* (KWOR-um)—the number of members who must be present in order to take action. The Committee of the Whole can approve or reject a bill by a majority vote. But the committee's action can then be overturned by the House in a regular session.

Except when the House sits as a Committee of the Whole, a majority of the members must be present for a quorum. Bills are then subject to the normal rules of the House of Representatives, unless special rules are allowed. The House Rules Committee almost always sets a limit on the time for debate. Equal time is allowed for representatives who favor and those who oppose a bill. Major bills usually get special rules.

In the Senate, a majority of the members must be present for a quorum.

Unlike the House, the Senate does not place a time limit on debate. For that reason, senators are able to *filibuster,* or try to block or delay action on a bill by talking until the majority of the Senate gives in and changes or withdraws the bill. A filibuster can include speeches or readings on any topic at all. Filibustering senators have given recipes for chicken soup and "pot likker"—the juice of cooked turnip greens. While a filibuster is going on, the Senate is unable to get any business done. That is how the minority hopes to bend the majority to its will. The filibuster was used successfully in blocking civil rights legislation until 1957.

There is only one sure way to stop a filibuster. A vote to limit debate can be taken and three-fifths of those voting must approve. This is called a vote for *cloture* or *closure.* After approval of cloture, no senator may speak for more than an hour on the bill under debate.

Under normal rules, any member may propose amendments to a bill while it is under debate in the House or the Senate. These amendments become part of the bill only if approved. *Riders* are also sometimes proposed. They are amendments that add something to a bill that is not related to the bill. Riders are used most often to rush through a provision that is not likely to be approved on its own.

While the House or the Senate is discussing a bill, visitors can watch from galleries or balconies above each chamber. The galleries are open to visitors at other times as well, except when the Senate goes into executive session. Visitors may not make demonstrations, take photographs, or read.

When discussion of a bill is ended and changes have been agreed on, the bill is printed in its new form. It then has its *third reading*—again by title only—and a vote on the bill as a whole is taken.

Votes on bills can be taken in one of three ways: by voice vote; by standing vote; or by roll-call vote or record vote. The voice-vote method, in which all those in favor call "Yea!" and all those opposed call "Nay!," is the most common. The standing-vote method, which requires all those in favor, and then all those opposed, to stand and be counted, is used on request. The roll-call or record vote means that a record of each member's vote is made, either by hand as each member answers yea or nay when his or her name is called, or by machine as each member, in turn, pushes a button. A roll-call or record vote is the only kind that permits the public to know how each representative or senator voted. It is required by Article I of the Constitution any time that one-fifth of the members request it (Section 5) or if the voting involves overriding a presidential veto (Section 7).

Given the weight of the legislative work load, members of Congress often know very little about the bills before them. As a result, they get their voting cues from others. The process leads to an exchange of votes that goes something like this: "I really have no strong feelings on this matter. I will defer to you in the expectation that you will reciprocate in the future on my bills." Sometimes the trade is more specific. It is then called *logrolling.* Members A and B agree that if A will support B's bill, B will support A's bill. Logrolling is often used to gain appropriations that will benefit each member's home district or state. The idea is: You help me and I'll help you.

In both houses of Congress, at least a majority of the members must vote in favor of a bill for it to pass that house. In practice, *a majority of those voting* is considered sufficient unless a member objects. That is why a visitor will find many routine bills being passed by the voice vote of a few members.

Final Steps

A bill that has passed one house is sent to the other house. There the process of approval or disapproval begins again. If the bill is passed with *any* changes, it must go back to the first

Chapter 6: How Congress Works

"IF WE WERE A TV SHOW, WE'D BE CANCELED."
HESSE IN *ST. LOUIS GLOBE-DEMOCRAT*

house. What if that house does not agree to the changes? Then a conference committee is formed with half of its members chosen from each house. If this committee can settle the differences, the bill will be sent back to both houses for approval.

A bill approved by both houses of Congress is not yet a law; it must next go to the President. The President can then choose to do one of the following things:

1. Let the bill become law—
   a. with the President's approval: by signing it;
   b. without the President's approval: by not acting on it for 10 days (not counting Sundays)—*provided* Congress remains in session throughout that period.
2. *Veto* (reject) the bill—
   a. directly: by returning it to the house that originated it with a message giving reasons for rejecting it;
   b. indirectly (the *pocket veto*): by not acting on it for 10 days (not counting Sundays)—*provided* Congress adjourns during that time.

Most often, the President will sign the bill. If choice *1b* is used, the bill still becomes a law. It might even become a law if choice *2a* is used. This is because *Congress can override a direct veto by a two-thirds majority vote of both houses. A pocket veto*—choice *2b*—*cannot be overturned* because Congress is no longer in session. Thus a pocket veto means sure death for a bill.

The one out of twenty bills that survives this long process and becomes a law is sent to the National Archives and Records Service. The law is given a number and is published in *Statutes at Large of the United States*. These statutes are codified from time to time. They are then printed in the *United States Code*. The next step is for the executive department to see that the new law is carried out.

Questions

1 What is a bill?
2 About what percentage of bills introduced in Congress become laws?
3 What is a filibuster? How can one be halted?
4 What purpose does the trading of votes serve?
5 Briefly explain how a bill can become a law.
6 How many ways have we seen in which a bill could become trapped and die?
7 How can *you* influence legislation?
8 In what ways does the process of making laws in Congress carry out the principle of checks and balances?
⌂ Do you think that logrolling can ever be justified? Explain.

Chapter 6: How Congress Works

PROBLEM: SHOULD OUR LAWMAKING PROCESS BE LESS COMPLICATED?

Our supply of petroleum is a continuing problem. We must import oil because not enough is produced in the United States to meet our daily needs. When the Arab nations in the Middle East cut off much of our imported oil in 1973, oil prices skyrocketed.

During that crisis, Congress set about to reduce the use of oil. An Emergency Energy Bill was introduced in both houses. It went to two standing committees—the Senate Interior and Insular Affairs Committee and the House Interstate and Foreign Commerce Committee. Some bills are passed by both houses without much opposition and are approved by the President. But many bills, like this one, have a difficult time. The stormy progress of the Emergency Energy Bill is reported in the following selection. In reading this account, you will discover how long and complicated the life of a bill can be. As you read the history of this bill, ask yourself:

- *What legislative steps did this bill go through?*
- *What, if anything, could have been done to simplify the process while still giving the bill proper consideration?*

It was October 18, 1973, when Representative Harley Staggers, from the coal areas of West Virginia, introduced a bill in the House of Representatives to: "Authorize and direct the President and state and local government to develop contingency plans for reducing petroleum consumption . . ." On the same day, Senator Henry Jackson introduced the same bill in the Senate.

In the beginning, everything moved smoothly and swiftly in the Senate. Jackson had the bill out of his Interior Committee and past the Senate on November 19, one month after its introduction. Staggers, meanwhile, made little progress in moving the bill to the floor of the House through the committee he chairs, the House Commerce Committee. "I've wanted to move," said Staggers, "but all my subcommittees were tied up and obligated."

House hearings did not even start on the bill until November 20. And as the pieces of the Emergency Energy Bill moved through the subcommittees toward the full Commerce Committee, a host of distractions pressed in. With all these distractions, the House members could hardly read the bill's all-important fine print. Lobbyists had been caught off balance by the speed with which the bill zipped through the Senate. They now focused on the House Commerce Committee. Each lobby had its own solution to some issue.

Meanwhile, key committee sessions were broken up by floor votes on all the other legislation moving through Congress. And there were arguments within the House. Members of the committee, for example, wanted to tax the excess profits of oil companies. But taxes are written by the Ways and Means Committee. So, to keep the bill in the Commerce Committee, the committee members had to work out a tax that was not called a tax. When the section was finally written, it referred to "windfall profits," which really meant a tax on a coal or oil company's profits regarded as above what was considered normal.

There was also the beginning of Christmas fever. Many members were eager to get home.

Next came what members called the "Christmas Tree," wherein they traded amendments to help their friends and hamper their enemies. Of 125 amendments that were offered in committee, 75 were accepted. Among those turned down were "a ban on disposable containers" and "free cash to insulate your house."

Finally, the bill came out of committee. It had been approved by a 25 to 13 vote—a division that indicated trouble ahead on the floor. The complex bill was rushed through the Rules Committee and to the House floor a day later, 2 weeks before Christmas. Debate began before many members had had a chance to read the bill.

Wednesday, December 12: The debate began calmly enough, the committee members explaining the bill on the floor of the House. There had been an agreement that the fifty-six additional amendments to the bill on file at the Speaker's table were not to be taken up until the next day.

Thursday, December 13: When the House convened at 11 A.M., members were standing, trying to get the Speaker's attention in order to have their amendments considered early while everyone was still fresh. They were all outfoxed by Tim Lee Carter of Kentucky, who said, "Let me go first. I just got a little ole amendment that changes one word." He did, too. Everywhere in the "windfall profits" section where the bill said "coal and oil," he moved to strike the word "coal," bringing the coal companies home free.

What could Staggers—from a coal area himself—do? He agreed to the amendment. Meanwhile, where there had been fifty-six amendments at the Speaker's table at the beginning of the debate, there were now sixty-seven.

John Dingell, a Democrat from Michigan, introduced an amendment that many members feared. It was a proposal to conserve energy by prohibiting busing to all but the nearest school. In effect, this would stop busing that was designed to achieve racial balance.

Dingell's amendment had been defeated in committee, and those managing the bill on the floor thought they had the bare handful of votes to turn back the amendment. But the amendment finally passed, 221 to 192.

Friday, December 14: The biggest problem now was that political killer, gas rationing. The Republicans wanted the Democratic-controlled Congress to vote for gas rationing. The Democrats wanted rationing to be a purely Republican move. In committee, John Heinz had fought to have the authority for gasoline rationing—to allow most families about 20 gallons of gasoline a week—rest with the Congress. And he had lost. Now, Heinz brought the matter to the floor. Enough Democrats split to pass the measure on a voice vote where no one had to go on record.

As Friday night rushed toward Saturday morning, there was no time left for members even to explain their amendments.

The scene shown here was common in many parts of the country during the 1973 oil crisis.

Chapter 6: How Congress Works

Finally, the House voted 265 to 112 to send the bill on to a joint conference committee with the Senate. Now it was up to the conferees from the House, led by Staggers, and those from the Senate, led by Jackson, to reconcile the two bills and to write the final legislation in secret.

Monday, December 17: "We're going to try and get a bill out today," said Jackson Monday morning. The conference recessed at seven that night with no bill.

Tuesday, December 18: "We're going to try and get a bill out today," Staggers said in the morning. The conference recessed at ten that night with no bill.

Several problems developed in conference. First the President had no bill. Normally, the White House sends to Congress the program or law it wants, and the two houses work from that. But Jackson and Staggers had created legislation without any certainty that it was what the other half of the government wanted. President Nixon did have an energy bill in reserve, but he had elected to keep it secret.

The Senate bill had given the President—through William Simon, head of the Federal Energy Administration—fairly broad powers to handle the crisis as he saw fit. The House bill hemmed in the President. It made him come back to Congress for authority to start his programs. Edmund Muskie, one of the Senate conferees, solved this problem by giving Simon different degrees of power until different dates. Simon would have broad powers until March 1 and then more restricted powers until the end of June. The House version of the bill would be followed after June 30. Some parts of the Christmas tree were taken out, and others were left in. The antibusing amendment vanished. Environmental standards were made stronger. The gas-rationing battle that the Republicans had won was now regarded by the President as one that should not have been fought. With the White House having suddenly changed its mind, Heinz's amendment, to have the authority for gasoline rationing rest with Congress, was killed.

Wednesday, December 19: The conference committee turned to "windfall profits," the tax that was not a tax. There was no mention of such a tax in the Senate bill. None of the senators and none of the House Republicans liked the language in the House bill. But all the Democrats agreed that there had to be an excess-profits tax. Again, Muskie provided the compromise formula. He recommended the same strategy that had been used on excess profits during the Korean war of 1950–1953. This was to hold off starting the taxes for 1 year but then to make them go back a year. The tax-writing committees of the House and Senate would then have a chance to produce a professional excess-profits tax rather than the ill-defined measure before them. Slowly, the final compromises began to be argued and gaveled out, line by line.

The conferees broke up shortly before midnight with what they thought was a final agreement.

Thursday, December 20: When the joint-committee staff went to work over breakfast sausages, the agreement fell apart over a minor issue of wording. Tempers were so short that the ruckus lasted a whole day before a final agreement was reached.

Friday, December 21: The House and Senate were scheduled to vote at noon on the bill the conference produced. But neither the members of Congress, the White House, the press, nor the industries and labor unions involved had seen copies of the bill. House and Senate members had sent their staffs to the printing office, but there were not any copies yet.

Most of the members had plans to leave for home later in the day, for the Christmas weekend. At 10 A.M., snow began to fall. Those who lived far away feared that their

Chapter 6: How Congress Works

Hearings on various energy bills were conducted from 1973 to 1978, when an energy bill was finally passed and signed.

travel plans might be messed up if the day's work dragged on. Meanwhile, at the White House, members of the President's staff were finding the bill unacceptable. They objected to three things. First was the funding of the Energy Agency's budget directly by Congress instead of through the White House budget office. Second was the "windfall profits" section. Third was the requirement that oil companies make public the figures on their reserves and refinery operations. The staff also wanted a "laundry list" of things the President's chief economic adviser would be able to do without Congressional approval.

White House staff members brought their demands to Jackson and his staff shortly after 11:00 A.M. Unless the demands were met, they said, there would be a Presidential veto. At the same time, Senator Russell Long of Louisiana was finally getting a copy of the "windfall profits" section of the bill and getting ready to fight, himself. He would not go along with the Korean war idea of taxing. The oil industry was so badly regarded, he told Jackson, that the Congress might not pass fair legislation. The industry would then be crippled by the tortured provisions of the House bill.

Long and two other senators began a mini-filibuster. While talk droned on the floor, the White House staff members went to work. The main action began in the office of the Vice President, right off the Senate floor, then shifted to the office of Mike Mansfield, the Senate majority leader. Representatives Staggers and Dingell told Mansfield that the House would never accept the "laundry list" and would insist on an excess-profits tax and public disclosure of oil company holdings.

The White House struck a final deal with Jackson, Muskie, Long and Republican Senate leader Hugh Scott. The deal was that the "laundry list" would be forgotten; the "windfall profits" section would be omitted; and the oil companies would give their data to the President's chief economic adviser, who would pass the information on to the departments of Interior and Justice only. In a meeting with the Senate leaders, Staggers said no to the deal.

The Senate approved the deal, 52 to 8. But by amending the conference report rather than accepting it, the Senate had created new legislation. Now the Senate had to find a way to get the package back to the House, while bypassing a further conference. The Wild and Scenic Rivers Bill, which had been agreed to by both Houses, was brought to the floor of the Senate. And the entire Emergency Energy bill was hooked on to it as an amendment, or "rider." At 6:35 P.M., the Senate passed the amended Wild Rivers Bill and sent it to the House, certain that, in a few hours, the House would approve it.

But Staggers, Dingell, and the other House conferees, who had been in and out of the Senate chamber all afternoon, wandered back dejected to the House side of Congress. There, the Republicans went back to their offices. The Democrats went to the Speaker's office to try to decide what to do next. "They felt they had been double-crossed and they were mad," said a staff member who watched them.

The tactic they agreed on was that Staggers would bring up the Wild Rivers Bill with his own amendment to the Senate amendment. The Staggers' amendment put the "windfall profits" tax back in the bill, but in a more workable form. This move required a suspension of the House rules. And to do that, a two-thirds majority would be required before the bill could pass. The Democratic House leadership took a quick count and felt it had that majority. Then Staggers—still angry at the White House, and leaning against the wall because he was so tired and was coming down with the flu—made his mistake. He thought he had enough votes without calling on the Republicans for help. So he never contacted his committee Republicans who had stuck with him throughout the conference. They walked out on the floor without knowing what was coming off. Several of them stuck with him out of friendship, but they did not do any arm twisting to help him get other Republican votes.

By then, many House members had left for home. When Staggers introduced his amendment, the vote was 196 for it, 95 against. A switch of only four votes would have given him his two-thirds majority to suspend the House rules. A total of 168 members were not present. "If I had realized it was so close . . . ," Staggers mused later.

"House Kills Energy Bill" read the headlines the next day. The House lost. The Senate lost but ducked the blame. The President lost. And those rivers that were to be protected certainly lost, dead innocent bystanders of the energy battle.

Adapted from Arthur Hadley, "The Agony and the Energy Bill," *New Times,* February 22, 1974, pp. 21–24, by permission of New Times Publishing Co. Copyright © New Times 1974.

Questions

1 According to this account, what difficulties did the Emergency Energy Bill meet?

2 Why do you think each of these difficulties arose?

3 What finally happened to this bill?

4 If you had been a member of Congress and wanted such a bill to become law, what could you have done to help pass it?

5 If you had been a member of Congress and did not want such a bill passed, what could you have done to help defeat it?

6 The threat of a presidential veto forced some changes that most members of

Congress did not want. Do you think it is a good idea for one person to be able, through the veto, to override the wishes of 352 elected members of Congress? Explain.

⌂ Do you think that our federal lawmaking process should be less complicated? Explain.

PROBLEM: DO OUR FEDERAL LAWMAKERS USE THEIR TIME WISELY?

James Boyd, who worked on a senator's staff for 6 years, describes a senator's typical day in the following account. The typical day of a representative would be much the same. As you read this account, consider:

- *What kinds of things did this senator do?*
- *Was each of these things a good use of the senator's time?*

The senator starts his typical day tired. He returned very late last night from a speech back home, and he had to get up early this morning to present himself at a breakfast sponsored by utility executives. In the cab, he gives his *New York Times* a 10-minute reading, hoping that his aides will let him know if anything important happened yesterday. The breakfast is a bore, naturally, but he hopes he convinced those Republican business leaders that *he* is one Democrat who understands their problems.

He arrives at his office at 9:30, already 30 minutes late. He goes in through his private door, so visitors will not see him. He has the usual committee meeting scheduled at 10 o'clock, and he remembers that yesterday he tried to accommodate his legislative assistant by agreeing to be briefed for half an hour on everything under consideration by the committee.

But a check confirms his suspicion: his waiting room is crowded with people he cannot ignore. He apologizes to his assistant and tells his secretary to "run them in." One of them helped him in an election back in the dim past. ("He just wants to say hello and show his wife that he has entree to a senator's office.") Then there is a delegation of labor union people who contributed to his campaign last time. They want to let him know they are watching what he does on a labor bill.

By now the committee hearing has already started. But there are more constituents, or self-proclaimed representatives of constituents, to be seen. He greets them, one after another, listens, nodding agreeably for a few minutes, and turns them over to his aides. But he worries. He gets a lot of votes by helping constituents, and this service is one of his major assets during campaigns. He knows it takes up half the time of his staff, time that he needs for help on the issues. And besides, even though he helps these people, he knows that most of the things they ask are not in the public interest.

If a call from his office to the Veterans Administration causes the disability file of John Jones to be pulled from the middle of the pile and placed on top, it only means that all the others are set back one.

Then there is the medical student from Nigeria. He was given a visa several years ago to study under a State Department program. Now he has completed his course. But he does not want to go back to Nigeria. He wants to be a specialist here in the United States, and the hospital he is attached to wants him to stay, too, for there is a shortage in his specialty. So a lot of people are writing letters.

Once in a while, some humble citizen with a legitimate complaint *is* rescued from the toils of the bureaucracy, and this is duly written up in the monthly newsletter. But senators know that the sum total of their efforts for constituents, instead of improving

Chapter 6: How Congress Works

Talking with fellow senators, and listening to their views, may help clarify issues—or obscure them.

bureaucracy for the benefit of all, is lowering its efficiency for the sake of a few.

It is past 11 o'clock when he gets to the committee hearing. During the walk over, his legislative assistant gives him a hurried briefing, just enough to confuse him. In the hearings, he asks the wrong questions. So do other senators who come and go every few minutes. By ten minutes of twelve he has picked up the thread, but it is time to get to the Senate floor to insert into the *Congressional Record* a number of press releases just handed him by his head speechwriter.

The luncheon with his campaign finance chairperson takes an hour and a half because he has to take his guest around the Senate dining room and introduce him to all the senators.

It is now 2 o'clock. The senator is back in his office, and the afternoon schedule shapes up like a nightmare. But somehow he gets through it. He signs the 1 percent of the outgoing mail that commits him to things too important to be signed on the autograph machine. ("I wish I had time to read them carefully.") He worries about the 100,000 letters that he never sees that go out over his name each year. And every once in a while when he is back home, some constituent approaches him and complains that he wrote a month ago and never got an answer. The senator writes the name down and tries to get to the bottom of the matter. But usually he does not.

He misses one vote on the floor because he is taping a discussion program downtown, but he does make three votes.

Each time it takes 20 minutes to get over to the floor and back, so there goes an hour.

There are two afternoon committee sessions on his schedule. He goes to the one that is being televised. By 4 o'clock, he leaves the hearing to have his picture taken on the steps of the Capitol with a high school class from back home. Afterwards, he takes them into the Senate Reception Room, makes a little speech, shakes hands, and presents each visitor with a ball-point pen. ("They'll all be voters in three or four years, and their parents are voters now.")

He is late for his 4:30 appointment at NASA, but he knows that the top people there will wait for a senator. He is accompanied by business people from his state who are bidding for a new government contract. The meeting is mercifully short.

He is back in the office at 5:45 for some paper work. But his secretary hands him a list of twenty phone calls that must be returned. He goes through the list. He picks out six from the home-state politicians, reporters, and contributors; he turns the rest over to his administrative assistant. He finishes the calls at 6:30 and asks his staff in. They have been waiting for a crack at him all day on matters they think are urgent. But those matters must wait; today is the last day he can name his state's quota to West Point and Annapolis. He finally scribbles down the prescribed number of names, and that's that.

By now his aides can tell that he is bushed, so they do not press him for decisions. The talk is pleasant and general, and gradually the chief's energy revives. His cleaning is brought in and he changes. He has dinner scheduled tonight with a columnist who has seven outlets in his state. And after that, he has promised to take his wife to a party. He has not seen her for three nights, and tomorrow night he will be speaking for a $1,500 fee in Pennsylvania. Maybe when he gets home, around midnight, he will take an hour to dig into his briefcase, to read that material on the population explosion, on starvation in Mississippi, on a new idea for housing in the ghetto, on the missile defense system, on the currency crisis, on the nuclear proliferation treaty. Yes, he has been trying to get to that briefcase for days, and maybe he will tonight. But he knows he won't.

Adapted from James Boyd, "Legislate? Who, Me? What Happens to a Senator's Day," *Washington Monthly*, February 1969, Reprinted with permission from The Washington Monthly. Copyright © 1969 by The Washington Monthly Co.

Questions

1 What were the different kinds of activities in this senator's day? List them.

2 What was the purpose of each?

3 Could any of these activities have been omitted or taken care of in some better way? Explain.

◌ Judging by this account, do you think that senators tend to use their time wisely? Explain.

Chapter 6 Review

Developing Your Political Vocabulary

Imagine that you are a member of Congress who has introduced a bill. How might each of the following affect the fate of your bill?

a a filibuster
b a rider
c logrolling
d a standing committee
e party whips
f a conference committee
g the Speaker of the House
h cloture

Recalling and Comparing

1 What is the main duty of Congress?

2 What do political parties have to do with the organization of Congress?

3 What part do legislative committees play in Congress?

4 At what points might you, as an individual, influence the fate of a bill?

5 In what ways can the President influence legislation?

6 How can experts in various fields influence legislation?

7 What are lobbyists? What part can they play in the making of laws?

8 What are the methods of voting on a bill? Which method is used most often in the House of Representatives? In the Senate?

9 Is this statement true or false? "A bill that has been vetoed can still become law." Explain.

Special Activities

1 Begin a special bulletin board of clippings about bills that are being considered in the present Congress and keep it up to date.

2 From the *Congressional Record*, the *Digest of Public General Bills*, or another source, make a list of several bills that have been introduced in the present Congress. Assign each bill to a standing committee.

3 Do research on, and discuss with others, a problem you have noted about the workings of Congress. Discuss your findings in class and send your suggestions to your representative and senators in Congress.

4 Make a study of a bill that is being considered in Congress, reading arguments for and against the bill in newspapers and news magazines. When you have formed your own opinion on the bill, write a letter to your representative or senators in which you give reasons for supporting or voting against the bill.

5 As a class project, form a mock Congress with two houses. Then have two small groups write different bills on a topic of school or local concern and try to work their bills through both houses. Keep a record of the steps taken to defeat the bills.

6 Consider arguments for and against the following statement: "Committees in Congress serve a useful purpose." Then decide whether you agree or disagree with the statement and why.

Unit II Review

Improving Your Reading Skills

Read the selection below and then answer the questions that follow it.

Congress is the legislative branch of the federal government. A new Congress meets in January of every odd-numbered year, and it has two sessions, one in each year of its life.

Article I of the Constitution states what powers Congress shall have. Most of these powers are expressed, but others are implied in Clause 18. Article I also states what powers Congress shall not have.

The Constitution provides for a Congress with two houses, the House of Representatives and the Senate. Each house has some powers which the other does not have. After each 10-year census, the 435 House members are divided among the states according to state population. Districts within states are now related to population as well. The 2-year terms of representatives all end in the same year. The 6-year terms of the 100 senators overlap. Only one-third of the Senate is elected at one time.

Though Congress has other powers, most of its day-to-day work is related to lawmaking. For this purpose, Congress is organized into standing committees.

The two major political parties form party caucuses in Congress to guide legislation along lines they desire. They select floor leaders and party whips to round up votes. The majority party has the largest number of members on the standing committees and names the committee chairpersons.

Laws begin as bills. Every bill follows its separate course through the House or the Senate. Each bill is assigned to a standing committee, and most bills die there. If a bill is approved by the standing committee, it goes back to the house from which it came. There it is debated and may be revised. At least a majority of the members of each house must approve a bill for it to be passed. A bill that passes the two houses in different forms is sent to a conference committee. Here members of both houses try to arrive at a single form for the bill. If they do, the final bill goes back to both houses for action.

Once approved, a bill goes to the President. The President's signature makes it law. A bill can also become law if the President does not act on it for 10 days while Congress is still in session. The President may veto a bill, but a direct veto can be overturned by a two-thirds majority in both houses. A pocket veto kills a bill.

Only about one bill in every twenty becomes a law. A bill that does not become law during a term of Congress dies at the end of that term.

1 In your own words, summarize this reading in no more than *four* sentences. Have your summary focus on what you regard as the most important points made in the reading.

2 The term *legislative* can best be used to describe which *one* of the following topics discussed in the reading?
  a The powers granted to Congress in Article I of the Constitution.
  b The meeting time of Congress.
  c The political party members in Congress.
  d Use of the pocket veto by the President.

Unit II Review: The Legislative Branch

3 Which *three* of the following topics discussed in the reading are related to the process of a bill's becoming a law?

    a Functions of standing committees in Congress.
    b Functions of conference committees in Congress.
    c Implied powers as granted by Clause 18 of the Constitution.
    d Presidential approval or disapproval of a proposed bill.

Developing Your Writing Skills: What Are Your Attitudes toward Government?

In this unit, you have considered the steps through which a bill must pass in order to become a law. Now think about these questions:

- *What makes a bill worthy of passage?*
- *What question or questions would you ask in order to decide whether a particular bill should be passed?*

Write a paragraph expressing your views. Begin with the sentence below, making it a complete sentence by selecting either "one" or "more than one."

I believe that there is (one/more than one) way in which to determine whether a law proposed in Congress is worthy of passage.

Recommended Reading

The Almanac of American Politics, Dutton, New York.
Congressional Digest (monthly).
Congressional Index (biennial).
Congressional Record (daily).
Richard F. Fenno, *The Power of the Purse,* Little, Brown, Boston, 1966.
Harrison W. Fox, Jr., and Susan W. Hammond, *Congressional Staffs: The Invisible Force in American Lawmaking,* Free Press, New York, 1977.
Walter Goodman, *The Committee: The Extraordinary Career of the House Committee on Un-American Activities,* Farrar, Straus & Giroux, New York, 1968.
Mark J. Green *et al., Who Runs Congress?,* Bantam Books, New York (paperback).
Sven Groenings and Jonathan P. Hawley, *To Be a Congressman,* Acropolis Books, Washington, D.C., 1973 (paperback).
Richard Harris, *The Real Voice,* Macmillan, New York, 1964.
Alvin M. Josephy, Jr., *The American Heritage History of the Congress of the United States,* McGraw-Hill, New York, 1975.
Ralph Nader Congress Report, *Ruling Congress: How the House and Senate Rules Govern the Legislative Process,* Penguin Books, New York, 1977.
Wright Patman, *Our American Government and How It Works,* Barnes & Noble, New York, 1974 (paperback).
Lawrence J. Pauline and Richard Gross, *Congress: The National Legislature,* Oxford Book Company, New York, 1973.
Robert L. Peabody *et al., To Enact a Law,* Praeger, New York, 1973.
Don Riegle, *O Congress,* Popular Library, New York, 1976 (paperback).
Ellen Switzer, *There Ought to Be a Law: How Laws Are Made and Work,* Atheneum, New York, 1972.
Washington Monthly.

The Executive Branch of the National Government

UNIT III

The Constitution created an executive branch to carry out the laws passed by Congress and to run the day-to-day business of government. That executive branch has several parts. Usually, though, when we think of the executive branch, we are thinking of the President.

People have always been curious about what kind of person their President is. Thomas Jefferson, for example, stirs people's curiosity. The nation's third President had lived grandly as a planter, but as President, he lived simply. His way of life led to stories like the following one about a visitor to the capital.

This visitor chanced upon a man who wore an ordinary brown suit, but rode a fine horse. The visitor asked if the man would trade his horse. "I want a good horse to get me out of town fast," said the visitor. "I hate that man Jefferson."

"Ever seen him?" asked the man in the suit.

"No, but I'd know him anywhere. The hypocrite pretends to be for the people, but he wears costly clothes, two watches, and rings on every finger," said the visitor.

"You may have been misinformed, sir. The President dresses no better than I do. It happens that business takes me to the White House tomorrow. Meet me there at ten, and you may see the man."

The visitor went to the White House the next day. He described what happened.

"My rider friend was near the door. But before he could speak to me, a servant approached him with a letter. 'Mr. President,' the servant began. I heard no more. I turned and ran—nearly killed myself on those rickety steps."

Based on Clara Ingram Judson, *Thomas Jefferson: Champion of the People*, Follett, Chicago, 1952, pp. 180–189. Copyright © 1952 by Follett Publishing Company. Used by permission.

Of course, it is not Jefferson's—or any President's—outward appearance that really matters. What matters is how a President carries out the powers and duties of the highest office in the land. Some of those powers can be delegated to others, but the President remains responsible for what is done. The President, the Cabinet, the President's staff, and a vast number of agencies make up the executive branch. It is their role in our national government that is the subject of this unit.

The unit contains three chapters. The first, Chapter 7, is concerned with individuals—the President and the President's chief advisers, including the Cabinet, members of the Executive Office of the President, and others. The next two chapters discuss the vast bureaucracy that helps to carry out the responsibilities of the executive branch. Chapter 8 discusses the role of the executive departments, each of which is headed by a Cabinet member and is responsible for carrying out certain executive functions. Chapter 9 turns to the many independent agencies that carry out other functions of the executive branch of the federal government.

Chapter 7

The Presidency

The President of the United States holds the highest office in our federal government. It is the President's duty to see that all federal laws, rules, and treaties are properly enforced. The President thus is our chief executive officer, and is sometimes called the Chief Executive. But the President has many other roles as well. The Constitution mentions several of them. For example, it provides that the President shall be our head of state, representing the United States in dealings with other countries, and also commander in chief of the armed forces.

Even so, the Constitution does not reveal much about what a modern President does. For the Presidency is an ever-changing office. Presidents in our day perform many functions that were not dreamed of in 1787. The office has grown to meet the nation's changing needs and desires. This chapter will focus on the many faces of the Presidency.

Goals

- To see how the nation chooses its Presidents.
- To learn the powers of the Presidency.
- To understand the roles of the President's advisers.
- To consider how public a President should be.
- To consider when a President should be declared disabled.

Chapter 7: The Presidency

AN OVERVIEW OF THE PRESIDENCY

The words are simple and solemn. They are spoken by each President upon assuming office, as required by the Constitution. Usually, the President's hand rests on a Bible to underline the seriousness of the occasion:

> I do solemnly swear (or affirm) that I will faithfully execute the office of President of the United States, and will to the best of my ability, preserve, protect, and defend the Constitution of the United States.

George Washington was the first to take that oath of office. He was standing on the balcony of Federal Hall, overlooking Wall Street in New York City. Nowadays, the oath is usually administered by the Chief Justice of the United States at the Capitol in Washington, D.C. That is where Jimmy Carter took the oath when he became the nation's thirty-ninth President on January 20, 1977.

By custom, after taking the oath of office, the President gives an *inaugural address.* This first speech by each President usually sets out a philosophy of government and a program to put those ideas into action. The task facing President Washington was impressive enough. He was to lead a nation of almost 4 million people, a new nation not yet settled in its traditions or its practices. As Washington wrote to a friend, he faced "an ocean of difficulties." The expression was apt at a time when sailing ships were the fastest means of long-distance travel and communication.

The tasks facing recent Presidents are vastly more complex. The United States is now a nation of more than 220 million people. It sprawls from the Atlantic Ocean to Alaska and across the Pacific to Hawaii. Enormous changes have taken place in the economy, communication, and transportation. The United States is now a leading world power. Changing needs and changing attitudes about the role of government have greatly enlarged the scope of the Presidency.

Electing a President

Every 4 years, the people of the United States line up to do battle. They divide into factions, each backing a candidate for the Presidency. Each faction cries that the country will go to rack and ruin unless its candidate is elected. Each promises that things will get better if its candidate is elected. Sometimes, things do get better. Sometimes, they get worse. Yet things are never quite so good as the promises, nor so bad as the worst predictions.

THE PROCESS OF ELECTING A PRESIDENT AND A VICE PRESIDENT

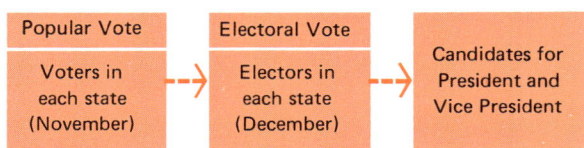

The popular vote for President and Vice President is commonly said to be for a particular candidate or party. Nevertheless, the vote is for electors, and their existence does sometimes influence elections. See the map on page 137.

The Founders did not foresee the exact nature of modern elections when they provided the framework for them. Some of the basic rules for electing a President that were spelled out in the Constitution were later changed. Here is how things work today:

A President and a Vice President are elected in November of every fourth year. President Carter was elected in 1976. Presidential elections are scheduled in 1980, 1984, and so on.

The voters cast their ballots on the Tuesday following the first Monday in November. They do not vote directly for the President and the Vice President. Instead, they vote for *electors* in each state. These electors are people chosen by each party to support its presidential

Chapter 7: The Presidency

PRESIDENTS OF THE UNITED STATES

No.	Name	In Office	Political Party	Native State	Age at First Inauguration
1	George Washington	1789–1797	(none)	VA	57
2	John Adams	1797–1801	Federalist	MA	61
3	Thomas Jefferson	1801–1809	Democratic-Republican	VA	57
4	James Madison	1809–1817	Democratic-Republican	VA	57
5	James Monroe	1817–1825	Democratic-Republican	VA	58
6	John Quincy Adams	1825–1829	National-Republican	MA	57
7	Andrew Jackson	1829–1837	Democratic	SC	61
8	Martin Van Buren	1837–1841	Democratic	NY	54
9	William Henry Harrison	March 4—April 4, 1841[a]	Whig	VA	68
10	John Tyler	1841–1845	Whig	VA	51
11	James K. Polk	1845–1849	Democratic	NC	49
12	Zachary Taylor	1849–1850[a]	Whig	VA	64
13	Millard Fillmore	1850–1853	Whig	NY	50
14	Franklin Pierce	1853–1857	Democratic	NH	48
15	James Buchanan	1857–1861	Democratic	PA	65
16	Abraham Lincoln	1861–1865[a]	Republican	KY	52
17	Andrew Johnson	1865–1869	Democratic[b]	NC	56
18	Ulysses S. Grant	1869–1877	Republican	OH	46
19	Rutherford B. Hayes	1877–1881	Republican	OH	54
20	James A. Garfield	March 4—Sept. 19, 1881[a]	Republican	OH	49
21	Chester A. Arthur	1881–1885	Republican	VT	50
22	Grover Cleveland	1885–1889	Democratic	NY	47
23	Benjamin Harrison	1889–1893	Republican	OH	55
24	Grover Cleveland	1893–1897	Democratic	NY	55
25	William McKinley	1897–1901[a]	Republican	OH	54
26	Theodore Roosevelt	1901–1909	Republican	NY	42
27	William Howard Taft	1909–1913	Republican	OH	51
28	Woodrow Wilson	1913–1921	Democratic	VA	56
29	Warren G. Harding	1921–1923[a]	Republican	OH	55
30	Calvin Coolidge	1923–1929	Republican	VT	51
31	Herbert C. Hoover	1929–1933	Republican	CA	54
32	Franklin D. Roosevelt	1933–1945[a]	Democratic	NY	51
33	Harry S Truman	1945–1953	Democratic	MO	60
34	Dwight D. Eisenhower	1953–1961	Republican	TX	62
35	John F. Kennedy	1961–1963[a]	Democratic	MA	43
36	Lyndon B. Johnson	1963–1969	Democratic	TX	55
37	Richard M. Nixon	1969–1974[c]	Republican	CA	56
38	Gerald R. Ford	1974–1977	Republican	NE	61
39	James E. Carter	1977–	Democratic	GA	52

a. Died in office (Lincoln, Garfield, McKinley, and Kennedy were assassinated).
b. Andrew Johnson, a former Democratic senator and then Union governor of Tennessee, had been nominated Vice President by Republicans in 1864, in an effort to gain Democratic votes. He had been elected with Lincoln on the "National Union" ticket.
c. Resigned August 9, 1974.

The use of voting machines has greatly reduced the length of time needed to know who was elected President.

and vice-presidential candidates. In most states, the electors are not legally bound to do so, however, and some have switched their votes.

A state may have anywhere from three to forty-five electors since each state has as many electors as it has senators and representatives in Congress. There are now 538 electors in all, including three from the District of Columbia. Together, the electors are known as the *electoral college*.

The electors in each state cast their ballots for President and Vice President in December. The electoral ballots from each state are sent to Washington, D. C., for a formal count. Early in January, they are certified before a joint session of Congress. This, properly speaking, is the point at which a President is actually elected. In reality, the nation usually knows who the next President will be by late on election night in November.

What if no candidate wins a majority of the electoral college votes? That has not happened since 1824, but when it does happen, the House of Representatives elects the President from among the top three candidates. Each state's delegation to the House gets only one vote. Thus there are fifty votes, of which twenty-six are needed to elect the President.

The new President takes office on January 20.

Congress sets the amount of the President's compensation. George Washington received a salary of $25,000 a year—a huge sum in 1789 when he took office. Presidents' salaries, like other people's, have since gone up. Nowadays a President receives $200,000 a year in salary and about $150,000 a year for official expenses, entertainment, and travel.

Congress has also seen to the needs of former Presidents by providing them a lifetime pension of $60,000 a year. They also receive free mailing privileges, free office space, and about $90,000 a year for office help. A President's surviving spouse is entitled to a pension of $20,000 a year.

The Vice President receives an annual salary of $75,000, free housing, and $10,000 a year for expenses.

Who Can Serve and How Long

What does it take to be President of the United States? It takes great political skill, certainly. Considerable knowledge and contacts with important people are necessary. So is a sense of history. No doubt it helps to have a sense of humor. But these are not formal requirements. The formal requirements are much simpler.

The Constitution states who is eligible to be President (Article II, Section 1). The President must be a natural-born citizen of the United States and must have been a resident of this country for at least 14 years before taking office. He or she must also be at least 35 years of age when taking office. The same qualifications apply to the Vice President.

Chapter 7: The Presidency

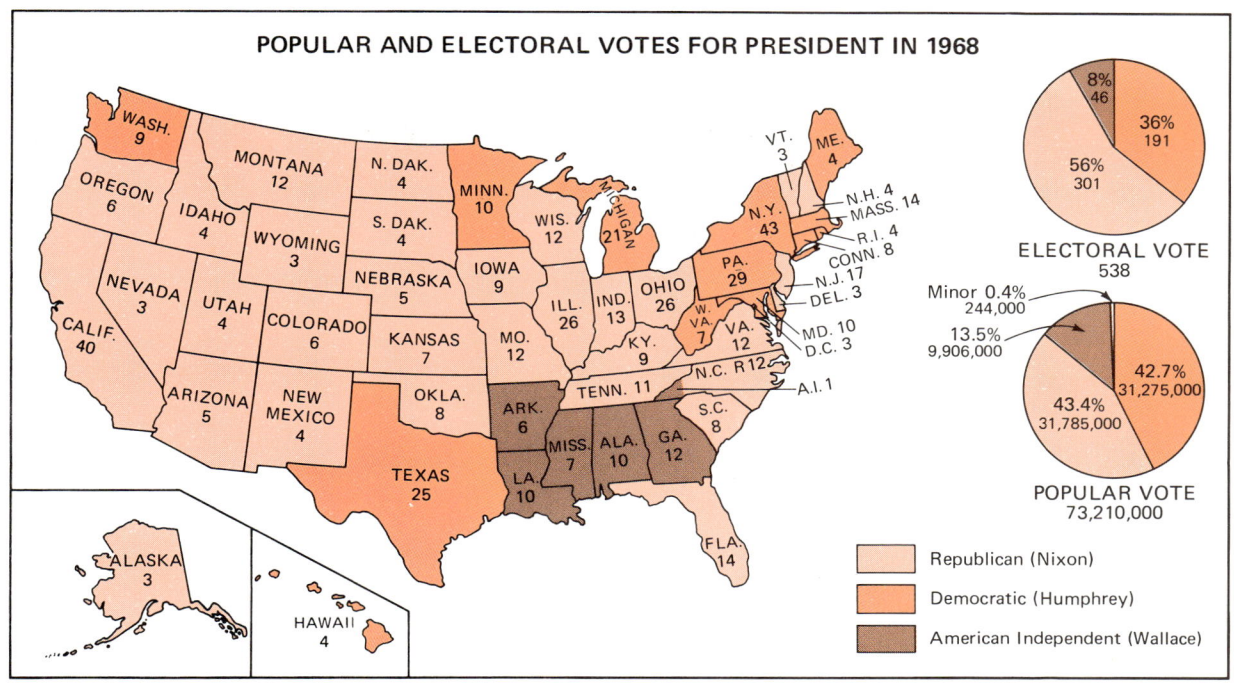

In 1968, the American Independent party received 13.5 percent of the popular vote and 8 percent of the electoral vote.

Jimmy Carter, shown here in a relaxed moment with two of his aides, was 52 years old when he was elected President.

As yet, there has been no President so young as 35. Theodore Roosevelt was the youngest person ever to assume the Presidency. He was 42 and serving as Vice President when President William McKinley died of an assassin's wound in 1901. John F. Kennedy was the youngest elected Chief Executive. He was 43 when he took office in 1961. When William Henry Harrison took office in 1841 at the age of 68, he was the oldest to assume the Presidency. But President Harrison died only a month later. The oldest President to serve was Dwight D. Eisenhower, who was 70 by the end of his second term.

The President is elected for a term of 4 years, and the same person may be elected only twice. George Washington set the pattern by serving 8 years and then stepping down. For more than a century afterward, no President served more than two terms. There was no formal rule about this. It was just tradition.

Chapter 7: The Presidency

> **President-Watching**
>
> As the top figure in the United States government, the President symbolizes the entire nation. People keep a close eye on, and sometimes copy, what their President is doing.
>
> Jimmy Carter was a peanut farmer before he became President in 1977. He liked to snack on peanuts. After his election, it became an "in" custom to serve peanuts to guests—at least to Democrats.
>
> Many recent Presidents have been golfers. They probably gave increased status to the game of golf—and some comfort to the ordinary player. Eisenhower kept his scores secret (they were only average). Kennedy accidentally hit a Secret Service agent with a golf shot in 1961. Ford hit a spectator the same way.
>
> Kennedy liked to play touch football on the lawn of the White House. When he stressed the need for people to keep physically fit, many people took a new interest in exercise. Schools introduced special programs to help "shape up" young people.
>
> Presidents and their spouses also help set fashion trends. Jacqueline Kennedy, for example, influenced hair and dress styles in the early 1960s. Carter's liking for sweaters and jeans helped to promote a casual style of dress.
>
> President Truman was an avid reader, and history was his favorite subject. He is said to have read every book in his hometown public library by the time he was 14. Yet there is nothing to show that Truman's interest in reading history led to any great increase in public library memberships among the voters.

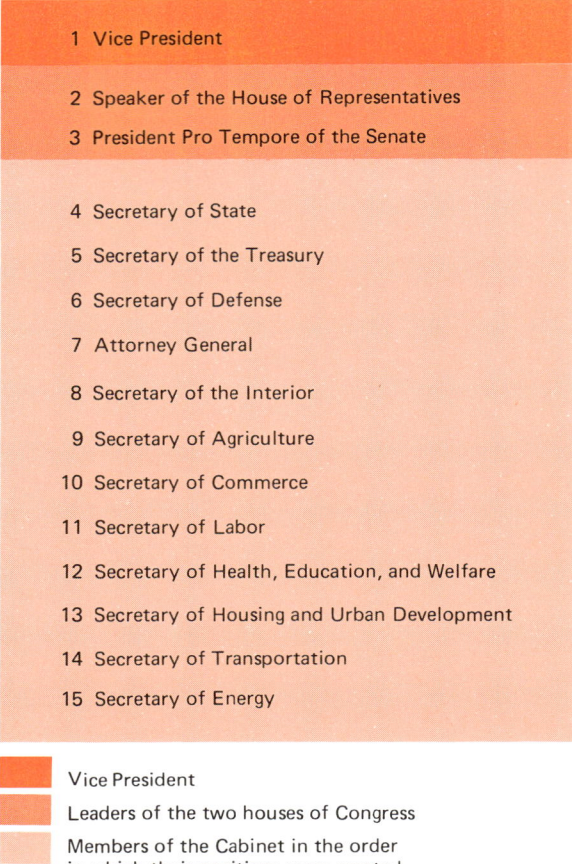

ORDER OF SUCCESSION TO THE PRESIDENCY
(Presidential Succession Act of 1947)

1. Vice President
2. Speaker of the House of Representatives
3. President Pro Tempore of the Senate
4. Secretary of State
5. Secretary of the Treasury
6. Secretary of Defense
7. Attorney General
8. Secretary of the Interior
9. Secretary of Agriculture
10. Secretary of Commerce
11. Secretary of Labor
12. Secretary of Health, Education, and Welfare
13. Secretary of Housing and Urban Development
14. Secretary of Transportation
15. Secretary of Energy

■ Vice President
■ Leaders of the two houses of Congress
■ Members of the Cabinet in the order in which their positions were created by Congress

In 1940, however, Franklin D. Roosevelt sought and won reelection to a third term. Then, in 1944, he won a fourth term. Because many people thought that was too many years for one person to serve as President, the Twenty-second Amendment was added to the Constitution in 1951 to limit Presidents' terms.

Under the Twenty-second amendment, no President may be elected for more than two terms. Thus, a President is normally limited to 8 years in office. But it is still possible for a President to serve up to 10 years. That can happen if the President assumes office during a term to which someone else had been elected. For example, if a President dies in office, becomes incapacitated, or resigns, the Presidency goes to the Vice President. If this happens more than half way through the term of office, the new President can still seek election twice.

William McKinley was the third of four Presidents to be killed by a political assassin.

Vacancies in the Office of President

If the position of President becomes vacant, the Vice President becomes President (Article II, Section 1; Amendment XXV, Section 1). As we have just seen, there are several reasons why the position might become vacant. William Henry Harrison, in 1841, was the first of several Presidents to die in office. So far, the office has not become vacant through illness or other disability. Richard Nixon, in 1974, was the only President to resign.

Congress has provided a line of succession in case there is no Vice President to succeed to office. (See the chart opposite.) So far, however, only Vice Presidents have taken over a vacant Presidency.

Public attention is focused on the problem of succession when a President dies or is seriously ill. This happened at least seven times since 1900. President William McKinley was shot and died in 1901. President Woodrow Wilson was disabled by a stroke in 1919. President Warren G. Harding died in office in 1923 and Franklin D. Roosevelt in 1945. President Dwight D. Eisenhower had a heart attack in 1955, followed by a major operation in 1956. Concern about succession resulted in action after President John F. Kennedy's assassination in 1963.

On Kennedy's death, Vice President Lyndon Johnson became President, and the Vice-Presidency was left vacant with more than a year remaining in the presidential term. What if something happened to Johnson during that time? The first two people in the line of succession were John McCormack, Speaker of the House of Representatives, and Carl Hayden, President pro tempore of the Senate. McCormack was 71 years old; Hayden was in his eighties. Both doubted their ability to meet the rigorous demands of the Presidency because of their age.

Congress soon began work on a constitutional amendment to provide for filling a vacancy in the office of Vice President. The amendment was proposed in 1965. It was ratified in 1967 and went into effect that year as the Twenty-fifth Amendment.

Section 2 of the Twenty-fifth Amendment provides a means of filling a vacancy in the Vice President's office. (For another aspect of that amendment, see p. 152.) The President is to nominate a person for the office. The nomination goes before both houses of Congress, and if a majority of each house approves, the person becomes Vice President.

This was the procedure followed when Spiro Agnew resigned as Vice President in 1973 after a scandal. President Nixon nominated, and Congress approved, Gerald Ford as Vice President. Ford, himself, became President when Nixon resigned the following year. Ford, in turn, nominated Nelson Rockefeller to be Vice President, and Congress again approved. In this rapid series of events, the nation found itself for the first time with a President and Vice President neither of whom had been elected to that office by the people.

Questions

1 What are the constitutional qualifications for anyone elected to be President or Vice President?

2 How many terms can a President serve? How many years? Explain.

3 Why did Congress see a need to provide some way to fill the Vice President's office if it became vacant?

⬠ Do you think it is a good idea to limit the number of terms a President may serve? Why or why not?

The President's Powers and Duties

The history of the Presidency has been a tug of war between those who tried to expand

Richard M. Nixon was the first person ever to resign from the office of President of the United States. His resignation in 1974 made headlines in newspapers around the world.

the President's powers and those who tried to limit them. Over the years, however, the powers have greatly expanded.

The Constitution gives only a short list of the powers of the President. Does this mean that the President has only those few powers? Some Presidents have thought so. William Howard Taft, for instance, argued that the President "can exercise no power which cannot be fairly and reasonably traced to some specific grant of power." That grant could be made only by the Constitution or by Congress, Taft believed.

Most Presidents have taken a broader view of the office. Woodrow Wilson, who succeeded Taft, believed that a President "is at liberty, both in law and conscience, to be as big a man as he can." Some Presidents have wanted to be big men indeed.

The President, first of all, has the executive power of our federal government. This is spelled out in Article II of the Constitution. That article begins, "The executive power shall be vested in a President of the United States of

America." Thus, *all* the executive power rests in the hands of the President. It does not rest in the hands of the Vice President, nor in the hands of anyone who works for the President. Naturally, that power is limited by what any one person is capable of doing.

The Constitution also gives the President certain powers related to lawmaking. We have already seen some of those powers. Each bill passed by Congress is sent to the White House, which is the President's home and office. The President then has 10 days, not counting Sundays, to act on the bill. The choices are three: to sign the bill, to veto it, or to ignore it. What happens in each case has been explained on page 119.

The President's power to recommend legislation (Article II, Section 3) is an extremely important one. Presidents have made much use of this power and now have a large staff to help write legislation. This staff can consult with other employees of the executive branch and with members of the Cabinet. On a major bill, the President may spend 20 to 25 hours working with the staff. Finally, the bill is ready to go to Congress. If it is a major bill, the President may seek television and radio time to publicize it. The ability to command national attention gives the President a major advantage in winning support through speeches and press conferences. Thus, the President has become one of the nation's leading lawmakers. Congress may change or reject the President's proposals, but it cannot completely ignore them.

The Constitution says that the President "shall from time to time give to the Congress Information of the State of the Union" (Article II, Section 3). The giving of this information has become a regular event. Each year, in January, the President delivers a State of the Union message to Congress. It presents the President's legislative program and arguments in favor of it. The message now gets national attention because it is usually read to Congress by the President and broadcast over radio and television. The President also sends Congress a budget for the federal government, as well as other messages from time to time.

Another power that the Constitution gives the President is that of calling Congress into special session. The special sessions are not limited to topics the President considers important. Congress may take up any measures it sees fit. There is no longer much need or opportunity for special sessions because Congress is in session most of the year.

One of the President's important powers relates to the judicial branch. It is the power to appoint the judges of the federal courts. These appointments must be approved by the Senate, with one exception: when an appointment is made while the Senate is not in session, the President's appointee may serve until the end of the next session of Congress. Otherwise, Supreme Court justices and almost all federal judges serve for life. Thus, they can carry on a

"PAGE ONE"

HESSE IN *ST. LOUIS GLOBE-DEMOCRAT*

Chapter 7: The Presidency

> **A President's Power Put to Use**
>
> The President's power to call a special session of Congress was meant to be used only in an emergency. But some Presidents have used this power for political purposes. President Harry Truman was one. In 1948, after the Republican National Convention, Truman ordered the 80th Congress back into session. Truman, a Democrat, challenged the Republican-controlled Congress to enact a program the Republican party had adopted. When Congress failed to do that, Truman campaigned for reelection against the "do-nothing 80th Congress." He won.

President's political views long after the President leaves office. An example was President John Adams's appointment of John Marshall.

The President has important powers in dealing with other nations. As chief of state, the President is the nation's top diplomat. One way the President represents the nation is by making treaties with other countries. A *treaty* is a formal agreement in which two or more nations promise to do certain things. For example, in recent years the United States and the Soviet Union have signed treaties to put controls on the arms race. Also, the United States and Panama have signed twin treaties that provide for a gradual turning over of control of the Canal to Panama.

Jimmy Carter, as President, here signs the Panama Canal treaties. Later, Jimmy Carter in the role of politician and leader of the Democratic party struggled to get the treaties approved by the Senate.

Any treaty signed by the President can go into effect only after it is approved by a two-thirds vote of the Senate. Once approved by the Senate, a treaty becomes part of "the law of the land," and can be enforced through the courts. Sometimes the Senate turns down a treaty. After World War I, the Senate voted against a treaty that President Woodrow Wilson all but staked his life on. It would have made the United States a member of the League of Nations. The United States never joined the League. More recently, each of the two Panama Canal treaties was approved with only one vote to spare though Panamanian extremists had threatened to blow up the Canal if the treaties were not approved.

The President can also make *executive agreements* with foreign nations. These agreements signed by the heads of states often deal with routine matters such as trade rules. But they can deal with more controversial matters, just like treaties. Because executive agreements do not require Senate approval, Presidents sometimes take important steps by means of executive agreements. That is what Franklin D. Roosevelt did in 1940 in order to trade ships of the United States Navy for permission to use some military bases controlled by Great Britain. At the time, Britain was fighting in World War II but the United States was still at peace.

As the nation's top diplomat, the President must decide whether or not the United States will recognize, or have dealings with, other governments. This is done by sending and receiving diplomats. The United States sends ambassadors only to countries the President has officially recognized. The President appoints ambassadors and other diplomats, subject to confirmation by the Senate.

The Constitution spells out certain powers of the President to conduct wars. The President is commander in chief of the United States armed forces and of all state militias. Though only Congress can declare wars, the President can use the armed forces to meet any sudden attacks from abroad or to halt any uprising at home.

The President also can order United States forces into foreign conflicts without a declaration of war. That happened in Vietnam and stirred a bitter controversy in this country. As a result, Congress passed a law to limit the President's power when war has not been declared by Congress. The law passed over a presidential veto in 1974. It limits to 60 days the time that a President can commit troops to a conflict overseas. Unless the President can get the approval of Congress within that time, the troops must be withdrawn. An extra 30 days may be allowed for this action. Also, the 1974 law requires that the President consult with key members of Congress before ordering any troops into battle. Congress can halt the President's use of troops at any time. All it has to do is pass a *concurrent resolution.* Such a resolution, passed by both the House and the Senate, requires a simple majority and cannot be vetoed.

The President has other powers and duties as commander in chief. One duty is to protect citizens traveling in other countries and, if necessary, use troops to do so. Another is to guard the safety of foreign visitors in this country. The President may also protect United States-owned property in other countries.

The President can issue pardons and reprieves (Article II, Section 2). A *pardon* is a legal document that frees a person from punishment for a crime. If it is an absolute pardon, it removes all charges against the person. A *reprieve* postpones the carrying out of a penalty for a crime. The President can also shorten federal prison terms and reduce fines.

The President can grant pardons to any person convicted of breaking a federal law, except in cases of impeachment. A pardon may also be granted to a person who has not been convicted of a crime. That is what President Ford did in 1974 when he granted a pardon to Richard Nixon shortly after Nixon resigned as President. Nixon had been in-

President Ford's pardon of former President Nixon was supported by some but opposed by others. Feelings ran high on both sides, and still do.

volved in a scandal known as the Watergate Affair. Some people had accused Nixon of committing crimes while President, but he had not been convicted or even formally charged with a crime. The pardon meant that Nixon could not later be charged with a crime relating to the Watergate Affair.

The President can also grant a group pardon, known as an *amnesty*. After the Civil War, President Andrew Johnson granted amnesty to some Confederate veterans. In 1889, Benjamin Harrison granted amnesty to members of the Mormon faith, some of whom had violated federal laws against polygamy, or multiple marriages. Presidents Ford and Carter granted limited amnesties to some persons who had broken draft laws and military rules during the Vietnam war.

The President has acquired a number of informal powers that are not specified in the Constitution. The President's informal powers have arisen from the size and complexity of modern government. Government growth is revealed by the number of people who work for the President. We now have 2.1 million men and women in the armed forces and 2.8 million civilians working for the executive branch of the federal government. All told, the President today is in charge of more people than were living in the United States of 1789.

One informal power is the power to issue *executive orders*, or presidential orders to agencies in the executive branch to carry out certain policies. Executive orders are sometimes used to impose policies on the executive branch. After World War II, President Truman used an executive order to end racial segregation in the armed forces. Executive orders must not conflict with any provision of the Constitution or with any other federal law. If they do, they can be overruled by the federal courts.

Presidents also use executive orders to establish *commissions*, or temporary groups to investigate important questions. George Washington appointed a commission to look into the causes of the 1794 Whiskey Rebellion, an uprising of Pennsylvania whiskey makers against the federal liquor tax. Lyndon Johnson appointed a commission to investigate the assassination of President Kennedy in 1963. Commissions are merely fact-finding bodies. Once they issue a report, their job is done. A President need not follow the proposals made in the report.

The President also has broad leeway in carrying out the laws passed by Congress. Often a law merely sets down certain goals desired by Congress and leaves it to the executive branch to decide how to meet these goals. Thus, when Congress decided to ban cancer-causing food additives, it did not make a list of banned items. It left that task to the Food and Drug Administration, which is part of the executive branch.

Chapter 7: The Presidency

> **A First Lady's Life**
>
> When Rosalynn Carter became First Lady, she had to decide for herself what her role would be. There are no rules or clear precedents for the role of First Lady. In the following selections from an interview, Rosalynn Carter describes a busy life.
>
> Q: Mrs. Carter, how do you view the role of First Lady?
>
> A: I'll handle it the only way I know how. I haven't looked to see what the past First Ladies did or how they operated. I'll be busy doing the things that are important to me. I learned when Jimmy was Governor [of Georgia] that you can be influential in almost anything that you want to be involved in.
>
> Right now I am putting together the Commission on Mental Health, and we're trying to work up some way to spotlight the needs of the elderly. So there are a lot of things that I want to do, and I'll be busy.
>
> Q: How many hours a day do you spend on your official duties?
>
> A: How many hours are there in a day? In the morning, Jimmy goes over to his office at 7 o'clock, but Amy [their young daughter] doesn't leave for school until 8:30, so I eat breakfast with her. I take Spanish lessons from nine to twelve 3 days a week.
>
> But most of the time I spend working on things I'm interested in, planning for foreign visitors, taking care of the correspondence. It's demanding and challenging. I get letters every day to be honorary chairperson of things that I just don't have time to get involved with. That's one of the hardest things—deciding what your priorities are. There are so many good causes and so many things that need help in the country. I like to really be involved, not just be an honorary chairperson. But I also realize that I can help just by lending my name.
>
> Q: You have an eighteen member staff. Just what do they do?
>
> A: I have a social secretary, a press secretary, my personal secretary, one in charge of my schedule, and a projects coordinator. Those are the main ones, and some of them have assistants. All of them are really working, too.
>
> My office is responsible for anything that goes on in the White House, whether it's a function of my own or not. We plan the format for the working visits by foreign visitors, with input from the State Department and the National Security Council. If it's a breakfast that Jimmy has for congressional leaders, a state visit on the lawn or whatever, my office handles it.
>
> Not only my staff is kept busy, but we have six volunteers, too, who come in and answer phones, type and do other work. I'm averaging forty-five or fifty invitations a day, and somebody has to answer those. The telephones ring all the time, and we need people to answer them. There is no way we could do it all without the volunteers.
>
> *U.S. News & World Report,* March 21, 1977. Copyright © 1977 by U.S. News & World Report, Inc.

A President can sometimes refuse to follow through on a law passed by Congress. This can happen when Congress appropriates money for a project that the President does not favor. The President might then hold the money and not allow it to be spent. This is known as the power to *impound funds*. The extent of that power depends, however, on the way a bill is written. A Democratic Congress proved this in the 1970s in a contest with President Nixon, a Republican. Congress passed a bill to assist state and local water pollution programs. The bill was vetoed by the President and then passed over his veto. President Nixon ordered most of the funds impounded. When New York City sued to force release of the impounded funds, the case went to the Supreme Court. The Court ruled in 1975 that President Nixon could not impound funds in this instance.

Presidents have also claimed executive privilege—that is, a special right to withhold information from Congress. Sometimes a claim of executive privilege is based on a need for secrecy. President Nixon made such a claim regarding certain conversations that had been tape-recorded in the White House during the Watergate Affair. Congress felt that it had a right to the information. The Supreme Court decided that, in this case, the President's claim of executive privilege was not valid. The Court ordered Nixon to give Congress most of the information it wanted, but the Court did not challenge the principle of executive privilege.

The President as a Political Leader

The President is not only the Chief Executive but also the leader of his or her political party. George Washington would have found this shocking. He thought that political parties—which he called "factions"—would lead to needless strife. But they have become a necessary part of modern democracy.

George Washington believed that the nation's Chief Executive should be above politics. On questions of foreign policy, some later Presidents have tried to follow Washington's advice. They have sought support from all citizens for their foreign policies so that the United States could speak with one voice to other nations. On matters within the United States, however, Presidents tend to be partisan. When they are urging new legislation, they try to get the support of members of their own party. Such efforts are made easier by the President's role of party chief. The President names the chairperson of his or her political party. Moreover, the President can fill many jobs by appointment and can use this power to reward political friends.

Thus, we have seen that the President has a wide range of powers, some formal and some informal. These powers are limited by Congress and the Supreme Court under our system of checks and balances. But a President's powers are flexible. To a large extent, they depend upon the President's willingness to use them. Those who use them to the utmost are known as "strong" Presidents. Those who do not are known as "weak" Presidents.

Questions

1 Who alone has the executive power of our federal government?

2 List the main powers that a President has. Which are formal powers and which are informal?

3 How are those powers limited? Give specific examples.

◊ Of all the powers of the President, which *one* do you think is the most important? Why?

THE PRESIDENT'S ADVISERS

The complexity of the President's job makes necessary a large assortment of advisers. The President also needs a large staff to do everything from helping to answer mail to arranging the President's schedule.

Much of the advice a President receives is from a Cabinet. The Cabinet is not mentioned by name in the Constitution. Yet the Constitution does say: "The President . . . may require the Opinion, in writing, of the principal Officer in each of the executive Departments, upon any Subject relating to the Duties of their respective Offices" (Article II, Section 2). The

The President's Cabinet and other advisers meet regularly in the White House to discuss a wide range of topics.

first three executive departments were created by Congress during George Washington's term of office. The heads of the departments became the President's *Cabinet*, or official advisers. The word *cabinet*, in this sense, comes from England. There, during the 1600s, a small group of advisers to the king used to meet in a private room called a cabinet. Later the word came to mean the group of advisers themselves.

There are now twelve executive departments, and the head of each is a member of the Cabinet. The members of the Cabinet are referred to as Secretary of their departments—for example, Secretary of State or Secretary of Labor. The only exception is the head of the Department of Justice, whose title is Attorney General. Besides advising the President, all Cabinet members are responsible for the operations of their departments. (The role of the executive departments will be discussed in the next chapter.)

Nowadays, the Cabinet meets in a large room in the office wing of the White House.

Chapter 7: The Presidency

The Vice President usually meets with the Cabinet, and other important officials are sometimes invited. The President is clearly in charge. Formal votes are rarely taken—probably because, as Abraham Lincoln once remarked, "The only vote that counts is the President's own." On one occasion, Lincoln presented his Cabinet with a proposal he favored. The Cabinet did not like it. Yet Lincoln declared, "Seven nays, one aye—the ayes have it."

A position on the Cabinet carries great prestige, in addition to a considerable salary ($66,000). The members of the Cabinet are appointed by the President, but they must be approved by the Senate. Approval requires a two-thirds vote. The Senate rarely rejects a Cabinet appointment, in part because the President picks the Cabinet with an eye to pleasing important groups. It is not unusual for a President to select a member of the opposition party for a particularly sensitive Cabinet post. There are no formal qualifications, such as being an expert in a particular field.

In addition to a Cabinet, some Presidents have assembled groups of informal advisers. Andrew Jackson had such a group, which reportedly met at first in the White House kitchen. Ever since, a President's informal advisers have been known as the *kitchen cabinet*. The number and types of informal advisers, and the extent of their influence, have varied widely from President to President.

The Executive Office of the President

Directly under the President is an office of several hundred persons called the Executive Office of the President. It is made up of individ-

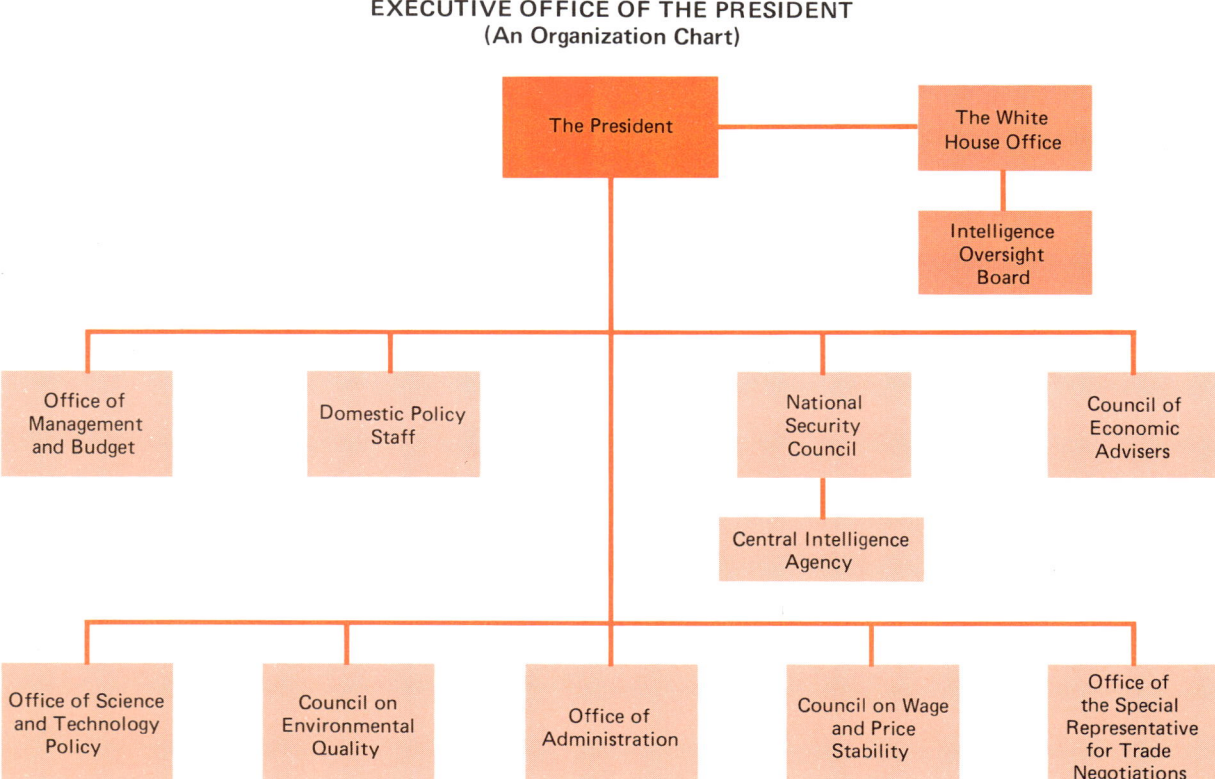

Chapter 7: The Presidency

uals and agencies that assist the President. (See the chart opposite.) When George Washington was President, his entire staff consisted of a few clerks. Today the members of the Executive Office of the President are scattered throughout the White House and nearby federal office buildings.

In closest contact with the President are the people in the White House Office. They are the President's closest advisers. One is the appointments secretary, who decides who will be permitted to see the President. Another is the press secretary, who deals with members of the press covering White House news. Others are top advisers on foreign policy, defense, and domestic problems.

Each President is free to create as big—or as small—a staff as he or she desires. President Nixon had as many as 630 White House aides. President Carter started with nearly 500 and reduced the number to about 340.

Several specialized agencies are also part of the Executive Office of the President. The most important is the Office of Management and Budget (OMB). The head of the OMB helps the President decide important spending policies. The OMB prepares a yearly national budget, which the President submits to Congress. (The federal budget and its preparation will be discussed in Chapter 18.) The OMB also evaluates the way the various departments spend their money and aids them in finding the most efficient ways to carry out government policies.

Another important agency is the National Security Council (NSC). It advises the President on defense and foreign policy. During President Nixon's early years, the head of the NSC was Henry Kissinger. He actually directed foreign policy, though the Secretary of State has formal responsibility for that task. Later, Kissinger became Secretary of State.

INSIDE THE WHITE HOUSE OFFICE WING

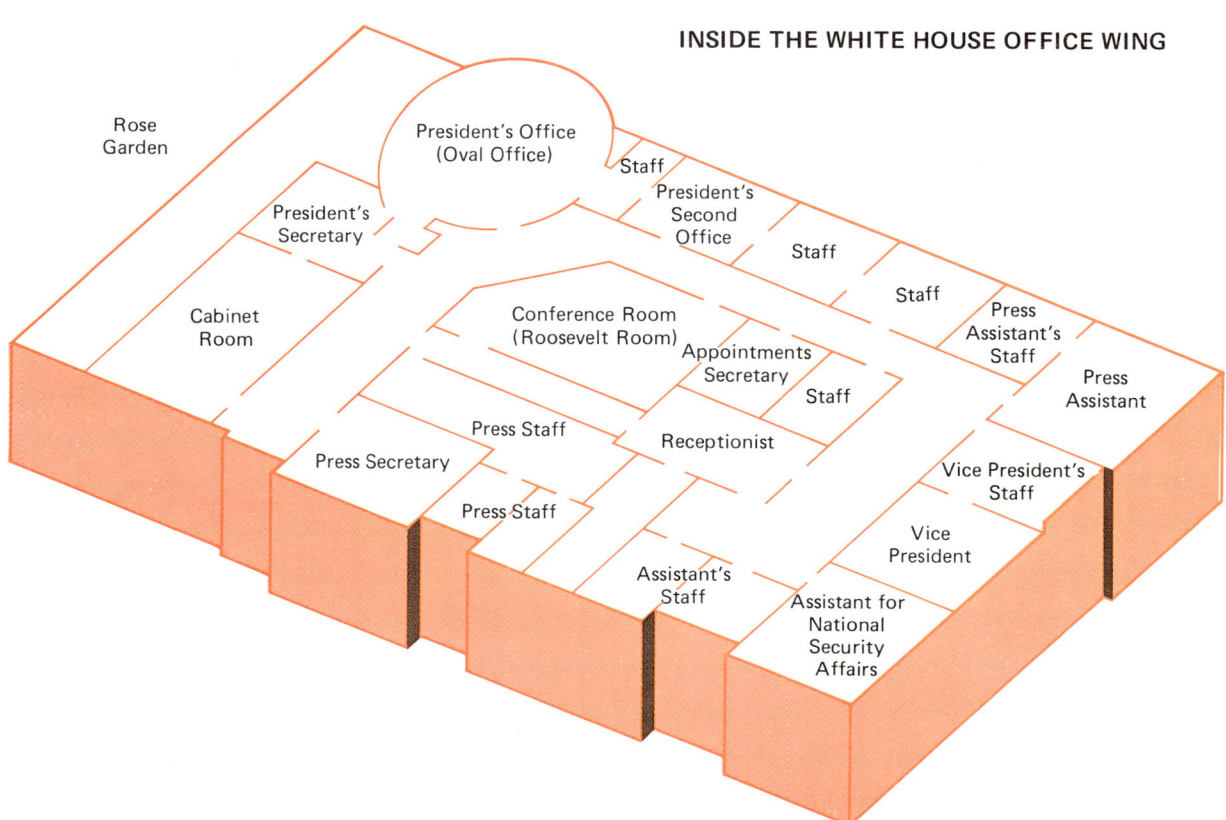

Questions

1 In what way does the Constitiution provide for a President's Cabinet?

2 How are Cabinet members appointed?

3 What is the Executive Office of the President?

4 Who determines how large a President's staff will be?

⬠ Do you think that the head of a Cabinet department should be required to be an expert in matters dealt with by that department? Explain.

PROBLEM: HOW PUBLIC SHOULD A PRESIDENT BE?

When Presidents go out in public, they expose themselves to danger. We have already noted that President Kennedy was assassinated in 1963. In September 1975, two attempts were made on the life of President Ford.

The cartoon below was published shortly after Ford's two narrow escapes. It also came after an auto accident involving a car in which President Ford was riding. Though Ford was not hurt in any of the incidents, a question had been raised: Should a President appear in public only when it is absolutely essential? How much can a President be expected to limit public activities in order to assure his or her own safety?

Three Presidents before Kennedy were assassinated: Abraham Lincoln (1865), James Garfield (1881), and William McKinley (1901). In addition, unsuccessful attempts were made on the lives of Andrew Jackson (1835), Theodore Roosevelt (1912, after he left office), Franklin D. Roosevelt (1933), and Harry Truman (1950). Moreover, people campaigning for nomination as presidential candidates have also been attacked. Two examples were Robert Kennedy, killed in 1968, and George Wallace, wounded in 1972.

Following are a number of arguments for and against isolating the President to protect his or her safety. As you read, ask yourself:

- *Is it realistic to expect a President to remain isolated from the public?*
- *Can the danger of a presidential assassination ever be completely eliminated?*
- *What measures can best be taken to protect the President?*

Arguments for Isolation

1. The President has an obligation to the nation to remain healthy and to take no unnecessary risks.

2. Fund-raising dinners and political rallies are frills. They are not part of a President's duties, yet they expose the President to danger. The President should avoid them.

3. It is especially dangerous for a President to venture into an open crowd. Even sharp-eyed bodyguards cannot spot every potential assassin.

4. It is impossible to determine in advance who might be a threat to the President. Even if prediction were possible, little could be done. It would violate our cherished freedoms if people were arrested on the mere suspicion that they *might* harm the President.

5. The President symbolizes the entire nation and is therefore a natural target for mentally unbalanced people with a grudge. Moreover, the President is always in the spotlight. A potential assassin knows that this means he or she would also become a public figure. The desire for public attention might motivate someone to attempt assassination.

6. If a President must venture into public, every precaution should be taken. This means bulletproof cars or vests, bodyguards, and close crowd surveillance.

7. It is impossible to keep all weapons out of the hands of potential assassins. Strict gun control would only keep guns out of the hands of law-abiding citizens. A potential assassin could still find a way to get a gun.

Arguments against Isolation

1. Presidents are supposed to represent the public's wishes. They cannot know those wishes without meeting the public—"pressing the flesh" and chatting with people.

2. Presidents are human, too. They need the psychological boost of cheering crowds.

3. A President is responsible for the well-being of his or her political party as well as of the nation. Public appearances are a necessary means of boosting that party.

4. One threat to a President's safety is the easy availability of handguns. Strict legislation to control handguns would help protect the President as well as other people.

5. The news media—newspapers, magazines, television, and radio—sometimes seem to glorify assassins by playing up their deeds. An effort by the media to tone down reports of incidents could help discourage publicity-seeking assassins.

6. Audiences can be kept back from a President. The greatest danger occurs when a crowd presses close to the Chief Executive. Also, audiences can be screened, or examined, before the President's arrival.

7. Officials could avoid announcing the time and route for a presidential appearance.

8. Individuals who are a clear threat to the President could be put in jail while a President is visiting an area, though constitutional safeguards must be followed.

Questions

1 Do you think that gun control would protect the President and presidential candidates? Why or why not?

2 Do you think that the news media encourage potential assassins? Explain.

3 Is it essential to the democratic process that presidential candidates campaign in public? Could they campaign on television instead? Explain.

4 Does the cartoon suggest other arguments for or against presidential isolation? Explain.

⬠ Imagine that the President has turned to you, as a close adviser, for advice in the following situation. The President is running for reelection, and Election Day is only 5 days away. A debate is scheduled later today between the President and the other major party's candidate. It will take place in a hall holding an audience of 2,000 and will be broadcast to the nation on radio and television. This debate is a chance to win needed votes in a close campaign, especially since the President is a skilled debater. An anonymous note has just arrived stating that an attempt will be made on the President's life at the debate. What is your advice to the President, and for what reasons?

This problem is based on an exercise copyright © 1976 by Gary Baumann, Deborah Gaschen, William Lynch, and Diane Temple.

PROBLEM: WHEN SHOULD A PRESIDENT BE DECLARED DISABLED?

Article II, Section 6 of the Constitution raised a potential dilemma. It said that a President's powers would pass to the Vice President in case the President were unable "to discharge the powers and duties" of office. But it did not say who decided when a President was disabled. What if a President were unconscious? What if mental illness affected a President's thinking?

The problem came to public attention three times during the Presidency of Dwight Eisenhower (1953–1961). He suffered three major illnesses while in office. He and his Vice President, Richard Nixon, talked the problem over and agreed on what circumstances might require Nixon to take over. But their agreement was not official.

Under President Lyndon Johnson, Congress proposed a constitutional amendment that provided ways to determine when a President is disabled. The amendment became the Twenty-fifth when it was ratified in 1967. We saw earlier in this chapter (page 140) that it also provides for filling a vacancy in the Vice-Presidency.

The Twenty-fifth Amendment answers the following questions about presidential disability:

1. *Who decides when a President is disabled?* The Vice President and a majority of the Cabinet, or another body designated by Congress.

2. *What process must be followed?* A written declaration must be sent to the President pro tempore of the Senate and the Speaker of the House of Representatives. The Vice President then automatically takes over as Acting President.

3. *What if the President recovers?* Then the President sends a written declaration to the same officials of Congress.

4. *What if there is disagreement over whether the President has actually recovered?* The Vice President and the Cabinet, or another body designated by Congress, may send a new declaration to the congressional leaders within 4 days of the President's. Then Congress must decide by a two-thirds vote of both houses. It has 21 days to act, plus 2 days if a special session must be called. Unless Congress decides in favor of the Vice President, the President may resume full powers.

Questions

1 What danger might arise if there were no legal procedures spelled out for determining when a President is disabled?

2 Why do you think the Twenty-fifth Amendment did not give the President absolute power to determine when a disability had ended?

⬠ In your opinion, what circumstances would require a President to be considered disabled? List as many as you can think of.

Chapter 7 Review

Developing Your Political Vocabulary

Define each of the following as used in this chapter:

a inaugural address
b electoral college
c treaty
d pardon
e reprieve
f amnesty
g impound

Recalling and Comparing

1 Why do you think the framers of the Constitution created the electoral college? Does the method of electing a President make sense today? Explain.

2 What do you think is the single most important duty of the President? Why?

3 Do you think it is a good idea to require that a President be a natural-born citizen of this country? Explain.

4 What are *two* main purposes of the Twenty-fifth Amendment?

5 If the majority of a President's Cabinet disagrees with a President's proposal, does that kill the proposal? Explain.

6 Do you think that it is necessary to limit a President's power in a democracy? Why or why not?

Special Activities

1 Prepare a chart that lists information in these categories: (a) powers of the President, (b) constitutional provision for each power (if there is one), and (c) ways in which the Constitution expressly limits any of these powers.

2 Imagine that the United States is at peace with all other countries. Which *three* formal presidential powers do you think might be used most often? List them. Now imagine that the United States is at war. Which *three* presidential powers do you now think might be used most? List them. Are different powers important in the two situations? Explain.

3 Make a study of news reports about the President for a period of a week. Classify the reports into categories, such as foreign relations, domestic economic problems, relations with Congress, and political activities. Summarize your findings.

4 On a map of the United States, plot locations that are associated with the Presidents, such as birthplaces, homes, burial places, and presidential libraries.

5 Make a study of four or five recent Presidents and choose one whom you would rate as either a "strong" or a "weak" President. Write a report explaining the reasons for your rating.

6 Make a study of four or five recent First Ladies and their roles in the White House. Prepare a report of your findings.

7 Make a study of four or five recent Vice Presidents and the roles they played in that office. Report your findings to the class.

8 Make a study of how the five Presidents from Harry S Truman through Richard M. Nixon used their presidential powers in connection with the war in Vietnam. Write a report of your findings.

9 Consider the following statement: "Like all other citizens of the United States, the President can never be above the law." Do you agree or disagree? Explain your answer.

Chapter 8

The Executive Departments

The President and the Cabinet are at the top of the executive branch, but they are only a small part of it. They oversee the work of the other 2.8 million civilian employees of the executive branch. This vast body of workers ranges from janitors and maintenance workers to high-level executives who may be almost as well known as the President. More than 98 percent of federal employees are in the executive branch. The legislative branch, by contrast, has about 40,000 employees.

People who work for the government are known as civil servants *but are more often called* bureaucrats. *They are workers in the* bureaucracy, *the pyramid-like organization that is characteristic of government service and of most large business organizations. In a bureaucracy, each worker is assigned specific duties and is part of a clear line of command. The line of command in the federal bureaucracy begins with the President, who is at the top of the pyramid.*

Both this chapter and the next are about the federal bureaucracy. This chapter deals with the part of the bureaucracy that makes up the executive departments, *the twelve Cabinet-level departments.*

―――― Goals ――――

- *To examine the question of who controls the bureaucracy.*
- *To look at what the bureaucracy does.*
- *To study the organization of a typical Cabinet department.*

155

Chapter 8: The Executive Departments

WHO CONTROLS THE BUREAUCRACY?

We have already seen that, as head of the executive branch, the President is responsible for everything that branch does. We have just noted that the executive branch is organized in a pyramid, with the President at the top. As we saw earlier, the framers of the Constitution thought that a government should be accountable to the people. One reason for the elaborate structure of the government bureaucracy is to make sure that each employee is accountable for her or his actions. Each employee reports to a superior within the bureaucracy, and the line of responsibility leads up to an elected official who is accountable to the voters.

Is it then a simple matter for the President to control what the executive branch does? Not at all. One President after another has complained how difficult it is to get a task carried out by the executive branch. Here is how Franklin D. Roosevelt spoke of the problem one time:

"Think of it! Presidents come and go, but we go on forever!"

The Treasury is so large and far-flung and ingrained in its practices that I find it is almost impossible to get the action and results I want—even with Henry [Morgenthau] there.

But the Treasury is not to be compared with the State Department. You should go through the experience of trying to get any changes in the thinking, policy, and action of the career diplomats and then you'd know what a real problem was.

But the Treasury and the State Department together are nothing compared with the Na–a–vy. The admirals are really something to cope with—and I should know. To change anything in the Na–a–vy is like punching a feather bed. You punch it with your right and you punch it with your left until you are finally exhausted, and then you find the damn bed just as it was before you started punching.

From Richard E. Neustadt, *Presidential Power*, Wiley, New York, 1960, p. 42.

There are many reasons for the difficulty of controlling the federal bureaucracy from the top. One is the sheer size of the bureaucracy. *Any* organization that large would be hard to control. Another reason is that the bureaucracy actually has many masters—not just the President.

Though the bureaucracy is formally part of the executive branch, Congress competes with the President for its control. The bureaucratic structure was created by Congress through legislation. In the first place, Congress passes the laws that the executive branch carries out. Second, Congress exercises a continuing power over the bureaucracy. It oversees the executive branch to make sure that the laws are carried out the way Congress intended. In exercising this power of legislative oversight, Congress may summon executive branch officials to explain or defend their policies.

In addition to the President and Congress, a third influence on the executive departments is special interests. The Agriculture Department, for example, was set up to help farmers. The Commerce Department, set up for purposes of control, came to represent the interests of businesses. Each department of the federal government serves its own constituency of special interests, just as a member of Congress serves his or her constituents—the people back home.

Thus, the bureaucracy serves three masters—the President, Congress, and special interests. No wonder it is sometimes hard to tell who runs the bureaucracy. The executive branch is a complicated network of people with interweaving responsibilities and conflicting loyalties.

Bureaucrats take an active part in the political process. They do not just follow orders from the top, but seek to influence all three masters and the public at large. Each government department employs a large public relations staff. Its job is to persuade the public that what the department is doing is of vital importance to every citizen.

One of the most successful public relations campaigns ever run by a government agency features Smokey the Bear.

> **Checks and Balances?**
>
> The complex workings of the federal bureaucracy are shown by an incident having to do with ice cream. The Food Safety and Quality Service in the Department of Agriculture decided that ice cream should be graded for quality. After consulting with ice cream manufacturers, the Food Safety and Quality Service proposed a grading system. The Office of Consumer Affairs objected that the system was confusing and would raise the price of ice cream.
>
> Meanwhile, the Department of Agriculture was receiving mail commenting on the proposed grading system. Almost one-half of the letters opposed the system and many of the others revealed a lack of understanding of it. The proposal was dropped.
>
> Later the Food and Drug Administration, which is part of the Department of Health, Education, and Welfare, issued a different labeling regulation. Effective July 1, 1979, it simply requires that the ingredients be listed on every ice cream package.

Bureaucrats can influence the kinds of policies Congress writes into law. If Congress nevertheless enacts legislation with which a bureaucrat disagrees, the bureaucrat may quietly sidetrack the policy. More than one top bureaucrat has learned to kill a policy by ignoring it. Here is what an aide to President Franklin D. Roosevelt once wrote about Cabinet officers:

Half of a President's suggestions, which theoretically carry the weight of orders, can be safely forgotten by a Cabinet member. And if the President asks about a suggestion a second time, he can be told that it is being investigated. If he asks a third time, a wise Cabinet officer will give him at least part of what he suggests. But only occasionally, except about the most important matters, do Presidents ever get around to asking three times.

Jonathan Daniels, quoted in Neustadt, *Presidential Power*, p. 41.

Similar tactics can be—and are—employed at each level of the bureaucracy. If you have ever conveniently "forgotten" to do what somebody asked you to do, you know how it is done. You may not always get away with it, but it works often enough to be a common tactic in a bureaucracy.

The fact that bureaucrats have such leeway is both a blessing and a curse. It is a blessing because it allows some flexibility in a tightly structured organization. It is a curse because some bureaucrats seem to be accountable to no one but themselves.

One safeguard against bureaucratic abuses is the federal court system. Most decisions of executive agencies are subject to review by the courts. The right to appeal the decisions, rules, and orders of bureaucrats to the courts protects individuals and corporations from arbitrary rulings. The courts have insisted that everyone has the same rights in dealing with the bureaucracy as in dealing with other parts of government. For example, the courts have required the Department of State to give fair treatment to all citizens who apply for passports to travel abroad.

Over the years, the terms *bureaucrat* and *bureaucratic* have taken on a negative meaning. When politicians are complaining about the federal government's complicated rules, these become "bureaucratic red tape." On the other hand, a politician who wants to praise a government employee speaks of a "civil servant" rather than a "bureaucrat." Technically, however, both terms mean the same thing. Any complex modern government requires large numbers of employees, whether we call them civil servants or bureaucrats. They are the people who deliver the mail, protect the nation, inspect the food, coin the money, and carry out all the services desired by the nation, as reflected in laws passed by Congress.

High-level bureaucrats often act as diplomats. Juanita Kreps toured Japan in her role as Secretary of Commerce. She is shown here meeting with Takeo Fukuda, Japan's Prime Minister. The purpose of Kreps's trip was to find ways to increase the sale of American goods to Japan.

Questions

1 What is a bureaucracy? A bureaucrat? A civil servant?
2 Why is the federal bureaucracy so hard to control?
3 How can Congress control what the executive branch does?
4 In what way can the courts control the federal bureaucracy?
⬠ Do you think it is good or bad that the bureaucracy serves three masters? Explain.

WHAT DOES THE BUREAUCRACY DO?

Except for contacts with a member of Congress, your dealings with the federal government are likely to be with the bureaucracy, and so mainly with the executive branch. Do you need to apply for a social security card? The person who helps you will be an executive branch employee. Do you want to join the Marines? The recruiting agent works for the executive branch. Do you need federal income tax forms? The Internal Revenue Service is part of the executive branch. Have you written a letter to the President? The person who answers your letter will be an employee of the executive branch. Do you want to camp in a national park? The park ranger who serves you is an employee of the executive branch.

The federal bureaucracy performs many functions, not all of which are purely "executive" functions. Some of them are similar to the functions of Congress and the courts. In other words, they are quasi-legislative or quasi-judicial. *Quasi* (KWAY-zigh) means "almost." The three types of bureaucratic functions are:

1. *Executive functions.* When the federal bureaucracy carries out laws or policies, it is performing an executive function. For example, an agency may send out notices to industries informing them of governmental regulations that affect those industries.

2. *Quasi-legislative functions.* When the executive branch is authorized by Congress to set standards in order to carry out a policy, the agency that does so is engaging in a quasi-legislative function. For example, the Agriculture Department sets standards for the purity of meat. This is a function that Congress delegated to the Agriculture Department. The legislative oversight power of Congress (page 000) provides a check on the bureaucracy's quasi-legislative functions.

3. *Quasi-judicial functions.* When a federal agency or department makes judgments about how a policy should be applied in a specific case, it is carrying out a quasi-judicial function. For example, a government department may decide to cut off funds to a city it decides is guilty of racial or sexist bias in using federal funds. The fact that such judgments can usually be appealed to the courts gives the judicial branch a check on these quasi-judicial functions.

Questions

1 What is one example of an executive function of the federal bureaucracy?
2 What is one example of a quasi-legislative function of the federal bureaucracy?
3 What is one example of a quasi-judicial function of the federal bureaucracy?
⬠ Do you think that it violates the system of checks and balances for the executive branch to have quasi-judicial and quasi-legislative functions? Explain.

ORGANIZATION OF EXECUTIVE DEPARTMENTS

The executive departments are a major branch of the bureaucracy. At the beginning, these departments were few in number and limited in duties. This was in keeping with the widely held belief that government should play only a limited role in national affairs, particu-

Chapter 8: The Executive Departments

Executive Departments and Their Role

Department of State (1789)
Top Official: Secretary of State
Duties:
Carries out the nation's foreign policy.
Supervises United States ambassadors and other diplomats abroad.
Issues passports to United States citizens.
Represents United States in United Nations.

Department of the Treasury (1789)
Top Official: Secretary of the Treasury
Duties:
Collects federal taxes.
Borrows money and pays bills for federal government.
Supervises printing of money and postage stamps.
Controls taxes on alcohol, tobacco, firearms.
Enforces customs laws (tariffs, quotas on trade).
Operates Secret Service to protect President and Vice President.

Department of Defense (1789; reorganized in 1947)
Top Official: Secretary of Defense
Duties:
Maintains armed forces—Army, Navy (including Marine Corps), and Air Force.
Conducts military intelligence.
Builds and maintains forts, bases, naval yards, canals, harbors.
Carries out military research and engineering projects.

Department of Justice (1870)
Top Official: Attorney General
Duties:
Investigates and prosecutes violations of federal laws.
Conducts suits on behalf of federal government in courts.
Supervises United States attorneys and marshals.
Supervises federal prisons.
Runs Federal Bureau of Investigation (FBI).

Department of the Interior (1849)
Top Official: Secretary of the Interior
Duties:
Supervises federal lands and parks.
Finances irrigation projects.
Investigates mine accidents.
Protects fish, wildlife, and other natural resources.
Conducts programs to benefit Native Americans.

Department of Agriculture (1862; Cabinet-level since 1889)
Top Official: Secretary of Agriculture
Duties:
Conducts programs to aid farmers.
Fights animal and plant diseases and insect pests.
Administers food stamp and school lunch programs.

Department of Commerce (1903)
Top Official: Secretary of Commerce
Duties:
Promotes business opportunities for United States companies here and abroad.
Makes loans to small businesses.
Conducts a population census every 10 years and gathers other statistics.
Grants patents for new inventions.
Maintains official weights and measures.
Operates United States Weather Service.
Makes surveys of coasts and reports on tides and currents.

Department of Labor (1913)
Top Official: Secretary of Labor
Duties:
Carries out laws on working conditions, minimum wages, and job discrimination.
Administers unemployment insurance and compensation for injured workers.
Sponsors job-training programs.
Keeps track of prices, unemployment levels, and other labor information.

Department of Housing and Urban Development (1965)
Top Official: Secretary of Housing and Urban Development
Duties:
Supports private-housing mortgage loans.
Finances housing for the elderly and for low-income families.
Makes grants for improvements to streets, sewers, and parks.
Department of Transportation (1966)
Top Official: Secretary of Transportation
Duties:
Finances interstate highways and improvements to railroads, airports, and some waterways.
Supports research on mass transit.
Sets safety standards for automobiles, trucks, buses, planes, trains.
Operates Coast Guard.
Department of Energy (1977)
Top Official: Secretary of Energy
Duties:
Promotes conservation and development of energy.
Promotes research on energy.
Regulates interstate gas and electricity sales.
Department of Education (1979)
Top Official: Secretary of Education
Duties:
Conducts programs to aid education.
Department of Health and Human Services (1979)
Top Official: Secretary of Health and Human Services
Duties:
Directs social security, Medicare, and other social service programs.
Administers programs to aid the handicapped.
Enforces pure food, drug, and cosmetics laws.
Conducts research into causes and treatment of diseases.

As Consul to Nice, France, Eleonore Hicks often had to go to Paris to confer with other State Department officials.

larly economic ones. As the nation's economy grew more complex, some parts of society began to seek more governmental action in their behalf. The new demands led to an increase in the number of executive departments.

In its first session in 1789, Congress created three executive departments. The Department of State was to handle foreign relations. The Department of War was to handle military affairs. And the Department of the Treasury was to handle finances. The Department of War controlled both the Army and the Navy. President John Adams set up a separate Department of the Navy in 1798 after an undeclared war with France had led to expansion of the Navy.

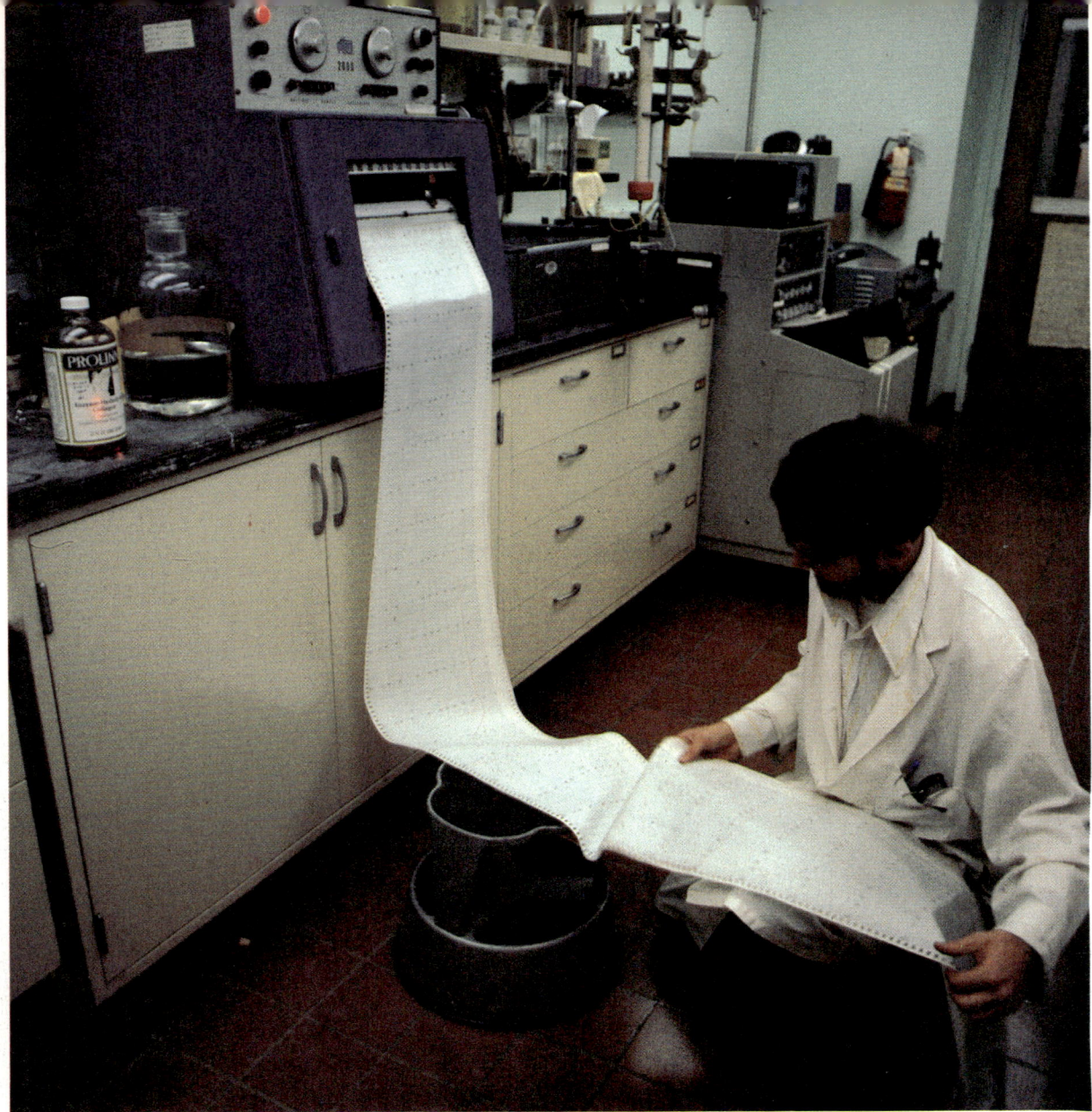

Many of the departments and agencies of the federal government employ scientists and use advanced technology to help them carry out the agencies' duties. This chemist is using a spectrophotometer to test liquid protein.

For many years, those few departments were all that were needed to do the work of the executive branch. But slowly the scope of government increased. In 1849, Congress created a Department of the Interior to manage federal lands. In 1870, Congress added the Department of Justice to handle legal matters. In 1882, the postal system became an executive department. (The post office system became an independent agency in 1971 and thus is no longer an executive department.)

As time passed, farmers, business leaders, and workers began to desire more services from the federal government. New departments were created to meet their needs. The Agriculture Departmemt came into being in 1862, the Department of Commerce in 1903, and the Department of Labor in 1913.

Chapter 8: The Executive Departments

More changes came after World War II. New military technology brought a return to the unified direction of the armed forces that the nation had had when George Washington was President. The Army Air Force, after being given independent status, was combined with the Army and the Navy in a single Department of Defense in 1947.

When the government tackled new types of social problems, it needed new forms of organization. In 1953, the Department of Health, Education, and Welfare was created, combining several agencies that already existed on a lower level. The Department of Housing and Urban Development was added in 1965 and the Department of Transportation was added in 1966. Amid growing talk of an "energy crisis," Congress established the Department of Energy in 1977. Congress also established a separate Department of Education in 1979. In each case, more efficient administration was sought by bringing various bureaus and services together in a single department.

Today there are twelve executive departments. They perform many functions that were undreamed of when Congress created the original three departments in 1789. The chart on pages 160–161 lists the principal duties of the present departments.

How much the federal government is involved in our lives is hinted at by this picture. The farmers who raised the food received federal aid. The meat was examined by federal inspectors. The meal was provided by the hot-lunch program.

Chapter 8: The Executive Departments

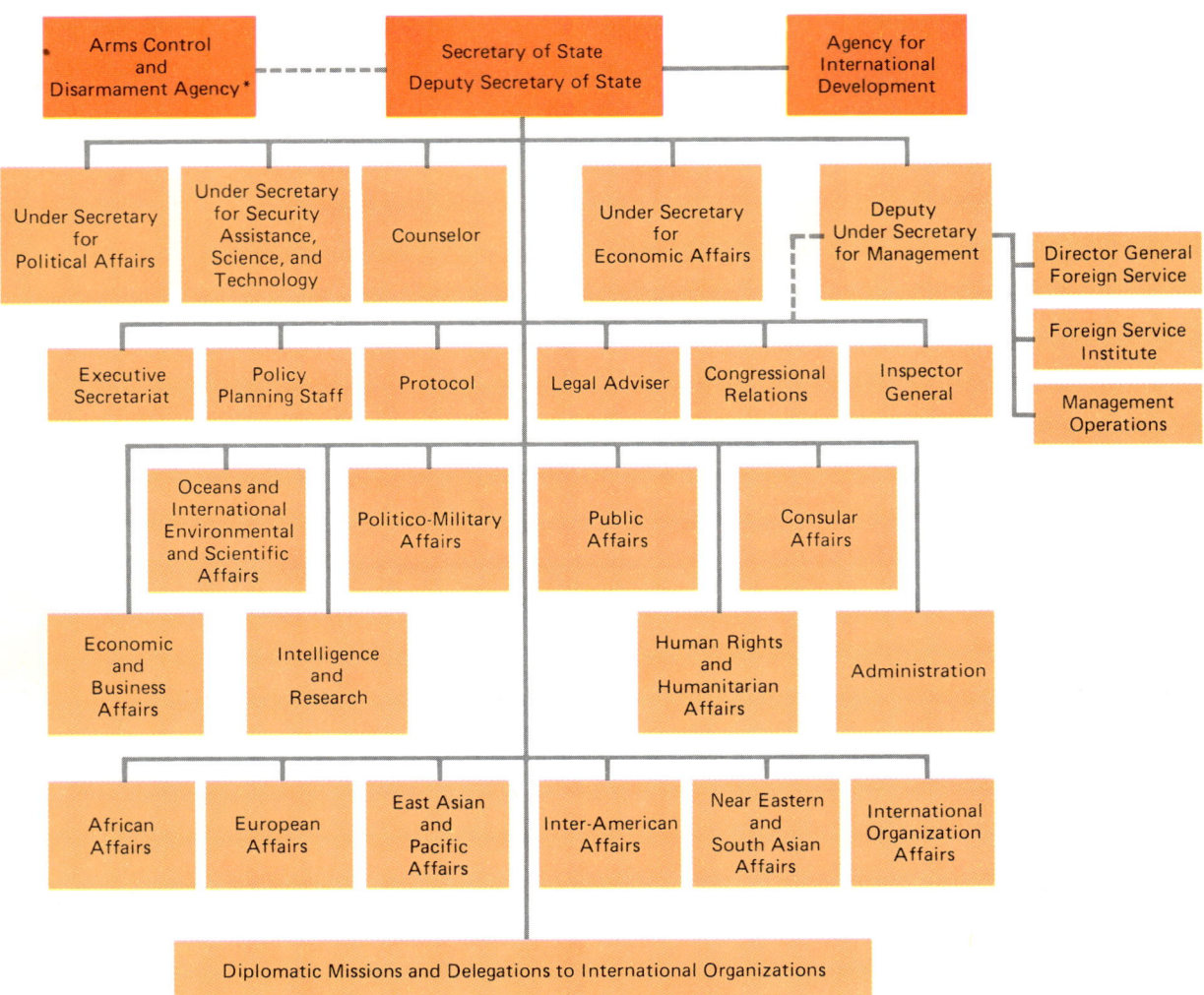

THE DEPARTMENT OF STATE
(An Organization Chart)

*A separate agency with the director reporting directly to the Secretary and serving as principal adviser to the Secretary and the President on arms control and disarmament.

To see how a typical federal department is organized, let us take a closer look at the Department of State. The chart above shows the line of command.

At the head of the department is the Secretary of State. As we have seen, the Secretary is a member of the President's Cabinet. In fact, the Secretary of State ranks first among Cabinet members because this office was the first Cabinet-level position created by Congress in 1789. The Secretary is responsible for carrying out the nation's foreign policy on behalf of the President.

The Secretary's principal assistant is the Deputy Secretary of State. During the Secretary's frequent absences from Washington, the Deputy Secretary handles the major business of the State Department.

Three Under Secretaries have responsibilities for three major aspects of foreign affairs.

Chapter 8: The Executive Departments

"I'm sorry, this is the West African desk, but I can take a message for the Central European desk."
Drawing by Ed Fisher: © 1978 The New Yorker Magazine, Inc.

These are the Under Secretaries for Political Affairs, for Security Assistance (military aid), Science, and Technology, and for Economic Affairs.

At each level, the organization chart of the Department of State can be broken down still further. You will find the Agency for International Development (AID) at the top right of the chart. AID has eight offices that report directly to its administrator and deputy administrator. It has ten other offices and bureaus that report to its executive secretary.

Remember, however, that the lines on organization charts do not tell the whole story. The lines show the *formal* organization only. There are also *informal* channels. Perhaps the leaders of two bureaus are close friends who play golf together on weekends. They may discuss business on the golf course and work out common approaches to a problem. Even though such contacts are informal, they may have an important effect on the way the bureaucracy actually works.

There are two lines of organization within the Department of State. One is *geographic*. As you can see in the chart, there are bureaus to handle each region of the world—Africa, Europe, East Asia and the Pacific, the Americas, and the Near East and South Asia. In turn, each of these bureaus is broken down into offices. Each office is responsible for a smaller area, such as a single country.

The second line of organization within the Department of State is *functional*. There are bureaus to handle specific functions, such as economic and business affairs, intelligence and research, or consular affairs. The work of these bureaus cuts across geographic areas.

At the bottom of the chart is a box labeled "diplomatic missions and delegations to international organizations." This represents the Foreign Service. The cartoonist's image of a diplomat is of a man in striped pants raising a cup of tea to his lips at a diplomatic reception. But the image is not very accurate.

True, some diplomats do wear striped pants and attend fancy receptions. But diplomats—women as well as men—perform many other functions, too. They help United States citizens in foreign countries to deal with such problems as a lost passport or an arrest on foreign criminal charges. Some diplomats serve in the consular services, which promote United States trade abroad. Some spend most of their time gathering information about foreign countries. Others spend long hours working out the details of treaties or executive agreements. Some make speeches to explain United States policies to business or student groups in other countries. Some help foreigners obtain the documents needed for travel to the United States as tourists or as business representatives. The duties are endless and they occupy a staff of at least 13,000 people in the 130 or so coun-

The National Park Service, a part of the Department of the Interior, provides services for an ever-growing number of visitors each year. National parklands occupy an area larger than the state of Pennsylvania.

tries with which the United States maintains diplomatic relations.

Altogether, the Department of State employs slightly more than 30,000 people. That may seem like a lot until you compare it with the number of employees in some other executive departments.

Largest of all is the Department of Defense. It employs more than 1 million civilians in addition to 2.1 million people on active military duty and 2.5 million in the reserves. The Defense Department receives a bigger share of the federal budget than any other department—about one-fourth of the total budget.

The Secretary of Defense is a civilian, just as are the heads of all other federal departments. This is because our nation has always followed a policy of civilian control over the military. Civilians also hold the top positions in the three major divisions of the Defense Department—the Departments of the Army, the Navy, and the Air Force. Each of the three is headed by a Secretary who does not hold Cabinet rank.

The largest department after Defense is the Department of Health, Education, and Welfare (HEW). It employs about 160,000 people to carry out its work.

Chapter 8: The Executive Departments

Perhaps the best-known agency within HEW is the Social Security Administration. This agency was set up in 1935 to administer the first large-scale federal program for social welfare. The social security program was created during the New Deal of President Franklin D. Roosevelt, in response to the hardship caused by the Great Depression. Later, the program was expanded to meet new needs. Since 1966, the Social Security Administration has also been in charge of the Medicare program, which helps people who are 65 or older pay for health care.

Among other agencies within HEW are the Public Health Service and the Social and Rehabilitation Service. This last agency provides assistance to the needy, the blind, and the disabled.

Typical of the smaller executive departments is the Department of Labor. It employs 17,000 people and is the smallest department of all. Much of the work of the Department of Labor involves collecting information on working and living conditions. One of its major agencies is the Bureau of Labor Statistics. This division compiles the cost-of-living index that is made public every month. The index is designed to show the rise and fall of the amount of money a typical family needs for everyday expenses. Another agency, the Employment Standards Administration, makes sure that eligible workers are paid at least the minimum wage set by Congress from time to time.

Whether it is large or small, each executive department is organized like a pyramid. Many attempts have been made to "streamline" the bureaucracy and make it work more efficiently. But all reform proposals keep the basic structure.

Questions

1 Why did it take so long for the number of executive departments to reach its present size?

2 How could you learn the formal line of command in a bureaucratic department?

3 How do informal lines of influence affect the workings of a bureaucracy?

⬠ Do you think there are too many executive departments, too few, or just the right number? Explain.

PROBLEM: WHO WOULD MAKE THE BEST HEAD OF EACH CABINET-LEVEL DEPARTMENT?

The head of each executive department performs a dual role. On the one hand, he or she is a member of the President's Cabinet.

Private concerns, such as Sandia Laboratories in New Mexico, often receive federal contracts for scientific research.

Chapter 8: The Executive Departments

One program run by the Department of Agriculture that affects many of the old and poor in our country is the federal food stamp program. People entitled to food stamps are able to buy groceries they otherwise could not afford.

This role of adviser is by its nature a political role involving the making of policy. On the other hand, a department head must also oversee the many activities carried out by the department. This is the role of an administrator. Both roles—policy maker and administrator—are essential parts of the job of department head.

As you know, there are no formal requirements for the Cabinet. Yet the activities of the executive departments are quite varied and specialized. For instance, the work of the Department of State differs greatly from the work of the Department of Agriculture. It stands to reason that the two departments would benefit by having leaders of different backgrounds and skills.

You have read a description of what each department does. Keep this in mind as you read the biographical sketches below. The sketches give some facts about twelve persons who were heads of executive departments in Jimmy Carter's first year as President. The persons are not identified by name in the sketches.

As you read each sketch, consider the following questions:

- *Which executive department is this person best qualified to head?*
- *What is his or her most important qualification for such a job?*

Individual One
Age: 45
State senator and governor
Former employee in timber industry and operator of a sawmill
Strong environmentalist

Chapter 8: The Executive Departments

Expert in consolidating or decreasing the number of government agencies
Head of National Governors Conference

Individual Two
Age: 55
Economist, specializing in labor force and working women
Vice President of a university
Vice President of National Council on the Aging
A director of the New York Stock Exchange and of several corporations

Individual Three
Age: 48
Economist, expert on problems of minorities and employment
Director of human resources research group at a university

Individual Four
Age: 45
Lawyer
General Counsel of the Army
Special troubleshooter for Defense Department

Aide to President Lyndon Johnson for civil rights, education, and poverty policies
Counsel to Democratic National Committee

Individual Five
Age: 48
Member of Congress from a farm district since 1971 and served on House Agriculture Committee
Owner and operator of a farm
Midwest administrator of Agriculture Department programs in 1960s

Individual Six
Age: 52
Lawyer
Law professor and dean of a law school
Attorney in Justice Department
Ambassador to Luxembourg
Alternate delegate to United Nations General Assembly
A director of several corporations
Civil rights champion

Individual Seven
Age: 50
Economist and lawyer

Attitudes affect how a department head does his or her job. Would someone who opposes low-cost housing run the Department of Housing and Urban Development in the same way as someone who supports the idea?

Member of Congress since 1964; served on House Commerce Committee and headed House Budget Committee
Drafted a plan for a new railway system, which Congress enacted

Individual Eight
Age: 50
Naturalized citizen
Economist and public administrator
Chairperson of a major corporation
Negotiator in nation's worldwide trade talks in 1960s
Deputy Assistant Secretary of State for Economic Affairs

Individual Nine
Age: 49
Physicist, expert in nuclear weapons
President of a leading institute of technology
Head of California Livermore Radiation Laboratory
Adviser to Defense Department in 1960s
Secretary of the Air Force
Member of Strategic Arms Limitation Talks with Soviet Union

Individual Ten
Age: 59
Lawyer
Expert in world affairs
General Counsel to Defense Department under Presidents Kennedy and Johnson

Secretary of the Army
Deputy Secretary of Defense

Individual Eleven
Age: 58
Lawyer
Judge of a United States Court of Appeals
Lifelong friend of President Carter

Individual Twelve
Age: 48
Economist, expert on national security and defense economics
Secretary of Defense in Nixon administration
Director of Central Intelligence Agency
Head of Atomic Energy Commission
Professor of economics

Questions

Select the person described in the sketches who you think is best qualified to head each executive department. Refer to the chart on pages 160-161. You may refer to other information about executive departments in this chapter. On a separate sheet of paper, list the name of each department and the number of the person you chose. State the reasons for your decisions. Later, your teacher will tell you the names of the persons and which department each was selected to direct.

Chapter 8 Review

Developing Your Political Vocabulary

1 Define each of the following as used in this chapter:
- **a** civil servant
- **b** bureaucrat
- **c** bureaucracy
- **d** executive department
- **e** Medicare
- **f** cost-of-living index

2 Use each of the words above in a sentence about the executive branch.

Recalling and Comparing

1 Which special interests would you think are served by: (a) the Labor Department; (b) the Department of the Interior; (c) the Defense Department?

2 Why do executive departments have public relations staffs? Do you think they could do their jobs just as well without such staffs? Why or why not?

3 In which of the following activities would you be dealing with the federal bureaucracy?
- **a** writing a member of Congress
- **b** requesting information about the federal minimum wage law
- **c** applying for Medicare
- **d** applying for a driver's license
- **e** requesting a federal income tax refund
- **f** seeking information about federal prison regulations
- **g** applying for a passport
- **h** getting food stamps
- **i** getting a government-backed small-business loan
- **j** appealing a lower court's decision to the Supreme Court
- **k** finding out the weather forecast
- **l** applying for a job-training program

4 Refer to the chart on page 164 and list *three* parts of the State Department that might be involved in a United States government grant to Brazil for an educational or cultural program.

Special Activities

1 Find out from your local office of the Social Security Administration what the present rules are for obtaining a social security card. Make a chart of the necessary steps.

2 Consult your local library and prepare an organization chart of one of the executive departments (other than the Department of State).

3 Suppose you have been asked to suggest changes in the organization of executive departments. Show on a diagram what new departments you might suggest. Include the name of each department and what two or three basic functions it might perform.

4 Prepare a special bulletin board display of news articles about one or more executive departments.

5 Compare news reports about two executive departments and identify differences in the roles these departments play. Report your findings to the class.

6 Make a poster advertising the services of one of the executive departments to the ordinary people in this country.

7 Consider the following statement: "The federal bureaucracy seeks to control too many aspects of our lives." Do you agree or disagree? Explain your answer.

Chapter 9

Independent Agencies

Besides the twelve Cabinet-level departments, the executive branch includes a large number of independent agencies. For administrative purposes, these agencies are counted as part of the executive branch. However, their decisions and actions are not under the President's direct control. Because of their independence, these agencies are sometimes referred to as "the fourth branch of government."

All told, the independent agencies employ more than 1 million of the 2.8 million employees of the executive branch. All these employees are part of the federal bureaucracy. The subject of this chapter is the independent agencies and the work they do.

Goals

- To learn the regulatory functions of independent agencies of our federal government.
- To examine criticisms of independent regulatory agencies.
- To learn the functions of independent service agencies.
- To consider how the operations of independent regulatory agencies affect our daily lives.

173

Chapter 9: Independent Agencies

INDEPENDENT REGULATORY AGENCIES

One important group of independent agencies is the regulatory agencies. Their job is to carry out the details of enforcing federal laws. In doing so, they make federal rules and regulations that have the force of law. The *Code of Federal Regulations* contains 75,000 pages.

A few regulatory agencies are part of the executive departments already discussed. One example is the Federal Energy Regulatory Commission, which sets wholesale rates for natural gas and electricity in interstate commerce. It used to be an independent agency, the Federal Power Commission, but in 1977 it was made part of the Department of Energy. Another example is the Occupational Safety and Health Agency, a part of the Department of Labor. It sets rules to protect the safety and health of people at their place of work. In this chapter, however, we are focusing on the *independent* regulatory agencies. These agencies are not under the authority of an executive department.

The decisions of the independent regulatory agencies affect the life of every one of us. If you have a baby sister, her sleepwear must meet safety standards set by the Consumer Product Safety Commission. If you own a CB radio, you must get a permit from the Federal Communications Commission. If you want to kill mosquitoes, you may no longer buy DDT because it has been banned by the Environmental Protection Agency. If you watch television, the commercials you see must meet standards of accuracy set by the Federal Trade Commission. If you buy a ticket for a bus or train to another state, the price is set by the Interstate Commerce Commission.

The regulatory agencies are part of the broadening role of the federal government in everyday life. It was not always so. In fact, for

Water pollution, such as the detergent foam in this fountain, is a concern of the Environmental Protection Agency.

Chapter 9: Independent Agencies

The establishment of the Interstate Commerce Commission did not immediately solve the problems of overcharging by the railroads. It was not until 1906 that the Commission was given the power to set standard rates nationally.

more than a century the United States did without any such agencies. During that time, the general rule in economic life was *caveat emptor* (KAY-vee-at EMP-tor)—a Latin phrase meaning "let the buyer beware." It was up to each person to look after his or her own interests in the market place. If you were cheated, it was your own fault.

By the last quarter of the nineteenth century, however, Americans were beginning to see that this would no longer work. The country's rapid economic growth had brought with it frequent major clashes of private interests. Often, it appeared, the exercise of a right by one interest, such as the big railroads, interfered with the rights of other interests, such as farmers and small-business people. Some means of regulation seemed necessary.

The first independent regulatory agency was created in 1887 to stop abuses by the railroads. Farmers felt that the railroads were charging outrageously high freight rates. Some state governments set strict controls on rates within their own states, but the states had no control over rates between states because the United States Supreme Court held that such rates fall within the "interstate commerce" clause of the Constitution. This clause, in Section 8 of Article I, gives Congress the right "to regulate Commerce . . . among the several States."

To meet the problem, Congress set up the Interstate Commerce Commission (ICC) in 1887. This agency was made up of five commissioners, each appointed by the President for a term of 6 years. (This has since been

Chapter 9: Independent Agencies

changed to eleven commissioners serving 7-year terms.) The ICC was given the task of regulating commerce between states.

At first, the ICC had only limited powers, but over the years Congress gave it further powers. Now the ICC regulates not only railroads but also truck lines, bus companies, and pipe lines—other than water or natural gas. Its wide powers include the power to fix rates, to prevent mergers between competing companies, and to assure safe travel.

As economic life became more complicated, Congress could not enact legislation on all the details of new products and services. New regulatory agencies were set up. Today there are fifty federal regulatory agencies, with an estimated 100,000 employees.

The independence of regulatory agencies is designed to shield them from political party control. The reason is that the agencies exercise a quasi-judicial function. They rule on specific cases, just as the courts do.

Congress has set certain rules to protect the regulatory agencies' independence. For example, each is headed by a group rather than an individual. These commissions or boards have five to eleven members, all appointed by the President with the consent of the Senate. The terms of these members are long (up to 14 years) and staggered—that is, they do not all expire at the same time. Generally, only a bare majority of the members may be from the same political party. Another safeguard is that the President cannot fire the members for political reasons, but only for certain causes specified by Congress. Thus, no President can gain control over an agency within one term of office.

Of course, it would be impossible to isolate the regulatory agencies from politics completely. The regulatory agencies are often subject to great political pressure because of the important decisions they make. Usually, the agencies reflect the prevailing political opinion. If they do not, new appointments by the President or changes by Congress in the laws under which the agencies operate will sooner or later bring them in line.

If It's KOOL in Phoenix, Can It Be WARM in Scranton?

The following selection is from an article about the federal rules for identifying radio stations.

They must consist of four letters. They must begin with K west of Mississippi and W east of the Mississippi. And they must be arranged in a unique combination. Call letters of all radio stations across the land must meet these rules set by the Federal Communications Commission. The rules would seem to put a strait jacket on creativity, but America's broadcasters have used ingenuity in identifying themselves.

A number of call letters are suggested almost automatically: WCAR in Detroit, KFOG in San Francisco, WIND in Chicago, WFUN in Miami, WLEE in Richmond, KPOI in Hawaii, WSUN in St. Petersburg, and WCOD in Hyannis on Cape Cod. Not so obvious are KICY in Nome, Alaska, and KYAK in Anchorage. There's KJIN in Houma, Louisiana, a country KUZN up the road at West Monroe, Louisiana, and a rambling WREK in Atlanta.

A few stations express a personal identification in their call letters. For example, we find WFDR in Manchester, Georgia, not far from President Franklin D. Roosevelt's home in Warm Springs. There's a KLBJ in Austin, Texas, owned by the family of the late President Lyndon Johnson.

This is all pure KORN, you say? That's a station in Mitchell, South Dakota.

Adapted from "If It's KOOL in Phoenix, Can It be WARM in Scranton?" by James McCrohan, *TWA Ambassador* Magazine. Copyright © Trans World Airlines 1974. Used by permission.

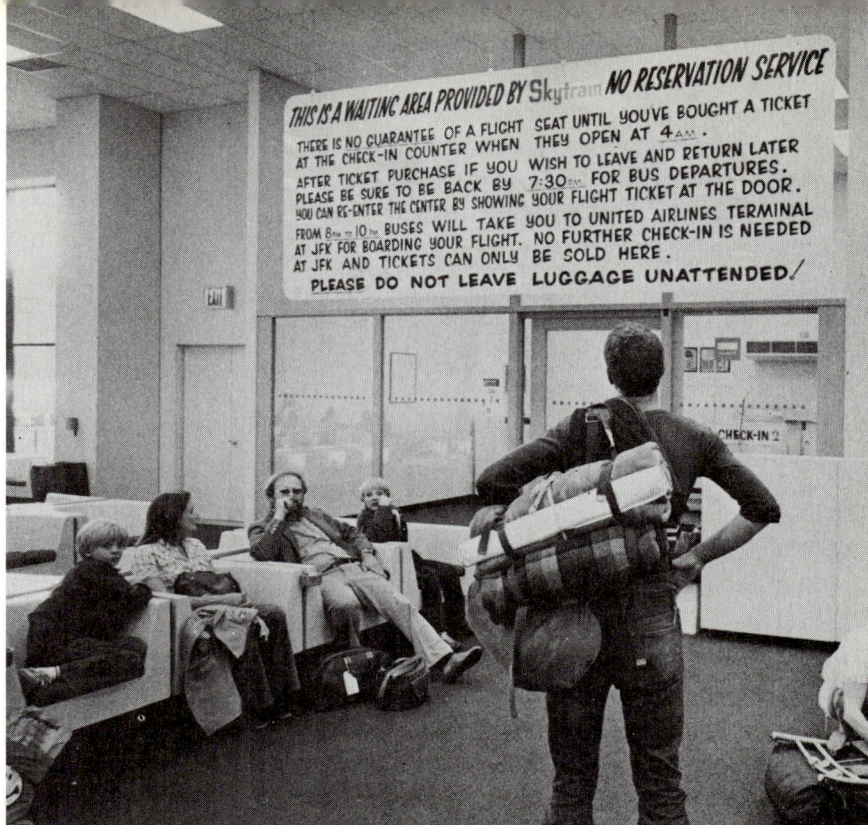

Recent changes in government policy have loosened the regulations that govern airlines in the United States. Controls over fares and air routes have been almost completely lifted.

In recent years, there have been repeated calls for reform of the independent regulatory agencies. In 1975, President Ford criticized "the Mulligan stew of government rules and regulations, often conflicting with one another, [which] has created a nightmare of red tape [and] paper shuffling." President Carter also called for reforms.

Some companies and industries wage war against regulatory agencies. They may print advertisements in newspapers. Some may ask their stockholders to protest to Congress.

Many of the agencies' critics believe that they stifle competition and create waste. Critics cite the case of a New Jersey manufacturer of building materials. Once a week, the company shipped three truckloads of goods from its main plant to Tampa, Florida. The trucks returned to New Jersey empty. A subsidiary of the company in southern Florida sent three truckloads a week to eastern Pennsylvania. The trucks returned empty to Florida. Why? ICC rules did not let a subsidiary's trucks carry goods for a parent company, or the other way around.

One university professor had a harsh solution for cases like this. He said: "The Interstate Commerce Commission should be abolished, its building torn down, and the ground sown with salt."

However, the ICC argued that its rule in the trucking case made perfect sense. To change it, the ICC argued, would take work away from independent truckers and lead to less competition in the trucking industry. That, in turn, would eventually lead to higher trucking costs, the commission maintained.

The regulatory agencies' leading defenders are often the very interests the agencies were established to regulate. Independent truckers are in favor of rules that protect their interests. Shipping companies and unions prefer rules that protect jobs and profits in this country's shipping industry. Many industries and labor unions become comfortable allies of the regulatory agencies and do not want any changes.

Chapter 9: Independent Agencies

Questions

1 What is the main job of the federal government's independent regulatory agencies?

2 Why are the independent regulatory agencies sometimes called "the fourth branch" of our federal government? Would you call them that?

3 Why have there been calls to reform our federal regulatory agencies?

⬠ Do you think that a President should be able to appoint all the commissioners of an independent regulatory agency at one time? Explain.

INDEPENDENT SERVICE AGENCIES

Some independent agencies perform a wide range of services other than regulation. The chart on this page shows the major independent service agencies. They can be divided into two main groups. We will discuss only a

---

Major Independent Service Agencies

ACTION (formerly Peace Corps; became an independent agency in 1971)
Commodity Futures Trading Commission
Community Services Administration
Export-Import Bank of the United States
Federal Deposit Insurance Corporation
Federal Home Loan Bank Board
General Services Administration
National Aeronautics and Space Administration (NASA)
National Foundation on the Arts and the Humanities
National Science Foundation
Panama Canal Company
Selective Service System
Small Business Administration
Tennessee Valley Authority
International Communication Agency
International Trade Commission
United States Postal Service (formerly an executive department; became an independent agency in 1971)
Veterans Administration

One of the independent service agencies is the International Communication Agency. Part of its job is to produce magazines written in many languages in order to portray our culture, history, politics, and scientific endeavors.

The efforts of ACTION are worldwide. Teachers like the one pictured above, engineers, farmers, and others provide services to help newly emerging nations acquire the skills and knowledge needed to raise standards of living.

few agencies within each group.

Some independent service agencies perform services for the executive branch. These federal agencies are independent so that they may cut across all parts of the executive branch.

One well-known agency in this class was the Civil Service Commission. It was set up in 1883 under the Pendleton Act in order to end the practice of giving the bulk of government jobs to the friends of the people in power. The Civil Service Commission was designed to create a *merit system* of hiring and promoting the most qualified workers. For this purpose, the commission held competitive examinations. Most of the jobs in the federal bureaucracy were within this commission's jurisdiction. The system continues, but in another form.

In 1978, President Carter proposed that the Civil Service Commission be replaced by two separate agencies. One would take over the hiring role of the existing commission and the other would be an independent regulatory agency to protect federal workers' rights on the job. The Office of Personnel Management and the Merit System Protection Board were then created by act of Congress.

Federal jobs are divided into two categories. *Classified* jobs are under the jurisdiction of the federal merit system. If you apply for such a job, you will be asked to take an examination to test your skills. Your score will determine how high on the hiring list your name appears. If you are a veteran, five points will be added to your score; and if you are a disabled veteran, ten points. Those with the best scores are hired first.

Chapter 9: Independent Agencies

This young woman takes part in the Villanueva (New Mexico) Stitchery Project. This project is intended to revive the traditional crafts of the area. The project received support from a federal service agency.

Once hired for a job, you cannot be fired unless you fail to do your work properly. You cannot be fired merely because you belong to the "wrong" political party. On the other hand, in a civil service job you would be forbidden by law to take an active part in politics. You could vote, but you could not collect money for a candidate or help in a candidate's campaign. This restriction was enacted by Congress in the 1930s. The Supreme Court upheld the law as constitutional when some civil service workers challenged it.

Jobs that are not under the jurisdiction of the merit system are known as *unclassified* jobs. Some of these jobs are filled by presidential appointment, with the consent of the Senate. These include the top positions in the executive departments and other high positions. Most people in unclassified jobs may be fired for a number of reasons, including political ones. They do not have job protection.

The General Services Administration (GSA) is another agency that serves all parts of the executive branch. The GSA is responsible

Chapter 9: Independent Agencies

for constructing government buildings, maintaining them, and supplying equipment to federal offices. If you wanted to buy surplus federal property, you would get in touch with this agency.

The GSA operates the National Archives and Record Service, which keeps the original copies of important documents. Among these are the originals of the Declaration of Independence and the Constitution, which you can see in the Archives Building in Washington, D.C.

The GSA also publishes all the rules and regulations that apply to various federal administrative agencies. One important part of the GSA is the Consumer Information Center. This office provides people with information of various kinds, mainly about products. Its goal is to help consumers save money and spend it more wisely.

Another group of independent agencies performs public services. These agencies have a wide variety of functions.

The largest is the United States Postal Service. Mail delivery was handled by an executive department, the Post Office Department, until 1971 when Congress made the

The huge United States Postal Service has one of the smallest public buildings in the country.

Chapter 9: Independent Agencies

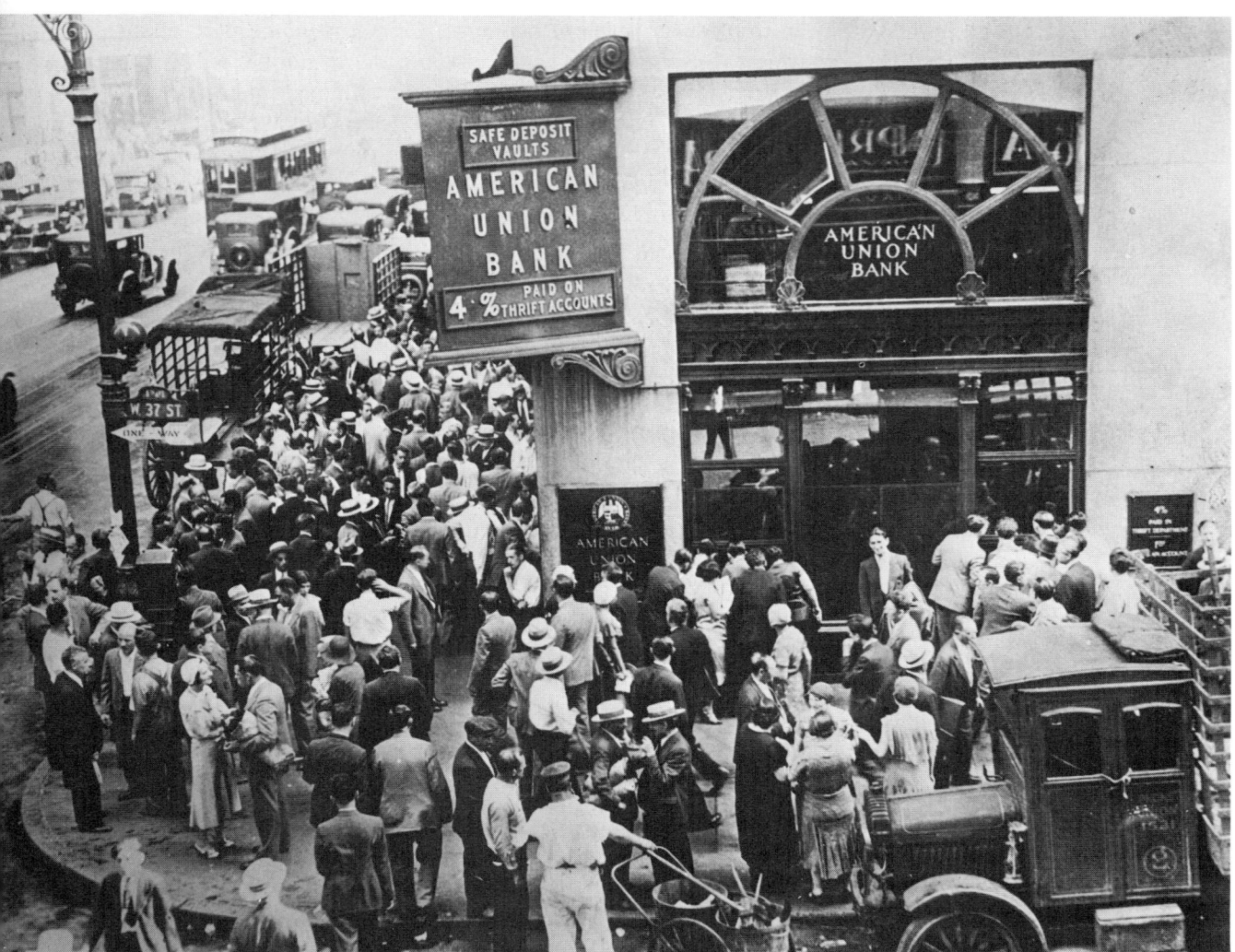

Bank failures in the 1930s led to the establishment of the Federal Deposit Insurance Corporation as a service agency.

Postal Service independent. The change was intended to isolate the agency from political pressures and to try to make it pay its own way, so it would not have to be subsidized with tax money. The Postal Service is the largest of the independent agencies, employing more than 680,000 people.

The second largest of the public service agencies is the Veterans Administration. It employs almost 220,000 people. The Veterans Administration operates hospitals and adminis-ters an insurance program for military veterans. It also provides other services to veterans, such as school benefits for many who served in the armed forces.

Another important independent agency providing a public service is the Federal Deposit Insurance Corporation (FDIC). If you have a savings account in a national bank or in a participating state bank, you may have seen a notice about the FDIC posted in your bank. The FDIC insures accounts up to a certain sum,

Each of us is affected in some way by the independent regulatory agencies, as in questions of product safety. Studies of injuries are made by the federal government to see whether products like skateboards should be regulated.

Chapter 9: Independent Agencies

	MAJOR INDEPENDENT REGULATORY AGENCIES			
Name of Agency	Date Created	Number of Commissioners	Length of term (years)	Functions
Interstate Commerce Commission	1887	11	7	Sets rates, routes, and practices for railroads, truck companies, bus companies, and pipelines (except water and natural gas) in interstate commerce.
Federal Reserve Board	1913	7[a]	14	Controls amount of money in circulation and amount of credit available; regulates commercial banks belonging to Federal Reserve System.
Federal Trade Commission	1914	5	7	Enforces some antitrust laws; protects businesses from unfair competition; enforces truth-in-lending and truth-in-labeling laws.
Federal Communications Commission	1934	7	7	Licenses radio and television stations; oversees interstate and international telephone and telegraph operations.
Securities and Exchange Commission	1934	5	5	Protects public against fraud in stock and bond markets; supervises stock exchanges; regulates holding and investment companies.
Civil Aeronautics Board	1938	5	6	Regulates the activities of interstate airlines.
Equal Employment Opportunity Commission	1964	5	5	Investigates charges of racial and other discrimination by employers and labor unions.
Environmental Protection Administration	1970	1[b]	[c]	Develops and enforces standards for the quality of air and water; sets rules on noise pollution, toxic substances, and pesticides.
Consumer Product Safety Commission	1972	5	7	Sets standards for product safety; issues recall notices for defective products.
Nuclear Regulatory Commission	1975	5	5	Issues licenses for the design, construction, and operation of nuclear power plants.

a. Called *governors*.
b. Called *administrator*.
c. No set term.

so that depositors will not lose their money if a bank fails. (Accounts in savings and loan associations are protected by a private insurance company.) The FDIC was set up in 1933, after the Great Depression had caused many banks to fail. Many people lost their life savings because there was no system to insure bank accounts in those days.

The FDIC acts much like a private insurance company. It charges a premium to each participating bank. If the bank fails, the FDIC takes over its assets, pays off the depositors, and reorganizes the bank.

Questions

1 How does the Civil Service Commission's merit system work?

2 Why was the Postal Service made an independent agency?

3 Why was some system of government bank insurance thought to be necessary? What government agency provides such insurance?

◌ Do you think that the Postal Service should make a profit or that it should be subsidized by general tax money? Explain.

PROBLEM: HOW DO INDEPENDENT REGULATORY AGENCIES AFFECT INDIVIDUALS?

Independent regulatory agencies, as we have seen, were established by Congress within the executive branch. The functions of some of these agencies have already been discussed. Further exploration of the federal regulatory agencies will shed light on the role of government in our complex society.

On page 184, you will find a table containing information about the major independent regulatory agencies. Study the table, especially the functions listed at the right. Try to relate these functions to your own life. To help you do so, ten actual situations are listed below. Consider which, if any, of the agencies described in the table would be involved in each of these situations. Then answer the questions following Situations 1 through 10.

Situation 1: You compare the ingredients listed on two packages of sandwich meat.

Situation 2: You buy a share of stock in a corporation and pay a brokerage fee.

Situation 3: A nuclear power plant is being built to supply electricity to your community.

Situation 4: You buy a ticket to travel across the United States by bus.

Situation 5: You buy a new car whose brakes do not work properly.

Situation 6: You want to borrow money in order to set up a business, and you find that the interest rate will be lower than it would have been last year.

Situation 7: You become a ham radio operator.

Situation 8: You take a job in a large company and find that you are being paid less than others hired at the same time and doing the same work.

Situation 9: You buy a chemical spray to use on fruit trees.

Situation 10: You want to make a complaint about an airline.

Questions

1 Which, if any, of the agencies described in the chart would be involved in Situations 1 through 10? List the numbers 1–10 on a sheet of paper and write your answer opposite each number.

2 What reasons do you see for having federal regulatory agencies? Give examples.

3 Do you think that the influence of federal regulatory agencies on our lives is likely to increase, decrease, or remain about the same? Explain.

Chapter 9 Review

Developing Your Political Vocabulary

1. What is a regulatory agency?
2. What is a merit system of employment?
3. What is the difference between a *classified* and an *unclassified* federal job?

Recalling and Comparing

1. This chapter deals in part with the independent regulatory agencies. There are also some federal regulatory bodies that are *not* independent. How do they differ from the independent regulatory agencies?
2. Briefly explain how the following seem to *differ* in their functions within the executive branch:
    a. the executive departments
    b. the independent regulatory agencies
    c. the independent service agencies
3. Briefly explain how the following seem to be *similar* in their functions within the executive branch:
    a. the executive departments
    b. the independent regulatory agencies
    c. the independent service agencies

Special Activities

1. Prepare a news bulletin-board about the regulatory agencies of the federal government. Divide the board into two parts, one for independent regulatory agencies and the other for regulatory agencies within executive departments.
2. Consult your local library to prepare a brief biography of the head of one of the independent agencies.
3. Make a study of one independent regulatory agency. First determine its field of responsibility and then track its activities as reported in the press. Note how often the agency acts in a quasi-judicial role.
4. Make a survey of public attitudes toward five or more independent agencies. Ask people in your community what, specifically, they think is good or bad about the work of each agency on your list. Then ask the people to rate the work of each agency from good to poor on a scale of 1 to 10. At the end of your survey, note whether attitudes tend to cluster at the favorable or the unfavorable side of the scale. Make a report of possible reasons for the responses and ratings given.
5. Ask an owner or manager of a business, industry, or farm to discuss with your class the ways in which federal agencies affect wages, hours, and working conditions in that enterprise.
6. As a group project, write to the Publications Sales Branch, National Archives and Records Service, Washington, D.C. 20408 for *Documents from America's Past*. This booklet lists reprints of famous documents sold by the National Archives. Make a list of the ones that you would like your school library to buy.
7. Consider what arguments might be made for and against the following statement: "The executive branch of the federal government has too many departments and agencies." Do you agree or disagree? Why?

Unit III Review: The Executive Branch

Unit III Review

Improving Your Reading

Read the selection below and then answer the questions that follow it.

A President must be a natural-born citizen of the United States and must be at least 35 years of age when taking office. A President must also have been a resident of the United States for at least 14 years.

The President heads the executive branch. In this role, the President has the responsibility of seeing that all federal laws are enforced.

Some of the President's other roles are stated in the Constitution, and others have developed informally over the years. The President has certain powers related to law-making. For example, the President can approve or veto any bills sent from Congress. The President can also recommend legislation to Congress and call Congress into special sessions. In regard to the judicial branch, the President has the power to appoint Supreme Court justices and the judges of other federal courts. Still other powers are related to the President's role as commander in chief of the armed forces and as the nation's top diplomat.

Because of these wide powers, the President needs the help of many advisers and assistants. The President's formal advisers are the Cabinet and the members of the Executive Office of the President. Sometimes a President also has informal advisers.

The executive branch employs about 2.8 million civilians. They make up all but a small part of the federal bureaucracy.

The bulk of this bureaucracy works for the twelve Cabinet-level departments known as *executive departments*. New departments have been created from time to time to meet the changing needs of the nation.

Another part of the bureaucracy works for specialized agencies that are not in any specific department. These independent agencies report directly to the President, though the President does not always control them. Some of the independent agencies perform regulatory functions. The rules and regulations set by these independent regulatory agencies guide the activities of private individuals and companies. The other independent agencies perform a wide variety of services.

1 In your own words, summarize this reading in *no more than four* sentences. Your summary should consist of what you regard as the most important points made in the reading.

2 Which *one* of the following topics discussed in the reading can best be described by the term *executive*?
   a the qualifications required of a President
   b the work of the independent agencies
   c the President's powers
   d the Cabinet's advice to the President

3 From which *three* of the following sources does the President receive advice or assistance?
   a judges of the Supreme Court
   b the Cabinet

Unit III Review: The Executive Branch

    c the White House staff
    d independent agencies of the executive branch

Developing Your Writing Skills: What Are Your Attitudes toward Government?

Writing a Paragraph

In this unit, you have considered many aspects of the executive branch of the federal government. You have seen how this branch has grown and changed over the years. Obviously, more changes can be expected in the future.

Think back over the changes that have been made since the federal government was first organized. Then think of what changes you might wish to make in any of the following:

- the manner of choosing the President
- the powers of the President
- the organization of executive departments
- the nature of the federal bureaucracy

Make a list of any changes you might wish to make. Try to think of at least *five* changes. Then decide which *one* change is most important, in your view. On a separate sheet of paper, write the following sentence. Complete the sentence and use it as your topic sentence in a paragraph. Give reasons why you think such a change is desirable and what difference you think it might make in life in the United States.

    The most important change that could be made in the executive branch would be to _____

Writing an Essay

Write an essay on the relationship between the democratic system and the development of a bureaucracy. In forming your ideas, consider whether a bureaucracy could exist under a monarch.

Recommended Reading

Lonnelle Aikman, *The Living White House,* National Geographic Society, Washington, D.C., 1973 (paperback).

James David Barber, *The Presidential Character,* Prentice-Hall, Englewood Cliffs, N.J., 1972.

Charles L. Black, Jr., *Impeachment: A Handbook,* Yale University Press, New Haven, 1974 (paperback).

Morton Borden (ed.), *America's Eleven Greatest Presidents,* Rand McNally, Chicago, 1971 (paperback).

James MacGregor Burns, *Presidential Government,* Avon Books, New York (paperback).

Thomas J. Fleming, "Great Moments in Presidential Inaugurations," *Reader's Digest,* January 1969.

John Hersey, *The President,* Knopf, New York, 1975 (paperback).

Emmet John Hughes, *The Living Presidency,* Penguin Books, New York, 1973 (paperback).

Ona Griffin Jeffries, *In and Out of the White House,* Funk & Wagnalls, New York, 1960.

Joseph Nathan Kane, *Facts about the Presidents,* Ace Books, New York, 1976 (paperback).

Gary E. McCuen and David L. Bender, *American Foreign Policy: Opposing Viewpoints,* Greenhaven Press, Minneapolis, 1972 (paperback).

Earl S. Miers, *America and Its Presidents,* Tempo Books, New York, 1970 (paperback).

The White House: An Historic Guide, National Geographic Society, Washington, D.C., 1975 (paperback).

The Judicial Branch of the National Government

As a necessary part of the federal government, and as a balance for the legislative and executive branches, the Constitution created a third branch: the judicial branch. This branch includes all the federal courts. At its top is the Supreme Court of the United States. An informal photograph of the justices of that highest Court in the land appears on the next page.

The role of the judicial branch was described only sketchily by the framers of the Constitution. That role, as we know it today, was worked out through actual practice during which the judicial branch sometimes clashed with the other branches over which one of them held the final power to decide a question. Following is a summary of one such clash.

In the 1820s, the Cherokee people were under pressure from white settlers who wanted the Cherokees' lands in Georgia. It made little difference to the settlers that the lands had been assured to the Cherokees by the United States in treaties. In 1827, the Cherokees set up their own government and declared themselves a nation.

The state of Georgia, which sided with the white settlers, outlawed the Cherokees' government and claimed ownership of their land. In its efforts to control the use of Cherokee land, Georgia went so far as to forbid whites to live in Cherokee country without a permit.

A white named Worcester had been living among the Cherokees with their permission but without the residence permit that Georgia required. When a state court sentenced Worcester to jail, he sued the state. The case, *Worcester v. Georgia,* came before the United States Supreme Court in 1832.

The Supreme Court decided the case in favor of Worcester and the Cherokees. Writing for the Court, Chief Justice John Marshall pointed out that Congress had approved many treaties that dealt with Native Americans as separate nations. Those treaties, he said, were part of the law of the land. Marshall declared that Georgia laws could not apply within the boundaries of the Cherokee nation because only the federal government could make laws dealing with Native American nations. The Georgia law in question could not stand.

The Cherokees thought they had won a victory, but they were soon bitterly disappointed. President Jackson refused to enforce the Court's decision. Instead, he decided to enforce a law that had been passed by Congress in 1830. This Removal Act gave the President the power to make a land trade with the Native Americans. In exchange for their lands, the Cherokees would get territory west of the Mississippi. If they did not want to trade, the President would have them removed by force.

Finally, the Cherokees gave in. In 1835, they signed a treaty accepting $5 million and some land in the West as payment for their lands east of the Mississippi. Nearly one-fourth of the Cherokees died on the "Trail of Tears" that took them to Oklahoma.

As this account shows, there have been times when the executive and judicial branches of the federal government have not agreed on the value of a particular act or treaty. Two things, however, have been agreed on since the early years of our federal government. One is that the judicial branch has the right to interpret the laws—to decide exactly what the laws mean. The other is that it is up to the federal courts to determine whether any law or treaty, or any action of the executive branch, violates the Constitution. How the federal courts carry out these powers will be the subject of the next three chapters.

189

Chapter 10

The Federal Court System and the High Court

The federal courts play a basic role in our federal system. Together, they make up the judicial branch of the federal government. That gives them a place equal to that of the President and Congress.

Yet, you will not hear about the federal courts on news broadcasts as often as you hear about the President and Congress. Most of the work of the courts is carried on quietly. When a federal court case does make news, it is usually because the case has a dramatic impact on some part of our national life.

Our federal system leaves many matters up to state and local governments. It should be no surprise, then, that state and local courts handle a far greater number of cases than the federal courts do.

Though the contrast between these numbers is striking, a frequent complaint is that our federal court system is overloaded with work. The responsibilities of that system and how it is organized to carry them out are the subjects of this chapter.

Goals

- To learn the main functions of the federal court system.
- To learn the organization and role of the United States Supreme Court.
- To consider the question of removing a disabled Supreme Court justice from office.

Chapter 10: The Federal Court System and the High Court

STRUCTURE AND ROLE OF THE JUDICIAL BRANCH

Article III, Section 1 of the Constitution declares: "The judicial Power of the United States, shall be vested in one supreme Court, and in such inferior Courts as the Congress may from time to time ordain and establish." Thus, the framers of the Constitution created the United States Supreme Court but gave Congress the power to create the lower federal courts. Note the words "from time to time." Congress is free to change the number of such courts as it sees fit. We now have eleven United States Courts of Appeals, nearly 100 United States District Courts, and a number of special federal courts. The present structure of the judicial branch is outlined in the chart below. Chapter 12 will tell in more detail how the lower courts are set up.

Functions of the Judicial Branch

The federal courts do not actively seek out cases. Instead, an individual or an organization involved in a dispute must make the first move. Let's say that you run a small business which has been hurt by a law passed by Congress, and you believe the law violates the Constitution. The courts will not act until you or someone else files a lawsuit challenging the law. Only then can court consideration begin.

Most of the main functions of the judicial branch are stated in Article III of the Constitution. Oddly, its best known function is not.

1. *The federal courts determine whether laws and treaties or other governmental actions are constitutional.* This is probably the first function that comes to mind. It means that the federal courts can decide that an act of Congress, a presidential decision, a rule of an executive agency, a state law, or a decision of a lower court is in conflict with the Constitution or with an established law. As we shall see, this function is not directly stated in the Constitution but has been accepted as part of the role of the federal courts since 1803.

2. *The federal courts must provide a fair trial for those accused of breaking federal laws.* Federal crimes include such actions as robbing the mails, filing false information on a federal income tax form, hijacking an airplane, or printing counterfeit money.

3. *On request, the federal courts must handle lawsuits between citizens of different states.* For example, let's say Citizen Paul of Arkansas owns a boat that has destroyed a fishing house owned by Citizen John of Mississippi. If the damage is more than $10,000, a federal court could be called upon to decide such a case. Each year the federal courts handle more than 30,000 lawsuits between citizens of different states. Congress has considered moving most of those cases to state courts to lighten the burden on federal courts.

THE JUDICIAL BRANCH

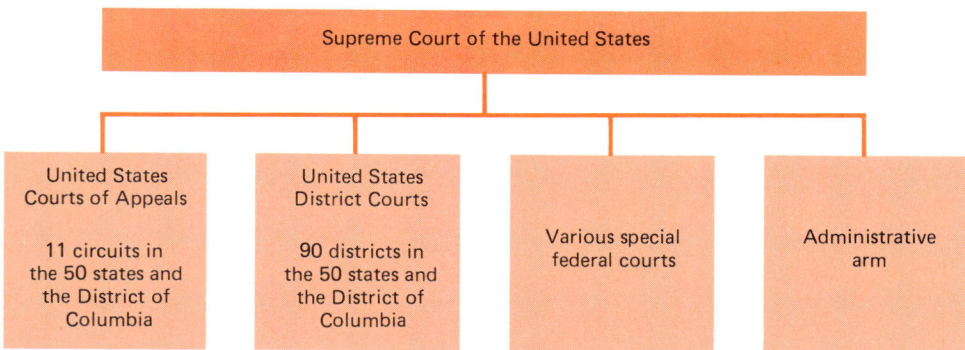

Chapter 10: The Federal Court System and the High Court

A DIFFERENCE OF OPINION!

ART WOOD
Courtesy U. S. Independent Telephone Assn.

4. *The federal courts handle disagreements between two or more states, or between a state and a resident of another state.* For example, if two states disagree on where the boundary between them lies, one of them may file a lawsuit in the United States Supreme Court.

5. *Disputes between one or more states and the federal government are handled by the federal courts.* Suppose the state of Wisconsin decided that lakes wholly within the state should not be subject to federal laws against pollution. And suppose the Environmental Protection Agency thought otherwise. Either the state or the agency could take the dispute to the Supreme Court, where the issue would be settled.

6. *The federal courts handle lawsuits filed by a state or a United States citizen against a foreign government or the citizens of a foreign country.* Say that the government of Mexico or one of its citizens damaged some property owned by the state of Texas. The state could file suit in a federal court. Can foreign governments or their citizens file lawsuits against one of our states in our federal courts? They cannot. This is specified in the Eleventh Amendment to the Constitution.

Under the Constitution, the federal courts also have power in two special situations. One is cases involving ambassadors, other public ministers, and consuls. The other is admiralty and maritime cases—that is, cases involving laws of the sea.

It is important to remember that Congress can extend and, in some ways, narrow the powers of the federal courts by legislation.

The power of a court to consider a case is called *jurisdiction*. All of the cases mentioned thus far are cases in which the federal courts have *original* jurisdiction. That is, the cases may begin in the federal courts. In addition, federal courts have *appellate* jurisdiction over certain cases that begin in local and state courts. That is, the cases may be taken to federal courts on appeal. In order to be appealed to a federal court, a case must involve either a federal law, a federal treaty, or an issue arising out of the Constitution.

Types of Cases

Cases within the federal court system can be broken down into a number of categories. We will mention three of them here: civil cases, criminal cases, and cases in equity.

Of the main functions described in the preceding section, only the second deals with criminal cases. All the others deal with civil cases. As we noted in Chapter 2, a civil suit is a dispute over the legal rights and duties of the parties to the suit. It is possible for the government to be a party to a civil suit, but in a criminal case, it is *always* the government that brings suit—that is, takes the case to court.

Usually, a civil lawsuit receives a title that includes the last names of the plaintiff, or the person who brought the suit, and the defen-

Thousands of legal cases are heard each year. The cases that attract the most attention are those involving famous people or controversial issues. William Kunstler, shown here being interviewed by the press, became famous himself for defending unpopular people and causes.

dant, who is the accused person. Let's say that Nancy Smith sues the Anderson Company. She accuses the company of refusing to hire her because she is a woman. Her case would be called *Smith v. Anderson Company.* (The *v.* stands for *versus,* a Latin word that means "against.") Or let's say that a state is involved. At the beginning of this unit, you read about a case entitled *Worcester v. Georgia.* Worcester, the person who filed the suit, was the plaintiff. The state of Georgia was the defendant; it was being sued. If Worcester had sued a federal agency, the title of the case might have included the name—say John Jones—of the head of that agency. The case might then have been called *Worcester v. Jones.* It might also have been called *Worcester v. United States,* with "United States" meaning the federal government. If Jones appealed the case to a higher court, the title would become *Jones v. Worcester* to indicate who made the appeal.

A *criminal case* involves an attempt to punish someone accused of breaking the law. If you do not pay the income taxes you owe the federal government, you are breaking a federal law. The government might file a criminal case seeking to put you in jail or make you pay a fine. (You might also face a civil suit in which the Internal Revenue Service would try to recover the money you owed it.)

Only a government agency may be a plaintiff in a criminal case. The defendant is the person accused of breaking a law. Suppose the federal government decides to *prosecute*—file a criminal case against—a person named Tom Brown, on a charge of hijacking an airplane. The case would be called *United States v. Brown*.

A *case in equity* involves an attempt to correct an unfair situation before it is too late. In this legal use, *equity* means "fairness." Again, an example will help. Imagine you own a ski resort in Montana. Someone in Idaho wants to seed the clouds to make rain or snow fall in Idaho. But you are afraid that this cloud seeding will mean less snow for Montana and will therefore hurt your business. Ordinarily, you would have to wait until you actually suffered some damage before you could file a lawsuit. But under the principle of equity, you might go into a federal court to request help. The court could issue an order forbidding any cloud seeding until the court has a chance to decide the issue. Such an order, forbidding (or, less often, requiring) a certain action, is an *injunction*. Cases in equity are intended to provide relief where the ordinary remedies of the law might come too late.

Appointment and Tenure of Federal Judges

In many states, judges are elected by the voters, but that is not so at the federal level. *All justices of the Supreme Court and all judges of lower federal courts are appointed by the President.* The Senate's approval is required. The appointments are voted on by the Judiciary Committee of the Senate and then by the full Senate.

Article II, Section 2 of the Constitution forms the basis of this practice. It provides that the President "shall nominate, and by and with the Advice and Consent of the Senate, shall appoint . . . Judges of the supreme Court, and all other Officers of the United States, whose Appointments are not . . . otherwise provided for."

Presidents generally appoint Supreme Court justices who share their own political beliefs. This usually means a person of the same political party. By tradition, senators take an active role in the choice of judges for the lower federal courts.

Justices of the Supreme Court and most other federal judges are appointed for life. They stay on the court until they resign, retire,

Associate Justice Thurgood Marshall was the first black appointed to the United States Supreme Court.

Chapter 10: The Federal Court System and the High Court

Only one Supreme Court justice, Samuel Chase, has ever been impeached (1804), and he was not convicted. Efforts by some people to impeach Chief Justice Earl Warren in the 1950s failed.

or die. Judges on a few of the lower federal courts serve only for a specified number of years.

Congress decides what salary shall be paid to federal judges. It cannot lower a judge's salary during the judge's term of office.

The only way a federal judge may be removed is by impeachment. Judges may be impeached for failing to maintain "good behavior," or for "treason, other high crimes or misdemeanors." As in all impeachments, the House of Representatives votes to impeach and the Senate then conducts a trial.

If Congress feels it necessary to remove a federal judge for not maintaining "good behavior," it must show that the judge has violated his or her oath. Each judge must take the following oath upon assuming office:

I, (name of judge), do solemnly swear (or affirm) that I will administer justice without respect to persons, and do equal right to the poor and to the rich, and that I will faithfully and impartially discharge and perform all the duties incumbent upon me as (position of judge) according to the best of my abilities and understanding, agreeably to the Constitution and laws of the United States.

Each judge is assisted in fulfilling that oath by a number of aides. Those who work most closely with federal judges are clerks, court reporters, stenographers, and marshals.

Checks and Balances

Like the other branches, the judicial branch operates within our federal system of checks and balances. As you have seen, the Senate can act as a check on the President's choice of a federal judge. Judges, by ruling on the constitutionality of laws passed by Congress and of actions of the executive branch, serve as a check on these two branches. Finally, by its impeachment power, Congress serves as an ultimate check on the judicial branch.

The relationship between the judicial and executive branches is an interesting one. Federal officials who bring cases to court are part of the executive branch, not the judicial branch. They are active parties on one side in court cases. Thus, a federal prosecutor, who works for the Department of Justice, goes to court to try to prove a case against someone accused of a crime. The judge's job is much different. The judge is expected to consider the case with an open mind, weighing all the arguments on both sides. In other words, federal judges can guard against too eager prosecution by the executive branch. This is another example of checks and balances at work.

Questions

1 What is the first step in bringing a case before the federal courts?

2 What are the main functions of the federal courts? Briefly describe each function.

3 What is a civil case? A criminal case? A case in equity?

⬠ Which do you think would be better: to have federal judges elected or to have them appointed by the President, as they are now? Explain.

THE SUPREME COURT OF THE UNITED STATES

At 10 A.M., a hush falls over the high-ceilinged courtroom on the main floor of the Supreme Court Building in Washington, D.C. "Oyez! Oyez! Oyez!" shouts a court crier, using an ancient English word meaning "Hear ye!" The crier continues: "All persons having business before the Honorable, the Supreme Court of the United States, are admonished to draw near and give their attention, for the Court is now sitting. God save the United States and this Honorable Court." With that, the black-robed justices file in and take their seats. The highest court in the land starts its work.

Public sittings of the Court sparkle with the pomp and ceremony of earlier centuries. If you were to visit this courtroom, you would see lawyers in striped trousers arguing weighty issues. You would see justices of the Court interrupting the lawyers with sharply worded questions. But you would not see the actual decision-making process, because that goes on behind closed doors. The deliberations of the Supreme Court are among the most closely guarded secrets in the nation's capital.

The Justices

Since 1869, the United States Supreme Court has been made up of nine justices. They are the Chief Justice of the United States and eight associate justices. Congress fixes the

Roosevelt tries to "pack" the Supreme Court in this cartoon.

number, which has varied from five (1801 to 1807) to ten (1863 to 1866).

A dramatic attempt to change the size of the Court was made in the 1930s. As we have seen, the President appoints the justices with the consent of the Senate. The Court, at that time, had a conservative majority. That majority had blocked many of President Franklin D. Roosevelt's New Deal laws by declaring them unconstitutional. Yet the voters had reelected Roosevelt by an overwhelming margin. Roosevelt's supporters argued that the "nine old men" on the Court were frustrating the popular will. In 1937, Roosevelt proposed to Congress a bill to enlarge the Court. The bill provided that for every justice over the age of 70 who decided not to retire after 10 years' service, the President could appoint one additional justice. The bill set a maximum of fifteen justices. Many people called Roosevelt a "dictator" and his proposal "court packing." Others applauded the proposal. It never passed.

Within months, however, two conservative justices on the Court began to vote with the liberal side. And President Roosevelt remained in office long enough to appoint eight new justices in traditional fashion. In the end, the Supreme Court accepted most of Roosevelt's New Deal measures as constitutional.

The Constitution mentions no minimum age or other special qualifications for federal judges. A judge does not even have to be a lawyer. Since the first meeting of the Supreme Court in 1790, however, all of its members have been lawyers. Some, not surprisingly, have been among the most eminent lawyers in the nation.

The Chief Justice receives a salary of $75,000 a year. Associate justices are paid $72,000.

A justice may serve as long as he or she feels capable of doing so. However, justices can retire with full pay at age 65 after 15 years of service. A justice who has been a federal judge for 10 years is eligible for the same retirement pension at the age of 70. The pension is intended to help solve the problem of justices who might try to hold their position after they are too old and feeble to perform adequately.

Jurisdiction of the Supreme Court

Only two kinds of cases may start in the Supreme Court: cases involving ambassadors and other foreign officials and cases in which a state government is one of the parties involved. These are the only cases in which the Supreme Court has original jurisdiction.

All other cases reach the Supreme Court only on appeal from a lower court. Cases such as those involving constitutional issues, charges of breaking federal laws, civil actions between citizens of different states, or a citizen's dispute with a foreign country (see the first three and the last of the judicial branch's main functions on pages 192–193) are among those in which the Court has appellate jurisdiction. Other cases may be appealed from state courts. Most Supreme Court cases are appeals.

The Supreme Court may not give advice about a proposed action or bill. How simple some things might be if it could! Such a power might help avoid uncertainty over whether a proposal was constitutional. But it would violate the constitutional separation of powers. At any rate, that seemed to be the opinion of our first Supreme Court when it refused to advise President Washington on a legal matter. He turned to his Attorney General for legal advice, and later Presidents have followed his practice.

The Supreme Court has work enough keeping up with the cases it has now. Each year, it is sent some 5,000 cases. In one recent year, the Court took up cases ranging from alleged sex discrimination, including "reverse discrimination" against males, to the constitutionality of environmental regulations. One dispute raised the question whether Native American tribal law could override an individ-

Supreme Court justices, such as Chief Justice Burger, must review each case to determine if they should hear it.

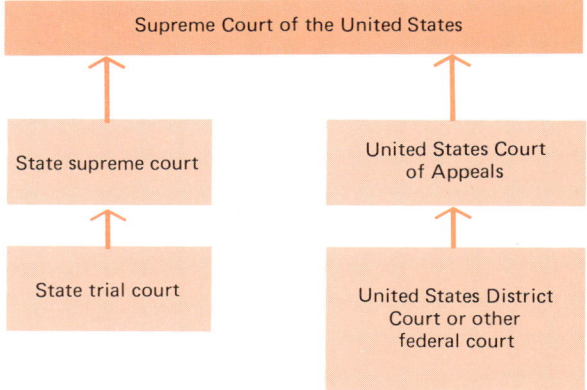

TWO MAIN PATHS TO THE UNITED STATES SUPREME COURT

Cases may follow either the state path or the federal path to the Supreme Court of the United States, depending on the nature of the case. Both paths are simplified in this chart.

ual's rights under the Constitution of the United States. Another case questioned whether a state could prohibit members of the clergy from serving in its legislature. Almost any question might end up before the Court if it meets one test: the justices must feel that the case involves a constitutional issue or a federal law or treaty.

Paths to the Supreme Court

We have already noted that most cases considered by the Supreme Court are under its appellate jurisdiction. There are two main ways in which such a case can reach the High Court: through lower federal courts or through state courts. The routes are summarized in the chart opposite. The federal route will be discussed further in Chapter 12.

Certain cases are said to reach the Supreme Court "on appeal." These are cases that the Court is required by law to consider if appealed from lower courts. Cases on appeal can rise from a lower federal court if the court has struck down a state law as contrary to a federal law, a treaty, or the Constitution. If a case on appeal began in state courts, it must already have been acted on by the highest state court. That court must have either (1) declared a federal law or treaty unconstitutional or (2) upheld a state law against a substantial challenge that it violates a federal law or treaty or conflicts with the United States Constitution. If the losing side wants to take the case to the Supreme Court, the Court *must* consider it.

In most cases, however, the person who loses in a lower court does not have an automatic right to appeal to the Supreme Court. Instead, the person must apply to the Court for a *writ of certiorari* (sur-she-uh-RAIR-ee), which is an order from a higher court to a lower court asking the lower court to hand up the records of a case for review. Usually, one of the parties has contended that an error was made. The Supreme Court turns down four out of five requests for a writ of certiorari. The only requests the Court grants are those that involve a significant public interest. That is, the issues in the case affect a number of people, and not just the parties to the suit.

Chapter 10: The Federal Court System and the High Court

The number of cases that reach the Supreme Court has been rising steadily. In 1945, only 1,460 cases were on the Court's *docket,* or schedule. By the mid 1970s, the docket had more than 5,000 cases. Most of the cases on the docket are rejected by the Court. This means that the decision of the lower court is left standing. The Supreme Court hears arguments on only about two hundred cases a year. Clearly, then, the public sessions of the Court are only the tip of the iceberg. Most of the Court's work goes on unseen.

Decision-Making

The Supreme Court meets each year from the first Monday in October until late June. The term of the Court follows a pattern outlined in the chart on this page.

For 2 weeks, the justices hold public sessions. During this time, they hear oral arguments in twenty-five or thirty cases. Lawyers

THE SCHEDULE OF THE SUPREME COURT

Monday–Thursday Opinions announced Cases heard Friday Private conferences of justices to discuss cases heard	} 2 weeks sitting
Study of cases heard Work on opinions Study of new questions arising; choice of those to be considered and acted on by the Court	} 2 weeks recess

People who wish to attend a Supreme Court session must go through a security check like those made in airports.

Chapter 10: The Federal Court System and the High Court

> **The Justices in Conference**
>
> Inside the United States Supreme Court's marble home on Capitol Hill, the Conference room stands ready. It is 9:30 A.M. on Friday. All week, lawyers from across the nation have presented their cases. Now clerks wheel in carts stacked with law books and briefs. An aide makes sure the silver coffee service is ready. A wood fire crackles in the black-marble fireplace, and from above the mantel a portrait of Chief Justice John Marshall peers down solemnly on the long oak table. The nine justices arrive, and by tradition each shakes hands with the other eight. The junior justice closes the door. The most secret meeting in Washington begins. For the next 6 to 8 hours these men will shape decisions affecting the rights of every American.
>
> Warren Earl Burger, fifteenth Chief Justice of the United States, opens the discussion by summing up his view of the case at hand. Then follows the senior justice, and on around the table. The justices frequently crack jokes, quote poetry, history, or Scripture. But the roaring debates that sometimes erupted in other years have reportedly vanished under Burger's gentle presiding. A seasoned mediator, he diverts an impending explosion by calling a coffee break or postponing the issue to another session.
>
> Adapted from Eugene H. Methvin, "Chief Justice Burger Balances the Scales," *Reader's Digest*, April 1975, pp. 121–125.

for each side stand at a lectern and speak, usually for half an hour. The justices may ask questions to clear up uncertain points. When a lawyer's time is up, a red light flashes. Also during these public sessions, the justices announce their decisions on cases they have heard earlier. These periods when the Court is in public session are called *sittings*.

Usually on Friday during their sittings, the justices hold a conference. They discuss cases among themselves and vote on specific cases. These votes in conference are kept secret until they are announced in open court.

For the next 2 weeks after a sitting, the justices "do their homework." They think over the arguments they have heard orally, study the decisions of lower courts, and read *briefs*—statements that lawyers have submitted about cases. They also handle other business. The periods during which all this takes place are called *recesses*.

Sittings and recesses alternate throughout the term. During the 3-month summer recess, new questions that arise are studied in preparation for the next term.

Some Supreme Court actions can be taken by one justice acting alone. For example, a single justice may order a *stay* of a lower court decision—that is, a delay in carrying out the decision—until the full Court is able to consider it. If the full Court decides not to accept the appeal, the stay is removed. If the Court does decide to accept the appeal, the stay remains in effect until the Court makes its ruling.

The Court's decisions are reached by majority vote. At least six justices must be present to decide a case. Usually, all nine are there, and there is a clear majority. Sometimes, however, a justice may be ill, and the remaining justices might split evenly, four to four. In this event, the decision of the lower court remains but does not become a national precedent.

Once the Court has voted, it must write up an *opinion*—a statement of the decision of the justices and the reasoning on which it is based. As we shall see, there can be two or more opinions.

Suppose the justices have split five to four on an important case, and the Chief Justice has voted with the majority. In this case, the Chief

Justice will assign one of the five majority justices to write a *majority opinion*. (If the Chief Justice votes with the minority, then this assignment is made by the senior justice on the majority side—that is, the justice who has been on the court the longest.)

The writing of opinions is a painstaking process. Legal points must be carefully checked in law books. Words must be chosen carefully so they convey the exact meaning intended. In a major case, an opinion may have to be revised and rewritten a dozen times.

During this process, the justices talk over the written opinions and suggest changes. Sometimes a majority opinion may be so skillful and logical that one of the justices who formerly voted on the other side will switch and support the majority. In other cases, it may be impossible for all of the majority justices to agree fully on the grounds for their decision. In that event, one of the majority justices may write a *concurring opinion* giving the justice's own reasoning in the case.

A justice who voted against the majority decision may also write a separate opinion. This *dissenting opinion* tells why the justice believes the Court's decision is wrong.

Sometimes months may go by while the justices write and rewrite their opinions. Eventually, however, the decisions are announced. The decisions are then published chronologically in a series of volumes titled *United States Reports.* For easy reference, a decision is identified by the volume and page number. For example, the famous decision in the case of *Brown v. Board of Education* is in Volume 347 of *United States Reports* and begins on page 483, so it is cited "347 U.S. 483."

How Supreme Is the Supreme Court?

The United States Supreme Court is the final authority on federal laws and treaties and the Constitution. The law is what the Court says it is. In the immediate sense, that gives the Supreme Court the final word. If you lose a case in the Supreme Court, you have nowhere else to go. About all you can do is apply to the Court for a rehearing. That usually will not do much good unless one of the justices has just left the Court, and you think the vote might now swing in your favor. Or you could apply to a lower court for a rehearing.

In the long term, however, the Supreme Court does not have the final word. The people do. Remember that the Court's job is merely to interpret the laws and the Constitution. Congress—representing the people—passes the laws. What if the public dislikes what the Supreme Court says about the meaning of the laws or their constitutionality? If a large number of people disagree with a decision of the Court, they can work for a new law or an amendment to the Constitution.

Generally, the Supreme Court does not go beyond the bounds of majority opinion. With changes in the climate of opinion, the Court has sometimes reversed itself. That is what happened with most of the laws of Roosevelt's New Deal, referred to on page 198. It also happened on the issue of racial segregation. From the 1800s until the early 1950s, the Supreme Court allowed racial segregation to exist. In 1896, in the case of *Plessy v. Ferguson,* the Court decided that separate railway cars for blacks and whites were constitutional, so long as they were "equal." Then, in 1954, in the case of *Brown v. Board of Education of Topeka,* the Court ruled that racial segregation in public schools was unconstitutional because segregated schools could never be "equal."

Was the Supreme Court "making law" in these two cases? Or was it merely reinterpreting laws and the Constitution in the light of changing public values? You may recall that English common law was known as "judge-made law." The law grew out of rulings that judges made over the years. So long as previous court decisions reflected current cus-

Though the Supreme Court can rule that a law is constitutional or unconstitutional, it has no power to enforce its decisions. Enforcement is left to the executive branch. Thus, President Eisenhower ordered troops into Little Rock, Arkansas, to ensure that the Court's school desegregation ruling was obeyed.

toms and opinions, they were upheld. When public opinion changed, the court decisions also changed.

Many federal judges today would agree with the comment of Jeremiah Smith, a former judge of the New Hampshire Supreme Court: "Do judges make law? 'Course they do. Made some myself." Yet, judges do not have a free hand to "make law." They are restricted by precedent (past decisions), by the wording of laws, and by legal principles and procedures. Congress can always pass a new law. It can take a law that has been declared unconstitutional and reword it so that it is constitutional. It can vote for a constitutional amendment, which must then be ratified by the states. Congress can also increase the number of justices on the Court, as Roosevelt tried to get Congress to do. Or the President can appoint justices with different views as Court seats become vacant.

In the next chapter, we will take up some of the Court's early and most far-reaching decisions.

Questions

1 Why is the Supreme Court called the High Court?

2 What happens when a Supreme Court vote is tied?

3 What can the public do if it does not agree with a decision of the Supreme Court?

◌ Do you think that the Supreme Court should reverse itself on a racial segregation or discrimination issue? Explain.

PROBLEM: SHOULD THERE BE A MEANS OF DECLARING A SUPREME COURT JUSTICE DISABLED?

In Chapter 7, we considered what might happen if a President were unable to carry on with the duties of office. In this exercise, we will consider what can be done when a Supreme Court justice becomes disabled.

Justice William O. Douglas was a constant supporter of the rights of the underprivileged during his time on the Court.

On December 31, 1974, at the age of 76, Associate Justice William O. Douglas suffered a stroke that left him confined to a wheelchair. In the following months, Justice Douglas was often absent from the Court. The following account relates to that experience.

As you read this account, consider these questions:

- *Is it possible to remove a disabled judge from office?*
- *Under what circumstances might a disabled judge remain on a court?*

The Constitution makes no provision for the removal of Supreme Court justices because of physical incapacity. Nor can Congress impeach a justice for reasons of failing health.

Members of the Court can try to persuade the incapacitated justice to retire voluntarily.

In 1869, Associate Justice Stephen Field persuaded Justice Robert C. Grier that he was too ill to continue. Some years later, Field himself became ill. Associate Justice John Harlan called on him and asked whether he remembered having persuaded Grier to retire. "Yes," Field replied, "and a dirtier day's work I never did in my life."

Occasionally, Presidents have been able to persuade Supreme Court justices to retire. President Kennedy apparently did so in the case of Justice Felix Frankfurter.

Finally, the Court can operate effectively without a full membership, or with a member able to carry less than a normal share of work.

For example, Justice Douglas himself was off the bench from October 3, 1949, until March 25, 1950. He had fallen from a horse and the horse fell on him, cracking twenty-three of his ribs. During that absence, the Court ruled on nearly seventy-five cases. In 1971, after the resignations of Justice Hugo Black and Justice John Marshall Harlan, the Court, for a time, had only seven justices. Before the year was out, however, Justice Lewis F. Powell and Justice William H. Rehnquist were sworn in.

Adapted from James Reston, "The Case of Justice Douglas," San Antonio *Express,* September 18, 1975, p. 18A. Copyright © 1975 by The New York Times Company. Reprinted by permission.

In November of 1975, 11 months after his stroke, Justice Douglas resigned from the Court. Justice John Paul Stevens was quickly appointed to take his place.

Questions

1 What does the Constitution say about the removal of a Supreme Court justice because of disability?

2 What can government officials do to have a disabled justice removed from office?

3 What difference might the absence of one justice make in the Supreme Court's decisions?

◇ Who do you think should decide when a Supreme Court justice or other federal judge is too ill to perform his or her duties? Explain.

Chapter 10 Review

Developing Your Political Vocabulary

Use each of the following terms in a sentence about our federal judiciary.
- **a** jurisdiction
- **b** original jurisdiction
- **c** appellate jurisdiction
- **d** civil case
- **e** criminal case
- **f** equity
- **g** plaintiff
- **h** defendant
- **i** docket
- **j** writ of certiorari

Recalling and Comparing

1 Review the three main types of cases considered by federal courts. How do they differ? Cite *one* thing about each type that sets it apart.

2 How are federal judges chosen, and how may they be removed from office?

3 What is the highest court in the land? Why is it called that?

4 Give *two* examples of how the judicial branch fits into our federal system of checks and balances.

5 What requirement must be met before a decision of a state court can be appealed to a federal court?

Special Activities

1 Prepare a poster in which you illustrate the main functions of our federal courts.

2 Find an article in a newspaper or magazine about a recent Supreme Court decision. Write a report about the decision, giving arguments for and against the Court's ruling. Do you agree with the Court's decision?

3 Use a library to do research and write a report on the impeachment in 1804 of Supreme Court Justice Samuel Chase. The impeachment was for political purposes, and the Senate refused to convict Chase.

4 Prepare an outline brief of a legal case as law school students are often asked to do. Select a case that interests you and as you read it, outline it as follows:
- **a** identification: title of the case, with the legal reference and date
- **b** background: How did the case reach the courts? Who did what to whom?
- **c** issues: legal questions involved in the case
- **d** decisions: What answer (yes or no) did the court give to each legal question?
- **e** reasons: What basic reasons did the court offer for its decision? Who wrote the decision?
- **f** dissent: If there was a dissenting opinion, what reasons were given for the dissent? Who wrote it?
- **g** significance: What was the legal significance of the case?

Conclude by giving your own opinions on the issue.

5 Consider what might be arguments for and against the following statement: "The United States Supreme Court has too much power." Do you agree or disagree? Explain your reasons.

Chapter 11

Some Historic Supreme Court Decisions

The Supreme Court acquired the important role that it plays today through the strength of its own decisions, not through the words of the Constitution. For the first decade of our federal government, the Court occupied an obscure corner of national life. Three Chief Justices came and went, disappointed with the lack of challenge in the job.

All of that changed in 1803. In that year, the fourth Chief Justice, John Marshall, pushed the Supreme Court into the limelight. Marshall wrote an opinion in 1803 that made the Court the number one referee in disputes involving the Constitution. Afterward, the Court could not be ignored. Over the next 61 years, opinions written by Marshall and his successor, Roger Taney, set down some of the basic rules of our federal system. Those rulings are the subject of this chapter.

Goals

- To understand the lasting impact of some early decisions of the Supreme Court.
- To learn about the justices who led the Court to those important rulings.
- To consider the basis for some Supreme Court decisions.

Chapter 11: Some Historic Supreme Court Decisions

Chief Justice John Marshall, a Federalist appointed by President Adams, established the power of the judiciary.

Parliament unconstitutional. The guardian of the British constitution is Parliament, not the courts.

Some of our nation's early leaders definitely thought that the courts should be our Constitution's guardian. Alexander Hamilton argued in *Federalist No. 78* that strong courts were needed as a check on Congress. Otherwise, Hamilton said, Congress might some day be swayed by the public to take away some of the property rights set down in the Constitution. Hamilton thought that the federal courts should have the power to curb Congress by declaring an act of Congress to be unconstitutional.

The power of a court to declare an act of Congress or an action of the executive branch unconstitutional is called the power of judicial review. It was Chief Justice John Marshall who established judicial review as a power of the federal courts.

The Democratic-Republicans, led by Thomas Jefferson, saw federal courts as a threat to the power of state courts.

HISTORIC DECISIONS BY JOHN MARSHALL

The Constitution does not specifically say who has the final authority to settle disputes about the provisions in that document. Nowhere in the Constitution is the Supreme Court given this authority. Yet the power to settle disputes about the meaning of the Constitution is the key to the Supreme Court's importance in our federal system today. How did the Court obtain that power?

It cannot be traced to our British political heritage. In Great Britain, the courts do not have the same authority to declare an act of

Marshall was born in a cabin on the Virginia frontier in 1755, the oldest of fifteen children. He was a soldier in the American Revolution, later a member of the Virginia legislature, then a member of Congress. For a brief period, Marshall served as Secretary of State under President John Adams.

Like Adams, Marshall was a Federalist, a believer in strong national government. At that time, the Federalists were opposed by a political party known as the Democratic-Republicans, or Jeffersonian Republicans. The members of this party believed that state governments were the best guardians of public liberties. It was a clash between Federalists and Democratic-Republicans that set the stage for Marshall's most famous decision.

The Federalists ran the federal government from 1789 to 1801. The Federalist party went down to defeat in November 1800 when Thomas Jefferson, leader of the Democratic-Republicans, was elected President. Several months passed between Jefferson's election and the time set for him to take office on March 4, 1801. During that time, the party in power did everything it could to prolong its strong voice in national affairs.

The outgoing Congress, dominated by the Federalists, had this purpose in view when it passed the Judiciary Act of 1801 early in the year. The new law increased the number of federal judges, marshals, attorneys, and clerks. Using his appointment powers, President Adams named Federalists to the new positions, and to many vacant positions. Congress quickly confirmed the appointments. The Federalists reasoned that with loyal Federalists in most judgeships, the party's belief in federal supremacy would be upheld by the courts.

One of the vacant positions President Adams wanted to fill was that of Chief Justice of the United States. The first person to whom he offered the position turned it down. The matter of a Chief Justice was weighing on the President's mind when Secretary of State Marshall went to Adams's office one day early in 1801. As Marshall later recalled, President Adams turned to him and asked, "Who shall I nominate now?" Marshall had no suggestion. After a moment's silence, the President declared: "I believe I must nominate you." No one could have been more surprised than Marshall was. He readily accepted and was confirmed by the Senate. It was an appointment that would mark the history of the federal system of government for decades to come.

When Jefferson took office as President on March 4, 1801, he learned that some of the new Federalist judges had not yet been handed their official commissions (fortunately, Marshall had received his). To keep these Federalists from taking office, Jefferson directed James Madison, the new Secretary of State, not to deliver the commissions.

William Marbury waited in vain for his commission as a justice of the peace in the District of Columbia. When Marbury learned what had happened, he went to the Supreme Court. There he filed for a *writ of mandamus* (man-DAY-mus)—a court order directing a public official or an officer of a corporation to perform his or her legal duty. Because, in this case, Marbury wanted Madison to hand over the commission, the case name was *Marbury v. Madison*. Marbury had gone directly to the Supreme Court because the Judiciary Act of 1789 gave that body original jurisdiction in cases involving writs of mandamus against federal officials. Not Marbury's rights, but that act of Congress, became the bombshell in the case.

In deciding Marbury v. Madison in 1803, Marshall declared that the act of Congress on which Marbury had relied was in violation of the Constitution. The Judiciary Act of 1789 was clear enough, but so was the Constitution. It stated in Article III, Section 2 that the Supreme Court has *original* jurisdiction *only* in cases involving foreign ambassadors or in which one of the parties is a state. Marshall's opinion, written for the Court, stated that the Judiciary Act of 1789 was in conflict with the

Constitution and was therefore void, or canceled.

The decision seemed to favor Jefferson's Democratic-Republicans since Marbury was denied the court order that he sought. (According to Marshall, Marbury had sought his writ of mandamus in the wrong court; he should have applied to a federal District Court.) In the long view, however, the Federalists won out since the ruling established the principle that the federal courts have the power to interpret the Constitution. Marshall's opinion was so carefully reasoned that, ever since, the right of judicial review has been an accepted part of the powers of the Supreme Court and all other federal courts.

John Marshall continued to make his mark on the Supreme Court. In the 34 years he served as Chief Justice, many of the decisions in which he took part became landmark cases. Following are some of the principles they helped establish.

A federal court decision takes precedence over a state law. This precedent was established in *United States v. Judge Peters* (1809) when Marshall and his fellow justices denied a state legislature the power to set aside a judgment or order of a federal court.

A state must comply with the contracts it enters into. Marshall and the Court established this principle in *Dartmouth College v. Woodward* (1819). The state of New Hampshire had granted a charter to Dartmouth College, a private institution, but had then decided to bring the college under public control. When the state issued a new charter and appointed a new set of trustees, the original trustees refused to turn over the college's records and money. Instead, they sued a state representative named Woodward.

The Supreme Court ruled in favor of the plaintiff, Dartmouth College. Marshall reasoned that the college's charter was a contract, and the state did not have the right to back out of a contract. This ruling, based on Article I, Section 10, which limits the powers of the states, preserved the legal obligations of contracts.

Congress has not only the powers specified in the Constitution but also "implied" powers. This doctrine of implied powers was established in *McCulloch v. Maryland* (1819). The state of Maryland had tried to collect a state tax from the Baltimore branch of the Bank of the United States. McCulloch, the bank's cashier, refused to pay the tax. The Supreme Court ruled that a state could not tax the bank, or any other agency of the federal government.

More important, in this case the defendant, Maryland, charged that the federal government did not have the right to set up a federal bank. Nowhere does the Constitution state that Congress has the power to charter a bank. Maryland based its position on a strict interpretation of the Constitution. Marshall denied this argument. Instead, he made a broad, or liberal, interpretation of the Constitution. He based his ruling on Article I, Section 8, Clause 18, which gives Congress the power "to make all Laws which shall be necessary and proper" to carry out the powers mentioned in the Constitution. This is the clause we know as the elastic clause. Marshall declared:

Let the end be legitimate, let it be within the scope of the Constitution, and all means which are appropriate, which are plainly adapted to that end, which are not prohibited, but consistent with the letter and spirit of the Constitution, are constitutional.

This milestone opinion represented Marshall's belief in a "living Constitution." The Constitution, he said, was "intended to endure for ages to come, and consequently, to be adapted to the various crises of human affairs." By recognizing Congress' possession of implied powers, Marshall laid the foundation for many further adaptations in our system of government. Much of the present structure of our federal government, from the Environmental

Federal interstate commerce regulations ended the steamship monopoly that Fulton's *Clermont* had on the Hudson River.

Protection Agency to the Department of Energy, has been built by Congress upon that foundation.

A decision of a state court is subject to review by the United States Supreme Court. This aspect of the power of judicial review was established in the case of *Cohens v. Virginia* (1821). The Cohens had sold tickets in Virginia for a lottery sponsored by Washington, D.C. Since Virginia had a state law prohibiting the sale of lottery tickets, a Virginia court convicted the Cohens of violating the state law.

In appealing to the Supreme Court, the Cohens pointed out that the lottery for which they had been selling tickets had been authorized by an act of Congress. They argued that Virginia's law conflicted with a federal law and was thus not valid. Virginia, on the other hand, argued that the verdict of a state court could not be appealed to the United States Supreme Court. Virginia pointed out that the Constitution did not specify who should be the final authority in disputes over its terms. So, argued Virginia, this authority could be exercised by the high courts of each state.

The Supreme Court firmly rejected Virginia's argument. The Court held, in an opinion written by Marshall, that in a case involving federal law or rights, a decision by a state court is subject to review by the Supreme Court of the United States. This gave the United States Supreme Court the final say in any dispute over federal law or rights. It meant that from then on the United States Supreme Court was to have more power than any state court.

The Cohens, incidentally, lost their case. The Supreme Court held that no act of Congress had authorized the sale of lottery tickets in states where lotteries were illegal.

States cannot interfere with the right of Congress to regulate commerce between the states. The Court established this principle in

Chapter 11: Some Historic Supreme Court Decisions

Gibbons v. Ogden (1823). The Hudson River begins at a lake in upper New York State and divides New York and New Jersey as it flows to the sea. It was on the Hudson, in 1807, that Robert Fulton successfully tested his new invention, the steamboat. The New York legislature gave Fulton and a partner a monopoly on steamboat transportation on the Hudson. The partners, in turn, named Aaron Ogden to operate a steamship between New York City and the New Jersey shore.

A competing line across the Hudson was later set up by Thomas Gibbons under a coasting license from the federal government. Ogden obtained an order from a New York state court requiring Gibbons to stop running his boats. Gibbons then took the case to the United States Supreme Court. He pointed out that his steamboat service linked one state with another, and was thus an interstate operation.

The Supreme Court agreed with Gibbons that New York's grant of a monopoly interfered with the power of Congress to regulate interstate commerce. The Court's decision cited Article I, Section 8, Clause 3, of the Constitution. That clause gives Congress authority "to regulate Commerce . . . among the several States." The Court's decision helped to expand the legal meaning of *commerce*. Today, the "commerce clause" is used by Congress to regulate a wide range of activities, including radio and television broadcasting and the building of dams.

Marshall's service as Chief Justice ended only with his death in 1835. His long career put into practice the Federalist strategy of 1801. Long after the Federalists had been ousted from power, their basic principle of a strong national government was being stamped indelibly upon the nation's legal system. Those who favored states' rights and a limited national government had lost the battle. The appointment that President Adams seemed to make offhandedly had proved to be a turning point for the nation.

Questions

1 What new precedents did John Marshall's Court set in the following decisions?
 a *Marbury v. Madison* in 1803
 b *United States v. Judge Peters* in 1809
 c *Dartmouth College v. Woodward* in 1819
 d *McCulloch v. Maryland* in 1819
 e *Cohens v. Virginia* in 1821
 f *Gibbons v. Ogden* in 1823

2 Which of these cases strengthened the power of the national government? How?

⬠ Do you think that all Chief Justices of the Supreme Court should be as forceful as John Marshall in forming judicial opinions? Explain.

The Supreme Court under Chief Justice Roger Taney tended to favor states' rights and private business interests.

HISTORIC DECISIONS BY ROGER TANEY

Marshall's successor as Chief Justice was Roger Taney, a Jacksonian Democrat. In some ways, Taney resembled Marshall. He had started out as a Federalist and had served in a state legislature, that of Maryland. Like Marshall, he was a firm believer in private property. But Taney was not so avid a supporter of federal rights over states' rights. He leaned toward a stricter construction of the Constitution.

Taney, a thin, stooped man, was an aristocrat. Born into a slaveholding family, he went to his grave a firm supporter of slavery. His views on slavery helped entangle him in the most controversial decision of his career. We will discuss that shortly.

After quitting the Federalists, Taney became a member of President Andrew Jackson's Cabinet in 1832 as Attorney General. In that position, he had two occasions to put forth his views on slavery. One was a legal opinion supporting a South Carolina law that prohibited free blacks from entering the state. The second was a legal opinion to the effect that blacks could not be United States citizens.

In his 28 years as Chief Justice, Taney often presided over a bitterly divided Court. Two of the Court's decisions under Taney are of particular note. They had far-reaching effects through the principles they affirmed.

There are no implied rights in a contract that would favor private enterprises over the public. This principle was established in *Charles River Bridge v. Warren Bridge* (1837). The state of Massachusetts had granted a charter to the Charles River Bridge Company to build a toll bridge over the Charles River. The tolls were high, but the bridge was a convenient route between Boston and Cambridge. Many people used it. Before long, the bridge company had paid off the costs of construction and was making a tidy profit.

In 1828, Massachusetts decided to build a free bridge across the river not far from the toll

In the Charles River Bridge case of 1837, the Supreme Court's decision to support a state's liberty to manage its own internal affairs made the Taney Court popular with the leaders of the business world. This engraving of the bridge is from 1787.

bridge. The free bridge was to be called the Warren Bridge. The Charles River Bridge Company sued to stop the new bridge.

The company's argument went like this: Massachusetts had granted the company a charter to operate a toll bridge. This charter was a contract. In its Dartmouth College decision, the Supreme Court had ruled that a state was bound by its contracts. The toll bridge company's contract with the state *implied* that the state would do nothing to destroy the value of the contract. By building a free bridge, the state would destroy the value of the toll bridge and thus violate its contract.

Chief Justice Taney wrote the Court's opinion in the Charles River Bridge case. The Court agreed that the charter was a contract and that the state of Massachusetts was bound by that contract. But the Court pointed out that the charter said nothing about a free bridge. The Court declared that the state was bound only by what was written in the contract, not by what somebody thought the contract implied. As a result, Massachusetts had the right to build a free bridge.

Taney's ruling pleased state officials. They were relieved that the Court had interpreted a state's obligations quite narrowly. Later Court decisions continued this trend. Owners of businesses—other than those holding state charters—were also pleased. Some people in business had feared that the Supreme Court would decide that there were implied powers in a contract as well as in the Constitution. The Court had not done so.

For more than 20 years, the Supreme Court under Chief Justice Taney followed a course that reassured the rising business interests. The Court was not extending its powers, as it had under Marshall, but clearing up questions that had caused confusion. This course was popular with leaders in the business world. The Court's prestige was growing.

Before the end of the 1850s, however, the Supreme Court faced an issue that divided the nation bitterly. This was the issue of slavery. Taney and his Court might have exercised judicial restraint and sidestepped the issue. But they tackled it head-on. The Court's decision split the nation further and brought the Court's prestige tumbling down. Here is what the Court ruled:

A black cannot be a citizen of the United States, and Congress cannot forbid slavery in United States territories. The Court handed down this opinion in the case of *Dred Scott v. Sandford* (1857). Dred Scott was a black who was born into slavery and lived for a time in Missouri where slavery was permitted. The neighboring state of Illinois was a free state. Scott's master, named Emerson, took him to Illinois for 2 years, and then to a territory where slavery was also illegal. Later Scott was returned to Missouri, where he came into the possession of a new owner. Scott went to a Missouri state court and sued for his freedom, maintaining that he was no longer a slave because he had lived for four years on free soil. The state supreme court declared that Scott was still a slave in Missouri. Scott's appeal, backed by Republicans who opposed slavery, came before the United States Supreme Court.

Though the Supreme Court had, in the past, avoided involvement in a state's actions if those actions had to do only with matters within the state, Taney and the four other Southern justices on the Court in 1857 chose another course. Apparently they thought that they could settle the issue of slavery by judicial action.

Years before, slavery had divided the Founders, and they had reached a compromise under which slavery was not challenged in framing the Constitution. Laws passed by Congress between 1789 and the 1850s continued to avoid a showdown on the slavery issue. One such law was the Missouri Compromise of 1820, which prohibited slavery in Western territories north of a specific line and permitted

Chapter 11: Some Historic Supreme Court Decisions

In the Dred Scott case, Chief Justice Taney argued that Congress did not have authority to prohibit slavery in the territories. This portrait of Scott was made from life.

it south of that line. Taney and his Court majority would have none of this delicate balancing of sectional interests. They turned to the Declaration of Independence and the Constitution for guidance.

First of all, said the Court, the stirring words of the Declaration of Independence had never been meant to apply to blacks. "The unhappy black race," said the Court, "had no rights which the white man was bound to respect." Therefore, the Constitution gave no rights to black people. Even free blacks were not citizens of the United States. They could not sue in federal courts. As for slaves, their owners could take them wherever they pleased.

Second, the Court continued, the Constitution was "the supreme Law of the Land" (Article VI), and it gave Congress no power to abolish slavery. That power was reserved to the states. Therefore, Congress had gone beyond its powers when it tried to interfere with slavery in such laws as the Missouri Compromise of 1820. Those laws were unconstitutional. It was the first time since *Marbury v. Madison* that the Supreme Court had declared an act of Congress unconstitutional. This time, the Court had taken the position on an issue that was highly controversial.

The Court's ruling in the Dred Scott case sent shock waves through the nation. It reopened the old wound of the slavery question. All Northern states had considered blacks to be citizens, though few blacks were eligible to vote. As citizens, blacks had often sued in state and federal courts. Now, suddenly, blacks were

The Dred Scott decision left blacks with no rights. And former slaves and free blacks were made a legal form of property.

CAUTION!!
COLORED PEOPLE
OF BOSTON, ONE & ALL,

You are hereby respectfully CAUTIONED and advised, to avoid conversing with the

Watchmen and Police Officers of Boston,

For since the recent ORDER OF THE MAYOR & ALDERMEN, they are empowered to act as

KIDNAPPERS
AND
Slave Catchers,

And they have already been actually employed in KIDNAPPING, CATCHING, AND KEEPING SLAVES. Therefore, if you value your LIBERTY, and the *Welfare of the Fugitives* among you, Shun them in every possible manner, as so many HOUNDS on the track of the most unfortunate of your race.

Keep a Sharp Look Out for KIDNAPPERS, and have TOP EYE open.

APRIL 24, 1851.

Chapter 11: Some Historic Supreme Court Decisions

Some abolitionists believed that political action might remove the curse of slavery without endangering the Union. This abolitionist meeting was held in Boston, "cradle of liberty," where the poster on the preceding page was also published.

told that they had no citizenship rights. The passions of factions for and against slavery were aroused.

Of course, the Court's decision did *not* settle the slavery question at all. The Civil War did that. The main points of Taney's decision were reversed after the war by amendments to the Constitution. In 1865, the Thirteenth Amendment abolished slavery in all states and territories. In 1868, the Fourteenth Amendment provided that "all persons born or naturalized in the United States . . . are citizens."

Taney did not live to see his opinion reversed by constitutional amendments. He died in 1864, while the war still raged. But he lived long enough to see the Supreme Court become the target of stinging abuse. Public opinion of the Court fell sharply in the aftermath of the Dred Scott case.

Questions

1 What was the issue in the Charles River Bridge case? In the Dred Scott case?

2 What principle was established by the Supreme Court's decision in the Charles River Bridge case? In the Dred Scott case?

⬠ Do you think that a Supreme Court decision should ever be based on what seems morally right rather than on the actual words of the Constitution? Explain.

Historians today consider both Marshall and Taney to have been strong Chief Justices. Though the Dred Scott decision is widely deplored, it does not detract from Taney's contributions to the Court in his younger years. Both Marshall and Taney strongly supported the rights of property owners. Where they differed was in the respective weight they gave to state rights and federal rights. Marshall, in general, set limits beyond which states might not go. Taney, on the other hand, set limits beyond which the federal government might not go. Together, they helped to clarify many constitutional principles that guided this nation in the decades after both chief justices were gone.

Chapter 11: Some Historic Supreme Court Decisions

By 1864, the Supreme Court had achieved much greater power than anyone in 1789 could have imagined. The Court had established the supremacy of federal law. It had assured its own powers through (1) the right of judicial review, (2) the precedence of Supreme Court decisions over state laws, and (3) the right of the Supreme Court to review decisions of state courts. Moreover, the Court had recognized (4) the implied powers of Congress and (5) the power of Congress to regulate interstate commerce. It had established (6) the obligation of contracts.

Other strong Chief Justices would follow in the traditions established by John Marshall and Roger Taney. Among those leaders of the Court would be William Howard Taft, Charles Evans Hughes, and Earl Warren. The standard against which they would be measured was the record of Marshall and Taney.

PROBLEM: WHAT WOULD YOUR DECISION BE?

The Supreme Court is called upon to decide a wide range of tough questions. There are no easy answers; the easy questions are settled in the lower courts and not appealed. Only the tough questions reach the Supreme Court docket. A hundred years after Taney's death, the Court was wrestling with a whole series of questions about individual rights. We will consider many of those questions later in this book (Chapter 16). The challenges they presented to the Court are merely suggested by the brief samples given here.

During the Reconstruction period after the end of the Civil War, blacks were granted the full rights of citizenship by means of amendments to the Constitution. The Freedmen's Bureau and other federal agencies tried to translate those rights into action. This wood engraving from an 1867 Southern newspaper shows both blacks and whites on a jury.

After busing of students was ordered by federal courts, the Supreme Court overruled it in at least one case.

Below are three cases that were presented to the Supreme Court after Warren Burger became chief justice in 1969. As you read about them, ask yourself:

- What decision was reached?
- For what reasons?

Case 1. From Florida comes James Gustafson claiming violation of his Fourth Amendment right against "unreasonable search." Driving at 2 A.M. in Orlando, he was stopped, questioned, and arrested because he had no driver's license. The officer patted him down, felt a cigarette package, and found marijuana. Gustafson was later convicted on this evidence. Reasonable enough, decide Burger and five other justices: even for minor traffic arrests, police may constitutionally conduct thorough body searches and use any evidence found in a criminal prosecution.

Case 2. From New York come Dolores Dublino and other able-bodied welfare recipients. They complain that the state violates the Thirteenth Amendment prohibition against involuntary servitude by requiring them to show up every 2 weeks at unemployment offices and take suitable jobs if available. Untrue, rule Burger and six other justices: the state is acting lawfully to promote self-reliance and civic responsibility, and to "assure that limited state welfare funds are spent on behalf of those genuinely incapacitated [disabled] and most in need."

Case 3. From Michigan come fifty-three suburban school districts. They complain that federal judges abused their power by ordering thousands of black and white children bused across county lines to reduce heavy black concentrations in Detroit city schools. Burger and four justices agree: without proof of specific official acts of racial discrimination, federal judges may not order busing to "produce the racial balance which they perceive as desirable."

Adapted from Eugene H. Methvin, "Chief Justice Burger Balances the Scales," *Reader's Digest,* April, 1975, pp. 121–125.

Questions

1 Who were the plaintiffs in these cases?

2 What was the complaint in each case?

3 What was the decision in each case? What was the basis for that decision?

◇ What would your decision have been in each case? Why?

Chapter 11 Review

Developing Your Political Vocabulary

Use each of the following terms in a sentence related to a court decision by either John Marshall or Roger Taney.

- a plaintiff
- b writ of mandamus
- c unconstitutional
- d judicial review
- e judicial restraint
- f contract
- g implied
- h jurisdiction

Recalling and Comparing

1 Look back over the major decisions made by John Marshall's Court and by Roger Taney's Court. In what ways are the decisions similar? In what ways do they differ?

2 What decision of the Supreme Court established the right of federal courts to interpret the Constitution?

3 What was one Supreme Court decision that was later changed by constitutional amendments?

4 What decision of the Supreme Court established the obligation of contracts? What decision of the Supreme Court established that there are no implied rights in a contract that is granted to a private party by a state?

5 What do you regard as Chief Justice Taney's single most important decision? Explain your answer.

Special Activities

1 Using library reference materials, prepare a chart showing the dates of office for all Chief Justices.

2 Using reference materials in a library, make a study of one of the cases discussed in this chapter. Seek out the arguments on both sides of the case and prepare an outline of those arguments.

3 In this chapter, you have read about Chief Justices John Marshall, Roger Taney, Earl Warren, and Warren Burger. Consult a library for information about one of these justices. Write an essay of one or two pages in which you answer the following questions about the individual you have chosen:

- *What are some of the most important facts about that person's life?*
- *How has that person influenced the way our federal system operates today?*

4 Some associate justices of the Supreme Court have been even more famous than the Chief Justices. Prepare a study of the role of one of the following associate justices: John Marshall Harlan, Oliver Wendell Holmes, Jr., Louis Brandeis, Hugo Black, or William O. Douglas. Each was voted "Great" or "Near Great" by a panel of sixty-five law experts in a poll carried out for *Life* magazine in 1971. See if you agree with the experts.

5 Invite a judge or lawyer from your community to speak to the class about the federal court power of judicial review. Allow time for questions and discussion.

6 Consider what might be arguments for and against the following statement: "In making a decision, a Supreme Court justice should not be concerned with social, economic, or political issues of the day." Do you agree or disagree? Why?

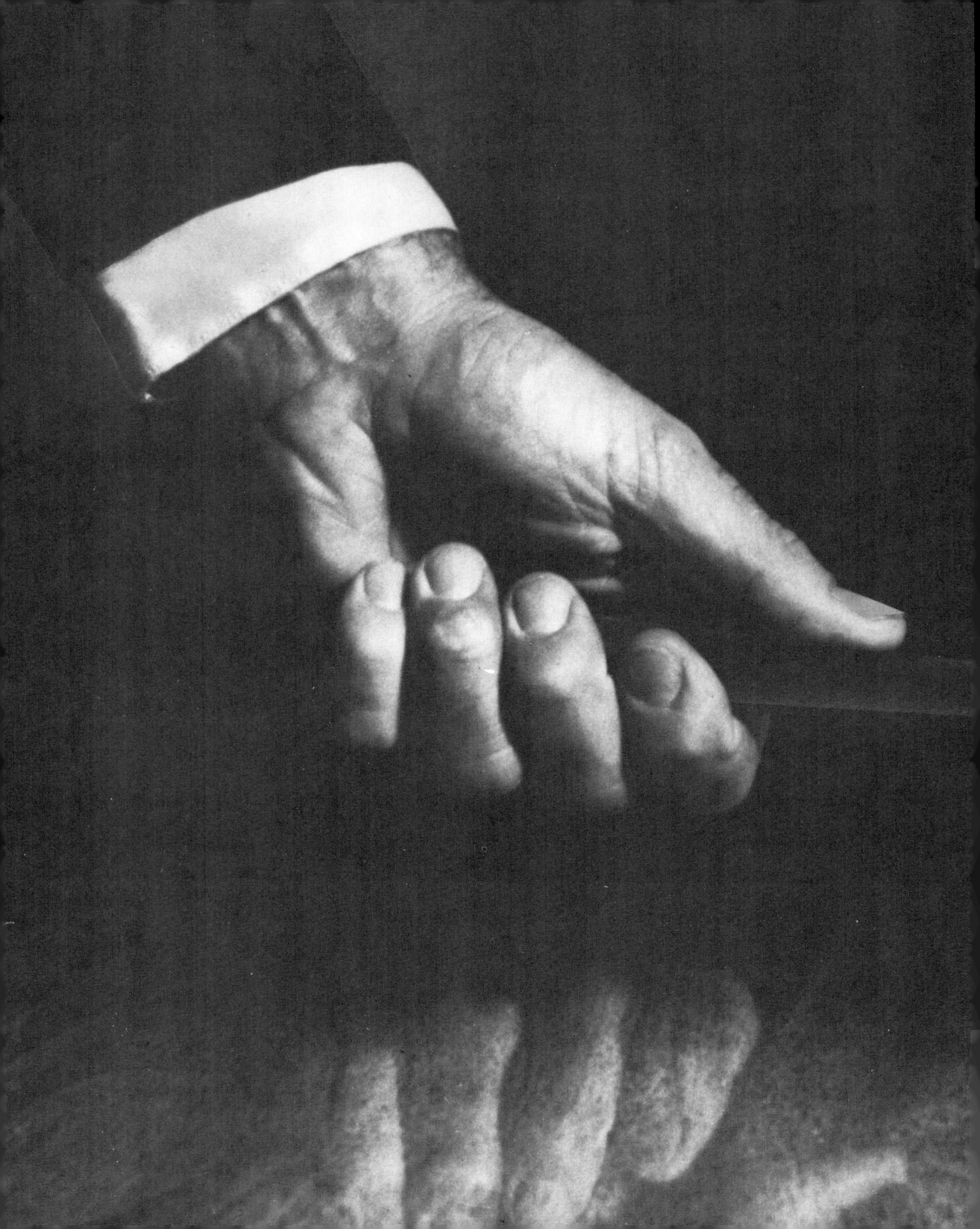

Chapter 12

The Lower Federal Courts

Though the Supreme Court is the "star" of the federal court system, it has a large supporting cast. These are the "inferior" courts provided for in the Constitution. They were created by Congress under the authority granted to it in Article I, Section 8, Clause 9.

Congress began to build the framework of these lower federal courts in the Judiciary Act of 1789. Over the years, the structure has grown more complex. This chapter describes that structure and the way it operates.

Goals

- To learn the organization of the lower federal courts.
- To learn the functions of the lower federal courts.
- To consider a proposed change in the present structure of the federal courts.

FEDERAL DISTRICT COURTS AND COURTS OF APPEALS

The most numerous of the lower federal courts are the United States District Courts. The vast majority of federal cases start and end in these courts. District Courts were first created by Congress in 1789. They have original jurisdiction over most federal cases and may also receive appeals from state courts.

Chapter 12: The Lower Federal Courts

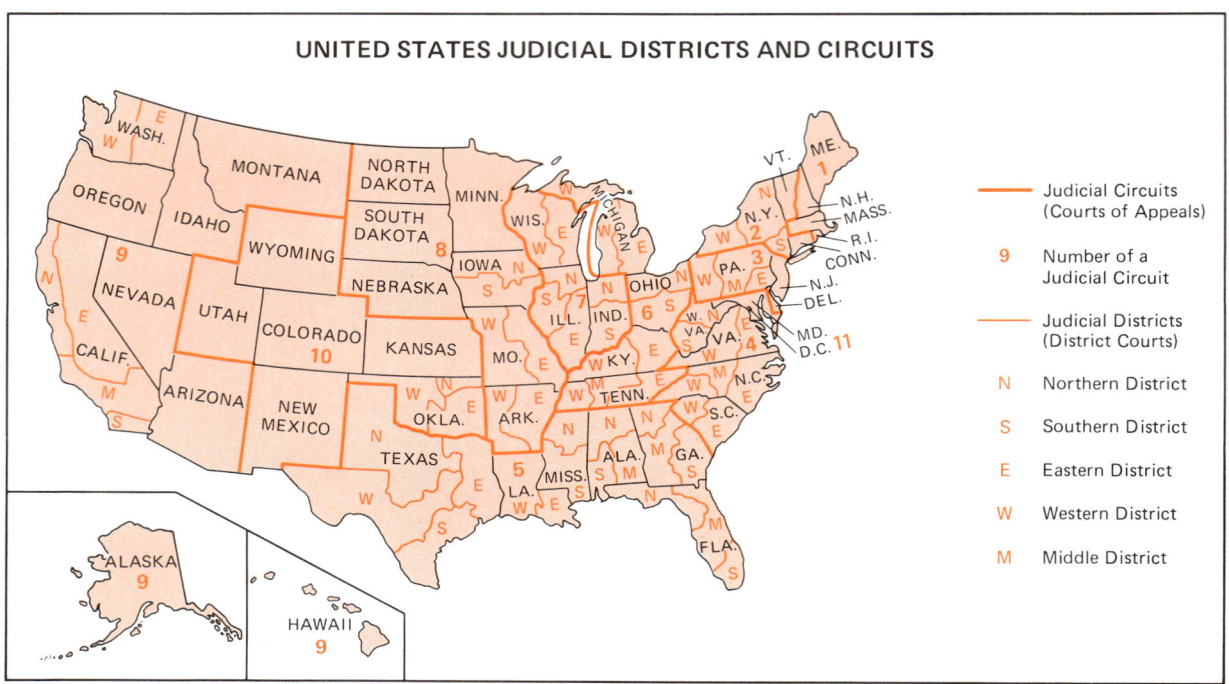

Thus, they are the workhorses of the federal judiciary.

At present, there are nearly one hundred United States District Courts and several hundred judges. Each state has at least one such court, as does the District of Columbia. Some states have as many as four. The districts are shown in the map above.

A District Court may have from one to twenty-seven judges. Like all federal judges, they are appointed by the President with the consent of the Senate. In practice, senators have a good deal to say about who shall fill any judgeships open in their states. The Senate has been known to withhold its consent to a District Court appointment because the President had not consulted the senior senator from that state. District Court judges, like Supreme Court justices, serve during "good behavior."

In addition to judges, each District Court has several other officials. One is a *United States marshal,* who delivers official documents and makes arrests. There are also *magistrates,* who hold preliminary hearings in criminal cases to decide if an accused person will be held for trial or released on bail. In some cases of lesser importance, magistrates may actually take the place of judges. Each court also has a chief clerk, who keeps the court records and helps the judges make up the *docket,* which is the schedule of cases to be tried. Finally, court recorders keep a word-for-word record of all testimony given during a trial. If the case is appealed, this record must be sent to the higher court.

Each District Court is assigned a *United States district attorney.* As we saw earlier, the district attorney works for the Department of Justice and is not a court official. In fact, the district attorney, or "D.A.," is a prosecutor, which means that she or he presents the government's side in criminal and civil cases.

Marshals, magistrates, and district attorneys are political appointees. Unlike judges, they serve 4-year terms. Presidents usually appoint people from their political party to fill these positions. The appointments are subject to Senate approval.

Chapter 12: The Lower Federal Courts

The Lady or the Lawyer?

Jill Vollner was employed for 7 years with the Department of Justice. The highlight of those years was her service as an assistant special prosecutor in the 1974 trial of some participants in the Watergate affair. In a speech to a group of government employees, Ms. Vollner recalled that it took a while for many people to think of her as first of all a lawyer.

"The first time I met with one of the accused and his lawyer, they assumed I was a secretary," she said. "When a male assistant prosecutor asked them if they wanted some coffee, the accused immediately turned to me and said, 'I'll take mine black." He later answered her cross-examintion in the courtroom with "Yes, sir" and "No, sir."

Further role confusion has come from judges who stood up when she entered the courtroom and male lawyers who did not know whether to help her with her briefcase or with the door.

But Jill Vollner stressed that equality "is not just a matter of words or small courtesies. It's a matter of being fair to men and women alike as individuals."

"We need to change many of our stereotypes and show we are not just lady doctors and lady lawyers but good lawyers and good doctors," Ms. Vollner said.

Adapted from "Jill Vollner: A Lawyer, Not a Lady Lawyer," *Dallas Morning News,* April 17, 1975.

Jill Vollner was an assistant special prosecutor in Watergate trials while employed by the Department of Justice.

District Courts hear both civil and criminal cases. Two out of three cases are civil cases. These may be lawsuits involving people from different states or involving such matters as the navigation of interstate waterways, bankruptcy, copyrights, taxes, and labor relations. Federal criminal cases involve alleged violations of federal laws.

Most cases are heard by a single judge. Three judges are required, however, in cases that challenge the constitutionality of a federal or state law.

Many cases in District Courts involve jury trials. Article III, Section 2, Clause 3 provides that all federal criminal cases except impeachment cases are to be heard by juries. These juries in criminal trials are composed of twelve persons. A jury trial is also possible in civil suits, if one party requests it. In a jury trial, both a judge and a jury listen to the testimony. The judge then explains the law to the jury. After deliberation in private, the jury returns a verdict based on the testimony in the case and on the judge's explanation of the law.

If the losing party is dissatisfied with a District Court decision, it may appeal to a higher court. (See the chart opposite.) Only about 5 percent of District Court decisions are appealed, partly because appeal is an expensive process.

Chapter 12: The Lower Federal Courts

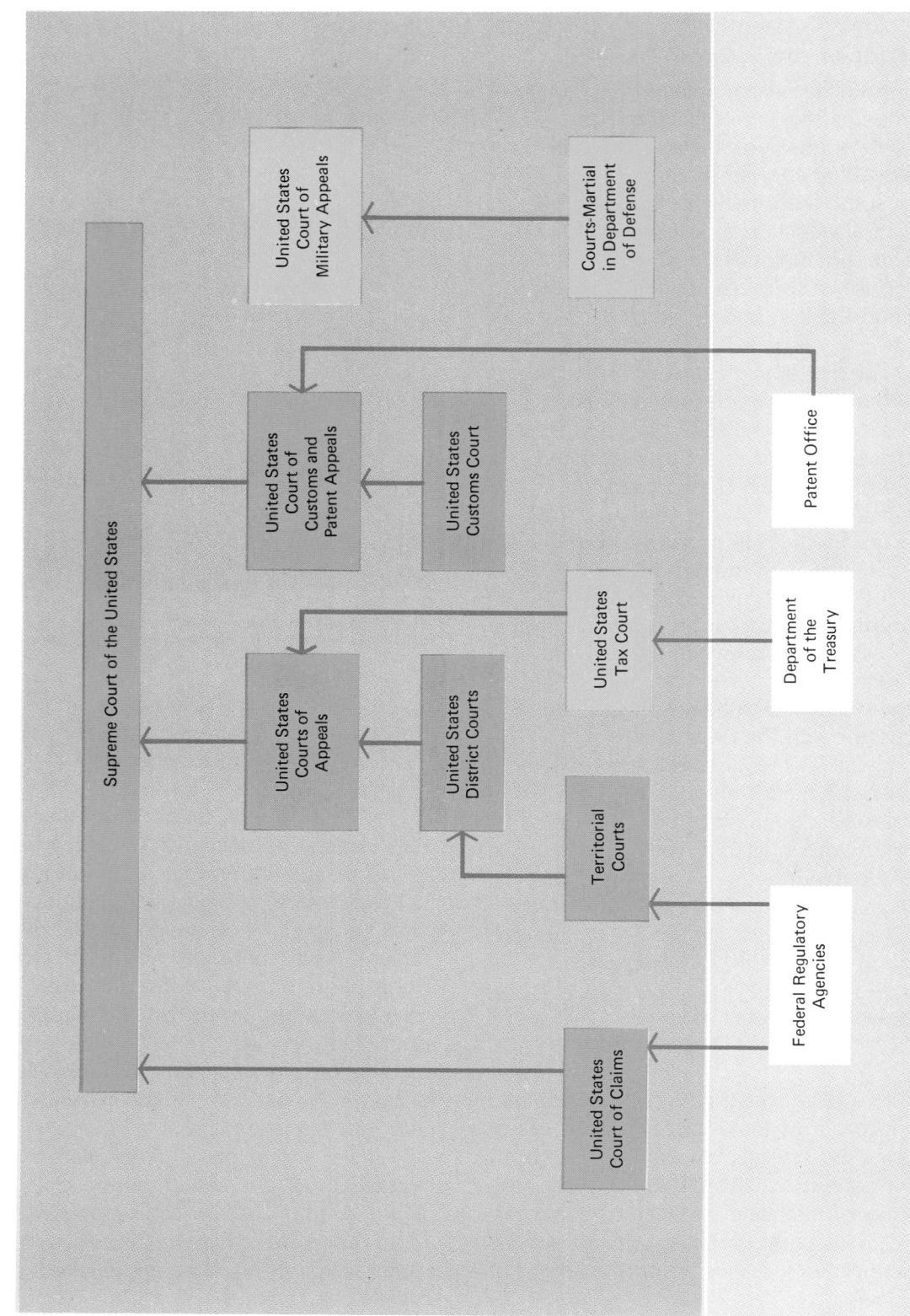

Most appeals from District Courts go to the United States Courts of Appeals. Some, however, go directly to the Supreme Court. This happens, for example, when a District Court holds an act of Congress to be unconstitutional and the decision is appealed.

The United States Courts of Appeals receive appeals from United States District Courts and certain other federal courts. They also hear appeals from the decisions of regulatory agencies, such as the Interstate Commerce Commission. Before the Courts of Appeals were created, all appeals from the United States District Courts went directly to the Supreme Court. There were too many appeals, and by 1891, the Supreme Court was 3 years behind in its work. When Congress created the United States Courts of Appeals in 1891, it greatly eased the pressure on the Supreme Court. In recent years, however, the Supreme Court's work load has again been growing. A proposal has been made to create a new appeals court below the Supreme Court (see Problem, pages 228–229).

The nation is divided into eleven regions, each of which has its own United States Court of Appeals. These regions are known as *circuits.* For example, the United States Court of Appeals for the Fifth Circuit considers cases from six Southern states. The Court of Appeals for the Eleventh Circuit handles cases only from the District of Columbia. (See the map on page 222.)

Depending on its work load, a Court of Appeals may have from three to fifteen judges. They are appointed by the President with the consent of the Senate and, like most federal judges, serve during "good behavior." A Supreme Court justice is assigned to each Court of Appeals, though the justice rarely takes part in cases. A judge from a District Court might also be assigned temporarily to a Court of Appeals.

Most appeals in these courts are heard by a panel of three judges. There are no juries in appeals cases. No new factual evidence is presented. The job of the judges is to review the decision of the District Court or the regulatory agency. The judges ask themselves: Did the lower court or agency follow the proper procedures? Did it apply the law correctly?

The Court of Appeals may uphold the decision of a lower court or agency, reverse it, or change it. The court may also send the case back down to the lower court to be tried again. In most cases, the decision of the Court of Appeals is final. But the United States Supreme Court may be asked to review a decision.

Questions

1 In what court would a person go on trial for the federal crime of kidnapping?

2 Would a kidnapping case be tried by a judge alone or by a judge and a jury? Explain.

3 To what court would a kidnapping verdict most likely be appealed?

⬠ Why do you think the Constitution requires jury trials in federal criminal cases?

SPECIAL FEDERAL COURTS

Congress has created a number of federal courts to hear special kinds of cases. Each of these courts has its own specialty.

The Court of Claims hears cases involving money claims against the federal government. There is an old saying: "The king can do no wrong." In modern times, this has been translated into the theory that a government cannot be sued without its consent. Until 1855, anyone who had a claim against the federal government had to persuade a member of Congress to introduce a bill directing the government to pay the claim. To provide an alternative to this awkward practice, Congress created the Court of Claims. Now, anyone with a claim against the federal government may take the claim to this court. A claim must be made within 6 years.

Decisions that customs inspectors make are subject to review by the Customs Court, based in New York City.

Suppose you run a business that sold a shipment of soap to a federal agency. The agency said that the shipment was damaged and refused to pay. You could file a claim with the United States Court of Claims. A trial would take place somewhere in your part of the country. It would be conducted by one of the fifteen trial judges. The trial testimony and legal briefs would later be submitted to the chief judge and nine associate judges of the Court of Claims. They usually sit in panels of three in Washington, D.C. If the court ruled against you, you might seek review by the Supreme Court.

Other plaintiffs who might take cases to the Court of Claims could include a federal employee seeking back pay, a person whose land had been taken by a federal agency, or a company that claimed a refund on an excise tax.

If the Court of Claims approves a claim of more than $1,000, Congress must vote to approve the payment.

The Customs Court hears cases involving taxes, or tariffs, on goods brought into the United States. If you import foreign goods into this country, they will probably be subject to a tax. The amount of this customs tax, or tariff, will depend on the value of the goods and on what kind of goods they are. A customs inspector examines imported goods to determine their value and the rate at which they will be taxed. If you disagree with the inspector's decision, you may file a case in the Customs Court.

The court is based in New York City, but may meet in other port cities, such as Boston, Los Angeles, or Houston. There are nine judges, no more than five of whom may belong to any one political party. An appeal from the Customs Court would go to the Court of Customs and Patent Appeals.

The Court of Customs and Patent Appeals hears appeals on customs and patent cases. Here are three people whose appeals it might hear:

1. someone who disputed a customs inspector's decision and lost the case in the Customs Court (as just described);
2. someone who was denied a patent on an invention by the Commerce Department or the United States Patent Office;
3. someone whom the Tariff Commission has found to be engaging in unfair import practices.

These are often highly technical cases.

This special appeals court usually meets in Washington, D.C., with all of its six judges hearing each case. If the court rules against you, you may seek review by the United States Supreme Court.

The federal courts discussed up to this point were created by Congress under Article III, Section 1 of the Constitution. The judges of those courts serve during "good behavior." We will now consider a group of special federal courts created by Congress under powers granted to it by Article I. The judges of these courts serve for fixed terms.

The Tax Court hears cases appealing the decisions of tax officers within the Treasury Department. Strictly speaking, it is part of the executive branch, having been created by Congress under its power to tax (Article I, Section 8). The Tax Court, however, operates much as any other court does and is counted as part of the judicial branch.

If you thought the Internal Revenue Service had overcharged you for federal income taxes, you could appeal to the Treasury Department. If the department ruled against you, you could then appeal to the Tax Court. Often an appeal to this court involves a disagreement over whether a certain expense can be taken off as a tax deduction—that is, whether the expense can be subtracted, or deducted, from taxable income. The more expenses you can deduct, the lower your income tax will be. If the Tax Court decides against you, you can appeal to the United States Court of Appeals.

The Tax Court is composed of nineteen judges. They are appointed by the President with the consent of the Senate and serve 12-year terms. The court's headquarters are in Washington, D.C., but it may hear cases anywhere in the country.

The Court of Military Appeals hears appeals only from people in the armed services who have been convicted in military courts. For example, it might hear the case of someone who was found guilty of a serious crime by a court-martial. (A *court-martial* is a court that

In a famous court-martial, Lt. William S. Calley, right, was charged with the murder of civilians in the Vietnam war.

tries a member of the armed forces who is accused of breaking a military or naval law. At the request of the accused person, enlisted personnel may be assigned to serve on the court. Otherwise, officers are normally assigned.) The Court of Military Appeals is the supreme court for members of the armed forces. Its decisions, like those of the United States Supreme Court for civilians, are final.

The Court of Military Appeals has three judges, all civilians. They are appointed by the President with the consent of the Senate for terms of 15 years. The court meets in Washington, D.C.

Four Territorial Courts—in Guam, the Virgin Islands, the Panama Canal Zone, and Puerto Rico—serve the same functions as United States District Courts. Except in Puerto Rico, the Territorial Courts also handle local matters such as those reserved to state courts. In Puerto Rico, the judges serve during "good behavior," but in the other Territorial Courts, judges serve 8-year terms. Decisions of the Territorial Courts may be appealed to the United States Courts of Appeals.

In addition to courts, the judicial branch includes two major business offices. They are the Administrative Office of the United States Courts and the Federal Judicial Center.

The Administrative Office of the United States Courts oversees the financial operations of all the lower federal courts. It is headed by a director and a deputy director appointed by the United States Supreme Court. The Administrative Office pays the judges and staff members of the lower courts, prepares the courts' budgets, keeps track of their case loads, and carries out other administrative tasks. The Administrative Office does not deal with the work of the Supreme Court, which has its own staff.

The Federal Judicial Center studies the operations of federal courts and seeks ways to improve them. It also carries on education programs for judges and other court workers from its Washington, D.C., headquarters.

Questions

1 Refer to the chart on page 224 and explain the role of each of the federal courts.

2 Imagine you had just lost a case in each of the following federal courts. To which court or courts might you appeal for review of the decision?
    a a Territorial Court
    b the Court of Military Appeals
    c the Tax Court
    d the Customs Court
    e the Court of Customs and Patent Appeals
    f a District Court
    g the Court of Claims
    h a Court of Appeals

⬠ What do you think a judge should take into account in deciding a case? Why?

PROBLEM: SHOULD WE HAVE A MINI-SUPREME COURT?

During our nation's first century, the Supreme Court received appeals directly from the United States District Courts. As we have seen, when the burden became too great, Congress created the United States Courts of Appeals. Now that the High Court's case load has again increased, Chief Justice Warren Burger has called for creation of one more appeals court. This National Court of Appeals would come between the United States Courts of Appeals and the Supreme Court. It would change the appeals route as follows:

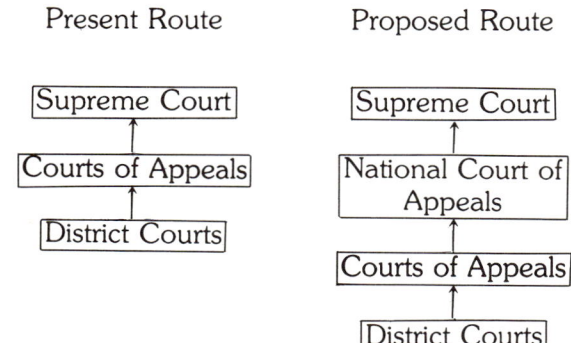

Following is a brief discussion of Chief Justice Burger's proposal. As you read it, try to determine the main arguments for and against a National Court of Appeals.

At present, a typical federal court case might begin in District Court, be appealed to a United States Court of Appeals, and finally be reviewed by the Supreme Court. A National Court of Appeals would add another step. The new court would be a super-Court of Appeals, or a mini-Supreme Court, depending on how you look at it.

One proposal would have the National Court of Appeals screen all cases that now go to the Supreme Court. The new court might reject some cases, hear less important ones itself, and send the most important ones on to the Supreme Court.

Chapter 12: The Lower Federal Courts

"Quasi-innocent, Your Honor."
Drawing by Joseph Mirachi; © 1977 The New Yorker Magazine, Inc.

The proposed National Court of Appeals would have seven judges. They would be senior judges from each of the eleven Courts of Appeals, who would take turns serving terms of 3 or 4 years on the new court. At the end of their terms, the judges would return to the United States Courts of Appeals.

Those who favor the proposed National Court of Appeals argue that the present burden on the Supreme Court is too great. By 1973, the docket listed 5,079 cases. The number dropped slightly to 4,668 cases in 1974. But some observers predicted it might reach 7,000 by 1980. This, it was argued, would be too many cases for nine justices to consider.

Those who want a National Court of Appeals believe it would reduce the Supreme Court docket to between 200 and 500 cases a year. These would be the "cream of the crop"—the cases that raise the most pressing constitutional issues. The Supreme Court justices could thus devote greater attention to the most important cases.

Those who oppose the new court argue that the Supreme Court is not really overworked. After all, they point out, the Court rejects most of the cases on its docket and hears only some 200 a year. This was the position of Associate Justice William O. Douglas, who resigned in 1975.

Some opponents argue that creation of a National Court of Appeals would unfairly restrict a citizen's right to make a final appeal to the Supreme Court. They argue that the Supreme Court must always retain the power to make final judicial decisions.

Some opponents also argue that the new court, by taking senior judges away from the United States Courts of Appeals, would increase the work load for the remaining appeals court judges. The number of those judges could be increased, but that would require an act of Congress.

Questions

1 What are the main arguments in favor of a National Court of Appeals?

2 What are the main arguments against a National Court of Appeals?

3 Before Congress adds any new agency, department, or court to our federal government, what do you think it should consider?

○ Do *you* favor creation of a National Court of Appeals? Why or why not?

Chapter 12 Review

Recalling and Comparing

1 In general, what are lower federal courts? What federal court or courts do not fall in this category?

2 By what authority did Congress create the lower federal courts?

3 Which of the lower federal courts has the most judges? Why do you suppose it does?

4 Name *two* lower federal courts on which judges serve a term of a fixed number of years.

Special Activities

1 Look at the map on page 222 and find your location. What are the boundaries of the United States District Court for your area? What circuit is your district in?

2 Make a bulletin-board display of newspaper and magazine articles about court activities in your federal court district.

3 Write an imaginary account of a court case that would be heard by one of the special federal courts. Discuss the issues involved and describe how the case would be handled, including any possible appeals.

4 Prepare a chart summarizing the main information about each type of federal court in categories such as the following: type of court; number of courts of that type; jurisdiction of that type of court; number of judges; length of terms of judges; and provisions for appeal.

5 Attend a session of a federal court and note the type of case being heard, the number of judges, and the procedures followed. Write a report of your observations.

6 Make a study of court-martial procedures and the rights of members of the armed forces. Report your findings to the class.

7 Consider what might be arguments for and against the following statement: "The judicial branch is a less important branch of our federal government than the legislative branch or the executive branch." Do you agree or disagree? Why?

Developing Your Political Vocabulary

Tell what the terms in *a–f* mean. Then match each term with a phrase in 1–6 and tell what the connection is.

patent	**a**	**1**	United States District Court
tax deduction	**b**	**2**	Court of Military Appeals
circuit	**c**	**3**	Customs Court
jury	**d**	**4**	Court of Customs and Patent Appeals
court-martial	**e**		
tariff	**f**	**5**	Tax Court
		6	United States Court of Appeals

Unit IV Review

Improving Your Reading

Read the selection below and then answer the questions that follow it.

The judicial branch of our federal government serves as a check on the legislative and executive branches. The federal courts have authority to interpret laws passed by Congress and by state legislatures. If a law is found to violate the Constitution, it is void, or canceled. The federal courts can also overrule any actions of the executive branch that violate the Constitution.

All federal judges are appointed by the President with the consent of the Senate. The judges on almost all federal courts serve during "good behavior." The exceptions are the Court of Military Appeals, the Tax Court, and the Territorial Courts.

The Supreme Court is the highest court in the land. There are nine justices, including a Chief Justice of the United States. Two early Chief Justices, John Marshall and Roger Taney, had a major impact upon the High Court and the lower federal courts. Their decisions helped to raise the judicial branch of the United States to a position of importance equal to that of the two other branches of the federal government.

According to Article III of the Constitution, the Supreme Court has two kinds of jurisdiction, or authority. The Court has original jurisdiction in any case involving ambassadors, other foreign officials, or states of the Union. Such cases *must* be tried first and only in the Supreme Court. The Court also exercises appellate jurisdiction. It hears appeals from state courts or lower federal courts on cases involving federal law or authority.

All decisions made by the Supreme Court are reached by majority vote and are final. In announcing their decisions, Supreme Court justices often offer both majority and minority opinions.

In addition to the Supreme Court, there are many other federal courts. The two main groups are the United States District Courts and the United States Courts of Appeals. Most federal cases begin and end in District Courts, which are the most numerous of the federal courts. Since 1891, the Courts of Appeals have handled many of the appeals from District Courts. There are also a number of special courts that handle cases on specific subjects, such as tax law or claims against the federal government.

1 In your own words, summarize this reading in *no more than five* sentences. Focus on what you regard as the most important points made in the reading.

2 In connection with the United States Supreme Court, the term *original jurisdiction* can best be applied to which *two* of the following:

    a cases involving ambassadors and other federal officials

    b cases appealed from lower courts

    c appointment of all federal judges by the President

    d cases in which a state is a party in a dispute

3 Which *one* of the following topics discussed in the reading can best be used to show the power exercised by the Supreme Court?

    a the process of appointing federal judges
    b the finality of decisions by the Supreme Court
    c the roles played by our lower federal courts
    d the number of justices on the Supreme Court

Developing Your Writing Skills: What Are Your Attitudes toward Government?

Writing a Paragraph

In this unit, you have learned that justices of the Supreme Court and all judges of other federal courts are appointed by the President. In many states, however, it is the custom to elect the judges of major courts. Consider the various arguments that might be made for either method of choosing judges—appointment or election. Then write the following topic sentence on a separate sheet of paper. Complete the sentence and fill out the paragraph with arguments in support of your position.

> I believe that judges in federal courts should be (elected/appointed).

Writing an Essay

Each chapter in this unit has examined a particular problem connected with the judicial branch of our federal government. Obviously, there are many other possible problems. Think back over what you have read, and as you do so, consider these questions:

- *What are* four *possible problems associated with the federal courts?*
- *Why might those things be problems?*
- *Which* one *of those problems seems most important to you?*

Write a brief essay that answers those questions. Your essay might begin as follows:

> Of the problems I have noted concerning the federal courts, I believe the one that requires attention first is _____

Recommended Reading

Patricia C. Acheson, *The Supreme Court: America's Judicial Heritage,* Dodd, Mead, New York, 1961 (paperback).

Theodore L. Backer (ed.), *The Impact of Supreme Court Decisions,* Oxford, New York, 1973.

Edmond Cahn (ed.), *Supreme Court and Supreme Law,* Simon & Schuster, New York, 1971 (paperback).

John R. Cuneo, *John Marshall: Judicial Statesman,* McGraw-Hill, New York, 1975.

James J. Flynn, *Famous Justices of the Supreme Court,* Dodd, Mead, New York, 1968.

Marjorie Fribourg, *The Supreme Court in American History,* Avon Books, New York, 1965 (paperback).

Gerald W. Johnson, *The Supreme Court,* Morrow, New York, 1962.

Alpheus T. Mason, *Brandeis: A Free Man's Life,* Viking, New York, 1946.

Edward C. Smith, *The Constitution of the United States with Case Summaries,* Barnes & Noble, New York, 1972 (paperback).

The Supreme Court: Justice and the Law, Congressional Quarterly, Washington, D.C., 1973 (paperback).

Our Living Constitution

Since the days of George Washington, it has been customary for patriotic orators to refer to our country as "the land of the free." People have pointed with pride to the many guarantees of individual liberty in the Constitution of the United States. They have drawn sharp contrasts between the rights of United States citizens and the tribulations of people in less favored lands.

What are the rights that have been the source of such pride? Are they the same today as they were in 1789, or 1860, or in 1950?

Think for a moment about yourself and your family. Imagine that you lived in 1800. What would your rights have been? If you were a black, you probably would have been a slave, but even if free, you could not have counted on many rights from the Constitution in 1800. If you were a female in 1800, you would not have been allowed to vote or hold a public office. Does your family own any land? If not, even your father would probably have been excluded from voting in 1800. Are you under 18 years of age? What rights would you have had in 1800—in school or on a job?

Now think of your rights today. Have they changed since 1800? Of course they have. They have changed because our Constitution is a living constitution. It is not the same today as it was in 1800 or in 1900 or even 5 years ago.

This unit is about the ways in which our Constitution has changed since it went into effect in 1789. Some of the changes are more obvious than others. Most obvious are the amendments we have added to the Constitution. New laws have also changed the way the Constitution works. As Congress became aware of new problems growing out of constitutional provisions, it passed laws to deal with these problems. The way the Constitution is applied has also been changed by the federal courts. As new problems arose, the courts took a fresh look at the words of the Constitution and interpreted those words in a different light.

In all these ways—and more—the Constitution of the United States has changed. It has grown—and it is still growing, as befits a living constitution.

Chapter **13**

Our Bill of Rights

The Founders of our nation were painfully aware of the dangers of oppressive government. They had led our War of Independence against one oppressive government, that of Great Britian. The Founders wanted to ensure that our own government would never become oppressive. They sought to provide this guarantee in framing the Constitution. At the same time, they provided means for changing the Constitution as the need might arise. A demand for changes was made almost before the ink was dry.

The Bill of Rights is designed to guarantee certain basic freedoms by placing limitations on the power of the national government. It was added to the Constitution in 1791, only 2 years after the Constitution went into effect. This chapter will discuss what those basic freedoms are and why they are important. First, however, it will take up the ways in which the Constitution can be changed.

Goals

- To learn how the United States Constitution can be changed.
- To learn how our Bill of Rights came into being.
- To consider what the Bill of Rights means in our lives today.

Chapter 13: Our Bill of Rights

METHODS OF CHANGING THE UNITED STATES CONSTITUTION

The Constitution is a living document because the Founders saw the need to make it so. They not only provided a formal method for changing the Constitution but also wrote the document in such a way that it could be adapted informally to changing circumstances.

There are at least three ways in which the meaning of the United States Constitution can be changed informally. As we have already seen in earlier chapters, it has been changed by *judicial interpretation.* Consider the implied powers of Congress. Nowhere in the Constitution are these spelled out; yet they are universally accepted today. This is because the Supreme Court, under John Marshall, ruled that Congress possessed certain powers besides those listed in the Constitution. The Court found such implied powers necessary to carry out the purposes of the Constitution. Many other decisions by the Supreme Court have adapted the Constitution by interpreting its principles in the light of new problems that the Founders could not have foreseen.

Informal changes in the Constitution have sometimes been brought about by *custom.* As you know, political parties are a vital part of our government today. But nowhere does the Constitution mention parties. They have developed through custom and long practice. Executive privilege is another example already discussed in Chapter 7.

Our constitutional structure has also been changed by *laws.* For example, the Constitution does not specifically provide for the United States Courts of Appeals, but the Constitution does grant authority for Congress to create federal courts. Under this authority, Congress passed a law creating the Courts of Appeals. All of the federal courts that are below the Supreme Court, and many other agencies of government, were created the same way. In a sense, one could say that all federal laws add to the Constitution by applying its principles to help meet the changing needs of our society.

The formal method that the Founders provided for changing the Constitution is the process of amendment. This provision appears in Article V. A *constitutional amendment* is a new article added to the articles of the Constitution. Articles of amendment have equal force with the original Constitution. Because ours is a federal system, the amending process requires action by the states as well as by Congress. Because it involves changing our basic rules of government, amending the Constitution requires more than simple majority votes by Congress and the states.

The Constitution provides four methods of amendment. First, there are two ways in which an amendment may be proposed. Second, there are two ways in which an amendment may be ratified, or approved, by the states. The four possible combinations for proposing and ratifying constitutional amendments are shown in the diagram below.

HOW THE UNITED STATES CONSTITUTION CAN BE AMENDED

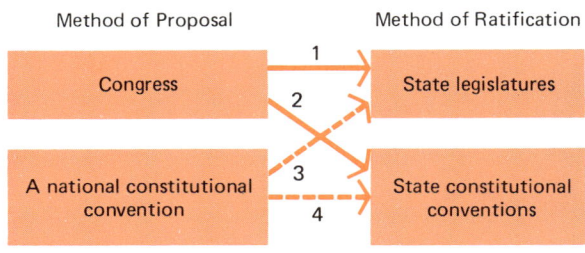

Proposal, Method One. The first method of proposal is by Congress. Two-thirds majorities are required in both the House of Representatives and the Senate. No presidential action is required.

Proposal, Method Two. The second method of proposal is by a *national constitutional convention.* If two-thirds of the state legislatures (thirty-four out of the present fifty states) request such a convention, Congress is

The Equal Rights Amendment is perhaps the most controversial amendment since the question of Prohibition in the 1920s. That explains why some state legislatures changed their position on the amendment after having approved it.

required to call one. The Constitution does not place any restrictions on the number of amendments that could be proposed by a national constitutional convention. Some people fear that such a convention would result in a new Constitution, just as happened at the Constitutional Convention of 1787. Though several efforts have been made since the 1960s to call a national constitutional convention, this method of proposing an amendment has not yet been used.

Regardless of which method is used to propose an amendment, it is up to Congress to determine the method of ratification. Congress has two choices:

Ratification, Method One: Congress can submit the proposed amendment to the *state legislatures.* The approval of three-fourths of the legislatures (thirty-eight out of fifty) is required. A state may turn down an amendment and later vote to accept it. It was long believed that once a state had voted to ratify an amendment, it could not later change its vote. In the 1970s, however, several states changed their vote on the Equal Rights Amendment after having approved it. A legislature's action on a constitutional amendment is not subject to a governor's veto.

Ratification, Method Two. Congress may also order *special state conventions.* Each state then calls its own convention under its own rules and chooses the delegates from among the people of that state. Again, at least three-fourths of the state conventions must ratify an amendment before it can take effect. This method of ratification is more expensive than

Chapter 13: Our Bill of Rights

"Get back there!" cried the Dry in this cartoon as the repeal of Prohibition let alcohol be bought and sold again.

the state-legislature method, but it is probably quicker because some state legislatures do not meet every year.

For all but one of the amendments that Congress has proposed since the Bill of Rights, Congress has called for ratification by state legislatures. The one exception was the Twenty-first Amendment in 1933. That amendment ended *Prohibition*—the banning of alcoholic beverages. Prohibition was required by the Eighteenth Amendment, which had been in effect since 1919. In this one case, Congress called for ratifying conventions in each state. One reason was a belief by Congress that state conventions would be more likely than state legislatures to repeal the Eighteenth Amendment and end Prohibition.

Congress may set a deadline for ratification. If the states do not complete ratification within a time limit—usually 7 years—the amendment dies. In 1972, when Congress proposed an amendment to guarantee equal rights to women, it set a time limit of 7 years. When it appeared that not enough state legislatures would ratify the amendment by 1979, Congress extended the deadline 39 months, until June 1982.

As you can see, the legislative branch is involved in amending the Constitution, but the executive branch is not. The President has no formal role at all. The President may not veto a proposed amendment.

Questions

1 How can the Supreme Court "change" the Constitution?
2 How can Congress informally "change" the Constitution?
3 What are the four methods in which a constitutional amendment may be put into effect?
4 How many states must approve an amendment to the Constitution before the amendment becomes effective?
⬠ Do you think that the procedure for amending the Constitution is too easy, too hard, or just about right? Explain.

OUR FIRST TEN AMENDMENTS: THE BILL OF RIGHTS

Ten amendments, known as the Bill of Rights, were added to the Constitution in 1791, only 2 years after the Constitution was declared in effect. These amendments fulfilled a promise made by supporters of the new Constitution. You will recall that some people opposed the new Constitution because it did not specifically guarantee the "natural rights"

"Convincing Juror Number Twelve" was the title of this early twentieth-century drawing. Trial by jury is guaranteed under the provisions of the Sixth Amendment, which is part of the Bill of Rights.

of the people against limitation by the federal government. In order to win support for the Constitution, the Federalists promised to propose a Bill of Rights. Action to fulfill that promise began as soon as the first Congress met.

The Bill of Rights guarantees some of our most basic freedoms, including freedom of religion, freedom of speech, and trial by jury. These and most of the other provisions derived directly from colonial experience with British government and can best be understood against that background. The ten amendments that make up the Bill of Rights are summarized in the chart on page 240. They will be discussed at more length later in this chapter.

As adopted, the Bill of Rights was understood to apply to the national government, but most of the provisions later were applied to the states. For example, nothing in the Bill of Rights required *state* governments to respect freedom of the press. However, in a series of decisions between 1925 and 1937, the United States Supreme Court held that state governments *are* bound by the First Amendment, which includes a guarantee of freedom of the press. The Court reasoned that a later amendment, the Fourteenth, guaranteed certain basic rights against abuse by state governments.

The ideas in the Bill of Rights can be traced far back in history. The idea of trial by jury was part of the Magna Charta in 1215, as was the idea that no person should be deprived of property without due process of law. The English Petition of Right in 1628 forbade the housing of soldiers without the consent of a homeowner. It also forbade jailing anyone without specific charges, and it required an orderly trial of accused persons. The English Bill of Rights of 1689 put restrictions on excessive bail, fines, and cruel or unusual punish-

Chapter 13: Our Bill of Rights

> **Summary of the Bill of Rights**
>
> *First Amendment:* forbids Congress from passing laws that interfere with religion, speech, or the press or with the right to assemble peaceably and to ask for remedy when treated unfairly by the government.
>
> *Second Amendment:* protects the rights of the people to have weapons so that a militia may be maintained.
>
> *Third Amendment:* forbids the lodging of soldiers in any private home, except with the consent of the owner in time of peace, or according to law in time of war.
>
> *Fourth Amendment:* forbids unreasonable search or seizure of persons or property without a warrant.
>
> *Fifth Amendment:* forbids (1) a trial for a serious offense without a grand jury indictment, (2) repeated trials for the same offense, (3) forcing one to accuse oneself, (4) taking life, liberty, or property without due process of law, and (5) taking property for public use without fair payment.
>
> *Sixth Amendment:* provides certain rights for persons accused of crimes: (1) a speedy and public trial, (2) a fair jury, (3) trial in the district where the crime was committed, (4) information about the accusation, (5) testimony by witnesses in the presence of the accused, (6) a summons to force witnesses to appear in the accused's favor, and (6) a lawyer to defend the accused.
>
> *Seventh Amendment:* provides the right of a jury trial in lawsuits for more than $20.
>
> *Eighth Amendment:* forbids too large bail or fines and cruel and unusual punishments.
>
> *Ninth Amendment:* provides that the mention of certain rights in the Constitution shall not be taken to mean that other rights do not belong to the people.
>
> *Tenth Amendment:* reserves to the individual states, or the people, all rights that the Constitution does not grant to the federal government nor deny to the states.

ment. All this was part of our early political heritage.

At the time the Constitution was adopted, some states already had guarantees of basic rights written into their constitutions. Others did not. In some states, people were complaining of abuses of rights by *state* governments. It seemed natural to many people to add a Bill of Rights to the federal Constitution. Thomas Jefferson and James Madison, in particular, were in favor of it as a means of curbing potential abuses of federal power.

Madison, then a member of the House of Representatives, made the first move on June 8, 1789. He proposed making nine amendments to the Constitution. They would have prevented both the federal and state governments from interfering with certain basic rights. Madison's idea was that the changes would be inserted in various places in the Constitution. In arguing for his proposals, Madison made two key points. One was that branches of government must be barred from abusing public rights. The other was that "the community itself"—meaning the majority—must not take rights away from a minority. As we shall see, the final Bill of Rights guarded against threats from both sources.

For more than 3 months, Congress worked on these and other proposals for changes in the Constitution. Finally, Congress agreed on a total of twelve changes and decided that they should be added as articles of amendment at the end of the original Constitution, not inserted into it. Congress also decided that no attempt would be made to apply restrictions to state governments—only to the federal government.

On September 25, 1789, Congress completed action on a joint resolution proposing twelve amendments. It specified that ratification should be by special state conventions. President George Washington sent copies of the proposed changes to each state.

The ratification process required more than 2 years. Two of the proposed amendments were not ratified. One of these would have set new limits on the number of people represented by each member of the House of Representatives. The other would have forbidden Congress to pay any of its members with tax money until the member had been duly elected. (This has been the custom, in any event.)

On December 15, 1791, Virginia became the eleventh state to ratify the other ten amendments. Since there were then fourteen states in the Union, the necessary three-fourths of the states had now ratified. The First through the Tenth Amendments were added to the Constitution. We know them today as our Bill of Rights.

Questions

1 Why was a Bill of Rights thought to be a necessary part of the United States Constitution?

2 How did each of the following serve as a precedent for freedoms found in our Bill of Rights?
   a Magna Charta (1215)
   b English Petition of Right (1628)
   c English Bill of Rights (1689)

3 James Madison believed that threats to our basic rights might arise from two sources. What were the sources?

4 How many amendments were submitted to the states in 1789? How many were finally approved by the states in 1791?

◌ Why do you suppose many of the provisions of the Bill of Rights have gradually been extended to the states?

PROBLEM: WHAT DOES OUR BILL OF RIGHTS MEAN?

The Bill of Rights forbids the federal government to violate certain basic rights of the people. Those rights are discussed in detail below. As you read about each separate right, ask yourself:

- *How is this right important in my own life?*
- *How might my life be affected if this right were taken away?*

Ten Basic Guarantees

Many people consider the First Amendment to be the most important part of the Bill of Rights. The purpose of the First Amendment is to guarantee *freedom of expression*. Without that freedom, other freedoms are largely meaningless. Here is what the First Amendment states:

> Congress shall make no law respecting an establishment of religion, or prohibiting the free exercise thereof; or abridging the freedom of speech, or of the press; or the right of the people peaceably to assemble, and to petition the Government for a redress of grievances.

First of all, the First Amendment guarantees our right to worship as we please, or not to have a religion if we prefer. There are two parts to this section of the amendment. One forbids Congress from making any law concerning "an establishment of religion," and the other states that Congress may not prohibit "the free exercise" of religion. Roger Williams and Anne Hutchinson were among the first people in this country to struggle for those principles (see Chapter 3, page 49–50).

In Great Britain, as we saw earlier, there was—and still is—a state-supported religion, the Church of England. There and in many other countries, public tax money may go to support a particular form of religion. In our country, the government is forbidden to favor one religion over another. We refer to this as *the separation of church and state*. The government is not an enemy of religion but treats all alike. We have laws that give certain privileges, such as tax exemption, to all religions.

The right to preach one's religious beliefs is not restricted to the pulpit. Sidewalk preachers and speakers for various religious groups are common sights in most of our big cities.

A free press is an important element in the democratic process. Without it, our other rights could be in danger.

The right to choose one's own religion, also part of Amendment I, implies the right to *advocate* a religion—that is, to try to persuade others to join it. In some countries, advocacy of any but the state-established religion is discouraged, and in the Soviet Union, advocacy of any religion is discouraged.

Second, the First Amendment guarantees freedom of speech and of the press. People often differ on public matters: one person may think X is true, while another thinks Y is true. The framers of Amendment I believed that if all people are free to state their opinions, the truth will eventually conquer. Some people will express opinions that are offensive to others. But in our system of government, people are free to express even those ideas. In the words of Supreme Court Justice Oliver Wendell Holmes: "The best test of truth is the power of the thought to get itself accepted in the competition of the market." Holmes maintained that we must allow freedom not just for the thought that we approve "but freedom for the thought that we hate."

Our country restricts freedom of speech in certain ways, however. Speech that harms others may be punished. For this purpose we have laws against *slander* and *libel*—spoken or written statements intended to damage someone's reputation. Speech that offends the moral sense of others may also be punished under our laws against obscenity. Speech that endangers the safety of the nation may be punished under laws, for example, that forbid telling military secrets to others.

Freedom of the press carries freedom of speech one step further; in addition to speaking freely, we may write down our opinions and circulate them to others. The framers of Amendment I had in mind newspapers, books, and pamphlets when they referred to freedom of the press. In modern times, magazines, radio, television, and movies have also become part of the press because they spread news and opinions beyond the reach of one person's unaided voice.

Freedom of the press protects not only our right to tell but also our right to know. In some countries, the government controls the press and may forbid any criticism of the government to appear. In our country, the press is owned by private individuals and corporations. The press is free to publish or broadcast what the owners want—a principle that began to be accepted in colonial times (see Chapter 3, page 49). There can be no *prior restraint*—that is, stopping the spreading of news or opinions before they are published or broadcast.

As with freedom of speech, freedom of the press does have limits. Obscenity, for example, may be punished—but only *after* it is printed or broadcast or made part of a movie.

Third, the First Amendment protects our right to assemble in groups for any peaceable purpose. This right of peaceable assembly does not exist in all countries. In some countries, people cannot even hold meetings in their own homes without obtaining permission. In our country, we are free to hold indoor meetings whenever and wherever we wish. Any political party or interest group—even if its views are unpopular—has the right to hold a meeting. We can also hold outdoor meetings and public demonstrations to make our views known, if these assemblies are peaceable and do not unduly interfere with the right of other people to be in public places at the same time.

Fourth, the First Amendment protects our right to petition government officials, or convey our opinions to them. Let us say you belong to a group that objects to plans for a new highway. You may prepare a petition, ask people to sign it, and then send or take the petition to the government officials who have the power to stop the highway. The right of petition also protects your right to send letters or formal written protests to public officials.

The Second and Third Amendments were written with past actions of the British in mind. In the years leading up to the American Revolution, some British officials had tried to take weapons away from the colonial militia. Soldiers had been sent to live in people's houses against people's will. The new nation wanted to make sure that such things never happened again.

The Second Amendment protects the right of the people to keep and bear arms. The amendment links this right with the need of a free state to keep a militia, or organized body of citizen soldiers. Because of this linking, Amendment II is generally held to apply to "the people" collectively rather than as individuals. The amendment is also regarded as applying only to the national government and as not limiting in any way the right of the states to restrict the ownership of weapons.

The Third Amendment protects people from having to keep soldiers in their homes. In peacetime, this right is absolute. Any homeowner may refuse to keep soldiers in peacetime. In wartime, the right is limited. A homeowner may be required to house soliders, but only under terms specified by law and not just at the will of military authorities.

The Fourth through Eighth Amendments protect the individual in dealings with police

Chapter 13: Our Bill of Rights

This group has used its right of peaceable assembly as a means of expressing its opposition to more nuclear power.

and the courts. Here again, the framers of the Bill of Rights remembered abuses by British authorities. They were also aware that officials of our own government might be tempted to take shortcuts that threaten individual rights.

The Fourth Amendment limits the conditions under which police may search for and seize evidence and people. In colonial times, it was not uncommon for authorities to enter private homes to search for stolen or smuggled goods. Sometimes the authorities were acting only on a hunch without any real evidence that the search would find anything. Amendment IV is aimed at stopping such "fishing expeditions" by public officials and at protecting any person's privacy.

The Fourth Amendment does not prohibit all searches and seizures, but it does lay down certain rules:

1. A search or seizure must be *reasonable*.

2. To be reasonable, a search or seizure must be based on *probable cause*. That is, the authorities must have enough information to expect that they probably will find what they are looking for.

3. In most cases, the authorities will need a *search warrant* or an *arrest warrant*. Those are documents authorizing a search or arrest by police officers, signed by a neutral judge, and based on information sworn to by a responsible person.

This group has used its right to assemble peaceably as a means of expressing its support of more nuclear power.

4. *A warrant must describe the specific place to be searched and the persons or things to be seized.*

In practice, the conditions under which a search or seizure is made usually determine whether or not it is reasonable. For example, a police officer may chase a suspect into his or her home. Also, if a police officer sees someone commit a crime, the officer may arrest the person without a warrant. In both situations, the officer would have "probable cause" for search or seizure.

The Fifth Amendment contains a number of protections of individual rights. They are:

1. *Nobody shall be made to stand trial for a serious offense unless a grand jury has voted an indictment.* We saw earlier that the grand jury is a feature we inherited from England. The grand jury hears the charges in a case and considers whether there is enough evidence to make a trial necessary. This provision does not apply to members of the military services in war or in time of public danger, nor does it apply to the states.

2. *Nobody may be tried twice for the same offense.* When a person is on trial, that person's life or freedom is in danger or jeopardy (JEP-ur-dee). This clause is known as the *double jeopardy clause* because it provides that no one may be put in jeopardy twice for the same offense. However, the same series of actions could lead to two trials—for exam-

When a Person Is Accused of a Federal Crime

To understand how the constitutional guarantees of justice work, let's look at what happens when a person is suspected of a federal crime. Let's say that person is you.

First, someone must formally accuse you. Imagine that a police officer claims to have heard you make a joking remark about hijacking as you board an airplane, and the officer arrests you. To make matters worse, let's say you are carrying objects in your hand luggage that, in the circumstances, could be regarded as weapons.

Next, the officer must take you before a judge. You will be informed of your right to see a lawyer and will be told of your right to a preliminary hearing before a judge.

If you choose to have such a hearing, the police officer will describe the evidence to the judge. You may question the police officer and any other witnesses against you. You may also offer any evidence that might support your side. If you convince the judge that you are innocent, the judge will dismiss the case right there. If not, you will be required to face further proceedings. The judge will set bail, but it cannot be excessive bail. If you can pay the bail, you can go free while waiting for your case to be decided.

Next, you will face formal accusation. In major federal cases and many state cases, a grand jury would consider your case. A grand jury consisting of from sixteen to twenty-three persons hears evidence presented by a public prosecutor. The grand jury might summon you to appear and answer questions, or it might not. The grand jury's job is only to decide whether there is enough evidence for a trial, not to decide whether you are guilty or innocent. Let's say the grand jury decides there is sufficient evidence. It will then issue an indictment.

Once indicted, you will be *arraigned* (uh-RAINED). This means that you will be called to appear in court in order to answer a legal charge. The indictment—or, in less serious cases, the "information"—will be read to you, and you will be asked to enter a plea. You may plead guilty or not guilty. With the judge's permission, you may instead plead "no contest," indicating that you will not fight the charge against you though you are not admitting guilt.

If you plead not guilty, you have a right to a jury trial. The jury that hears your case will be a *petit jury,* or a trial jury. A federal petit jury contains twelve persons. (State petit juries sometimes have as few as six jurors.)

At the trial, you will have the right to question any witnesses against you and to call your own witnesses. You do not have to testify if you do not want to. But if you do testify, the prosecution lawyer will be allowed to ask you questions, and you will have to answer them.

Before the jurors start to talk over the case, the judge will explain the meaning of the law to them. The jury cannot convict you unless all of the jurors agree that you are guilty "beyond a reasonable doubt."

If you are convicted, the judge will give you an opportunity to make a statement. Then the judge will set your sentence, or punishment, in accordance with the seriousness of the crime. You will have a right to ask a higher court to review your case.

The right to a fair trial is one of our basic freedoms. The purpose of a trial is the determination of guilt or innocence. It is just as important that innocent people *not* be punished as that guilty people *should* be punished.

Chapter 13: Our Bill of Rights

ple, one for murder and one for conspiracy to murder. Also, if someone commits an act that violates both federal and state law, there are two offenses. Such a person may be tried once in a federal court and once in a state court.

3. *Nobody may be forced to testify against himself or herself.* If you are questioned by the police, you may refuse to answer. If you are on trial, you do not have to take the witness stand. If you are called to testify at a congressional hearing, you may refuse to answer certain questions about your own conduct. In no case can you be required to say things that might be used against you in a criminal proceeding—in other words, required to *incriminate* yourself. Nor can you be required to incriminate your spouse. You may, however, be required to testify against other people.

4. *Nobody may be deprived of life, liberty, or property without due process of law.* This means that you must be given a fair trial, conducted according to proper procedures by an unbiased judge. This clause has also been interpreted to mean that the laws, themselves, must be reasonable. We will examine judicial interpretation of this clause in Chapter 16.

5. *No private property may be taken for public use without a fair price being paid.*

The Sixth Amendment protects an individual's right to defend himself or herself in a federal court trial. It gives an accused person the following rights:

1. *The right to a speedy and public trial before an impartial jury in the state and district where the crime was committed.* An accused person is not *required* to have a jury trial. He or she may ask to be tried by a judge alone. An accused person may also ask to have the case transferred to another place. Such a transfer is sometimes granted when a crime has received much publicity and public feelings are running high.

2. *The right to be told plainly what crime one is accused of.* It is not possible to defend yourself unless you know just what you are accused of.

Anyone accused of a crime is provided certain rights by the Fifth and Sixth Amendments, including a speedy and open trial, a fair jury, a trial in the district where the alleged crime was committed, and the services of a defense lawyer.

3. *The right to hear and question (usually through a lawyer) all witnesses against one.*

4. *The right to compel witnesses to appear at a trial to tell the accused's side of the story.*

5. *The right to have a lawyer to question witnesses and argue the case.*

The Seventh Amendment guarantees the right to have a civil lawsuit tried by a jury. The amendment specifies that this right applies to all disputes about property worth more than $20.

The Eighth Amendment puts restrictions on bail, fines, and punishments. It contains the following provisions:

1. *A person who is awaiting trial must not be required to put up excessive bail in order to be set free.* Bail is a sum of money that a person deposits with court officials. Its purpose is to assure that the accused person will appear in court, and the money is returned only if the person does appear. A judge may set the bail low or high depending on the seriousness of the offense.

2. *A person who is convicted of breaking a law may not be required to pay an excessive fine.* As in the case of bail, what is "excessive" depends on what the crime was. For a serious crime, the fine may be higher than for a less serious one.

3. *A person who is convicted of breaking a law may not be punished in a cruel and unusual way.* This provision bars such punishments as torture. It is up to the federal courts to determine what is "cruel and unusual." Note that a punishment does not fall under this ban unless it is *both* cruel and unusual. The Court of Military Appeals has abolished an old Navy punishment of 3 days on bread and water as being both cruel and unusual.

The Ninth Amendment makes clear that we have more rights than those listed in the Bill of Rights. This amendment was included because some people feared that a Bill of Rights might come to be considered a complete list of rights. Amendment IX states that other rights not listed in the Constitution are "retained by the people."

The Tenth Amendment limits the power of the federal government. It provides that any powers not granted to the United States, or specifically taken away from the states by the Constitution, "are reserved to the States respectively, or to the people." These words recognize the states and the people as full partners in our federal system.

Both the Ninth and the Tenth Amendment echo the theory of the social contract: if the people have not agreed to delegate their powers, then the people still have them.

Questions

1 What do we mean by *freedom of expression*? Give examples.

2 What requirements must be met before a police officer may constitutionally search someone's home?

3 What are eight ways in which the Bill of Rights guarantees the right to a fair trial?

4 What do the Ninth and Tenth Amendments guarantee to the people?

◇ It is sometimes said: "Better that ten guilty people should go free than that one innocent person should be convicted." Do you agree or disagree? Explain.

Chapter 13 Review

Developing Your Political Vocabulary

1 How would you define *the press*? How would you define *prior restraint*? Write a sentence using both terms.

2 How do the terms *bail* and *fine* differ in meaning? Use each term in a sentence that provides an example.

3 What does *double jeopardy* mean? Write a sentence using the term and providing an example.

Recalling and Comparing

1 Describe some ways in which the Constitution can be "changed" without being formally amended.

2 Briefly describe *two* methods by which our Constitution has been formally amended. Briefly describe *two other* methods that can be used to formally amend the Constitution but that have never been used.

3 List *three* possible restrictions on freedom of speech.

Special Activities

1 Prepare a walking skit in which you and some of your classmates illustrate ways in which the United States Constitution can be formally amended. Have "stations" which represent Congress, state legislatures, state conventions, and a national convention.

2 The First Amendment guarantees several basic rights. Think it over; then write a brief report telling which *one* of those rights is most important to you and why.

3 Write and act out a short play with some of your classmates. Imagine that it is 1789. Have the characters in your play debate whether or not the Bill of Rights should apply to state *and* federal governments or only to the federal government.

4 Prepare a poster or cartoon that illustrates one of the first ten amendments to the Constitution.

5 Prepare a chart comparing the provisions of the Bill of Rights and those of the English Bill of Rights of 1689 (page 35). Use library sources to obtain information beyond that included in the text.

6 Make a study of the Virginia Bill of Rights, adopted by a convention in Virginia in June 1776 and said to be the parent of the Bill of Rights in the United States Constitution. Report your findings to the class.

7 Consider what might be arguments for and against this statement: "The amendment process required in our federal Constitution is too complicated and difficult." Do you agree or disagree? Explain.

Chapter 14

Our Growing Constitution

The Bill of Rights, added in 1791, was only the first addition to our federal Constitution. Since then, there have been several more amendments. The total reached twenty-six in 1971. The very next year Congress proposed another amendment, one that would guarantee equal rights for women. Before it had been ratified by the necessary number of states, Congress proposed still another amendment to the Constitution. This one would give the District of Columbia the voting powers of a state in Congress. Several other amendments have been under discussion.

Some of the amendments approved since 1791 added to the basic rights set down in the Bill of Rights. This is true of the Thirteenth, Fourteenth, and Fifteenth Amendments; the Nineteenth; and the Twenty-third, Twenty-fourth, and Twenty-sixth.

Some other amendments brought changes in our institutions or procedures of government. This is so of the Twelfth Amendment; the Sixteenth and Seventeenth; the Twentieth, the Twenty-second, and the Twenty-fifth.

Still others—the Eleventh, Eighteenth, and Twenty-first—fall in a miscellaneous category.

Clearly, our Constitution is a living document and is still growing. It adjusts to new needs in new times. This chapter will discuss the amendments that have been made to the Constitution since 1791, and

Chapter 14: Our Growing Constitution

how they have affected our system of government. The amendments will be discussed in the order in which they were ratified.

Goals

- *To learn what amendments have been made to our Constitution since 1791.*
- *To consider how the "due process" clause of the Fourteenth Amendment has been put into practice.*
- *To consider why the Sixteenth Amendment, which allows an income tax, applies to people who are too young to vote.*

AMENDMENTS XI THROUGH XV

As people began to put the Constitution into practice, they found that the machinery of government did not work exactly the way its designers had expected. Slight changes were therefore made in 1798 and 1804. More changes became necessary for other reasons in the 1860s, after the Civil War. By 1870, the Bill of Rights was followed by Amendments XI through XV.

The Eleventh Amendment (1798) removed from the federal courts all lawsuits by individuals against states. Generally, states do not allow individuals to sue the state without the state's consent. This was true also at the time the Constitution was adopted, and most people thought the Constitution would change nothing. However, they were overlooking Article III, Section 2, which allowed citizens of one state to sue another state in the *federal courts.*

The issue arose in 1793 when two citizens of South Carolina sued the state of Georgia. They were heirs of Alexander Chisholm, to whom Georgia owed money. In *Chisholm v. Georgia,* the United States Supreme Court ordered Georgia to pay the debt.

Many people objected strongly to this ruling because they felt that it meant a loss of state power to the national government. Georgia simply denied that the Supreme Court had any right to interfere in its affairs, and it refused to pay the debt. The Supreme Court did not challenge Georgia's refusal. Five years later, in 1798, the Constitution was changed by the adoption of the Eleventh Amendment. It says:

The Judicial power of the United States shall not be construed [interpreted] to extend to any suit in law or equity, commenced or prosecuted against one of the United States by Citizens of another State, or by Citizens or Subjects of any Foreign State.

The Twelfth Amendment (1804) changed the electoral system for choosing the President and Vice President. This amendment was added because the original electoral college system did not work as it was intended to work.

Under the Constitution, an electoral college, composed of electors from each state, elects a President and a Vice President. Originally, there was no distinction between candidates for President and Vice President. All candidates appeared on the same list. Each elector voted for two candidates, at least one of whom was not from the elector's state. If one candidate had a clear majority, that candidate became President and the runner-up became Vice President. If no one had a clear majority, the House of Representatives decided.

The Founders had expected that the House would usually elect the President and Vice President. It had been thought that voting would be along sectional lines and that the electors would split their votes among many candidates. By 1800, the system broke down because two national political parties—the Federalists and the Democratic-Republicans—had been formed.

Under the political party system, the electors voted for the two candidates of their own

This engraving of 1879 shows a group of Southern refugees arriving at St. Louis. Many former slaves left the South in search of a new life elsewhere. Some had no choice because the Civil War had disrupted the South's economy.

party. That concentrated the vote. In 1800, the Democratic-Republicans won a majority of the electoral votes. Each Democratic-Republican elector cast one vote for each of the party's candidates—Thomas Jefferson and Aaron Burr. The result was predictable: the two candidates tied. It was up to the House to break the tie. The House was controlled by the other party, the Federalists. Though the Democratic-Republicans wanted Jefferson to be President, some Federalists preferred to see Burr as President. The House took thirty-six ballots before electing Jefferson as President and Burr as Vice President. The balloting lasted a whole day and a whole night.

Before the next election, the Twelfth Amendment was proposed and quickly ratified. Now there are separate candidates for President and Vice President. If no presidential candidate receives a majority of electoral votes, the House chooses from the top three candidates. If no vice-presidential candidate receives a majority of electoral votes, the Senate chooses from the top two candidates.

After the Twelfth Amendment, more than 60 years passed before the Constitution was changed again. Then the Civil War called into question the parts of the Constitution that related to slavery. Between 1865 and 1870, three more amendments were added. Each of these "Civil War amendments" had to do with wiping out slavery. In some respects, however, the amendments came to have an even wider application.

The Thirteenth Amendment (1865) banned slavery and involuntary servitude, except as punishment for a crime. This amendment followed up on President Abraham Lin-

These foreign-born residents of the United States are taking an oath of allegiance and will now be naturalized citizens.

coln's Emancipation Proclamation of 1862, which declared that slaves in the Confederate States were free. To abolish slavery throughout the nation, Congress proposed Amendment XIII in 1865. By the end of that year, the amendment had been ratified. Slavery, a practice that had divided the nation from the very first, was finally outlawed.

The longest and most detailed of the Civil War amendments is the Fourteenth Amendment. It is also the one most often invoked today. This amendment grew out of a complex battle in Congress over how the former Confederate states should be brought back into the Union. Two successive Presidents, Abraham Lincoln and Andrew Johnson, wanted to readmit the states at once in order to heal the nation's wounds. The Republican majority in Congress, on the other hand, wanted to "reconstruct" the South first. The Republicans insisted that the Southern states agree to the Fourteenth and Fifteenth Amendments before they were readmitted. The Southern states did not comply willingly.

The Fourteenth Amendment (1868) granted citizenship to freed slaves and guaranteed their rights.

In settling the debate over whether slaves and other blacks could be citizens, Amendment XIV provided a definition of citizenship. The amendment says that all persons born in the United States and subject to its jurisdiction are citizens, and that foreign-born persons who are *naturalized*—formally granted citizen-

Citizens and Noncitizens

The rights set down in the United States Constitution and its amendments are generally guaranteed to citizens and noncitizens alike. For example, the Fifth Amendmant begins: "No person shall be . . ." The word *person* includes everyone within the United States whether a citizen or not.

Yet the 5 million residents of this country who are not citizens do not share *all* the privileges of citizenship. For example, they cannot vote. They are barred from jobs in the defense industry and, in some states, from professions such as the law. Though they must pay federal taxes, noncitizens in some states are not allowed to draw unemployment insurance and other benefits.

Those who are not citizens are known as *aliens*. Aliens who were admitted legally carry documents showing their right to be here. An alien who enters illegally—with false documents, for example—is subject to expulsion.

Many aliens come to this country with the intention of becoming citizens. To do so, they must reside here for at least 5 years (3 years if the alien is married to a citizen) and meet various other requirements. Then they may apply for naturalization, take an oath of allegiance, and become United States citizens.

Between 1820 and 1976, more than 47 million aliens entered this country legally from abroad. Most of our citizens today are descended from these immigrants.

A "green card," or alien registration document, grants aliens special permission to live and work in the United States.

ship—are also citizens. (Congress has since made laws to give citizenship to the people of Puerto Rico, Guam, and the Virgin Islands.)

The Fourteenth Amendment also extended the Bill of Rights in two ways. It required all states to follow "due process" and to give "equal protection" to all. You will recall that the Fifth Amendment required that no person be deprived of life, liberty, or property without due process of law. That amendment was believed to apply only to the federal government.

Amendment XIV applied this same rule to the states. (Most other provisions of the Bill of Rights were later extended to the states through Supreme Court decisions.) The "equal protection" provision of Amendment XIV was something new. It provided that no state shall "deny to any person within its jurisdiction the equal protection of the laws." The Bill of Rights had not mentioned "equal protection." The phrase was to prove a very significant one.

The Fourteenth Amendment also gave Congress the right to reduce a state's representation in the House of Representatives if the state denied the vote to any adult male citizen except one guilty of crime. (The amendment named "rebellion" as a crime.) This amendment applied only to males over 21. Today, the same provision would apply if a state denied the vote to women or to anyone 18 years of age or more. Congress has never enforced this provision of Amendment XIV even though many states had restrictive voting laws for a long time.

The Fourteenth Amendment had certain other provisions that were resented by many

Former slaves were guaranteed the right to vote by the Fifteenth Amendment. But only men could vote at that time.

Southerners. It denied the right to hold a state or federal office to any former federal or state official who had supported the Confederacy. It also declared that debts owed by the Confederate government had no legal force.

The Fifteenth Amendment (1870) guaranteed the right of freed slaves to vote. It states:

The right of citizens of the United States to vote shall not be denied or abridged by the United States or any State on account of race, color, or previous condition of servitude. The Northern states approved.

All of the former Confederate states except Tennessee rejected Amendment XIV at first. Congress then imposed military rule on the other ten Southern states. It required the states to hold conventions to draft new constitutions that guaranteed blacks the right to vote, as provided in the Fifteenth Amendment. The new state constitutions had to be ratified by a majority of the voters. The constitutions passed, and the Southern states eventually ratified the federal amendments. Amendment XIV took effect in 1868 and Amendment XV in 1870.

The Fifteenth Amendment, providing suffrage for blacks, was the last of the post-Civil War additions to the Constitution. Its language seems clear, but there were ways of getting around it. Some states continued to keep many blacks from voting for almost another century. We will examine various aspects of this problem in the next chapter and in Chapter 26.

--- Questions ---

1 Briefly describe why each of the following amendments was added to the Constitution:
  a Eleventh Amendment (1798)
  b Twelfth Amendment (1804)
  c Thirteenth Amendment (1865)
  d Fourteenth Amendment (1868)
  e Fifteenth Amendment (1870)

2 How did the Fourteenth Amendment extend the Bill of Rights?

3 What provision of the Fourteenth Amendment has Congress never used?

⬠ Which of the five amendments discussed in this section seems to you to have the most importance in our lives today? Why?

AMENDMENTS XVI THROUGH XXVI

After 1870, there were no additions to the Constitution for 43 years. Then, between 1913 and 1971, eleven more amendments were adopted. Let us now turn to them.

The Sixteenth Amendment (1913) gave Congress the power to pass income tax laws. Congress had enacted an income tax during the Civil War, and the United States Supreme Court had ruled that the tax was an

"That means we assist you in preparing your return—not in paying your tax."

indirect tax. But when Congress passed another income tax in 1894, the Court, in a 5–4 decision, declared it to be a direct tax. Under Article I, Section 9 of the Constitution, any direct tax must be collected according to the population of each state. In other words, if a state has 10 percent of the nation's population, then its citizens must pay 10 percent of a direct tax. An income tax does not work that way, since income is divided unequally among the states. Thus, a majority of the Court ruled that an income tax is unconstitutional.

To solve this problem, Congress proposed the Sixteenth Amendment, which the states ratified in 1913. It provides:

The Congress shall have power to lay and collect taxes on incomes, from whatever source derived, without apportionment among the several States, and without regard to any census or enumeration.

Kegs of beer or liquor are being smashed by a federal agent in this 1920 photograph. During the Prohibition period, federal agents all over the country sought out and destroyed alcoholic beverages and equipment used to make them for sale.

The income tax is now the federal government's biggest single source of income. Without it, our nation would have had great difficulty financing the growing federal government.

The Seventeenth Amendment (1913) provides that United States senators shall be elected by the people. Originally, the Constitution provided that senators should be elected by state legislatures (Article I, Section 3). Because many people came to feel that this method was undemocratic, Amendment XVII changed the rules in 1913. Since then, the voters have had a direct voice in choosing the upper as well as the lower house of Congress.

The Eighteenth Amendment (1919) prohibited the manufacture, sale, or transportation of alcoholic beverages. A number of people who had long called attention to problems caused by the abuse of alcoholic beverages succeeded in getting Amendment XVIII added to the Constitution in 1919. It began a period known as Prohibition. The nation found, however, that Prohibition did not stop drinking, nor did it stop people from making and selling beer, wine, or whiskey. Instead, a new class of criminals, called *bootleggers,* became rich by selling illegal liquor and bribing government officials. In 1933, the Eighteenth Amendment was canceled by the Twenty-first Amendment, discussed later.

The Nineteenth Amendment (1920) gave women the right to vote. Women in this country had sought this right for many years. In 1648, Margaret Brent went to the Maryland

House of Burgesses with a petition claiming two votes, one because she was a landowner and the other because she was a lawyer representing Lord Baltimore. The burgesses gave her none. Abigail Adams raised the issue of women's rights with her husband, John Adams, at the time of the Declaration of Independence.

After the Fourteenth Amendment was adopted in 1868, the struggle for woman suffrage intensified. Some women were enraged because that amendment for the first time included the word "male" in the Constitution. In Section 2, the amendment protected only the right of adult *males* to vote. When women claimed the right to vote in national elections as part of the "equal protection" provision of the same amendment, the Supreme Court turned them down.

The woman suffrage movement fared better in the states than at the national level. Beginning with Wyoming in 1869, some state legislatures approved woman suffrage in state and local elections. Virginia Woodhull dramatized the continuing struggle in 1872 by running for President on the ticket of the Equal Rights Party. The party won few votes.

Many men, and some women, ridiculed the woman suffrage movement. Slowly, however, public opinion changed, and in 1920 the Nineteenth Amendment was adopted. It says:

> The right of citizens of the United States to vote shall not be denied or abridged by the United States or by any State on account of sex.

The Twentieth Amendment (1933) set new dates for the start of terms of Congress and for the inauguration of the President and Vice President. Article I, Section 4 of the Constitution provided for Congress to convene on the first Monday in December unless Congress named a different day by law. Presidents traditionally were installed in office on March 4,

These women—and, quite possibly, the grandmothers of some of the ERA supporters pictured on page 237—turned out to march for ratification of the Nineteenth Amendment that would give all women the right to vote.

four months after the November election. The Twentieth Amendment, adopted in 1933, provides for new members of Congress to meet on January 3, two months after their election. The inauguration of the President and Vice President was moved up to January 20.

The Twentieth Amendment also provides for filling the Presidency if the office is vacant when a new presidential term begins. For instance, if a President-elect dies before starting his or her term, the Vice President-elect will become President. The amendment gives Congress the power to provide by law for choosing someone to "act as President" if neither a President nor a Vice President has qualified. (See pages 138 and 139 on the Presidential Succession Act of 1947.)

The Twenty-first Amendment (1933) repealed the Eighteenth Amendment. Thus, the sale of alcoholic beverages again became legal in this country wherever the states chose to permit it. The new amendment allowed each state to decide for itself whether or not to ban liquor, and it prohibited the taking of alcoholic beverages into any state in violation of state laws.

The Twenty-second Amendment (1951) limited the number of times any person can be elected President. As we have seen, this amendment was adopted mainly in reaction to Franklin D. Roosevelt's having been elected to four terms as President (in 1932, 1936, 1940, and 1944). It provides that no one can be elected more than twice as President or serve more than a total of 10 years.

The Twenty-third Amendment (1961) gave citizens living in the nation's capital the right to vote for President and Vice President. Until this amendment was adopted in 1961, residents of the District of Columbia could not vote for any national officials. Later, in 1970, Congress passed legislation allowing the capital's residents to elect one nonvoting delegate to Congress.

The Twenty-fourth Amendment (1964) abolished all taxes on voting in federal elec-

The cartoonist pictured President Franklin D. Roosevelt trying to make a choice that Presidents can no longer make.

tions. In spite of the Fourteenth Amendment, some states were requiring citizens to pay a tax before they could go to the polls to vote in any election. These *poll taxes* were one means used to keep low-income blacks, especially, from exercising their right to vote. The Twenty-fourth Amendment prevented states from applying poll taxes in federal elections. Poll taxes in *state* elections were ruled out in 1966 when the Supreme Court held that such taxes violate the "equal protection" clause of the Fourteenth Amendment.

The Twenty-fifth Amendment (1967) provides new procedures for determining when a President is disabled. It also provides for the filling of a vacancy in the office of Vice President. These provisions were discussed on pages 152 and 139–140 respectively.

The Twenty-sixth Amendment (1971) lowered the voting age in all elections to 18. The Constitution had left it up to each state to decide the age at which voting rights should start. Most states set that age at 21, but a few states set it lower. Beginning in the 1960s, the war in Vietnam focused national debate on the issue of the minimum voting age because many 18-, 19-, and 20-year-olds were being drafted to serve in the war. Was it fair, some people asked, to deny voting rights to young people who might be asked to risk their lives for the nation? In 1971, Congress proposed the Twenty-sixth Amendment lowering the voting age to 18 in all states. This amendment was ratified the same year.

Thus, the right to vote has been greatly expanded since our nation began. At first restricted by most states to property-owning white male citizens who were at least 21 years of age, suffrage now extends nationally to citizens of all races and both sexes who have reached the age of 18. A few restrictions do remain under state laws. Insane persons and those convicted of serious crimes may not vote. Some states disqualify people who have been dishonorably discharged from the armed forces. Each state also requires that a voter have lived in a state or the voting district for a specified time, generally 30 days. Under a law passed by Congress in 1970, 30 days is the maximum time that a state may require a voter in a *presidential* election to have lived in a locality.

Proposed Amendments

At almost any time, several proposed amendments to the Constitution are under consideration. Most prominent of those proposed in recent years are the so-called Equal Rights Amendment and an amendment that would give the District of Columbia voting representation in Congress.

The Equal Rights Amendment, proposed by Congress in 1972, is intended to protect the rights of women. It provides that "Equality of rights under the law shall not be denied or abridged by the United States or by any State on account of sex." This amendment would take effect 2 years after ratification.

As already noted, the Twenty-third Amendment gave the District of Columbia a nonvoting delegate in the House of Representatives. An amendment proposed by Congress in 1978 provides for repeal of Amendment XXIII and for treatment of the District as if it were a state for purposes of representation in

With passage of the Twenty-sixth Amendment, a member of the Myers Park Mustangs and other 18-year-olds in North Carolina registered to vote for the first time in a national election.

Congress, election of the President and the Vice President, and amendment of the Constitution. Ratification of the amendment would give the District two senators and, based on population, probably one member of the House—all with the same powers as other members of Congress.

Questions

1 How has the Sixteenth Amendment been important in the development of our national government?

2 Do you think that the United States Senate would be any different today if it were elected by state legislatures? Explain.

3 Briefly describe what seemed to be the main reason for adoption of the following amendments:
 a Nineteenth Amendment (1920)
 b Twenty-third Amendment (1961)
 c Twenty-fourth Amendment (1964)
 d Twenty-sixth Amendment (1971)

◯ The Eighteenth Amendment placed the federal government in the position of trying to control people's drinking habits. Do you think this is a valid purpose for a constitutional amendment? For a federal law? Explain.

PROBLEM: HOW SHOULD "DUE PROCESS" APPLY TO NATIVE AMERICANS?

We have seen that both the Fifth and the Fourteenth Amendments provide that no person shall be deprived of "life, liberty, or property" without "due process of law."

Just what is "due process"? Some historians trace the idea to the Magna Charta. In that thirteenth-century English document, King John promised to obey "the law of the land." This meant, in part, that the nation's usual legal process had to be followed in each case. If the law called for certain procedures, then those procedures had to be followed, or the king's actions were illegal. From this idea came our own constitutional provisions binding the government to follow the procedures set down in its own laws. If it takes shortcuts or fails to follow the prescribed procedures, it is not following "due process."

The reading below deals with due process. It involves a claim by two Native American groups that they were deprived unconstitutionally of their territories. In March 1977, with the help of the federal court and the Department of Justice, those Native Americans took a long stride toward asserting their claim over a large part of the state of Maine. The area of the claim is now occupied mainly by whites and includes busy towns and thriving industries. Many Maine residents feared that the dispute might lead to economic disaster for the state. But when a cash settlement was finally reached, the two groups said they would buy timberlands at fair market value.

As you read, consider these questions:

- *In what way does the claim of these Native American groups reflect the principle of due process?*
- *How could the dispute be resolved in accordance with due process?*

The Long Shadow of a 1790 Law

As Maine goes, it used to be said, so goes the nation. The legal challenge by Maine's Passamaquoddy and Penobscot Indians does typify a new surge of tribal nationalism around the United States. In particular, the Maine case reflects the activism of about half a dozen Eastern tribes that lately have won the right to seek redress under a 1790 federal law. The law required that all state and local treaties be approved by Congress. These tribes now are claiming millions of acres of land, in several states, that were taken during the past 200 years without congressional approval.

These members of the Penobscot Tribal Council were taking political action to obtain what they considered to be their rights. The Penobscots and the Passamaquoddys claimed that their land had been taken without due process of law.

For sheer size, the Maine claim leads all the rest. It began in 1957, when a Passamaquoddy woman opened an old trunk and found a copy of a 1794 treaty between local tribes and Massachusetts, from which Maine later broke away. She called in tribal leader John Stevens. He spent years trying to get compensation for some small portions of the Indian land that had been lost to whites. Finally, with the help of Tom Tureen, a lawyer, the Indians forced the United States government to take up their cause. In 1975, Tureen won a federal court ruling that gave Eastern tribes the same protection under the 1790 law that previously was granted only to Western tribes.

Maine's Native Americans also raised the ante. Tureen discovered that the long-forgotten 1794 treaty itself had never been cleared with Congress as required by the 1790 law. Accordingly, he stepped up the Indians' claim to cover all tribal land originally held by the Passamaquoddy and neighboring Penobscots. This is a total of 12.5 million acres, nearly 60 percent of all the land in Maine. Still, few whites took the case seriously until 1976. Then state and local bond issues were held up by the pending lawsuit.

The battle lines have now emerged. The Justice Department and the Indians returned to court with an amended claim of about 5 million acres. Federal Judge Edward T. Gignoux gave the claimants until June 1, 1977, to work out a legal strategy or reach an out-of-court settlement. The state continued to oppose the claim. The Maine congressional delegation submitted legislation to wipe out the Indians' rights to the land—although permitting them to seek compensation through civil suits. If no deal is struck, the Indians plan to file suits against "a limited number of major landowners"—including several paper manufacturers. But Congress may well legislate a compromise, leaving all or most of the land with current owners and providing federal compensation for the Indians. "Only Congress can correct past injustices to the tribes without causing new hardships to other citizens of Maine," said a Justice Department memo. How generous the great white fathers in Washington would be in this and similar cases, however, remained to be seen.

Adapted from "Indians: This Land Is My Land," *Newsweek,* March 14, 1977, pp. 18, 23. Copyright © Newsweek, Inc., 1977. Reprinted by permission.

Questions

1 What were the Passamaquoddy and the Penobscots asking for? Why?

2 What might due process of law have to do with those claims?

3 The present owners of the Maine land paid someone for the land they now own. How can *they* be guaranteed due process of law?

4 Can due process of law sometimes cause problems for all concerned? Explain.

⬠ Do you think that it is important for a government to follow procedures set down in a law? Explain.

PROBLEM: SHOULD YOUNG PEOPLE HAVE TO PAY TAXES?

The American colonists coined many slogans in their struggle for independence, including the famous one, "No taxation without representation." The colonists had in mind mainly tariffs and excise taxes. Since passage of the Sixteenth Amendment, our main tax has been levied on individual incomes.

A few years ago, a young man wrote a letter to a United States senator. The writer explained that he was 17 years old and was not allowed to vote because of his age. Yet, when he had a job, the federal government took taxes from his paycheck. Wasn't this "taxation without representation"? Why should he have to pay taxes if he could not vote?

The senator who received the letter was Alan Cranston, a Democrat of California. His reply is printed below. As you read it, ask yourself:

- *Is the 17-year-old's situation similar to or different from that of the American colonists?*
- *Are the senator's points valid ones?*

A Senator's Answer

Think of the 4- and 5-year-old child stars earning thousands of dollars in movies, television, and commercials. I don't think you would favor giving them, and all other 4-year-olds, the right to vote because some of them earn taxable incomes.

Nor do I think you would want them to go tax free. Everyone who enjoys the benefits and protections of our society, and those who earn, should help pay their own way, at whatever age. But remember that 17-year-old workers are covered by our unemployment compensation, social security, occupational health and safety laws, among other things. So while they do not get the vote, they get a lot else. You must admit that even though 18 is an arbitrary cutoff (as was 21) there has to be a reasonable limit to how much we can lower the voting age.

Adapted from "Ask Them Yourself," *Family Weekly,* July 13, 1975, p. 2. Question by Mark Waggoner of Alta Loma, California. Reprinted by permission of Family Weekly magazine, Copyright © 1978.

Questions

1 What are two arguments used by Senator Cranston in favor of taxing people who are too young to vote?

2 Do you think that taxing such people is taxation without representation? Explain.

3 Do young people have any ways other than voting to influence the decisions of their government? Did the colonists? Explain.

⬠ Do you think that it is fair for people who are not eligible to vote to have to pay taxes? Explain.

Chapter 14 Review

Developing Your Political Vocabulary

What do the following terms mean? Use each one in a sentence about any of the amendments added to the Constitution since the Bill of Rights.

    a electoral votes
    b "Civil War amendments"
    c naturalized citizen
    d due process of law
    e suffrage
    f Prohibition
    g inauguration
    h poll tax

Recalling and Comparing

1 How many amendments have been added to the Constitution as of the present time?

2 How many of those amendments concern the rights of individuals? List by their number all amendments that do.

3 List the amendments that deal with the right to vote. Do you think that everyone who should have a right to vote now has it? Should any persons who now have the right to vote be denied it? Explain.

4 Though citizens under 18 cannot vote, do they have other rights under the Constitution? Explain.

5 Would you say that the Constitution has been amended quite often or rarely? Explain.

6 Do you suppose that as our society becomes more complex, more amendments will be added to the Constitution? Explain.

Special Activities

1 Prepare a poster in which you illustrate basic freedoms found in the Thirteenth, Fourteenth, and Fifteenth Amendments.

2 Make a special bulletin-board display that shows how the Fifteenth, Nineteenth, Twenty-third, Twenty-fourth, and Twenty-sixth Amendments have extended the right to vote.

3 Consult your library and prepare a brief history of *one* of the amendments discussed in this chapter.

4 Using the *Reader's Guide to Periodical Literature* or another source in your library, look up magazine articles telling about recent efforts to add further amendments to the Constitution. Describe these efforts in a written report.

5 Consider what might be arguments for and against the following statement: "Any time the people of this country disagree with a decision of the Supreme Court, they should propose a constitutional amendment to change that decision." Do you agree or disagree? Explain.

Chapter 15

Rights and Legislation

The Constitution, with the Bill of Rights and other amendments, contains some high-sounding words about rights and liberties. Yet there is room for argument about the meaning of some of those words. Moreover, individuals or groups of people may feel at times that the rights and liberties provided under the Constitution are not being put into practice. Constitutional amendments and appeals to the Supreme Court can help to solve disputes arising from these sources. But the disputes can also be solved in another way.

Disputes over the meaning of rights and how they should be put into effect are often carried to the floor of Congress. By using its legislative powers, Congress can give clearer meaning to our rights. Especially in the past two or three decades, Congress has passed laws spelling out detailed civil rights for more and more people. This chapter will look at some of those laws and how they affect our lives today.

―――――――― **Goals** ――――――――

- To examine some laws by which Congress has attempted to strengthen people's rights.
- To learn of attempts to end discrimination against groups of people.
- To consider whether workers should be forced to retire because of age.
- To consider our right to know what government is doing.

Discrimination comes in many forms. Sometimes it is obvious—as it is in the sign shown above. Sometimes the loss of rights is less quickly understood—as was the case in the past practice of giving only white males positions of authority.

CIVIL RIGHTS AND CIVIL LIBERTIES

Our rights may be threatened either by the government or by private individuals. The Constitution concerns itself mainly with the threat of *government* to individual liberties. Its wording shows this. The First Amendment begins: "Congress shall make no law . . . ." The Fourteenth Amendment says: "No State shall make or enforce any law . . . ."

Government is not the only possible abuser of rights. Private individuals may also keep us from exercising our rights, by denying us equal opportunity because of the color of our skin, because of our sex, because of our age, or for other reasons. Such actions are *not* clearly banned by the Constitution, but they have been increasingly attacked in recent years by court decisions and by acts of Congress.

The unequal treatment of black people was one of the first targets of congressional action as part of the steps taken since the late 1950s to eliminate discrimination. Deeply entrenched attitudes and social customs had led to unequal treatment of blacks. It is important to recall that history.

Though the Thirteenth Amendment abolished slavery, it did not abolish attitudes that had their roots in the practice of slavery. Though the Fourteenth Amendment promised "equal protection of the laws" to all people, it did not say just what "equal protection" meant. Nor did it say that private individuals had to treat all others equally.

Blacks were rarely treated as equals. They were treated as inferiors—not because of any personal qualities, but because they were black. When someone treats any group of people differently from other groups of people, we say that person *discriminates,* or practices *discrimination.* Discrimination is singling out people for special treatment because of the group to which they belong, not because of their individual characteristics.

In the Civil Rights Act of 1875, Congress sought to end some kinds of discrimination based on race. The act said that people of all races had a right to equal use of such public accommodations as restaurants, inns, theaters, and public conveyances, such as railroads. The act had little effect. In 1883, in the Civil Rights Cases, the Supreme Court declared the act unconstitutional. The Court pointed out that such establishments were privately owned, and said that Congress had no authority to stop discrimination by private individuals.

Later, the Court upheld certain forms of racial discrimination by government, as well. In *Plessy v. Ferguson* (1896), the Court ruled that Louisiana was not violating the Constitution in requiring railroad companies to provide separate facilities for blacks and for whites. Segregation was constitutional, the Court held, as long as the facilities were "equal."

So matters rested for many decades. Federal law largely avoided the question of racial discrimination. Social custom and state laws worked together in many parts of the nation to keep the races segregated. "Separate but equal" was the law of the land. Even the armed services were segregated, with separate units for blacks and whites.

Slowly, however, conditions and attitudes were changing. A series of victories in court cases chipped away at the walls of segregation in the 1930s and 1940s. In 1948, after the end of World War II, President Harry Truman issued an executive order desegregating the armed forces. Then, in 1954, the Supreme Court reversed its 1896 decision on segregation. In *Brown v. Board of Education of Topeka,* the Court held that separate facilities could never be "equal." In this landmark case, the Court declared that racially segregated schools violated the Fourteenth Amendment guarantee of "equal protection of the laws." It ordered that schools must be *desegregated.*

The black civil rights movement, which had been struggling for years with little public attention, suddenly burst into the national spotlight. Further court decisions spurred the movement on. Congress, which had long been unsuccessful in passing laws to combat racial discrimination, began to stir into action. In 1957, Senate Majority Leader Lyndon Johnson pushed through the first civil rights bill enacted by Congress in 82 years. After Johnson became President, major laws were passed in 1964, 1965, and 1968 to protect people against discrimination based on race or color. Most of these laws banned discrimination on the basis of religion, national origin, or sex as well. The laws attacked discrimination not only by government but also by private individuals. These were cases in which a private individual was offering something to the public, such as meals in a restaurant or lodging in an apartment. The Supreme Court upheld these laws of the 1960s on various grounds. In effect, the

The arrest of Rosa Parks for her refusal to give up her bus seat to a white man set the stage for a boycott of the buslines by the black residents of Montgomery, Alabama, in 1955. The boycott became a model for the civil rights movement of the next decade.

Mexican Americans have rallied and demonstrated for civil rights in a pattern set by the black civil rights movement.

Court gave Congress wide leeway to pass laws against private discrimination that affects the public at large.

The chart on this page gives a brief summary of those laws. As you study it, remember that all of the actions barred by the legislation were common practices in many states—especially in the South but often elsewhere in the country, too. The legislation regarding voting rights will be discussed further in Chapter 26. As you will see, Congress extended the Voting Rights Act in 1970 and 1975. The 1975 revisions protected the voting rights of many Spanish-speaking Americans, Native Americans, Alaskan natives, and some Asian Americans who had been unable to vote because they could not read English.

Just because a law is on the books does not mean that it is obeyed or that a problem is solved. Federal agencies cite many examples

Major Civil Rights Legislation of the 1960s

The Civil Rights Act of 1964

1 Forbids discrimination in voter registration, public accommodations, public facilities, and public schools on the basis of race, color, religion, or national origin, or on the basis of sex.
2 Forbids discrimination in employment opportunity on any of these bases.
3 Forbids the use of federal funds in programs that practice discrimination on any of these bases.
4 Allows certain civil rights cases to move from state into federal courts.

The Voting Rights Act of 1965

1 Provides that federal officials will control voter registration in areas where people have been denied the right to register or vote on the basis of race or color.
2 Forbids literacy tests in determining qualifications for voting.
3 Prohibits anyone from depriving another of the right to register or to vote.

The Civil Rights Act of 1968
Open Housing Act

1 Forbids discrimination in the sale or rental of all housing except privately owned single-family homes sold or rented by the individual owner.
2 Forbids discriminatory advertising in housing sales and rentals.
3 Forbids violence or intimidation to prevent anyone from exercising his or her civil rights, including civil rights work.
4 Forbids travel between states for the purpose of inciting a riot, manufacture of weapons to be used in a riot, or instruction in the use of weapons for the purpose of a riot.

of continuing violations. In 1977, for instance, the Justice Department reported that many restaurants continued to turn away blacks and other minorities. That same year, the department charged fifty-seven people with criminal violations of other people's civil rights. Most were cases of alleged police brutality against racial minorities. Probably the greatest obstacle to full political participation of all groups is an economic one. In spite of the great legislative reforms during the 1960s, many people are held back because of poverty.

Congress also has passed laws to guarantee more rights to handicapped persons. In the past, for instance, something as obvious as a high curb or a stairway might prevent someone in a wheelchair from being able to use a public building unaided. The Rehabilitation Act of 1973 helps the handicapped by requiring, among other things, the elimination of such barriers in any buildings or grounds for which federal funds are used.

The Rehabilitation Act of 1973 applies to the estimated 35 million physically and mentally handicapped people of this country. Its basic provisions are carried out through detailed regulations issued by federal agencies. For example, if you are an employer who receives federal funds, you may not discriminate against a handicapped person who applies for a job. If a blind applicant can do a job as well as a sighted applicant, you must give equal consideration to both. You must also provide reasonable accommodations for a handicapped person whom you might hire.

To take another example, suppose you are a doctor who treats Medicare or Medicaid patients. According to the regulations issued by the Department of Health, Education, and Welfare, handicapped people must have ready access to your office. Otherwise, you must make house calls or provide service at some place that *is* accessible to handicapped patients.

Other HEW regulations had a major effect on schools, colleges, and state and local health agencies because many of them receive funds from HEW. It has been estimated that, before

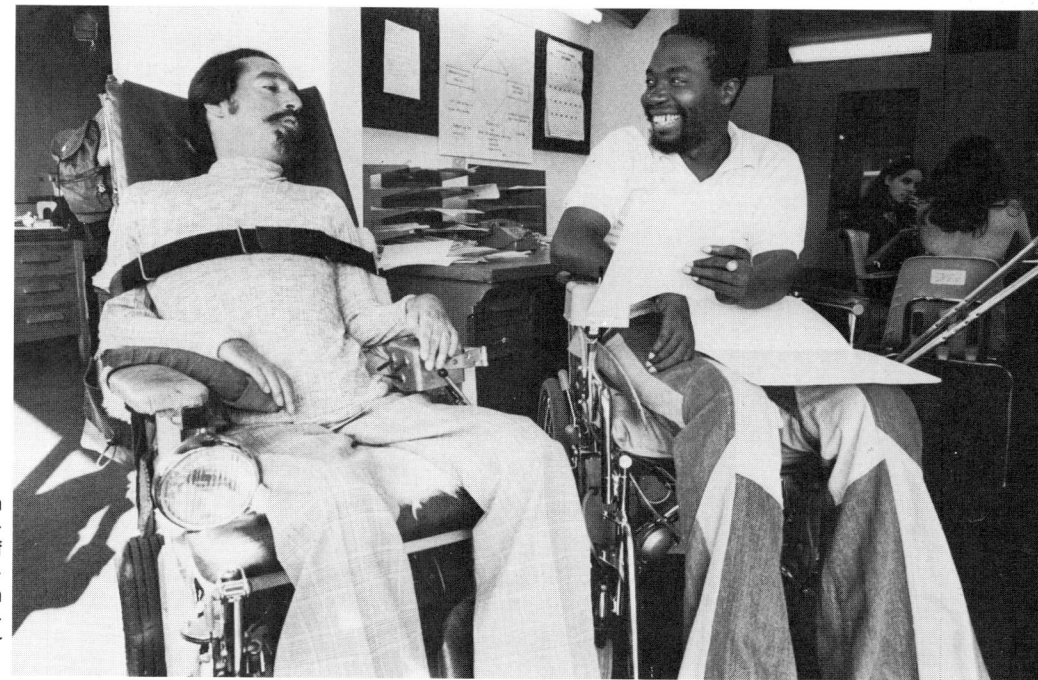

Edward V. Roberts, seated in the wheelchair with a headlight, was appointed Director of the Department of Rehabilitation by Governor Jerry Brown of California in 1975. Mr. Roberts has been paralyzed for more than 20 years.

Chapter 15: Rights and Legislation

The requirement of a speedy trial is based on the belief that justice delayed is justice denied. More than 20 years ago, the Supreme Court made the same point when it used the words "with all deliberate speed" in its decision calling for an end to racial segregation in schools.

the regulations, a million handicapped children of school age were receiving no education and millions more were in separate classrooms or institutions. Now, except in special circumstances, such children are entitled to go to the same schools and classrooms as others.

Congress has also acted to protect the rights of people accused of federal crimes. Those rights have received increasing attention in recent years, both from the courts and from Congress. Here we will mention one example of congressional action on rights of the accused: the Speedy Trials Act of 1975. That act tries to give concrete meaning to the provision of the Sixth Amendment that guarantees an accused person a "speedy and public trial."

In the past, federal justice often creaked along very slowly. Sometimes a person accused of a federal crime had to wait more than a year to be brought to trial. This was a long time to someone free on bail, and seemed even longer to anyone held in prison. The 1975 law set deadlines to speed things up.

Here is what the law required when a person was accused of violating a federal law: Within 60 days, the person had to be indicted. Within 10 more days, the person had to be brought before a federal judge to enter a plea to the charge. If the plea was "not guilty," a trial had to start within 6 months (180 days).

The law provided for stepping up the pace even more after 1979. Now no more than 100 days may pass from the time a person is arrested until he or she is brought to trial.

Questions

1 What is the difference between *public discrimination* and *private discrimination*?

2 What *four* provisions in laws passed by Congress to help assure the rights of members of minority groups do you consider to be most important? Explain.

3 How have the rights of handicapped persons been advanced by federal laws?

4 What was the main reason for passage of the Speedy Trials Act of 1975? Do you think that was a good reason? Explain.

◌ Do you think the laws mentioned in this section went too far? Do you think they went far enough? Explain.

Chapter 15: Rights and Legislation

THE RIGHT TO KNOW AND THE RIGHT TO PRIVACY

An essential part of democracy is the right of citizens to know what their government is doing. Freedom of the press is one way our system tries to provide this knowledge. Now that government is so complex, however, it has vast stores of information beyond the usual concern or reach of the press.

In the Freedom of Information Act of 1966, Congress gave the individual a tool to break through government red tape and find information that he or she might need. The law was amended in 1975 to make it more effective. It provides that any person has a right to see records of the executive branch of the federal government. That right may be enforced by the federal courts. There are some exceptions, of course. The government is not required to make public such things as trade secrets, military secrets, or the minutes of Cabinet sessions with the President. Moreover, the law does not apply to the records of Congress or of the federal courts.

People have used the act for many purposes. Some people were curious to know whether the Federal Bureau of Investigation kept a file on them. Interest grew after a Senate committee reported in 1976 that the FBI kept files on more than 500,000 persons, many of them law-abiding. Others wanted to know if their names were on a list of 1,500,000 individuals compiled by the Central Intelligence Agency by illegally opening first-class mail to and from United States citizens. (Both the FBI and the CIA were later ordered to respect citizens' rights.) Still other people requested information about how regulatory agencies made their decisions. Some consumer groups used such information to support their arguments in favor of reform plans. Reporters used the law to pry out information about federal actions that might affect their communities.

Congress passed the Government in Sunshine Act of 1976 to open closed meetings to the public. Often meetings and hearings of the federal bureaucracy had been held "in the dark"—that is, in closed sessions. The purpose of the new law was to "let the sunshine in."

The law applies to some fifty federal agencies, boards, and commissions, including the Securities and Exchange Commission and the National Science Foundation. Not only must

Among those who have made use of the Freedom of Information Act are Robert and Michael Meerpol, shown here talking with reporters. The Meerpol brothers obtained records in the hope of clearing their parents, Julius and Ethel Rosenberg, of wrongdoing. The Rosenbergs were executed in 1953 after having been found guilty of giving United States atomic secrets to the Russians.

meetings be public, but there must be at least a week's advance notice. A few exceptions are allowed, but when a closed meeting is held, transcripts or summary-records must be kept. A federal court can order public disclosure of the proceedings if necessary.

Some members of Congress have agreed to their own Sunshine Rule. The House Democratic Caucus, which helps set the Democratic party's policy in Congress, is one such group. In 1975, it decided that all its meetings must be public unless a majority voted in a public session to go into a closed session.

Congress has also given parents the right to look at their children's school files and to correct any inaccurate information there. Until 1974, many schools would not let parents know what was in their children's files. For example, Mrs. Connie Gomes had a teenage son who had been handicapped by an attack of encephalitis. She asked school officials in Providence, Rhode Island, about the results of special tests the school gave to her son to determine his educational needs. The officials would not give the results to her.

Then Congress passed the Family Educational Rights and Privacy Act of 1974, which opened school files to parents. Now Mrs. Gomes would have the right to see the test results she had asked about. Parents can now check the results of personality tests, the reports of psychiatrists or social workers, and all other information in their children's school files. If a school refuses to comply with the law, it can lose all federal funding.

One reason Congress passed the law was that some parents feared that school files might contain false information. In some cases, such information had harmed a child's chances to get a job or to get into college. Under the 1974 act, a parent can demand a formal hearing before a school official who has no direct interest in the outcome. The school official is then supposed to issue a written decision summarizing the evidence and stating the reasons for the decision.

The law gives a school 45 days to respond to a parent's request. A student who is 18 years old or older may make a request on his or her own behalf.

The law raised one tricky question: What about letters of recommendation? Suppose a student asks a teacher for a letter of recommendation to help the student get into college. Such a letter would become part of the student's file. Would a teacher write a frank letter, knowing that the student could later read it? To settle this question, the law allows a student to give up the right ever to see letters of recommendation.

Congress has at times had to walk a tightrope. In protecting the public's right to know, it has not wanted to destroy the individual's right to privacy.

The Family Education Rights and Privacy Act of 1974 also limits the amount of information a school or government official can give out about an individual. Supporters of the act

Copyright © 1977 by Herblock in *The Washington Post*
"Personal Profile"

said that school systems, while keeping parents from seeing their children's files, had turned files over too freely to law enforcement agencies and other outsiders. The act places strict controls on who may see an individual's school records. For example, only faculty or staff members with a legitimate educational reason may examine a college student's files.

The act also applies to federal agencies that keep files on individuals. Most agencies must keep a list of the names and addresses of anyone who looks at an individual's file. The act also seeks to let people know what kinds of information the government collects. It requires that the names of all record systems kept by the federal government be listed each year in the *Federal Register*, a government publication.

Suppose you consult a file that a federal agency has been keeping on you, and you find an error. You want it corrected. You may write the agency a letter, which it has 10 days to answer. If the agency refuses your request, you have 30 days to appeal or to explain your side of the story. Your statement about the disputed information becomes part of your file. If you still are not satisfied, you may bring a complaint in a United States District Court. If you can prove that your records have been purposely misused, you can sue for damages.

The law restricts access to your file. For example, with certain exceptions, one agency cannot transfer information about you to another agency. Such transfers are permitted, however, for routine uses, law enforcement purposes, and statistical use of the Census Bureau. You may sue public officials for unlawful possession or disclosure of personal information about you. If you win, you can collect damages, and the official can be fined up to $5,000.

Questions

1 What is the purpose of the Freedom of Information Act?

2 What are Sunshine Laws? Do you think we should have them?

3 What are two purposes of the Family Educational Rights and Privacy Act?

◌ To what extent do you think we should have the right to keep our lives private? Explain.

EQUALITY OF THE SEXES

In 1776, the Declaration of Independence declared that "all men are created equal." Ever since, women in this country have been fighting to be included in that lofty sentiment. During the nineteenth and early twentieth centuries, suffragists led the fight for women's rights. In 1920, they succeeded in getting men to add the Nineteenth Amendment to the Constitution, granting women the right to vote. In the 1960s and 1970s, a new women's movement campaigned for nothing less than full equality. This movement brought about many changes. For the first time, females were given a nearly equal role in the armed forces, admitted to space flight training, hired for such formerly "male" jobs as mining and construction, and permitted to play on Little League baseball teams. Some of these changes were brought about by court decisions or informal persuasion. Many, however, resulted from new laws passed by Congress.

In 1967, Congress outlawed job discrimination based on sex. The Civil Rights Act of 1964 had banned job discrimination based on race, color, religion, or national origin and had created an Equal Employment Opportunity Commission (EEOC) to enforce its provisions. In 1967, Congress added sex discrimination to the list. The EEOC began to help women, too, in overcoming job discrimination.

The Equal Employment Opportunity Act of 1972 expanded the terms of the earlier laws. It covers a wide range of activities—from hiring and firing through promotion, pay, and other working conditions.

Chapter 15: Rights and Legislation

The entry of young women into Little League baseball was opposed in some places and warmly accepted in others.

An employer is required to pay a woman just as much as a man if both do the same kind of work. The fact is that women do not often do the same work as men because of traditional restrictions on women's job opportunities. As a result, men's and women's pay scales are still far apart. Working men received a median income of $13,859 in 1976. Half of all men received more than that and half received less. That same year, the median income for working women was $8,312.

The Depository Act of 1974 gave women new rights in dealing with banks. Women had previously complained that many banks made it harder for single women to borrow money than for single men to do so. They also complained that married women were treated differently from married men. The 1974 law requires banks not to discriminate on the basis of sex or marital status.

The Civil Rights Act of 1968 and the Fair Housing Act of 1974 seek to guarantee women equal rights in finding housing.

The Equal Credit Opportunity Act of 1975 outlaws discrimination against women seeking credit. It applies to any *creditor*—any company, bank, or government agency that extends credit. The credit law was expanded in 1977 to bar discrimination based on age, race, color, religion, or national origin.

Previously, a credit application often asked a person's sex or marital status. Now those questions are illegal. Previously, when a married couple applied for credit, the creditor might refuse to take into account the fact that

Each year, more and more women are employed in types of work formerly believed to be suitable for men only.

Chapter 15: Rights and Legislation

The First Women's Bank, located in New York City, first opened for business in 1975. The purposes of the bank were, first, to enable women to obtain banking services more easily and, second, to provide banking for both women and men.

both the wife and husband had jobs. Now a creditor must consider both incomes. Previously, a creditor might refuse to let a husband and wife have separate accounts. Now, this is no longer legal, so long as each can meet the creditor's normal standards.

Other discriminatory practices were also outlawed. For instance, a married woman might previously have been denied a loan on grounds that she had "no credit record," even though she and her husband had borrowed money jointly and paid it back on time. Creditors commonly counted those credit records in the husband's name only. Now, the past history of an account used by both must be credited to both.

Congress has also sought to give women equal opportunity in school sports. It did this in a 1976 amendment to an earlier law, the Omnibus Education Act of 1972. As amended, the act applies to all levels of school, from elementary grades through college. Besides sports, the act covers segregated classes (not allowed), employment (women teachers cannot be discriminated against), and admissions (a school cannot discriminate against a student who is pregnant, married, or already a parent).

Rights of Borrowers and Creditors

Any time a person is refused credit, the person must be informed of the reason and of his or her rights under the law. Suppose a department store has refused you credit and you want to know why. The store tells you it received a bad credit report on you from a local credit bureau. Under the law, you have a right to see what the credit bureau's files say about you. If there is inaccurate information in your file, you have a right to challenge it. You may also file a complaint about a credit refusal with a federal agency such as the Federal Trade Commission.

The law seeks to protect both the rights of individuals and the rights of creditors. For example, no creditor is required to lend to a bad credit risk. All who are covered by the law must establish that they are willing and able to pay the money back.

Thus, the mere fact that you are refused credit does not mean that you are being treated unfairly. And if unfair treatment does exist, you have to be able to prove it.

Colleges used to have separate teams for men and women. Now, men and women sometimes play on the same team.

Any school that fails to comply with the act can have its federal funds cut off.

The law does not require schools to spend equal amounts on sports programs for boys and girls. It does require that girls and boys have an equal opportunity to participate in sports programs. The gap between the sexes was quite wide before the law took effect. In 1970–1971, for example, 3,666,000 boys competed in interscholastic sports but only 294,000 girls did so. By 1976–1977, participation by girls had already increased a whopping 460 percent. Many of these girls were on newly formed soccer or cross-country teams or were participating in newly expanded track and field events.

The federal law makes it clear that schools do not have to require girls to join in contact sports. These would include football, basketball, boxing, wrestling, rugby, or ice hockey.

The law allows schools to maintain separate teams for boys and girls. It provides, however, that a single team open to both sexes may exist when selection is based on competitive skill. For example, in 1977 two girls played on the formerly all-boy football team of Bogue High School in Kansas. Because the school had only 30 students and not enough boys to fill out the team, Tina Irby played tackle and Tammy Thompson played safety. Some people thought the game would be too rough for the girls. Tina Irby said it wasn't. "Girls' basketball is rougher," she declared.

Just as the struggle for racial equality reached a high point in the 1960s, the women's rights struggle reached a high point in the 1970s. In spite of a series of new laws promoting equality of the sexes, many people felt that sex discrimination could not be wiped out except by an amendment to the Constitution. The Equal Rights Amendment, passed by Congress in 1972, was designed to bar sex discrimination by the federal and state governments (see Chapter 13).

Questions

1 List four types of discrimination against women that are barred by existing federal laws. What are the laws?

These members of a basketball team at a girls' high school in Iowa play as hard at the game as any boys' team does.

2 Can you think of any types of discrimination against women that might be legal under *existing* federal laws? Explain.

⬠ Do you think that Congress should bar *all* types of discrimination? Explain.

PROBLEM: SHOULD WORKERS BE FORCED TO RETIRE BECAUSE OF AGE?

An employer cannot fire someone for having black skin or yellow skin, or for being a woman, or for being Yugoslavian, or for being Jewish or Buddhist. That would be discriminatory. It would be illegal under various laws passed by Congress. But an employer *can* fire someone for being old. Is that discriminatory? Is it fair?

Those questions set off a vigorous debate in Congress in the 1970s. Some people argued that any discrimination based on age should be illegal. They called for a federal law to ban *mandatory retirement*—the widespread practice of forcing an employee to retire at a certain age.

In 1977, Congress went part way toward that goal. Congress passed a bill to make it illegal to force someone to retire before the age of 70. That was 5 years beyond the usual mandatory retirement age of 65. Some organizations of the elderly continued to press for a ban on mandatory retirement at *any* age. They maintained that the right to work should be based, not on chronological age, but on pure and simple ability.

The selection below presents some of the arguments against mandatory retirement. As you read, ask yourself:

- *Does mandatory retirement violate the rights of the aged?*
- *Why might some employers consider it necessary to have a policy of mandatory retirement?*

'I'm sorry, Blakely, but you know perfectly well there can be no exceptions to our policy of mandatory retirement'

Drawing by Richter; © 1977 The New Yorker Magazine, Inc.

Retirement as Nightmare

Mention retirement to the average person and the image that usually springs to mind is that of a handsome, vigorous elderly couple like the ones who keep turning up in advertisements for special retirement "sunshine" communities. Unfortunately, this picture of the golden years is distorted.

Make no mistake. There are some people who are healthy, creative and rich enough to benefit from the leisure provided by retirement. But most retirees find it a nightmare of boredom, poverty, and insecurity. Take a look at these statistics:

- The average white male dies 30 to 40 months after retirement.
- Men over 65 account for one-fourth of all suicides.
- One-third of all marriages decline after retirement, according to a National Institute of Mental Health study.
- Alcoholism and mental illness plague a large number of retirees.

Not all of these woes can be blamed solely on retirement, of course. The physical infirmities that often come with increasing age obviously play a role.

Yet many authorities think that retirement hastens physical and emotional decline. Among such authorities is Dr. Frederick C. Swartz, head of the American Medical Association's Committee on Aging. "After retirement," says Dr. Swartz, "many men collapse into a state of lethargy and boredom. And once this happens, they start down the road to bad health."

Psychiatrist Robert Butler agrees. Dr. Butler defines what he calls the "retirement syndrome." Men and women who are otherwise perfectly healthy will suddenly develop headaches or stomach disorders. They will oversleep. They will become irritable. They will suffer from mental confusion and nervousness.

A job gives purpose to a person's life. The loss of a job, says Dr. William Reichel of the American Geriatrics Society, may prove "traumatic" (stressful) for retirees.

The American Medical Association has labeled retirement a health hazard. It declares flatly that forced retirement and the denial of work opportunity—whether the work is for pay or for the pleasure of giving—seriously threaten the individual.

But there is a big distinction between voluntary and forced retirement. "Usually those who are able to make their own decision to retire fare better than those forced out by a mandatory policy," says Dr. Butler. He thinks that those who retire voluntarily look forward to more leisure time. They are equipped financially and emotionally to put it to creative use. Those who are forced out have no idea what to do.

Unfortunately, more and more Americans are going to find themselves in this second category. At the turn of the century, only a handful of workers were forced to retire. Today, 50 percent are forced out. The result has been a steady decline in the percentage of over-65s in the work force. In 1900, two-thirds of them worked.

Of course, not everybody who is forced to retire is unhappy. But recently a study of the attitudes of retirees was done for the National Council on Aging by pollster Louis Harris. Seventy-four percent of the respondents said they missed the money their job brought in, 73 percent missed the people at work, 62 percent missed the work itself, and 59 percent just missed the feeling of being useful.

It is not surprising that money worries ranked first. About 55 percent of retirees enter retirement in debt.

The average social security benefit for an elderly couple in the mid 1970s, for example, was $341 a month, or $4,092 annually. This was a little more than half the money needed to live on what the Bureau of

Chapter 15: Rights and Legislation

Labor Statistics called an Intermediate Budget. Such a budget allots only $30 a week for groceries, $170 a month for housing costs, and $27 a month for clothing costs.

Pensions do not help much, either. The median monthly pension benefit in the mid 1970s was $200 for people who worked till 65 and $224 for those who retired because of a disability. And many people do not have pensions.

What all this means is that an estimated 4.8 million people aged 65 or over are living in poverty. That makes the elderly the fastest growing poverty group in America.

Supporters of mandatory retirement contend that, without it, men and women would remain in jobs long after they passed their physical and mental prime. This would block the advancement of younger, more aggressive employees. But, in Dr. Butler's opinion, this argument overlooks one important fact. "Chronological age," he says, "is an inaccurate measure of how old someone is. Aging occurs unevenly. One may be at very different ages at the same time in terms of mental capacity, physical health, endurance, creativity, and emotions. Thus, while one person may be 'old' at 60 or 65, another may remain vigorous well into the late 70s."

Adapted from John Kelly, "Is Retirement Fatal?" *Family Weekly*, September 28, 1975, pp. 4, 7.

Questions

1 What are *three* problems many retired people have? Do you think that banning mandatory retirement might affect those problems? If so, how?

2 What are *two* reasons why many people are forced to retire? Do you think those are good reasons for retirement? Explain.

3 Should people have the right *not* to retire? Why or why not?

◇ Imagine you own a business. Would you force any of your employees to retire? If so, how would you decide who would have to retire and who would not? Would you want someone else to use those same reasons to force your retirement? Why or why not?

PROBLEM: HOW MUCH SHOULD THE PUBLIC HAVE A RIGHT TO KNOW?

As this chapter has shown, recent laws passed by Congress have increased public access to government documents. Yet some people say we still do not know enough about what our government does. They want new and broader laws. Others say we are prying too deeply into what should be confidential aspects of government. They believe that government cannot work smoothly without a certain amount of secrecy. Since the days of the American Revolution, our government has struggled with this problem: Where to draw the line between secrecy and openness?

Our government has always kept some of its workings a secret. George Washington, as commander of the Revolutionary Army, did not publicly reveal his battle plans against the British. Lydia Darragh, a young Philadelphia woman, kept secret her intention of smuggling British battle plans out of that city to Washington's army. The Constitutional Convention of 1787 kept its deliberations confidential until after it had adjourned.

Recently, some of the things that government officials have tried to keep secret have become public. For example, we now know that the Federal Bureau of Investigation used illegal techniques, such as burglary, to spy on law-abiding citizens, and that the Central Intelligence Agency opened mail illegally. When these acts became public, top officials promised they would not happen again.

Some people argued that such abuses of private rights might better be prevented in the future if the FBI and CIA operated under less secrecy. Others took a different stand. They argued that secrecy is essential to the FBI in investigating crime and to the CIA in gathering intelligence. To "let the sunshine in" would make both agencies useless, these people said.

Following are arguments on two sides of this complicated issue. As you read them, ask yourself:

- *In what circumstances does the public have a broad right to know what the government is doing?*
- *In what circumstances does the government have a right to maintain secrecy?*

A Right to Know

1. We have a representative form of government. We have a right to know what our representatives and all of our government agencies are doing. After all, they are our "public servants."

2. Government officials often misuse the right to classify documents as "military secrets." They do so to protect themselves, not to protect the country.

3. Excessive secrecy allows government officials to do what *they* want to do—not what the people want them to do. It opens the way to bribery, corruption, and violations of our basic rights.

4. We rightly scorn other forms of government for employing secret police. To protect our freedoms, we must abolish secret police actions in our own country—especially those that violate the law.

5. Government secrecy is often used to protect special interests. The public should know who benefits from such government policies as tax loopholes, subsidies to business, and welfare payments.

A Right to Secrecy

1. Our government must be able to defend the nation against its enemies. Military planning often requires secrecy. An enemy that knew all our plans could find ways to break through our defenses.

2. Our government must find out what other nations might be plotting against us. To do this, we need spies. Their lives would be endangered by too much openness.

3. Our government has agencies that fight crime. They must be able to collect information about criminal activities. Unless much of this information is kept secret, the criminals might escape punishment.

4. Sometimes it would do more harm than good to reveal past government actions that violated the law. Such violations should be discouraged, but if they turned up valuable information, the government should be able to make use of it.

5. Innocent people might be deprived of their rights if some government records are revealed. For example, individual income tax records should be kept secret. So should the names of people who receive welfare.

Questions

1 What do you think is the strongest argument in favor of the public's right to know? Why?

2 What do you think is the strongest argument in favor of the government's right to secrecy? Why?

3 What might happen if the government revealed *all* its operations? If it kept *all* of them secret?

◌ Where would *you* draw the line between the right to know and the right to secrecy? List examples.

Chapter 15 Review

Developing Your Political Vocabulary

1 How would you define *discrimination*? Name a type of discrimination that is forbidden by federal law. Name a type of discrimination that is not forbidden.

2 What does the phrase *separate but equal* mean? Use it in a sentence.

3 Define the following terms. Then use each in a sentence about the federal government.
    a segregated
    b median income
    c creditor
    d mandatory retirement

Recalling and Comparing

1 Name *three* ways, now illegal, in which federal or state governments discriminated against blacks.

2 Name *two* ways, now illegal, in which federal or state governments discriminated against women. Name *three* ways, now illegal, in which private individuals discriminated against women.

3 What categories of people besides blacks and women have gained more rights as a result of laws discussed in this chapter? Explain.

4 Of all the laws discussed in this chapter, which *three* do you think have the most meaning for you. Why?

Special Activities

1 Make a special bulletin-board display that illustrates recent actions by Congress on civil rights or basic freedoms.

2 Make a scrapbook of newspaper and magazine cartoons dealing with laws against discrimination.

3 Using your library, research and write a paper on the topic, "Continuing Discrimination against————." Choose any group that you think is discriminated against.

4 Choose a congressional bill now in the news that deals with basic freedoms. Write both senators from your state requesting their opinion about the proposed legislation. Write a report evaluating their positions.

5 Draw a poster or cartoon that illustrates a problem involved in the right to know and the right to secrecy in government.

6 Make a study of laws that prohibit discrimination in housing. Then study the difficulties in applying the laws. Report your findings to the class.

7 Make a comparative study of laws affecting the rights of children and old people. Summarize your findings in a chart.

8 Consider what might be arguments for and against the following statement: "Since 1964, Congress has not passed enough legislation on individual rights and liberties." Do you agree or disagree? Why?

Chapter **16**

Rights and Court Decisions

Decisions of the federal courts have played a vital role in giving meaning to our constitutional rights. In Chapter 11, we saw that Chief Justice Marshall believed in a "living Constitution," one that could be "adapted to the various crises of human affairs" (page 210). We have now examined the basic principles set down in the Constitution. We have seen how laws passed by Congress have embodied those principles in rules concerning one major field of human affairs—individual rights. But it is the application of those rules that counts. How well the application fits both the principles and the rules is a matter for the federal courts to decide.

Since the 1960s, the federal courts have taken the lead in guaranteeing individuals certain basic rights. United States District Courts and Courts of Appeals have handed down some landmark decisions, just as the Supreme Court has done. Because of limits of space, this chapter will concentrate on Supreme Court decisions. Those decisions can affect every one of us. Like the Constitution itself, they are "the law of the land."

―― **Goals** ――

- To learn how the courts have interpreted our basic freedoms.
- To see how the exercise of our basic freedoms has changed over time under the influence of court decisions.

Chapter 16: Rights and Court Decisions

- *To consider the rights of news reporters.*
- *To consider whether the use of lie-detector tests should be allowed.*

JUDICIAL INTERPRETATION OF FIRST AMENDMENT FREEDOMS

The First Amendment is one of the key parts of the Bill of Rights, and one of the most difficult to interpret. What does this amendment mean when it says: "Congress shall make no law respecting an establishment of religion" and no law "abridging the freedom of speech, or of the press"? Does a law banning obscenity abridge the freedom of speech? It is up to the federal courts, and ultimately the United States Supreme Court, to decide.

One thing the Supreme Court has decided is that all parts of the First Amendment now are binding on state governments as well as on the federal government. This is because of the Fourteenth Amendment, which requires "due process of law" and bars states from making laws that "abridge the privileges and immunities of citizens of the United States." The Court held that these words cover all rights that are "basic or essential to the American concept of liberty." First Amendment rights, the Court said, are definitely covered. So are some—but not all—of the other parts of the Bill of Rights.

Following are a few of the questions about the First Amendment that the Supreme Court has been called upon to settle. You can see that the issues involved are varied and often complex.

Freedom of Religion

School Prayers. In 1962, the Court ruled that it is unconstitutional to have public school students recite a prayer written by school officials, even though the prayer was nondenominational and students could ask to be excused

Parochial schools like this one in Albuquerque, New Mexico, can receive state aid, but only for nonreligious purposes.

from saying it *(Engel v. Vitale)*. The following year the Court struck down a state law that required Bible verses to be read in schools each day *(School District of Abington Township v. Schempp)*. In each case, the Court said that the practice violated the separation of church and state.

Parochial Schools. Many religious denominations conduct their own elementary and secondary schools. The purpose of these parochial schools is to give students religious training along with a general education. In general, the Court has held that states may provide money that aids students attending the schools but that does not advance the teaching of religion. Thus, states can provide free bus rides and *secular*—that is, nonreligious—textbooks to parochial school students. Also per-

Chapter 16: Rights and Court Decisions

Militant groups like the American Nazi Party are granted the freedom of speech and assembly provided to all under the First Amendment.

In the early 1950s, Senator Joseph McCarthy, below right, publicly accused many people of being Communists. Many were accused just because of things they had said or groups they had joined in their youth. These people suffered even though all they were accused of was legal under the First Amendment. McCarthy was later censured by the Senate.

mitted are hot lunches as well as remedial training and counseling outside the school.

But in *Meek v. Pittenger* (1975), the Court ruled that states may *not* provide church-related schools with films, magazines, charts, recordings, maps, laboratory equipment, projectors, or similar equipment.

Church-Related Colleges. The Court has been slightly more lenient in allowing states to aid church-related colleges. For example, colleges may receive state money for constructing buildings, so long as the buildings are for nonreligious instruction. In 1976, the Court upheld a Maryland program granting state money to private colleges for general use.

Freedom of Speech

Speech against the Government. The right to speak against the government has at times been restricted, particularly in wartime and when public feelings run high. The Supreme Court has tip-toed along a wavering line in deciding which restrictions to permit and which to rule out.

During World War I, Congress passed the Sedition Law of 1918. It banned any "disloyal, profane, scurrilous, or abusive language about the form of government, the Constitution, soldiers and sailors, flag or uniform of the armed forces." The Supreme Court held the law constitutional. The Court upheld the punishment of people responsible for leaflets that opposed the war or intervention in Russia by the United States after the 1917 revolution.

By World War II, however, the Court was beginning to question such restrictions. It imposed a *clear-and-present-danger* rule that had been stated in 1919 by Justice Oliver Wendell Holmes in the case of Schenck v. United States. Holmes used the example of a person falsely crying fire in a crowded theater and causing panic. The cry itself was not wrong, but the circumstances made it wrong. Thus, said Holmes, freedom of speech should not be limited unless there was "a clear and present danger"—one that was obvious and immediate—that what was said would bring about actions "that Congress has a right to prevent." Holmes's clear-and-present-danger rule is now used as a general guideline in cases involving freedom of speech.

The Smith Act of 1940 made it unlawful for anyone to advocate the violent overthrow of the United States government or to knowingly be a member of a group with that aim. The United States Communist Party supported passage of the Smith Act since it seemed to be aimed at Nazis and Fascists. But when eleven Communist party leaders were tried and convicted under the act in 1949 they appealed on the ground that the law violated their First Amendment rights. In 1951, the Supreme Court upheld their conviction (Dennis v. United States).

In a later case, however, the Court was guided by the clear-and-present-danger rule (Yates v. United States, 1957). Again, leaders of the Communist party were involved. This time the Court upset their conviction. The Court held that no one could be punished just for advocating communism. That was within the right of freedom of speech. What could be punished, the Court said, was speech that incited others to specific actions trying to overthrow the government by force.

Freedom of the Press

High School Newspapers. There are some 35,000 high school newspapers in this country. In the past, many of them were routinely censored by school officials. Contro-

The Supreme Court has ruled that high school students are entitled to the same First Amendment rights as adults. These workers on a student newspaper have freedom of the press.

A federal judge ruled that this *New York Times* reporter, Earl Caldwell, had to reveal his sources before a grand jury.

Reporters' Rights. Many news reporters maintain that freedom of the press protects their right to refuse to reveal the names of people who have given them confidential information. This claim sometimes conflicts with the right of grand juries to call reporters as witnesses to testify about possible crimes by others.

Earl Caldwell, a reporter for the *New York Times*, wrote a story based on confidential sources. When a grand jury subpoenaed Caldwell and asked who his sources were, he claimed a First Amendment right not to answer. In 1972, the Supreme Court rejected Caldwell's claim by a vote of 5–4. The majority argued that grand jury proceedings are secret, and that this serves as a protection of a reporter's sources.

Some states have since passed laws specifying certain circumstances in which reporters may keep their sources confidential. These are known as *shield laws.*

"Gag Orders." Which is more important: the First Amendment guarantee of freedom of the press or the Sixth Amendment guarantee of a right to a fair trial? Sometimes the two rights seem to be in conflict.

In October 1975, Erwin Charles Simants was charged with murder. It was a big story, and the press covered it in detail. Judge Hugh Stuart, fearing that Simants' right to a fair trial might be damaged by such publicity, issued a "gag order" forbidding the press to report testimony that was taken before the trial. Finally, Simants went on trial, was found guilty, and was sentenced to death.

The press meanwhile appealed the judge's "gag order," and in 1976, the Supreme Court declared it unconstitutional. The justices did not deny that pretrial publicity might threaten a person's right to a fair trial. The Court held, however, that Simants could have gotten a fair trial without the judge's limits on press freedom. The justices suggested other methods, such as carefully screening jurors for prejudice *(Nebraska Press Association v. Stuart).*

versial material, such as criticism of school board policies, was often removed. When students complained, school officials replied that school newspapers are supported by tax money. They are owned by the public, not by the students. Besides, said many officials, the First Amendment does not apply to high school students.

A few years ago, the Supreme Court decided differently. It held that high school students enjoy the same First Amendment rights as adults. The justices declared: "Students do not shed their constitutional rights to freedom of speech and expression at the schoolhouse gate." The Court said that students could express their views on any topic in school so long as they did not "materially and substantially" interfere with the operation of the school.

Chapter 16: Rights and Court Decisions

The question of free press or fair trial is one that cannot be settled once and for all. It requires the same delicate balancing of rights that so many other freedoms do.

Questions

1 What are *four* decisions of the U.S. Supreme Court since 1962 that deal with First Amendment freedoms? Of these, which *two* do you think most important? Explain.

2 In what way might the First Amendment guarantee of freedom of the press clash with the Sixth Amendment right to a fair trial? How would *you* resolve such a conflict? Explain.

⬠ Choose *one* ruling of the Supreme Court discussed in this section and tell why you agree or disagree with it.

JUDICIAL INTERPRETATION OF FOURTH AMENDMENT FREEDOMS

As we have seen, the Fourth Amendment forbids "unreasonable searches and seizures." But what is reasonable and what is not? Again, it has been up to the federal courts to decide.

Illegally Seized Evidence. For many years, the courts gave great leeway to law enforcement officials. The courts put only mild restraints on how authorities could conduct searches and seizures. The main requirement was that no undue violence be used. Even if a search was conducted illegally, the evidence obtained might be used in a trial.

In 1914, however, the Supreme Court cracked down. The case, *Weeks v. United States,* involved a seizure of some papers. There was no question that the seizure had violated the Fourth Amendment. In such a case, ruled the Court, the evidence could no longer be admitted in federal courts. This became known as the *exclusionary rule,* because it excluded illegally seized evidence from the courts. It applied only to federal courts until 1961 when the Court extended it to the states in the case of *Mapp v. Ohio.*

Wiretapping and "Bugging." Modern technology has raised new questions about the Fourth Amendment. When the Bill of Rights was adopted, there were no telephones. The tapping of phones was not an issue then and did not become one until the 1920s when many people had phones. Then federal agents tapped the phones of a group of bootleggers in the state of Washington. The agents took notes of conversations they overheard, and the notes helped to convict the bootleggers of violating federal law.

The bootleggers appealed their conviction on the ground that the phone taps amounted to an unreasonable search. In *Olmstead v. United States* (1928), a 5–4 majority on the Supreme Court rejected that argument. Writing for the majority, Chief Justice William Howard Taft said: "The [Fourth] Amendment does not forbid what was done here. There was no searching. There was no seizure. The evidence was secured by the use of the sense of hearing and that only. There was no entry of the houses or offices of the defendants."

An opposing view was set forth in a dissent by Justice Louis D. Brandeis. He said that Amendment IV had not been designed merely for the narrow purpose of protecting private homes against trespass. It was designed, he said, to protect an individual's "right to be let alone—the most comprehensive of rights and the right most valued by civilized men. To protect that right, every unjustifiable intrusion by the Government upon the privacy of the individual, whatever the means employed, must be deemed a violation of the Fourth Amendment."

Brandeis's view eventually won out as phone-tapping equipment and eavesdropping devices became more and more effective. In 1967, the Court ruled that Amendment IV

Searches for wiretapping and bugging devices, as shown here, are means of guarding our constitutional freedoms.

Fourth and Fifth Amendment rules provide protections against the use of wiretapping and bugging except in special cases.

protects *people,* and not just buildings, against unreasonable searches and seizure. No wiretaps or electronic "bugs" are now permitted unless they are authorized by a court, in advance. As with search warrants, their limits must be defined clearly.

Other issues raised by wiretaps continue to come before the Court. Sometimes, for example, wiretaps produce information that can be used to convict people who are not themselves being investigated. Suppose that officials get a warrant to tap the phone of Jane Doe and through the tap hear evidence that her friend Mary Jones has committed a crime. Can such information be used in court? In a 1974 case, the Supreme Court said it can.

Self-incrimination. The Fourth Amendment's rules on search and seizure are sometimes linked to the Fifth Amendment's protection against self-incrimination. Can a seizure sometimes have the effect of forcing one to give testimony against oneself? In some cases, the Supreme Court has ruled that it can. Yet there are exceptions.

A defendant contested the use of evidence seized in a lawful search, with a warrant naming the items to be seized. The claim was that the use of such evidence violated the defendant's right against self-incrimination. The Court, in a 7–2 decision, rejected the claim on the grounds that there was no violation of the Fifth Amendment because the accused had not been required to aid in obtaining the evidence *(Anderson v. Maryland).* And in a later case, the Court upheld the right of police to make an unannounced search on the basis of a court-approved warrant even if there is no suspicion of crime.

"Stop and Frisk." When police officers are making an arrest, they often search the suspect for weapons. But can they "frisk" someone they do not plan to arrest? For example, can they stop and frisk someone in an unruly crowd? In *Terry v. Ohio* (1968), the Supreme Court upheld Ohio's "stop-and-frisk" law. The Court said such searches are permissible when they seem necessary for the safety of the police and others present.

The Supreme Court has upheld the right of law officers to "stop and frisk" when this is required for public safety.

Mass arrests made at this demonstration in Washington, D.C., were declared illegal by the federal courts.

Mass Arrests. In May 1971, thousands of demonstrators moved through the streets of Washington, D.C., and sat down in the streets to block traffic. They were protesting the Vietnam war. The police swooped through the city, arresting anyone who looked like a demonstrator. They picked up some 13,000 people, most of whom were held for a few days and then released without being charged. The federal courts held that such mass arrests were illegal and that those arrested and not charged were entitled to compensation.

Sometimes people object that the federal courts "handcuff" the police. They say it would be much more efficient to let the police do their job the way they see fit. In their opinion, the police cannot operate efficiently unless they can arrest and question people at will, eavesdrop, or break into a criminal's room if they feel that this is necessary.

Such tactics might be more "efficient," but efficiency is not the first goal of our legal system. Justice is. The federal courts have held that justice can only be assured when the police are required to respect the constitutional rights of all citizens.

Questions

1 What are at least *five* decisions that the Supreme Court has taken about Fourth Amendment freedoms? Which *two* of these decisions do you think are most significant? Explain.

2 When do you think the government should be allowed to search a person's property? Why?

3 When do you think the government should be allowed to wiretap or "bug" private conversations? Why?

◇ Do you agree or disagree with this statement: "Innocent people have nothing to fear from a police search, so the police should be allowed to search when and where they want"? Explain.

Ever since the Miranda case in 1966, law enforcement officers have had to show the Miranda card when making an arrest.

SELF-INCRIMINATION, A FAIR TRIAL, AND CRUEL AND UNUSUAL PUNISHMENT

Among the many rights guaranteed in the Bill of Rights is the right not to have to testify against oneself (Fifth Amendment). Another is the right to a fair trial (Sixth Amendment). The Eighth Amendment forbids cruel and unusual punishments.

Self-incrimination. In 1950, Congress passed the Internal Security Act, aimed at the Communist party. The act required communist organizations and their officers to register each year with the federal government. At the same time, the act made advocacy of communism a crime. Officers of the Communist party refused to register, and the case reached the Supreme Court. In 1965, the Court ruled the act unconstitutional. The Court said the government could not force a person to register as a Communist because, under the law as written, that amounted to self-incrimination.

A second aspect of self-incrimination was involved in the famous Miranda decision of 1966 *(Miranda v. Arizona)*. Miranda had been arrested for a crime and had confessed after extensive police questioning. The Supreme Court overturned his conviction because the police had not told Miranda of two specific rights: (1) the right to remain silent and (2) the right to have a lawyer present during questioning.

The second of these safeguards for accused persons had been set down in 1964 in *Escobedo v. Illinois*. In that case, the Supreme Court threw out a murder conviction based on a confession. The defendant had asked repeatedly to see a lawyer during questioning. The Court held that a suspect being questioned in custody had a right to see a lawyer.

The rights of juveniles in police custody are more complicated. Does a juvenile have a right to talk to his or her parents? Should an adult be advised of the juvenile's rights?

In 1971, a 6-year-old was beaten to death in Philadelphia. Police arrested a fifteen-year-old, who confessed to the crime during questioning. He was later tried and convicted. According to testimony, police officers had advised the youth four times of his right to have a lawyer and to remain silent during the questioning. The last time, the youth's mother was present—but that was after the confession.

The Pennsylvania Supreme Court overturned the conviction on the grounds that the boy's mother should have been allowed to see him earlier. The court cited a previous ruling

293

that, when a parent is present, the parent, and not just the juvenile, must be advised of the suspect's rights. The United States Supreme Court let the Pennsylvania ruling stand.

Right to a Lawyer. Often a suspect in a criminal trial is too poor to be able to afford a lawyer. Can a suspect be tried without one?

In *Gideon v. Wainwright* (1963), the Court held that a person accused of a *felony*— a major crime—in a state court is entitled to free counsel if he or she cannot afford a lawyer. But what about a person convicted of a *misdemeanor*—a less serious crime? In 1972, the Court answered that question. It held that a defendant has a right to a lawyer in any trial that might result in a jail term. Before a trial, the judge must determine if a jail term might result. If so, the judge must see to it that a lawyer is available. A defendant does not have to use a lawyer and has a right to conduct his or her own defense.

The right to a lawyer does not normally apply in an *appeal,* the Court has ruled.

Right to a Jury Trial. How serious does a crime have to be for a defendant to have a right to a jury trial? It depends on what the punishment may be, the Court ruled in 1970. If the punishment could be 6 or more months in jail, then a defendant has a right to a jury trial.

How large should a jury be? Traditionally, criminal juries have contained twelve members. But when some states reduced the size of juries for some criminal cases to six members, the Court held that this was constitutional. In a unanimous 1978 decision, the Court declared that the number could not be reduced below six. The Court has also upheld the use of six-member juries in civil trials in federal courts.

Cruel and Unusual Punishment. Since the Eighth Amendment was adopted, public ideas about what kinds of punishments are "cruel and unusual" have been changing. Some people have argued that the death penalty is "cruel and unusual" and thus unconstitutional. But the Supreme Court has rejected that argument.

In 1972, however, the Court held that the *way* the death penalty was then applied violated the Eighth Amendment *(Furman v. Georgia).* The Court said the death penalty was imposed "capriciously"—that is, in a way hard to explain or predict. As a result, the federal government and most states revised their laws dealing with the death penalty. They set down narrow guidelines that gave judges and juries little leeway. The laws specified that in some circumstances—for instance, a murder committed by someone previously convicted of murder—the death penalty was required.

In 1976 and 1977, the Supreme Court accepted some of these new laws. The majority decision made clear that the Court did not consider the death penalty to be "cruel and unusual punishment" when carried out under proper guidelines. Even so, the Court later overturned an Ohio law on the grounds that the guidelines it set were too narrow.

Another type of punishment—paddling—also came under Supreme Court scrutiny. In 1977, the Court held that a teacher may paddle an unruly pupil. A student has no constitutional right to an informal hearing before the paddling.

Questions

1 According to the Supreme Court, what is *one* form of self-incrimination under the Fifth Amendment?

2 What was specially important about each of these Supreme Court decisions?
 a *Miranda v. Arizona* (1966)
 b *Escobedo v. Illinois* (1964)
 c *Gideon v. Wainwright* (1963)

3 How has the Supreme Court distinguished between laws on the death penalty that violate the Eighth Amendment and those that do not violate it?

4 What do you think is "cruel and unusual punishment"? Cite an example.

◌ Do you feel that the death penalty is ever necessary? Explain.

EQUAL PROTECTION OF THE LAWS AND DUE PROCESS

Of all the provisions in the Constitution and its amendments, perhaps none have received so much attention as those that guarantee equal protection of the laws and due process of law. These rights are expressed in the Fourteenth Amendment.

The Fourteenth Amendment places two very important restraints on state governments: they must observe "due process of law," and they must grant everyone "equal protection of the laws." As you know, a due process clause also appears in the Fifth Amendment. The Court's attitude toward these provisions has changed dramatically over the years. Let's look first at due process.

Until late in the nineteenth century, the Supreme Court held, with few exceptions, that due process dealt only with the *procedures* of government. These procedures had to follow the law; they could not be arbitrary. This concept of *procedural due process* was involved in the Native American land claim case discussed in Chapter 14 (pages 262–264).

Gradually the Court came to apply the due process clause to the *substance* of laws—in other words, the content of laws rather than the legal process. Was a law's purpose unreasonable? Did a law allow unreasonable interference with a person's property rights? This was the concept of *substantive due process*. It placed Supreme Court justices in a position of determining some of the most basic elements of social policy.

Beginning in the 1890s, the Supreme Court used this concept of substantive due process to protect property rights against government regulation. Here is an example: Nebraska had a law setting rates on freight shipment within the state. The railroads appealed in the federal courts, presenting evidence to support their argument that the rates were unreasonably low. The Supreme Court agreed. It ruled that the Nebraska law was

Due process was suspended under wartime conditions when Japanese Americans were relocated in the 1940s.

unconstitutional because it deprived a person—in this case, a corporation—of property without due process of law (*Smyth v. Ames*, 1898).

This use of substantive due process was in line with the economic policy of *laissez faire* (LESS-ay-FAIR). This was a policy, followed at the time, of minimum government interference in business matters. But attitudes changed. By the 1930s, a majority in Congress and in many state legislatures believed that the government had a right to restrict private enterprise for the good of the whole society.

Finally, the Court stopped using the concept of substantive due process to protect property rights from government regulation. In recent years, it has linked substantive due process with the "equal protection" clause and used those clauses to protect individuals' civil rights.

The equal protection clause has had an equally varied history. In *Plessy v. Ferguson* (1896), as we have seen, the Supreme Court ruled that racially segregated facilities did not

An end to housing segregation is a measure that some people think necessary in order to end school segregation.

deprive blacks of "equal protection of the laws." That decision was reversed in the 1954 ruling in *Brown v. Board of Education of Topeka*. The Court declared that school segregation deprived black children of "the equal protection of the laws guaranteed by the Fourteenth Amendment."

The Court has continued to use both the due process and the equal protection clauses to ban various forms of discrimination. A recent case came to the Court from Chicago. A group of blacks had sued the Chicago Housing Authority. They argued that the Housing Authority was keeping blacks out of white neighborhoods. The Housing Authority received some of its money from the Department of Housing and Urban Development (HUD). So the black group sued that federal agency, too.

In 1976, the Supreme Court found both housing agencies—city and federal—guilty of illegal racial discrimination. It ordered sweeping remedies. Lower courts, said the Supreme Court, could now order HUD to promote desegregated housing throughout a six-county area. That area, within the jurisdiction of the Chicago Housing Authority, was populated mainly by whites in 1976.

The Court has also relied on the equal protection clause in sex discrimination cases. For example, it was common in the past for states to discriminate between the sexes in setting the age at which children become adults. Utah's laws set 18 as the age for girls and 21 for boys. In 1975, the Supreme Court ruled the Utah law unconstitutional.

Sometimes laws discriminated against men. For years, the federal government did not pay social security benefits to a man when his working wife died and left children in his care, even though, then as now, a surviving wife in the same circumstances received benefits. Stephen C. Wiesenfeld was turned down when he applied for social security benefits after his wife died in childbirth. He sued, the case went to the Supreme Court, and he won. In an 8–0 decision in 1975, the Court said the government was guilty of unconstitutional sex discrimination against men.

Other Supreme Court decisions have expanded the rights of students. In a series of decisions, the Court has ruled, for instance,

Recent Supreme Court rulings, as well as actions by Congress, have helped to clarify students' rights.

that public school students are entitled to certain procedural rights before they can be suspended. They must be told the nature of the charges against them, given an explanation of the evidence, and allowed to tell their side of the story. In a 1978 decision, the Court said that no injury need be proved because "the right of procedural due process is absolute." If this right is violated, students can sue and collect "nominal" damages of less than one dollar.

As we have seen, the issues involved in federal rights cases are almost endless. We have mentioned only a sampling of court rulings. There are many more. Each year, state and federal courts hand down many decisions, spelling out in detail what our rights and liberties mean in practice. That is why we call our Constitution a living document—one that is ever growing, ever changing.

Questions

1 How has the Supreme Court's use of the concept of substantive due process changed from the 1890s to the present?

2 What constitutional guarantee did the Supreme Court cite as the basis of its 1954 ruling that school segregation is unconstitutional?

3 What have been two key rulings by the Supreme Court about sex discrimination?

4 Discuss a recent ruling by the Supreme Court about the Fourteenth Amendment rights of students.

◌ What is most important to *you* about the Fifth and Fourteenth Amendments? Why?

PROBLEM: TO WHAT EXTENT SHOULD REPORTERS BE ALLOWED TO PROTECT THEIR NEWS SOURCES?

All of the court cases discussed in this chapter have been hotly debated. In each case, people disagreed about the legal and constitutional issues. The same disagreement has accompanied our Constitution at every step of the way. When it was being drawn up, people

Chapter 16: Rights and Court Decisions

clashed over what it should say. When it was amended, people argued over each amendment. There were at least two sides and often several. The give and take of such public debate is at the heart of our democratic process.

The fact that the Supreme Court has ruled is rarely enough to settle a debate. Often, the ruling leads to further questions. Take the Court's 1972 ruling in the Caldwell case (page 289). As we saw, the Court declared that the First Amendment does not give journalists the right to refuse to name their sources to a grand jury in secret. But what if reporters are questioned in open court? Should they have to identify sources then?

Since the early 1960s, more than 200 reporters have refused to identify sources. Many have served time in jail as a result.

The following account discusses two cases and public attitudes on the issues involved. As you read, ask yourself:

- *What are the key arguments in favor of forced disclosure of reporters' sources?*
- *What are the key arguments against forced disclosure?*

To Tell or Not to Tell

Twice in the early 1970s, reporters were jailed for not disclosing sources. Both cases received wide publicity.

Peter J. Bridge, a newspaper reporter in New Jersey, wrote a story about an attempt to bribe a commissioner of the Newark Housing Authority. The story named the commissioner and quoted her as saying she had been offered $10,000 if she would vote "right" on a new executive director for the authority.

A New Jersey grand jury subpoenaed Bridge to testify about his story. When he went before the grand jury, all he would do was confirm the truth of what he had written. He refused to answer further questions. He

Myron Farber, a newspaper reporter, was jailed for refusing to turn in his notes for use in a murder trial.

said if he did he might be revealing confidential sources.

A second case involved William T. Farr, a Los Angeles reporter. He wrote an article about the 1970 murder trial of Charles Manson. When Farr refused to answer questions about the article, he was jailed for contempt of court.

Both reporters had been doing *investigative reporting*. They had tried to dig out facts about important issues. In doing so, they had reported information about possible crimes that had been committed.

Two conflicting rights were at stake. The reporters had a right to do their job— reporting the news. The government had a right to uncover and punish crime. Courts often have to balance these rights. They must weigh the First Amendment rights of the press against the needs of the criminal justice system.

A number of people were asked what they thought about forcing reporters to reveal confidential sources. Here are some of their answers:

A 25-year-old newspaper reporter: "A reporter should not be forced to divulge his sources. If he has to, he won't be able to get any more inside information. The information he provides is more important than the person who gave it, anyway. So why should the court insist on names?"

A 66-year-old mover and hauler: "Why should the reporter who is trying to get inside dope be made to reveal it and become a target of criminals? He should be kept safe from retaliation."

An elderly male homeowner: "I don't like the 'big brother' approach of requiring someone to reveal his sources. How's the newspaper reporter going to get information if he doesn't protect his sources?"

A 23-year-old student: "Such procedures intimidate people and undermine the system. They are against the spirit of the Constitution."

A 32-year-old mail carrier: "If the court forces a man to reveal who gave him information, this is an invasion of one's privacy—a breach of confidence."

A 38-year-old telephone repair worker: "The reporter is under oath to tell the truth—the whole truth. He shouldn't be given special privileges."

A 27-year-old data processor: "If information is available that can help deal with a crime, then it should be revealed. The courts protect criminals enough as it is."

A 29-year-old banker: "If a newspaperman is going to offer information, he ought to be able to back it up and reveal his source. How else can the courts tell if his information is true or not?"

In 1972, pollsters interviewed 1,462 people aged 18 and older in all parts of the nation. They asked the following question:

"Suppose a newspaper reporter obtains information for a news article he is writing from a person who asks that his name be withheld. Do you think that the reporter should or should not be required to reveal the name of his man if he is taken to court to testify about the information in his news article?"

Here are the responses, broken down according to educational experience:

	Should %	Should Not %	No Opinion %
National total	34	57	9
College background	27	68	5
High school	37	55	8
Grade school	35	48	17

Adapted from "Reporters' Right to Protect Sources Backed," A Gallup Poll Exclusive, San Antonio *Express-News,* December 3, 1972, p. 20A, © Field Enterprises, Inc.

Questions

1 What are two arguments *against* having reporters reveal their sources?

2 What are two arguments *for* having reporters reveal their sources?

3 Do you think reporters should always have to tell their sources, if ordered by a judge? Explain.

○ Should all people have the right to refuse to reveal the source of a story they have told? If so, in what circumstances?

PROBLEM: SHOULD LIE DETECTOR TESTS BE ALLOWED?

Many experts maintain that polygraph, or lie detector, machines can show whether someone is telling the truth or not. But some experts say lie-detector tests can be inaccurate. They may indicate a person is lying when the person is telling the truth. Often, lawyers seek to introduce lie-detector tests as evidence in court. The courts have no uniform policy on the matter. Some courts allow the tests as evidence, and some do not.

The following account discusses the use of lie detectors in one state. As you read, ask yourself:

- *What are some arguments in favor of using polygraph tests?*
- *What are some arguments against using such tests?*

The Truth Machine

Thousands of people in Texas are hooked up to polygraph machines every year. Then an examiner starts asking questions:

"Have you ever done anything to be ashamed of?"

"Have you ever lied in your life?"

"Have you stolen any merchandise from a place where you have worked?"

"Have you ever been placed in jail?"

"Have you ever used narcotics?"

As the people answer, moving pens make lines on paper. The examiners say that the lines show whether or not the answers are truthful.

Many of the people hooked up to these machines are not suspected of any crime. They are applying for jobs. In San Antonio, at least fifty firms use lie detectors to screen potential employees.

"Employee dishonesty is a big problem," said the manager of a grocery.

Many firms use the tests on existing employees as well as new ones. According to a polygraph operator, one chain discovered that 90 percent of its employees were taking home at least small amounts of cash or merchandise. Those "small" amounts were said to add up to more than $1.5 million a year. When the employees were tested again 6 months later, only 3 percent turned up as repeaters.

"Our company does not fire employees for small thefts the first time they are caught by the machine," a supermarket manager said. "Spot checks serve as a psychological deterrent. The best employees are those who have been caught once. They won't take the chance to get caught again."

Critics charge that the lie detector tests are an invasion of rights and privacy. "I was asked about very personal matters," claimed one man applying for a job. The man said he told a polygraph operator about some traffic warrants he had not paid. "He told me to go in another room and wait. Next thing I knew, police were arresting me for the warrants." Answers to polygraph tests are supposed to be kept confidential.

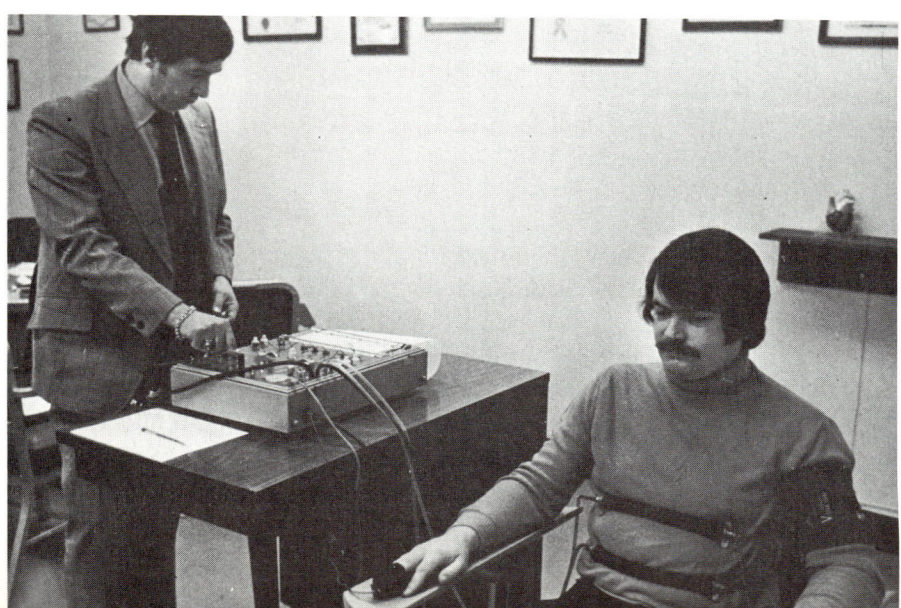

Polygraphs work on the principle that when people lie, their bodies undergo physical changes. The polygraph records such changes as they occur during questioning.

Chapter 16: Rights and Court Decisions

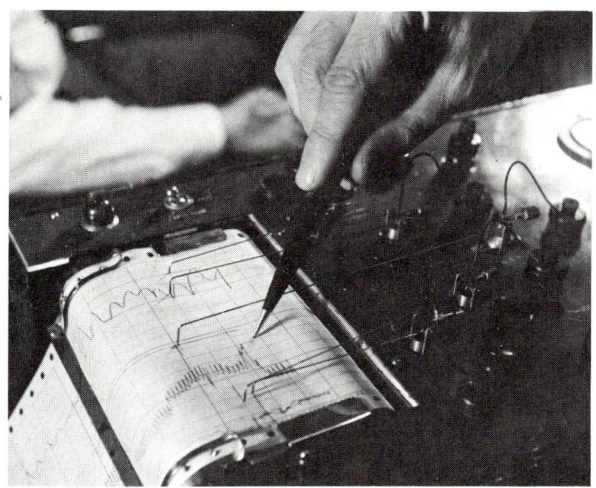

In this test, the bodily changes show up as wave patterns.

"A lot of people have been unjustly hurt by incompetent polygraph examiners," said attorney Freeman L. Mittenthal. He once represented a man who had been turned down for employment by two companies as the result of a polygraph examination. One of the companies told him why. The polygraph report had indicated the man lied about his drinking habits, about thefts of property, and about narcotics.

The man went to another polygraph examiner. The second examiner said the tests showed he had not lied about the matters. The companies still refused to hire him, so he filed suit against the first polygraph examiner. He won $4,000 in damages. "This was strictly a case of negligence, and we know it happens all the time," said attorney Mittenthal.

Critics of the tests make a number of other charges. They say the tests are prejudiced against minorities. They say examiners are ill-trained, without a necessary background in such things as sociology. And they say that some examiners abuse their positions by obtaining unnecessary personal information.

Dan R. Barnes, a polygraph examiner, pointed out: "A person may refuse to answer any question asked."

"Sure a person can refuse to answer," said an attorney, "but it is then assumed you have something to hide. If a person feels that certain personal information is none of [the examiners'] business, he should have a right to privacy."

Another examiner, Joe Low, noted that Texas law requires polygraph operators to be licensed. "Texas was the fourth state to get a licensing law, and it is one of the strictest in the country," he said.

According to Low, polygraph operators must either have a college degree or 5 years' experience in investigative work acceptable to the Texas Polygraph Examining Board. In Low's view, a polygraph operator is an expert to whom others come for opinions. He compared polygraph operators to doctors and handwriting analysts.

Polygraph operator Barnes argued that businesses must be satisfied with polygraph tests, since they keep using them. He said much of the opposition stems from public misunderstanding of the polygraph.

Can polygraphs make mistakes? Yes. Estimates of their accuracy range from 85 to 95 percent.

Adapted from Jerry Deal, "Polygraph Called a Liar," San Antonio *Express-News,* February 29, 1976, pp. 1A, 8A, and "Polygraph Tests Save Millions of $s," San Antonio *Express,* March 1, 1976, p. 3A.

Questions

1 What are two arguments in favor of using polygraph tests?

2 What are two arguments opposed to the use of polygraph tests?

3 In what circumstances, if any, do you think polygraph tests should be allowed? Explain.

4 Do you think that the results of polygraph tests should be admitted as evidence in court? Why or why not?

◇ Do you think people should ever be *forced* to take a polygraph test? Explain.

Chapter 16 Review

Developing Your Political Vocabulary

1. How would you define *judicial interpretation?* Use the term in a sentence about individual rights.
2. What is the difference between *procedural due process* and *substantive due process?* Give an example of a claim that an individual might make under each concept.
3. Define the following ideas discussed in this chapter:
   a. clear-and-present-danger rule
   b. "gag orders"
   c. exclusionary rule
   d. investigative reporting

Recalling and Comparing

1. How could a decision of the United States Supreme Court extend or decrease the civil liberties we enjoy? Cite one example for an extension and one for a decrease.
2. Cite one example of a Supreme Court decision that reversed an earlier Supreme Court decision. Why do you think the Court reversed itself in that particular case?
3. Of all the Supreme Court decisions discussed in this chapter, which *two* do you think affect you the most? Explain.
4. Of all the amendments to the Constitution, which *three* do you think affect you the most? Why did you select those three?

Special Activities

1. Prepare a skit on a police arrest that illustrates an issue dealt with in this chapter. You may want to focus on the moment of arrest, the questioning of a suspect, or some other aspect of the case.
2. Ask members of the clergy of various faiths what their opinion is of United States Supreme Court decisions regarding religion and the public schools. Write a report giving the major points made both supporting and opposing the Court's decisions.
3. Make a special bulletin-board display that illustrates recent decisions by the United States Supreme Court about basic freedoms.
4. Prepare a report on a major United States Supreme Court decision on individual rights that has been made within the past year. Use newspapers, magazines, and other sources at a local library.
5. Consider what might be arguments for and against the following statement: "Since 1954, the United States Supreme Court has not done enough to protect our basic rights and personal freedoms." Do you agree or disagree? Explain.

Unit V Review

Improving Your Reading

Read the selection below and then answer the questions which follow it.

The United States Constitution may be amended in several ways. One way is for Congress to propose an amendment by a two-thirds vote of each house. Then the proposed amendment is sent to the states.

Another way is for the legislatures of at least two-thirds of the states to ask Congress to call a national constitutional convention. If this happens, Congress must call the convention, which then prepares the amendment.

No matter which way an amendment is proposed, at least three-fourths of the states must ratify it.

Many of the basic rights we enjoy today can be found in our first ten amendments. Together they form our Bill of Rights. They guarantee such things as freedom of religion, freedom of speech, freedom of the press, freedom of assembly, the right to petition, protection against unreasonable searches or fines, protection against cruel and unusual punishment, and trial by jury.

Other amendments also guard our freedoms. The Thirteenth Amendment, for example, forbids slavery. The Fourteenth Amendment guarantees various rights against abuse by state governments. The Fifteenth, Nineteenth, Twenty-third, Twenty-fourth, and Twenty-sixth Amendments extended the right to vote.

Congress has passed legislation that protects our rights in many ways. Congress has forbidden various types of discrimination, has protected the rights of persons accused of crime, and has set out rules to protect privacy.

The United States Supreme Court is the final interpreter of our rights. Over the years, the Court has changed its interpretation of some rights we have under the Constitution. Since the late 1950s, the Court, through its interpretation of the Constitution, has expanded our civil rights in various ways—and in the process it has stirred up many controversies.

1 In your own words, summarize this reading in *no more than four* sentences. Have your summary focus on what you regard as the four most important points made in the reading.

2 The term *individual liberties* can best be used to describe which *two* of the following topics discussed in the reading?

   a the process of amending the Constitution
   b the number of states required to approve an amendment to the Constitution
   c the Bill of Rights
   d the Thirteenth, Fifteenth, Nineteenth, Twenty-third, Twenty-fourth, and Twenty-sixth Amendments

3 Which *two* of the following topics discussed in the reading show ways in which our individual rights can be altered, other than through amendments?

   a laws passed by Congress
   b national constitutional conventions
   c ratification by three-fourths of the states
   d judicial interpretations by the federal courts

Developing Your Writing Skills: What Are Your Attitudes toward Government?

Writing a Paragraph

In this unit, you have considered some of the problems involved in defining our basic rights and putting them into practice. We have seen that people often disagree about just what our rights should be.

Think back over some of the disputes mentioned in this unit. See if any other disputes over fundamental rights occur to you. Then ask yourself:

- *What are four major questions about individual rights that people often disagree on?*
- *Why are these questions so controversial?*
- *Which one of those questions is most important to you?*

Complete the following topic sentence. Fill out the paragraph with arguments in support of your position.

Of the controversial questions about individual rights that I have noted, the one that is most important to me is _____
_____

Writing an Essay

In this unit, you have seen that Congress and the federal courts play a major role in defining our individual rights. Actions by the President and the state governments can also affect our rights. Write a brief essay, beginning with one or the other form of the following sentence: "Our governmental institutions (can/cannot) be counted on to protect our individual rights."

Recommended Reading

M. Glenn Abernathy, *Civil Liberties under the Constitution,* Dodd, Mead, New York, 1972.

Michael Dorman, *Under 21: A Young People's Guide to Legal Rights,* Dell, New York, 1970 (paperback).

Joel M. Gora, *The Rights of Reporters,* Avon Books, New York, 1974 (paperback).

Sylvia Law, *The Rights of the Poor,* Avon Books, New York, 1974 (paperback).

Alan Levine, *The Rights of Students,* Avon Books, New York, 1973 (paperback).

Anthony Lewis, *Gideon's Trumpet,* Vintage Books, New York, 1964 (paperback).

Robert S. Rivkin, *The Rights of Servicemen,* Avon Books, New York, 1972 (paperback).

Oliver Rosengart, *The Rights of Suspects,* Avon Books, New York, 1974 (paperback).

Susan C. Ross, *The Rights of Women,* Avon Books, New York, 1973 (paperback).

David Rubin, *The Rights of Teachers,* Avon Books, New York, 1968 (paperback).

David Rudovsky, *The Rights of Prisoners,* Avon Books, New York, 1973 (paperback).

Robert A. Rutland, *The Birth of the Bill of Rights,* Collier, New York, 1962.

Edward C. Smith, *The Constitution of the United States with Case Summaries,* Barnes & Noble, New York, 1972 (paperback).

The Story of the Bill of Rights, National Archives, Washington, D.C., 1966.

Growth of the National Government

In each of the preceding units, we examined the national government from a different point of view. The last unit provided an opportunity to sum up where we stand as a nation in terms of rights and liberties. Now it is time to sum up where we stand in terms of the size and the cost of our national government.

The federal government is big, and it has been growing bigger over the years. Those are the facts, but what do those facts mean? We have seen that the size of the federal government is most apparent in the huge bureaucracy that carries out the responsibilities of the executive branch. In a sense, therefore, we are talking about the executive branch when we talk about the size of the national government. But in another sense, we are talking about the legislative branch. For it is Congress that makes the laws that are carried out by the federal bureaucracy.

Why did those laws come into being? They did not come about by accident; rather, people seemed to need and want more and more services from the national government. It is easy to say that we should reduce the size of government, but not so easy to do it. When Congress does try to cut the size of a federal program, interest groups rise to defend the program. As a nation, we have been calling for sacrifices, but no one wants to be the sacrificial victim.

The two chapters in this unit will be about the growth of the national government. In discussing this subject, we will try to keep facts in perspective. The following selection indicates the importance of perspective.

There is an old saying (and if there isn't, there should be) that "You can't control the growth of weeds and government bureaus by just picking at them."

Nothing could be truer.

But actually, the number of people on the federal payroll has not expanded as much in the past 20 years as it may seem. Would you guess that we had added a million new people on the federal staff in the past 20 years? You would be overestimating.

According to government figures, taxpayers had a little over 2 million civilian employees on their federal payroll in 1950, here and in "outlying areas of the United States and in foreign countries." By 1970, there were 2.9 million. About 45 percent more employees after 20 years agrowing, under four different Presidents of different political persuasion. Not bad!

Adapted from Dwight Bohmbach, *What's Right with America*, Concept Productions, Minneapolis, 1972, pp. 143–145.

A bigger federal payroll requires more tax money, and most people do not like to pay taxes. Still, an increase in the size and cost of the federal government does not always mean an increase in the amount of taxes collected per person in the population. Remember, the population has been growing. The nation's economy has been growing too, and a growing economy means a greater return from taxes even if the tax rate stays the same.

We will examine these and other factors as we explore the size and cost of the federal government in the next two chapters.

Chapter 17

The Size of the National Government

Whatever one's opinion of government, it is hard to avoid contact with it nowadays because government is all-pervasive. Everywhere you look you see signs of government action: rules to follow, taxes to pay, aids and benefits to be obtained. This applies especially to the federal government. Until 50 years ago, an ordinary person did not have to think much about the federal government. Personal contact with a government was more often with a local or state government. That is not so any more.

A great change in the size and activities of the federal government took place during and after the Great Depression in the 1930s and World War II in the 1940s. The two periods together seem to have been a watershed. Ever since, the federal government has been deeply involved in our economy and in our society. The growth in that period was extreme, but there had been a gradual build-up over many years in the nation's needs and in its demands upon government. This chapter will take a look at those changes and what brought them about.

Goals

- To understand how the nation's needs have changed over the years.
- To understand why new demands have been placed upon the federal government.
- To examine the growth of federal employment and the federal payroll.
- To consider some problems posed by big government.

Chapter 17: The Size of the National Government

ECONOMIC AND SOCIAL CHANGES

To understand the growth of the federal government, we must think about how the world has changed since 1789 when the government of the United States began operating. Today's government must meet economic and social needs very different from those of 1789. Government now operates in a vastly changed economy and society. The changes are so many and so complex that we can only give a sample of them here.

Population Increase. In the first place, there are many more of us now. George Washington presided over a nation of not quite 4 million people. When President Jimmy Carter assumed office in 1977, the nation had 216 million inhabitants. Those 216 million were spread over a land area four times the size of the original United States. Government needs had grown accordingly. The Census Clock in the Department of Commerce Building in Washington, D.C., geared to show estimates, was ticking off a birth every 10 seconds. The Census Bureau was going to have to hire hundreds of thousands of workers simply to take an accurate population count in 1980. To maintain a representative democracy in a nation so much greater in size required a vast increase in the scale of governmental operations of all kinds.

Industrialization. In 1789, the United States was largely a nation of farmers. Indeed, Thomas Jefferson and some other Founders thought that an agricultural society was the only kind in which democracy would work. As more factories were built, the nation gradually became *industrialized*—its economy was no longer based mainly on agriculture, but on industry. As industrialization advanced, companies became bigger. They could buy and sell across the nation as well as in local markets. Big companies and big markets meant large concentrations of power. New needs for public decision-making were necessary to keep the nation's great experiment in democracy alive. Just to gather necessary information on trade, investment, incomes, and employment required much more work by the federal government.

Growth of Transportation and Communication. In 1789, people and goods traveled on dirt roads or on rivers. Today the United States

Small farms were the rule rather than the exception when the United States government began operating in 1789. This farm was in the state of Connecticut.

Chapter 17: The Size of the National Government

Big cities are now the rule rather than the exception in the United States. They create new economic and social needs.

population, and the size of cities has grown. In 1790, Philadelphia—which was then the nation's capital—had 28,500 residents. In 1970, Philadelphia had 1,950,000 residents. Other cities grew even more. *Urbanization* is the name given to this change from a rural to an urban way of life.

Urbanization has brought dependence on money income. Back in 1789, few farmers made much money, but most of them grew the food that they ate. In our present urban and industrial society, most people work for others and have to buy their food rather than grow it. Loss of a job means loss of a paycheck. Hundreds or thousands of workers in one area may be thrown out of work when a plant shuts down. Nor is it so easy to find another job when work is highly specialized. Changing jobs often requires retraining. Who will supply an income meanwhile? *Income insecurity* became a serious threat.

Income insecurity created new human problems across the nation. These, in turn, created new needs for federal income-security programs, such as retirement and disability insurance, unemployment insurance, and public assistance.

Technical Nature of Decisions. Industrial growth went along with changes in methods and processes. One result of these changes in *technology* is that decisions became more complicated. They are increasingly technical. Problems of food purity, for example, no longer resemble those of 1789. Then a city shopper might have sniffed the milk to see if it were sour. Today technology has helped to keep milk from souring. That same technology has poured thousands of chemicals into foods, posing grave questions about long-term health and environmental hazards. You cannot tell if a processed food is safe by just sniffing the plastic container it comes in. Consumers are left with fewer obvious clues to the safety and purity of foods. The risks are greater and less easy to determine. Complex technical decisions have to be made for the entire nation's benefit.

is crisscrossed by networks of highways, rail lines, and air services in addition to canals and other waterways. None of these were possible without federal rules and regulations.

Our present society is not only more mobile but also better informed. Newspapers and magazines provide us with far more information than our ancestors ever had to deal with. Radio and television bombard us with electronic messages from the time we wake until the time we fall asleep. Rules and regulations for these sources of information, too, have had to be made by the federal government.

Income Insecurity. A society of farmers is a rural society. An industrial society is largely an urban society. Three out of four people in this country live in towns or cities of 2,500 or more

Chapter 17: The Size of the National Government

An Interconnected World. While all these changes have been taking place within the nation, the world has changed too. The United States is no longer isolated—thirteen former colonies huddled at the edge of an ocean half a world away from the centers of world power. Today all nations depend on one another whether they wish it or not.

World trade forms economic and financial links between the nations. Foods, manufactured goods, and natural resources are exchanged worldwide. A squeeze on oil supplies from the Middle East forces policy decisions by the United States government. The ebb and flow of imports and exports of all kinds throws national currencies out of balance. This happens when, for instance, Americans spend more on Japanese products than the Japanese spend on American-made products. The value of the dollar then drops in relation to the yen. The federal government must consider how such financial changes around the world will affect the immediate and future welfare of all people.

National defense has grown infinitely more complicated. In 1789, national defense involved mainly soldiers, horses, ships, and guns. Now there are vast defense industries turning out planes and bombs and missiles of ever more intricate design. Their cost swells the national budget.

The first Volkswagen produced in the United States was a symbol of the interconnected world in which we now live.

All of these changes in our own country and in the world around us have created new needs for government services. Not only the federal government, but also state and local governments have grown dramatically. This growth itself has added to the complexity of our society. Government agencies have had to be formed to keep track of what is going on in other agencies.

Questions

1 What are *five* major changes within this country that have created needs for more federal services?

2 What major change in the relationship of the United States to the rest of the world has created needs for a larger federal government?

3 What are some differences in the role of the federal government that have resulted from economic and social changes? Give examples.

⌂ What *one* change in American life do you think has most affected our needs as a nation? Explain.

GROWTH IN OUR EXPECTATIONS OF GOVERNMENT

The economic and social changes since 1789 have resulted in changes in the way we view the role of government. The average citizen of 1789 expected little of the national government. People expected to have to fend for themselves, and most people were able to do so.

When people's lives changed, so did their expectations. As the growing complexity of life made it harder for people to fend for themselves, they sought more help from government. They turned more to the federal government because problems were often national in scope.

As a growing economy brought increased competition, demands for federal aid were heard from various groups. Farmers were one. The fact that farming was a business with many small-scale producers became a disadvantage as the economy grew. Farmers found themselves dealing with big railroads and big marketing companies. When railroads raised their freight rates, farmers could not fight back. They sought help from government, and the federal government began to regulate railroad rates. Federal help was later sought in leveling out the "boom and bust" nature of farming. In a year of good weather, almost all farmers have good crops. Food is plentiful, so prices drop. However, in a year of bad weather, prices rise but many farmers lose money anyway because they have poor crops. So the federal government tried various schemes to help tide farmers over the bad years.

Other economic interests also sought help from the federal government. Large businesses wanted information to make planning possible. So the government began to collect such information. Smaller businesses wanted protection against unfair competition. So the federal government began trying to put limits on *monopolies*—companies with total, or nearly total, control over certain products or services. Labor unions wanted protection for their efforts to organize workers into new unions. So the government took steps to guard workers against unfair practices used by employers.

Consumers wanted the government to keep prices down and help people cope with decisions in the market place. You say you cannot tell if a product is safe by just sniffing? Government can help by requiring tests of products' safety.

People turned to the national government for help in putting an end to economic hardship. The Great Depression of the 1930s had shocked the nation. Businesses failed, savings were wiped out, and local resources were unable to deal with hardship on that huge scale. The federal government established a national program to regulate banks and insure bank deposits. It started programs to protect people who lost their jobs or who became disabled. It set up a social security system to help assure working people an income after retirement. Economists devised theories about how governmental action might protect against economic depression and inflation. Congress passed laws to put some of the theories into practice.

The Works Projects Administration (WPA) was a 1930s program to create jobs for the unemployed. These marchers were seeking an extension of the program, which was the first major federal effort to shoulder unemployment problems.

Chapter 17: The Size of the National Government

Other people sought federal action out of concern for disadvantaged groups and individuals. Only the federal government, some argued, could wipe out local racial discrimination. Others sought federal action to ensure the rights of a wide range of people—women, military veterans, people accused of crimes, the young, the aged, various ethnic groups, the poor, and those who are the mentally or physically handicapped.

Overburdened cities turned to the federal government for help. People fleeing rural poverty ended up in city slums, and the cities had too few jobs for the newcomers. Businesses and industries were moving out of the big cities as suburbs and highway systems grew. The cities could no longer collect enough in taxes to pay for necessary services. Downtown sections were crumbling. City leaders argued that urban decay was a national problem. So the federal government stepped in with money.

States, too, sought federal help. A state with a depressed economy was unable to raise as much money in taxes as a state with booming industries. Couldn't the federal government help equalize the states? Yes, it could. Increased federal-state cooperation poured money from federal coffers into the states.

People concerned about the environment sounded an alarm about increasing damage to land, water, and air. These *environmentalists* argued that leaders in industry, farming, and ranching had too much power over state and local governments. Environmentalists also pointed out that pollution was a national problem because bad air from St. Louis, for example, could drift over Illinois and Indiana and cause problems far from the source of pollution. So the federal government began a national attack on a deteriorating environment and depleted resources.

The nation's increased involvement in world affairs led to new demands on the federal government. While World War II raged, many groups in this country were already planning how to avoid future wars. Proposals of many kinds were made for national action. The United States became a leader in organizing the nations of the world to preserve peace once it had been reestablished. The result was the establishment of the United Nations in 1945. Ever since, the United States has worked within the United Nations to reduce international frictions, promote the development of poor countries, and pursue other goals.

Two great world powers emerged from World War II—the United States and the Soviet Union. Many people urged the nation to hold back what they saw as a world threat of communism. The United States built a huge and costly defense system, set up foreign bases, and stationed military forces overseas. It enlarged its intelligence-gathering services. It expanded its diplomatic efforts, trying to help

Israeli Prime Minister Begin (left) and Egyptian President Sadat were brought together at Camp David, in Maryland, by President Carter for peace talks.

other nations work out their differences peacefully.

Many people thought a rich nation like the United States had a responsibility to provide aid to less fortunate nations. The United States began various foreign aid programs. In part, they were aimed at making friends abroad, and in part, they were humanitarian.

In all these ways, and many others, the role of the federal government grew as the nation's life became more complex. Much of the growth came in response to specific demands at specific times. One group after another said, "The federal government should do this job . . . and this job . . . and this job." Before the nation quite knew what had happened, the responsibilities of the federal government were widely accepted as being very broad indeed.

Questions
---

1 What are *two* ways in which the federal government has responded to demands from farmers and other economic interest groups?

2 What are *two* ways in which the federal government helps protect individuals against economic hardship?

3 What are *two* arguments used by environmentalists to support their demands for federal action?

4 What are some other sources of demands for federal action?

⬠ Do you think that the federal government tries to do too much? Not enough? Name one change you would like to see in the scope of governmental action. Explain.

SIZE OF THE NATIONAL GOVERNMENT

If you were to count the people employed by the federal government and counted 24 hours a day at the rate of one number every second, it would take you more than a month to count all the civilian employees. It would take you almost another month to count the members of the armed forces.

Suppose you were counting out the federal payroll in $10 bills. If you peeled off two bills every second, you would count out $1,728,000 every 24 hours. If you did this work around the clock every day, with no weekends or holidays, it would take you almost 65 years to peel off enough bills to pay the annual wages of all federal civilian employees at 1975 rates.

Of course, those examples are farfetched, but they may give you some idea of the size of the federal government.

As a more realistic example, consider what the size of government means to one small-business operator. A consulting chemist who operated a small firm in New York City with only five regular employees once figured out how much paper work he had to do to meet government regulations. He calculated that he had to file eighty-eight separate forms with thirty-six different agencies—federal, state, and city.

Paper work. All told, more than two billion forms are filed each year with the federal government. Most of those forms are filed by individuals rather than by businesses or by state and local governments.

Filling out forms or preparing reports requires both time and money. An application for a student loan can take 35 hours to fill out. A special Commission on Federal Paper Work did a 2-year study of possible improvements. It estimated the total cost of federal paper work at $100 billion a year. This included the cost of the paper as well as the government and private time involved. The commission made recommendations for saving $10 billion a year. Half of those suggestions had already been adopted, and the saving that resulted was estimated at $3.5 billion.

As you might expect, many people complain about government forms. They see many

Chapter 17: The Size of the National Government

Getting the System to Work

Even a huge bureaucracy can operate efficiently in the right conditions. What conditions are right? The following selection throws some light on that question. It is drawn from a report written for the *New York Times* by Deborah Rankin after a tour of a huge center that processes federal income tax returns.

It is an assembly line operation that could rival any industrial line, and it takes in more money each year than any company in the nation.

The low brick building here is the home of the Brookhaven Service Center. It is one of ten regional processing facilities operated by the Internal Revenue Service (IRS). Security is tight as the center goes into high gear for its peak season.

The center covers the smallest geographical area of any IRS service center, but it collects more taxes than any of its sister facilities.

Calling in its cadre of seasonal workers, the center will more than double its full-time staff to absorb the deluge of work expected on the deadline for filing tax returns. Last year the April 15 mailing deadline fell on a Friday. The center received 800,000 pieces of mail on Friday and another 700,000 pieces on Monday.

"I don't know if we'll get one and a half million pieces of mail on 1 day this year," said Thomas J. Laycock, director of the service center, "but it sure will be a lot."

What happens to a tax return after it enters the service-center processing pipeline is an example of time-study techniques developed to a fine point.

A passion for operating at peak efficiency permeates the center. In every section, there are charts that plot the performance of Brookhaven against its nine sisters. "It's a very competitive thing," Mr. Laycock said.

He recalled the situation a few years back, when he worked at the Andover, Massachusetts, service center. The rival Philadelphia center was riding high on the charts. "They were murdering us," he said. He hopped a plane to Philadelphia, found out the center's secret, returned home, and instituted the time-saving process.

"It was a good use of taxpayer's money," he maintains.

The color-cued line that represents Brookhaven on charts displayed in each processing area indicated on a recent visit that the extractors were equal with Memphis after a slow start. (First place among the five centers charted, that is.)

But the charts spelled a different story in the clearing and deposit section. Here, seventy-five clerks record on a central register the dollar amounts of checks that accompany returns and then detach them.

"I was afraid you'd ask," said the section chief when he was asked to explain why Brookhaven's wavering production line had plunged below those of the other service centers in some areas. (The reason: There is a "learning curve," or break-in period, associated with the processing cycle. Since Brookhaven receives most of its returns later than the other service centers, workers get a later start in learning the procedures.)

The charts are more encouraging at the data conversion section. Here information on the tax returns is put into language that can be understood by the computer. Kansas City is the star—processing an average of 32 long forms an hour. Brookhaven averages almost 30.

The section is doing even better at processing short forms. It ranks third in the country at 54.2 an hour.

(Continued on next page)

Chapter 17: The Size of the National Government

> The end of the tunnel is now in sight. Data is fed into the computer by two different terminal operators, working independently as a safeguard. Errors nevertheless crop up. Discrepancies are spewed out on long computer printouts that go to another section.
>
> Each examiner—there are 400 or so in this section—"perfects" twenty-five or thirty returns an hour. "These people are at war with the computer," said Mr. Laycock. "If a mistake doesn't get corrected after three times around it is sent to the rejection unit—the ultimate banishment, where the center admits defeat and starts examining the return afresh."
>
> The cycle that started on the mail loading dock is now complete. A tax return's stay in the center's pipeline ranges from about 5 days, early in the year, to a maximum of 16 days, according to the IRS. "We get slapped on the wrist if it's any longer," Mr. Laycock said.
>
> Adapted from *New York Times*, April 6, 1978. © 1978 by The New York Times Company. Reprinted by permission.

of them as makework for the bureaucracy, or as government meddling in things that are none of its business. Yet, others defend the paper work as necessary. We have given the government many tasks, they say, and to do those tasks, the government needs information that has to be collected on forms.

Whether all of the federal paper work is or is not justified, it symbolizes for many people two major failings of big government. These people say that government is too impersonal, and that a bureaucrat could not care less about your individual problems. The same people say that big government is not truly efficient. One arm of government may not know what another arm is doing. As a result, the argument goes, the federal government often is unresponsive to the nation's true needs. That the nation's needs are vast is not denied. How best to meet them and where to place our priorities is a matter of ongoing debate.

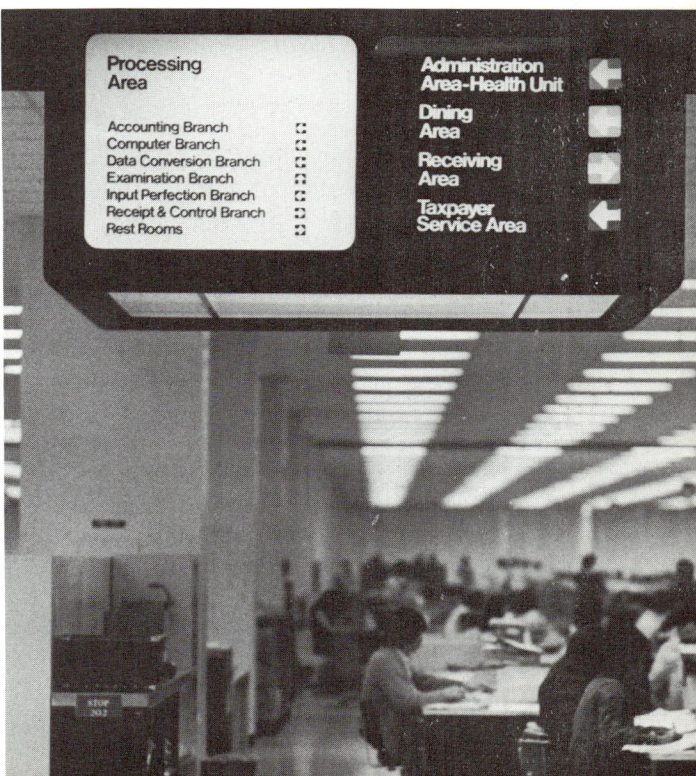

Federal income tax forms are processed in this huge assembly line operation of the Internal Revenue Service.

"DO YOU SOMETIMES GET THE FEELING...?"

Chapter 17: The Size of the National Government

> **Making Rules for Business**
>
> Despite the huge size of today's government, there *are* ways to deal with it. Many federal agencies allow the public to take part in rule-making.
>
> Let's say you believe that certain toys are unsafe. How could you help the Consumer Product Safety Commission make a rule about those toys?
>
> First, you could send a petition to the Commission asking for a rule about toy safety. Your petition should cite a specific problem and suggest solutions.
>
> The petition would go to the office of the Commission's general counsel. If that legal office finds that the Commission has jurisdiction, it sends your petition to the technical staff. That staff looks into the risk you pointed out. It collects data about the risk—whether it is minor or serious, how often injuries have occurred, and so on. Then the technical staff makes recommendations to the Commission itself. The Commission decides whether or not to grant your petition.
>
> If your petition is granted, the staff prepares a rule for the Commission's approval. This is printed in a daily publication called the *Federal Register*.
>
> Now you and other members of the public have another chance to give your opinion. Will the rule solve the problem? Is the rule too soft? Too harsh? You usually have 30 to 60 days to make your views known. Then the technical staff reviews the comments on the rule and may decide to make changes in it.
>
> The Commission reviews the staff's evaluation and any proposed changes. It makes a final decision. The rule is then published in the *Federal Register* with the date on which it will take effect.
>
> Adapted from "Making Rules for Business: How It Is Done," *U.S. News & World Report*, May 9, 1977, p. 61. Copyright © 1977 U.S. News & World Report, Inc.

Employment

The federal government is the largest single employer in the nation. All told, it employs 5 million people, or about one out of every forty-four persons. Of that total, 2.1 million are on active duty in the armed forces. The remaining 2.9 million are civilians. If all federal civilian employees were put in one place, they would make up a city the size of Los Angeles.

Each time the federal government expands its services, it hires more people. Thus, the trend over the years has been toward more and more employees. You can see this in the graph below. You can also see that the upward movement has been uneven.

CIVILIAN EMPLOYEES OF THE FEDERAL GOVERNMENT

Source: U.S. Civil Service Commission data

The biggest spurt took place in the wartime decade after the depressed 1930s. This was, first, because of new economic and social services taken on during the Great Depression. Second, it was because of war. A huge civilian force was employed as the federal government geared up for battle even before the nation entered World War II in December 1941. The level of federal civilian employment reached 1 million for the first time in 1940 and was over 2 million a year later. In 1945, the last year of World War II, the figure reached 3.8 million, its highest point ever. Though the total dropped by almost half in the 5 years after the war ended, it never again dropped below 2 million. Bear in mind that the armed forces are not included in any of these figures.

The federal government has generally tried to be a pacesetter in employment practices. It was a pioneer in giving special preferences to military veterans. After the Civil War, Congress voted to give extra points on civil service examinations to people who had served in the armed forces. The policy continued, and now about 50 percent of all federal jobs are held by veterans.

One unforeseen side effect of this policy, however, was discrimination against women. Veterans' preferences have tended to favor men over women because male veterans far outnumber female veterans. Partly for this reason, less than one-third of those working in federal jobs are women. In recent years, the federal government has sought to set an example for private employers by removing its own employment barriers against women, racial and ethnic minorities, and the handicapped.

As we saw in Chapter 7, almost all the people hired by the federal government work for the executive branch. In 1977, for example, civilian employment totaled 12,471 in the judicial branch, 40,715 in the legislative branch, and 2,840,000 in the executive branch. It should be noted, too, that the numbers of employees in the Central Intelligence Agency and the National Security Agency, both of which are part of the executive branch, are kept secret. Within the executive branch, the biggest employers are the Defense Department (35 percent of all federal civilian employees), the Postal Service (23 percent), and the Veterans Administration (8 percent).

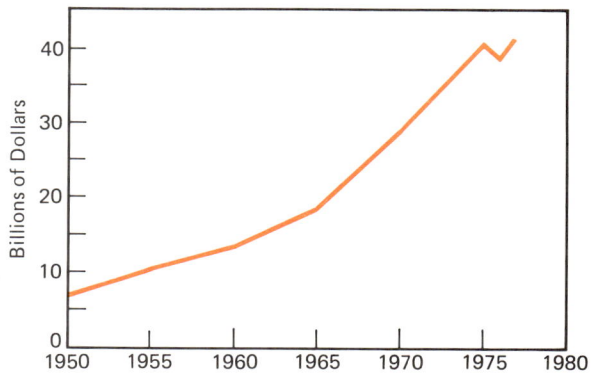
FEDERAL CIVILIAN PAYROLLS

Source: U.S. Civil Service Commission data

Payrolls

The federal civilian payroll has risen over the years and is still rising. It now amounts to more than $40 billion (see the graph above).

For several reasons, the average federal worker earns more than the average worker in

A woman at work in an aircraft factory was the symbol of the World War II civilian labor force. The war effort required millions of workers in government as well as in private industry during the 1940s.

Chapter 17: The Size of the National Government

the nation as a whole. Built-in inflation is partly responsible. Inflation is built into federal salaries because Congress passes cost-of-living raises from time to time. Many workers for private employers do not have this wage protection as prices rise. Second, the government has sought to attract highly qualified people for federal jobs. To do so, it has tried to offer salaries that are at least as high as those offered by private employers. Another factor—which people who complain of federal pay levels often overlook—is that federal workers are a special group. Few federal employees do the kind of unskilled work that occupies many people in the nation's total work force. Low pay for unskilled work holds down the national average figure of wages and salaries.

The result of all these factors is that the average civilian employed full time by the federal government earned $14,576 in 1976. The average employee in the United States as a whole received $11,623 that year. Since both figures are averages, many workers earned less.

From Washington to the Grass Roots

The federal government and the people who work for it can be found in every state of the nation and in most foreign countries. News reporters sometimes use the word "Washington" to refer to the federal government, as when they say: "Washington ordered. . . ." or "Washington announced. . . ." That custom should not mislead us into thinking that our federal government is to be found only in Washington, D.C.

Only about 13 percent of the federal government's employees work in the nation's capital. The remaining 87 percent work in regional or local offices in other parts of this country or abroad.

The federal government owns some 405,000 buildings around the country for

---

If You Want to Work for the Federal Government

The following selection applies to federal civil service jobs, but much of what it says is true also of civil service jobs in state, county, and city government.

Federal jobs once offered little except job security. Pay was low. Now, however, things have changed.

If you take a federal white-collar job, you will receive raises each year pegged to the increases given to similar workers in private jobs. Blue-collar workers get wages pegged to rates prevailing for similar jobs in the local area.

You can also look forward to generous fringe benefits, such as vacations and a pension. After 15 years on the job, you will be eligible each year for 26 leave days—that is, days off and vacation. Full retirement benefits can be claimed when you have at least 30 years of service and have reached age 55. If you have spent part of your career in private industry, you might be able to draw social security benefits as well as your federal pension.

How can you get into government work? Several federal agencies do their own hiring. Most jobs, however, are awarded through a merit system. The applicant is rated by the results of a test or by a review of education or work experience.

The federal civil service system has offices in most major cities. After testing or review, an applicant is listed with others qualified for the same kind of work. When an agency has a vacancy, it asks for names of qualified persons. Normally it chooses from the three candidates rated highest on the list.

Adapted from "If You Want to Go to Work for the Government," *U.S. News & World Report,* May 9, 1977. Copyright © 1977 U.S. News & World Report, Inc.

Chapter 17: The Size of the National Government

those employees to work in. It rents thousands of other buildings. If all these buildings were put together, they would have 300 times as much floor space as the twin towers of the World Trade Center in New York City.

In addition, the federal government owns about one-third of the nation's land. The map below shows where that land is located. Almost all of it is managed by the Department of the Interior or the Department of Agriculture. Some of the lands are leased to ranchers for grazing or to coal companies and other industries for mining. National parks and monuments are maintained on other lands.

The federal government's presence is felt by the entire country in many ways. No wonder people say that it is "all-pervasive."

Questions

1 What is the purpose of many of the federal forms that people have to file? What complaints do some people make about the necessary paper work?

2 What are some reasons why the average civilian working for the federal government earns more than the average employee in the nation as a whole?

3 On the basis of the line graphs in this section, which has risen faster in recent years: the number of federal employees or the size of federal payrolls? Explain.

◌ Do you think that a government could ever have too many employees? Too few? Explain.

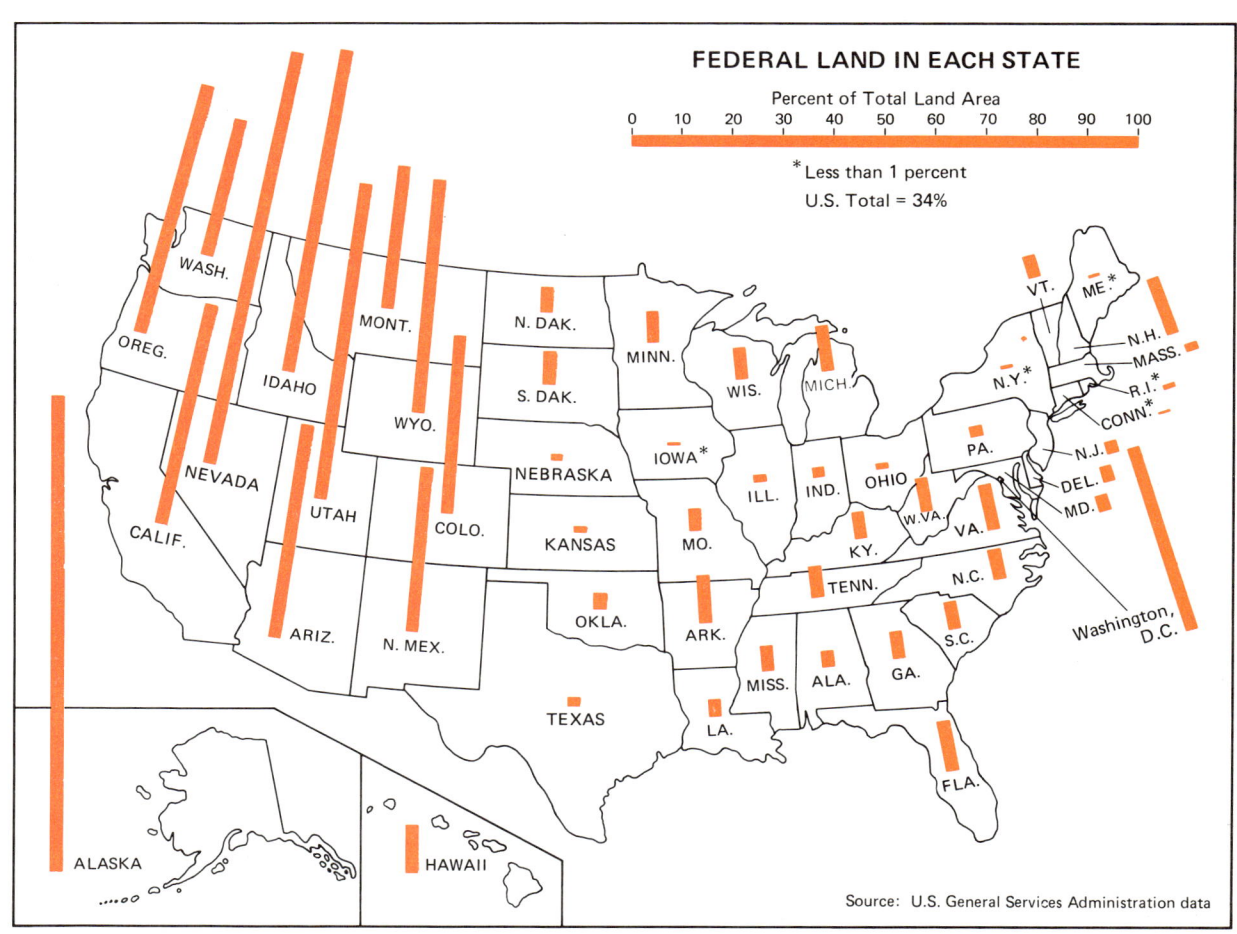

FEDERAL LAND IN EACH STATE
*Less than 1 percent
U.S. Total = 34%
Source: U.S. General Services Administration data

Chapter 17: The Size of the National Government

PROBLEM: HAVE WE TOO MANY FEDERAL RULES?

The Department of Health, Education, and Welfare (HEW) not only has a very large budget and work force, it also issues thousands of new rules and regulations each year.

The problems with such a bureaucracy are illustrated in the two selections that follow. The first is in the form of an imaginary reply by HEW to a letter asking whether there is a Santa Claus. This selection was written by Art Buchwald, a well-known humorist. The second selection is from a column by Meg Greenfield for *Newsweek* magazine.

As you read these selections, consider the following questions:

- What were some problems noted by Buchwald and Greenfield?
- Why were they problems?
- Why might HEW have made the regulations described?

A Fable about Bureaucracy

Dear Virginia:

We regret we are unable to process your request for an answer to your question until you have filled out Form B1897 and Impact Application R9004567 as well as submitting Certification 459K as outlined in Paragraph 6, Page 198, Section 11 of Volume Four HEW Regulations. Once you have fulfilled these requirements, your question shall be forwarded to the appropriate department.

But because of the pressure of work, we advise you not to contact us again for 8 months at the minimum. When you do, please refer to Serial 145923, which is the number your letter has been assigned.

Respectfully yours

From Art Buchwald, "Back to Virginia's Question," *San Antonio Express-News*, December 25, 1975, p. 18A. Copyright © 1975 Los Angeles Times Syndicate.

Thoughts of a Bureaucrat

A few months ago, when he was fairly new in office, I had lunch with F. David Mathews, [who was then the] Secretary of HEW. Mathews described the role he saw for himself in his job. He would be a sort of people's helper, as I got it, an "intermediary" between the public and the government in the growing conflict over the billions of dollars' worth of social programs—and rules and regulations—that HEW administers.

A group of foster parents were telling him, Mathews observed, that their allowances for their kids permitted them to buy only *square* eyeglasses. But the kids kind of wanted *round* glasses like those their friends had, which did not cost so much more. What about that? he asked.

And what about grandma? he added. Grandma? Well, yes: "I recently had to decide how long your Grandma gets to come home for from the nursing home at Christmas. She can be out a total of 18 days a year. What I had to decide was whether Grandma could blow the whole 18 days at once, or whether she had to take it in 3- or 4-day bites, so you might have to say on Christmas Eve: 'Well, sorry, Grandma, it's 12 o'clock and the government says you've got to go now.'"

Mathews paused. "What am I doing making that decision?"

Adapted from Meg Greenfield, "Jerry Brown—East," *Newsweek*, January 19, 1976, p. 84. Copyright © Newsweek, Inc., 1976. Used by permission.

Questions

1 Buchwald was trying to be funny in writing his imaginary letter from HEW. But what problem was he illustrating?

2 What problems did Meg Greenfield note about the operations of HEW?

◌ Do you think that any government could have *too many* rules for its citizens to follow? Could it have *too few* rules? Explain.

Workers at one federal agency posed with their files on moving day. Government agencies exist as physical realities, with buildings, desks, papers, and telephones. Abolishing an agency is no easy matter.

PROBLEM: WHEN SHOULD A FEDERAL AGENCY BE ABOLISHED?

Between 1960 and 1976, Congress created 236 new federal agencies. During that time, it did away with only twenty-one agencies. The following excerpt tells how one of those agencies was abolished. As you read, ask yourself:

- Why did Congress create this agency?
- Why did Congress abolish it?

Life and Death of a Federal Agency

This is the story of one bureaucrat in Washington, D.C. His story is not intended to be representative of bureaucratic Washington. Still, it reveals important truths about our federal government.

Jubal Hale is a 47-year-old government lawyer with an engaging smile and unruly salt-and-pepper hair. In May of 1975, he found himself on front pages and television programs across the nation. Why? He admitted to a reporter that since he had no work to do in his $20,000-a-year job, he whiled away the 8 hours a day in his office listening to Beethoven records and reading.

The story began in 1971 when Jubal Hale was hired as executive secretary of the newly created Federal Metal and Non-Metallic Mine Safety Board of Review, funded by a $167,000 congressional appropriation. His job was to hear appeals from mine operators whose mines were shut down by the Interior Department for safety reasons. Hale and his secretary, Mary Burke (with a $14,125-a-year salary), were nicely housed in a six-room office suite in Washington. The five board members gathered only for annual meetings—and when there was a case to decide.

But there were no appeals. Hale and Miss Burke sat and waited. Although the Department of the Interior had issued more than 3,200 mine closing or closure orders in 4 years, not one was appealed. The board of review spent only $50,489 in 1973, turning back $109,511 of its appropriation.

Chapter 17: The Size of the National Government

This remarkable happening did not inspire the usually alert watchdogs in the Office of Management and Budget to suggest doing away with the board. Indeed, they recommended yet another $160,000 appropriation for the following year. Congress did reduce the generous sum to $60,000, but still did not bother to start any kind of action to abolish the agency. Jubal Hale gave up much of the board's office space, keeping only a reception room, a supply and coffee room, and a large office for himself.

To pass the time, Hale equipped his office with his own stereo system. He and his secretary chatted over coffee. They processed the board's expense vouchers and set up annual meetings. In 1972, for instance, the board had met in San Francisco, spending $3,302.74 to discuss such measures as the design of an official seal for themselves. At the 1974 board meetings in Las Vegas—billed to taxpayers for $1,885.99—it was proposed they ask Congress to abolish their agency. The proposal lost by a 4-to-1 vote. In the required year-end report to Congress, Hale clearly stated: "Though 1,998 mine closure orders were issued in 1974 under the Federal Metal and Non-Metallic Mine Safety Act, none of these orders was appealed by a mine operator to this board."

Finally, these reports attracted the attention of Representative Ken Hechler, a Democrat from West Virginia. He was a careful student of mine safety laws and enforcement. Last May, he called at the board's office. It was empty, the phone off the hook. Hechler noted the stereo system, waited 20 minutes and returned to Capitol Hill. Several days later, Hechler, at an Appropriations Committee hearing, denounced the Federal Metal and Non-Metallic Mine Safety Board of Review as "a useless, toothless, do-less government agency which has never earned its pay."

Associated Press reporter Tom Raum followed up Hechler's revelation by visiting Jubal Hale. Only slightly embarrassed, Hale explained that his secretary had been out ill when the Congressman had called earlier, and he himself had been at the Interior Department. Yes, he confirmed, in 4 years his board had never had a case. And yes, he whiled away his working hours reading and listening to records in his office. That afternoon reporter Raum rapped out his story.

Next day, it hit Page 1. CBS put Hale on its evening network news, photographed behind the spinning turntable of his stereo and smiling amiably. Almost overnight, the "Beethoven bureaucrat" became the most famous government worker in America.

On June 30, 1975—about a year after Hechler's opening blast—the board was finally abolished and its functions were transferred to the Secretary of the Interior. Hale found a job with higher pay on Interior's Board of Indian Appeals. Miss Burke retired after 30 years' government service. The total taxpayers' cost for this tragicomic escapade in bureaucratic futility: over $250,000, the yearly federal taxes paid by sixty-six average American families.

Adapted from Eugene H. Methvin, "Tale of Two Bureaucrats," *Reader's Digest,* December 1975, pp. 207, 209, 211.

Questions

1 Briefly describe how Jubal Hale spent most of his working hours as a federal bureaucrat. Do you think that he was typical of bureaucrats? Why or why not?

2 Do you think that Hale's agency should have been abolished? Explain.

3 Why wasn't Hale's agency abolished earlier?

◌ Do you think that there is any way Congress could prevent such an experience from happening again? Explain.

Chapter 17 Review

Developing Your Political Vocabulary

Define each of the following terms and then use each in a sentence about the growth of the federal government.
- a industrialization
- b urbanization
- c income insecurity
- d technology
- e monopoly
- f environmentalist

Recalling and Comparing

1 Name *five* changes in life in this country between 1789 and the present, and *five* ways in which the federal government has adapted to these changes.

2 How might an agricultural society differ from an urban society in the needs it raises for action by government?

3 What trends have there been in the growth in the number of civilian employees of the federal government since 1910?

4 What trends have there been in the growth of federal civilian payrolls since 1950?

5 During what periods did the federal government grow the most? Why?

6 What general pattern do you see in the growth of our federal government? Explain.

7 How do the demands placed upon the federal government illustrate democracy at work? Give examples.

Special Activities

1 Begin a class bulletin-board chart and fill it in for 1 week. Write down all the contacts by students, family members, and friends with the federal government.

2 Make a chart of the six aims of government in the Preamble of the Constitution and some ways in which federal agencies help carry out each today.

3 Interview one or more persons who experienced the Great Depression of the 1930s and ask which of the present government services were not available then. List those services.

4 Follow letters-to-the-editor columns in newspapers and magazines for a week. What arguments do you find expressed in support of and opposed to the present size of government? Do you think that the arguments are good or bad? Chart your findings.

5 Invite someone who is employed by a large private corporation to visit your class and discuss paper work and bureaucracy in the business world as compared with the situation in government. Allow time for class discussion of possible underlying causes.

6 Obtain copies of federal civil service requirements for jobs in a field that interests you. Consider what training you would need.

7 Consider what might be arguments for and against the following statement: "So long as our nation keeps changing, the federal government will keep growing." Do you agree or disagree? Why?

Chapter 18

Financing the National Government

Q: How long would it take to spend $1 billion?
A: If you had spent $1,000 a day, every day since Christ was born, you would not yet have spent $1 billion. —David Wallechinsky and Irving Wallace, *The People's Almanac*

When we talk about spending by the federal government, we are talking about billions of dollars. We are no longer dealing with numbers in the millions, as when we talk of federal employment.

Since 1976, our federal government has spent at a rate of more than $1 billion a day. In this chapter, we will see where that money comes from, how it is spent, and the various steps in between.

Goals

- To learn how the annual budget of the federal government is prepared.
- To learn the nature of the federal government's expenditures.
- To learn how funds are obtained to meet the federal government's expenditures.
- To learn the nature and origin of federal budget deficits and the federal debt.
- To consider budget problems related to national defense and to welfare programs.

Chapter 18: Financing the National Government

THE FEDERAL BUDGET

The federal budget is an annual list of the amounts of money that the government expects to take in from various sources and the amounts it expects to pay out. In some ways, the federal budget is like any budget, even one you might keep. You would estimate how much money you might receive over the next year, and its sources. How much from after-school jobs? From summer jobs? From allowances? Then you would list all the expenses you expected to have in the year. How much for transportation? School supplies? Snacks? Special projects? A budget would help you decide whether you had enough income to cover your expenses.

The federal budget tells how the nation's spending will be divided among various government programs. That depends on the nation's *priorities*—its preferences as revealed by policy decisions. Which is more important: to build more highways or give more help to cities? Thousands of these decisions have to be made each year.

Some federal expenditures affect our lives directly and some indirectly. The budget sets aside money for three main purposes:

1. *Purchase of goods and services.* Some of the goods are supplies and equipment, like computers for government offices or airplanes for the military. The term *goods* also covers construction. For example, the federal government constructs post offices and other federal buildings, highway and waterway improvements, parks, and military bases. Services would include such things as the federal payroll and expenses for research.

2. *Payments to individuals.* A number of federal programs provide money directly to individuals. Such payments include retirement benefits under the social security program, unemployment insurance, welfare payments, and health care, among others.

3. *Payments to state and local governments.* These payments eventually are used for one of the two purposes already mentioned.

The federal budget also tells where the money will come from. The government receives money from two main sources—taxes and borrowing. We will examine these sources at greater length shortly.

The federal budget covers a 12-month period called a "fiscal year." This year differs from the calendar year, with which we are most familiar. The calendar year begins on January 1 and ends on December 31. A *fiscal year* starts anywhere in one calendar year and ends 12 months later, in the next calendar year. It is a concept widely used for budgeting and accounting. For example, a farmer might file tax returns for a fiscal year based on a crop year.

The federal government's fiscal year begins on October 1 and ends on September 30. The fiscal year 1985, for example, begins on October 1, 1984 and ends on September 30, 1985. (Until 1977, the federal fiscal year began on July 1 as the fiscal year of most state and local governments still does.)

Freshly printed copies of the Budget of the United States government are here being packaged for delivery.

Drawing Up the Budget

The executive branch and the legislative branch share in the work of preparing the budget. Under our system of checks and balances, the President is responsible for drawing up a proposed budget. Congress then examines, revises, and finally approves it. The constitutional responsibility for taxing and spending lies with Congress. It must make the necessary appropriations.

The President starts the budget process by deciding on general goals. Will the budget hold the line on spending? Or will federal spending grow? By how much? Once these decisions are made, the President enlists the help of all parts of the executive branch. The Office of Management and Budget (OMB) supervises the task. Each executive department and independent agency draws up a list of its own spending plans. It spotlights programs that it wants to introduce or expand, and others that should be cut back or dropped. OMB has the unpopular task of squeezing the various spend-

"THIS IS GOING TO BE EXCITING!"

Speaker of the House Thomas P. ("Tip") O'Neill, Jr., here discusses the federal budget with a task force.

ing plans into the overall budget. Often this means chopping back the proposals of a department or agency. The President sometimes has to help settle a dispute over how much a department will get.

Meanwhile the President receives estimates of receipts prepared by the Treasury Department. It, the Council of Economic Advisers, and the OMB also supply information about the outlook for the economy.

This process ends with the President's budget message to Congress. The message is delivered within 15 days after Congress convenes each January. The budget message does not make light reading. It is accompanied by some 1,000 pages of details, set forth in a series of "budget books."

Congress has its own machinery for dealing with the budget. The House and the Senate each have a budget committee. These committees help set broad goals for spending and taxes. Other committees in each house work on the actual taxes and spending plans. In addition, there is a Congressional Budget Office, created in 1974. This looks at each part of the budget and tells Congress how it would affect the nation's economy. The Congressional Budget Office also sounds a warning if Congress passes bills that would require more money than the budget allows.

Congressional review of the budget ends with the passage of bills to appropriate money for federal spending. Under the Constitution, all appropriations bills start in the House (Article I, Section 7). The Senate can, and often does, amend them. Congress has from mid-January until the start of the new fiscal year on October 1 to complete action on appropriations. If Congress has not acted by then, an agency may find itself without funds.

Finally, the executive branch takes over again. The President may sign or veto an appropriations bill. Not until such a bill has been passed by Congress and signed by the President, or passed over a veto, can the Treasury Department pay out money. The Treasury

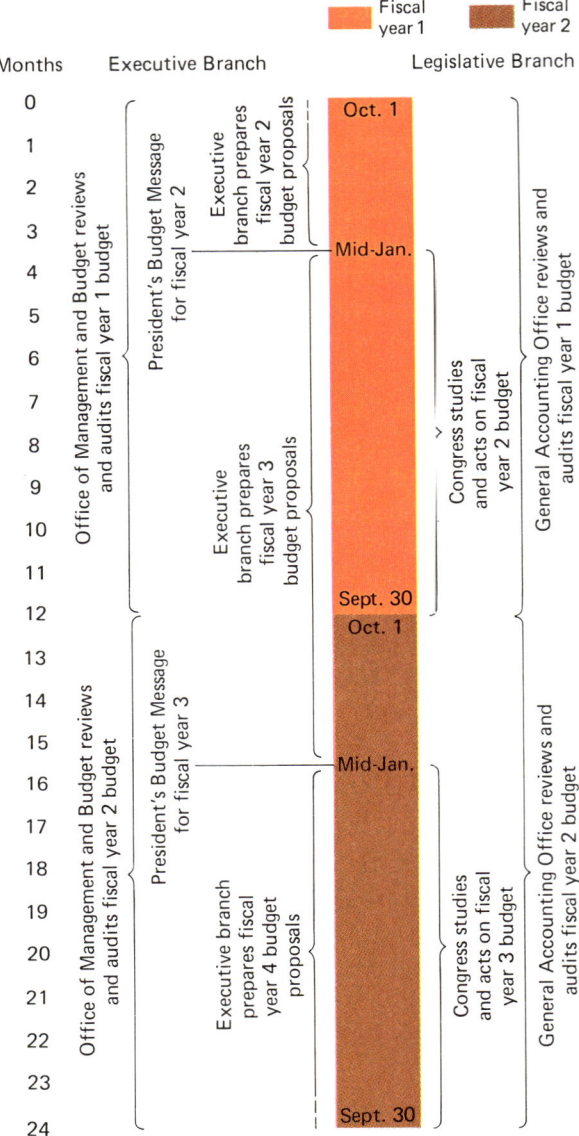

Department also collects taxes and arranges, if necessary, to borrow money.

The entire budget process seems endless. Usually, at least 18 months go by from start to finish. Before one year's budget is complete, work is already under way on the next year's budget. The time line on this page illustrates the lengthy process.

The Budget as an Economic Tool

The government often uses its spending and taxing powers as a means of controlling the stability of the nation's economy. This is known as *fiscal policy*. A rise or fall in government spending or taxing sets off ripples throughout the economy. For example, if the government raises personal taxes, people have less money to spend. Their *purchasing power* is reduced. If the amount of goods and services available for purchase does not decrease at the same time, prices tend to fall. Usually, therefore, a rise in personal taxes cuts down inflation. To prevent an economic depression, fiscal policy would stress tax reductions or increased government spending. Because the national economy is so complex, it is difficult to predict the results of any measures taken to control it. Federal officials do not always agree among themselves on how to use fiscal policy to make the economy run smoothly.

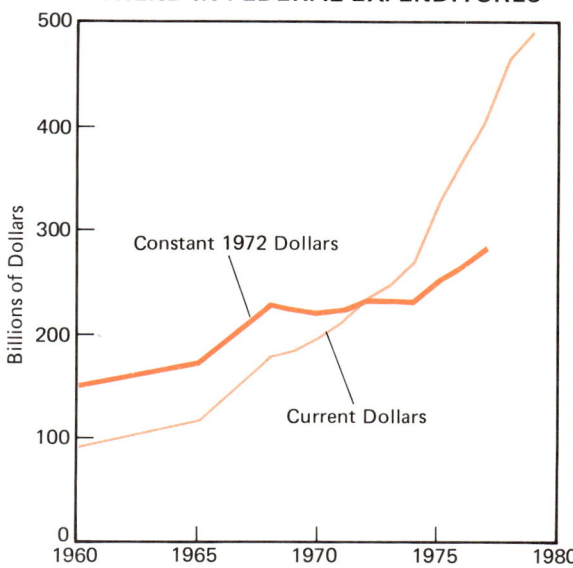

Money figures in constant dollars rule out the effects of price changes over the years, permitting better comparisons.

Questions

1 In what way does the federal budget set the nation's priorities?
2 How do the executive and legislative branches share responsibility for the federal budget?
3 What is fiscal policy and how does the government use it?
⬠ Do you think that the preparation of the annual federal budget involves the people as much as it should in a democracy? Explain.

FEDERAL BUDGET EXPENDITURES

The federal government is by far the biggest spender in the United States. Its spending amounts to more than one-fifth the value of all goods and services produced by our economy.

Growth of Spending

The size of the federal budget keeps going up. From around $4 million a year during George Washington's first term, federal spending had soared to nearly $500 billion at the end of the 1970s. Federal spending doubled from 1960 to 1969, and had already doubled again by 1976. In only 3 more years, it increased by one-third.

Inflation is one reason for the growth in federal spending. Above is a line graph showing the growth in federal spending since 1960. The graph shows federal spending in terms of both current and constant dollars. *Constant dollars* are dollars whose puchasing power remains unchanged because of a statistical adjustment that removes the effects of price changes over a period of years. When inflation is thus ruled out, the rise in federal spending is

Chapter 18: Financing the National Government

seen to be only about half as great as it had appeared.

Other reasons for the growth in federal spending are the changing role of government and the expansion of our economy. In the last chapter, we saw how the federal government's enlarged role has caused a growth in federal employment and payrolls. Other expenditures have grown for the same reason. Economic expansion has a different effect. It is measured by *gross national product* (GNP)—the value of all goods and services produced in the nation. As the national output grows, federal receipts grow because there are more dollars to be taxed. Larger receipts make it possible to increase expenditures. A good example can be drawn from the 1960s. In 1960, federal expenditures of more than $92 billion were 18.5 percent of GNP. Five years later, federal expenditures had risen to more than $118 billion, but the percentage of GNP had dropped slightly to 18.0 percent.

Allocation of Expenditures

The executive branch accounts for all but a small part of federal spending. In 1977, a fairly typical year, total budget expenditures were $402 billion. The legislative branch spent $1.0 billion and the judicial branch $0.4 billion. All the rest was spent by the executive branch.

Within the executive branch, independent agencies spent about $34 billion in 1977. The executive departments spent much more. Ignoring some offsetting receipts, they spent $367 billion in 1977 (see the table on this page). The bulk of executive department spending was done by just three departments—Health, Education, and Welfare (HEW), Defense, and Treasury. HEW alone accounted for about 40 percent of the $367 billion.

HEW is in charge of many of the social service programs run by the federal government. The biggest of these, social security,

Budget Expenditures of Executive Departments, 1977

	Billions of dollars
Department of Health, Education, and Welfare	$147.5
Department of Defense	98.0
Department of the Treasury	49.6
Department of Labor	22.4
Department of Agriculture	16.7
Department of Transportation	12.5
Department of Housing and Urban Development	5.8
Department of Energy	5.2
Department of the Interior	3.2
Department of Commerce	2.6
Department of Justice	2.3
Department of State	1.1
Total	$366.9

U.S. Office of Management and Budget data

began during the Great Depression of the 1930s. Most of the others have been added since the 1950s.

Another way to look at federal expenditures is by function. Instead of grouping expenditures by agency or department, we can group them according to how they are used. The two broad functions that account for the largest share of spending are national defense and human resources. Human resources include such items as income security, health, veterans' benefits, and education and training. Almost all HEW expenditures fall under the heading of human resources.

Most human resources spending is in the form of *transfer payments*—that is, payments to individuals. The rest are grants-in-aid to state and local governments.

Here is how spending broke down by broad function for 1977: defense, $97.5 billion; human resources, $214.8 billion; and other expenditures, $89.6 billion. Over the years, the share going to human resources has increased. As the graph in the next column

Chapter 18: Financing the National Government

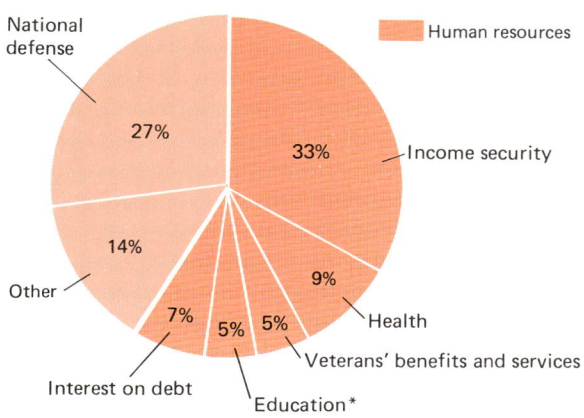

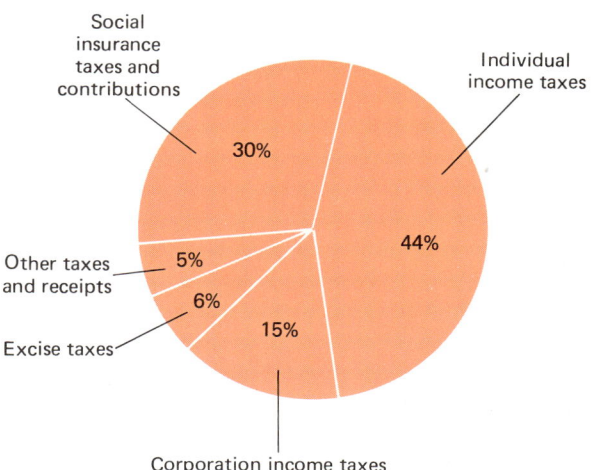

shows, defense expenditures have averaged a little more than one-fourth of the total during the past 5 years while human resources has averaged more than one-half of the total.

Questions

1 How has inflation affected federal spending in recent years?

2 Which branch of the federal government spends the most money?

3 What broad function does the federal government spend the most money for?

○ Do you think that the federal government divides its spending wisely among the major functions? Explain.

FEDERAL BUDGET RECEIPTS

As federal spending goes up, so does federal income. But, as we noted earlier, income does not always keep up with spending. How the government makes up any shortfalls will be discussed later. In this section, we will examine where federal budget receipts come from.

In 1978, the federal government took in a total of $400 billion. That compares with $2 billion as recently as 1932. Federal budget receipts were $92.5 billion in 1960, and had doubled by 1969. They had doubled again by 1978.

The money the government takes in comes from a variety of sources. The main sources are shown in the pie graph above.

The bulk of the government's income is from taxes. The job of collecting most of these taxes belongs to the Internal Revenue Service, which is a subdivision of the Treasury Department.

People in this country pay federal taxes in a number of ways. The main tax—and the one that has many people tearing their hair every April, when it falls due—is the individual income tax. This tax amounts to a certain percentage of an individual's income from salary or wages, interest on savings, and other sources. The percentage rises as income rises, so that wealthier people pay at a higher rate. Because the tax rate rises (progresses) with income, the federal income tax is a *progressive tax*. However, individuals do not actually pay the tax on their full incomes. Their incomes are

Chapter 18: Financing the National Government

Loopholes make it possible for some people to pay less than the rate of income tax for their income bracket.

first adjusted according to various formulas permitting deductions of many kinds. These formulas are complex and may result in the payment of no tax at all by some people, even among those with large incomes.

When the federal individual income tax was made possible in 1913 by the Sixteenth Amendment, the tax amounted to a tiny percentage of income. It has been raised many times since then, and by big jumps in wartime. Mainly for this reason, a full-time worker now has to work 4 months out of every year just to pay all of his or her taxes—federal, state, and local.

Anyone who has watched the steep rise in taxes in recent years finds small comfort in knowing that the rise has been even steeper in other industrial countries of the Western world. When the tax burden is compared with gross national product, or the value of the total output of goods and services, the people of this country are less heavily taxed than the people of Europe. By the mid 1970s, taxes amounted to about 30 percent of GNP in the United States, 35 to 45 percent in most industrial countries of Western Europe, and 45 to 50 percent in the Scandinavian countries.

In addition to individual income taxes, the federal government levies a number of other taxes. One is a *corporate income tax,* on the income of businesses organized as corporations. Receipts from this source were once about the same as those from the individual income tax but are now generally about one-third as much.

Another major federal tax is a *payroll tax,* paid by workers and their employers to finance social security. Only workers in jobs covered by the Social Security Act pay this federal tax. The worker's share is the "FICA tax" on employers' statements of deductions from pay. (The initials stand for Federal Insurance Contributions Act.) With the growth of the social security program and benefits, this payroll tax has risen. It was stepped up sharply in the 1970s in order to keep the social security program from running out of funds.

Among other federal taxes are *excise taxes,* which are taxes on the manufacture or sale of certain items, including liquor, cigarettes, firearms, and gasoline. Since excise taxes are included in the price of the product, every purchaser pays the same amount of tax. But a tax that is the same for everyone in money amount takes a bigger share of small incomes than it does of large incomes. Such a tax is called a *regressive* tax. Still other money comes from such sources as unemployment insurance contributions, estate and gift taxes, and customs duties.

Questions

1 What tax contributes the most to federal budget receipts?

2 What is a progressive tax? Name one.

3 Who pays the tax that finances the social security program?

4 Give an example of a federal excise tax. Is it a progressive tax? Explain.

◇ Which do you think is fairer—an income tax or an excise tax? Why? Are both needed? Explain.

The destruction of naval vessels in the bombing of Pearl Harbor in 1941 set off an explosion of wartime spending.

DEFICITS AND THE FEDERAL DEBT

Every budget has two sides—income and outgo. If income is as large as or greater than outgo, we are said to have a *balanced budget.* This means that income and outgo are in balance. Since the 1930s, we have been living with unbalanced federal budgets most of the time. The government has had to borrow money to pay its bills.

When the federal government spends more money than it receives, it is said to have a deficit. The same would apply to an individual. Suppose you had a part-time job that paid $20 a week but you managed to spend $25 a week. Your deficit would be $5 a week.

Federal deficits are figured in billions of dollars. In 1978, for example, the federal government spent nearly $451 billion and received $402 billion. The difference between these figures left a 1978 deficit of $49 billion. You can see the 50-year trend in deficits on the graph on the following page. Huge deficits occurred during World War II when the costs of military operations were far greater than the federal government's annual income. (President Franklin Roosevelt proposed large tax increases to reduce deficits during that war but was unable to get Congress to go as far as he wanted.) As we have seen, the government also uses budget deficits in times of peace as a tool of fiscal policy in an effort to achieve economic stability. Budget deficits are also

Chapter 18: Financing the National Government

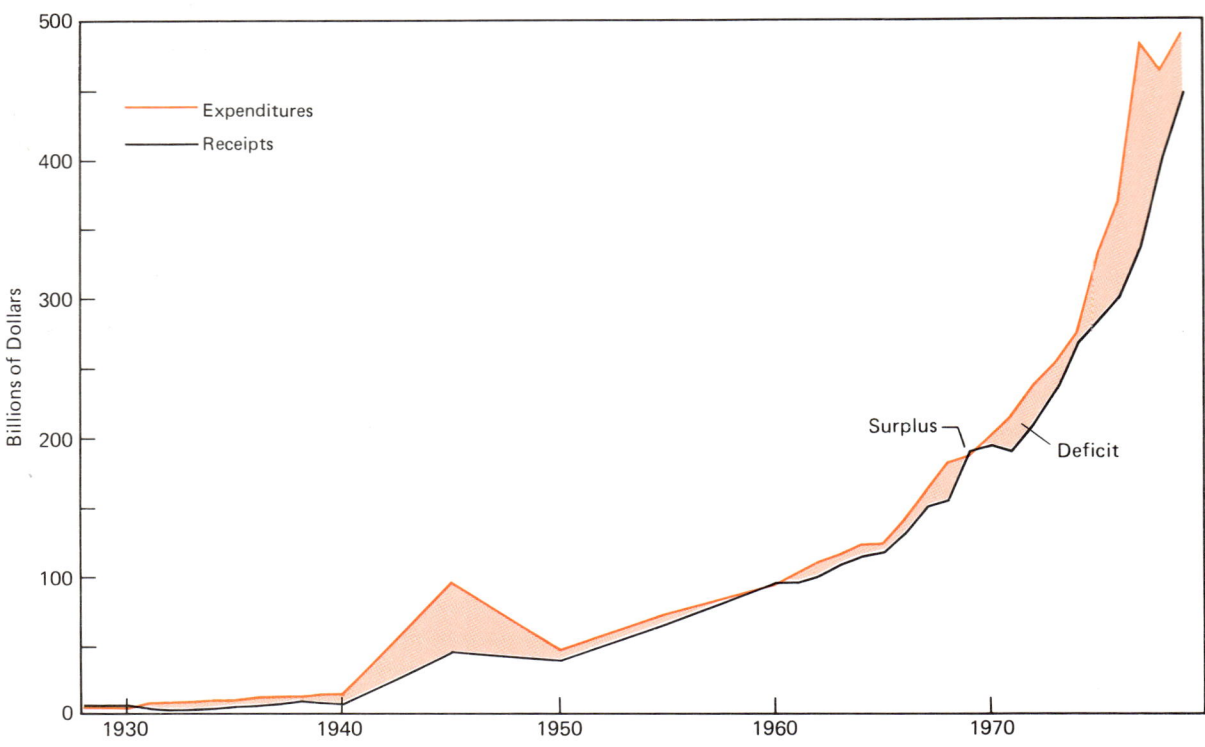

TREND IN FEDERAL BUDGET SURPLUSES AND DEFICITS

Source: U.S. Office of Management and Budget data; 1978 and 1979 estimated

undertaken as a matter of social policy in order to aid disadvantaged groups. Large deficits in the 1970s were due to policy decisions of both types. As the graph shows, surpluses have been few and slight.

What can the government do to deal with a deficit? There are some obvious ways. First, it can *use a surplus*—if there is one—from earlier years. Second, it can *increase taxes*—as it often has done. Third, it can *reduce expenditures*—which seems harder to do.

Still another way to deal with a deficit is to *print more money*. The Constitution gives Congress the power "to coin Money [and] regulate the Value thereof" (Article I, Section 8). Congress has delegated the power to coin money to the executive branch. Coins are turned out by the Bureau of the Mint, and paper money by the Bureau of Engraving and Printing. Both agencies are within the Treasury Department. Paper money has been *legal tender* since 1863. That is, if you offer (tender) it in payment of a debt, the person to whom you owe money is obliged to accept it. (Nowadays, 90 percent of money transactions in this country are not by cash but by checks.)

The Treasury Department does not actually put more money into circulation. That is the job of an independent agency, the Federal Reserve Board, which supervises the Federal Reserve System. The number of one of the twelve banks within the Federal Reserve System appears on almost every piece of paper money. Only about 5 percent of paper money is not issued by a Federal Reserve bank.

The decision to issue money is an important policy decision. Congress wanted to shield such decisions from shifting political winds. That is why it assigned them to an independent agency.

United States Savings Bonds give the people of this country a means of lending money to the federal government.

The Federal Reserve System has two main ways of influencing how much money is available in the economy. First, as we have just seen, it can issue more currency. Second, it can change the rules that tell banks within the Federal Reserve System how much money they may loan out and how much they must keep in reserve. Letting banks loan more money has the same effect as issuing currency—it puts more money into circulation.

A change in the amount of money in circulation is one means of stabilizing the economy. This regulation of supply of money and credit to achieve selected goals is known as *monetary policy.* Like fiscal policy, monetary policy is used to "tune" the economy. You should note that monetary policy is set by the Federal Reserve Board and fiscal policy by Congress and the President. Usually, both types of policy work toward the same goal. An example would be putting the brakes on inflation by raising taxes (fiscal policy) and cutting the amount of money in circulation (monetary policy). Sometimes, however, monetary and fiscal policy have worked at cross purposes because the exact effects of any single policy decision are very difficult to predict in an economy as complex as ours.

Borrowing money is a fifth way of dealing with a budget deficit. Borrowing is an element of fiscal policy, which is determined by the actions of Congress and the President. The Constitution expressly grants to Congress the power "to borrow money on the credit of the United States" (Article I, Section 8).

The federal government borrows money much the same way a business does—by giving, in effect, an I.O.U. This I.O.U. is a promise to pay the money back on a certain date, with interest. The most common of these I.O.U.s are *bonds,* which are certificates containing a promise to repay borrowed money with interest. Like a business, the federal government asks people to loan it money by offering bonds for sale.

The federal government sells two kinds of I.O.U.s—long-term (for many years) and short-term (for 30 days to 7 years). There are two kinds of long-term bonds—savings bonds and Treasury bonds. *Savings bonds* are bought mainly by individuals. You can buy a savings bond for as little as $25.00. *Treasury bonds* are bought mainly by banks and other large investors, such as insurance companies and trust funds. The government's short-term borrowing is done mainly with Treasury notes (for periods of 3 months and up) and Treasury bills.

Foreigners can and do buy United States government bonds, but the people of this country buy most of them. Most federal borrowing, therefore, is from the people themselves. The borrowed money has to be paid back sometime, but in most years the government borrows more money than it pays back. So long as this happens, the government is running up a debt.

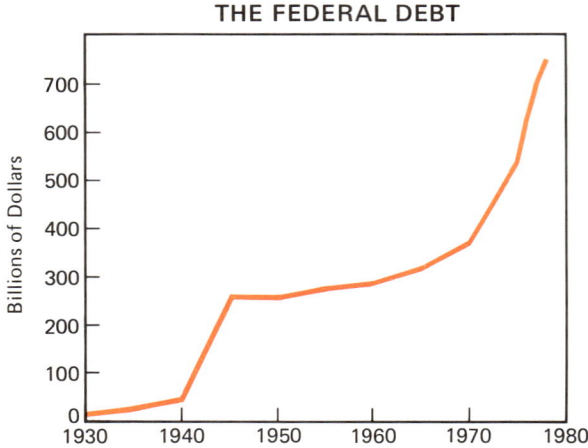

Source: U.S. Department of the Treasury data; Alaska and Hawaii included beginning in 1960; 1978 and 1979 estimated

The Federal Debt

The amount of money owed by the federal government is known as the *federal debt,* the *public debt,* or the *national debt.* In 1978, it amounted to about $750 billion. That averaged out to more than $3,400 for every man, woman, and child in the nation. The average debt per person in the population is the *per capita debt.*

The Constitution puts no limit on the amount of money the government may borrow. However, Congress passes laws that do put such an upper limit, or *ceiling,* on the national debt. Congress often engages in bitter debates when bills are introduced to raise the debt ceiling. Some members of Congress believe that a federal debt on the present scale is unwise and dangerous. They compare federal practices to those of an individual who spends more than he or she earns and has to borrow money to make ends meet. Other members of Congress believe that a federal debt is an essential tool of fiscal policy. They say that public debt cannot be compared to individual debt for that reason. Some members also point out that the federal debt is smaller than the total debt of individuals and corporations.

Most of the federal debt is the result of wars. The graph on this page bears this out.

Notice the steep rise in the World War II period, 1940–1945. In more recent years, the rise in the federal debt has been due to two other factors—inflation and increased outlays for human resources. As we noted, outlays for human resources have grown more rapidly than total federal outlays mainly because of expansion of social security and other income security programs. Since most of the benefits under these programs are related by law to changes in the cost of living, their rise shows the force of inflation as well as the growth of the programs.

The large federal debt has certain repercussions on the nation's economy. One is that the federal government must pay interest on the debt, and money for interest payments must be taken out of federal tax receipts. The bigger the debt, the more interest we must add to the expenditures side of the federal budget. Net interest on the federal debt amounts to $30–$40 billion a year. It accounts for 7 to 8 percent of all federal spending. The money to pay the interest has to be obtained from taxes or from additional borrowing.

Is the federal debt too high? This is a topic that can lead to almost endless debate. Some people say that the United States may one day reach the limit of its credit. Like a free-wheeling gambler after a streak of hard luck, it may suddenly find that no one wants to lend it money any more. This was the idea behind a challenging headline in *Forbes,* a business magazine: "Would you lend money to this outfit?" In fact, the people of this country have readily lent to their government, and they continue to do so. The bonds and notes of the United States government are a form of savings and investment for individuals and businesses. United States bonds and notes have proved to be the safest of all investments because the federal government has always kept its promise to pay. The interest that lenders collect on federal I.O.U.s is a part of their income.

Whether they are willing to lend money to the federal government or not, many people are concerned about balancing the federal budget and reducing the federal debt. When we question the figures, though, what are we really questioning? The size of the budget and the national debt represents decisions that the people in this country have made—decisions about national defense, unemployment, retirement, inflation, and many more subjects. We cannot change the decisions already made. For the future, however, the nation can make other choices. Whatever they are, they will be your choices. Those choices about public policy will be reflected in the federal budget and debt.

Questions

1 What are *five* ways of dealing with a budget deficit?

2 Which executive department has the job of coining and printing money? Which part of the executive branch puts money into circulation?

3 What is monetary policy? What part of government controls it?

4 What is a savings bond? Who might own one?

5 What are some problems related to our large federal debt?

◯ What do you think could be some problems with trying to eliminate the federal debt by raising taxes? By cutting back federal programs?

PROBLEM: HOW MUCH IS ENOUGH FOR NATIONAL DEFENSE?

More than one-fourth of all federal outlays go for national defense. That money pays the salaries of civilians who work for the Defense Department and all members of our armed forces. It also buys guns, bullets, planes, missiles, as well as other supplies, equipment, and services.

The cost of national defense has been going up. In 1960, it was $45.2 billion. In 1969, during the Vietnam war, it was $80.2 billion. It passed the $100 billion mark in 1978. Other nations have also seen their defense budgets rising.

As you read on, ask yourself these questions:

- *Do we spend too much on defense?*
- *Do we spend enough on defense?*

Should Defense Spending Be Increased or Not?

Here are some of the typical arguments for increasing our defense budget:

1. We need to remain militarily strong in order to protect our way of life from foreign invasion.
2. Everything now costs more than it did 10 or 20 years ago; so why shouldn't national defense cost more?
3. A country that is militarily weak invites aggression and invasion from stronger nations.

Chapter 18: Financing the National Government

Typical arguments against increasing our defense budget include the following:

1. With the great power of modern weapons, we are now militarily strong enough to halt any foreign invasion.
2. The taxpayer in this country already has too many taxes to pay; so why pay even more for national defense?
3. We should use more of our tax dollars o feed, house, educate, and, in general, care for our own people.

What Do the People Think about Defense Spending?

In 1973, the American Institute of Public Opinion, better known as the Gallup Poll, conducted a nationwide poll on attitudes toward defense spending. The poll asked people the following question: "There is much discussion as to the amount of money the government in Washington should spend for national defense and military purposes. How do you feel about this? Do you think we are spending too little, too much, or about the right amount?" The table on this page shows how various groups of people responded.

Questions

1 What are three arguments used *in favor of* an increase in defense spending? Can you add other arguments?

2 What are three arguments used *against* an increase in defense spending? Can you add other arguments?

3 What patterns do you see in the answers to the Gallup Poll? How would you explain those response patterns?

4 How would you respond to the question posed by the Gallup Organization? Why?

◇ What do you suppose might happen if the United States spent too little money for defense? If it spent too much money?

Responses to the Gallup Poll

	Too Much	Too Little	About Right	No Opinion
National	46%	13%	30%	11%
By region:				
East	48%	11%	29%	12%
Midwest	50%	10%	32%	8%
South	40%	15%	30%	15%
West	48%	12%	30%	10%
By political party:				
Republicans	31%	14%	43%	12%
Democrats	55%	11%	22%	12%
Independents	47%	15%	21%	17%
By age:				
Under 30	56%	11%	26%	7%
30–49 years	43%	14%	32%	11%
50 and over	41%	13%	31%	15%

Adapted from "Should Defense $s Be Cut?" George Gallup, San Antonio *Express,* October 7, 1973, p. 1B. Reprinted by permission of the American Institute of Public Opinion (The Gallup Poll).

PROBLEM: WHAT SHOULD WE DO ABOUT WELFARE PROGRAMS?

A second controversial area of public spending is welfare. The term *welfare* covers a wide variety of federal programs that provide help to people who are deemed to need it.

People sometimes differ as to just what expenditures to label as "welfare." Are federal subsidies to businesses and farmers a form of welfare? What about certain tax laws that aid mainly middle- and upper-income citizens? What about social security benefits to which people have contributed from past earnings? Some people would include these under "welfare," and some would not. On the other hand, nearly everybody would agree that the term *welfare* does apply to such programs as Aid to Families With Dependent Children.

Defense spending goes for new weapons as well as for conventional ones. This is an artist's drawing of an Advanced Strategic Air Launched Missile, designed for both air-to-ground and air-to-air missions.

As you read the following two selections, ask yourself:

- What problems are raised by certain kinds of welfare?
- How can one distinguish between facts and myths about welfare?

Do Welfare Programs Really Work?

James J. Kilpatrick is a nationally published newspaper columnist. In the following selection adapted from one of his columns, he criticizes some aspects of our welfare programs.

Taxpayers invest billions of dollars each year in programs designed to distribute cash, food, housing, and medical services. Congressional committees and social agencies know how these programs are intended to work. But how do they really work?

A joint House-Senate subcommittee, headed by Martha W. Griffiths of Michigan, has explored that question. The papers released to date provide some insights into the mazes of the welfare world.

This is a world occupied, for one example, by Mary Doe, the 17-year-old mother of two children. Mary is not doing badly. She earns $56 a month in private employment. She gets $542 a month from eight different programs of public assistance. This gives her an income equivalent—all of it tax-free—of $598 a month, or about $7,200 a year. Will Mary ever go off welfare? Don't hold your breath.

Also living in this welfare world is a couple in an Eastern city, John and Susan Roe. They support a young child and Susan's teenaged brother. They have earnings in private employment at the rate of $5,148 a year. On this, they pay federal

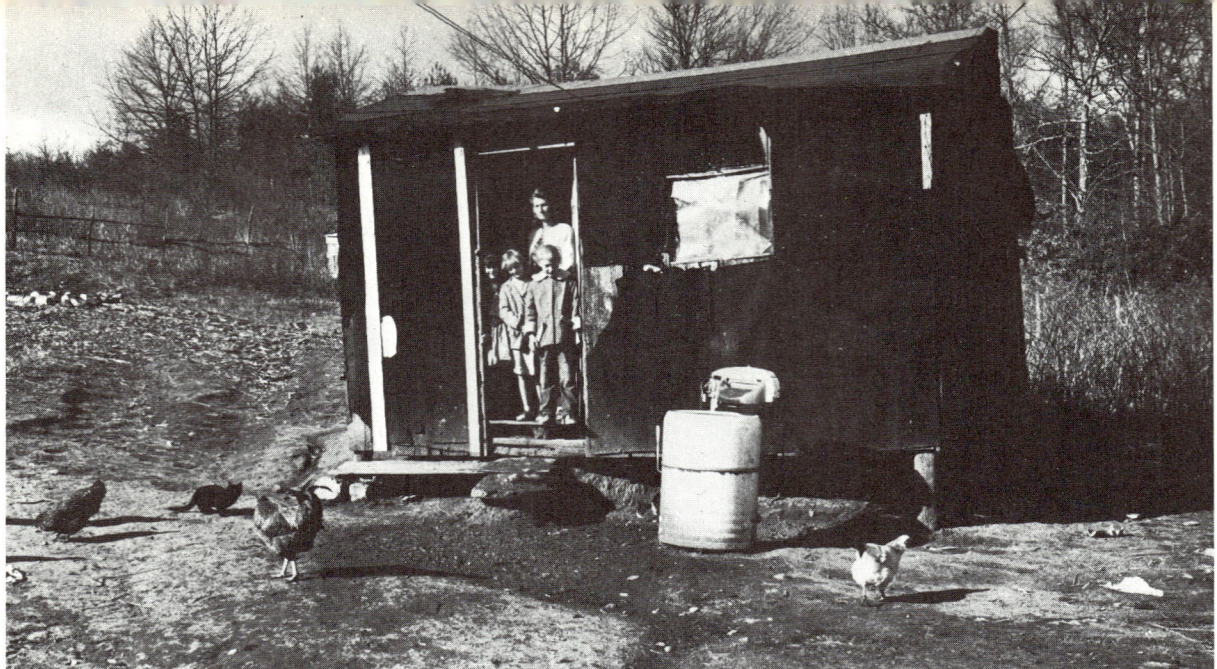

Welfare myths tend to make us forget that poverty does not exist only in cities and densely settled areas.

taxes of $116 a year. This leaves them a net of $5,032.

To this net private income of $5,032, the Roe family add $4,620 a year in tax-exempt benefits from various welfare programs. They live in public housing having a rental value of $106 a month. They get $21 a month in aid to dependent children, $83 in general assistance, $34 in food stamps, $123 in Medicaid, and $18 from a neighborhood youth corps. They are thus making do, after taxes, on $9,652 a year.

The two households are not necessarily typical. But they are not unique, either. The subcommittee staff based its study on a random study of 1,758 households drawn from six sites designated by the Census Bureau as "low income" areas. About one in four of all families in these areas are statistically "poor." Over the 12-month period of the study, at least 1,154 of the households received some public benefit.

One-fifth of the 1,154 households received only a single public benefit—nothing but social security, for example. The rest were collecting from two or more programs. The study turned up one three-generation family of five, living in a Southern city, which received $8,300 over a 12-month period from eleven federal programs.

In many cases, welfare families plainly do better by not working than by working. Their combined tax-free benefits in cash, food, and housing—not counting medical care, manpower training, and the like—exceed the income they might earn in private employment. In a typical welfare family, a job can become a calamity: as private income goes up, public benefits go down. Too much income can bring eviction from a housing project, the loss of food stamps, and the loss of Medicaid. In the real world of public welfare, why work?

Adapted from James J. Kilpatrick, "How Messy Welfare Really Is," San Antonio *Express*, August 27, 1973, p. 16A. Copyright© Washington Star Syndicate, Inc.

What Are Truths about Welfare and What Are Myths?

Joseph A. Califano, Jr., became Secretary of Health, Education, and Welfare in 1977. In the following selection adapted from one of his speeches, he suggests that some people who criticize welfare programs use misleading arguments.

The gap between the realities of poverty and the public perception of the poor population is one of the major barriers to effective welfare reform. We must work to dispel the myths and misconceptions about the poor. The five most common myths are:

Myth No. 1. People are poor because they do not work and do not want to work. This is the most pernicious and widespread myth. The facts are quite different. Nearly 71 percent of the 26 million poor are people that we do not normally ask to work. They are children and young people under 16, the aged, the severely disabled, students, or mothers with children under 6. In addition, 19 percent of the poor population work either full-time or part-time. Thus, 90 percent of the poor either work at least part-time or are people no civilized society would force to work.

Only 2 percent of the 26 million poor people even resemble the mythical welfare stereotype—males who are neither aged nor disabled but who do not work. And census figures show that most of this group are between 62 and 64, ill, or looking for work.

The facts are that the vast majority of household heads who live in poverty are working; that nearly one-third of these work full-time, all year around, and still remain poor. The poor are poor, not because they will not and do not work, but because when they do work, they do not earn enough money to lift them out of poverty.

Myth No. 2. Most of the poor are poor for life. The fact is that sizable numbers of people move in and out of poverty with remarkable frequency. Each year, about 7.5 million to 10 million people move above the poverty line, and a like number become poor. Most of those who are poor are poor, not because of some character flaw or personal failing, but because of events they cannot control. And many of them do, in fact, regain higher incomes and climb back again out of poverty.

Myth No. 3. The poor are mostly black and nonwhite. The fact is that 69 percent of the poor people are white.

Myth No. 4. The poor do not know how to spend their money. The evidence shows that low-income people spend a somewhat greater proportion of their income on food, clothing, housing, medical care, and transportation than do people with higher incomes.

Myth No. 5. Many welfare families receive payments that are far too high. The fact is that in twenty-four states the combined benefits of Aid to Families with Dependent Children and the food stamp program total less than three-fourths of the official poverty-income level. And that poverty level was only $5,500 for a family of four in 1975.

Adapted from a speech by Joseph A. Califano, Jr., Secretary, Department of Health, Education, and Welfare, before the Washington Press Club, April 27, 1977.

Questions

1 What seems to be Kilpatrick's principal criticism of the way welfare programs work?

2 What change in those programs could you suggest that might meet his criticism? Do you think such a change would be fair? Fair to whom?

3 In what way does Califano's approach to the welfare question differ from Kilpatrick's? Do you think the two might agree on any aspect of welfare? If so, what aspect?

4 The federal government has put up money to help large corporations, such as aircraft manufacturers, get out of financial trouble. Would you call such help "welfare"? Why or why not?

◌ Do you think the idea of federal welfare in general is good or bad? Explain.

Chapter 18 Review

Recalling and Comparing

1 List at least *six* steps in the preparation of a federal budget.

2 What *three* departments of the executive branch spend the most money?

3 What are *three* sources of income for our federal government?

4 Both the Bureau of Engraving and Printing and the Federal Reserve System deal with our national currency. What is the main difference in their roles?

5 Has the federal government usually had a balanced budget? Why or why not?

6 In what ways do you think borrowing by the federal government resembles borrowing by an individual? In what ways do you think it is different?

7 Do you think it is more important to reduce the federal debt or to reduce taxes? Explain.

Special Activities

1 Make a special bulletin-board display about the most recent federal budget. Use pie graphs to show where the federal budget dollar comes from and what it goes for.

2 Prepare a skit containing three characters: a Welfare Individual, a Federal Bureaucrat, and an Angry Taxpayer. Have them present arguments for and against the present federal welfare system.

3 Look up the word *money* in an encyclopedia or other reference book. Write a report giving a brief history of money.

4 Take your own opinion poll on defense spending and chart your findings.

5 Consider what might be arguments for and against the following statement: "Every federal budget should be balanced." Do you agree or disagree? Why?

Developing Your Political Vocabulary

Tell what the terms in *a–e* mean. Then match each term with an entry in 1–5 and tell what the connection is.

appropriations	**a**	**1**	Internal Revenue Service
transfer payments	**b**	**2**	House of Representatives
budget	**c**	**3**	Department of Health, Education, and Welfare
progressive tax	**d**		
legal tender	**e**	**4**	Federal Reserve System
		5	Office of Management and Budget

Unit VI Review

Improving Your Reading

Read the selection below and then answer the questions that follow it.

Over the years, economic and social changes have brought changes in the nation's needs. Our federal government has grown as a result of those needs. Economic and social changes have also brought changes in our expectations about government. We have put new demands upon government, and it has grown to meet them.

Our national government has grown tremendously. This growth is shown, for one thing, in the increased number of people employed by the federal government. Second, it is shown in the rising federal payroll. In our daily lives, it is shown in the increased paper work required to comply with federal rules and regulations.

The federal budget has grown along with the role of government. This summary of income and expenditures is prepared annually. The executive branch and the legislative branch share the job of drawing up the budget. The budget takes 18 months to prepare.

Federal spending goes for a wide variety of activities. In recent years, the largest amounts have gone to pay for human resources and defense. Almost all the expenditures are made by the agencies of the executive branch.

Money to pay for our federal budget comes from many sources. Much of it is from taxes on individual or business income. An important payroll tax goes to finance the social security program. The federal tax burden on the average individual has increased over the years as federal government activities have broadened.

The federal government does not always take in as much money in taxes as it spends. When this happens, the budget is said to run a deficit. In most years of this century, our federal government has operated at a deficit.

Both fiscal and monetary policy are employed to deal with deficits. Fiscal policy includes changes in the budget, such as raising and lowering taxes, raising and lowering spending, and borrowing. Monetary policy includes such activities as printing more money or otherwise increasing the amount of money in circulation.

Over the years, our national government has borrowed extensively. The total amount that it now owes is known as the federal debt.

1 In your own words, summarize this reading in *no more than five* sentences. Focus on what you regard as the five most important points made in the reading.

2 The term *fiscal policy* can best be applied to which *three* of the following terms as they appeared in the reading?
   a budget
   b federal debt
   c taxes
   d deficit

3 Which *one* of the following four descriptions can best be used to define the term *federal budget?*
   a source of federal income
   b plan for federal receipts and expenditures
   c expenses for the upkeep of the nation's health, education, welfare, and defense

d amount of money borrowed by the federal government

Developing Your Writing Skills: What Are Your Attitudes toward Government?

Writing a Paragraph

In this unit, you have considered some of the problems associated with the size and cost of the federal government. Think back over what you have read. As you do so, consider these questions:

- *What are four possible problems associated with the size and cost of our federal government?*
- *How could those things seem like problems to some people?*
- *Which one of those problems seems most important to you?*

On a separate sheet of paper, write the following topic sentence. Complete the sentence and then fill out the paragraph with arguments in support of your position.

Of the problems I have noted about the size and cost of the federal government, I believe the one that should receive the most consideration is _____
_____

Writing an Essay

1 Write a short essay in favor of or opposed to the federal government's present fiscal policy. Do library research for background information.

2 Write an essay commenting on the statement: "Taxes are the price we pay for civilized society." This statement was made by Oliver Wendell Holmes (1841–1935), who was an associate justice of the United States Supreme Court. Consider the statement against the background of Holmes's lifetime and our own times. Do you think it was true in his lifetime? Do you think it is true today?

Recommended Reading

Patricia C. Acheson, *Our Federal Government: How It Works,* Harper & Row, New York, 1970 (paperback).

F. M. Bator, *The Question of Government Spending: Public Needs and Private Wants,* Macmillan, New York, 1962 (paperback).

Facts about United States Money, U.S. Government Printing Office, 1976.

Harold M. Groves and R. Bish, *Financing Government,* Holt, New York, 1973.

Richard Hofstadter, *American Political Tradition,* Knopf, New York, 1973.

Henry Owen and Charles L. Schultze (eds.), *Setting National Priorities in the Next Ten Years,* Brookings Institution, Washington, D.C., 1976.

Austin Ranney and Willmoore Kendall, *Democracy and the American Party System,* Greenwood Press, Westport, Conn., 1975.

Ruth Leger Sivard, *World Military and Social Expenditures* (annual), WMSE Publications, Leesburg, Virginia; available from The Rockefeller Foundation, New York.

United States Government Manual (annual), U.S. Government Printing Office.

State Government

The state governments seem to have grown naturally, as the country grew. First there were 13, then 14 . . . 48 . . . 50. Who can imagine a United States without a Massachusetts or a Texas or a California? Some people can, and several of them have proposed changes in the number of states.

G. Etzel Pearcy is a geographer who thinks that the states are put together wrong. Pearcy has suggested fitting the fifty states into a new pattern with only thirty-eight pieces. His reasons are explained in the following account.

Why the need for a new map? Pearcy says that many of the state boundaries were drawn while the areas were scarcely populated. Boundaries were fixed by using the land's physical features, such as rivers and mountain ranges, or simply by using latitude and longitude. The usefulness of the old state lines is now questionable. For example, some urban areas cross state lines.

One of the advantages of Pearcy's state regrouping is the money that it would save taxpayers. According to Pearcy, about 25 percent of state spending goes for maintaining state government itself. He has estimated the annual savings in such costs at $100 per person if thirty-eight states replaced the present fifty.

In realigning the United States, Pearcy gave high priority to population density, location of cities, lines of transportation, land relief, and size and shape of individual states. Where possible, he located his lines in less populated areas. Each major city that now spreads across state lines was neatly tucked within the boundaries of a new state. Pearcy tried to place a major metropolitan area in the center of each state.

Pearcy did not attempt to consider all factors. Other factors he thinks worth considering are sources of water supply, location of resources, and composition of population.

Adapted from "A 38-State Nation," *The People's Almanac*. Copyright © 1975 by David Wallechinsky and Irving Wallace. Reprinted by permission of Doubleday and Company, Inc.

For the present, Pearcy's proposal for redrawing state lines seems unlikely to catch on. Most of us are attached by history and by personal and political experience to the present system of fifty states. This unit is about those fifty states. It will consider how they are governed, what they do for us, and what problems they face. But keep Pearcy's proposal in mind as you read. We will return to it at the end of the unit.

Chapter 19 takes up structure and goals. Chapter 20 turns to government in operation.

Chapter **19**

Formation and Goals of State Government

States existed in this country before there was a federal government. Any discussion of the system of government in the United States must recognize this fact. Our federal system was set up in 1787 by thirteen states that delegated certain powers to the national government and kept all other powers for themselves.

The thirteen original states served as a laboratory for democratic government. At first, these states tried to band together loosely in a confederation, but the Articles of Confederation did not work. The thirteen states then decided on a federal government modeled on their own state governments. In turn, that federal government and the Constitution on which it rests served as a model for the government of the other thirty-seven states that are now part of this nation. It is not surprising, then, that our state governments are similar in many ways.

It is not surprising, either, that there are important differences within these broad similarities. Even at the beginning, the states differed from one another in size, number of people, and way of life. A federal government was achieved only by painful compromise. The addition of more states brought an even greater range of state size, traditions, and needs. The fifty state governments reflect these differences. How those state governments came into being, their functions, and their sources of income will be the subject of this chapter.

Chapter 19: Formation and Goals of State Government

Goals

- *To learn how our state governments came into existence.*
- *To learn the various roles of state governments.*
- *To study how state governments are financed.*
- *To consider how state governments can introduce new political ideas.*

FORMATION OF OUR STATE GOVERNMENTS

The Declaration of Independence in 1776 cut the thirteen colonies adrift from their political moorings. Until that year, each had been firmly anchored to a colonial charter. The charters provided a link to British rule and set the framework within which the colonies passed laws and governed. In 1776, the colonies-turned-states began to replace their charters with state constitutions. Each of these constitutions provided for a representative form of government.

Basic ideas about government in the original state constitutions reappeared in the United States Constitution in 1787. Representative government was one such idea. Another was the separation of government into three branches—legislative, executive, and judicial. All of the original state constitutions had such a separation of powers. Seven of those state constitutions included a bill of rights, as the United States Constitution was to do in its first set of amendments.

Looking at the original thirteen state constitutions, one can also find some differences from the United States Constitution. The states generally gave the legislatures the biggest share of power. Only two of the original thirteen states, Massachusetts and South Carolina, gave the governor a power of veto. But the greatest difference between state constitutions and the federal Constitution has come about over time.

Since this difference is due to the amendment process, let's consider how state constitutions are amended. Amendments can be proposed by the legislature in every state. Nearly all states provide for constitutional conventions. Some states even require that the voters be asked every 10, 20, or other specified period of years whether a constitutional convention should be held. One-third of the states permit initiative petitions for amending their constitutions. Whichever of the three methods is used, a majority of the voters must approve proposed changes for them to take effect.

As we have seen, no convention for the purpose of amending the United States Constitution has yet been held. Many states, however, have amended their constitutions—and a few have even replaced them—as a result of constitutional conventions. New constitutions have been adopted as many as six, eight, and, in Louisiana, eleven times. Nevertheless, a complete overhaul is not the general practice. Instead, states have tended to add amendments rather freely, with predictable results.

Unlike the Constitution of the United States, which merely lays down general principles, the present state constitutions tend to go into the details of government. The United States Constitution is concise and brief (7,000 words). One-half of the state constitutions have 20,000 words or more. New York's constitution has 47,000 words; Georgia's has 500,000. Some people maintain that great detail results in confusion and causes a constitution to become quickly outdated so that further amendment is needed. For years, reformers have been urging the replacement of detailed state constitutions with shorter ones. Some states have done so; most have not.

The Powers of the States

When the original thirteen states formed a federal government, they agreed that the Constitution of the United States would be the supreme law of the land. That document sets

These New Mexico delegates are working on revisions of the state's constitution. Some states hold periodic statewide conventions to propose amendments to their constitutions.

the limits within which each state in the Union may operate.

The Constitution places certain restrictions on the states, just as it does on Congress. Article I, Section 10 declares that states cannot:

1. make treaties
2. coin money
3. pass a bill of attainder or an *ex post facto* law
4. pass a law impairing the obligation of contract
5. grant titles of nobility
6. tax imports or exports without the consent of Congress
7. keep troops or warships in time of peace
8. sign agreements with other states or with foreign nations without the consent of Congress
9. engage in war unless invaded

Some of these powers are reserved to the federal government. Others are forbidden to it, too. (See pages 86–87.)

Several amendments to the Constitution also limit the power of states. Thus, states cannot:

1. permit slavery (Thirteenth Amendment)
2. abridge "the privileges or immunities" of United States citizens (Fourteenth Amendment)
3. deprive anyone "of life, liberty, or property without due process of law," nor deny anyone "the equal protection of the laws" (Fourteenth Amendment)
4. deny anyone the right to vote because of race or color (Fifteenth Amendment), sex (Nineteenth Amendment), or age beyond the age of 17 (Twenty-sixth Amendment)
5. deny anyone the right to vote in a national election because of failure to pay a poll tax or other tax (Twenty-fourth Amendment)

What *can* the states do? That question is not answered directly by the Constitution. No article lists state powers in the way that the powers of Congress are listed. That is why the first set of amendments includes one, the Tenth Amendment, that declares:

The powers not delegated to the United States by the Constitution, nor prohibited by it to the States, are reserved to the States respectively, or to the people.

The Tenth Amendment is the last one in the Bill of Rights. The states that had created the federal government wanted to remove any doubts about the source of power. Power flowed from the people and the states to the federal government. It did not the other way around.

Members of the Pennsylvania National Guard are helping people during a flood at Johnstown. Every state has a National Guard unit to protect the life and property of its residents.

By now, tradition and court rulings have made it clear what powers belong to states, under the Constitution.

Certain powers are shared by the states and federal government. These shared powers are known as *concurrent powers*. Thus, not only Congress but also each state has the power:

1. to make and enforce laws
2. to establish courts
3. to tax
4. to borrow money
5. to spend money for the general welfare
6. to take property for public purposes, so long as payment is made

It would be difficult, if not impossible, for any government to operate without these powers.

The states have some powers that the federal government does not have. These *reserved powers* give each state the power:

1. to protect life and property and maintain order
2. to protect health, safety, and morals
3. to regulate commerce within the state
4. to establish local governments
5. to conduct elections
6. to ratify amendments to the United States Constitution
7. to change its own constitution

The Constitution provides certain guarantees to the states. These protections are stated in Article IV.

1. Each state will give "full Faith and Credit" to every other state's "public Acts, Records, and judicial Proceedings." This means that the laws, legal papers, and court rulings of one state are recognized in all other states. Examples are birth certificates, marriage certificates, wills, and contracts.
2. The rights a United States citizen has in one state will be respected by all other states.
3. Every state will return a fugitive who is wanted for a serious crime or for escaping custody. This surrender of a fugitive is known as *extradition*. There is no way of forcing extradition, and state governors have refused it in a few cases.
4. No new state will be formed within an existing state or by joining together existing states or parts of states unless the legislatures of the states involved and Congress agree to it.

The Fifty States and Their Origins

State	Source of State Lands	Admission as a State Year	Rank Order
Alabama	Mississippi Territory, 1798	1819	22
Alaska	Purchased from Russia, 1867	1959	49
Arizona	Ceded by Mexico, 1848; small portion of land obtained by Gadsden Purchase, 1853	1912	48
Arkansas	Louisiana Purchase, 1803	1836	25
California	Ceded by Mexico, 1848	1850	31
Colorado	Louisiana Purchase, 1803; portion of land ceded by Mexico, 1848	1876	38
*Connecticut	Fundamental Orders, January 14, 1638; English charter, 1662	1788	5
*Delaware	Swedish charter, 1638; English charter, 1683	1787	1
Florida	Ceded by Spain, 1819	1845	27
*Georgia	English charter, 1732, from George II to Trustees for Establishing the Colony of Georgia	1788	4
Hawaii	Annexed 1898	1959	50
Idaho	Treaty with Britain, 1846	1890	43
Illinois	Northwest Territory, 1787	1818	21
Indiana	Northwest Territory, 1787	1816	19
Iowa	Louisiana Purchase, 1803	1846	29
Kansas	Louisiana Purchase, 1803; portion of land ceded by Mexico, 1848	1861	34
Kentucky	Part of Virginia until admitted as state	1792	15
Louisiana	Louisiana Purchase, 1803	1812	18
Maine	Part of Massachusetts until admitted as state	1820	23
*Maryland	English charter, 1632, from Charles I to Calvert	1788	7
*Massachusetts	English charter, 1629, to Massachusetts Bay Company	1788	6
Michigan	Northwest Territory, 1787	1837	26
Minnesota	Northwest Territory, 1787; portion of land obtained by Louisiana Purchase, 1803	1858	32
Mississippi	Mississippi Territory; portion acquired from Spain in 1813	1817	20
Missouri	Louisiana Purchase, 1803	1821	24
Montana	Louisiana Purchase, 1803; portion obtained from Oregon Territory, 1848	1889	41
Nebraska	Louisiana Purchase, 1803	1867	37
Nevada	Ceded by Mexico, 1848	1864	36
*New Hampshire	Grants from Council for New England, 1622 and 1629	1788	9
*New Jersey	Dutch settlement, 1618; English charter, 1644	1787	3
New Mexico	Ceded by Mexico, 1848	1912	47
*New York	Dutch settlement, 1623; English control, 1664	1788	11
*North Carolina	English charter, 1663	1789	12
North Dakota	Louisiana Purchase, 1803; portion acquired by treaty with Great Britian in 1818	1889	39
Ohio	Northwest Territory, 1787	1803	17
Oklahoma	Louisiana Purchase, 1803	1907	46

*One of the original thirteen colonies.

Continued on next page

Chapter 19: Formation and Goals of State Government

The Fifty States and Their Origins (continued)

State	Source of State Lands	Admission as a State Year	Rank Order
Oregon	Settlement and treaty with Britain, 1846	1859	33
*Pennsylvania	English grant, 1681, from Charles II to William Penn	1787	2
*Rhode Island	English charter, 1663	1790	13
*South Carolina	English charter, 1663	1788	8
South Dakota	Louisiana Purchase, 1803	1889	40
Tennessee	Part of North Carolina until land ceded to United States in 1789	1796	16
Texas	Republic of Texas, 1845	1845	28
Utah	Ceded by Mexico, 1848	1896	45
Vermont	From lands of New Hampshire and New York	1791	14
*Virginia	English charter, 1609, from James I to London Company	1788	10
Washington	Oregon Territory, 1848	1889	42
West Virginia	Part of Virginia until admitted as a state	1863	35
Wisconsin	Northwest Territory, 1787	1848	30
Wyoming	Louisiana Purchase, 1803; small portions of land from Mexican Cession and Oregon Territory, 1848	1890	44

*One of the original thirteen colonies.

5. The federal government will guarantee every state a republican—that is, representative—form of government.
6. The federal government will protect every state against invasion.
7. At the request of the state legislature or governor, the federal government will protect a state against "domestic violence." An example would be rioting and looting.

Each state constitution sets out rules for that state within the limits of the United States Constitution.

Admission of New States

The United States Constitution gives Congress the final say in admitting new states to the Union (Article IV, Section 3). We have just seen the guarantees this section provides. The procedure for admission is set out in federal laws.

Suppose a group of people living in an area that is not now a state want to set up a new state. They ask Congress for permission. Congress then passes an enabling act, calling for the preparation of a state constitution that sets up a representative government conforming to the United States Constitution. A convention is held to draw up a constitution that is then submitted to a vote of the people living in the proposed state. It passes. Then Congress, by majority vote, grants statehood. (Of course, Congress may also reject statehood.)

Thirty-seven times over the years, Congress has exercised its power of admission. Some of the new states were formed by dividing old states. Maine, for example, separated from Massachusetts in 1820 with the parent state's consent. Another state, Texas, was an independent republic before joining the Union in 1845. The terms of its admission provide that Texas can divide itself into as many as five states if it wants. Other states were formed on land that the federal government had bought from other countries or gained by war or treaty. These areas were governed for a time as territories. The two newest states, Alaska and

A Honolulu news vendor expressed Hawaii's pride and joy as a bill making Hawaii a state was sent to the President.

Hawaii, were territories before being admitted to the Union in 1959.

Questions

1 What is *one* way in which state constitutions sometimes differ from the United States Constitution?

2 What are some activities forbidden to the states by the Constitution?

3 What are some rights that are guaranteed to the states by the United States Constitution?

4 How can a territory become a state?

⬠ Do you think that a constitution—state or federal—could ever put too many restrictions on a state's powers? Explain.

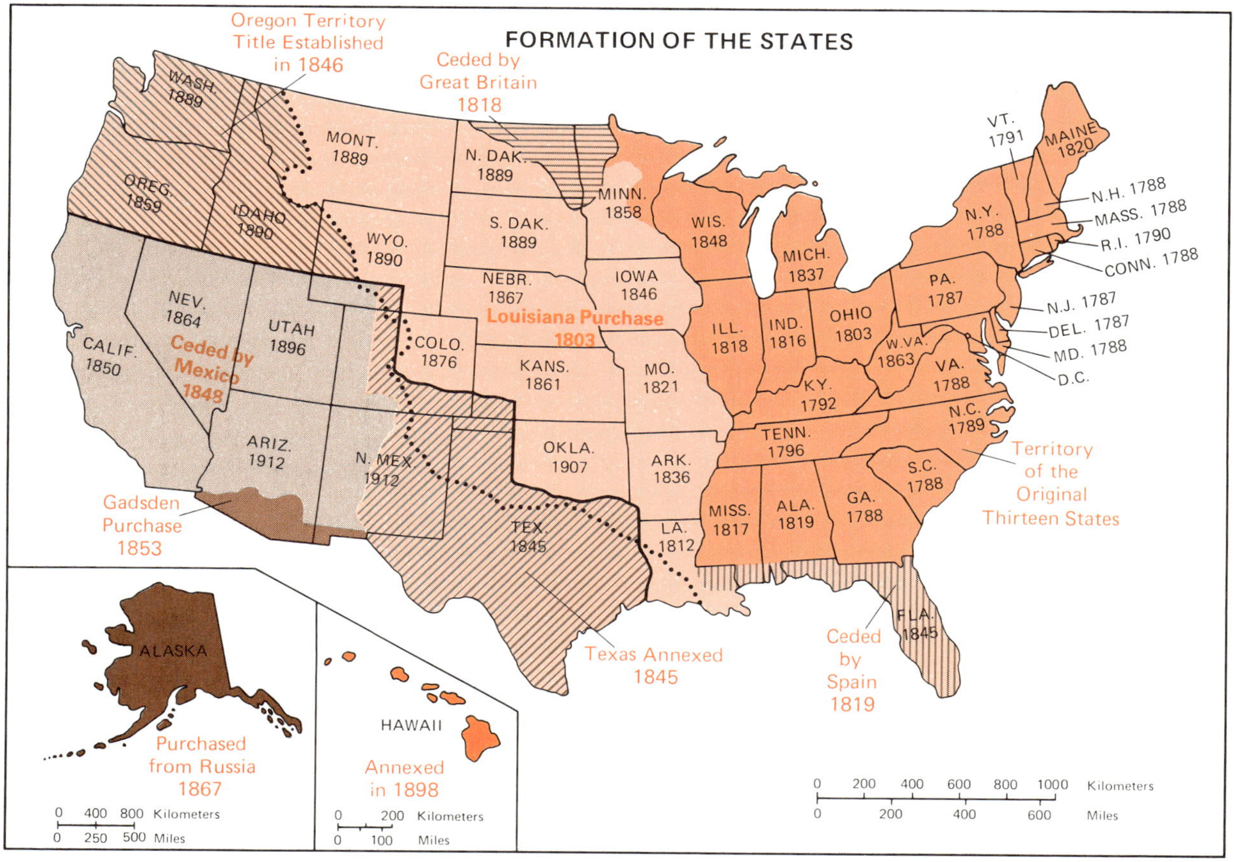

Chapter 19: Formation and Goals of State Government

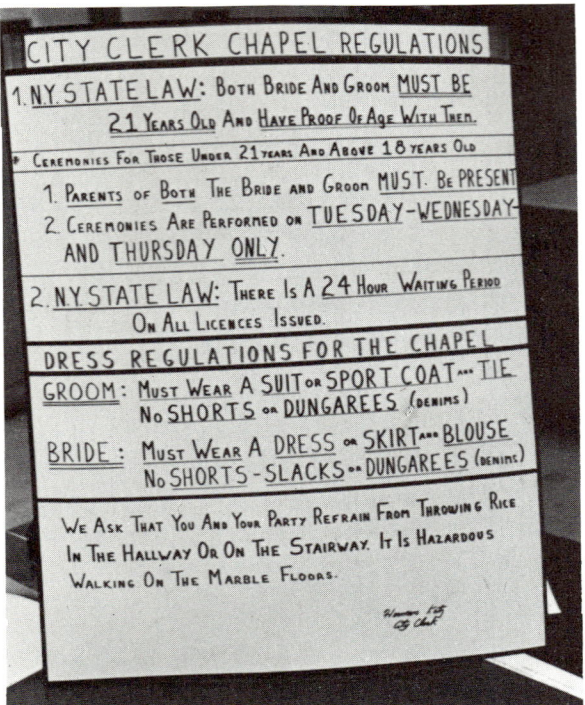

Marriage laws are among the state laws that closely affect our lives. Local regulations are subject to state review.

FUNCTIONS OF STATE GOVERNMENTS

The main functions of state governments are similar to those of the federal government. The original thirteen states did not change their own government apart from turning over certain powers to the federal government. Remember that at the time of the Constitutional Convention in 1787, people looked to the states to perform most governmental functions. The federal government was to do only those things that the states could not do by themselves. As time went on and conditions changed, the federal government assumed more and more responsibilities.

Even today, though, the federal government carries on many of its activities through the states. It leaves certain decisions to be made at the state or local level, closer to the people. For example, the federal government set up a system of unemployment insurance in the 1930s. But the states administer this system. The federal government provides much of the money for the nation's highways. But state governments decide where the roads should go and build the roads.

The Declaration of Independence tells us that governments exist to assure people of life, liberty, and the pursuit of happiness. In the states, we see these functions in a direct way. The laws that affect our daily lives are usually made at the state level. State laws define what is a crime, and they also provide various forms of police protection. State laws provide for our systems of education and decide at what age we may marry or drive a car. State laws also control most property transactions. The limits within which county, city, and other local governments may operate are set by state constitutions and laws.

The Size and Growth of State Governments

The size of state governments has been increasing at a more rapid rate than the size of the federal government. This fact surprises many people because of frequent reports that the federal government is getting bigger and bigger. But the state governments are growing even faster as people demand more service from their state and local governments.

To carry out their functions, state governments now employ more people than the federal government. Compared with a federal total of 2.9 million civilian employees, states employ 3.3 million.

State spending has also been increasing faster than federal spending. In the 15 years from 1960 to 1975, spending by state governments increased from $26 billion to $117 billion, or by 450 percent. During the same 15 years, spending by the federal government went up 300 percent from $100 billion to $300 billion. (Federal expenditures have been adjusted to match the state system of reporting for the purposes of this comparison.)

High school courses, such as this foreign language laboratory, must meet minimum statewide standards in many states.

Where does all the state money go? The answer gives a clue to the major functions of state government. Pie graph A on page 356 shows the average distribution for all states.

The biggest portion of state expenditures goes for education. One-third of all the money spent by the fifty states goes for education. State-operated colleges and universities receive by far the largest part of this money. Only a small part goes to elementary and secondary schools because they are supported mainly by local taxes in most states. As we shall see in the next unit, the battle that began in the 1970s over local taxes may change the picture of state finances in the future. The state constitutions and laws make the rules for school taxes. The states also set minimum statewide standards for elementary and secondary schools, leaving final decisions about education to local school boards. For example, a state government may require each school to hold classes a minimum number of days each year. It may set qualifications for teachers. It may require certain courses to be offered in all public schools.

Another large share of state money goes for public welfare, to help people in need. Much of this money is paid out for medical care. The states also provide cash assistance to the needy—the elderly, the blind, the disabled, and the unemployed. Each state sets its own rules for welfare, and the rules vary greatly.

Insurance benefits account for a major share of state expenditures. These benefits are cash payments from *insurance reserves.* Unemployment insurance, pensions for state employees, and workmen's compensation are the main insurance systems. Payments into these systems and interest on this money provide the reserves.

Public welfare and insurance benefits together account for nearly one-third of every dollar spent by the states.

One-tenth of every dollar spent by the states goes to maintain state highways and secondary roads. From this nation's earliest days, the building of roads has been an important function of government. Roads are necessary not only for travel but also to get products to markets. Roads are highly visible; when snow or potholes make the going difficult, people are quick to complain. The states also set rules for the use of roads—what qualifica-

Chapter 19: Formation and Goals of State Government

tions a driver must have and, on state highways, what vehicles are permitted and what the speed limit is.

The next largest share of state money goes for hospitals and health. State governments maintain certain specialized hospitals, promote the health of the people, and try to prevent the spread of disease. Each state regulates the practice of medicine and the sale of drugs. The states also set rules for restaurants and other places that handle food, so as to halt the spread of disease. States require health examinations for school pupils.

A large number of other functions account for the rest of the state dollar. These other functions can be grouped into four broad categories, as follows:

States protect the lives and property of their inhabitants. A state police force or a state highway patrol enforces state laws outside of cities. Units of the National Guard are maintained in each state. Any governor can order

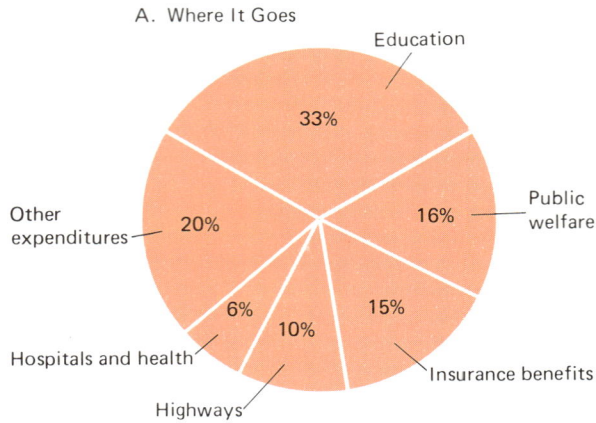

THE STATE GOVERNMENT DOLLAR

A. Where It Goes

- Education 33%
- Public welfare 16%
- Insurance benefits 15%
- Highways 10%
- Hospitals and health 6%
- Other expenditures 20%

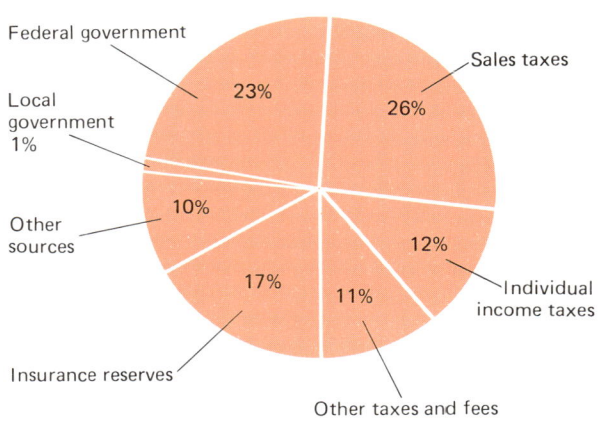

B. Where It Comes From

- Sales taxes 26%
- Federal government 23%
- Insurance reserves 17%
- Individual income taxes 12%
- Other taxes and fees 11%
- Other sources 10%
- Local government 1%

Source: Both; U.S. Bureau of the Census data for 1976

the state's National Guard to help put down riots or respond to natural disasters, such as floods and violent storms. States also operate court systems and maintain state prisons.

States seek to conserve natural resources. Since early in this century, states have played a major role in preserving land, forests, and wildlife. Efforts are made to prevent waste that occurs through soil erosion, reckless cutting, and uncontrolled killing of animals. In recent years, states have joined the federal government in combating pollution.

States regulate business activity in various ways. Many states have commissions or other agencies to regulate the activities of banks,

Despite federal aid, states spend heavily on highways and roads. States pay 10 percent of federal road construction.

insurance companies, public utilities, and transportation companies. States often require licenses for the operation of certain professions or trades. Doctors, lawyers, teachers, electricians, and plumbers are among those licensed. A license may also be required to operate a bar, an auto repair shop, or a television repair shop. States have laws regulating working conditions or requiring safety inspections in mines, factories, or stores. States may also regulate collective bargaining between management and unions.

Many states have agencies to protect the rights of their residents. These rights include the freedoms of speech, press, religion, and assembly guaranteed in state constitutions. Some states pioneered in civil rights legislation, long before the federal government acted to end discrimination. States may, and often do, grant broader rights than the United States Constitution does.

Each state decides on its own "mix" of functions. Some states spend heavily on education, while others spend more sparingly. Some states have strict regulations on business activities, while others have much looser regulations. In our federal system, it is up to the citizens of each state to decide how their state government will go about its business.

Questions

1 Give an example of cooperation between the federal government and state governments.

2 What are *three* ways in which your state government affects your daily life?

3 On what activity do state governments spend the most money? What other activities account for significant shares of state spending?

4 What are *three* kinds of insurance benefits paid by the states?

◌ How well do you think your state government meets the needs of the people of your state?

HOW STATE GOVERNMENTS GET THEIR MONEY

The states obtain money from three main sources. The largest of these is state taxes. Contributions to insurance funds are another major source of state revenue. The states receive the rest of their income mainly from the federal government. Pie graph B on page 356 shows the share received from each major source.

The state governments depend on state taxes for about one-half of their income. The states have a variety of taxes, including some kinds that the federal government does not have.

The biggest single revenue-producer in most states is the sales tax. As already mentioned, the sales tax is a regressive tax because the rate is the same for everyone regardless of ability to pay. One-fourth of all state income is from this source. When you go to a hardware store to buy a hammer, do you pay the amount marked on the hammer? Or do you pay a few cents more? If the clerk adds a small sum to your bill, it is probably a sales tax. Like federal excise taxes, state sales taxes are figured as a percentage of the price of each item. The amount might be as litttle as 2 cents on each dollar or as much as 7 or 8 cents. Often there are local sales taxes as well.

Sales taxes are of two types. If the tax is charged on all except a few purchases, it is a *general sales tax.* General sales taxes often exempt medicines, food, or other necessities. If a tax is charged only on certain purchases, it is a *selective sales tax,* which is a form of excise tax. A tax on motor fuel is an example of a selective sales tax or an excise tax. If you have traveled by car across the country, you know that the tax on gasoline varies from state to state. There is also a federal tax on gasoline. So each time you fill up the tank, you are paying taxes to two levels of government.

Personal income taxes bring in about half as much state income as sales taxes do. Many

Tolls paid to use state turnpikes and roads, bridges, ferries, and docks provide a good deal of income for some states.

states have a personal income tax. This tax, like the federal income tax, is usually progressive—that is, people with larger incomes pay at a higher rate. State income taxes apply to income derived from sources within the state. Thus, you might live in state A but pay income taxes to state B because you work there.

In addition to sales taxes and individual income taxes, many other taxes and fees are used. One large group of these taxes may be called *business taxes*. States tax businesses in several ways. The fees charged for the licenses mentioned earlier (page 357) are a form of business tax. In addition, all but a few states levy taxes on the income of corporations. *Severance taxes* on the removal of natural resources, such as oil or timber, are a large source of income for some states.

A *property tax* is sometimes levied, either on *real property*, consisting of land and buildings, or on *personal property*, such as cars, furniture, and stocks and bonds. Some states use a personal property tax in place of a personal income tax. At one time, property taxes were the main source of state income, but local governments have now mainly taken over the property tax. It will be discussed further in the next unit.

Nearly all of the states collect an *inheritance tax* on the property of people who die. This "death tax" is in addition to the federal inheritance tax. In many states, anyone who makes a large gift of money or property to another person must pay a *gift tax*.

Fees are charged for the ownership and operation of motor vehicles and other purposes. When you apply for a driver's license or register an automobile, motorcycle, truck, or bus, you pay a fee in exchange for a license issued by your state. Besides license fees, states usually collect a small fee for recording legal documents, such as mortgages and deeds. Fees called *tolls* are charged at some docks, canals, bridges, and ferries operated by state governments, as well as state toll roads.

Apart from taxes, states obtain a large part of their money from insurance reserves. These reserves, as noted earlier (page 355), are accumulated from employers' payments into special funds set aside for insurance benefits and from the interest on those payments. The money in insurance reserves can be used only for the purpose for which it was collected.

Some states operate certain businesses, such as liquor stores and power or water companies. Any net income a state receives from these businesses is part of the state's revenue.

Significant amounts of money flow to the states from the federal government. This means that part of the money the federal government collects from taxpayers is redistributed among the states. About one-fourth of all state revenue now comes from the federal government. The states receive some of this federal money from *grants* for specific purposes, such as roads or education, and some from the federal *revenue-sharing program*. The states may use revenue-sharing money for any purpose except education. While the federal government has long given grants to state governments, the present program of revenue sharing began only in 1972.

As a contributor, the federal government is often a partner in the activities of state government. Most federal grants have strings attached. Not only must the money be used for a specific purpose, but it must be used according to federal guidelines. Thus, states that want to receive federal grants for education must obey federal rules against discrimination in education. States that build highways with federal money must meet strict safety standards. State officials often complain that the federal grants have "too many strings." But since most taxpayers feel that they need the money, a way is usually found to meet the rules.

Questions

1 Suppose that you buy a pair of jeans while traveling in another state. The price of the jeans is $20.00 and the sales tax is $1.60. You know that the *local* sales tax is 3 percent. What is the *state* sales tax rate?

2 Why do many states that have sales taxes exempt items like food and medicines?

3 Why do you think states depend less on individual income taxes than on sales taxes?

4 What are *three* ways in which states might receive revenue from the drivers of automobiles?

5 What types of business taxes do various states collect?

◇ Do you think that federal aid to the states should or should not have strings attached? Explain.

PROBLEM: CAN STATE GOVERNMENTS SHOW THE WAY?

Where do new political ideas first take hold in our nation? Many, of course, begin at the federal level. But there is only one federal government, and there are fifty state governments. Moreover, the differences among states tend to stand in the way of legislative pioneering by Congress. It is not surprising, then, that many ideas are tried first at the state level.

Consider the idea of woman suffrage. Long before the Nineteenth Amendment was adopted, several states had given women the right to vote. Or consider the minimum age for voting. Georgia lowered its voting age to 18 in 1943, and Kentucky followed in 1955. It was not until 1971 that the Twenty-sixth Amendment extended a minimum voting age of 18 to all of the states. These are only two examples of how states have paved the way for national action.

In recent years, several states have taken the lead in cleaning up the environment. The selection below describes an approach to litter that was first adopted by Oregon in 1971.

Chapter 19: Formation and Goals of State Government

Within 7 years, Vermont, Michigan, South Dakota, and Maine had similar laws. And Congress had begun to consider a national law along the same lines.

As you read, think about these questions:

- Why are the states able to serve as a testing ground for new ideas in politics?
- In what ways did Oregon pioneer in this case?

Putting a Lid on Bottle Litter

One day in 1968, Richard F. Chambers, a machinery salesperson in Oregon, found a mess of empty beer cans and bottles tossed on his lawn. He was outraged.

At his instigation, a bill was introduced in the Oregon legislature to outlaw both pull-tab beverage cans and nonreturnable bottles. Beverage and container interests killed Chambers' proposal that year. But the more Oregonians thought about the idea, the more they liked it. By 1971, there was enough popular support to overcome all resistance. Oregon banned pull-tabs and required that refunds be given for the return of all plastic, metal, and glass containers for soda and beer. The goal was to persuade people to turn such containers in for the money, rather than carelessly discard them.

Results have been dramatic. Summer litter rates for cans and bottles covered by the law have dropped by an estimated 90 percent. "We're losing the habit of littering," says John Kadaja, an Oregon park management assistant. "In any picnic crowd, Oregonians are the ones with empty bottles and papers stuffed under car seats. When there is no litter receptacle handy, the popular thing is to take the trash with you until you find one."

It's true. On a 2-hour walk through Devil's Elbow State Park, for example, amid big crowds, we found just one cigarette butt, one fragment of a facial tissue, one bottle cap.

Oregon has long taken a lead in cleaning up the environment. During the 1930s, voters became tired of the foul smells that resulted from raw sewage pouring into the Willamette River. Using the right to get issues on the ballot through initiatives, the voters demanded action. By a 3-to-1 margin, they told the politicians to get on with the job of giving the Northwest's dirtiest waterway a scrubbing. The result: one of America's first statewide laws to restore and maintain purity in public waters.

Ever since, Oregon's environmental achievements have offered example and hope to the rest of the country. From 1968 to 1974, the state adopted some 100 laws dealing with the environment. To control air pollution, for instance, Oregon now requires permits, so that it can keep out polluting industries. Also, the state allocates 1 percent of its highway budget to build bike paths; 112 miles of them, costing $4 million, have been completed.

As the nation's eleventh-fastest-growing state, Oregon still faces some tough environmental decisions. But it has come a long way. Says Tom Garrett, wildlife/conservation director of Friends of the Earth: "Oregon is now ahead of any state in action to preserve and restore its environment, and far ahead of the federal government."

Adapted from Earl and Miriam Selby, "How One State Fights to Stay Livable," *Reader's Digest,* April 1975, pp. 11–16.

Questions

1 In what ways has Oregon pioneered in cleaning up the environment?

2 How did Oregon's "bottle bill" help to reduce litter?

⬠ Do you think that such an approach would work in every state? Why or why not?

Chapter 19 Review

Developing Your Political Vocabulary

Below are five pairs of phrases. For each pair, explain the difference between the two terms. Then use each term in a sentence about state government.

1 concurrent powers/reserved powers
2 general sales tax/selective sales tax
3 real property/personal property
4 property tax/inheritance tax
5 federal grant/federal revenue-sharing money

Recalling and Comparing

1 Why did basic ideas about government in the earliest state constitutions reappear in the United States Constitution?
2 Why is great length considered by some to be a weakness in a state constitution?
3 Why does the United States Constitution place certain restrictions on the states?
4 Why is the Tenth Amendment important to our state governments?
5 How do Article I, Section 10, and Article IV of the Constitution differ in their provisions about the states? Why do you think Article IV was necessary?
6 Is the general purpose of state governments the same as or different from the general purpose of the federal government? Explain.
7 Which spends more money: the federal government or the fifty state governments? Which employs more people?
8 Is it correct to say that the largest single share of state spending goes for elementary and high schools? Explain.
9 What are *four* state taxes that are similar to federal taxes? Refer to Chapter 18 if necessary.
10 In what way can the federal government be called a partner in the activities of state government? Explain.

Special Activities

1 Consult your local library and write a brief history of how your state became a part of the Union. In your report, note people who played key roles and tell what problems they faced.
2 Choose three functions of state government and prepare a special bulletin-board display showing what services your state government provides in carrying out those functions.
3 Keep a record for a week of the various kinds of state taxes you have to pay.
4 Prepare a pie graph showing where your state gets it revenue.
5 Make a poster showing the three major taxes in your state and describing how they are calculated.
6 Arrange a panel discussion at your school inviting a member of the governor's staff, your state representative or senator, and a state court judge. Ask each panel member to describe his or her role in state government. Then have the panel tell what they think is the problem facing state government and how they would suggest solving it.
7 Consider what might be arguments for and against the following statement: "Funds for state government should come only from income taxes." Do you agree or disagree? Why?

Chapter 20

The Operation of State Governments

Like the federal government, each of the state governments is based on the principle of a separation of powers. Each state government has three branches—legislative, executive, and judicial—none of which is all-powerful. As in the federal government, each branch is checked by the powers of the other two branches. This was so in the thirteen original states before they formed a federal government. Yet the separation of powers was not perfect. James Madison found "not a single instance in which the several departments of power have been kept absolutely separate and distinct." The same could be said about the overlapping of powers in the states today.

In this chapter, we will see how state governments work in practice. We will examine the three branches of state government in turn. We will also see in what ways each branch is similar to the parallel branch of the federal government, and in what ways they differ.

Goals

- To learn the organization and duties of the legislative branch of state governments.
- To learn the organization and duties of the executive branch of state governments.
- To learn the organization and duties of the judicial branch of state governments.
- To consider the problems in passing a state law.

363

THE LEGISLATIVE BRANCH OF STATE GOVERNMENTS

In the early years after the Revolution, the legislative branch wielded most of the power in state governments. The colonists, having seen strong governors abuse their power, wanted to keep the governors of the new states weak by making the legislatures strong. But the balance of power has been shifting in the twentieth century. Now state legislatures and governors are more nearly equal.

Legislature is the general term for the lawmaking body of a state. Many state lawmaking bodies are indeed called legislatures, but others have different names. A few states use the name *general assembly* or *legislative assembly*. In Massachusetts and New Hampshire, the legislature is called the *general court*.

Nebraska is the only state with a unicameral legislature. All of the other state legislatures are bicameral. In these two-house legislatures, the upper house is called the *senate;* its members are state *senators*. In most states, the lower house is called the *house of representatives,* but in a few states the lower house goes by the name of *assembly, general assembly,* or *house of delegates.* Members of the lower house are generally called state *representatives* or *members of the assembly.*

Until now at least, no state has a legislature as large as the Congress of the United States. Yet the size of a legislature is not related to the size of a state. New Hampshire has 400 members in its lower house, but California has only 80 though its population is more than twenty-six times the size of New Hampshire's. The state senate is always smaller than the house, generally ranging from thirty to fifty members.

Every state elects its legislature by popular vote. The states are divided into voting districts, with smaller districts for the lower house and larger districts for the upper house. These arrangements are parallel to those for elections to Congress. For years, many states based their senate districts on county lines. This practice led to dominance of the legislature by lightly settled rural districts. District lines were redrawn after 1962, when the United States Supreme Court ruled that grossly unequal election dis-

The forty members of the upper house of the California legislature meet in this chamber.

Members of the lower house of the New York State legislature are at work in the chamber during a regular session.

tricts violate the Constitution. Each state must now maintain districts of nearly equal population for each house of the legislature.

Like the United States Constitution, state constitutions set the qualifications for state legislators. Most states require every legislator to be a resident of the district from which he or she is elected. In addition, there are age and citizenship requirements. Some states have set a minimum age of 18 for state legislators. Usually, however, a member of the lower house must be 21 years old and must have been a citizen of the state for 2 years. Usually a senator must be 25 years old and must have been a citizen of the state for 5 years. A few states have set a minimum age of 30 years for senators.

In most states, the members of the lower house serve 2 years, and the senators serve 4 years. In a few states, members of both houses serve the same number of years. The table on pages 366–367 gives figures for each state. Though members of Congress tend to seek reelection, rapid turnover of legislators is a problem in the states. Low pay, coupled with the high cost of frequent campaigning for reelection, helps to explain the problem.

State legislatures do not meet as regularly as Congress does. But this difference is not as marked as in the past. At one time, being a state legislator was an undemanding job. A legislator could practice law or run a business and spend only 1 or 2 months every second year in the state capital doing "the people's work." Now most state legislatures meet annually, and for steadily increasing periods, because they have more work to do. The average length of a regular session is 60 to 90 days. Between sessions, some legislators serve on research and policy-making committees. Legislatures may also be called into special sessions. The governor of each state (like the President)—and sometimes the legislature itself—may call special sessions.

A legislative session usually starts slowly and then picks up speed. The first weeks are devoted to getting organized and drawing up a legislative calendar. Then the hard work be-

Chapter 20: The Operation of State Governments

Facts About State Legislatures

State	Name of Legislative Body	Total	Number of Members Upper House	Number of Members Lower House	Term, in Years Upper House	Term, in Years Lower House
Alabama	Legislature	140	35	105	4	4
Alaska	Legislature	60	20	40	4	2
Arizona	Legislature	90	30	60	2	2
Arkansas	General Assembly	135	35	100	4	2
California	Legislature	120	40	80	4	2
Colorado	General Assembly	100	35	65	4	2
Connecticut	General Assembly	187	36	151	2	2
Delaware	General Assembly	62	21	41	4	2
Florida	Legislature	160	40	120	4	2
Georgia	General Assembly	236	56	180	2	2
Hawaii	Legislature	76	25	51	4	2
Idaho	Legislature	105	35	70	2	2
Illinois	General Assembly	236	59	177	a	2
Indiana	General Assembly	150	50	100	4	2
Iowa	General Assembly	150	50	100	4	2
Kansas	Legislature	165	40	125	4	2
Kentucky	General Assembly	138	38	100	4	2
Louisiana	Legislature	144	39	105	4	4
Maine	Legislature	184	33	151	2	2
Maryland	General Assembly	188	47	141	4	4
Massachusetts	General Court	280	40	240	2	2
Michigan	Legislature	148	38	110	4	2
Minnesota	Legislature	201	67	134	4	2
Mississippi	Legislature	174	52	122	4	4
Missouri	General Assembly	197	34	163	4	2
Montana	Legislature	150	50	100	4[b]	2
Nebraska	Legislature	49	— 49 —		— 4 —	
Nevada	Legislature	60	20	40	4	2
New Hampshire	General Court	424	24	400	2	2
New Jersey	Legislature	120	40	80	4[c]	2
New Mexico	Legislature	112	42	70	4	2
New York	Legislature	210	60	150	2	2
North Carolina	General Assembly	170	50	120	2	2
North Dakota	Legislative Assembly	150	50	150	4	2
Ohio	General Assembly	132	33	99	4	2
Oklahoma	Legislature	149	48	101	4	2
Oregon	Legislative Assembly	90	30	60	4	2
Pennsylvania	General Assembly	253	50	203	4	2
Rhode Island	General Assembly	150	50	100	2	2
South Carolina	General Assembly	170	46	124	4	2
South Dakota	Legislature	105	35	70	2	2
Tennessee	General Assembly	132	33	99	4	2
Texas	Legislature	181	31	150	4	2

Continued on next page

Chapter 20: The Operation of State Governments

Facts About State Legislatures

| State | Name of Legislative Body | Number of Members | | | Term, in Years | |
		Total	Upper House	Lower House	Upper House	Lower House
Utah	Legislature	104	29	75	4	2
Vermont	General Assembly	180	30	150	2	2
Virginia	General Assembly	140	40	100	4	2
Washington	Legislature	147	49	98	4	2
West Virginia	Legislature	134	34	100	4	2
Wisconsin	Legislature	132	33	99	4	2
Wyoming	Legislature	92	30	62	4	2

a. All senators run for election every 10 years. Senate districts are divided into three categories. One group elects senators for terms of 4 years, 4 years, and 2 years; the second group for terms of 4 years, 2 years, and 4 years; the third group for terms of 2 years, 4 years, and 4 years.
b. One-half of the senators, chosen by lot, serve only 2 years after each reapportionment following a national decennial census.
c. Senate terms beginning in January of the second year following a national decennial census are for 2 years only.

gins. Often the closing days of a session are hectic, with all-night sessions and tough bargaining as tired legislators struggle to meet a closing deadline.

To avoid this last-minute crush, some states have removed all limitations on the length of sessions. Some other states have split their legislative sessions into two parts. Legislators meet for perhaps 30 days to introduce bills and start work on them. Then the legislators go home, listen to what their constituents have to say, and mull things over. Later the legislators return to the capital and complete action on the various bills. States that have these so-called *split sessions* have rules against introducing new bills in the second part of the session, except in urgent cases.

State legislators are not paid as much as members of Congress, and the range of their pay is extremely wide. Alaska, Illinois, New York, and California pay their legislators more than $20,000 a year. Some states pay by the day, and a few of these pay $10 or less. Inflation and the increased amount of time legislators spend on public business are likely to push salaries up. Most legislatures have the power to fix their own salaries, with or without review by a special board.

Each house has a presiding officer. Like the United States House of Representatives, the lower houses elect their chairperson—who is called the *speaker*—from among their members. Often the speaker is quite powerful, having the right to appoint committee heads and control the rules of debate. (In the United States House of Representatives, the speaker no longer has the power to appoint committee heads.)

In most states, the lieutenant governor serves as presiding officer in the senate, just as the Vice President presides over the United States Senate. Some states have no lieutenant governor. These, and a few other states, provide for the election of a senate president by the senate's members.

Various employees of the legislature are appointed by the majority party, usually as a reward to loyal party workers. A sergeant-at-arms is in charge of keeping order. Doorkeepers prevent unauthorized people from entering. Clerks and typists keep records. Page girls and boys run errands.

Like Congress, state legislatures are organized into committees. Committee members are chosen at the beginning of each session. Political party caucuses and the presiding offi-

The Senate Finance Committee in New Mexico, like any other legislative standing committee, enables its members to gain knowledge and skill in a particular field. Committees do most of the work in any legislature, state or federal.

cer in each house usually make the selection. Some states require that at least one person from the minority political party be named to each committee. Each committee specializes in a particular subject, such as highways or taxation. These standing committees continue from session to session, and many of them work between sessions as well. Subcommittees, special committees, and select committees are set up when the need arises. There also may be joint committees that include members of both houses.

Special committees are sometimes chosen to conduct legislative studies between sessions. Kansas pioneered this practice in 1933. *Legislative councils* or *interim committees,* as such bodies are called, may conduct research, hold hearings, and issue reports. Such committees can thus lay the groundwork for the regular session and help the legislature get off to a quick start.

The making of a law in a state legislature follows much the same procedure as in Congress. (See the chart on page 113 of Chapter 6.) First a member of the legislature must introduce a bill. The bill is then referred to a committee, which may hold public hearings. If the committee fails to approve it, the bill will die unless some means can be found to extract it from the committee.

If the committee approves a bill, with or without changes, it returns the bill to the house from which it came. That house debates the measure, perhaps adding amendments, and then votes on it. If the bill passes, it is sent to the other house, where it goes through a similar procedure.

Sometimes the second house may make changes in a bill before passing it. A conference committee, made up of members of both houses, is then appointed to work out the differences between the two houses. The revised bill must be voted on in each house.

A bill that passes both houses in the same form is sent to the governor for signature or veto. (Only the governor of North Carolina lacks the veto power. There, a bill becomes law 30 days after the legislature adjourns.) Like Congress, state legislatures may override a veto. Usually a two-thirds vote is required, but some states require only a simple majority.

The exact provisions of state laws vary from state to state. What is legal in one state may not be legal in another. But one thing is certain: any state law that conflicts with the Constitution of the United States, the laws of

Congress, or treaties with foreign countries can be challenged in the federal courts.

Questions

1 What might be an advantage of a small legislature? What might be a disadvantage?

2 What is a split session? Why are such sessions held in some states?

3 Do you think it is a good idea to have the speaker of the house appoint committee heads? Explain.

◯ Do you think that all state legislators should be full-time lawmakers? Why or why not?

THE EXECUTIVE BRANCH OF STATE GOVERNMENTS

Just as the President is the head of the federal executive branch, the governor is head of the state executive branch. The governor of a state occupies a position of leadership much like that of the President of the United States. It is notable, therefore, that several states have had women and minority chief executives though the United States has not. As early as the 1920s and 1930s, women were elected governors to succeed their husbands in office. The first was Miriam A. Ferguson, who was elected governor of Texas in 1924. Nellie T. Ross of Wyoming and Lurleen Wallace of Alabama also succeeded their husbands in the governor's office. The pattern was not broken until 1974 when Ella Grasso was elected governor of Connecticut in her own right.

Members of minority groups have served as governors in Hawaii, New Mexico, and Arizona. Hawaii elected Japanese Americans as governor and lieutenant governor in 1974 when George Ariyoshi and Nelson Doi won on the Democratic ticket. Arizona's first Mexican American governor was elected in the same year. New Mexico has had several Mexican American governors, the most recent being Jerry Apodaca. A black, former State Senator Mervyn Dymally, was elected lieutenant governor of California in 1974.

As the state's chief executive, the governor carries out a variety of roles—executive, legislative, and judicial. He or she gets frequent attention from the state's newspapers and radio and television stations.

Yet the appearance of power is sometimes deceiving; governors rarely exercise the same degree of power within their states as the President exercises within the nation. In most states, the governor must share executive power with other elected officers. These other officers may represent a different political party. Even if they belong to the governor's party, they may compete rather than cooperate with the governor. While governors are more powerful today than in the past, they still cannot fully control the executive branch.

Unlike the President, the governor of each state is elected directly by the voters. Many states set a minimum age, commonly 30

Governor Ella Grasso of Connecticut relaxes in her home. Governor Grasso was elected to a second term.

Length of Term of Governors

State	Term in years	Number of Consecutive Terms Allowed	State	Term in years	Number of Consecutive Terms Allowed
Alabama	4	2	Montana	4	–
Alaska	4	2	Nebraska	4	2
Arizona	4	–	Nevada	4	2
Arkansas	2	–	New Hampshire	2	–
California	4	–	New Jersey	4	2
Colorado	4	–	New Mexico	4	0
Connecticut	4	–	New York	4	–
Delaware	4	2	North Carolina	4	2
Florida	4	2	North Dakota	4	–
Georgia	4	2	Ohio	4	2
Hawaii	4	–	Oklahoma	4	2
Idaho	4	–	Oregon	4	2
Illinois	4	–	Pennsylvania	4	2
Indiana	4	2	Rhode Island	2	–
Iowa	4	–	South Carolina	4	0
Kansas	4	2	South Dakota	4	2
Kentucky	4	0	Tennessee	4	0
Louisiana	4	2	Texas	4	–
Maine	4	2	Utah	4	–
Maryland	4	2	Vermont	2	–
Massachusetts	4	–	Virginia	4	0
Michigan	4	–	Washington	4	–
Minnesota	4	–	West Virginia	4	2
Mississippi	4	0	Wisconsin	4	–
Missouri	4	2	Wyoming	4	–

years, and all states require that the governor be a resident of the state. In all but four states, the term of office is 4 years. As the table above shows, the governors of four states serve 2-year terms. Many states place a limit on the number of terms a governor may serve. Seven Southern states and New Mexico do not allow a governor to succeed himself or herself in office.

The governor's salary is generally much higher than that of state legislators—as high as $85,000 in New York. At least twelve governors receive $50,000 or more a year. All but a few of the states provide an executive mansion for the governor to live in. Most also pay part of the governor's living expenses.

A governor's main powers are executive in nature. Like the President of the United States, the governor must see to it that laws passed by the legislative branch are put into effect. To do this, the President oversees the activities of the executive branch. Governors do so to a lesser extent.

Usually a governor can appoint the heads of many executive departments. Some departments, however, may have elected heads who are not directly answerable to the governor. Some governors cannot appoint the heads of specialized agencies, boards, and commissions. For a long time, most state executive branches were split into so many uncoordinated parts that it was impossible for them to

Chapter 20: The Operation of State Governments

A governor's powers over prisoners include the powers to grant pardons, to reduce sentences, and to release prisoners on parole.

work effectively together. In recent years, there has been a trend toward reorganizing state governments, grouping specialized agencies into a small number of departments, and giving the governor a more effective leadership role.

One role the governor now plays in some states is that of budget maker. Like the President, the governor in these states supervises the drawing up of a budget to set spending figures for each part of the state government. This can greatly increase the governor's power.

The governor also serves as commander in chief of state units of the National Guard. He or she can call the Guard into action to help fight forest fires or dig out from massive snowstorms or restore peace after civil disturbances. However, the governor does not have complete control over the National Guard. The President may call up state units of the Guard for service to the federal government.

Many governors have still another power, the importance of which is mainly political. The Seventeeth Amendment authorizes a state legislature to grant the governor power to make a temporary appointment to the United States Senate when one of a state's Senate seats becomes vacant between elections. At times, a governor has resigned and then accepted a senatorial appointment from the succeeding governor.

The governor also exercises important legislative powers. The governor may recommend bills to the legislature. Besides recommending specific bills, most governors shape a broad legislative program and propose it to the legislature at the start of each session. As we have seen, the governor may call the legislature into special session. Except in North Carolina, the governor may veto bills passed by the legislature. More than forty states give the governor an *item veto*. This means the governor may veto one or more items in certain bills—usually appropriations bills—without killing the whole bill. The President of the United States does not have this power.

Finally, the governor has certain judicial powers. Governors appoint certain judges. In all states, the governor has one or more of the following powers over prisoners: to reduce sentences, to release prisoners on parole, or to grant pardons.

Assisting the governor—or, in some cases, competing with the governor—are a variety of other important executive officials. Their roles and powers vary greatly from state

Chapter 20: The Operation of State Governments

> **Typical Powers of Governors**
>
> *Executive*
>
> Supervising the execution of laws passed by the legislature
>
> Appointing department heads and members of state boards and agencies
>
> Overseeing the activities of state boards and agencies
>
> Drawing up and submitting a state budget
>
> Serving as commander in chief of state units of the National Guard
>
> *Legislative*
>
> Recommending laws to the legislature
>
> Approving or disapproving bills passed by the legislature
>
> Calling special sessions of the legislature
>
> *Judicial*
>
> Appointing judges
>
> Reducing criminal penalties and granting pardons

dies. Most of the forty-two states that have lieutenant governors call upon them to preside over the senate.

In only about one-half of the states does the governor run on a single ticket as the President and Vice President do. In other states, the candidates for the two top state offices are voted on separately. If the victors happen to belong to different political parties, the governor's power is weakened, especially if the lieutenant governor presides over the senate. Friction may exist even when the two top officials belong to the same party. Governor Hugh Carey of New York was made acutely aware of this when Lieutenant Governor Mary Anne Krupsak decided not to join him in running for reelection in 1978. She ran *against* him in the Democratic primary for governor—and lost.

Some high state officials have titles similar to those of Cabinet members but play a different role. Because these state officials are usually elected, they are not responsible to the governor as Cabinet members are to the President. Nor do they serve as advisers in the way that Cabinet members do.

A *secretary of state* keeps the official records and publishes state laws. He or she usually sends out notices of elections and officially reports the results of any state election. In 1974, March Fong Eu, a Chinese American, was elected California's secretary of state after

to state. The fact that these officials are usually elected by the voters gives them a high degree of independence.

A *lieutenant governor* usually serves in the governor's place when the governor is absent and replaces a governor who resigns or

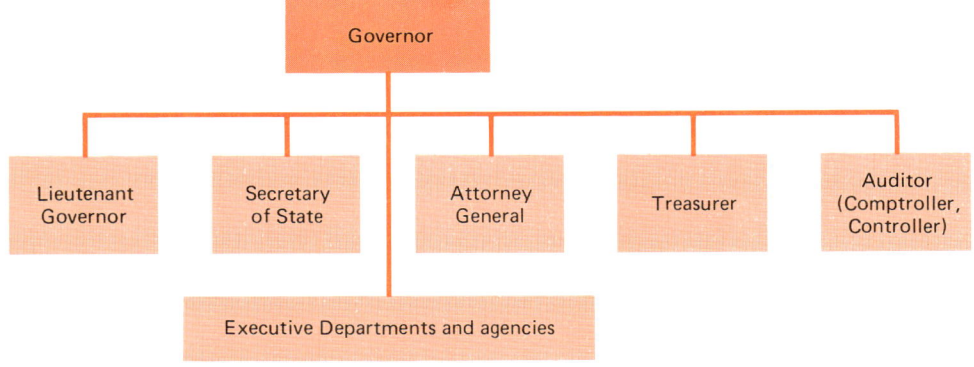

A TYPICAL STATE EXECUTIVE BRANCH

Chapter 20: The Operation of State Governments

As New Mexico's attorney general and chief legal adviser, Toney Anaya spoke at a meeting on nuclear wastes.

she had served as a member of the California legislature.

An *attorney general* is usually the chief legal official of the state. The attorney general advises the governor and other state officials about legal questions. The attorney general, or an assistant, also represents the state in court cases.

A state *treasurer* takes care of money that comes to the state from taxes, fees, and other sources. The treasurer also pays the state's bills upon receiving a *warrant,* or order, from the proper official.

An *auditor* or a *comptroller* or a *controller* watches over the spending of state money. After making certain that a proposed expenditure is legal, the auditor issues a warrant authorizing the treasurer to pay. The auditor keeps a record of all money paid into or out of the treasury and of all money that the legislature has voted to spend. Some states divide the work and have both an auditor and a comptroller or controller.

A bureaucracy is an important part of every state government. As in the federal government, the state bureaucracies are mainly within the executive branch. Consolidation of departments and centralization of budgeting have brought the state bureaucracies more under the governor's control than they were in the past.

The growth of government activity at all levels is reflected in the state bureaucracies. Huge departments of human resources now coordinate such activities as public assistance, health, and vocational rehabilitation in some states. Environmental protection and transportation departments have also been formed. Meanwhile, the traditional activities are still carried on. A department or commission of education—often headed by an elected official—supervises the state school systems. A labor board may be responsible for labor problems. A banking commission usually regulates the banks. A public utilities commission is part of the bureaucracy in most states. Special boards give examinations for every profession or trade that a state chooses to license.

In staffing government offices, the states do not rely on the merit system as fully as the federal government does. This is true even though Wisconsin began the merit system in civil service. If you are seeking a job in a state agency or department, how you go about it depends on which state you live in. Most states hire employees under a merit system, much like the federal civil service system. In those states, you would have to take an examination. If you got a job, you could probably keep it as long as your work was satisfactory. In other states, however, many state jobs are political prizes handed out by the majority party. If you live in such a state, you might have to help out in an election campaign or do other political work to qualify for a job. And if the state government changed hands, you would probably have to look for another job.

With federal prodding, state governments have been improving their hiring and promotion practices. For one thing, the federal government will not give grants for activities unless the employees carrying them out are hired under a merit system. For another, federal pressure and court decisions have forced states to make greater efforts to remove discriminatory practices.

Questions

1 In what ways do governors have less executive control than the President?

2 What is *one* power that some governors have but the President does not have?

3 What is *one* example of a governor's executive power? Of a governor's legislative power? Of a governor's judicial power?

⌂ How much power do you think your state governor should have? Explain.

THE JUDICIAL BRANCH OF STATE GOVERNMENTS

Each state maintains a system of courts to administer justice. These courts handle all cases or disputes that arise under that state's constitution and laws. Local courts are part of the state system.

By far the greatest number of legal cases are settled by state and local courts rather than by federal courts. This is because the United States Constitution reserves general police powers to the states. The jurisdiction of federal courts is quite limited (see Chapter 10, pages 192–193). If you ever have to go to court, chances are that it will be a state or local court. If you get a traffic ticket, it will be handled by a state or local court, depending on whether you are accused of violating a state highway law or a local traffic rule. If you file a complaint against a neighbor who is annoying you, it will be handled by a state or local court, depending on whether you have brought suit under a state law or a local ordinance. If you are robbed at gunpoint, you may have to go to a state court to testify when a suspect is brought to trial because most trials of violent crimes are held in state courts. In almost any state or local case, you would probably find the wheels of justice grinding slowly because court dockets are so crowded.

State courts follow principles similar to those followed by federal courts. Cases are generally divided into two classes—civil and criminal. There are two main levels of state courts, just as there are of federal courts. Trial courts are at the bottom, and appeals courts are at the top. At the trial level, however, few state court systems were arranged in an orderly fashion until recent judicial reforms.

Unlike federal judges, who are appointed by the President, most state judges are elected by the people. In Virginia and South Carolina, supreme court judges and major trial court judges are elected by the state legislatures. Many states, however, provide for the appointment of judges by the governor with or without the consent of the senate. In such states, a special board usually prepares a list of candidates from which appointments are made.

The question of popular election of judges has been hotly debated. Those who favor election argue that it produces judges who are attuned to the voters' wishes. Opponents argue that voters rarely have enough information to make a careful judgment of judicial candidates. It is also argued that political party machines usually select party candidates for judgeships and that this leads to inferior choices.

Though lifetime appointments are usual for federal judges, they are rare for state judges. More often, a state judge's term runs for 4 to 15 years.

The states often allow the removal of judges by impeachment, just as the federal government does. In addition, many states allow voters to remove a judge by *recall*. First a certain number of residents must sign a petition demanding a recall election. The recall question is then put before the voters. If a majority

Chapter 20: The Operation of State Governments

At the age of nineteen, Rita Cargill presided over the local trial court in Granbury, Texas, as justice of the peace.

vote against the judge, then he or she loses office.

After the judge, the principal judicial official is the *clerk of the court*. The clerk keeps court records and maintains the docket, or schedule of cases. Another duty of the clerk is to collect fees and fines. Many states provide for the election of clerks of the courts.

Court systems are similar among the states though the names of the courts may differ. The chart on this page shows the general pattern.

Local Trial Courts. Minor legal matters are often handled by a *justice of the peace*, who is usually not required to have any legal education. A justice of the peace performs marriages, witnesses documents, and also handles petty offenses, such as domestic disturbances and charges of drunkenness. A "JP" may also handle minor civil cases, such as a claim over a "bounced" check. Justices of the peace long fulfilled a valuable function in rural areas. More and more, however, they are being replaced by more specialized officials and courts.

In urban areas, the role of "JP" is usually taken over by *police courts, magistrate courts,* or *municipal courts*. These courts sometimes have separate divisions to handle traffic cases, criminal cases, and other types of cases.

Often, local courts themselves are specialized. *Probate courts* handle cases involving the property of a person who has died. *Juvenile courts* try young people accused of law violations. *Domestic relations courts* settle squabbles between husbands and wives. *Small claims courts* settle civil disputes over small sums of money and usually operate without a lawyer.

General Trial Courts. Cases in general trial courts may be heard by a judge and a jury. Many defendants choose to dispense with a jury trial, because of the time and expense it involves, and rely on the decision of a judge. The cases vary from minor criminal cases (misdemeanors) to major criminal cases (felonies), such as murder, robbery, and burglary. General trial courts also handle civil cases, or disputes between individuals.

TYPICAL ROUTE OF APPEAL IN A STATE COURT SYSTEM

STATE SUPREME COURT
↑
Intermediate Court of Appeals
↑
General Trial Courts
(county or superior courts, district courts, circuit courts, and others)
↑
Local Trial Courts
(justice of the peace courts, police courts, municipal courts, and specialized courts)

In states without an intermediate court of appeals, an appeal is made directly from a trial court to the state supreme court.

Among the general trial courts are *county courts* (called *superior courts* in some states), *district courts,* and *circuit courts.* As their names suggest, district or circuit courts often cover more than one county. (State districts and circuits are, of course, separate from the federal districts and circuits shown on the map on page 222.) General trial courts have original jurisdiction over many cases and also hear appeals from lower courts.

Appeals Courts. Every state provides for the appeal of some cases to a top state court. Someone who loses in a lower court may thus get a rehearing on the legal issues.

An appeal must be based on a point of law or a claim that new evidence has turned up. A point of law would be a claim that the original trial was unfair or that a state law is unconstitutional. Appeals courts do not have juries and do not hear witnesses as trial courts do. Instead, the judges read the transcript of lower court proceedings, read briefs prepared by lawyers, and listen to oral arguments by lawyers. The judges have two choices. They may either uphold the trial court's decision or send the case back to be tried again.

In nearly every state, the highest court is an appeals court, called the state supreme court. In New York, though, the highest court is the state court of appeals, and the so-called supreme court is a trial court with an appellate division.

About one-third of the states have an appeals court between the general trials courts and the state's highest court. These intermediate appeals courts handle many appeals and thus ease the load on the state's highest court.

Most cases that involve state or local law can be appealed no further than the state's high court. However, a case that raises a question of conflict with federal law may be carried to the United States Supreme Court. Such a question would be a claim that a state law violates the Constitution of the United States, an act of Congress, or a treaty. In practice, though, the United States Supreme Court tends to let the high court in each state have the final say on what that state's laws mean. One famous exception, as we noted on page 214, was the Dred Scott case in 1857.

Questions

1 How does the method of selecting state judges differ from that of selecting federal judges? How do their terms differ?

2 What are two kinds of local courts? Describe their responsibilities.

3 What are two grounds for appeal to a state's high court?

⬠ Which do you think is better, to have state judges elected by the voters or to have them appointed by the governor? Why?

PROBLEM: WHAT ARE SOME PROBLEMS IN GETTING A BILL THROUGH A STATE LEGISLATURE?

There is only one way to get a bill through a state legislature: work for it. Each session, a state legislature turns out dozens or hundreds—in a few states, even thousands—of new laws. Somebody had to think each one up. Somebody had to argue for it, and somebody had to keep the pressure on until the bill passed. State legislatures are not self-activating. Somebody has to wind them up.

The selection that follows is an imaginary account of one bill's adventures in a state legislature. The story demonstrates the importance of organized groups in getting bills passed. Corporations and labor unions frequently speak up for legislation; citizens' groups do so less frequently. Our story is somewhat more fast-paced than legislative action usually is.

As you read, ask yourself the following questions:

- *What can an ordinary citizen do to get a bill passed in a state legislature?*
- *What steps must a bill go through?*

Citizens in Action

Mr. and Mrs. Citizen have six children, a house in Center City, a large mortgage, and ulcers. Their oldest child will soon be ready for college. Tuition at the state university is high. Still, the Citizens think they can scrape it up. The problem is that the university is 300 miles away—too far to commute. The Citizens could not afford to pay room and board at a dormitory. Is there any alternative?

"What if the state university built some branches around the state?" the Citizens ask themselves. In Center City, for instance. Then the Citizen children could live at home while going to college. The Citizens talk to their friends and neighbors. A few go with them to talk to their state representative. "Great idea," says the representative. The state senator is also enthusiastic, though he cautions that university branches can be expensive.

The legislature for State X (as we shall call it) soon starts its session.

The representative from Central City takes the Citizens' idea and writes it out in bill form. The bill provides for the establishment of 2-year community colleges in every major city in the state. He takes his bill to the clerk of the House of Representatives, who assigns it a number, House Bill 1678 (or HB 1678 for short), and the speaker refers it to the Joint (House and Senate) Education Committee.

Meanwhile, the state senator also introduces a bill, a modified version of the Citizens' idea: legislation providing for 2-year junior colleges in three of the largest cities in State X. This bill also receives a number, Senate Bill 123 (SB 123 for short). It is referred to the same committee as HB 1678.

Early in the legislative session, the Education Committee schedules a public hearing on the two bills. The Citizens know that if they go to the committee meeting by themselves, nobody in the legislature will pay much attention to them. They have already lined up support behind HB 1678 (the bill they prefer to SB 123) among a number of organizations. For instance, they belong to the Parents of More Than Five Children Club in their town, and they know that all those parents are just as worried about college bills as they are. The club hires a bus and drives to Capital City as a group, to support the bill. Mrs. Citizen is president of her local Parent-Teachers Association. She has persuaded that group to vote to support the bill. She has also taken the idea to the annual conference of the State PTA. There she received a vote in favor of branch colleges. The legislative chairperson of the state PTA promised that the members will go to the hearing to testify for the bill. Mrs. Citizen has also been seeking help from other organizations to which she belongs.

Mr. Citizen has discussed the idea at a meeting of his local union. The union steward agreed to take the idea to the state union convention, which endorsed HB 1678 by acclamation. Mr. Citizen was less successful with the president of the Central City Chamber of Commerce, made up of business leaders. The Chamber's president agreed that some higher education facility would be good for Central City, but he thought HB 1678 would cost the taxpayers too much. He agreed, however, to urge his membership to support SB 123, the more limited of the two bills.

When the day of the Joint Education Committee's hearing arrives, many organizations send people to testify for the bill. Organization members, present in large groups, applaud loudly every time someone speaks in favor of HB 1678. Mr. Citizen testifies as an individual (not as a representative of a group) and tells the committee about the problem he will have financing his children's education. He says that the very thought of paying six separate sets of college bills aggravates his ulcer, and members of the committee and the audience (except those who have ulcers) laugh loudly. But they also look sympathetic.

Opponents of the bills come to the hearing too. One is a representative of an organization called the Hardworking and Pennypinching Concerned Citizens. He tells the Education Committee that the state is spending too much money on education already. He feels that the legislature should forget about branch colleges and cut taxes. A representative of the Central City Taxpayers' Association feels that taxes are too high and services too generous. "I got along without a college education and so did my grandfather," this speaker tells the Committee. "I think too many kids go to college these days, anyhow." Members of a Central City Homeowners Association fear (quite accurately, it turns out) that the community college might be built on a large empty lot near their neighborhood. They tell the committee that they don't want an institution with all those "loud radicals" in their section of town. This is because, in their opinion (inaccurate, it turns out), the construction of the college will depress real estate values.

The sponsors of the two bills tell their reasons for favoring their bills. Other senators and representatives testify for or against one or both bills. By late afternoon, the head of the Education Committee declares the open hearing closed.

The next time the Education Committee discusses HB 1678 and SB 123, it does so in closed (executive) session. Only the committee members are present. The committee now has several options.

1. It can give both bills a favorable report. This would leave it up to the full house and senate membership to decide which should pass.

2. It can select one of the two bills for a favorable report.

3. It can issue an unfavorable report on both bills, or it can issue no report on either bill. No report is as bad as an unfavorable report. In either case, the bill will not get to the floor of the House or Senate for discussion unless enough representatives or senators feel strongly enough about the issue to sign a petition demanding a vote. This happens very rarely. Since most legislatures receive several thousand bills every session, the vast majority of bills get no committee report. This is called, very accurately, "dying in committee."

However, the members of the Education Committee have been swamped with letters from parents who want community colleges. So they vote to issue a favorable report on SB 123. The representative from the Citizens' district explains to the Citizens that the committee members felt HB 1678 was too expensive. "Money is tight this year," he adds apologetically. (Legislators have been saying that since the first legislature met in colonial days.) The Citizens are a little disappointed. But they agree with their representative that a compromise bill is better than nothing. "Will the bill go to the House or the Senate first?" they ask. "Neither," says the representative. "First we go to Appropriations."

Appropriations committees or finance committees exist in every state legislature. Some have the more accurate name of Finance and Control. These committees do indeed control the fate of any piece of legislation that requires the expenditure of state funds. More bills die there than in any other committee of the legislature. No more testimony from the public is taken. "We can always look at the transcript of testimony from the Education Committee," the

Appropriations Committee chairperson explains.

Actually, only a few committee members look at hearing transcripts. Many just count their letters from constituents. If there is a huge outpouring of support for or against a bill, a committee member will probably join the bandwagon. Also, the Appropriations or Finance Committee is where much "log-rolling" goes on. "If you'll vote for the community college in my district, I'll vote for the road resurfacing program in yours," the senators and representatives say to each other. Many of the legislators are a little embarrassed about this wheeling and dealing. But it is an important part of the political process. At any rate, SB 123 receives a favorable report from the Appropriations Committee. However, the amount of money recommended by the sponsor of the bill is cut in half.

At this point, the original sponsors revise their bills to conform to the version recommended by the Appropriations Committee. Either or both might have stuck to the original version. That might have meant a long and probably useless fight on the floor of one or both houses of the legislature. The bill might not have passed before adjournment.

The house and senate bills are now the same. They still keep their own numbers and probably have the word "amended" added to the title. They are scheduled on the calendars of both houses. After a brief debate, in which only house and senate members can take part (though the public and the press are allowed to watch and listen from the galleries), the bills are passed. Of course, either or both houses might have rejected the bills. But once bills have passed the two important committees with favorable recommendations, that doesn't happen often.

Next the bills go to the governor, who in State X is a woman. She has three options. She can sign either of the bills. It doesn't matter which one since they now are identical. She can veto the bills, thus pleasing the Concerned Citizens, Taxpayers, and Homeowners. This would send the legislation back to both houses of the legislature. There it would have to pass again with a much larger majority (usually two-thirds). Or she can allow the bill to become law without her signature. That happens automatically after the bill has been on the governor's desk for several days to several weeks, depending upon the state, without being vetoed. In this case, the governor signs the bill before television and newspaper cameras. A smiling Mr. Citizen is there, too, to shake the governor's hand and be given the pen with which she signed the bill. The governor is willing to balance the goodwill of the community college supporters against the wrath of the Concerned Citizens at the next election.

The bill is now no longer a bill, but a *law*. It receives a new name and number, Public Act (or Public Law) 23456 (PA or PL 23456 for short). Everyone hopes that the establishment of 2-year junior colleges in three major cities in the state (including Center City) will begin promptly.

Copyright © 1972 by Ellen Switzer. From *There Ought to Be a Law! How Laws Are Made and Work*. Used by permission of Atheneum Publishers.

Questions

1 What steps did Mr. and Mrs. Citizen take to get the legislature to accept their idea?

2 On what occasions might the legislature have rejected their idea? Briefly describe each time.

3 How was their idea changed in the process of becoming a law? Why were the changes made?

◌ Do you think that organized support is necessary for *any* bill to become a state law? Explain.

Chapter 20 Review

Developing Your Political Vocabulary

Classify the words below as belonging either to the legislative, executive, or judicial branch of state government.

- a governor
- b general trial court
- c criminal case
- d attorney general
- e override
- f standing committee
- g magistrate
- h unicameral
- i civil case
- j executive powers

Recalling and Comparing

1 Briefly describe three ways in which state government is *similar to* our federal government.

2 Briefly describe three ways in which state government is *different from* our federal government.

3 How are state legislatures elected? How does this procedure compare with elections to Congress?

4 What might be *two* reasons for a rapid turnover of state legislators?

5 In state government, what is *one* check of the legislative branch on the executive branch?

6 In what ways can a governor check the legislative branch? The judicial branch?

7 How does the election of governors differ from the election of Presidents?

8 How has the balance of power between governors and state legislatures changed since the early years of our nation? Why?

9 Give one example each of a criminal case that might be heard by a justice of the peace and by a county court.

Special Activities

1 Draw a cartoon that illustrates a problem associated with getting a bill through a state legislature.

2 Make a chart showing the titles and names of the top elected officials in your state, your state representative, and your state senator.

3 Consult your local library and write a biographical sketch of the governor of your state.

4 Make a chart showin the powers of the governor of your state.

5 Make a special bulletin-board display of news items about the activities of the three branches of your state's government.

6 Ask a local leader of each of the main political parties in your area to describe to your class the role of political parties in your state legislature. Allow time for questions.

7 Trace the progress of one bill through your state legislature and prepare a chart showing each major step with the date it began.

8 Make a study of your state legislature and prepare a chart showing the differences between it and Congress. Refer to Chapters 5 and 6 if necessary.

9 Consider what might be arguments for and against the following statement: "All state officials should be elected for specific terms of office." Do you agree or disagree? Why?

Unit VII Review

Improving Your Reading

Read the selection below and then answer the questions that follow it.

Each of the fifty states enjoys certain privileges under the federal Constitution. Each state, for example, can expect its court proceedings to receive full faith and credit in all other states. Its citizens' rights are to be recognized by all other states. It is assured of a representative form of government. It is to be protected by the federal government against foreign invasion or domestic violence.

There are, however, some things the states cannot do. For example, they cannot make treaties. They cannot coin money or engage in war unless invaded. They cannot pass any bills of attainder or *ex post facto* laws. They cannot tax imports or exports without the approval of Congress.

State governments share many common functions. One is protecting the rights of each of their citizens. Others are guarding the health, lives, and property of their people; providing education; maintaining highways; caring for the needy; protecting natural resources; and regulating business.

Money to support such services is derived mainly from taxes. The chief of these are sales taxes and individual income taxes. In addition, the federal government provides part of the money spent by each state.

Each of the fifty states has three branches of government—legislative, executive, and judicial.

The main duty of the legislative branch is the passage of laws for the state. A bill in a state legislature follows a path similar to that of a bill in Congress. In all states except Nebraska, a bill must pass both houses of the legislature. Nebraska's legislature has only one house; it is unicameral.

Each state's executive branch is headed by a governor. The governor's primary duty is to see that all laws are properly enforced. The power of governors varies among the states.

The judicial branch of state government has the duty of hearing state-related legal cases and interpreting the state constitution and laws. Each state has a high court to hear appeals from lower state courts.

1 In your own words, summarize this reading in *no more than five* sentences. Have your summary focus on what you regard as the five most important points made in the reading.

2 Which *three* of the following topics discussed in the reading can be used to best show the similarities among state governments:

   a rights granted to the states by the Constitution of the United States

   b restrictions on states in the United States Constitution

   c the number of branches in state government

   d the method in which state legislatures are organized

3 Which *one* of the following four topics noted in the reading can best be used to show a difference that exists among our state governments:

   a the number of branches in state governments

   b rights granted to the states by the United States Constitution

- c the powers of state governors
- d the functions of state governments

Developing Your Writing Skills: What Are Your Attitudes toward Government?

In the introduction to this unit, you read about a proposal by G. Etzel Pearcy. He proposed reducing the number of states from fifty to thirty-eight. Among Pearcy's arguments in favor of the proposal are these: (1) Each state would be more uniform geographically. (2) There would be twelve fewer state bureaucracies. (3) Costs would be lower because some duplication of facilities could be avoided. Keep these arguments in mind as you think about the following questions and form your own opinions:

- Would it be good or bad for a state to have geographic uniformity? Why?
- Should our states be more nearly equal in population? Why or why not?
- Would having fewer states necessarily result in fewer bureaucracies? In fewer state officials?
- Would Pearcy's proposal really save state tax money?
- How might a reduction in the number of states affect representation in Congress? Could it affect our nation in other ways?
- Would having fewer states result in greater or in less centralization of government in the nation?
- Could there be better ways to solve the problems of state bureaucracies and duplication of services?

Now write a brief essay on Pearcy's proposal. Discuss advantages and disadvantages of reducing the number of state governments as well as advantages and disadvantages of not reducing their number. Explain why you agree or disagree with Pearcy's proposal.

Recommended Reading

The Almanac of American Politics (latest edition), Dutton, New York.

The Book of the States (latest edition), Council of State Governments.

Braddock's Federal-State-Local Government Directory (latest edition), Braddock Publishers, Washington, D.C.

Daniel R. Grant and H. C. Nixon, *State and Local Government in America,* Allyn and Bacon, Boston, 1972.

Donald G. Herzberg and Alan S. Chartock, *Our State Legislatures: They Are at a Crossroads,* Center for Information on America, Washington, Conn., 1969 (paperback).

State Blue Books and Reference Publications: A Selected Bibliography (latest edition), Council of State Governments.

State Government Finances (annual), U.S. Bureau of the Census, Washington, D.C.

Statistical Abstract of the United States (annual), U.S. Bureau of the Census, Washington, D.C.

Alfred Steinberg, *The Bosses,* New American Library, 1972 (paperback).

Lincoln Stephens, *The Autobiography of Lincoln Stephens,* Harcourt, New York, 1937.

Who's Who in American Politics (latest edition), Bowker, New York.

Who's Who in Government (latest edition), Marquis Who's Who, Chicago.

Almanacs and yearbooks.

Local Government

UNIT VIII

Not all government activities are carried out by highly paid—or even poorly paid—bureaucrats. Some of the work that keeps the governmental machinery going is done by volunteers, especially in local communities. Consider what happens when the fire alarm sounds in Hometown, Illinois (population: 6,700):

As soon as the alarm starts to sound, Marlene Swiney puts down her housework and grabs her gear. She knows that a neighbor will be right over to watch her four children. Speed is of the essence. Mrs. Swiney must get to the firehouse, where she and seven other women will join the few male firefighters who are available to answer the alarm.

The eight women make up a third of the town's firefighting force. During the daytime, their presence is especially important because most of the male firefighters are away at their jobs.

Fire Chief Richard Christopher recruited the women through an advertisement in the community's weekly newspaper. "Ten responded to the notice and eight stayed on for 160 days of training," he says. "They can do everything. They wear boots, helmets, and bunker coats, just like the men."

The women go on an average of one ambulance call a day and one fire call a week. Most fire calls are for overheated furnaces or minor garage blazes. But some calls are for major fires.

All eight women have children. The husbands of three are volunteer firefighters, and the husbands of two others are police officers.

"I really enjoy the duty," says Mrs. Swiney. "It is a lot of work, but it is interesting. And we have the satisfaction of doing good for the community."

Adapted from an Associated Press report, May 5, 1975.

Of course, most of the work of local government is done by paid employees. But even then, local governments are close to the people. Residents of a county, city, or township can easily attend meetings and hearings held by these units of government. The people are likely to take an active part in debating local issues. Like Mrs. Swiney, they can actively benefit the community.

The next two chapters will discuss the various political units into which states are divided. Chapter 21 will explore the types of local government and their functions. Chapter 22 will focus on cities and the special problems involved in financing and governing them.

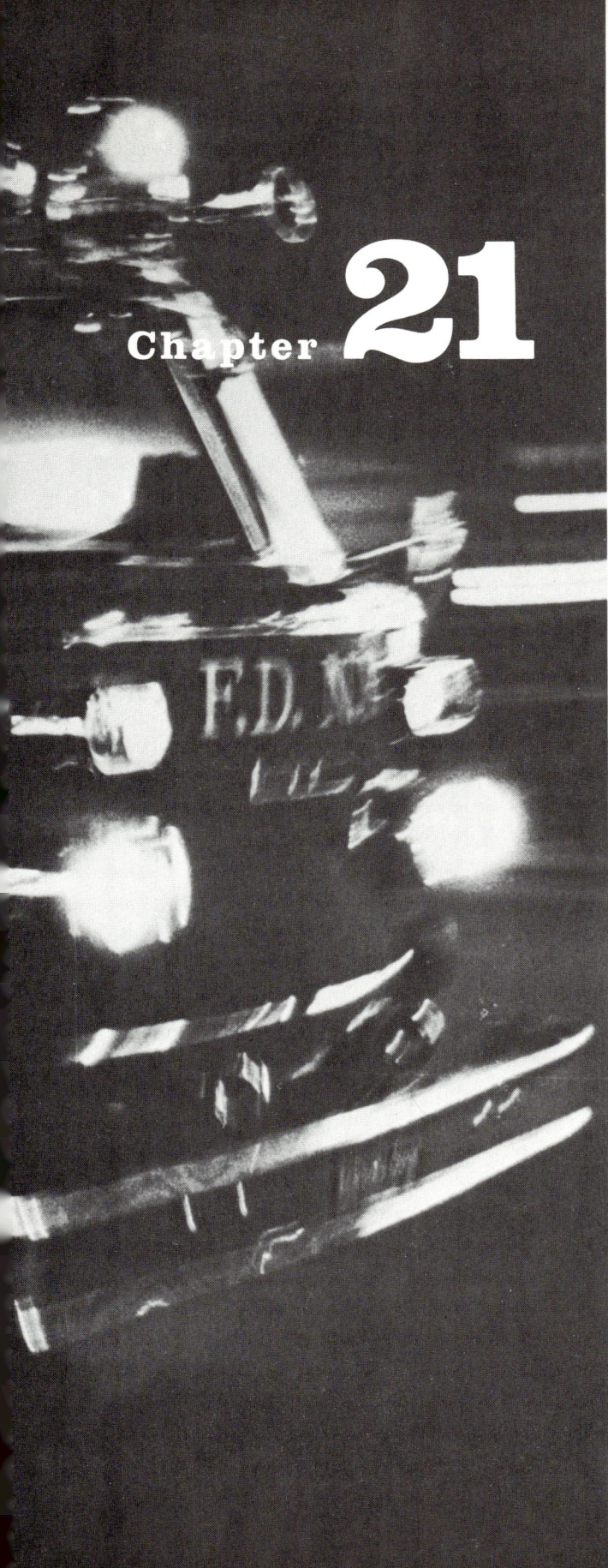

Chapter 21

Functions and Types of Local Governments

There are more than 78,000 different local units of government today. You yourself are probably served by at least three or four—perhaps by a county or a city and certainly by several special districts of various kinds. These units of government exist so that local people can manage local affairs. Local governments are much closer to us than state governments or the federal government. They can have a direct influence on our lives—from the kind of school we attend to the way our garbage is collected to the amount of police protection we have.

The state governments set the ground rules for all local governments. State legislatures determine what types of local governments will exist in the state and what powers they will have. Note that the flow of power is the reverse of that in the federal-state relationship. There, power flows upward from the smaller units—the states—to the larger unit. In the states, power flows down from the larger to the smaller units of government.

In this chapter, we will discuss the services local governments perform and the way they carry out those services.

Goals

- To learn what services local governments provide.
- To learn how county governments operate.

385

Chapter 21: Functions and Types of Local Governments

- *To learn three main types of city government.*
- *To learn the functions of smaller communities and special districts.*
- *To consider how police relations with communities might be improved.*

FUNCTIONS OF LOCAL GOVERNMENTS

Local governments perform many of the same functions as state governments, with an emphasis on local services. Compare pie graph A on page 388, showing *local* government expenditures, with the graph in Chapter 19 (page 356) showing *state* expenditures. In these graphs—which are based on nationwide averages—most of the same categories stand out. Yet they are not all in the same order.

As we shall see, some units of local government, such as school districts, provide a single service. Others, such as counties and cities, have broad responsibilities. Thus, the range of local functions is very wide. Yet some generalizations can be made.

Some functions belong almost entirely to local governments. Some of these functions are relatively inexpensive. *Record-keeping* is one of these. Local governments—usually counties—keep birth certificates, marriage licenses, property deeds, and many other kinds of records.

Another relatively inexpensive function is *regulation of local activities.* Local governing units regulate everything from door-to-door sales to the supplying of electric power and water. Perhaps the most important type of local regulation is *zoning.* This is the practice of dividing an area into zones and restricting property uses within each zone. For example, one zone may be for residence only and another may be for industry only.

Some expensive services are provided by local governments. They require special buildings, equipment, and other capital expenditures. Among services of this kind are police and fire protection as well as sanitation and sewerage.

Of all the services that local governments perform, the most expensive is public education. As we saw in Chapter 19, a state may set minimum standards and provide some money for elementary and secondary schools. But the burden of running those schools and paying for them falls mainly on the local community in most states. Usually this means on a school district. Education expenditures take the largest single share of the average local government dollar.

An important political issue in recent years has been the amount of local control of public schools. Parents and other taxpayers often take a lively interest in how schools are run. Some people would like their school district to have complete freedom to set its own policies. But many other people feel that the states must continue to set minimum standards in order to

Up to now, local property taxes have been the main source of support for public high schools and elementary schools.

assure all students of an equal education, free from discrimination.

There are many functions that both local and state governments perform. Like the states, local governments build and maintain hospitals. They also strive to improve public health and welfare. Like the states, local governments keep up streets and roads, provide recreational facilities, and protect natural resources. But in all these services, the state has the more important role.

To perform their functions, local governments hire more employees than federal and state governments combined. Local governments employ more than 8.8 million people. The federal government employs about 2.9 million civilians, and the state governments, 3.3 million. About half of local government workers are in education, and most of those are employed by school districts. Teachers are the largest single group of local government workers.

More than three-fourths of the income of local governments comes either from taxes or from the states and the federal government. By the mid 1970s, all taxes and fees together made up about 38 cents of the local government dollar. Property taxes, mainly taxes on real property, accounted for the largest share, by far. We noted earlier that the real property tax is almost entirely a local tax. States obtain little income from this source, and the federal government obtains none.

A tax on real property is based on the *assessed value* of the property. The assessed value is either the market value of the property or, more often, a fraction of the market value. Imagine that John and Jane Smith bought a house for $40,000 ten years ago in a town that assesses property at 50 percent of its market value. Let's say the town's tax rate is $15.00 for each $1,000 of assessed value. Ten years ago, the Smiths' property tax was $225. If the Smiths' house is now worth $80,000, their property tax is now twice as high even though the town has not raised its tax rate. The Smiths'

A Year without Local Taxes

Nelliston is a New York State village with 723 persons. In 1978, it was able to look forward to a year without local taxes. A news report told why.

They sipped champagne at the Village Hall here to celebrate a zero local property-tax rate for the coming year.

The village's mayor, Harvey Gramps, announced the tax break because of a surplus of revenues. Mayor Gramps is on the three-member village board that determines the extent of any property taxes for this community. The mayor and two trustees gave the village a financial boost when they discovered that they had $23,000 accumulated in surpluses. The village budget is $50,000.

While residents will not pay property taxes to the village, they are still taxed by the county, the school district, and other tax authorities.

Adapted from an Associated Press release, June 5, 1978.

---

school taxes may also have doubled, since school taxes are often based on the assessed value of property.

The property tax falls directly not only on homeowners but also on the owners of business properties. Others pay the tax indirectly. If you rent a house or an apartment, the rent includes a part of the property tax that the landlord must pay. The price of the food you buy in a store includes a part of the property tax paid by the store owner or operator.

Growth in the size and cost of government brought a "taxpayers' revolt" in some places in the late 1970s. The residents of school districts often refused to approve bond issues for the support of schools. The property tax was a special source of complaint as inflation drove up house prices and assessments with them. Unlike the income tax, the property tax is a regressive tax, one for which the rate is the same for everyone. Nor is the property tax deducted from paychecks week after week like the income tax. Instead, a bill arrives in the mail once a year. As assessments rose, these bills increased rapidly in size. Increased taxes meant more income for local governments, but louder complaints from taxpayers.

Potholes are a familiar sight in city and local streets as income from taxes fails to keep up with rising costs.

Spurred by these complaints, some states amended their constitutions to limit the growth of taxes and spending. A movement was begun to obtain a similar amendment to the Constitution of the United States.

The cutbacks in taxes pinched local governments. They tried to hold down the number of their employees and the size of their payrolls. They reduced services and maintenance. And they turned to the states and the federal government for more money. Until the "taxpayers' revolt," local governments received about as much money from the states as they received from property taxes.

Federal aid to local governments is often channeled through state governments. But some states permit local communities to deal directly with the federal government. In that case, local governments may receive direct aid under the same federal programs that furnish aid to state governments (see Chapter 19, page

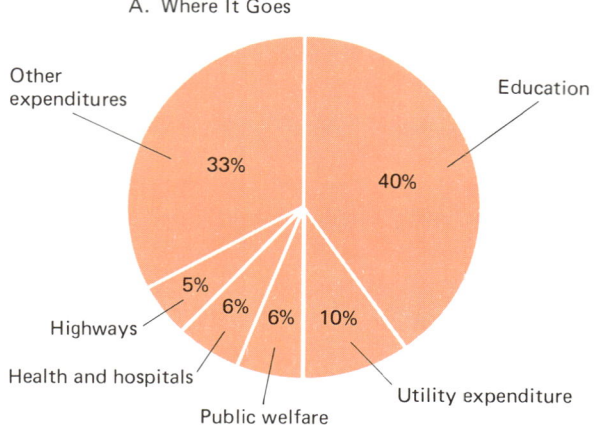
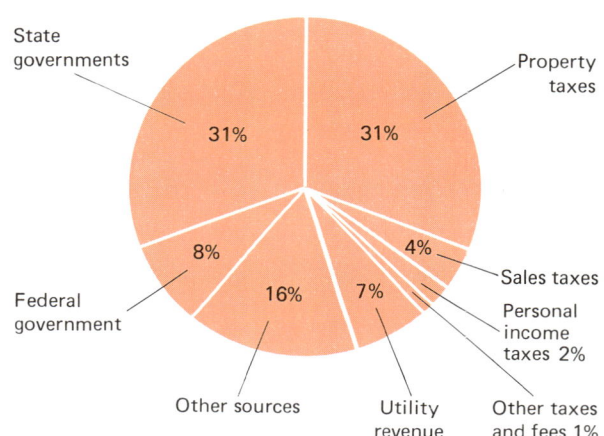

THE LOCAL GOVERNMENT DOLLAR

A. Where It Goes
- Other expenditures 33%
- Education 40%
- Highways 5%
- Health and hospitals 6%
- Public welfare 6%
- Utility expenditure 10%

B. Where It Comes From
- State governments 31%
- Property taxes 31%
- Federal government 8%
- Other sources 16%
- Utility revenue 7%
- Sales taxes 4%
- Personal income taxes 2%
- Other taxes and fees 1%

Source: Both; U.S. Department of Commerce data for 1976

Both pie graphs are based on total figures for counties, cities, school districts, and special districts combined. The percentage distributions for any single local governing unit might differ markedly from these broad averages.

359). Such direct federal aid is often received by cities, as we shall see in the next chapter.

Both federal and state governments have sought to use aid as a means of encouraging cooperation among local units of government. One way of doing this is by requiring several counties to agree to use a single facility before giving any funds toward its construction. An example would be a juvenile detention center.

Questions

1 On what function do local governments spend the most money?

2 What are *four* functions that are performed almost entirely by local governments? Give examples.

3 What are *four* functions that local governments share with state governments?

4 What are the *two* main sources of local government income?

⬠ Do you think that each school district should have full control of its own educational policies? Or should the national and state governments continue to set minimum standards? Explain.

COUNTY GOVERNMENTS

All but four of the fifty states have divided themselves into units of local government called counties. Two of the remaining states have units of local government that are similar except in name. Louisiana calls its units *parishes* and Alaska calls its units *boroughs*. The two states that have no organized county governments are Connecticut and Rhode Island. Their "counties" are merely divisions of the state court systems.

The idea of counties came to this country with the English colonists. England was parceled into shires, later called counties because each was the domain of a count or earl.

Memphis is the county seat of Shelby County, Tennessee's most populous county. All but two states have counties or local governing units similar to counties.

In this country, the county was designed as a unit of government to serve rural areas. Counties are still the only form of local government for some people, especially in the rural South. Elsewhere most counties now have to share jurisdiction with smaller governing units within their borders. However, some counties have been swallowed by cities that occupied the same area. Denver, San Francisco, and Honolulu are examples. New York City is made up of five counties. A few cities, such as Baltimore and St. Louis, have set themselves off from any county.

Where counties exist, under whatever name, they are *administrative* subdivisions of a state. They do not make laws or ordinances of their own but take care of the functioning of government within the county.

The United States contains 3,040 counties. The largest in area, San Bernardino County in California, is nearly 800 times the size of the smallest, New York County in New York City. Eighteen counties have populations of 1,000,000 or more, while 102 have populations of fewer than 2,500 people.

The number of counties varies greatly from one state to another. Texas has the most, 254. Delaware and Hawaii have only three.

In each county, there is a town or city known as the *county seat*. Like a state or national capital, a county seat is the headquarters of government. County officials have their offices there, usually in the county courthouse or county building.

County Boards and Other Officials

Counties are generally governed by elected boards. The members are sometimes elected at large—that is, by all voters in the county—but more often they are elected by district. The county governing board may be called the *board of commissioners* or the *board of supervisors*. Among other titles used are *board of freeholders* and *board of revenue*.

Most county governing boards hold both legislative and executive powers. The separation of powers has been largely ignored in the traditional county government.

The main legislative power of county boards is setting taxes and appropriating money. Other legislative functions include zoning, setting rules to safeguard public health, and regulating places of amusement.

The executive functions of a county board are similar to those of the state and federal executive branches. The board itself supervises the departments that carry out the board's regulations. One such department might manage the county's road-building program. Another department might be in charge of county hospitals or fire protection. In some places, counties operate the school system, but usually the cities or separate school districts take over this job.

Besides the board members, many other county officials are elected. A *county clerk* keeps records of births, deaths, and marriages in the county. She or he also keeps copies of deeds and other documents dealing with the ownership of property.

A *county treasurer* is usually in charge of taking in and paying out money for the county. A *county auditor* has the duty of examining the accounts of all county offices. A *county assessor* is in charge of determining the value of all property within the county that is taxed. A special board may be available to hear appeals from taxpayers who think that the assessed value of their property has been set too high.

In many states, each county has a *coroner* who investigates violent or suspicious deaths. To help in such an investigation, the coroner may call together a jury of citizens, or coroner's jury. The coroner must issue an official report stating the cause of death after having made an investigation.

A *prosecuting attorney,* or *district attorney,* or *county attorney* represents the county in court cases. As the title suggests, this official's job is to prosecute people accused of crimes.

Those crimes might be violations of county ordinances or of state laws.

Each county has officials with judicial powers. These officials, as already explained (pages 374–376), are part of the state court system. Each county has one or more local courts run by *justices of the peace* or *magistrates*. In some states, each county also has a county court. This general trial court is presided over by a *county judge,* who is usually elected. Some states group counties into judicial districts or judicial circuits. In that case, a *district judge* or *circuit judge* might hold court in one county's courthouse for a week or two, then move on to another county.

Counties also have law enforcement officers. The chief county law enforcement officer is the *sheriff.* He or she maintains order, notifies witnesses and jurors when to appear in court, and supervises the county jail. When ordered by a court, the sheriff may sell the property of people who have not paid their local taxes.

The sheriff is usually assisted by *deputy sheriffs.* In the Old West, the sheriff called a group of local people together in an emergency to form a *posse* (POSS-ee). This custom has largely died out now that a sheriff has deputies and can obtain help from other governing units. The governor can be asked to send the National Guard. City and state police forces can be called on for aid. In many areas, the sheriff's law enforcement functions have been largely taken over by city and state police agencies.

Proposals for Government Reform

Many people feel that power is too fragmented in traditional counties. They say there are too many elected officials for the voter to have any real control over the government. If something goes wrong, it is hard to pin the blame on anyone. Where so many people share responsibility, no one is responsible. Because many people hold these beliefs, two

Sheriff Luscius Amerson of Macon County, Alabama, was the first black sheriff elected in the South since Reconstruction.

alternative systems are in use. Both involve the establishment of a county executive office.

Under the *county mayor or president plan,* the voters continue to elect the county board but also elect a chief executive. This county mayor or president appoints other administrative officers.

Under the county manager plan, the voters elect the county board only. The board then appoints a county manager who has experience in administration. Normally the county manager is chosen after competitive examination and is hired for a specified period of time, under contract. The county manager appoints administrative heads for most or all of the departments of county government. The manager is responsible for carrying out policies set by the board. She or he can be dismissed by the board, but would have to be paid for any unexpired portion of the contract.

Both plans have been tried mainly in urban areas and are said to work well. But there is great resistance to change. Moreover, many state constitutions require that certain county offficers be elected. Those constitutions would have to be amended before different forms of county government could be tried. About three-fourths of all counties still have traditional county boards.

Questions

1 Who holds the executive power in most county governments? Explain.

2 What are *four* important county officials? What are their duties?

3 Why have reforms in county governments been sought?

4 What is the county manager plan? Why do some counties use it?

○ Which plan of county government do you feel is the best plan? Would you recommend it for all counties? Explain.

CITY GOVERNMENTS

The importance of city governments has grown as the population has shifted from rural to urban. It is hard to imagine today what people thought of as a "big city" at this nation's birth. In 1790, the biggest city was New York's Manhattan, with about 33,000 residents. Goats and pigs wandered muddy city streets. Horses were the principal means of transportation. At the edge of the city, farms nestled among rolling hills that have since been obliterated by skyscrapers. In all the nation, only one person in twenty lived in a city. For most people, the only unit of local government was the county.

Today our cities have swelled into vast expanses of concrete and brick and scattered greenery. To us a "big city" is a place with a population of at least 100,000. The United States has more than 160 cities of that size. Horses are no more likely to wander the streets of our big cities than are goats and pigs.

The nature as well as the size of cities has changed over the years. At first, the cities were largely places of commerce and trade. The Industrial Revolution in the middle and late nineteenth century brought factories to the cities. Waves of immigrants arrived to work in the factories, and the cities became congested. Then the automobile, early in the twentieth century, made it possible for people to live farther from their places of work. Suburbs were built farther and farther from the center of large cities.

Today each city lies at the hub of a vast built-up area. Where farms once nudged up against city boundaries, suburbs sprawl. Fifteen people out of twenty now live in or near cities of 50,000 or more population. (See graph below.) The federal government calls these large urban concentrations *Standard Metropol-*

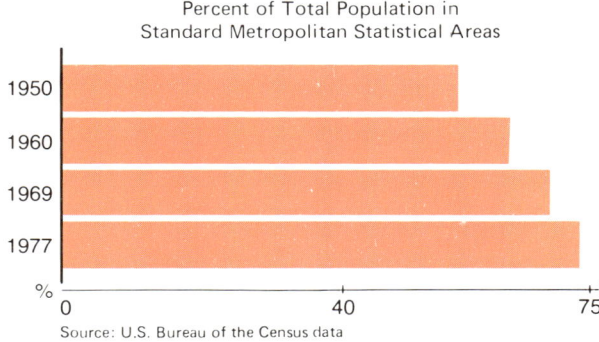

GROWTH OF URBAN POPULATION
Percent of Total Population in Standard Metropolitan Statistical Areas

Source: U.S. Bureau of the Census data

itan Statistical Areas (SMSAs). There are more than 270 SMSAs, each containing a large city and its suburbs. Some SMSAs extend into two or more states. The SMSAs are not governing units, but merely densely settled areas. As such, they point up some of the problems of local government.

Chapter 21: Functions and Types of Local Governments

Forms of City Government

Governing today's cities requires far more complex machinery than governing sparsely settled rural areas or small eighteenth-century cities. Some city functions, such as police and fire protection and street maintenance, date back to the earliest years. But others are the result of changing needs and demands. Large concentrations of population created needs for city water and sewer systems, public transportation, and so on. Changes in ideas about what government should do brought demands for other services. Cities now spend vast sums of money to protect public health, aid the needy, provide recreational facilities, and do many other things that were formerly left to private charity.

All these functions are carried out under rules set down by a state government. State constitutions spell out some of the rules, and state legislatures add others from time to time.

For a city to exist as a unit of government, it must have a charter issued by the state legislature. A *city charter* is a plan of government authorized by a state legislature for a city. Legislatures issue charters in response to petitions from citizens who want their community to have a government separate from the surrounding area. The charter establishes the community as a corporation and enables it to have its own government. The legislature can increase or decrease the city's powers by changing its charter.

Some states draw up a single charter for use by all cities or a set of charters for cities of different sizes. Some other states provide for individual charters tailored to each city's needs. A third system is gaining in popularity. This is *home rule,* a system in which the state legislature grants cities wide powers of self-government. Even under the home-rule system, the important point is that cities are "creatures of the state."

The form of a city's government is set down in its charter, which may be regarded as

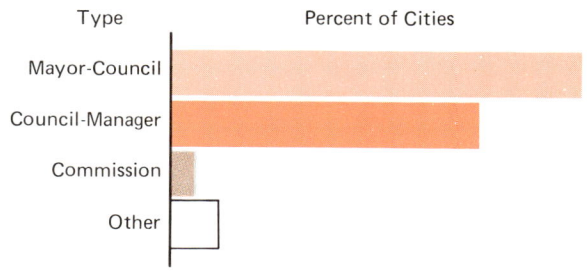

About 95 percent of the cities in this country use one or another of the three main types of city government.

the city's constitution. Three major types of city government have emerged in this country. They are the *mayor-council,* the *council-manager,* and the *commission* systems. (See the graph above.) Many cities have combinations of these types.

The mayor-council type of government is the most common type. In this system, the voters elect both a council and a mayor. The members of the council are elected at large or by districts known as *wards.* Council members are elected for terms of 1 to 6 years. The mayor's term may differ; usually it is from 2 to 4 years.

The council exercises the legislative power. By passing city laws, known as *ordinances,* the council sets basic policies. The council also sets local taxes and allocates tax revenues to various services.

The mayor is the chief executive, but sometimes in name only. Departments to provide city services—a police department, a fire department, a garbage-collection department, a health department, and so on—may or may not be under the mayor's supervision. Mayor-council governments can be divided into two main categories depending on how much power the charter gives to the mayor. Many cities fall somewhere between the two extremes.

Strong-Mayor System. Under this system, the mayor has strong executive powers. Usu-

MAYOR-COUNCIL TYPE OF CITY GOVERNMENT

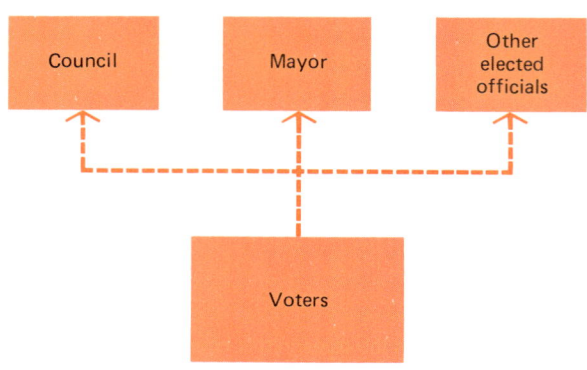

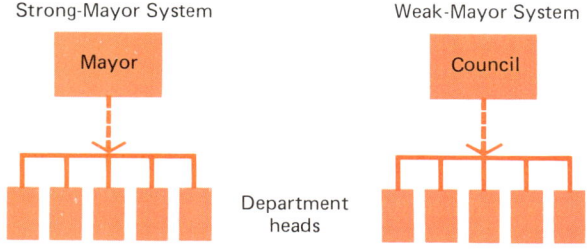

In the mayor-council system, the voters elect a council, a mayor, and certain other officials, such as judges. Heads of departments are appointed by the mayor in a strong-mayor system, but by the council in a weak-mayor system.

In the commission type of government, the voters elect a commissioner to head each department. The commissioners together make up the board of commissioners. Certain other officials, such as judges, are independently elected.

ally the mayor can appoint and dismiss the heads of city departments, prepare the city budget, and otherwise oversee city affairs. The mayor may recommend legislation to the council, over which she or he sometimes presides. In some cases, the mayor may vote to break a tie in the council. Usually the mayor can veto measures passed by the council.

The strong-mayor form is most common in large cities. By centralizing executive power, it often makes for efficiency. It also gives voters a clear target for praise or blame—the mayor. But the strong-mayor form of city government also has drawbacks. For one thing, it depends on a skillful and honest mayor. For another, it may bog down in clashes between the mayor and the council.

Weak-Mayor System. The mayor has only limited power in this system. The council shares the executive power, and usually appoints the heads of city departments. Whatever powers the mayor retains are watered down. For example, vetoes may be allowed only on certain types of council actions, and may be readily overridden by the council. The mayor may be left with only ceremonial duties such as snipping ribbons and making speeches.

The weak-mayor system is usually found in smaller cities (with the notable exception of

COMMISSION TYPE OF CITY GOVERNMENT

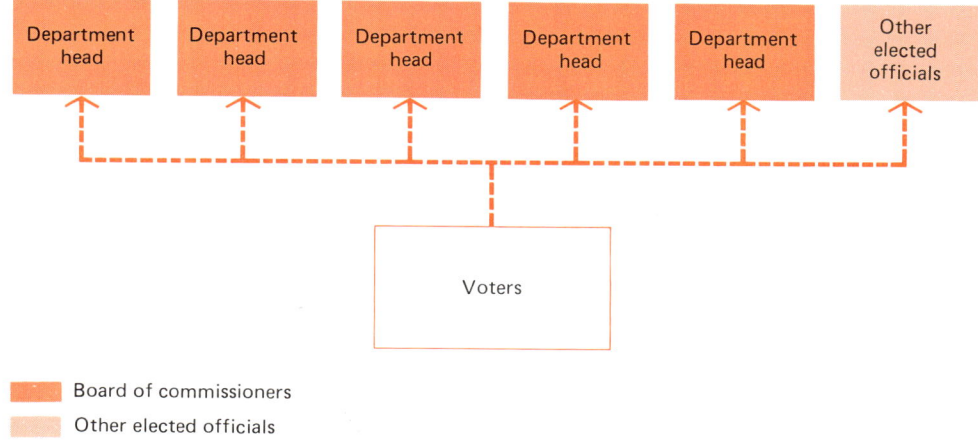

Chapter 21: Functions and Types of Local Governments

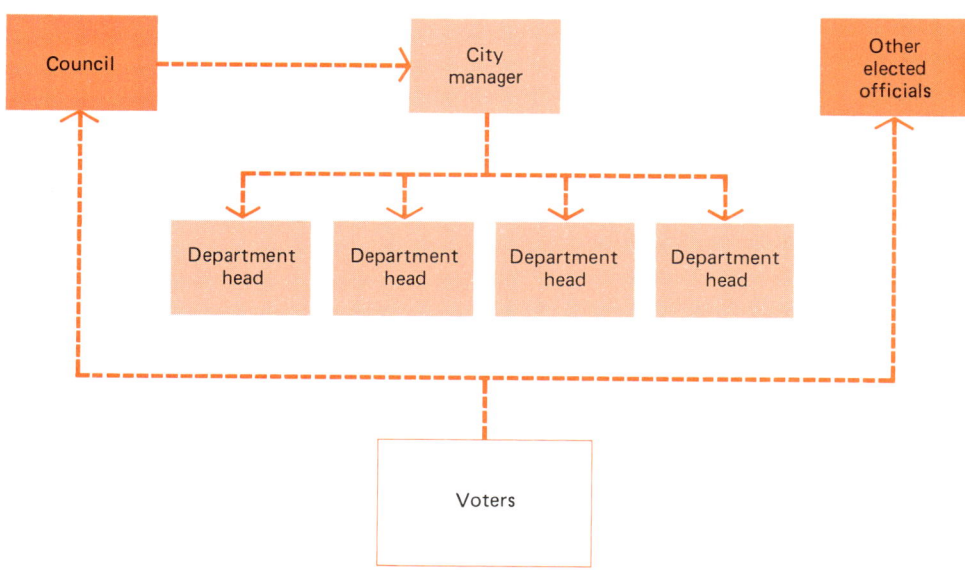

COUNCIL-MANAGER TYPE OF CITY GOVERNMENT

In the council-manager type of city government, the voters elect a council, which then appoints a city manager. In turn, the city manager appoints the heads of departments. Certain other officials, such as judges, are independently elected.

Carol Bellamy, president of the New York City Council, shakes hands with State Senator Carl McCall on a tour of Harlem.

Los Angeles). By spreading out the executive power, it reduces the chances that one person may become too powerful. But divided power may make it harder to coordinate city policies. And if things go wrong, the voters often have trouble deciding whom to blame.

A second type of city government is the commission form. The voters elect one person to head each department of city government. Together, the department heads constitute a commission. The commission performs the duties of a city council—setting taxes, voting ordinances, and appropriating money.

Usually, there is no mayor in the commission system, or else one of the commissioners serves as mayor for ceremonial purposes. In some cities, however, the voters do elect a mayor, who heads a department like other commissioners.

The commission form gained popularity after it was adopted in 1901 by Galveston, Texas. That city had just been devastated by a hurricane, and its previous weak-mayor government was unable to handle the problems of recovery. Many other cities then adopted the plan. In recent years, it has fallen into disfavor, and even Galveston has abandoned it. Today only about 3 percent of cities use the commission form. In most of these cities, commissioners are elected at large, usually for terms of 2, 3, or 4 years.

The chief advantage of the commission form is its clear fixing of responsibility for particular services. The voters know which person is in charge of roads, for example. If the roads are not well maintained, then that person can be voted out of office. Moreover, there is little chance of a clash between legislative and executive powers because the powers are combined in the hands of one set of people. The commissioners have both powers.

On the other hand, commissioners may be good at legislating but poor at administering. And problems may arise from the fact that the commissioners vote the money that they spend for their departments. In some cities, this financial arrangement has led to waste and corruption.

A third major type of city government—and the type that is gaining most in popularity—is the council-manager system. The council is usually elected at large and possesses wide powers. It hires—and can fire—the city manager, who is a specialist in public administration just as a county manager is. The council exercises legislative powers and sets basic city policies. There is usually also a weak mayor.

The city manager can be compared to the general manager of a corporation. He or she carries out policies set by the council. The city manager appoints the heads of city departments and sees that they carry out the council's policies. The manager may make recommendations to the council for policy changes, but it is the council that decides.

The council-manager system is now used in nearly 40 percent of the nation's cities, including such large ones as Cincinnati, Fort Worth, and Dallas. The chief advantage of this system is that an experienced administrator has complete responsibility for carrying out city policies. If the policies are not carried out, the administrator can be replaced. The council, which sets the city's policies, is elected and presumably responsive to public opinion. On the other hand, critics argue that city managers sometimes lack the political skills necessary to carry out sensitive policies in cities where racial or ethnic tensions are high. Whatever the case, most writers about government think the council-manager form is the best all-around method of city government.

Whatever its form of government, each city has a system of courts. Sometimes the judges are elected. Sometimes they are appointed—either by the city council or commission or by the state governor. City courts are part of the state court system discussed on pages 374–376.

A widespread problem with local government, of any type, is patronage. We noted earlier that patronage is the giving of government jobs to faithful party workers who helped to elect public officials. Patronage, or the spoils system, exists at all levels of government where there is no merit system of employment. And civil service merit systems are less common in local than in state and federal employment. Even in the absence of a merit system, some local governments discourage partronage by their form of election ballot. Their ballot lists candidates as individuals rather than as party members. The more common type of ballot makes it easy for voters to vote a straight party ticket. Recently the Supreme Court dealt a blow to the patronage system. The Court held that local government bodies that violated civil rights could be sued for damages. But patronage has a strong hold.

Those who defend the patronage system say that it makes government more responsive. Employees who hold their jobs through patronage respond to pressure from their political party. Thus a voter with a problem can go to the party's local leader, and the leader will see that a public employee deals with the problem. Critics says that, for the same reason, the patronage system creates political "bosses" and often leads to graft and bribery. In many places, one political party dominates local elections because of the strong backing it has built up through past patronage.

―――― **Questions** ――――

1 What are *two* ways in which cities changed in the nineteenth and early twentieth centuries? How did these changes affect city government?

2 In what ways are cities "creatures of the state"?

3 What are the *three* main types of city government? Give one advantage and one disadvantage of each form.

◯ Imagine that you are in charge of drawing up a plan of government for a large city. What features would you choose? Why?

OTHER TYPES OF LOCAL GOVERNMENT

Local government includes many other units besides counties and cities. In this section, we will examine the most important.

Towns, Villages, and Boroughs. Small built-up areas go by many names in various parts of the country. What is called a village in one state may be a town in the neighboring state, and a borough elsewhere.

Many towns and villages, like cities, are incorporated. They have petitioned the state for permission to form a local government and have received a charter. Incorporated towns and villages operate much as cities do. As with cities, the form of government is controlled by the state.

In many ways, town or village government is a simplified version of city government. The weak mayor-council form is widely used. The mayor goes by many names—*mayor, president,* or *burgess,* for example. The council may be called a *town board* or a *board of trustees.* Both the mayor and the council are elected by the voters. Various other officials may also be elected.

Because towns and villages are smaller than cities, their government is much simpler. There are fewer departments and fewer powers. Mayors and council members usually serve without pay.

In New England, towns are a special unit of government that takes the place of county government. The New England states are divided into counties, but the counties have never become important units of government. Instead, the counties are divided into towns, and these towns are the basic units of local government. Each town covers a certain geographic area. The area may be rural, or it may be heavily settled, but unincorporated.

New England town government is a form of direct democracy, based on an assembly of the town's qualified voters. These assemblies, or town meetings, are held annually or more frequently. In the assembly, voters discuss and vote on policy matters such as taxes and town ordinances. The assembly usually elects town officers, though in some larger towns these officers are chosen at an earlier election. Administrative matters are handled throughout the year by a board of selectmen and selectwomen.

New England town government dates from colonial times when communities were closeknit. In those times, the annual assembly was a major political and social event. Today many of the assemblies are poorly attended or find it difficult to act because of sharp divisions among the people. Elected town officials are assuming more and more responsibilities. Still, many New Englanders take great pride in their unique form of local government.

Townships. The subdivision of counties into geographic units spread westward from New England, but in different form. The county was the main unit of local government and was divided into *townships.* Government by direct democracy was put aside. In the Midwest, townships were part of the settlement pattern under the Land Ordinance of 1785. Each township was a huge square. It, in turn, was divided into smaller squares for individual farming. Thus, a unit of local government called the township still exists in states from New Jersey to the Dakotas. The township form of government did not spread to other areas, such as the South.

In general, townships now include only the rural parts of counties. Communities of any size have usually incorporated and formed separate governments.

Townships are usually governed by a board of trustees or a board of supervisors. The voters may elect this board, or they may elect individual officials—such as a clerk, a treasurer, a supervisor, and a justice of the peace—who then form the board.

School Districts and Other Special Districts. Often a unit of local government is formed to perform a single function. The boundaries of such a unit may cut across towns, counties, or other units. The most common form of special district is the school district.

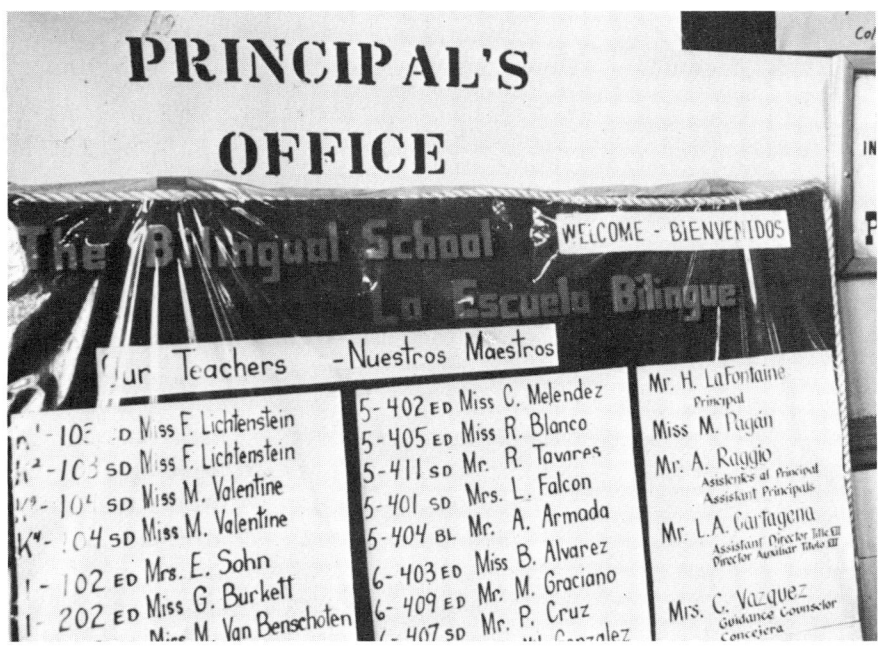

La Escuela Bilingue is a bilingual public school where classes are taught in English and in Spanish. Like most other public schools, it is under the direction of the school board in its school district.

Most of the educational functions of local governments are carried out by school districts. While some county and city governments build schools and hire teachers, those functions are more often performed by school districts.

School districts are usually governed by boards elected by the residents. In small districts, the school board members are not paid, but in larger districts they may be salaried. School boards have the power to set taxes, borrow money, and approve expenditures for the district. A school board usually appoints a superintendent, who directs the schools. In rural areas, an elected county superintendent is more often in charge. Or schools from more than one county may be grouped in an *intermediate district*.

In the past, rural school districts were small and so were schools. The "one-room schoolhouse," with one teacher in charge of many grades, served all pupils who lived within walking distance. As roads and transportation improved, pupils could travel greater distances by bus. Federal and state funds now help to even out the differences between rural and urban schools.

Other special districts provide individual services. Special districts are common in rural and suburban areas. Two or more townships or other units may form a special district in order to provide better services than any one of them could afford by itself. Libraries, hospitals, water, sewerage, parks, firefighting, irrigation, and drainage of marshlands are often provided in this way. Like school districts, these special districts can usually levy taxes to finance their operations. The rules under which special districts can operate are set by each state.

Questions

1 In what way is the government of towns and villages similar to city government? In what *two* ways is it different?

2 What is unusual about New England town governments?

3 Why are special districts created? How are they financed?

◌ Do you think that a form of government suitable for a rural community of 200 people would also be suitable for a city of 20,000? Why or why not?

PROBLEM: HOW CAN POLICE RELATIONS WITH COMMUNITIES BE IMPROVED?

Police officers must deal with all kinds of people, many of them unlike themselves. In some communities, the police do not represent a cross-section of the population. Such groups as youths, women, and racial and ethnic minorities may be underrepresented on police forces. In many communities, relations are strained between the police and some residents. This has been particularly true of minority groups.

The following account discusses one attempt to help police and community residents get along better together. It concerns a program aimed at helping police to become acquainted with Mexican Americans, or Chicanos, in a *barrio*—a city area with a large population of Chicanos. As you read, ask yourself:

- *Why was this program started?*
- *Is it worthwhile?*

Knowing Each Other

An interesting police-community relations experiment is going on in Riverside, California. Its purpose is to get police and the barrio population to know each other.

Police in Riverside often view the barrio as a high crime area filled with real and imagined danger. Chicanos often view the police as brutal oppressors who do not understand the barrio way of life.

Police departments in some cities give police classes to high school students. This student is getting her grade.

The theory behind the project is simple: when people get to know each other as people, not as stereotyped images, the individual benefits and society benefits.

The police department's get-to-know-the-barrio program starts with a 40-hour course in Chicano history and culture. Police learn about Mexican character, art, music, food. They live in Mexico for 2 weeks and study Spanish. As a further option, the police can be placed in barrio homes, where they live like the families there for up to 2 weeks.

The purpose is twofold: the barrio learns about the police; the police learn about the barrio.

The Riverside program is worthy of consideration in other cities. And let's not limit it to white police visiting poor brown homes. What about brown, black, and white police visiting rich white homes? The idea is to set up lines of communication, understanding, and empathy in the community.

This is a very small program. It alone will not cement together the various factions in a divided city. It is not presented as a solution, but as one tiny step in the right direction.

Adapted from Gus Clemens, "Talking Point: Knowing Each Other," San Antonio *Express*, April 24, 1975, p. 13A.

Questions

1 What is the purpose of the Riverside program?

2 How does the program work?

○ Can you think of other ways of handling the problem of community relations? Explain.

Chapter 21 Review

Developing Your Political Vocabulary

Briefly explain the *difference* between the following pairs of terms:
1. state government/county government
2. county government/city government
3. city government/township government
4. mayor-council system/council-manager system
5. commission system/council-manager system

Recalling and Comparing

1. What is one main reason why local government units exist?
2. Of the three levels of government—federal, state, and local—which has the largest number of employees? What do most of these employees do?
3. Is it possible to live in the United States and not in a county? Explain.
4. Give examples of *two* kinds of local government in which legislative and executive powers are held by the same people.
5. Why are local governments likely to have a patronage system? What are some arguments for and against that system?

Special Activities

1. Prepare a diagram of your county's or city's government. Identify the form of government.
2. Consult your local library and write a biographical sketch of the head of your city, county, or other local government.
3. Invite a member of your county, city, or town government to visit your class and describe the functions of that unit of government.
4. Invite a member of your school board to visit your class and explain the problem of financing public schools in your district.
5. Make a special bulletin-board display of news stories about your local govenment.
6. Prepare a diagram of your city or county court system. Explain the basic functions of each court.
7. Visit a session of a local or county court and write a report on it for your class.
8. Visit your local police or fire station and ask about job qualifications, pay rates, benefits, and conditions of work. Try to determine the level of job satisfaction and the reasons for it.
9. Identify the major services offered by your county or equivalent unit of government. Make a list of those services, and the government departments offering each of them.
10. Make a study of the different groups that have settled in your area and the extent to which they are now represented in local government. Report your findings to the class.
11. Consider what might be arguments for and against the following statement: "The best form of city government is the council-manager form." Do you agree or disagree? Explain.

Chapter 22

The Special Problems of Big Cities

The helter-skelter growth of cities brought some disturbing problems. Crowded slums, decaying downtown areas and soaring city budgets are only a few of the symptoms. From time to time, popular magazines run stories with such titles as "Crisis in the Cities" and "Can Our Cities Survive?" Cities seem able only to deliver less service for more money.

Just as worrisome is the growing number of governing units in urban areas. The boundaries of these local governments overlap, and problems spill across all boundaries. Local governing units compete for tax revenues and for federal and state aid.

This chapter will explore the special problems of big cities and some measures that are being taken to deal with them.

Goals

- To examine the problems of raising funds for big cities.
- To explore new approaches to urban government.
- To consider who should pay school taxes.

FINANCING OUR BIG CITIES

Big cities are not just grown-up villages. They are a special type of community with their own special needs and problems. You have

Chapter 22: The Special Problems of Big Cities

Cultural centers have sprung up in many cities to provide a focus for such urban attractions as drama and dance.

Rundown neighborhoods and slums continue to be problems of urban life and, in turn, lead to loss of local tax income.

only to walk through a big city to see how much it differs from a village. Start in a comfortable residential area. The broad lawns and spacious houses here are not unlike those in a village. But keep walking toward the center city. You will pass factories. Sooner or later you will pass slums. The streets will begin to be congested. Finally you will reach a downtown area with taller buildings and more traffic. The busy city center offers more excitement—opportunities for entertainment, for shopping, and for culture.

It is the attractive features—the jobs, the cultural opportunities, the excitement—that draw people to cities in the first place. But it is the unattractive qualities—the poverty, the crowding, and the crime—that make cities so difficult to govern.

Think for a moment of the problems that press so much more urgently on big cities than on rural areas or villages. There is the clash of ethnic groups and cultural traditions. There is the concentration of "people problems" such as alcoholism, drug addiction, and juvenile delinquency. There is the run-down housing, the traffic congestion, the air pollution. There is the poverty, revealed in slums and in unemployment figures.

In Chapter 21, we saw how cities have taken on a variety of functions in the course of their growth. The exact "mix" of functions in each city varies. Small cities have different priorities from big cities. The chart below shows

Five Biggest Categories of Expenditures, by City Size[a]

Small Cities (under 50,000)	Big Cities (over 1,000,000)
Sewage and sanitation	Public welfare
Highways	Education
Police protection	Health and hospitals
Education	Police protection
Fire Protection	Sewage and sanitation

a. Problems ranked by descending order of expenditures per person. U. S. Bureau of the Census data for 1976

Chapter 22: The Special Problems of Big Cities

how spending priorities in small and big cities differ. Note that the costs of public welfare are at the top of the list for cities of more than 1,000,000 people. Education, health and hospitals, and police protection follow. The need for all of these services increases in big cities.

How do big cities manage to pay for their services? Pie graph B on page 388 gives the broad answer, since the budget dollar is divided up in much the same way for all local governments. Big cities have some special problems, however.

Cities have depended heavily on the property tax as a source of income. Property taxes are higher in bigger cities. The average city collected $96 in property taxes for each of its residents in a recent year, while cities of 1,000,000 or more collected $198 per resident.

Some big cities operate utilities such as water companies, electric or gas companies, and transit systems. Some cities operate liquor stores. Generally, cities do not make a profit on any of these enterprises. They are more likely to take a loss.

Big cities sometimes levy sales taxes similar to the sales taxes levied by state governments. City sales taxes brought in an average of $20 for each city resident in a recent year.

Some big cities have an income tax or a payroll tax on all people working in the city, even those who live outside the city limits. The cities justify the tax on nonresidents by pointing out that everybody who works in the city benefits from its services.

Big cities have a hard time collecting enough revenue to pay for their expenditures. Of course, officials at any level of government sound the same complaint. But cities have some special problems.

The shrinking of city tax bases has reduced the income of big cities. At one time, most of the people who benefited from city services lived within the city limits. The city could easily tax them to pay for its services. But the automobile lured many middle-class fami-

These taxpayers are protesting the size of property taxes, which have been the biggest source of local tax income.

These taxpayers are opposing a change in property taxes that they feel will do them more harm than good in the long run.

Sprawling suburbs in Marin County, California, repeat a pattern that can be seen clearly from the air near most urban centers. Revenue-raising problems are worsened for cities as they lose their taxpayers to the suburbs.

lies to the suburbs. Though many of these people commuted to the city to work, the property tax they paid on their new homes went to the suburban government, not to the city. Meanwhile poorer people often moved into city dwellings vacated by the new suburbanites. The buildings deteriorated. Property values fell—and so did city tax collections. To compensate, many cities raised their property tax rate, but that just increased the flight to the suburbs. In recent years, the population of many big cities has been dropping.

As city taxes increased and conditions declined, industries began to feel the pinch. Many of them, too, moved to the suburbs. The flight of industries caused the tax base to shrink further. For one thing, there were fewer industries to tax. For another, the loss of industries meant a loss of jobs. The big cities were in a bind. The more they raised property taxes, the worse their troubles became.

Big cities suffer from state restrictions on local revenue raising. As we have seen, the states control what all units of local government may do. States often exempt certain property from taxation—for example, churches and schools. Many states have other strict rules. For example, the state constitution may set a maximum property tax rate that a local government may not exceed. Or a state may forbid local governments to use certain kinds of taxes, such as sales and income taxes. In addition, states may restrict borrowing by local governments. Michigan is an example. No local government there may borrow money until it has approval from the state's Municipal Finance Commission. Many states set a maximum amount that a local government may borrow.

State and federal governments are providing increasing help to city governments. In 1960, only about 15 percent of city revenue came from other governments. By 1974, that

Chapter 22: The Special Problems of Big Cities

figure had topped 31 percent, and by 1978, it was over 60 percent in some large cities. The proportion is likely to rise even more as the "taxpayers' revolt" reduces the income that cities obtain from property taxes.

The bigger the city, the more assistance it receives from federal and state governments. In one recent year, cities having up to 50,000 residents received $63 per resident, while cities with 1,000,000 or more received $438 per resident.

States make grants to cities for education and some other specific purposes. In addition, the revenues from certain state taxes are sometimes shared with cities. But until now, states have borne only a small part of the burden of financing cities.

Cities get most of their financial aid from the federal government. Federal aid to cities began with the Housing Act of 1949. Since that first "urban renewal" program, the federal government has taken an increasing part in meeting the "crisis of the cities." As we have seen, federal grants help finance specific programs. Among these are job creation, community development projects, and many others besides new housing. The federal government also provides revenue-sharing funds to be used for general purposes.

Federal money for urban renewal and housing is supposed to be used mainly for the direct benefit of lower-income neighborhoods. A city can use only 25 percent for general maintenance, such as street repair and sewer improvements. Moreover, most federal funds are provided only if the receiving unit puts up money of its own. Thus, a city that wants to build a water treatment plant with federal aid must pay 25 percent of the cost. Some federal money must be matched fifty-fifty. Cities must bear 50 percent of the costs of food stamps, medical assistance, and certain other federal programs. As a result, federal aid is no simple answer to city needs. The poorest cities can afford it least. And efforts made to cut down local taxes risk leaving cities with less income to meet their share of federal grants.

Questions

1 What are *three* differences in the spending priorities of small and big cities?

2 What are *three* kinds of taxes used by big cities?

3 Why has the flight to the suburbs affected the income of big cities?

4 How do states limit the sources from which big cities can raise revenue?

5 What assistance do cities get from federal and state governments?

◌ Do you think that the federal government has a responsibility to aid the cities? Explain.

Detroit, like many other large cities, has been rebuilding its downtown in the hope of attracting more businesses and residents.

A passenger waits to board a train at a BART (Bay Area Rapid Transit) station. The public transit line was built to help relieve the problems caused by automobile traffic congestion in the San Francisco Bay area of California.

NEW APPROACHES TO URBAN GOVERNMENT

If you were to look at a highway map of your state, you would see some clear-cut political divisions. First you would notice the boundaries that separate your state from neighboring states. Then a series of lines would probably divide your state into counties. Next you would see dots, circles, and irregular boxes that mark the locations of towns and cities. It all looks very simple. But the reality is much more complicated, as you would find if you tried to draw in the boundaries of *other* units of local government.

Overlapping Jurisdictions

In most areas of the United States, local governing units form a hodgepodge of overlapping jurisdictions that confuse voters and government officials alike. The voters are confused because they must help elect so many officials and pay taxes and fees to so many units of government. A single family may be subject to a dozen units of local government, from a county to a fire district. Public officials are confused because of all the overlapping jurisdictions. A county may include all of one sewer district and fragments of two more sewer districts. The same is true of other districts. It is hard for officials to coordinate activities among so many overlapping units.

The problems are most severe in large cities and in the built-up areas that surround them. Within the more than 270 Standard Metropolitan Statistical Areas, there are 24,800 local governing units. That includes counties, townships, municipalities, school districts, and other special districts. The 7 million people in the Chicago area were served by 1,171 local governments at last count. Small wonder there is confusion.

Usually no single unit of government handles the problems of an entire metropolitan area. This divided responsibility makes long-range planning difficult. It often leads to wasteful duplication of facilities and creates conflicts between local units of government.

Approaches to Problems

A number of approaches have been tried in attempting to solve these problems. No single approach offers "the" solution, but several approaches, alone or in combination, have brought good results.

Chapter 22: The Special Problems of Big Cities

Consolidation of Governing Units. Consolidation is a time-tested approach. Five major cities—Boston, Philadelphia, New Orleans, San Francisco, and New York—were formed by consolidating smaller units of government in the nineteenth century. More recently several cities have consolidated with their surrounding county. Nashville, Baton Rouge, and Indianapolis are among cities that did this. The most common form of consolidation is the joining together of two or more school districts to form one new school district.

State laws set the rules for consolidation. Usually the laws require the approval of voters in each governing unit involved. There is often strong resistance to consolidation from residents of small units that are being joined with large ones.

One variation on consolidation is a "federal" form of county government used in Dade County, Florida. Some powers are delegated to the county government and some are reserved for other units of government within the county. The county is in charge of planning, tax assessment, and tax collection. It also takes care of county-wide services—mass transit, major streets and highways, prisons, hospitals, welfare services, flood control, and water conservation. Communities within the county—even the huge city of Miami—handle only local affairs. An elected commission sets policies for the county and appoints a county manager to administer county affairs.

Consolidation of Services. Often two or more governing units join forces to provide a service across political boundaries. Suppose that two counties lie on opposite sides of a river that has no bridge. Each county wants a bridge, but neither wants to build the bridge by itself. So they may form a *joint bridge authority* to build and operate a toll bridge.

This organization is an example of a *public service authority*. Its purpose is to provide a service and charge for that service. Such an authority has no power to tax. Instead, it resembles a private corporation in many ways. It may own property and make contracts, and usually may sell bonds to raise money in addition to the tolls and fares it charges. Unlike a private corporation, a public service authority issues no stock. Its directors are appointed by officials of the government units that set it up.

A public service authority may have a limited lifetime. That is, the act or charter that establishes it may specify that it will last only until it has performed the job it set out to do. In our example, the joint bridge authority might sell bonds, build a bridge, and collect tolls for perhaps 30 years until the bonds are paid off. Then the bridge authority would be dissolved. Tolls would be abolished and state highway officials might assume responsibility for maintaining the bridge.

Sometimes two or more states go together to create an interstate public authority. New York and New Jersey, which are neighboring states on New York Harbor, created such an authority in 1921. It is called the Port of New York Authority, and its purpose is to deal with common transportation and shipping

GRANT IN OAKLAND TRIBUNE

"HANG IN THERE—I'LL THINK OF SOMETHING."

problems. The authority builds and operates bridges, tunnels, shipping piers, bus and truck terminals, and even airports. The authority is run by commissioners, half of whom are appointed by the governor of each state.

There are now more than 4,800 public authorities in this country. Some 3,000 of them are set up to take care of housing and urban redevelopment. Others operate transit systems, utility systems, flood control facilities, irrigation systems, and water supply and sewer systems. Some others are on a smaller scale. They run hospitals, recreation areas, public markets, and parking garages. There is at least one that operates a cemetery.

Regional Cooperation. In many metropolitan areas, neighboring communities cooperate voluntarily on common problems. Thus, a large city might agree to provide fire protection for small communities nearby. The governments involved might sign a formal written agreement, or they might cooperate informally.

Sometimes, several local governments join together in a *regional council of governments*. The council takes action on area-wide problems and promotes consultation among local governments. It may also provide shared services. Federal and state governments have been encouraging the formation of these councils. More than 600 are now operating. Federal or state aid to local areas is sometimes funneled through these organizations in an effort to discourage duplication of facilities.

Minnesota pioneered the formation of regional councils of government. The state legislature created a Metropolitan Council to promote cooperation among 120 municipalities and 7 counties in the area of the Twin Cities, Minneapolis and St. Paul. The members of the Twin Cities Metropolitan Council are appointed by the governor. The council sets planning priorities, coordinates the work of regional service agencies, and controls budgets. When a shopping center or other commercial development opens in the region, 40 percent of the additional tax income is turned over to a tax pool. This novel arrangment allows all local governments to share in the increased tax revenue resulting from urban growth.

Some regional councils may pave the way for actual consolidation. The Association of Bay Area Governments in the San Francisco Bay area of California has considered going in that direction.

Two or more states often cooperate on a common problem. They may enter into an *interstate compact,* a formal agreement to attack a problem jointly. The United States Constitution requires such compacts to be approved by Congress (Article I, Section 10).

One compact might regulate activities on a river that passes through two or more states. Another might concern conservation of natural resources. Sixteen Southern and border states have a compact to promote regional cooperation in using colleges and university facilities. More than 200 different compacts have been created in all.

Questions

1 What is the chief difficulty in governing metropolitan areas?

2 What are *four* broad approaches to solving the problems of metropolitan areas? Give one example for each approach.

3 What can be done when metropolitan problems cross state boundaries? Give two examples.

◇ What do you think is the best approach to the problem of overlapping local governments in metropolitan areas? Explain.

PROBLEM: WHO SHOULD PAY FOR PUBLIC SCHOOLS?

Our system of public schools began in Massachusetts in the 1600s. Ever since, people have been arguing over the fairest way to pay for public schools.

Today a large share of local governments' budgets goes for education. In most areas, the property tax is the principal means of financing public schools. Some people believe this is unfair. They argue that an income tax, a sales tax, or some other tax would be fairer. Efforts to change the method of financing schools have been made in several states.

But some people raise another objection. They say that certain kinds of property owners should not have to pay school taxes at all. Below are arguments on both sides. As you read, ask yourself:

- *Whom do property taxes hit most heavily?*
- *Who benefits from the public schools?*

At least five arguments are made by some people who are *against* the payment of school taxes by certain groups.

1. People without children in school should not be required to help pay for the schools.
2. People who disagree with a school's programs should not be forced to help pay for them.
3. Retired people should not have to pay for increased school taxes because the largest part of the income of most retired people is fixed income.
4. Many older people had children in schools long ago and paid for their education. They should not have to pay to educate someone else's children.
5. Requiring people without school-age children to pay school taxes is taxation without representation.

Five arguments are often made by some people who are *in favor of* payment of school taxes by all property owners.

1. All people in a community benefit when children are educated. Our representative form of government is based on educated voters.
2. Without tax-supported public schools, only about 30 percent of people aged 16–18 could attend school.
3. Democracy does not require that a person pay only those taxes whose use he or she approves. Many who pay federal income taxes disapprove of some things those taxes pay for.
4. Many public schools are open evenings to provide community education programs. People without school-age children may use these programs.
5. Any district resident who is displeased with a school's curriculum or with the size of school taxes can make his or her opinions known in a school-board election.

Questions

1 Of the five arguments against having some people pay property taxes to support public schools, which *one* do you think is strongest? Why?

2 Of the five arguments favoring the requirement that all property owners pay school taxes, which *one* do you feel is the strongest? Why?

◇ Do you think that a compromise might resolve this issue? Explain.

PROBLEM: WHAT SPECIAL PROBLEMS DO MAYORS OF BIG CITIES FACE?

Some people look at the problems of big cities and throw up their hands in despair. But not everybody. Each election year produces a new crop of eager candidates for mayor.

The last several years have seen a big change in the kind of person who seeks—and wins—the office of mayor in our big cities. In the past, most mayors were white males. Recently there have been growing numbers of women mayors. San Jose, California, elected Janet Gray Hayes. Oklahoma City chose Patience Latling. San Antonio, Texas, elected Lila Cockrell. Even more striking has been the rise in numbers of black mayors. According to the Joint Center for Political Studies, there were 40 black mayors in 1970, 82 in 1973, and 130 by 1975. About half were in Southern and border states. Major cities with black mayors included Los Angeles, Detroit, and Atlanta.

The following selection describes some of the difficulties faced by blacks and others who took office as mayors in recent years. As you read, consider these questions:

- *What specific troubles do many mayors face?*
- *How might these troubles be overcome?*

The Increase in Black Mayors

The political influence of blacks in United States cities has grown with startling speed. Why this sudden increase?

In some places, the flight of whites to the suburbs has left a black majority in control. In others, the city seems so hopeless that whites appear to be abandoning responsibility and power the way they previously abandoned neighborhoods that were on the decline. But a new white trust in black politicians also seems to be a factor. In almost every case, blacks have won against white opponents.

Raleigh, the capital of North Carolina, is only 23 percent black. Yet Clarence Lightner, a black, became mayor by defeating a white candidate. In Chapel Hill, North Carolina, in 1969, Howard Lee became the first black mayor elected in a majority white community in the South. He squeezed into office with 52 percent of the vote. But he became so popular that he was reelected with 64 percent of the vote in 1971, and 89 percent in 1973.

Most of the new mayors are middle-class blacks. "They are not militants," says Robert Brisbane, head of the political science department of Morehouse College in Atlanta. "No way. Many never carried a picket sign."

Black mayors face the same troubles as any other mayors—crime, corruption, finance, education, housing. But, in addition, they are confronted with a special problem. They must walk a tightrope between the demands of the blacks, who have been shortchanged for centuries, and the concerns of wary whites, who still are not certain how to react to black mayors—and who still wield economic, if not political, power.

The election of a black mayor is a boost to the pride of all the blacks in a city. The high hopes, however, are a mixed blessing. "Black people expect more than I can reasonably deliver," complains Detroit's Coleman Young. Right after the election of Tom Bradley in Los Angeles, a group of powerful and prominent blacks announced to all blacks who would listen: Unless you want to destroy this city's first black mayor, do not ask him to erase in a year all the injustices and brutalities imposed upon black people in three centuries. Give him a chance. And in Atlanta, a campaign aide to Maynard Jackson declares: "Blacks don't want to live in an all-black city. They know that Jackson campaigned for the sharing of power, not taking over."

One problem black mayors probably face more often than whites is that they come to power in cities which are already in trouble, if not in ruins. The middle and upper classes are moving to the suburbs. They take with them a large chunk of the tax base. They leave behind a crippled education system, deteriorating housing, and a tight job market.

But two problems especially worry black mayors: how to cut crime, and how to handle the police. Black mayors see these matters as crucial to their tenure as well as to the well-being of their cities.

Mayor Coleman Young, for example, says that Detroit is a troubled city because the police department is predominantly white. Blacks make up almost half of

Detroit's population, but less than 20 percent of the police force.

Young took office trying to make clear that he is not "soft on crime." He warned the drug pushers to get out of town, which pleased most of the black and white communities. He also expressed the belief that a lot of police corruption had to lie behind the drug traffic, which did not please police.

One of Young's first acts as mayor was to banish an undercover arm of the police department called STRESS (Stop the Robberies, Enjoy Safe Streets). In a short period, it had killed 17 persons, all black. Young said that STRESS used "methods bordering on entrapment" and was "improperly supervised." He knew that the organization had become a target of black hatred. Young insists that crime can never be curbed until the people trust their police and become involved in fighting crime.

Similar police-related problems exist in almost every major city. Being for law and order is simple; whether Coleman Young and the other black mayors can make peace with their police forces is a much more complicated matter.

It would be both unfair and foolish to expect all black mayors to be supermen or wonder women. We must not demand of them miracles that white mayors have found to be beyond their powers. Some crucial urban problems are beyond immediate solution no matter what the skin color of the person in the mayor's chair.

Why, then, is it of such special note that we have these black mayors? One reason is that so many whites in Los Angeles, for example, now refer to Bradley as "our mayor," instead of "our black mayor." It means that more and more whites are thinking of blacks as individuals and peers. It can mean the lessening of white fear of blacks in general and black politicians in particular. And for minority citizens, these

The mayor of Atlanta, Georgia, Maynard Jackson, gives the oath of office to a newly appointed city official.

mayors may both inspire and symbolize a restoration of faith in the "American system." Says Maynard Jackson, "Politics is the last nonviolent hurrah for the masses of people and, especially, for black people."

Adapted from Carl T. Rowan and David D. Mazie, "The Boom in Black Mayors," *Reader's Digest,* July 1975, pp. 179–184.

Questions

1 What have been some reasons for an increase in black mayors in the cities in recent years?

2 What have been some problems faced by mayors of big cities?

3 What have been *three* special problems faced by black mayors? Explain.

◇ How do you think mayors can be helped to solve their problems?

Chapter 22 Review

Developing Your Political Vocabulary

Use each of the following terms in a sentence describing how governments in a metropolitan area sometimes cooperate with one another.

1. overlap
2. public authorities
3. compact
4. consolidation
5. interstate

Recalling and Comparing

1. What problems do big cities suffer from more than other local governments?
2. What are *two* problems connected with federal aid to cities?
3. What are *two* ways in which local governments might consolidate services?
4. What are *three* ways in which regional cooperation between governing units might be carried out?

Special Activities

1. Draw a map of your own city or county showing overlapping jurisdictions of local units of government. Get information from a local library or from local government offices.
2. Draw up a list of all the things you can think of that might attract people to your city or to the nearest metropolitan area. Make another list of things that might turn people away. How can some of the things in each list cause problems for local governments?
3. Interview one or more local government officials and prepare a report on regional cooperation in your area.
4. Find out how one city government in your area gets its revenues. Make a graph to illustrate your findings.
5. Learn how your local tax assessments are determined. Illustrate your findings in a chart.
6. Find out what kinds of civil service examinations are given by your city or the nearest big city. Make a chart showing each main job category, the frequency of the examination, and the requirements for taking the examination.
7. Make a study of the zoning laws in your city or the nearest big city. Summarize your findings in a map, a chart, or a written report.
8. List the sources of pollution in your city or the nearest big city. Find out which city departments or agencies are attempting to regulate each source of pollution.
9. Some magazines occasionally publish articles that rate cities on various factors, such as air quality, quality of schools, and amount of land devoted to parks. Make your own list of factors that you would look for, in the order of importance, in choosing your "ideal city." Write a report explaining how well or how poorly your own city meets those standards. Add suggestions for improvements in your city.
10. Make a study of the career of county or city manager and of college programs designed to prepare people for this field of employment.
11. Consider what might be arguments for and against the following statement: "People who live in a metropolitan area but outside the boundaries of the central city should help pay for that city's government." Do you agree or disagree? Why?

Unit VIII Review

Improving Your Reading

Read the selection below and then answer the questions that follow it.

There are many kinds of local government in the United States. The constitution and laws of each state set the ground rules for local governments.

Local governments carry out a wide variety of functions. Some functions they share with state governments. Other functions, such as fire protection and sanitation, are provided almost exclusively by local governments.

Almost every state has some form of county government. The most common is that in which a board performs both legislative and executive functions. The board members are elected by the voters.

County governments were originally designed to serve rural areas. As our nation has become more urban, city governments have taken on more and more of the responsibilities of local government.

There are three basic forms of city government. Some cities have worked out combinations of these three.

The most frequent form of city government is headed by a mayor and a city council. In a weak-mayor system, the mayor has few executive powers. In a strong-mayor system, the mayor exercises broad executive powers.

A second basic version of city government is the commission form. Each commissioner heads a department of city government. The commissioners exercise both legislative and executive functions. This type of city government is losing popularity, and only a small percentage of cities now use it.

A third type of city government is the council-manager form. The council sets policies and hires a city manager to carry out the policies. An increasing number of cities are using some variation of the city-manager system.

Many other units of local government exist. Among them are towns, villages, boroughs, townships, school districts, and other special districts. Most elementary and secondary education is carried out by school districts.

Governments in big cities and metropolitan areas have been faced with special problems. The need for services has increased while the property tax and other revenue-raising methods have provided insufficient income. Recently, federal and state aid has become an important source of revenue for cities.

The increased number of local governments has resulted in overlapping jurisdictions. No single government has been able to make decisions for an entire metropolitan area. To solve this problem, some areas have tried regional cooperation or consolidation of governments or of services.

1 In your own words, summarize this reading in *no more than five* sentences. Have your summary focus on what you regard as the five most important points made in the reading.

2 Which *one* of the following four topics noted in the reading can best be used to show the differences among city governments?

   a a shift of population from rural to urban areas

Unit VIII Review: Local Government

  b mayor-council, commission, and city manager systems
  c problems in raising revenue
  d cooperation among local governments

3 Which *one* of the following topics discussed in the reading can best be used to show how local governments are not fully independent political units?
  a the officials of county government
  b the three basic types of city government
  c rules set by state constitutions and laws
  d federal aid to local governments

Developing Your Writing Skills: What Are Your Attitudes toward Government?

Writing a Paragraph

In this unit, you have considered some of the problems faced by local governments. Many more could have been mentioned. Now think about the problems described and any other problems you may be aware of. Then ask yourself these questions:

- *What problems are faced by one unit of your local government?*
- *Which of those problems do you think should receive the most attention?*

Now complete the following sentence on a sheet of paper. Fill out the paragraph with arguments in support of your position.

  Of the problems faced by my (identify your local governing unit here), the one that should receive the greatest attention is _____
  _____

Writing an Essay

Now that you have examined the various levels of government and the services they provide, write a short essay on the desirability of centralized government. Do you think that the states and the federal government should have greater power than they do? Or do you think that more power should rest with local governments? Why?

Recommended Reading

The County Year Book (annual), National Association of Counties and the International City Management Association.

Governmental Finances (annual), U.S. Bureau of the Census.

John D. Haeger and Michael P. Weber, *The Bosses,* Forum Press, St. Charles, Mo., 1974 (paperback).

Glen R. Peterson, *Public Office at the Local Level: How Does One Get Elected? Who Should Try?* Center for Information on America, Washington, Conn., 1962 (paperback).

Mike Royko, *Boss: Richard J. Daley of Chicago,* Dutton, New York, 1971.

Jonathan Rubinstein, *City Police,* Farrar, Straus, New York, 1973.

John T. Salter, *Boss Rule: Portraits in City Politics,* Arno Press, New York, 1974 (paperback).

Statistical Abstract of the United States (annual), U.S. Bureau of the Census.

Lincoln Steffens, *The Autobiography of Lincoln Steffens,* Harcourt, New York, 1937.

Annmarie Hauck Walsh, *The Public's Image* (a study of public authorities), Twentieth Century Fund, New York, 1978.

Political Parties and Campaigns

UNIT IX

Why would anyone want to run for President of the United States? Is the prize worth the grueling effort required? That is what United States Senator Lloyd M. Bentsen of Texas asked himself as he began an ultimately unsuccessful drive for the 1976 Democratic nomination for President. Here are his thoughts:

> Citizens who announce their candidacy for President undergo a period of armchair psychoanalysis before they even have a chance to submit their credentials. What are their motives? Are they on an ego trip? Are they power-starved? Or are they some kind of masochists to subject themselves to the tortures of the campaign trail?
>
> Those tortures are well known: the 24-hour day, the sleepless nights, the split-second scheduling, the jet lag, the handshake paralysis, the aching vocal chords, the kaleidoscope of airports, hotel rooms, traffic, crowds—and the inevitable chicken dinner at every stop.
>
> Who needs it? Is it worth all this? Why run?
>
> The answer may be incredibly simple. It could lie in an earnest desire to do something for the country—and the rather uncomplicated conviction that the survival of democracy depends on personal sacrifices. Ego also plays a part. It takes a healthy ego and a base of self-confidence to aspire to the most demanding elective office in the world.
>
> But I think impatience has more to do with it: impatience with things done badly or left undone, impatience with a bureaucracy that stifles competition rather than encourages it.
>
> Fortunately, there are citizens who prefer to be in the thick of the action rather than seething on the sidelines while someone else fumbles the ball.

Adapted from Lloyd M. Bentsen, "The Reasons They Run," San Antonio *Express*, August 19, 1975.

In this country, "the thick of the action" is the world of political parties and political campaigns, of races for office, appeals to voters, appeals to campaign contributors, appeals to history.

Our democratic system is organized around two poles. At one pole are the political parties. At the other is the public to whom those parties appeal. Unit IX will explore how political parties fit into our system of government. The three chapters in this unit will take up, in turn, the role of parties, their involvement in primaries and conventions, and the role of the candidate who is seeking nomination and election. The next unit, Unit X, will focus on the people's political participation.

Chapter 23

The Role of Political Parties

For more than a century, every President of the United States has worn one of two political labels. Either he has been a Democrat, or he has been a Republican. We have become so accustomed to this either/or division that it seems as natural as night and day. But it is not. Our two-party political system grew out of specific historical circumstances and specific political choices. This chapter is about how that system came to be, and how it works in practice.

--- Goals ---

- To understand the origins and main features of our two-party political system.
- To learn the functions and organization of our political parties.
- To consider how our political parties operate at the local level.

OUR TWO-PARTY SYSTEM

The most important fact about our national political party system is that it is a two-party system. If the Democrats are in power, the Republicans are waiting impatiently in the wings. If the Republicans are in power, the Democrats are itching to replace them. These two major parties have the national stage pretty much to themselves.

Democracy does not *require* a two-party system. Many democracies have three or more parties seriously contending for power. In Eu-

419

Chapter 23: The Role of Political Parties

By 1798, the nation had split into two opposing political parties. Federalist Roger Griswold here battles Democratic-Republican Matthew Lyon in the House. Theirs was the first physical fight in Congress.

rope, for example, governments are often *coalitions,* or temporary alliances, of two or more parties.

In the United States, however, alternative parties—often called *third parties*—have never had much luck. One reason is historical. Our two-party system developed early in our history. Despite the fact that George Washington and others were against *any* political parties, the nation soon split into two opposing political camps—the Federalists and the Democratic-Republicans, who had been the Anti-Federalists. Party names have changed over the years, but a two-way division has remained.

Our electoral rules encourage the two-party system. There are two ways of holding democratic elections—by allowing one person to win or by allowing more than one to win. The first way is used in most elections.

In *single-member districts,* only one candidate can win. Voters cast their ballots for a list of candidates. The one with a *plurality* (more votes than any other candidate) wins. All other candidates lose. In *multimember districts,* two or more candidates are elected from one list. Each voter has one vote. The two or more top vote-getters are elected. This system gives representation to political parties in accordance with the proportion, or share, of the vote their candidates receive. For that reason, it is called *proportional representation.*

A close look will tell us that proportional representation encourages a multi-party system. Even small parties have a chance to win a seat on a governing body without placing first in any district. Our system of single-member districts, on the other hand, *discourages* small parties. Few voters are interested in supporting a party that has little chance of winning. This does not mean that third parties have played no great role in this country. As we shall see, they have made major contributions.

The two-party system has an important side effect: political parties tend to be broad coalitions of diverse forces. Each party tries to build a majority following. To do this, it must appeal to both business and labor, to both farmers and consumers, to both rich and poor. Each party tries to bring together diverse sectional groups. Southern Democrats differ from Northern Democrats. "Eastern Establishment" Republicans differ from Midwestern Republicans. Conservatives and liberals are found in both parties. Differences between the parties become blurred. Neither party carves out a single set of ideas for itself.

Some people see this as bad. They say that Democrats and Republicans are as alike as Tweedledum and Tweedledee. In this view, the voters have no real choice, since each party tries to be all things to all people.

Other people see the parties' similarities as a vital strength. They say that the two parties are similar enough to promote national harmony, but different enough to offer a choice to the voters. In this view, our nation benefits from the *moderate* choices offered by our two-party system, in contrast to the more extreme stands often taken by parties in multi-party systems.

It should be noted that, while the two-party system predominates nationally, it is not as firmly fixed at the state and local level. In some states and cities, a third party holds the balance of power between the two major parties. It may even be strong enough to win elections on its own. More commonly, states and cities are under single-party domination. For almost a century after Reconstruction, the Democrats had a solid grip on the South. Few Republicans even bothered to run for office. In some areas of the North and Midwest, the reverse was true. Republicans had such a strong hold that few Democrats bothered to run. Even today many areas lean strongly toward one or the other major party, and many elections are uncontested.

The Two Major Parties

The Democrats formed our first major national party and have the broadest base of support today. At first called the Anti-Federalists, or Democratic-Republicans, the Democrats took their present name in 1825. The Democratic party led national politics until 1860, then took a back seat to the Republicans until 1932, when they again took the lead.

The Democratic party began as the party of Thomas Jefferson. It favored strong state governments and weak national government—the position taken by the Anti-Federal-

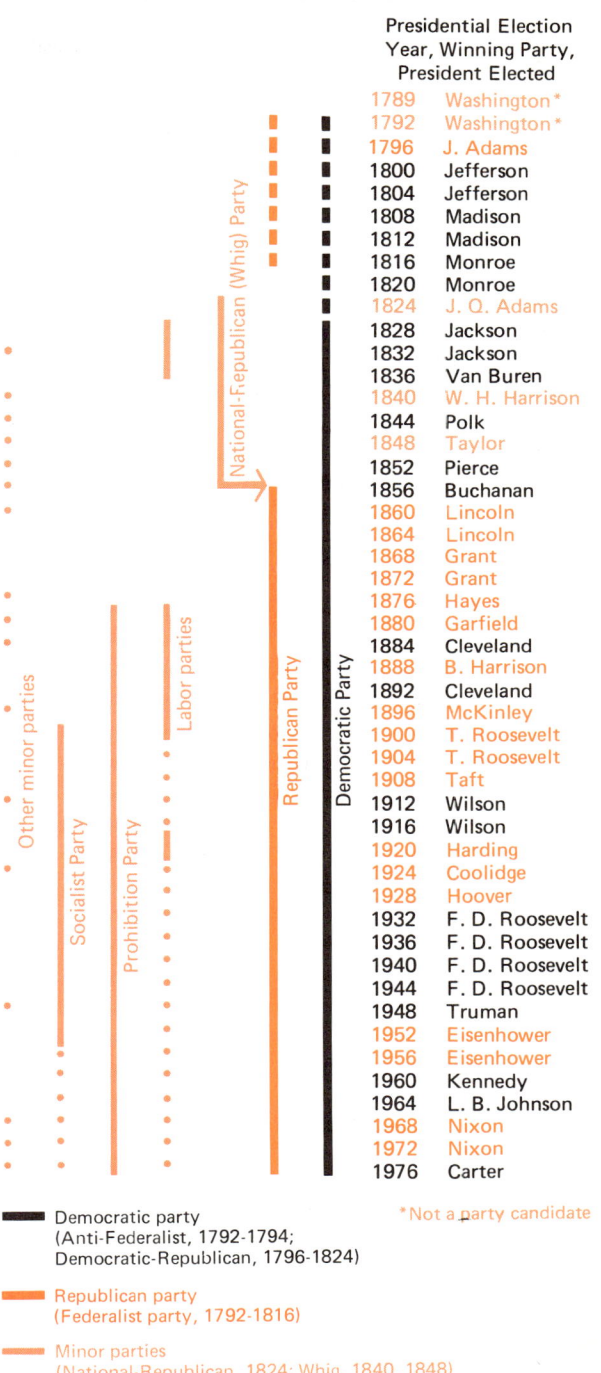

NATIONAL POLITICAL PARTIES

Presidential Election Year, Winning Party, President Elected

1789 Washington*
1792 Washington*
1796 J. Adams
1800 Jefferson
1804 Jefferson
1808 Madison
1812 Madison
1816 Monroe
1820 Monroe
1824 J. Q. Adams
1828 Jackson
1832 Jackson
1836 Van Buren
1840 W. H. Harrison
1844 Polk
1848 Taylor
1852 Pierce
1856 Buchanan
1860 Lincoln
1864 Lincoln
1868 Grant
1872 Grant
1876 Hayes
1880 Garfield
1884 Cleveland
1888 B. Harrison
1892 Cleveland
1896 McKinley
1900 T. Roosevelt
1904 T. Roosevelt
1908 Taft
1912 Wilson
1916 Wilson
1920 Harding
1924 Coolidge
1928 Hoover
1932 F. D. Roosevelt
1936 F. D. Roosevelt
1940 F. D. Roosevelt
1944 F. D. Roosevelt
1948 Truman
1952 Eisenhower
1956 Eisenhower
1960 Kennedy
1964 L. B. Johnson
1968 Nixon
1972 Nixon
1976 Carter

▬ Democratic party
(Anti-Federalist, 1792-1794;
Democratic-Republican, 1796-1824)

▬ Republican party
(Federalist party, 1792-1816)

▬ Minor parties
(National-Republican, 1824; Whig, 1840, 1848)

*Not a party candidate

The Presidents included in this chart are those who were elected to the office. Those who served only as a result of another's death or resignation are not included.

Cheers arose at the 1878 state convention of the Democratic party as George B. McClellan stepped up to accept his party's nomination as governor of New Jersey. McClellan had been general of the Union armies early in the Civil War.

ists in the debate over the Constitution. The issue of federalism faded as the Democratic party grew into a broad coalition of diverse interests. Andrew Jackson, the President from 1829 to 1837, identified the Democrats with the "common people" and solidified their support in the South and West. But the party split over the issue of slavery. With the beginning of the Civil War, it was greatly weakened by its identification with the South. From 1860 until 1932, only two Democrats were elected President.

The Democratic party made a national comeback during the Great Depression of the 1930s. The party's presidential candidate, Franklin D. Roosevelt, who promised the voters a New Deal, was elected four times in a row. Democrats have controlled Congress in all but two sessions since 1932—the sessions of 1947–1948 and 1953–1954. Democrats served as President from 1933 to 1953, 1961 to 1969, and again in 1977. (See the table on page 135.)

Today, when people in this country are asked which political party they prefer, almost twice as many say "Democratic" as say "Republican." But the Democrats' lead is not always clear from the votes cast in elections, particularly presidential elections. A popular candidate who gives major attention to a question that is of high interest can often win votes across party lines.

The Republican party originated as a third-party movement in 1854. It is the only third party in the United States that has ever blossomed into a major party. Within 7 years, it had placed a candidate—Abraham Lincoln—in the White House.

To attain big-party stature, the Republicans had to win votes away from two other parties of the time, the Democrats and the Whigs. The Whigs had been organized in the 1830s to oppose Andrew Jackson's policies, but they had never really gotten off the ground. The Whigs elected Presidents only twice, in 1840 and 1848, and then only by nominating war heroes. By 1856, the Whigs were dividing over slavery, just like the Democrats.

The Republicans ran a former Democrat, John C. Frémont, as their first presidential candidate in 1856. He finished second, behind the Democratic candidate. In the 1860 elec-

Chapter 23: The Role of Political Parties

The young Republican party used torchlight parades in 1860 to drum up support for its presidential candidate, Abraham Lincoln. Here a parade of Wide-Awakes passes the buildings of two major New York City newspapers.

tion, the Republicans had the advantage of a three-way split among their opponents. The Republicans won with Lincoln and a platform that opposed further extension of slavery.

The Republicans became known as the GOP, for "Grand Old Party," and a grand time they had for many years. They emerged from the Civil War with a reputation as the "party of the Union." Unlike the Democrats, whose supporters were now concentrated in the South, the Republicans won support from all sections of the country. They had a firm hold on the Presidency from the late 1860s through the 1920s, winning 12 out of 16 elections.

Since 1932, the Republicans have fared less well. They have had three Presidents—Dwight Eisenhower (1953–1961), Richard Nixon (1969–1974), and Gerald Ford (1974–1977)—but have rarely controlled Congress. While Republicans have made gains in the South in recent years, they have lost ground in industrial areas of the North. Still, a band of strong supporters stands by the Republicans.

Minor Parties

Minor parties have often played a key role by raising new issues that the major parties had ignored. The Democratic and Republican parties tend to appeal to voters in the middle of the political road. Often this means straddling divisive issues and stressing safe issues. This wins elections, but it leaves many problems unsolved.

Third parties have long served as a safety valve. They attract voters whose concerns are not being handled by the major parties. You can detect this in some of the third-party names: Vegetarians, Prohibitionists, Equal

Chapter 23: The Role of Political Parties

The Socialist party was in its infancy when it named Eugene V. Debs its presidential candidate in 1904. This minor but enduring party nominated Debs in each presidential election campaign for the next 20 years.

Righters, Greenbackers, and States' Righters. But if the issue is important and enough voters show an interest, the major parties usually adopt the issue. As a result, most third parties eventually fade away.

Among the important issues first taken up by third parties were the abolition of slavery, woman suffrage, the progressive income tax, abolition of child labor, old-age pensions, and railroad and banking regulation.

Occasionally, third parties start as spinoffs of major parties. For example, Theodore Roosevelt, who had served as a Republican President from 1901 to 1909, ran as a Progressive in 1912. He drew enough votes away from the Republican candidate, William Howard Taft, to enable a Democrat, Woodrow Wilson, to win. In 1948, Strom Thurmond of South Carolina led many Southern Democrats into the States' Rights party. He received thirty-nine electoral votes, but the Democrats still won the election. George Wallace of Alabama left the Democratic party to run under the label of the American Independent party in 1968. He won forty-six electoral votes (see map, page 137).

Because they are issue-oriented, minor parties are often criticized as dogmatic and extremist. Certainly they are more willing than the major parties to appeal to the left and right of the political spectrum. This has been evident in recent elections. The Communist, Socialist Labor, Socialist Worker, and Peace and Freedom parties have campaigned on leftist, or "radical," issues. Some of these parties have opposed the nation's foreign policy as "imperialist" or have proposed a greater redistribution of income in favor of poor people. Other parties, such as the American Independent and America First parties, have stressed rightist, or conservative issues. Rightist parties have called for such things as giving more power to the states and cutting out many federal programs.

Minor parties must struggle against great odds to get a hearing. The Democratic and Republican parties have put up legal barriers, such as state laws that require large numbers of signatures on election petitions. Just as important are the informal barriers. The mass media usually do not take minor parties seriously, nor do the media give them attention. Thus, many voters may be unaware until they enter the voting booth that they have a choice among more than two candidates.

Questions

1 In what way can the two-party system be said to reflect our historical experience?

2 What is one argument *in favor of* and one argument *against* our system of two broadly based parties?

3 How have minor parties been important in our nation's history?

⬠ Do you think that the nation could ever have too many political parties? Explain.

FUNCTIONS AND ORGANIZATION OF POLITICAL PARTIES

Though the Constitution does not mention political parties, they are an essential part of our way of government. Without them, we would have a far different political system.

Political parties seek to put their ideas about government into action by capturing elective office. In working toward that goal, the parties fulfill a number of functions in our political system.

Nominating Candidates. A party that wants to win elections must put up candidates. It does this by nominating the people who will bear the party's label on the ballot. The party also supports its candidates with money and propaganda. These important party activities will be examined in Chapters 24 and 25.

Focusing Issues and Informing the Public. Our federal, state, and local governments deal with so many issues that even the best-informed person would have a hard time following all of them. Political parties help make government meaningful by simplifying issues. That is, they choose certain issues as a focus of debate and state them in terms that make sense to most people. One result is to inform the people about what government is doing, or could be doing. Another result is to offer choices between alternative approaches to those issues.

Governing. Once a party's candidate has been elected, the party shares responsibility for the way government is run. The party's role is weaker in our system than in parliamentary systems. In England, for example, the majority political party actually runs the government and can replace a prime minister between national elections. In our system, candidates have party support but are elected as *individuals*. The President may retain office until the next election, even after losing the support of his or her party. But parties play an important role in governing, nonetheless. We have seen that they help to round up support in Congress for a President's policies. And parties furnish a group of individuals from whom Presidents, governors, and mayors appoint people to important positions.

Whistle-Blowing. An important function performed by parties out of power is to oppose the party in power. This "whistle-blowing" or "watchdog" function involves guarding against abuses of power. For example, the Democrats blew the whistle when President Nixon's White House staff stepped out of bounds in the Watergate scandal in the early 1970s. Likewise, Republicans have blown the whistle on Democratic scandals. Closely related to whistle-blowing is the function of offering alternatives to the programs of the party in power. The opposition party is always ready to criticize shortcomings and to suggest changes.

Moderating Conflicts. Our broadly based political parties tend to take the edge off divisive issues by promoting compromise. For example, Democrats who want to get a bill through Congress may have to compromise opposing views held by Northern and Southern members of their party. The same holds true for the Republican party, which is often divided between liberal and conservative wings.

Political candidates who are viewed as extreme have trouble winning the middle-of-the-road votes needed to win elections. In 1964, the Republicans chose Senator Barry

Hopeful supporters greet Senator Barry Goldwater of Arizona during his unsuccessful 1964 campaign for President.

Goldwater as their presidential candidate. Goldwater took some clear stands, wanting to offer "a choice, not an echo." But many Republicans would not vote for him on grounds that he was too conservative—too extreme. He lost by a wide margin. Senator George McGovern suffered the same fate after winning the Democratic nomination in 1972. Many Democrats thought he went too far in the other direction. Most successful presidential candidates have worked for compromise within their party in order to build the widest possible base of support. Both Gerald Ford and Jimmy Carter took careful middle-of-the-road positions in the 1976 presidential election with a resulting close vote.

The organization of our major political parties is basically decentralized and undisciplined. On organization charts it does not seem so. The parties have what appears to be a chain of command stretching from a national party organization at the top to local party officials at the bottom. But this chain of command has many missing links. Any command from the top would most likely be ignored.

This is because our parties reflect the federal structure of our government. State party organizations are only loosely linked to national party organizations. Local organizations often are quite independent of state organizations. Each level of a party is concerned mainly with elections at one level of government—local, state, or federal. (See the chart on the facing page.)

The highest authority in each party is the *national convention,* a meeting of party delegates held every 4 years. In Chapter 24, we will explore the place of the national convention in presidential campaigns.

The national convention elects a *national committee.* This committee includes at least one man and one woman from each state. Various other members are also provided for. The Republicans, for instance, include the state Republican chairperson from each state that went Republican in the last election. The Democrats include representatives of Democratic governors and members of Congress, and some members chosen from the party at large. The main job of the national committee is to choose the city where the next national convention will be held.

In theory, each party's national committee picks the *national chairperson.* In practice, this official is handpicked by the presidential candidate. The chairperson directs the party's presidential campaign and raises money for the national party. He or she names an *executive committee* to run party affairs for the 4 years between presidential elections.

Each party has a *Senatorial Campaign Committee* and a *Congressional Campaign Committee* to help the party's candidates for Congress. The people on these committees are chosen by each party's members of Congress in order to prevent the President or presidential candidate from having too much influence.

TYPICAL ORGANIZATION OF A MAJOR POLITICAL PARTY

- National Committee and Executive Committee
- Campaign committees for Senate and for House of Representatives
- State committees
- County, city, or town committees and ward committees
- Precinct captains or district leaders

Political parties at the state level are independent of the national organization. At the top is a *state central committee.* Its members represent congressional districts, state legislative districts, or counties. The committee is headed by a *state chairperson,* who may be a figurehead or a powerful boss.

Below the state committee, party organization varies greatly, depending on state laws and customs. Usually there are county committees, city or town committees, and sometimes ward committees. At the bottom are precinct captains. A *precinct* is a polling district and is the basic unit of party organization. The precinct captains, or district leaders, are the ones most responsible for getting out the party's voters. Often the precinct captain is a volunteer member of a local party club. Anyone can organize a Democratic or Republican or other party club, but to be official it must have a charter from the party's county, city, or town committee. Since a major function of these committees is to encourage the formation of party clubs, such charters are easily obtained.

Chapter 23: The Role of Political Parties

In theory, power in each political party is organized from the bottom up. Thus, party members in each precinct may elect representatives to go to ward, city, or county party conventions. There, delegations to a state party convention are chosen. This theory does not always work out in practice because party committees often are tightly organized. A central leadership or party boss with loyal supporters can control party elections at the precinct or other levels. As with any form of politics, the winners are those who can marshal the most votes.

Questions

1 What is the primary goal of a political party?

2 How do political parties bring issues into focus?

3 Who chooses the top official in a major political party?

⬠ Do you think that the national party leaders should have control over state party organizations? Why or why not?

PROBLEM: HOW DO OUR POLITICAL PARTIES OPERATE AT THE GRASS ROOTS?

At the bottom of the official ranks of a political party is the precinct captain or district leader. The exact role of this official varies from place to place. Often it depends upon the personality of the individual officeholder. It also depends on whether he or she is part of a powerful political machine.

The job of district leader is unpaid and unglamorous. Usually this spare-time job is a stepping-stone for someone who wants to move up in party politics. Some people think the job is pointless and should be abolished. Others say it is important precisely because it is so close to the people—the point where party organization and individual needs make contact.

The following selections are from statements that were made by two individuals seeking district leaderships in separate areas of New York City. The statements show how each candidate viewed the job. As you read, ask yourself:

- What does the district leader do?
- How would this candidate perform the job?

The Political Party in the Neighborhood

Dennis P. Casey, Democrat:

As I see it, the role of a district leader is one of service to the community. People today, though better educated than in the past, still have problems with increasing rents, inadequate housing, insufficient sanitation, unsafe streets, and unresponsive elected officials.

It is the duty of a district leader to ensure that the people of the district get the services they are entitled to and the attention they deserve from the various agencies and institutions throughout the city. A district leader should be an ombudsman for his or her constituents and a gadfly to our often inert, unresponsive city government.

To be of service, however, a district leader must be accessible to everyone in the district. A district leader needs to be able to work with and foster the growth of community and civic organizations.

Our club is the one with the open door. We don't have a back room, we don't impose loyalty tests on our membership, nor do we have an "official line." We do, however, harness the intelligence and good will of our neighbors in behalf of our area. That, to me, is the most effective as well as the most democratic way to provide needed services to our community.

Patricia Conaty, Republican:

The role of the district leader is to organize the party in the district and select candidates by an open process. As an elected official, the district leader should use his or her influence to assist and protect the interests of the people in the district.

As associate district leader, I would work with the resources available to me, channeling them in the direction of the two groups of society—namely, youth and senior citizens—that I feel are being overlooked. I would try to get private associations and businesses to help with programs for these people.

An individual should have a person to go to in order to get action on legitimate complaints. I would be such a person. This suggests a great deal more power and authority than is common in this position. But, as associate district leader, I would have access to authorities.

I would like to focus on encouragement, planning assistance, and the numerous opportunities available for fund raising for building up the community.

If we strive for objectives at this level of community life, it will reflect on our national life, for ours is a nation of many neighborhoods.

Adapted from *Our Town* (a New York City community newspaper), September 9, 1977.

Questions

1 What do you think Dennis Casey considers to be the most important job of a district leader?

2 What do you think Patricia Conaty considers to be the most important job of a district leader?

◯ Do you think the job of district leader is an important job? Would you want it? Why or why not?

Chapter 23 Review

Developing Your Political Vocabulary

Use each of the following terms in a sentence about our political process:
- a political party
- b proportional representation
- c coalition
- d major party
- e third party
- f Grand Old Party
- g national committee
- h precinct

Recalling and Comparing

1 How does a multimember district differ from a single-member district? How does the type of voting process in these two districts tend to encourage different forms of party systems?

2 How did our two major political parties develop? Briefly describe the development of each.

3 List *five* issues first popularized by minor parties.

4 What are *two* obstacles faced by minor parties in seeking votes?

5 What are *five* functions performed by political parties?

Special Activities

1 Visit the local headquarters of a political party in your area. Ask the person in charge to outline the main problems faced by that party locally. Write a report describing those problems and possible remedies.

2 Draw a cartoon illustrating at least one problem faced by a minor party in our political system.

3 Make a special bulletin-board display that illustrates recent activities of political parties in the United States.

4 Identify the members of your state committee for one of the major political parties. Write a brief biographical sketch of each, stressing their occupational and political backgrounds.

5 Make a study of one of the minor political parties in this country's history and write a report explaining the party's aims and achievements.

6 Review the political organization of Congress (Chapter 6) and draw up a set of recommendations that meet your ideas of what the role of political parties in Congress should be.

7 Make a study of the majority and minority parties in your state legislature over the years. Describe in a chart or a report what parties have been in a majority position during this period. Compare the political organization of your state legislature with the political organization of Congress (Chapter 6).

8 Identify a set of issues that you think need more national attention than any political party is giving them. Describe the issues and the kind of political party organization you would recommend to bring the issues into focus.

9 Consider what might be arguments for and against the following statement: "Political parties have much to offer in the way of new ideas and possible solutions to problems." Do you agree or disagree? Why?

Chapter 24

Primaries and Conventions

How do political parties choose their candidates? In smoke-filled rooms? In secret deals? In open elections? In some combination of those ways? The success of our democracy depends to a large extent on the way in which candidates for office are chosen.

Nomination is the first step toward election to public office. The final step is the general election, when the candidates of both major parties and of any minor parties are listed on one ballot for the voter to choose from. This chapter is about how political parties choose their candidates for that general election ballot.

Goals

- To learn what role the primary election plays in our political process.
- To learn how national conventions of our political parties are organized and what role they play in our political process.
- To learn the problems of minor parties in getting on a general election ballot.
- To consider whether we should have a national presidential primary.

THE PRIMARY SYSTEM

Two methods of nominating political candidates are common in our nation today: the primary election and the nominating convention. This section will deal with the first of these methods.

Chapter 24: Primaries and Conventions

For a few weeks in February or March of every presidential election year, New Hampshire is the center of the nation's political life. Presidential candidates stand at factory gates in Manchester and Nashua, stamping their feet in the cold, shaking hands with men and women—potential voters—coming to work. Reporters and television camera crews stop passersby on the snowy streets to ask what they think of the presidential candidates. Each evening in homes across the nation, the day's events in New Hampshire are retold. Why all the attention on this one state—a state with fewer than half a million registered voters? The reason is that a primary election is taking place. New Hampshire's is the first primary election of the long presidential season.

The word *primary* comes from the Latin root for "first," and that is what a *primary election* is—a first election, preparing the way for another. The New Hampshire primary, like most primary elections in this country, is a *party primary*. That is, it is used by political parties as a step in choosing their candidates for a later election. But a primary may also be a step in a nonpartisan election, where candidates run without party sponsorship. The purpose of a *nonpartisan primary* is to thin out a field of several candidates. The winners of the primary—generally the two candidates with the most votes—then run against each other in the final, or general, election.

Primary elections have other purposes beyond narrowing the field of presidential candidates. They also help to choose delegates to the presidential nominating conventions, where the actual choice of presidential candidates is made. Primaries play a part in elections for many lower offices as well. They are used in all fifty states to choose nominees for some or all local and state offices, and usually for positions in Congress.

Primary elections became a major part of our national politics only in the twentieth century. They were seen as a way to give more people a voice in choosing party candidates.

Previously, candidates were chosen by small groups of politicians. Until 1828, presidential and vice-presidential candidates were named by party caucuses in Congress. Candidates for Congress and for state offices were usually named by party caucuses in each state's legislature. Beginning with the election of 1832, candidates for President and Vice President were officially chosen in national party conventions. Within each state, conventions also began to choose candidates for statewide and local offices. These conventions widened the pool of politicians who helped to choose the party's candidates, but party bosses and political machines ran the conventions.

Reforms started at the state level. Around the turn of the century, several state and local governments adopted the *direct primary* as the main method of nominating candidates for state and local offices. In a *direct primary,* the voters themselves choose the nominees who will run in the general election. Later, the direct primary was extended to congressional races.

The most common type of primary is the *closed primary,* which is limited to voters who have registered as members of the party. Anyone who is registered as a Democrat may vote only in the Democratic primary. Anyone who is registered as a Republican may vote only in the Republican primary. Any voter who has not registered as a party member is barred from participating in a closed primary. The closed primary is sometimes used to pick party leaders as well as nominees for public office.

The other main type of direct primary is the *open primary.* It is open to all voters, regardless of whether or not they belong to the party. A registered Republican, for example, may vote in either the Republican or the Democratic open primary—but usually not in both. Two states, Alaska and Washington, have a variation of the open primary. In this variation, a voter may switch back and forth between parties on the primary ballot, voting on the Republican ballot for one position and on the Democratic ballot for another.

433

Chapter 24: Primaries and Conventions

The voters in this direct primary will nominate the state and local candidates who will run in the general election.

places, there may be two or more levels of conventions. For example, voters may elect delegates to a county convention that elects delegates to a state convention that, in turn, elects delegates to a national convention.

Since early in this century, indirect primaries have played an important role in the selection of presidential nominees by the two major parties. In 1976, about thirty states had *presidential primaries.* The New Hampshire primary was one example. In states that do not have presidential primaries, delegates to presidential nominating conventions are chosen at state conventions or by state party committees. More will be said about this later.

Presidential primaries usually have two purposes. The first is the *election of delegates* to the national presidential convention. The second is *finding out voters' preferences for a party's presidential nomination.* The voting can be done in a number of ways.

In most states, a primary election is won by the candidate with the most votes, whether or not that candidate has a majority. But some states provide for runoff primaries when no candidate has a majority. A *runoff primary* is a second election between the two persons who received the most votes in the first primary. The winner of the runoff is then the party's nominee in the general election.

Some states allow party leaders or conventions to endorse a candidate in a party primary. But voters may—and often do— reject the "official" candidate in the primary.

In an *indirect primary,* the voters do not actually choose their party's nominees. Instead, the voters elect delegates to nominating conventions, and the selection of nominees is made by the convention delegates. In some

Delegates to a party's national presidential convention are chosen directly or indirectly in primaries.

In the first method, only the delegates' names are on the ballot; there is no indication of which candidate the delegates will vote for at the national convention. This method may confuse the voter because the delegates are likely to be politicians whose names have little meaning to the average voter. Sometimes, however, the delegates will have made an announcement before the primary saying which candidate they support, or at least which way they are leaning.

In the second method, the delegates' names are listed on the ballot along with the name of the candidate they support. Sometimes the delegates must sign a pledge promising to support that candidate.

The other three methods involve a *preference poll*. In one version the presidential candidates' names are listed on one part of the ballot and the delegates' names on another part. The voter then casts separate votes for a presidential candidate and for a slate of delegates. In this method, it is possible for one presidential candidate to win the preference poll and for another presidential candidate to win the most delegates.

A variation of this method is a *mandatory preference poll*—one that is binding on the delegates. Voters cast separate votes for a presidential candidate and for delegates in this system. All of the delegates elected are then required to vote at the convention for the presidential candidate who won the state's preference poll.

Another type of mandatory preference poll is held in some states. Voters cast ballots only for presidential candidates and not for delegates. The delegates are elected separately, at a state party convention. But, as in the previous system, the delegates are required to vote for the candidate who won the state's preference poll.

As a result of these various types of presidential primaries, some state delegations and some individual delegates go to the convention "bound" to one candidate. Usually, this obligation holds only for the first round of convention balloting. After that, the delegates are free to use their own judgment, or to follow the judgment of the delegation's leader.

In presidential primaries, it is not always the number of delegates that a candidate wins that counts the most. Take the New Hampshire primary, for instance. It includes a preference poll (not mandatory) and a separate election of delegates. Conceivably, a candidate could win the preference poll and not get a single delegate vote. The victory then would be purely psychological, but still very important. Though New Hampshire is a small state and has only a few delegates, it can influence voters in other states because it is the first state to hold a presidential primary. Jimmy Carter's victory in New Hampshire's Democratic primary in 1976 gave a big boost to his campaign by making Carter the leading Democratic candidate. The lead helped him win financial contributions, votes in later primaries, and votes at the national convention.

With thirty states holding presidential primaries, the 1976 race was an exhausting one for all the candidates. The first primary was on February 24 in New Hampshire, and the last primaries were on June 8 in California, New Jersey, and Ohio. In between, the candidates crisscrossed the country endlessly in their search for votes. Some widely separated states held primaries on the same day.

In most states, a candidate must formally enter the primary in order to appear on the ballot. Thus, the candidate has the choice of entering only in states where she or he seems to have a good chance. By not entering the primary, the candidate can avoid poor showings in other states. But then the voters are deprived of a chance to express a preference among all the candidates. In twelve states, therefore, state law provides for *all* active or likely candidates in the major parties to appear on the ballot. An individual can get off the ballot in most of these states by signing a statement denying any intent of running.

Because each state sets its own rules for presidential primaries, voters—and even candidates—often become confused. Some people have suggested a single presidential primary for the entire nation. Woodrow Wilson proposed such an idea in 1913. More recently it has been revived as a potential constitutional amendment (see pages 443–444). Other people have proposed a series of regional primary elections. Voters in New England would vote in one primary, then the Midwest would vote, then the South, and so on. A system of regional primaries would mean that candidates would no longer have to hop from New Hampshire to Florida to Wisconsin, and to other states, campaigning in several regions at the same time.

Despite quibbles over the way the presidential primary works, it seems to be here to stay. It was widely popular around the time of World War I and then lost ground. It regained popularity in the early 1970s when the political parties sought new ways of increasing democracy in party operations.

--- **Questions** ---

1 What is a primary election? Briefly define the term.

2 What are *five* types of presidential primaries?

⬠ What kind of system do you favor for selecting delegates to presidential nominating conventions? Why?

THE NATIONAL CONVENTION SYSTEM

Summer is usually a time of beach parties and baseball games, of repose and relaxation. But every fourth year, the summer is punctuated by political conventions. The television screen is filled with flags and speeches, political

Iowa may have wanted Ronald Reagan, but most delegates chose Gerald Ford at the Republican national convention in 1976. And when the choice of President was put to the nation, it turned out that America wanted Jimmy Carter.

promises, and political attacks on the opposing party. People may sit glued to their sets into the wee hours of the morning to see who is finally nominated. Or, put off by the speeches and bickering, they may flick off the switch in disgust and go fry a hamburger. Whatever the television viewer does, the politicians are in their element, wheeling and dealing and choosing the presidential candidates for whom or against whom the voters will cast their ballots in November. The presidential nominating convention is a national event unlike anything in other countries.

At first, conventions merely ratified the choices of candidates that had already been made at congressional caucuses or by informal means. But by 1840 the Whig convention, and by 1844 the Democratic one, had rejected the handpicked candidates because they were thought likely to alienate many party voters. The Democratic nominee in 1844 was what is called a *dark horse*—an obscure candidate who has little popular following. This "dark horse" was James K. Polk of Tennessee, the Speaker of the House. Polk went on to win the election and to become President. After that, nominating conventions called the shots.

Arrangements for the national conventions are made by the national committee of each major party. The most important decision is where the convention will be held. Usually, the deciding factor is political: the convention city must be in a state with enough votes to make wooing its voters worthwhile. Another factor is financial: business groups offer large sums of money to attract conventions to their city because they expect a rise in business during the convention.

The national committee also sets the date for the convention. It is usually between mid-June and late August of the election year. Before the days of air conditioning, convention halls were hot and sweaty places.

Among other preparations made by the national committee are deciding the rules of procedure, drawing up a temporary roll of delegates, and choosing temporary officers for the start of the convention. One further important job may fall upon the national committee. If a party's presidential or vice-presidential nominee should win the general election but drop out or die before the electoral college met, the national committee would name a replacement.

Each party has its own rules for deciding how many delegates a state may send to a convention and how many votes those delegates may cast. Conventions, unlike primary elections, are largely unregulated by government. (Some states, however, do set certain rules on how delegates must be selected.)

In the first nominating conventions, each state was alloted as many convention votes as it had electoral college votes. However, the Republican party decided that Southern states, which rarely voted Republican, had too big a voice in the convention. So in 1916, the Republicans began to give extra, or "bonus," votes to states that had gone Republican in the previous election. As the Northern and Western states received these bonus votes, they gained a greater voice in Republican matters. The Democrats began their own form of bonus votes in 1944. The Democrats give extra votes on the basis of a state's vote for the party's presidential candidate in the three previous presidential elections.

Each party also gives convention seats to the District of Columbia, Guam, Puerto Rico, and the Virgin Islands.

Not all of those who attend a convention have a full vote. The Democrats often allot more delegates to a state than there are votes for that state, so some of the delegates are given only one-half of a vote. Each party has alternate delegates.

The number of delegates varies from year to year. In 1976, the Democrats had 3,048 delegates and the Republicans had 2,259 delegates plus alternates. With so many in attendance, a convention is often unwieldy, if not unruly.

There is no uniform method of choosing delegates to presidential nominating conventions. Many states provide by law for primary elections to choose the delegates. Other states leave the method of choosing delegates up to each party. In some states, one party may choose its delegates in a primary, and the other party may use a state convention. In a few states, the state party committee chooses some or all of the delegates.

The Democrats appointed a commission in 1968 to reform the method of choosing the party's convention delegates. At the time, there were widespread abuses—discrimination against minorities and women, tightly controlled state conventions, and periods of as much as 2 years between the choice of convention delegates and the actual convention. In 1972, the Democrats introduced new rules designed to end such abuses. In each congressional district, a meeting is held to nominate national convention delegates. The state level of the party organization then chooses among the nominated delegates after the presidential primaries have been held. The choice is made from among those nominees who favored the presidential candidates who received the largest number of votes in the primaries. In making the choice, an effort is made to give women, minorities, young people, and older people a voice in the convention proportionate to their numbers in the electorate.

Republicans have traditionally given their national conventions more control over state selection methods. When the Republican national committee sends out its call for a convention, it sets the time and method by which delegates should be selected in states where state law does not provide otherwise.

A nominating convention has two main purposes: writing a party platform and choosing the party's nominees for President and Vice President. But some other matters must also be taken up in the 3–5 days a convention lasts.

A *keynote speech* is usually one of the first events. This is a stirring address by a prominent member of the national party. Its purpose is to whip up enthusiasm for the party's election campaign. This is done in part by pointing out the presumed failures of the opposing party.

One early piece of business is settling any contests over convention seats. At times, two rival delegations may claim a state's seats. In 1912, the Republican credentials committee had to choose between rival delegations pledged to President Taft and Theodore Roosevelt. In 1952, the Republican convention was faced with rival delegations pledged to Senator Robert Taft and General Dwight Eisenhower. In 1964 and 1968, the Democratic convention had to choose between all-white and interracial delegations from some Southern states. At some conventions, charges of voting fraud in state delegate selection may have to be resolved.

A second important matter of business is deciding the rules of the convention. From 1832 until 1936, the Democrats had a rule requiring that a candidate must get two-thirds of the convention votes in order to be nominated. This rule gave the South a veto over Democratic nominations and led to many deadlocks. In 1924, the Democrats took 103 rounds of voting to nominate John W. Davis, a compromise candidate, for President. Since 1936, the Democrats—like the Republicans—have required only a majority for the nomination.

The Democrats abolished another rule in 1968. This was the *unit rule,* which allowed any state's delegation to require that all votes for that state be cast as a unit. Thus, a majority of a state's delegation could determine how all of the state's votes would be cast. The Republicans had barred the unit rule in 1876, and neither party allows it today.

After settling the rules, the convention usually chooses its permanent officers. Then it turns to the party platform.

The *platform* is a statement of the party's principles and policies. Each principle or policy is called a *plank.* A committee of the national convention fits the planks into a platform designed to win votes for the party's candidates, who are expected to run on the platform. Of course, the platform is made not of wood but of paper. Its promises are carefully written and rewritten so as to appeal to as many voters as possible and to alienate as few voters as possible.

Many people criticize party platforms as vague and meaningless. They advise voters to be skeptical of platform promises. But others contend that platforms actually do make meaningful promises, and that the promises are often put into effect by winning candidates. One study of platforms since 1954 found that 79 percent of the specific promises made in platforms of winning parties had been carried out. Certainly a President who goes back on a platform promise can expect to hear about it. President Carter was severely criticized for firing some Republican United States attorneys after having promised that his appointments to such positions would be "nonpolitical."

The struggle over a party's platform is often as bitter as that over the party's nominees. Usually the platform struggle begins long before the convention does. Each party has a platform committee. Its members include delegates from each state and territory. The head of the committee is appointed by the national party chairperson, generally several months before the convention.

A week or more before the convention, the platform committee holds hearings to sound out the views of party officials and ordinary citizens. In 1972 and 1976, the Democratic platform committee held hearings in various parts of the country and Republicans sent questionnaires to some 60,000 people. A President who is running for reelection will probably submit a draft platform. Other candidates for the nomination may do the same.

The committee then hammers the platform into shape. About midway through the convention, the committee makes its report. Sometimes the convention votes to accept the platform as reported. Or there may be a debate over a controversial plank in the platform. Often the vote over a platform plank is a preliminary test of the strength of rival candidates for the nomination.

The climax of the convention is reached when the delegates choose the party's candidate for President. The lengthy process begins with a roll call of the state delegations. As each state is called, it may place the name of a candidate before the convention. Nominations are usually made with flowery speeches followed by noisy parades around the convention floor. Both parties put a time limit of 15 minutes on speeches and try to restrain the demonstrations to singing and cheering.

Sometimes a state nominates a *favorite son* or *favorite daughter*—that is, a prominent party member from the state itself, often the governor or a United States senator. Such a nominee is not expected to win the party's nomination. The state's delegation may vote for the favorite son or daughter on the first round to see how the voting is shaping up. Then it is in a position to swing its vote to a more promising candidate and win special favors in the process.

By the time all of the states have been called, there have usually been several nomi-

'THAT MUST BE PRESIDENT FORD AGAIN.... MERLE'S AN UNCOMMITTED DELEGATE, Y'KNOW...'

nating speeches and more speeches to second the nominations. Then the first round of voting—called the first *ballot*—begins. Again the clerk calls the roll, state by state in alphabetical order. If no candidate receives a majority on the first ballot, voting begins on a second ballot. In recent years, most nominations have been decided on the first or second ballot.

The person being nominated remains modestly on the sidelines until the convention voting is over and the nomination assured. In former times, the candidate was expected to wait at home for a committee from the convention to bring news of the nomination. Franklin Roosevelt broke that tradition when he flew to Chicago in 1932 to accept the nomination in person. Nowadays presidential candidates' modesty does not prevent their presence in the convention city. The candidates hold press conferences and interviews throughout the convention.

After the balloting, the nominee appears before the convention to make an acceptance speech and to indicate a choice for vice-presidential running mate. Another round of voting, purely formal this time, is held to officially choose the nominee for Vice President. An exception to this practice occurred in 1956 when the Democratic presidential candidate, Adlai Stevenson, left the choice of a vice-presidential candidate to the convention from the beginning.

Many of the recent changes in nominating conventions can be traced to the rise of television. All major-party conventions since 1952 have been televised. The parties have used several means to put their best faces forward for the potential voter at home. They have juggled schedules so as to restrict dull or divisive matters to late night or midday when few people are watching. They have clamped time limits on speeches. They have taken pains to schedule the nominee's acceptance speech in prime viewing time.

The parties have also tried to keep their conventions from degenerating into bickering and "family quarrels." In the past, Democrats were prone to disputes at conventions because of the sharp contrasts between different segments of the party—business and labor interests, blacks and Southern whites, urban and rural members. The Democrats have been trying to iron out some convention problems ahead of time by holding a midterm convention halfway between their presidential conventions. They did so for the first time in 1974 and again in 1978. The session sets basic rules for the next regular convention and gives party members a chance to speak out on national issues.

Questions

1 How does the method of allotting convention votes to state delegations differ in the Republican and Democratic parties?

2 What was the two-thirds rule at Democratic conventions? What problems did it cause?

3 What is a political platform? What is a plank in a platform?

4 How has television changed political conventions?

◯ Do you think that national conventions should be made more democratic? If so, how?

NOMINEES ON THE BALLOT

Once a party has nominated its candidates, there are regular procedures to follow to place their names on the ballot. For the major parties, these procedures are purely formal. The party need only inform the proper official in each state of the official candidates. Most states automatically provide a place on the ballot for parties that received a significant share of the votes at the previous election.

But minor parties may face a series of hurdles before getting on the ballot. First, they must circulate nominating petitions to be

What It's Like to Be a Delegate to a National Convention

Lynn Bureta was one of the delegates to the Democratic national convention of 1972. She was then a 21-year-old junior at the University of Wisconsin at Milwaukee. In the following diary, she describes her convention experiences. (The convention nominated Senator George McGovern of South Dakota. He later lost to the Republican candidate, Richard Nixon.)

Monday: Our Wisconsin delegation caucused at the hotel at 9 A.M. Frankly, it was boring—just housekeeping details like guest passes and bus service. I got invited to the women's caucus, but I wasn't interested. All issues should pertain to women.

Being part of this convention really didn't hit me until tonight. I came into Convention Hall and saw thousands of people running around. I started to psych up. I had seen it so many times on television and never thought I would become part of it. All of a sudden I had all this work that had to be done. Maybe I was a little bit afraid. A fellow delegate told me, "The expression I can see on your face is the same way I feel inside."

During the national anthem, it kept going through my mind that so many older people say young people don't care about this country. It wasn't that way for me because I felt it deep inside. There is something great about this country and we lost it and we have to go back and find it.

I understood what was going on because our leaders went through and explained what it meant to vote yes and no. They never really told us how to vote, just gave us advice.

I knew that Governor Patrick Lucey was gone from our section, but I didn't know where he was. He is a floor leader and part of his job was to be away from the delegation.

I know that I am just one vote, but that one vote is still important. I am just a tiny part of so big a puzzle. Yet that little part is important because without it you cannot finish the puzzle. I think, in my own way, I am changing the system slightly.

Tuesday: After almost 12 hours on the convention floor last night, I have learned to be patient. Yeah, and I have learned to sit. I got to bed around 7:30 this morning, got up at 12:30 and we caucused at 2 o'clock. At 4, there was a meeting to introduce the platform issues.

The McGovern people told us to vote no on a proposal to guarantee every family a minimum annual income of $6,500. I don't know why. All I know is the word came down. I understood from my floor leader that they worked out something with the welfare group. They also said that we could vote our conscience.

I voted my conviction. To me, $6,500 is a great deal of money. There is something that bothers me about giving people that much to do nothing. It is much better to give people a job. Some teachers' starting salaries are about $6,500, and here is a person with four years of college education. My father is a school principal. It isn't easy living on a teacher's salary. It seems to me a deep injustice. You reward people for doing nothing, yet penalize somebody for having a job.

Many of the proposals drawn up by the platform committee were controversial. Often a minority of the committee made a

Chapter 24: Primaries and Conventions

Hats and buttons announce the preferences of delegates.

separate report. I went through all the minority reports and I jotted down little notes at the top—yes or no. I deliberated a lot. I couldn't support most of the minority reports.

I don't know if I am part of the new politics or the old. I suppose deals have to be made. If McGovern goes through it all and does get into office and does what he said he would do, I suppose all that deal-making was worth it. I guess I am saying that the ends justify the means.

This convention has been an extension of the course on political parties that I took last semester. The opening ceremonies were like a homecoming pep rally. All those cheerleaders come out and it's, "Give me a D, give me an E, give me an M . . . ." It's getting ready for the big Republican football game. Larry O'Brien, Chairman of the Democratic national convention, comes out and says, "OK, team members. This is what I want you to do. When in doubt drop back 30 yards and punt." I think the whole election year would kind of go blah if it weren't for the convention.

Wednesday: It seemed impossible that McGovern could lose the nomination. But I was ready to go down to the last ballot. I am committed but it is not just my being for McGovern. That is what the people in Wisconsin wanted. That is why they voted for him. I think McGovern people are more loyal than others are to their candidates, because so many of us worked so hard for him.

Tonight I wore my yellow McGovern T shirt and a straw McGovern boater. I felt like I was going into battle. I followed the roll call. When our Wisconsin delegation voted, I was tense. Then came the Illinois vote, and when McGovern got it, I went wild. I was tired. Yet I had to go out and celebrate my personal victory. We went back to the hotel. There were several parties in the hotel. We went to somebody's room. From there we went out to eat.

Thursday: I slept until afternoon. I awoke in time to hear that Senator Thomas Eagleton of Missouri had been selected as the vice-presidential nominee. I have never seen the man, never heard him speak, never seen him on television. I don't even think I ever read anything about him. Eagleton should have gone around talking to the delegates. I would have liked to sit down and talk to the man before saying I am going to vote for him.

I really don't want to go home. My father gave me the money to come here because he figures this will be my greatest educational experience so far. I think I'll drop out of school and work on the campaign, I told my father. He said I could make up my own mind—and I have.

Adapted from "Diary of a Young Delegate," *Newsweek,* July 24, 1972, pp. 30–31. Copyright © Newsweek, Inc., 1972. Used by permission.

signed by a minimum number of state residents. Second, these petitions must meet other specific state requirements. Often a state sets a time limit for gathering the signatures. It may also require that the petitions be circulated in several areas of the state. Third, the party's candidates may have to put up a considerable filing fee. In some states, this fee is returned if the candidate wins a certain percentage of the votes.

Leaders of minor parties have long complained that such state requirements are discriminatory. In 1968, Ohio supporters of the third-party candidate, George Wallace, gathered more than 400,000 signatures on his nominating petition. But Ohio officials refused to place Wallace on the ballot because he did not have 15 percent of all registered voters' signatures, as required by state law.

When the case came before the United States Supreme Court, the Court declared that a state could require evidence of some minimum level of public support before granting a party a place on the ballot. But the Court ruled that the Ohio law was unconstitutional because it did not give minor parties a "fair" opportunity to appear on the ballot. The Court did not say what type of rules would be fair.

Since then, the Supreme Court has upheld a state law that required the signatures of 5 percent of registered voters. But the Court has indicated that a reasonable time must be allowed for gathering those signatures. Candidates in some states are now being allowed more time—up to 6 months—to get the required number of signatures.

In California, some minor-party candidates sued over the question of the large fee required by the state to be listed on the ballot as a candidate for a state office. The suit was upheld in California court, and today signatures on petitions may replace the required fee.

The jockeying over party nominations and getting on the ballot is only the beginning of most election races. Many people try for elective office, but in each race only one can win. In the next chapter, we will examine the way a candidate campaigns for elective office.

George Wallace campaigns at the California state convention of the American Independent party in 1968.

Questions

1 In what ways have states restricted the access of minor parties to the ballot?

2 How has the United States Supreme Court strengthened the rights of minor parties?

◌ What requirements, if any, do you think a party should have to meet before its candidates are placed on the ballot? Explain.

Chapter 24: Primaries and Conventions

PROBLEM: SHOULD WE HAVE A NATIONAL PRESIDENTIAL PRIMARY?

The "presidential primary season" is a punishing event. For months, candidates travel around seeking votes in state primaries that are scattered around the country. The season wears out many a politician. It also exhausts many voters.

In the past and again in recent years, there have been proposals to abolish this scatter-shot approach to presidential primaries. The object would be to stage one national presidential primary for both parties, early in August. This was the essence of a constitutional amendment proposed during the 1970s in the United States Senate. Though the amendment was soon shunted aside, it touched off a renewed debate over the merits of a national primary.

Such a primary would replace the present series of indirect primaries with a single direct primary. If the top candidate won 40 percent or more of the votes cast in a party's primary, that candidate would be the party's nominee. If no candidate received as much as 40 percent of the votes, a runoff between the two top candi-

National political conventions receive the full attention of the press. Reporters cover every detail and candidate.

dates would be held 4 weeks later. The tasks of nominating vice-presidential candidates and adopting platforms would still be performed by national party conventions.

The following selection presents some pros and cons on the proposed amendment. As you read, ask yourself:

- *What would be the advantages of a national primary?*
- *What would be the disadvantages?*

A national primary would reduce the total campaigning time and spare all of us the fatigue that generally sets in by September of a presidential election year—just when we should be listening most closely to the candidates. It would cut campaign costs. It would compel candidates to formulate national policies, rather than policies tailored to tiny audiences. A national primary would, moreover, discourage those who simply want to pick up some inexpensive publicity by entering a few primaries.

But consider the drawbacks. With only one shot at the nomination (two, counting the possible runoff), most candidates would undoubtedly jump the gun and, one way or another, begin campaigning long before the official starting date. That would ensure their—and our—utter exhaustion long before polling day. In a national primary, the underdog candidate would probably have less, rather than more, of an opportunity to score an upset. Under the present system, an underdog at least has time to become known by doing well in the early primaries. With only one shot at winning, an underdog would have almost no chance unless he or she proved to be an absolutely compelling television figure.

This raises what may be the most important point of all. A national primary, by its very nature, would force candidates into an almost total reliance on television. To the extent that this would reduce the freak-show aspects of current primary campaigns, it might be a good thing. But it might also saddle us with presidential nominees chosen more for their mellow voices, good looks, and smooth on-camera performances than for their intellectual qualities.

Adapted from Ronald P. Kriss, "A National Primary: Building a Bigger Circus?" *Saturday Review,* April 1, 1972, p. 28.

Questions

1 What are two arguments in favor of a national presidential primary?

2 What are two arguments against a national presidential primary?

3 When asked his views during a television interview, former President Truman objected to a national primary on the grounds that few people could afford the costs of such a campaign. Might there be ways of overcoming that problem? Explain.

⬠ Do you think we should have a national presidential primary? Why or why not?

Chapter 24 Review

Developing Your Political Vocabulary

Briefly explain the difference between the terms in each pair:
1. caucus/convention
2. convention/primary
3. party primary/nonpartisan primary
4. direct primary/indirect primary
5. delegate/candidate for public office
6. political platform/political plank

Recalling and Comparing

1. What are *two* purposes of presidential primaries?
2. How might a candidate benefit by winning a preference poll in a presidential primary, even if the candidate did not win many convention delegates?
3. What is *one* proposal for changing the way presidential primaries are conducted?
4. Of the two methods of nominating candidates—primary elections and party conventions—which is more closely regulated by state governments? How?
5. How might the nomination of a "favorite son" or "favorite daughter" give a state's delegation political leverage in a presidential convention?

Special Activities

1. If your state uses a primary election system, illustrate it on a poster. Include the type of primary, its basic organization, the date it is held, and the qualifications voters must meet.
2. Imagine that you are a delegate attending a presidential nominating convention. Write a letter home, telling what impresses you and why.
3. Consult your local library and compare the platforms of the two major political parties in the last presidential election. Write a short report describing the similarities and the differences. You may also wish to find out the extent to which the winning party has kept its platform promises.
4. Draw a cartoon that shows either a problem with the national presidential primary plan or an advantage of it.
5. Through a local party organization locate one or more persons who have served as delegates to a national convention. Ask one of the former delegates to describe to the class the advantages and disadvantages of national conventions.
6. Invite a representative from each of the major political parties in your area to discuss with your class some of the problems of nominating state and local candidates.
7. Interview people in your community in order to find out whether they approve or disapprove in general of the system of nominating presidential candidates in your state. Also ask for opinions on specific aspects of the nominating system. Report your results to the class.
8. Consider what might be arguments for and against the following statement: "A President who seeks reelection should have a major part in writing the platform of his or her party." Do you agree or disagree? Explain.

Chapter 25

The Candidate in the Race

A candidate for elective office faces a long and trying ordeal. A political campaign does not begin a month or two before the general election. Usually it begins months—even years—earlier.

The two most pressing problems for a candidate are how to organize the campaign and how to pay for it. This chapter discusses a way of going about those two tasks and the kinds of winners that tend to emerge.

Goals

- *To understand the problems of organizing and financing campaigns for elective office.*
- *To learn how the federal government regulates national election campaigns.*
- *To examine the kinds of candidates who win elections.*
- *To consider the demands a campaign makes on a presidential candidate.*

CAMPAIGN ORGANIZATION AND OPERATION

Organizing a political campaign may be very simple or incredibly complex. It depends on the importance of the office being sought and on the intensity of opposition from other candidates.

Whistle-stopping was once the only way for presidential candidates to be seen and heard by people across the country.

A good campaigner will eat with people, speak with them, shake their hands—all in an effort to get votes.

At the local level, campaign organization may be almost nonexistent. Consider, for example, a person running for treasurer of a rural township. She or he might personally take a nominating petition around to friends for signatures. Once on the ballot, the candidate might drive from house to house, talking to voters individually and asking their support. There might be no written campaign materials at all. Probably there would be no organization, as such—just one individual using spare moments to campaign. Costs would be low. But of course, the prestige and pay—if any—of the position sought would be low as well.

As the political office becomes more important, the competition becomes stiffer and requires a more organized campaign. A person running for mayor of a big city, for governor, or for Congress must have some sort of campaign organization. This requires money—the fuel on which campaigns run. The problems involved in raising and spending money for political campaigns will be discussed in the second section of this chapter.

All these problems become infinitely more difficult for the person who wants to run for President. Such a person may begin assembling a campaign staff years before the actual election. Jimmy Carter, who was almost unknown outside of Georgia when he decided to run for President, had the beginnings of a campaign organization 4 years before the 1976 election. Before Carter had any chance at all to be President, he had to become known.

The methods used by Carter are typical of those any candidate might use. First, Carter gathered a staff to do research on public issues and help him decide what stands to take on those issues. Next he began making speeches to get his name before the public. It helped that he already held an elective position—governor of Georgia. Third, he courted the news media. A member of his staff drew up a list of prominent reporters and columnists for special attention. Other staff members made sure that newspeople assigned to report on Carter had

frequent chances to meet with the candidate and ask questions. Fourth, Carter courted politicians. He volunteered to help other Democrats running for Congress in 1974. He made speeches, met eager young party workers, and—most important—made friends. One high Democratic official remarked: "He must have spent a fortune in the last 2 years on flowers. At every wedding, birth, and funeral in a Democratic family, there were flowers and a card from Jimmy."

Formal Campaign Organization

At some point, a candidate for a major office must establish a formal campaign organization. Sometimes, especially in a presidential race, this point comes during the effort to be nominated. Sometimes it comes only after the nomination is won and the general election campaign is under way. The chart on this page shows the sort of campaign organization that a candidate for Congress might use. Similar organizations would be assembled by candidates seeking other major offices.

Any election campaign depends heavily on volunteers. Some are attracted by the candidates' positions on political issues. Others have political ambitions themselves and are seeking political experience and good contacts.

Some volunteers perform routine tasks like keeping a coffee pot steaming at campaign headquarters or stuffing envelopes. Others do more important work. One major task assigned to volunteers is *canvassing.* This involves asking individual voters how they plan to vote and urging them to support the candidate. In presidential primaries, a candidate may fly hundreds of college students and other volunteers into a state to do canvassing from door to door. In New Hampshire's 1976 Democratic primary, more than one thousand such canvassers were at work. One candidate, Birch

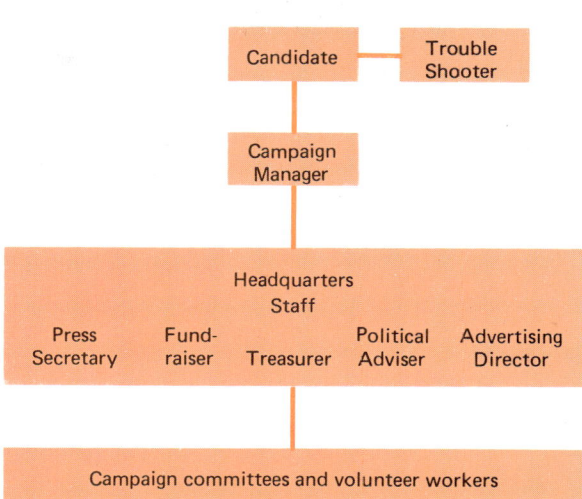

Bayh, had to depend on weekend volunteers for "crash canvasses." They spent all day on the streets, talking to voters. At night, they spent several exhausting hours writing notes to voters they had contacted.

Some members of a campaign organization receive a salary. Often, this salary is barely enough to pay for living expenses during the race. Even that salary may be jeopardized if campaign money runs low and the candidate has more pressing bills to pay. Campaign workers hope for future glory, not for here-and-now financial rewards.

A major campaign requires many committees to see to all the details. Each committee has its own job to do. One arranges campaign teas, another organizes "get-out-the-vote" drives, still another arranges travel schedules.

At the top levels, a campaign organization is usually staffed by men and women who have long worked with the candidate. Many are close personal friends of the candidate—people whom the candidate can trust. It helps if the top people read the candidate's mind and anticipate wishes before they are spoken.

Closest to the candidate is the *campaign manager,* who with the candidate decides

Chapter 25: The Candidate in the Race

Campaign officials, like this one, have to be dedicated people in order to stand the pace of their work.

overall strategy and plans. Another top official is the *press secretary,* who serves as a spokesperson for the candidate and handles the campaign's dealings with the news media. Usually there is a *fund-raiser* in charge of seeking contributions and a *treasurer* in charge of paying the bills. The campaign may have a *political director* to handle the candidate's relations with politically important organizations. There will be an *advertising director* in charge of campaign advertising, perhaps even a staff *pollster* to conduct opinion polls to see how well the campaign is going. And, with or without a title, there will be a *troubleshooter,* or senior adviser, to deal with the crises that always arise during a campaign.

A candidate may receive help, such as money and campaign workers, from his or her political party. A presidential nominee actually takes charge of the party's national committee by appointing the chairperson. A governor or United States senator may similarly be able to command a state party organization. Candidates for lesser offices can usually count on some form of support from state or county-level party organizations, at least in a general election campaign.

Campaign Techniques

Candidates may choose from a number of techniques in conducting their campaigns. Each candidate must decide three important questions: What "pitch" will I make to the voter? How shall I use my campaign time? How shall I use the news media?

"The Pitch." The candidate's main job is to convince a plurality of the voters to vote for her or him on election day. There are a number of possible approaches. One is to stress *issues.* The candidate tells the voters how he or she would decide important policy matters once in office ("I will build more highways . . . fight crime . . . make peace . . . ."). Another approach is to stress *personal qualities* ("I have worked for the people of this state for 30 years . . . ."). Another is to *attack the opponent* ("Mayor Grunch has turned our city over to crooks and swindlers . . . ."). There are many variations on these and other themes.

Campaign Time. Each candidate must also decide how to spend the limited campaign time available. In former years, personal contact was all-important. A candidate tried to shake as many hands as possible, speak to as many civic groups as possible, appear in as many cities as possible. Presidential candidates made "whistle-stop" campaigns. They rode a train across the country, stopping in every small town along the way for a speech from the train platform. Today a candidate can reach more voters with a one-minute appearance on a television news program than in several days of whistle-stopping. This does not mean that candidates can forget about personal contacts altogether. Nor would they want to. Most candidates for major offices feel the need for interaction with the public.

The News Media. The rise of television has been accompanied by the appearance of *media consultants* on campaign staffs. Most

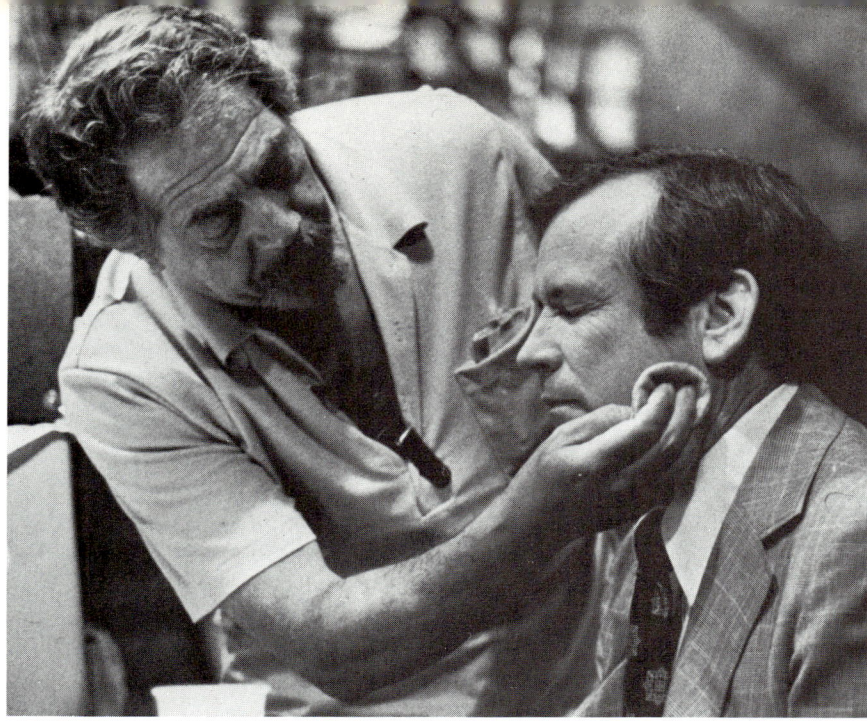

Senator Howard Baker being prepared for a national television appearance. Television enables politicians to become known to millions of potential voters.

advisers believe that a candidate's television image is as important as what the candidate has to say. Media consultants help candidates choose the right clothes to wear, the proper makeup to apply, and the way to speak clearly and with expression.

In most major races, candidates buy television time to get their message to the voters. Some political advertisements on television stress campaign issues, explaining a candidate's platform. Others seek merely to promote a favorable mood or image, much like commercials for personal-care products or oil companies. One candidate may run an advertisement showing the candidate relaxing in blue jeans and shirt sleeves, to show a "just folks" image. Or, if the candidate is already in office, the advertising may stress the importance of the position and the great duties that weigh on the candidate's strong shoulders.

Some political observers are concerned about the effects of television on the election process. They argue that campaigns should be fought over issues, not images. They point out that television has reduced the importance of political parties, which once served as the bridge between the candidate and the voters. Now a candidate can appeal directly to the people, building a personal following that is largely independent of political parties.

Other observers believe that television may help make political campaigns more meaningful to the average citizen. In the presidential elections of 1960 and 1976, the major-party candidates held televised debates on important issues. These debates helped to publicize the candidates' positions on major issues and gave viewers an opportunity to see how well the candidates handled politically sensitive questions. Candidates for state and local offices have made frequent use of television debates.

Questions

1 What are some tasks that might be performed by a volunteer in a political campaign?

2 What are the top positions in a campaign organization?

3 Why are "whistle-stop" campaigns less important now than formerly?

◇ In general, do you think that the importance of television in modern political campaigns is good or bad? Explain.

Chapter 25: The Candidate in the Race

CAMPAIGN COSTS AND FINANCING

Raising the money to run a campaign is one of the most important jobs facing a candidate. It takes a lot of money to run for an important office. First there is the need for *campaign offices.* Telephones must be installed, equipment must be rented, and rent, heat, and light bills must be paid. A candidate for Congress may need campaign offices in several cities. A candidate for President needs them all over the country.

Then there are *travel expenses.* Even a candidate who travels in a personal car must buy gasoline. Some candidates rent buses or planes to transport their staff. There are hotel bills for nights away from home and restaurant bills for meals taken on the run.

Perhaps most expensive is *advertising.* A one-minute commercial on local television in prime time may cost thousands of dollars. Then there is the cost of hiring a professional company to prepare the commercial. Next there may be radio ads, newspaper ads, billboards, campaign buttons, and even matchbooks bearing the candidate's name. Many candidates also use direct-mail advertising—for instance, a letter to every voter registered as a member of the candidate's party. Some candidates rent computers to deal with the high volume of mail sent out. Computers can turn out hundreds of letters in an hour, each looking as if it had been typed by hand and signed personally by the candidate.

Sources of Contributions

Contributions are sought in a number of ways. Direct-mail appeals are used by individual candidates and party organizations alike. Fund-raising dinners are held. People pay anywhere from $10 to $1,000 to attend these social functions. For example, the Democrats kicked off their 1978 congressional campaign with a $1,000-a-plate dinner in Atlanta addressed by President Carter. Special fund-raising committees are formed. The President Ford Committee in 1976 was a temporary committee set up to raise funds for a specific election campaign. Such special committees are also established to seek support from particular groups. Thus, Republican candidate named Bill Jones who is trying to win Democrats to his side might have a committee called Democrats for Bill Jones.

Most of the money used for political campaigns is contributed by private individuals and groups. The main exception is presidential elections. Beginning with the 1976 election, public funds have been made available for presidential candidates. Public financing will be discussed later in this chapter. First, we will consider the private sources of money.

Most candidates put up money of their own to help pay for their campaigns. Other people contribute for a variety of reasons. Many—perhaps most—contributors are people who think that a particular candidate is the one most likely to help bring about the sort of government the contributor favors. The many small checks of $10 or $20 that candidates receive are likely to be from such people. A further motive for small contributions is the allowance or deduction permitted for them on federal income tax returns.

Most of the contributors of large sums probably are hoping for something in return. That something may be merely a returned phone call from a successful candidate who will listen to what they have to say. Government workers who hold their jobs at the will of elected officials are major contributors for obvious reasons. Other individuals, organizations, or companies may have deeper motives for making political contributions. Those whose affairs are directly affected by government actions may be seeking an officeholder who will remember their support when the time comes to decide a controversial matter. Those who make things the government uses—munitions makers, airplane manufacturers, road contractors, and the like—may be hoping to have friends in high places who will help them get government contracts. Political-action groups formed by doctors, teachers, contractors, unions, and others are important contributors.

Common Cause, an organization that lobbies on public-affairs questions, has made studies of contributions to congressional campaigns. It found that in 1976, the biggest contributors among special-interest groups were groups sponsored by the American Medical Associations and the dairy industry. Early reports filed for the 1978 campaigns showed the same two groups at the head of the list. (See the table below.)

Leading Interest-Group Contributors to the 1978 Congressional Campaigns (preliminary data)

Rank Order	Interest Group	Amount[a]
1	American Medical Associations	$2,413,121
2	Dairy committees	1,097,369
3	National Education Associations	951,972
4	Maritime-related unions	929,427
5	Coal, oil, and natural gas interests	807,498
6	National Association of Realtors	769,402
7	United Auto Workers	672,461
8	AFL-CIO COPEs	661,082

a. Information based on campaign finance reports filed by registered interest groups for the period from January 1, 1977 through February 28, 1978. Federal Election Commission data compiled by Common Cause.

One important fact noted by Common Cause is that *incumbents*—officeholders seeking reelection—receive by far most of the money contributed by special-interest groups. It is a fact of life in politics that the incumbent has a long head start in any campaign. Partly this is because the incumbent's name is more likely to be familiar to the voters. But the advantage in raising money also lies with the incumbent. Common Cause reported that 96 percent of the members of the House of Representatives who sought reelection in 1976 were successful.

Preventing Corruption

Political observers have long been worried about the potential for corruption in the way election campaigns are financed. Can a contributor "buy influence" with a contribution? Is a candidate "bribed" if he or she depends too heavily on a narrow source of campaign funds? Is democracy well served by a system that depends so heavily on financing by special interests?

Both state and federal governments have passed laws to reduce the possibility of abuses in campaign financing. Each state has its own laws covering contributions to candidates in state and local elections. These laws and the regulations of the agencies that administer them may set up a maze of financing and reporting rules. Their effects are influenced as well by court decisions. In this section, however, we will focus on *federal* laws. These apply only to elections for Congress and for the Presidency and Vice-Presidency.

Until recently, federal laws on campaign financing took three approaches. They required candidates to report the amounts of certain contributions and the names of certain contributors. They placed upper limits on the amount one source can contribute or on the amount a candidate can spend. And they prohibited certain types of people or groups from contributing. Recently a fourth approach—public financing of presidential campaigns—was added to the others.

Congress began regulating federal election campaigns in 1907. At that time, Congress barred federally chartered corporations from making contributions. By 1911, there were ceilings on how much a candidate for the House or Senate could spend. The Federal Corrupt Practices Act of 1925 added new regu-

Dennis Renault, Sacramento Bee

'Your honor, my client believes that campaign spending limitations are a curb on free speech because everybody knows money talks!'

lations, which have since been superseded by other laws.

The Hatch Acts of 1939 and 1940—still in effect—put an upper limit of $3 million on the amount a national committee can spend in one campaign. The Hatch Acts also bar any individual from giving more than $5,000 to one committee or candidate. In addition, the acts ban many political activities (but not voting) by federal employees.

The Hatch Acts had many loopholes that reformers have since sought to plug. For instance, the Hatch Acts did not bar a candidate from creating several campaign committees. Many candidates do just that. Under the Hatch Acts, an individual could legally contribute $5,000 to *each* campaign committee. Moreover, the Hatch Acts said nothing about multiple gifts from the same family. Thus, a family of six—father, mother, and four children—could contribute $30,000 to *each* campaign committee. As a result of such loopholes, the Hatch Acts did little to free federal election campaigns from dependence on wealthy contributors.

In 1947, Congress banned contributions to federal election campaigns by all corporations and by all labor unions. But corporation executives and officers and members of labor unions may contribute to campaigns on their

Chapter 25: The Candidate in the Race

Campaigns for governor often cost enormous sums. New York State Governor Hugh Carey waged a costly primary campaign against Lieutenant Governor Mary Anne Krupsak in order to win nomination for a second term. Here Krupsak campaigns in New York City.

own behalf. Some corporations have given special bonuses to executives, with the understanding that the executives would donate the money to desirable candidates. This practice is illegal, but it is hard to stop. Also, business and labor groups can legally set up so-called *political action committees* to collect money for candidates in federal elections. Most of the money given by special-interest groups to federal election campaigns now comes from political action committees.

The Federal Elections Campaign Act was passed in 1972 after a series of scandals had pointed up the weaknesses of federal campaign laws. Many people believed that wealthy individuals and interest groups were able to wield too much power in the election process. In response to the public outcry, Congress put stiffer regulations into effect by passing the Federal Elections Campaign Act of 1972. Further provisions were added in 1974 after it was revealed that the Committee to Re-Elect the President had raised more than $60 million for President Nixon's 1972 campaign. Here is what the law now provides:

Ceilings on Contributions. An individual or a group may not give more than $1,000 to a presidential primary candidate. This is the ceiling regardless of how many primaries the candidate enters. An individual or a group may not give more than $1,000 to any other candidate in any one election. Thus, you may contribute as much as $1,000 to a congressional candidate for a primary election, another $1,000 for a primary runoff, and a third $1,000 for the general election. An individual may not give more than $25,000 to all candidates for federal office in any one election year.

A contribution is not necessarily a gift of money. Any loan other than a regular bank loan is considered to be a contribution. Thus, if you made a loan, its value would count toward your total contributions. The services of a volunteer are *not* counted as a contribution unless someone is paying the volunteer a salary for the time spent in the campaign. In that case, the salary counts as a contribution.

These ceilings apply only to individuals. There is no ceiling on the amount of money that a business or labor political action committee can spend to help a candidate so long as the candidate does not control the way the money is spent. For example, if such a group runs ads in favor of a certain candidate, the

Chapter 25: The Candidate in the Race

candidate must have no control over what the ads say.

Government contractors and builders are forbidden to make contributions for federal elections. So are people who are not citizens of the United States.

Ceilings on Spending. For presidential candidates, the law offers two options during the race for a party's nomination. A candidate who accepts public funds must also accept a spending limit. A candidate who does *not* accept public funds may spend unlimited amounts in seeking the nomination. *Once nominated, a presidential candidate of a major party is required to rely solely on public funds and to observe a spending ceiling.*

The law sets limits on the amount any candidate for Congress may spend. In a primary race, Senate candidates may spend $100,000 or 8 cents per resident of voting age, whichever is higher. In a general election, Senate candidates may spend 12 cents per voter. Candidates for the House may spend $70,000 for the primary and another $70,000 for the general election. In states that have only one House member, the higher Senate limits apply.

National, state, and local party organizations may spend additional sums on a candidate's behalf. Those sums are: senator, 2 cents per voting-age resident or $20,000, whichever is higher; representative, $10,000; President, 2 cents per voting-age resident.

Disclosure. Candidates and political committees must keep a record of all contributions, no matter how small. The names, addresses, and occupations of all persons or groups contributing more than $100 are made public. No gift of cash may exceed $100.

Public Financing. The 1976 election was the first one in which public subsidies were paid to presidential candidates. In primary campaigns, a candidate who raised a certain amount of campaign funds became eligible for federal matching funds. The more money a candidate's own fund-raisers could attract from private sources, the more money the government would contribute.

This line on the federal income tax form can be checked to allow $1 of taxes to go to the presidential campaign fund.

For the November general election in 1976, each major party received a public subsidy of $21.8 million. The party could spend only that amount and no more on the presidential campaign.

Federal campaign funds for the general election are paid only to parties, not to individuals. An independent candidate for President is not eligible for a subsidy. In theory, a minor party might qualify for a partial subsidy. But to do so, it would have to have received at least 5 percent of the vote in the last presidential election. Only three minor-party candidates in this century have done so.

If a minor party *did* qualify for a subsidy, it would receive a smaller one than the Democratic or Republican party. To qualify for a full subsidy, a political party must receive at least 25 percent of the vote.

Money for presidential campaign subsidies comes from a special checkoff on the federal income tax form. Each taxpayer has the option of checking a box that allows $1 of his or her taxes to go into the campaign fund. The taxpayer's taxes are neither raised nor lowered by the checkoff. A Federal Election Commission was created by the 1974 law to distribute the public subsidies and monitor compliance with the campaign laws.

The public financing law has raised a great deal of controversy. Some people argue that it should be extended to cover elections for the House and the Senate as well as the Presidency. Some go as far as to say that public financing of campaigns should be carried all the way down to the city council level. On the other hand, some people believe that tax money should not be used to support election campaigns. Others question the cost of the law and its fairness.

The chief argument in favor of public financing is that it removes an election from the influence of special interests. This, it is argued, reduces the danger of corruption and makes elections more democratic. Moreover, advocates of public financing say that it reduces the unfair advantage of incumbents and gives challengers a more even chance. One of the leading advocates of public financing for congressional races is Common Cause, the public-interest lobby.

Supporters of minor parties and independents protest that campaign subsidies favor the major parties. One outspoken critic of the present law is Senator Eugene McCarthy, who sought the Democratic nomination for President in 1968 and 1972 and ran as an independent in 1976, getting 0.9 percent of the vote. He was not eligible for a subsidy and was no longer able to accept large contributions from wealthy supporters. Senator McCarthy criticized the subsidies as undemocratic. He accompanied his appeal for private contributions with this refrain: "The American Revolution was not financed with matching funds from the Crown."

The final answer to the problem of the high cost of political campaigning has not yet been found. And the cost will probably rise as the population increases and inflation drives up prices. New suggestions are bound to be put forward.

On the basis of his experience as an independent candidate, Senator Eugene McCarthy has criticized public funding.

Questions

1 What kinds of people and groups are most likely to contribute to election campaigns? Why?

2 What are *four* ways in which the federal government has sought to control abuses in campaign financing?

3 Explain how a minor party might qualify for federal subsidies for its presidential campaign.

○ Do you think that federal subsidies to presidential candidates are a good idea? Why or why not?

THE WINNING CANDIDATES

A certain type of victor has traditionally emerged from the national electoral process. Almost always the victor is male. Most of the time he is white. At least in federal elections, victory usually goes to a member of the middle class who is in business or the law.

There have been exceptions, and they are worth noting. Some Southern blacks won elective office in the Reconstruction period after the Civil War. The first blacks to serve in Congress

Though most winning candidates have been male, March Fong Eu was elected Secretary of State of California. Here she celebrates with her husband after the swearing-in ceremony.

were elected at that time. Both Senator Hiram R. Revels of Mississippi and Representative Joseph H. Rainey of South Carolina were elected in 1870.

Later in the nineteenth century, political parties began to draw working-class candidates from the immigrant groups that were settling in big cities. This was because many big-city political machines depended on the votes of the immigrants. From this beginning, such groups as the Irish, the Germans, and the Italians gained a place in national politics.

More recently, Hispanic Americans and Oriental Americans have been among winning candidates. We have seen some examples in state and local government. Congress has had several members with Spanish surnames in the twentieth century. Members of Congress from Hawaii have included Senator Daniel K. Inouye and Representatives William B. Paul and Patsy Mink, all Japanese Americans.

After almost a century, blacks began winning major elective positions again in the 1960s. When Edward W. Brooke was elected in Massachusetts in 1966, he was the first black to win a seat in the Senate since Reconstruction. Two years later, Representative Shirley Chisholm became the first black woman elected to Congress.

Even now, however, the number of Hispanic, Oriental, and black political victors is small. They were still less than 5 percent of the membership of Congress as the 1970s drew to an end. (See the table on page 96.)

A few women ran for national office even before women could vote in national elections. One was successful. Representative Jeanette Rankin of Montana became the first female member of Congress in 1917, three years before the Nineteenth Amendment was passed. She served again in the 1940s. The first women to win election to the United States Senate were Margaret Chase Smith and Maurine Neuberger, both of whom served in the 1950s. By 1979, the House had sixteen women members and the Senate had one.

Women, as we saw earlier, have also won state and local elections in recent years. By 1978, about 10 percent of all holders of state-wide executive offices were women.

The gains, though dramatic, are still small. Yet voters are apparently getting used to the idea of women candidates. Though being a woman is often regarded as a political handicap in the South and the Midwest, some women candidates in the East and the West believe that their sex is an asset in elections. Polls taken over the years show a growing acceptance of women in politics. Asked if they would vote for a qualified woman for President, only about one-third of the people questioned in 1937 answered yes. Forty years later that total had risen to about three-fourths.

Questions

1 What sort of candidate has traditionally won elections in this country?

2 What other kinds of candidates have emerged more recently?

◇ Do you think that we should ever have a woman President? Explain.

Hispanic American Raul Castro not only was elected governor of Arizona but was later named Ambassador to Argentina.

Representative Shirley Chisholm opened new doors in 1968 when she became the first black woman elected to Congress.

PROBLEM: WHAT ARE THE CAMPAIGN DEMANDS UPON A PRESIDENTIAL CANDIDATE?

In 1964, Senator Barry Goldwater of Arizona was the Republican party's presidential nominee. After a hard-fought campaign, he lost to Lyndon B. Johnson, the Democratic nominee. Later Senator Goldwater described some of his feelings about his long campaign for the Presidency. As you consider Goldwater's observations, ask yourself:

- *What problems did he find?*
- *How did he seem to feel about campaigning for the Presidency?*

Primary campaigns for President are a lot like the weather. Everybody talks about them but nobody does anything. As a one-time participant in this crazy spectacle, I

Chapter 25: The Candidate in the Race

should like to go on record as saying that it is downright disgraceful. It is an obstacle course of formidable proportions.

The most important advice I could offer to another candidate would be to retain a sense of humor at all costs—because if you lose this in the midst of a hectic campaign marathon, you are lost. One of the first things a candidate has to become accustomed to is the idea that despite the best laid plans, the campaign will be marked by mass confusion and multiple mistakes.

Any candidate who picks up a nicely typed shedule of campaign events for the day and expects it to be followed as written is asking for trouble. One day in New Hampshire my campaign schedule called for a stop in a town square, but I was shunted off to a schoolhouse in another part of town. When the car stopped, I got out and the Republican county chairman from the district led me into a room filled with first to sixth graders. I couldn't believe it. My audience not only was not old enough to vote, some of its members hadn't even learned to write.

Such surprises are bound to occur, and the candidate must be ready to take them in stride. In this instance, I took one look at my audience, scuttled all the important political remarks I had in my notes and launched into a 20-minute talk about cowboys and Indians. My audience applauded happily. While I was walking out, I asked the county chairman why this stop had been added to the schedule. He smiled a bit shamefacedly and said, "Gee, Senator, I didn't think you would mind since my son is in that class."

The candidate at all times is subject to the pulling and hauling of people. Some of them are important people who believe you should change your plans to make a detour and see some special individual or group that hadn't been included when the schedule was arranged.

I wish I had a dollar for every time some good friend pulled me by the arm and said, "Barry, it won't take us more than five minutes to hop across town and see this man. He could be very important in your campaign."

Decisions must be made. A lot of them have to be made personally, For example, when there is only so much time, only so much can be done. The things that are left out are bound to leave some bruised feelings. Time and again I have had to ignore last minute pleas for changes in the itinerary to make room for something or someone who had been overlooked when the original plans were made.

Needless to say, when you are working on a schedule that involves something like two press conferences and twenty speeches in a single day, your digestion is going to suffer and your vocal chords will begin to show strain.

One of the discouraging things about it all is how little the general public understands about campaigning. If a candidate is late at a meeting the crowd can't understand why. If the candidate has to cut a speech short to get to a larger meeting, this, too, will be misunderstood.

And of course every stop produces its share of local politicians who want special favors from the person running for President. Some will be satisfied with a handshake and a picture. But others will want a special kind of picture taken at a special place, and after that they would like the candidate to stop off and say hello to their families.

Every stop also produces politicians who believe that extra time should be found for a newspaper interview, or a TV appearance, or a radio interview. The plea usually goes something like this: "Gosh, Barry, this station has the biggest audience in the district. It's a real break to have a chance to go on this program." Then you have to decide how much time you have to play with, whether the interview is important enough to keep another crowd waiting 45 minutes.

Chapter 25: The Candidate in the Race

I have always had an excellent digestive system that seems to put up with all kinds of hastily gobbled sandwiches, soft drinks, and other food that can be eaten on the run. Another attribute which I seem to have is the ability to take 10-minute naps almost anywhere I happen to be sitting down—in the back seat of a car, in a plane, or at a rest stop in some strategically located motel along the campaign route.

Rest is important to any candidate. Lack of it affects not only an individual's judgment but also his nervous system. If there is one thing the candidate learns early, it is that people expect you to be smiling all the time—even if your shoes are killing you. It is easy when you have gone for a long stretch of intense campaigning on little sleep to become irritable and even lash out occasionally at minor irritants.

Recent history is, of course, strewn with examples of what the physical strain of a campaign often does to the candidates. With Wendell Wilkie, it affected his voice. Of course, in his time there weren't public address systems and microphones to help out. By the end of the 1940 campaign, poor Wendell was croaking so bad, you could hardly understand him.

And I believe that Dick Nixon got too tired in his presidential campaigns. In the 1960 race, Nixon insisted on going to every state. It proved almost physically impossible. As a result, the man looked tired and his judgment suffered.

There were times in 1964 when interruptions seemed to become the rule rather than the exception. I can't remember how many times local police or FBI representatives advised us about bombing threats and other possible assassination attempts. And I'll never forget the not-so-fresh eggs that were thrown at me in New Hampshire and California. Also, there was one time when I got caught in a crowd and had my sleeve ripped off. And I can't begin to remember the number of sets of cuff links I lost to the campaign souvenir hunters.

But it's all part of the great American game. It's tough and it's disconcerting and it's annoying. It also has its moments of glory.

I should like to advise all of today's harried candidates to hang in there. It won't last forever—even if it seems that way right now.

Adapted from Barry Goldwater, "America's Ordeal by Primary," San Antonio *Express-News*, April 30, 1972, p. 76.

Questions

1 What were *four* problems Senator Goldwater noted? Why were they problems?

2 Did Senator Goldwater seem to enjoy any of his campaign? Tell why or why not.

◌ What sort of person do you think would be required to successfully cope with a presidential campaign? Would you like to accompany such a person on the campaign?

Chapter 25 Review

Developing Your Political Vocabulary

1. Briefly explain the difference between the terms in each pair.
   a. campaign manager/press secretary
   b. fund-raiser/campaign treasurer
   c. campaign advertising director/campaign pollster

2. Tell the meaning of the following terms and use each one in a sentence.
   a. media consultant
   b. incumbent
   c. campaign spending ceiling
   d. political action committee
   e. public financing

Recalling and Comparing

1. List *four* steps that a candidate might take in beginning a campaign for a presidential nomination.

2. What are *three* possible "pitches" that a candidate might use in a campaign? Which of these do you think would be most effective? Explain.

3. Name *three* provisions of the Hatch Acts of 1939 and 1940.

4. How do federal campaign financing laws restrict corporations and labor unions?

5. What are *two* jobs of the Federal Election Commission?

Special Activities

1. Make a special bulletin-board display that illustrates highlights of a current or recent local, state, or national political campaign. Include in your display the names of the candidates and the major issues they have raised. Give examples of three or more types of "pitch" made by the candidates.

2. Prepare a poster showing what restrictions your state places on the financing of state and local elections.

3. Consult your local library and prepare a report on the political successes of a minority or woman politician from your state.

4. Plan a campaign for a candidate for student council membership.

5. Make a collection of cartoons about political candidates. Prepare a report on the attitudes expressed in the cartoons and your opinions about the fairness or unfairness of the cartoons.

6. As a class project, arrange a panel discussion on the problems of obtaining good candidates, of running for office, of financing a campaign, and of obtaining voter support. Invite a local party leader, a former candidate for public office, a member of the press, and a member of the general public. Prepare a list of discussion topics in advance.

7. Find out what laws your state has about the financing of political campaigns. Report your findings to the class.

8. Volunteer to help in a campaign. Apply to the office of a candidate or a political party. Write a report of your experience.

9. Consider what might be arguments for and against the following statement: "The law providing federal subsidies for candidates in presidential elections should be extended to cover congressional elections as well." Do you agree or disagree? Explain.

Unit IX Review

Improving Your Reading

Read the selection below and then answer the questions that follow it.

A political party has one overriding goal: getting members of the party into public office. For nearly two centuries, political parties have managed to elect almost all members of Congress, Presidents, and Vice Presidents.

Two major parties—the Democratic party and the Republican party—dominate our electoral system. Minor parties have nevertheless played an important role in our history. They have raised many important issues that major parties had ignored. Most such issues have eventually been dealt with by the major parties.

The major political parties in this country are decentralized, in the sense that the national party has little control over state and local parties. But an order of rank does exist, beginning at the precinct level and moving up through ward, city, county, and state committees and finally to a national committee.

Political parties select candidates by two main methods—primary elections and nominating conventions. A primary is a preliminary election in which members of a political party select candidates who will run on the party's ticket in a general election. Primaries are also used to choose party leaders and delegates to political conventions.

A political convention is a meeting of party delegates. It decides on party policy and strategy. It also nominates candidates for elective office. National party conventions are held during the summer of every presidential election year.

Candidates for major public offices usually form organizations to run their campaigns. A candidate who has won a party's nomination can expect party aid in campaigning.

Raising money for campaigns poses a special problem for candidates—and a crucial issue for the public. Traditionally, candidates have depended on contributions from private individuals and special interests. This tradition sometimes leads to corruption. Over the years, federal and state governments have passed laws to prevent corrupt campaign practices. Limits have been placed on contributions and on campaign spending. Candidates have been required to disclose the names of certain contributors and the amounts they contributed. Some persons or groups have been barred from making any campaign contributions at all. More recently, federal money has been made available for the presidential candidates of major parties. Those who accept such money may not receive private contributions except in primary elections.

1 In your own words, summarize this reading in *no more than five* sentences. Have your summary focus on what you regard as the five most important points made in the reading.

2 Which *one* of the following four topics discussed in the reading can best be used to show the main reason for the existence of political parties:

   a the organization of primary elections

b a need to influence government
c the structure of politcal conventions
d restrictions on campaign finance

3 Which *two* of the following topics noted in the reading can best be used to show something about the organization of political parties:
  a levels from precinct committees to a national committee
  b a need by a group of people to influence government
  c national conventions
  d laws about campaign financing

Developing Your Writing Skills: What Are Your Attitudes toward Government?

Writing a Paragraph

Below are four words that describe attitudes that you as a citizen might have about candidates for public office. Choose any of the words to finish the topic sentence following. Write your topic sentence on a separate sheet of paper and then complete a paragraph with arguments supporting your topic sentence.

trust/respect/skepticism/distrust

As a citizen, my attitude toward candidates for public office should be one of _____.

Writing an Essay

In this unit, you have considered some of the main aspects of our political process. Among the subjects you have studied are political parties, primary elections, national conventions, and campaign finance.

What seems to you especially noteworthy about each of these subjects? In a brief essay, tell what importance you think each subject has in our political process and describe at least one way in which each of the four subjects is related to each of the others.

Recommended Reading

The Almanac of American Politics (latest edition), Dutton, New York.

James S. Chase, *The National Party Convention: Retrospect and Prospect,* Forum Press, St. Charles, Mo., 1974.

Shirley Chisholm, *The Good Fight,* Harper & Row, New York, 1973 (paperback).

Jack Dennis, *Socialization to Politics: A Reader,* Wiley, New York, 1973.

Virginia and James Eisenstein, *Presidential Primaries of 1972*, Center for Information on America, Washington, Conn., 1971 (paperback).

Judith Harris, *Political Party Platforms: Rhetoric or Reality?* Center for Information on America, Washington, Conn., 1972 (paperback).

Donald G. Herzberg, *The Citizen and Political Parties: What is Their Function? Should You Belong?* Center for Information on America, Washington, Conn., 1965 (paperback).

Stephen Hess, *The Presidential Campaign,* Brookings Institution, Washington, D.C., 1978 (paperback).

Samuel A. Johnson, *Essentials of Political Parties,* Barron's Educational Series, Woodbury, N.Y., 1974 (paperback).

Burt Neuborne and Arthur Eisenberg, *The Rights of Candidates and Voters*, Avon Books, New York, 1976.

Theodore H. White's series of books on *The Making of the President*, Atheneum, New York.

UNIT X

The Voice of the People

In a democracy, the people rule. One way they exercise their rule is by voting in regular elections. In a representative democracy, those elections are the mechanism by which people choose leaders to make laws and conduct the business of government. In a direct democracy, the people themselves make decisions on public policy at the ballot box and in open meetings. Our system of government combines elements of both representative and direct democracy. The people choose representatives in the election process, yet the system also provides means for direct participation in government by individuals and groups.

This unit is about the voice of the people in government. The following selection tells about a way in which the people of one state make their voices heard.

The state of Nevada is offering its voters one of the most ingenious ballot-box reforms in many years. It is called a positive-negative vote. Instead of presenting just a choice of candidates, Nevada ballots give the voter another option entitled "None of the above." You can tell the candidates that you reject the lot of them. Thus, the so-called silent majority, the people who do not vote or vote with mounting distaste, will be handed a voluntary measuring rod. We will be able to find out whether they are really a majority or not. The percentage of eligible voters who take the trouble to go to the polls has been disturbingly low in this country. The positive-negative vote will give voters a new incentive to vote with their fingers instead of their feet, and will enable them to put a show of spirit behind their party.

If the positive-negative vote should be large, it still would not prevent someone from being elected. But it could certainly qualify the winner's claim to a popular mandate. It could also warn both political parties that they had better put up an attractive slate the next time around. At the very least, it would give a more accurate reading of true voter sentiment, and very few politicians should object to that.

Where did the idea come from? According to Erwin Canham, the former editor of the *Christian Science Monitor,* it was offered to him by a young man at the University of California at Santa Barbara. Canham wrote a favorable column about it in the *Monitor.*

Adapted from John K. Jessup, "A Voice for the 'Silent Majority'?" ©1976 CBS Inc. All Rights Reserved. Transcript reproduced from Spectrum broadcast over the CBS Radio Network on January 5, 1978.

In at least one election, more Nevada voters chose "None of the above" than either of the candidates listed. Nevadans are not the only people who sometimes feel that they are faced with an unacceptable choice. And Nevada is not the only state where many people have not bothered to vote. What causes low voter turnout and low voter interest? Are they signs of weaknesses in our democracy or signs of strength?

These are among the questions that we will consider in the next three chapters. We will also consider how people take part in politics through direct action and pressure groups, and how public opinion is measured and shaped. These topics are part of the subject of political participation on which this unit focuses.

Chapter 26

The Voting Process

Voting is the official process by which the voice of the people is heard in a democracy. It therefore is important to examine the methods by which elections are conducted, the laws that determine who may vote, and the relative weight of each person's vote in influencing governmental decisions. All of these matters will be discussed in this chapter. In addition, we will consider the implication of efforts to arouse more voter interest in order to "get out the vote" for elections.

--- Goals ---

- To learn the origins of the ballot system in this country and the types of balloting now in use.
- To learn who may or may not vote in various elections.
- To understand how the principle "one person—one vote" applies to elections.
- To gain insight into voting behavior.
- To consider the arguments for and against get-out-the-vote campaigns.

BALLOTS

Voting is the expression of a choice, and in our country that choice is expressed by choosing among lists of candidates that appear on a ballot. In addition to candidates, a ballot may contain public issues—such as proposed

Monitors like these check voting lists and help guard against fraud by voters on Election Day.

amendments to a state constitution—on which the voter is asked to express an opinion. All fifty states use the secret ballot in state and local elections, and under federal law the secret ballot *must* be used in federal elections.

The methods of voting that were in most common use in the early years of our nation did not provide secrecy. The voter was subject to pressure or intimidation from neighbors or public officials.

In some communities, voting was conducted by a show of hands or by voice vote. In *viva voce* (VIGH-vuh VO-see), or "living voice," voting, an official might ask each voter in turn to name out loud the candidate for whom the vote was being cast. Sometimes the candidates were present in the room and thanked voters as they stated their choices. Voice voting was still used in Missouri and Virginia as late as the 1860s and in Kentucky until 1890.

Most states were using paper ballots by the middle of the nineteenth century. At first, these ballots were prepared by the voters themselves or by candidates or political parties. The ballots contained only the names of the candidates favored by the person or party that prepared the ballot. There was no guarantee of secrecy since each political party commonly used a distinct color on its ballots. Even a casual observer could tell how someone was voting. The paper-ballot system was also subject to abuse. A voter could cast two ballots by folding one within the other. Political parties could buy votes by paying voters to use favorable ballots. A political party could even print counterfeit ballots made to look like an opposing party's ballot, but omitting key names. These faults led to demands for a kind of ballot that would be both uniform and secret.

The Australian ballot, first used in Australia and introduced in this country in 1888, is the standard form of ballot today. It has three major features:

1. It is secret.
2. It is a uniform ballot printed by the government and used by all voters.
3. It lists all candidates and issues that have met the requirements for a place on the ballot.

While adoption of the Australian ballot solved certain problems, it created others. When the government prints a ballot, it must not seem to favor one candidate or public option over another. Thus, the design of the ballot became an important consideration.

About thirty states use a ballot in which the candidates of each party are listed together in one column with the party's name at the top. This *party-column ballot* makes it easy for a voter to vote a *straight ticket*—that is, to vote for all of the candidates of one party. In some states, the voter does not even have to cast separate votes for each of the party's candidates but only has to make a single mark or pull one lever to vote a straight ticket.

About twenty states use an *office-block ballot,* which groups together all candidates for a single office. The names of the candidates of the various parties are thus mingled together, and the voter who wishes to vote a straight ticket must take greater care to avoid mistakes. For this reason, the office-block ballot encourages people to vote a *split ticket*—that is, to vote for candidates of more than one party.

At one time, candidates on the office-block ballot were listed in alphabetical order. But it turned out that the candidates near the top of the list tended to get the most votes. Most states now use some method designed to make the listing random—for example, drawing lots to determine the order or rotating the names so that not all ballots have the same order.

Regardless of which ballot form is used, the length of the ballot may have an effect on voter participation. Thus, controversy has often arisen over the relative merits of the *long ballot* and the *short ballot.* Obviously, the greater the number of officials to be elected, the longer the ballot must be. Likewise, the greater the number of issues to be submitted to voters, the longer the ballot must be.

Those who favor a long ballot argue that democracy works best when the voters have a voice in as many public matters as possible. This means making most government positions elective and submitting many public issues to the voters. Those who favor the short ballot argue that it is unrealistic to expect voters to take an interest in minor public offices and issues. They maintain that democracy is better served by having lower officials appointed and by reducing the number of issues presented to the voters. This, they say, allows voters to concentrate their attention on the most important offices and issues.

Since each state controls its own voting procedures, the length of ballots varies greatly from state to state. But in this century, there has been a trend to shorter ballots.

Voting machines have been introduced in many areas, especially in cities, to speed up voting and the counting of ballots. Voting machines also reduce the possibility of mistakes in adding up the vote. The machines take the place of paper ballots for about one-third of all voters. The Australian ballot is used on machines as it is on paper ballots.

Whether paper ballots or machines are used, voting is now commonly done in privacy. The voter marks the ballot in a booth, behind a curtain. If a voting precinct uses paper ballots, the voter takes the ballot into a booth, places an X or a check mark beside the names of the desired candidates, then folds the ballot, and deposits it in a closed container. If the precinct uses machines, the names of the candidates are usually listed beside a series of levers on the machine. The voter enters the booth, pulls a handle to close the curtain, then pulls down a lever beside the name of each candidate desired. After finishing with all the candidates and all the public issues, the voter again pulls the handle to open the curtain. This action records the vote and clears the machine for use by the next voter. Election officials later read the total tally for each machine.

Some counties have introduced computer voting. The voter inserts a computer punch card into a small slot beneath pages listing the names of the candidates. To vote for a candidate, the voter punches a hole in the card in the space provided beside the candidate's name and then drops the card into the ballot box. At the end of the balloting, all cards are taken to a central computer where the votes are recorded quickly.

Questions

1 How does the Australian ballot differ from other types of ballot?

2 What form of Australian ballot makes it easy to vote a straight ticket? How?

3 What is the difference between a short ballot and a long ballot?

⬠ Which do you think is preferable—the short or the long ballot? Why?

WHO MAY OR MAY NOT VOTE

Each state sets its own qualifications for voters, but all states must follow certain basic guidelines set down by the Constitution, federal laws, and decisions of the United States Supreme Court. Thus the voting laws of the fifty states have certain basic similarities.

Rights and Guarantees

The Constitution provides that citizens 18 years of age or older have the right to vote, and this right may not be taken away because of race, color, or sex. If a person reaches the age of 18 on or before the date of an election, he or she is eligible to vote in that election.

The states may not place certain types of requirements upon voters. Among them are the following:

Poll Taxes. From the late nineteenth century until 1966, various Southern states required anyone who wanted to vote to pay a tax. This poll tax was not large—perhaps a few dollars. But it was a burden on low-income citizens and especially on blacks, who were its main target in the South. In 1964, the Twenty-fourth Amendment barred the use of poll taxes as a requirement for voting in *federal* elections. Two years later, the Supreme Court declared poll taxes in *any* election to be in violation of the equal protection clause of the Fourteenth Amendment.

Lengthy Residence Requirements. Most states require that a person have lived in the state or local voting district for a certain period of time before becoming eligible to vote. This is known as a *residence requirement.* At one time, residence requirements commonly ranged up to 1 year in a state. Then, in 1972, the United States Supreme Court declared such lengthy residence requirements to be unconstitutional. The Court did not specify a maximum permissible length. But most states have since cut their residence requirement to 30 days or less (see the table opposite).

Most states deny the vote to temporary residents, or transients. Two groups commonly affected by such efforts have been members of the armed forces and college students. The restriction has been based on the theory that legally they are still residents of the community where they formerly lived. In 1965, however, the United States Supreme Court threw out a Texas law that had prevented service personnel from voting in the area where they were stationed. The Court ruled that Texas must apply the traditional test for residency to members of the armed forces. That is, if they are physically present in a voting district, have the intention of staying there for the foreseeable future, and are otherwise eligible, they must be allowed to vote. Many state courts have ap-

Residence Requirements for Voting (minimum number of days in state)

State	Days	State	Days
Alabama	30	Montana	30
Alaska	30	Nebraska	—
Arizona	50	Nevada	30
Arkansas	—	New Hampshire	30
California	29	New Jersey	30
Colorado	32	New Mexico	—
Connecticut	—	New York	30
Delaware	—	North Carolina	30
Florida	30	North Dakota	30
Georgia	—	Ohio	30
Hawaii	—	Oklahoma	—
Idaho	—	Oregon	30
Illinois	a	Pennsylvania	30
Indiana	b	Rhode Island	30
Iowa	—	South Carolina	—
Kansas	—	South Dakota	—
Kentucky	30	Tennessee	30
Louisiana	—	Texas	30
Maine	—	Utah	30
Maryland	30	Vermont	—
Massachusetts	—	Virginia	—
Michigan	30	Washington	30
Minnesota	20	West Virginia	30
Mississippi	30	Wisconsin	10
Missouri	30	Wyoming	—

a. 30 days in district.
b. 30 days in precinct.

plied a similar rule to college students, thus allowing many to vote in the community where they attend college.

Early Registration. In most parts of the United States, citizens who wish to vote are required to *register*—that is, have their names placed on a list of eligible voters. Registration is designed to prevent fraud. It also provides a means of checking to see that a voter actually resides in a certain election district and is thus eligible to vote on local matters.

At one time, many states stopped registering voters many months before an election. The Supreme Court has ruled that this is unconstitutional. Now the cutoff date is generally 10 to 30 days before an election. But in some states it is longer—up to 50 days in Arizona.

For presidential elections, Congress has required that officials continue to register new voters until 30 days before the election. This was a provision of the Voting Rights Act Amendments of 1970. For people who move too late to register in their new community, Congress required that convenient *absentee ballots* be made available, allowing them to vote at their former place of residence. An absentee ballot must be made available early, on request, to people who would otherwise be unable to vote. Absentee ballots can also be used by people who plan to be away on Election Day or who are physically unable to go to the place of voting.

Property Ownership (except in certain elections). At one time, almost all states allowed only property owners to vote. Even after property requirements were dropped for general elections, they continued to be imposed for certain other types of elections. Most of these uses are no longer permitted. For example, New York had a law that limited voting in school board elections to persons who either owned or leased taxable property or were parents of school-age children. In 1969, that law was overturned by the United States Supreme Court. Some states restricted voting on municipal bond issues to those who paid property taxes. These laws, too, have been banned by the Supreme Court.

The Court has permitted property restrictions on voting in a narrow class of elections. These are elections held by such governing units as water irrigation districts, which have a limited purpose and which make decisions that affect property owners more than others.

Literacy Tests. Over the years, a number of states adopted literacy tests aimed at preventing people who could not understand English from voting. The various tests used were supposed to measure the ability to read, or to both read and write, or to read, write, and "understand" English. Often, the judgment of literacy was made by an election official, without using a written test. Literacy tests were widely used in the South to keep blacks from voting. In the Voting Rights Act Amendments of 1970, Congress ordered an end to the use of literacy tests for 5 years, until 1975. The law was later extended to August 6, 1982. It applies to all elections—federal, state, and local. The United States Supreme Court has upheld the right of Congress to include state and local elections in this law in order to prevent discrimination based on race.

So far we have been discussing federal rules that apply to all states and communities. Two other federal rules apply to certain areas where discriminatory voting practices occurred in the past.

Federal Control of Voter Registration. In the Voting Rights Act of 1965, Congress made interference with voting rights a federal crime. The act provided for the United States Attorney General to order a federal takeover of voter registration in any area where (1) there was discrimination against some voters, (2) a literacy test was required, and (3) less than 50 percent of the voting-age population was registered to vote.

Bilingual Voting. In the Voting Rights Act Amendments of 1975, Congress sought to end voting discrimination against non-English-speaking minorities. The law applied special rules to areas where (1) a language minority made up 5 percent or more of the voting-age population, and (2) less than 50 percent of the voting-age population was registered to vote. In such areas, registration and voting must be conducted in two languages—English and one other. Election notices and voting rules also must be printed in two languages.

The law was found to apply for various language groups in three entire states and parts of twenty-seven other states (see map opposite). The language groups identified as meeting the requirements of the law were Alaskan Native languages, Native American languages, Chinese, Filipino, Japanese, and Spanish. The map shows where each group was identified.

Federal legislation to protect voting rights was one of the major goals of the black civil rights movement in the 1950s and 1960s. As laws began to lift the long-standing barriers to voting by blacks, efforts were made to register blacks in the Southern states. Comparison of registration figures in the presidential elections of 1960 and 1976 shows the results of those efforts and the new laws (see graph on page 474). In Mississippi, only 5 percent of blacks of voting age were registered in 1960. That figure had risen to 61 percent by 1976. In North Carolina, black registration increased from 39 percent to 55 percent while white registration *decreased* between the two elections. By 1976, the percentage of blacks registered to vote in seven of eleven Southern states exceeded the percentage of blacks registered in the nation as a whole.

Until recently, non-English-speaking minorities stayed away from the polls. Now, many states get a better turnout by printing ballots and voting rules in more than one language.

BILINGUAL ELECTION REQUIREMENTS
(states in which bilingual election requirements were identified under the Voting Rights Act Amendments of 1975)

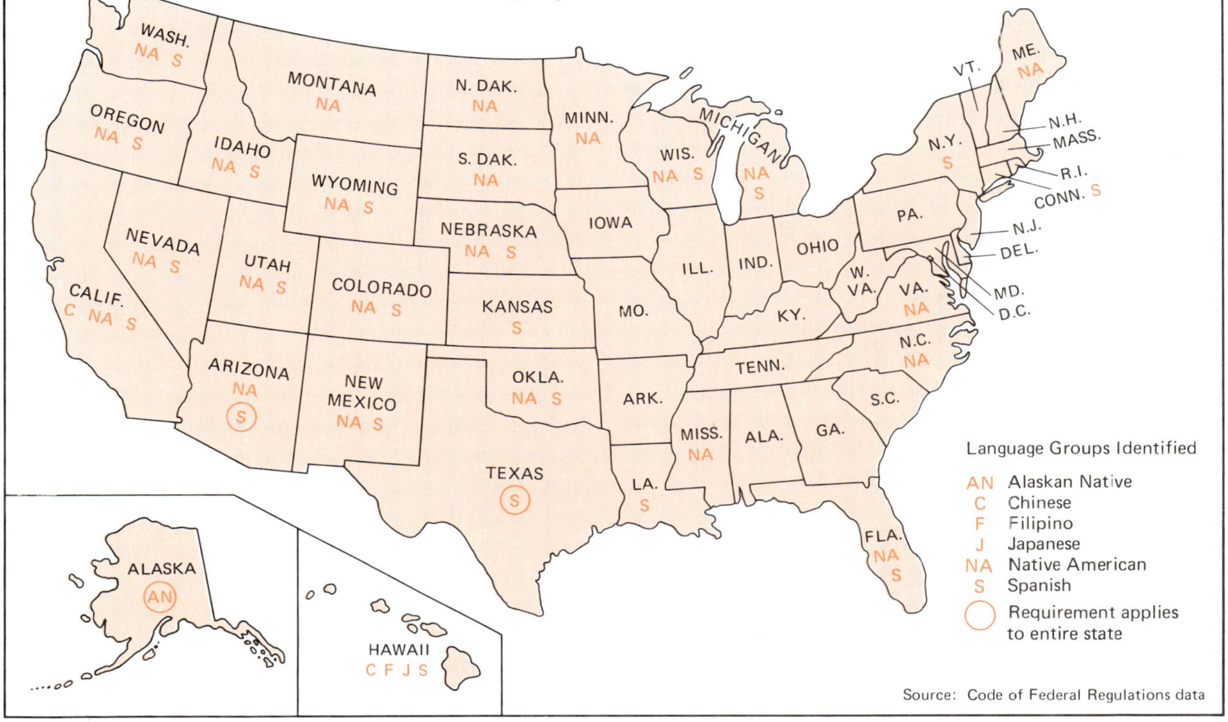

Language Groups Identified
- AN Alaskan Native
- C   Chinese
- F   Filipino
- J   Japanese
- NA Native American
- S   Spanish
- ◯   Requirement applies to entire state

Source: Code of Federal Regulations data

Chapter 26: The Voting Process

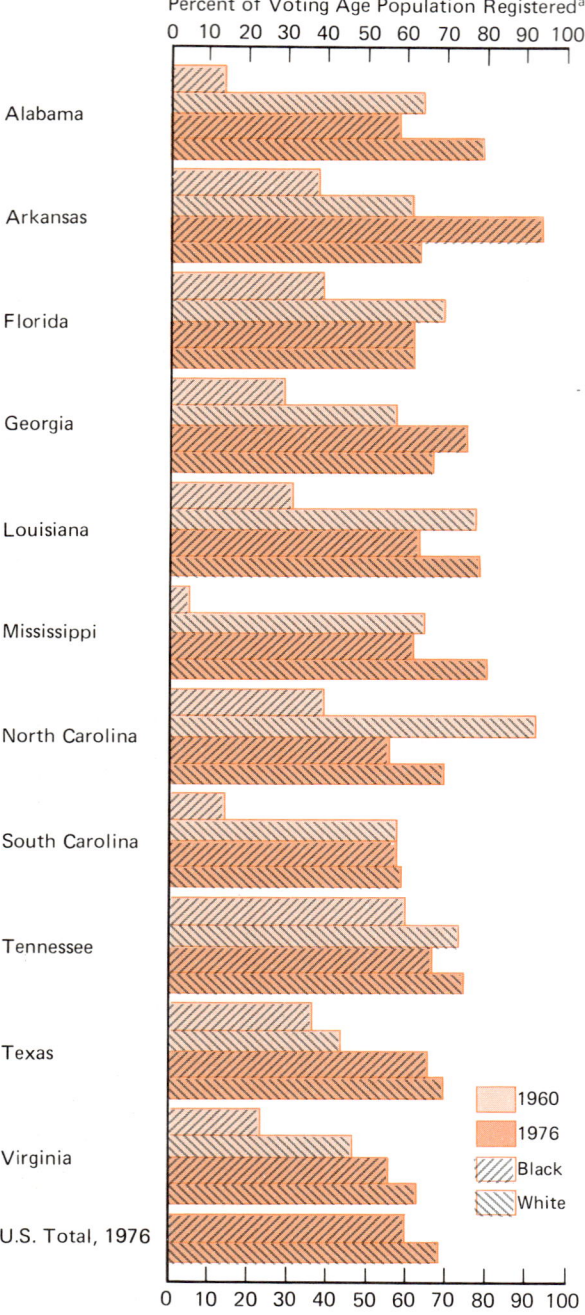

VOTING REGISTRATION IN ELEVEN SOUTHERN STATES, 1960 and 1976

Percent of Voting Age Population Registered[a]

Legend: 1960, 1976, Black, White

[a] For 1960, population aged 21 and over except Georgia, aged 18 and over. For 1976, population aged 18 and over.
Source: Data from *Statistical Abstract of the United States, 1977*

Restrictions on Certain Groups

While federal law is concerned with protecting the voting rights of all citizens, various restrictions on voting and election activities *are* allowed. Commonly, the states deny the vote to people who are mentally ill or who have been convicted of a serious crime. Some states also deny the vote to anyone who has been dishonorably discharged from the armed services.

The most widespread restriction on voting is that which applies to people who are less than 18 years of age. Under the Twenty-sixth Amendment, the age requirement for voting cannot be higher than 18. But there is nothing to prevent its being set lower. Some communities permit persons younger than 18 to vote in certain elections, but no state has adopted a lower voting age statewide. If Congress wished to lower the voting age in federal elections, it could do so by legislation. A constitutional amendment would be necessary, however, for the federal government to lower the voting age in state and local elections.

Federal law also places certain restrictions on election activities by one group of people—federal employees. As we noted in Chapter 25, the Hatch Acts of 1939 and 1940 bar federal employees from taking an active part in political campaigns or in party politics. The purpose is to remove the federal bureaucracy from partisan political activity.

Two groups of employees are affected by the Hatch Acts: civil service employees of the federal government and any employees of state and local governments who are paid from federal funds. The acts do not apply to federal officials who are appointed by the President.

Here are some things that federal employees may *not* do:

1. Run for any political office as the candidate of a political party.
2. Openly endorse the candidate of a political party.

3. Serve as a campaign manager of a candidate of a political party.
4. Circulate nominating petitions for a candidate of a political party.
5. Hold office in a political party.
6. Actively solicit votes for a candidate of a political party.
7. Serve as a delegate to a political party's convention.
8. Organize a new political club or party.

You should note that all the banned activities have to do with political parties.

Federal employees *are* allowed to do the following:

1. Vote.
2. Express political opinions.
3. Join a political party already in existence.
4. Sign nominating petitions.
5. Make a contribution to a political party or candidate.
6. Wear a campaign button when off duty.
7. Display a political bumper sticker.
8. Serve in a nonpartisan political office. (For example, a federal employee may run for election as a local judge or a member of a city council, so long as the employee does not run as the candidate of a political party.)

While the Hatch Acts do not apply to most state or local employees, many states have "Little Hatch Acts" that do. These laws apply to special groups, such as police officers, firefighters, teachers, and sanitation workers. The state laws are usually patterned on the federal Hatch Acts.

The federal Hatch Acts were passed at a time of rapid growth in government employment. The laws were designed to keep elected officials from rounding up the federal bureaucracy in support of their own reelection campaigns. In that sense, their purpose was to protect government employees from coercion.

But some employees have complained that the acts restrict their right of free speech. The United States Supreme Court has rejected this argument on two occasions, though each time by a split decision.

Questions

1 What two devices—now banned—were formerly used by some states to keep many blacks from voting?

2 In what ways have Congress and the Supreme Court protected the voting rights of people who change their place of residence?

3 In what sort of election might property ownership be a qualification for voting?

4 In what ways are the election activities of federal employees restricted by law?

◌ Do you think that a student who goes away to college should be allowed to register and vote in the college town? Why or why not?

"ONE PERSON—ONE VOTE"

All voters are entitled to an equal voice in the election of members of local governing bodies, state legislatures, and the United States House of Representatives. This is known as the *"one person—one vote"* rule. Each vote is to count as much as any other vote. The rule was not widely obeyed until the 1960s.

The United States Constitution calls for a census every 10 years to be used as the basis of apportioning seats in the House of Representatives. Most state constitutions call for reapportionment of other districts as well to take into account changes in population. Before the 1960s, the states often ignored these provisions. It was common for many years to go by without reapportionment of congressional, legislative, or other districts. Meanwhile population was decreasing in rural districts and increasing in urban districts. (See page 94.)

Chapter 26: The Voting Process

Beginning in 1962, the United States Supreme Court made three landmark decisions that forced reapportionment. Here is what the Court decided:

1. *The federal courts have the power to consider whether the apportionment of state legislatures is constitutional.* This was the Supreme Court's finding in *Baker v. Carr* (1962).

Charles W. Baker had complained that he was denied equal protection of the laws because of the way votes were counted in electing members of the Tennessee legislature. Baker's legislative district in Memphis had 627,019 residents and eight legislators. That was one legislator for every 78,000 people. Yet one rural district had 3,454 residents and one legislator. That meant, Baker pointed out, that the vote of a rural Tennesseean might be worth more than twenty-two times as much as Baker's vote.

The Court agreed with Baker that such an apportionment might violate the Fourteenth Amendment, which says that no state shall "deny to any person within its jurisdiction the equal protection of the laws." Chief Justice Earl Warren considered the decision in *Baker v. Carr* the Court's most basic reform in his sixteen years as head of the Court. He believed that if elected representatives represented the entire community, most problems could be solved through the political process rather than through the courts. The *Baker v. Carr* case reversed the position taken by the Supreme Court in *Colegrove v. Green* (1946). In that case, the Court had held that the question of apportionment was "political" and not up to judges to decide. After the 1962 decision, the Tennessee legislature set new boundaries for state legislative districts, and other states soon followed. The *Baker v. Carr* decision was confined to districting for state elections.

2. *Congressional districts must be roughly equal so that each person's vote has equal weight.* The Supreme Court took this stand in *Wesberry v. Sanders* (1964). The Court said: "We hold that, construed [taken] in its historical context, the command of Article I, Section 2 that representatives be chosen by the people of the several states means that as nearly as prac-

ticable one man's vote in a congressional election is to be worth as much as another's." In 1967, Congress passed a law requiring congressional districts to be substantially equal in population.

3. *The seats in both houses of a two-house state legislature must be apportioned on the basis of population.* The Supreme Court made this decision in *Reynolds v. Sims* (1964).

It is now widely recognized that the "one person—one vote" principle applies also to all representative bodies of local government, including county, town, village, and municipal legislatures and local school boards. Reapportionment must take place after every 10-year census in congressional and most state legislative districts.

The Court's ruling in *Reynolds v. Sims* came as a surprise to those people who had looked upon the upper house of a state legislature as parallel to the United States Senate. The Constitution specifically provides for each state to have two United States senators, regardless of the number of people in the state. Some people feel that *state* senates should also be exempt from "one person—one vote." They say that so long as one house of a bicameral legislature is apportioned by population, the other house need not be. It should be allowed some other basis of apportionment, such as geography.

However, the Supreme Court has turned down this argument on the ground that the United States Constitution does not provide for such an exemption. The Court has noted that the United States Senate is a special case because of the compromise reached by large and small states in writing the federal Constitution of 1787. The special historical factors that applied to the United States Senate apportionment do not apply to state legislatures, the Court has held.

While the Supreme Court has not said so specifically, most authorities believe that "one person—one vote" also does not apply to elections of judges. That is because judges are not part of a lawmaking, representative body.

Questions

1 How does the "one person—one vote" principle apply to the apportionment of legislatures? Give an example of a legal and an illegal apportionment.

2 What representative body is exempt from "one person—one vote"? Why?

⬠ Do you think that *all* public elections should be guided by the "one person—one vote" rule? Why or why not?

VOTING BEHAVIOR

As each Election Day approaches, politicians worry over what lies ahead. How will the election turn out? What will the voters do? Before an election, no one can predict with certainty what will happen. But after an election, and especially after a long series of elections, it is possible to look back and detect certain patterns in voting behavior.

Nonvoters

A significant proportion of people who are eligible to vote do not do so. Many people do not bother to register to vote, and many who do register fail to go to the polls on Election Day. Even in presidential election years, when people are more likely to vote than in other years, less than two-thirds of the voting-age population is likely to vote (see the graph on page 479).

Why do so many people fail to vote? Some of them are sick on Election Day, or away from home, or in jail, or in mental institutions. A small part of the voting-age population—including all noncitizens—is not eligible to vote. But the main reason for not voting is lack of interest. Many people say that they find

Will Your Vote Count?

Have you ever thought that the vote of just one person did not count for much in an election? If so, consider how many elections have been decided by one or a few votes. There are dozens of examples, ranging from votes for school board members to races for mayor, representatives, and senators.

In the presidential election of 1976, if about 9,000 voters in five key states had voted for Gerald Ford instead of Jimmy Carter, Ford rather than Carter would have had a majority of the electoral college votes and would have won the election.

Earlier, in a suburb of Cincinnati, Ohio, a candidate for one of the seats on the town council was suddenly hospitalized with an attack of appendicitis and was not able to vote. When the votes were counted, he had lost by one vote. Similar one-vote defeats have occurred elsewhere.

The following selection is about the elections of November 1974. It shows how close many elections can be.

If a bare handful of the near-record number of citizens who stayed away from the polls had voted in 1974, many who lost cliff-hanger elections might have been elected to high government offices. Five races for state governorships were decided by fewer than 5,000 votes. In a sixth close contest, a candidate conceded that he had lost, only to learn later that he was the winner.

There were also cliff-hangers in five United States Senate races that year. In one, the final unofficial returns had the candidates less than 100 votes apart—too close for the outcome to be decided before an official canvass. In another race, the spread was less than 300. In a third, it was about 600. The two others were decided by fewer than 5,000 votes.

Republican Paul Laxalt, the former governor of Nevada, in 1974 narrowly won his race for the United States Senate by some 600 votes out of about 158,000 cast in the race. United States Representative Louis C. Wyman, another Republican, won by fewer than 300 votes in a New Hampshire race where 220,000 ballots were cast.

Incumbent United States Senator Henry Bellmon, an Oklahoma Republican, got by a little more easily. Even though some 777,000 persons voted in the race, Bellmon won by a little more than 3,000 votes.

Democrat Patrick J. Leahy of Vermont went to the Senate with a 4,042-vote margin of victory in a race that attracted 136,000 voters.

Then there is North Dakota, where Senator Milton R. Young, a Republican, led his challenger in unofficial returns by fewer than 100 votes out of more than 236,000 cast. It took an official canvass to confirm Young's victory.

The winning margins in 1974 were somewhat wider in four of the cliff-hanger races for governorships. Had 5,000 persons voted the other way, Democrat Raul Castro of Arizona, Republican Robert Bennett of Kansas, incumbent Republican Meldrim Thompson of New Hampshire, and Democrat Jerry Apodaca of New Mexico would have been looking for other work. Their winning margins really were not as wide as they look since hundreds of thousands of votes were cast in these races.

Adapted from an Associated Press dispatch, November 8, 1974.

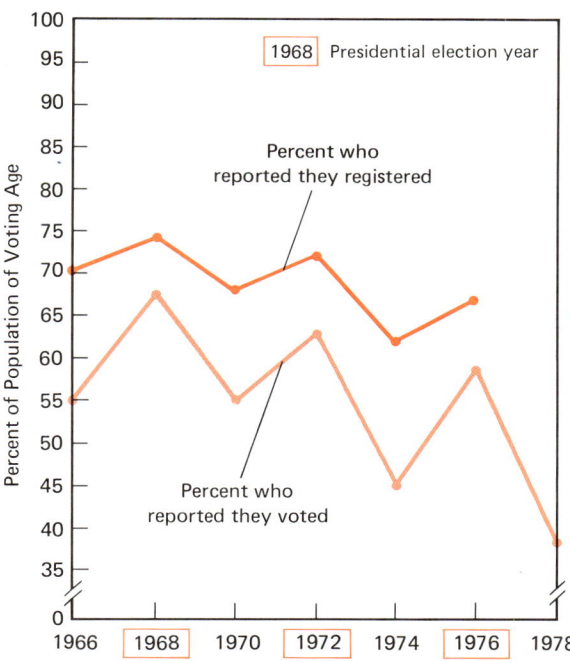

VOTER TURNOUT IN NATIONAL ELECTIONS

Source: U.S. Bureau of the Census data

politics "dull" or "boring." Others think that it is useless to vote, because "my one vote wouldn't make a difference" or because "nothing would change anyway."

Studies have shown that certain people are more likely than others to fail to vote. Nonvoters tend to have lower incomes and less education. They are more likely to be women or members of racial minorities. They are more likely to be young. When the Twenty-sixth Amendment gave 18- to 20-year-olds the right to vote in national elections for the first time, many people expected them to start voting in large numbers. But experience has shown this age group to be less likely to vote than most. One other finding has been that voting is highest where there is strong competition between political parties, and lowest in areas where one party is dominant.

Political observers disagree sharply on what failure to vote means. Some see it as a sign that our democracy is working well. In this view, if people were unhappy they would show their discontent by "voting the rascals out." Others see nonvoting as a sign of weakness in our democracy. They say that nonvoting means that many people feel powerless to change things that they do not like.

Voting Patterns

Family and group characteristics often influence the way people vote. Political observers have noted that people tend to vote for the same parties as their parents. Moreover, certain groups of people tend to vote in certain ways. These findings have enabled political observers to draw a picture of how certain groups will vote.

For example, women, Protestants, older people, and business persons are more likely than others to vote Republican. Men, Catholics, Jews, younger people, and union members are more likely to vote Democratic. This, of course, does not mean that *all* people in those categories will always vote the same way. But it does reveal certain patterns in the way people vote.

An individual's party preference greatly influences the way she or he will vote. At election time, people often ponder whether to "vote for the party" or "vote for the best candidate." Every election sees large numbers of people abandoning their party to vote for the candidate they prefer. But over long periods of time, most people tend to favor one party over another most of the time.

Voters in presidential elections are likely to favor other candidates in the same party as the leading presidential candidate. In political jargon, many candidates ride into office on the coattails of a successful presidential candidate. This *coattail effect* is due to the fact that a large part of the electorate votes a straight ticket, choosing one party's candidates for all offices. The presidential race is usually the one that most interests the voters, so it can strongly influence the vote in other races. This is why

Chapter 26: The Voting Process

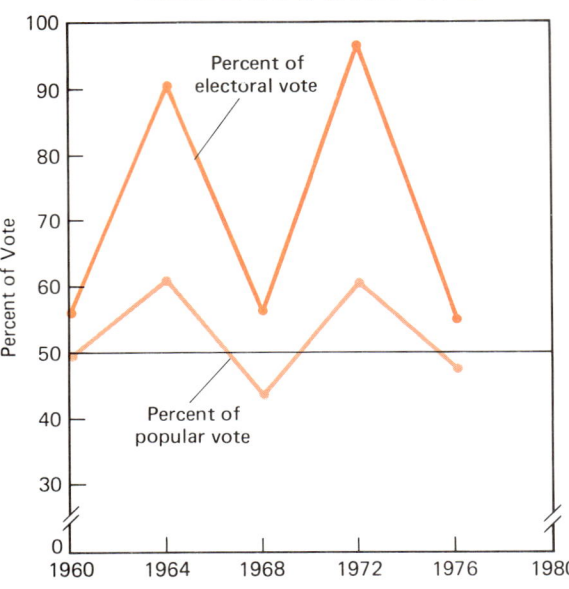

PERCENT OF POPULAR AND ELECTORAL VOTE RECEIVED BY WINNING PRESIDENTIAL CANDIDATES

Source: Data from *Statistical Abstract of the United States, 1977*

politicians always prefer a strong vote-getter at the top of their party's ticket. It is also why the party in power usually loses congressional seats in off-year elections, when there is no presidential candidate to head the party ticket.

As you know, the popular vote for President is not always accurately reflected in the electoral college vote. In the elections of 1876 and 1888, the candidate who came in second in popular votes was the winner in the electoral college and thus became President. In recent years, some elections have been quite close in popular votes but not so close in electoral votes. Winning candidates who received less than 50 percent of the popular vote received 55 to 56 percent of the electoral vote (see the graph above). In the 1968 election, there was a difference of only 0.7 percentage points between the Republican and Democratic presidential candidates in popular vote, but a difference of 20 percentage points in electoral vote. A third-party candidate, George Wallace, received 13.5 percent of the popular vote but only 8 percent of the electoral vote. (See the map of the 1968 presidential vote on page 137.)

Questions
---

1 What is the main reason for low voter turnout in elections in this country?

2 What are some of the factors that help political observers predict how certain groups of people will vote?

3 What is the coattail effect? Whom does it benefit?

⬠ Do you think that nonvoting is a sign of strength or of weakness in a democratic system? Explain.

PROBLEM: SHOULD WE TRY TO GET OUT THE VOTE?

In recent presidential elections, only about 60 percent of the voting-age population has voted. In "off-year" elections, participation is even lower. Only 38 percent of the voting-age population voted in the November 1978 elections, for example. Such low turnouts have caused many people to call for ambitious get-out-the-vote drives. But other people feel that it is better to let uninterested citizens stay home from the polls.

Following are two opposing views on the issue. As you read, ask yourself:

- What arguments are made in favor of drives to get out the vote?
- What arguments are made against ambitious efforts to get out the vote?

Yes! Get Out the Vote

Suppose they held an election and nobody came? Would anybody care? Does it matter?

It has become the custom in election years to urge everyone to vote. National

481

Chapter 26: The Voting Process

In an effort to "get out the vote," this campaign worker phones registered voters offering transportation to the polls.

advertising campaigns popularize slogans like "Vote for the Candidate of Your Choice—But Vote." It is considered somewhat of an embarrassment that, among all the Western democracies, the United States turns out the lowest percentage of voters on Election Day. And whatever a candidate might secretly prefer, none is heard to say, "Unless you intend to vote for me, please stay at home." Even a vote for the opposition is presumed to be better than no vote at all.

Illogical as this presumption might appear, it springs from a sound historical instinct. For the history of democracy has been the continual rediscovery that all members of a society—rich and poor, wise and foolish—contrive a better life for themselves when their political decisions are made collectively than when they are left to any one group in the society, acting alone.

A citizen who fails to vote is, in effect, denying fellow citizens the benefit of his or her opinion. Were every citizen to behave likewise, the democratic process would grind to a halt. Thus, intentionally or not, the voter who chooses to "sit this one out" is indulging in conduct that is not democratic.

Subversion of democracy consists of nothing more than placing the ultimate power to decide in the hands of some one citizen, or some group of citizens, to the exclusion of all the others. Whether the decision-making power comes to rest in the hands of a few because they conspire to seize it or because others let it slip from their grasp, the result is the same. This is a point apparently overlooked by large numbers of citizens. For despite our relatively poor performance at the polling place, in opinion polls we continue to regard our own democracy as healthier than most others.

A common excuse for not voting is dissatisfaction with the candidates and the issues put forward by our two major parties. "If they want me to vote, let them put up somebody worth voting for."

The citizen who feels this way is confusing the role of a voter with that of a consumer. In a free-market economy, the consumer's disinclination to buy is a powerful creative force, eliminating wasteful surpluses and inspiring ceaseless innovation. But an election is not a banquet hall. If we succeeded in turning it into one, and left the

Chapter 26: The Voting Process

Will she vote as her parents do? Political observers try to forecast the vote even as new voters register for the first time.

catering to others, the result would not be a more elaborate buffet to choose from, but one dish for everyone, with no substitutions allowed. This has, in fact, been known to happen. It is called the one-party state.

To return to our question: Suppose they held an election and nobody came? Perhaps the best answer is that, in real life, it will never happen. For—you may depend on it—somebody *will* come. Somebody always does. And there is still safety in numbers.

Adapted from *Citiviews*, Citibank N.A., August 2, 1976.

No! Let Sleeping Dogs Lie

We should never plead with the people to get out and vote. It is wrong to beg the uncaring, uninformed, and ignorant to "vote for the candidate of your choice." ("Who? What is the candidate running for?")

Somewhere in the middle of the twentieth century, perhaps because of a guilt complex about the bad old days when not all persons could vote, we acquired an obsession that if only we could get all eligible people to register and vote, we could attain some sort of political goodness. If all voted, then all would be free.

Not so. Why should we encourage those who do not care and do not know, those whose vote can be bought for a catchy jingle, to dominate elections? We know that among the caring and informed there are strong differences of opinion. Must we deliberately court the lowest common denominator among us by drafting the uncaring to vote?

Volunteers are the heart of our system. So let's halt this foolishness of trying to browbeat, brainwash, or cajole people to get out and vote. If individuals have to be begged to vote, the chances are excellent that they do not know what is going on. They must be shown a ballot, told how to mark it, told who is running for what office before they share with us a blind guess based on ignorance.

Let us make voter registration easy and reasonable, open to all persons. Then let's leave the people to take part and vote if they want to and leave them alone if they do not.

Historians, viewing expansion of the right to vote in this country during our first 200 years, will speak wisely about how, in 1976, every person had the opportunity to vote. Very good. That is how it should be.

Adapted from Francis P. Lynch, "Let's Not Get Out the Vote," *Newsweek*, October 18, 1976, p. 15. Copyright © Newsweek, Inc., 1976. Used by permission.

Questions

1 What are *three* reasons given in the first article why eligible persons should vote?

2 According to the first article, how does an election differ from a free-market economy?

3 What reasons does the second article give for *not* encouraging all eligible persons to vote?

◌ Do you think that eligible persons should be encouraged to vote in public elections? Explain.

Chapter 26 Review

Developing Your Political Vocabulary

1 Briefly explain the *difference* between the terms in each pair:
   a Australian ballot/voting machine
   b party-column ballot/office-block ballot
   c split ticket/straight ticket

2 Define the following terms and use each one in a sentence about the voting process:
   a poll tax
   b residence requirement
   c absentee ballot
   d "Little Hatch Acts"

Recalling and Comparing

1 What has the United States Supreme Court ruled about the validity of property restrictions on voting?

2 What are *two* kinds of special rules that Congress has laid down for areas in which voting discrimination is held to have occurred?

3 What are *two* restrictions that prevent some people from voting?

4 What powers does the federal government have over voting qualifications? What powers do the state governments have?

5 What is the meaning of the "one person—one vote" rule? In what way was this principle established?

6 On what grounds did the Supreme Court rule that federal courts can determine whether state legislatures are apportioned properly?

Special Activities

1 Consult your local library or agencies of local government and determine if your state has any form of "Little Hatch Act." If it does, prepare a report that explains how the act restricts the political activities of state or local employees.

2 Prepare a drawing of how "one person—one vote" works in practice.

3 Consult local officials to secure a copy of a ballot from a recent election. Use the ballot in a bulletin-board display that gives a step-by-step explanation of how a person votes in your community (for example, by paper ballot or by voting machine).

4 Find out in what ways your state restricts the right of certain groups to vote. Write a report on these restrictions including your own opinion on their fairness.

5 Make a study of the controversy over the presidential election of 1876. Samuel J. Tilden had a majority of the popular votes, but four states filed multiple sets of electoral votes. Report on how Congress dealt with the problem.

6 Make a survey of attitudes toward voting in your community. Ask such questions as the following: Do you think that voting is a duty? Should strong efforts be made to get out the vote? Do you think that people are more likely to vote if they are (a) in favor of a candidate or an issue or (b) opposed to a candidate or an issue? In each case, ask reasons for the opinions expressed. Chart your findings.

7 Consider what might be arguments for and against the following statement: "Anyone who does not vote should be subject to fine and punishment." Do you agree or disagree? Why?

Chapter 27

Pressure Groups and Direct Actions

Taking part in the election of public officials is only one of many ways in which a citizen can have a voice in our government. People in this country have other means of political action. One way is by forming a group of like-minded people and pressing for a common political interest. By putting pressure on the legislative branch, groups of this kind often help to bring about new laws or change old ones. Such groups also put pressure on the executive branch and often influence its decisions.

Many states also give citizens other ways of having a voice in government, apart from elections. Some states allow voters to offer constitutional amendments, state laws, and local ordinances. Some states also allow voters to remove public officials before the end of their term of office.

This chapter will deal with pressure groups and direct voter actions as part of the means by which the people rule in the United States.

---- Goals ----

- To understand the operation of pressure groups and lobbying in our political process.
- To learn three examples of direct political action.
- To consider whether there should be a national initiative and recall.
- To consider how lobbying works in action.

485

After "The Longest Walk," these Native Americans met with Marlon Brando, rear center, in the nation's capital.

PRESSURE GROUPS AND LOBBYING

When people with common goals organize into groups in order to try to change government policies, they are said to be forming *pressure groups*. Unlike political parties, pressure groups are not mainly interested in winning control of public *offices*. Rather, they aim to put pressure on government in order to bring about certain *policies*.

Pressure groups have been around since this nation was born. Merchants and property owners formed pressure groups to push for adoption of the Constitution of 1787. Abolitionists formed pressure groups to fight for an end to slavery. Suffragists formed pressure groups to win the vote for women. Prohibitionists formed pressure groups—and then a political party—to stop the sale of alcoholic beverages.

The most obvious sorts of pressure groups are those that represent business, labor, and other economic interests on a regular basis. Pressure groups of this type include long-term organizations of teachers, doctors, lawyers, farmers, or federal workers, among others. But many other organizations act as temporary pressure groups at one time or another. Religious groups sometimes try to influence public

Ralph Nader, left, was the nation's first well-known consumer advocate. Here he lobbies in Washington, D.C.

policy on civil rights, abortion, and foreign policy. A group of hunters may lobby for conservation measures or against gun-control legislation. A garden club may seek to get a city council to create more parks. Whenever an organization tries to influence the policies of a unit of government, it is acting as a pressure group, even though the group's main purpose may be recreational or social or religious.

"Harm to one is harm to all," says this Mexican American wall slogan. Wall paintings are one means used to exert political pressure.

In addition, temporary pressure groups may be formed by people who join together for the sole purpose of getting action on a single issue in which they have a common interest. One example of such a pressure group in action could be seen on the streets of Washington, D.C., in the spring of 1968. Poor people from all over the country came to the nation's capital as part of a Poor People's Campaign. They set up tents, listened to speeches, and visited members of Congress, trying to draw attention to their plight and their proposals for governmental action.

Ten years later, a group of about twenty Native Americans walked from San Francisco to Washingtion, D.C., in a protest movement. By the time they reached the national capital, three to four hundred other marchers had joined what they called "The Longest Walk." The purpose of the walk was to protest bills in Congress that the group saw as threats to their way of life.

Now it is not unusual for people who feel that they have a common interest or a common problem to organize into a pressure group and try to influence government. Pressure groups often run up against other pressure groups with conflicting purposes. These days, much of the give-and-take in politics is the struggle between conflicting pressure groups to impose their policies upon national, state, and local governments. Indeed, political parties have been worried that pressure groups may be weakening their own role in government.

Pressure groups pursue their goals by seeking to influence government both directly and indirectly. Direct approaches are aimed at government officials. Indirect approaches are aimed at public opinion, which in turn helps to influence government officials.

Pressure groups can often influence lawmakers by offering campaign support or by threatening opposition. This sort of influence begins long before a specific bill becomes an issue. Some pressure groups can afford contributions of money to a campaign fund, as we saw in Chapter 25 (pages 452–455). Others have little money but lots of members, and they may be able to deliver votes. Both money and votes are two-edged swords. A member of Congress who ignores a pressure group can usually expect to see the group switch its support to an opponent.

A common tool used by pressure groups is lobbying. One or more persons act as the group's lobbyist or agent in trying to influence government officials—to get them to act in a certain way. A lobbyist may be paid or unpaid. Some lobbyists are paid far more than the people they are hired to influence.

Leaders of the Poor People's Campaign made their protests known at a press conference held in "Resurrection City." Ralph Abernathy is flanked by Chief George Crows Fly High and Mexican American leader Reies Lopez Tijerina.

We Demand

Among the thousands in the 1968 Poor People's Campaign were several hundred Mexican Americans led by Reies Lopez Tijerina of New Mexico and Rodolfo "Corky" Gonzales of Colorado. This group issued a statement with the title "We Demand." Below are some excerpts from this statement by one Mexican American pressure group.

We demand that our schools be built in the same fashion as our neighborhoods and that they be warm and inviting and not jails. That the teachers and other personnel live in the neighborhoods of the schools they work in.

We demand a completely free education from kindergarten to college with no fees, no lunch charges, no supplies charge, no tuition, and no dues. This is in payment for decades of poor education given to our people.

We demand that from kindergarten through college, Spanish be the first language and English the second language and that the textbooks be rewritten to emphasize the heritage and contributions of the Mexican Americans in the building of the Southwest. We also demand the teaching of the contributions and history of other minorities who have also helped build this country.

We demand the necessary resources to plan our living accommodations so that it is possible for family homes to be built around plazas or parks with plenty of space for the children. We want our living areas to fit the needs of the family.

We demand training and placement programs that would develop the vast human resources available in the Southwest. For those of our people who want further choice in employment and professions, we wish training programs that would be designed and run by our own people.

We demand an end to discrimination in employment by all private and public agencies.

We demand money to organize the necessary trade, labor, welfare, or housing unions to represent those groups.

We demand training and low-interest loans to set up small industries in our own communities. These industries would be co-ops, with the profits staying in the community.

Adapted from Rodolfo "Corky" Gonzales, "We Demand: Statement of Chicanos of the Southwest in the Poor People's Campaign," as reprinted in *Aztlan: An Anthology of Mexican American Literature,* edited by Luis Valdez and Stan Steiner, Knopf, New York, 1972, pp. 219–221.

Lobbyists focus their main attention on legislative bodies, such as Congress, state legislatures, and city councils. But they also seek to influence the executive branch of government. For example, lobbyists may form friendships with officials in regulatory agencies in an effort to influence the decisions of those agencies. Lobbyists also may go to court to challenge legislative or executive deeds.

Though lobbyists are at work at all levels of government, the largest concentration of them—between 5,000 and 10,000—can be found in Washington, D.C. As the activities of the federal government have broadened, lobbying activity in the nation's capital has increased. The list of registered lobbyists in the nation's capital includes several former members of Congress, hired because they know the legislative ropes.

Let's look at some of the ways in which Washington lobbyists pursue their goals.

Lobbyists keep a close eye on bills introduced in Congress in order to spot "good" bills that would help their clients and "bad" bills that would harm them. The lobbyists' job is to see that the good bills pass and the bad bills either fail or are amended to take the sting out of them.

An example would be a bill to require tough pollution controls on factory smokestacks. A pressure group for the steel industry might consider this a bad bill because it would raise costs and might cut profits. An environmentalist pressure group might think the bill was a good bill because it should help reduce air pollution. Lobbyists on both sides would go to work in several ways to influence the fate of the bill.

The lobbyists might actually help to write the bill or amendments to it. Members of Congress and their staffs often depend on advice from lobbyists, especially on detailed technical questions.

Lobbyists on each side might speak at congressional hearings on the bill. The steel industry experts might tell of technical difficul-

Professional lobbyist Richard Viguerie, center, runs a service that sends out 100 million pieces of mail a year.

ties and high costs that the bill might cause. The environmentalist experts might tell of the dangers of air pollution and of the steps taken in other countries to clean up factory smoke.

Lobbyists for both pressure groups might organize letter-writing campaigns. The steel industry might encourage workers in steel plants to write their members of Congress expressing fears for job losses if the bill passes. The environmentalist group might print an article in its newsletter asking people to write letters to members of Congress telling why they favor the bill.

Lobbyists also pursue social contacts with influential people. Some lobbyists have large expense accounts and can "wine and dine" members of Congress. A lobbyist may make it a practice to drop by the office of a member of Congress regularly, just to say hello and chat. Others join the best country clubs and other social organizations to be able to meet influential people in informal settings.

Chapter 27: Pressure Groups and Direct Actions

How a law is put into practice is often just as important as what the law says. Thus, many lobbyists concentrate on seeking to influence the decisions of agencies of the executive branch. Here again, lobbyists may testify in official proceedings and make informal social contacts to pursue their goals.

Lobbying, like campaign contributions, may be subject to abuse. Sometimes lobbyists resort to bribing or other illegal tactics. But even legal activities of lobbyists are often called in question. Some people say that lobbying gives big business, organized labor, and other large pressure groups power that is out of all proportion to the number of members in these groups.

Efforts to control lobbying at the federal level have centered on bringing it out into the open. The Regulation of Lobbying Act of 1946 provides that any lobbyist or pressure group engaged in lobbying must register with the Clerk of the House of Representatives and the Secretary of the Senate. Four times a year, each lobbyist must report all receipts and expenditures, telling the purposes for which the money was spent.

As with most laws, this one has loopholes. The law defines a lobbyist as a *paid* professional who *seeks*, whether directly or indirectly, to influence the vote of a member of Congress. It applies only to organizations whose *principal* purpose is to influence legislation. Thus, it does not apply to many pressure groups that have other purposes besides lobbying. Then, too, the law does not attempt to stop lobbying, but only to bring it out into the open. Any attempt to stop lobbying might run up against the Constitution's guarantees of free speech and the right of petition.

Under the First Amendment, the right of petitioning government belongs to every citizen, and a large number of special-interest groups have been formed in recent years to take advantage of it. The Poor People's Campaign and the Longest Walk were both undertaken by such single-interest groups. Other single-interest groups might represent people who live near a polluting factory or people who want to curb the growth of nuclear power. The people in a single-interest group attempt to speak with an *organized* voice on one issue, regardless of their differences on other issues.

Chapter 27: Pressure Groups and Direct Actions

An aide to Senator Lawton Chiles sorts out heaps of telegrams that resulted from a successful lobby campaign.

A few broader groups, such as Common Cause and Ralph Nader's Project for Corporate Responsibility, try to speak for consumers or some of the general public.

Consumer or single-interest groups can rarely match the financial resources of pressure groups for economic interests. But there are many ways in which groups of citizens try to influence government policies. The first step—which is not always followed—is to study the issues, listen to all sides, and seek the advice of experts. After gaining knowledge and insight, the next step is to organize. Once organized, such groups go after the twin goals of influencing the public and influencing government officials.

Following are some methods used by existing groups in seeking to influence the public.

1. Writing letters to the editor of a local newspaper, a national magazine, or some other publication.
2. Inviting members of the press to cover a newsworthy event that gets the group's story across. (Thus, a group trying to get more city parks might spend a day cleaning up a vacant lot and creating its own "mini-park.")
3. Doing research projects in order to gather evidence to support the group's cause. (Thus, a group seeking stricter laws on water pollution might gather samples of river water at several locations and have the samples analyzed for pollutants.)
4. Staging a public demonstration with signs and speeches to publicize the group's cause.
5. Seeking out other organized groups as possible allies and getting them to issue statements that support a group's view.
6. Offering to provide speakers for social and civic organizations.

Existing groups have used various means in their efforts to influence government officials. Examples are:

1. Writing representatives in Congress and the state legislature, especially the heads of committees, describing specific legislation for which support is desired and asking for copies of relevant bills.
2. Offering to send a representative to a hearing to testify on behalf of legislation and having other members of the group in the audience.
3. Visiting a legislator in person or the staff members in a legislator's local office and explaining the group's position, giving facts to support it.
4. Inviting candidates to meet with the group.
5. Sending a questionnaire to candidates for public office asking their positions on matters that interest the group.
6. Offering the assistance of volunteers to candidates who seem likely to further the group's goals.

This is only a partial listing of techniques. Most groups have found that the most important things are knowledge, organization, and enthusiasm. Organization magnifies influence: ten citizens acting together are more than ten times as powerful as one person acting alone. That is why pressure groups can have power out of proportion to their size. It is why pressure groups have taken an important place in our way of government.

Questions

1 In what way other than lobbying do pressure groups seek to influence government policies?

2 Why might a lobbyist be interested in influencing the executive branch?

3 In what way does federal law seek to control lobbying? In what way is lobbying protected under the Constitution?

4 Why are pressure groups that represent economic interests often more effective than others?

⬠ Do you think that pressure groups have a place in a democracy? Explain.

THREE METHODS OF DIRECT ACTION: REFERENDUM, INITIATIVE, AND RECALL

In a wave of reform early in the twentieth century, a number of states adopted measures giving voters a more direct voice in goverment. None of the measures is in effect at the federal level, though efforts have been made to extend them to the federal goverment (see Problem, pages 495-496).

Two measures allow voters to have a direct say in making laws. The third allows voters to remove public officials from office.

Referendum. The *referendum* is a device by which voters are asked to approve or reject a measure passed by the state legislature. In twenty-four states, a referendum may be demanded by a petition of the people. Usually, a state law does not take effect until 90 days or so after it is signed by the governor. During that period, citizens in these twenty-four states have the right to circulate petitions opposing the law. If a certain number of people sign the petitions—usually a number equal to 5 or 10 percent of the total votes cast in a preceding election—the law is submitted to the voters in a popular referendum. If a majority of the voters reject the law, it is killed. In most states, referendums may not be used on emergency or financial bills.

Another kind of referendum is a referral from the legislature *to* the people. It may be either optional or mandatory. Many states and local governments use the *optional referendum,* which allows a lawmaking body, if it wishes, to refer a measure to the voters for approval or rejection. In addition, some states provide for a *mandatory referendum* that applies only to certain measures, such as a law authorizing a public debt. Measures of the specified type must be referred to the voters. A *constitutional referendum* is a special type of mandatory referendum. Every state except Delaware gives voters an opportunity to approve or reject state constitutional amendments that are proposed by the state legislature. In Delaware, the legislature can amend the state constitution on its own.

Initiative. The *initiative* is a device by which voters themselves may propose state laws or amendments to a state constitution. Again, action is started by circulating a petition. The signatures of 3 to 15 percent of the voters may be required. Usually the percentage depends on whether a law or a constitutional amendment is involved. What happens next depends on whether the state has the *direct initiative* or *indirect initiative.* In states with the direct initiative, the proposal goes on the ballot at the next election, to be decided by the voters. If a majority approves, the proposal becomes law. In states with the indirect initiative, the proposal goes first to the legislature. Only if the legislature fails to pass it within a reasonable time is the proposal submitted to the voters. Thirteen states have the direct initia-

Availability of the Initiative Process

C: For constitutional amendments   L: For legislation   I: Indirect initiative (all others are direct)

State	At State Level	At Local Level	State	At State Level	At Local Level
Alabama	—	—	Montana	C,L	L
Alaska	L	L	Nebraska	C,L	L
Arizona	C,L	L	Nevada	C/I: L	L
Arkansas	C,L	L	New Hampshire	—	—
California	C,L	L	New Jersey	—	L
Colorado	C,L	L	New Mexico	—	—
Connecticut	—	—	New York	—	—
Delaware	—	—	North Carolina	—	—
Florida	C	—	North Dakota	C,L	L
Georgia	—	L	Ohio	C,L/I: L	L
Hawaii	—	—	Oklahoma	C,L	L
Idaho	L	L	Oregon	C,L	L
Illinois	C	—	Pennsylvania	—	L
Indiana	—	—	Rhode Island	—	—
Iowa	—	—	South Carolina	—	L
Kansas	—	—	South Dakota	C/I: L	L
Kentucky	—	L	Tennessee	—	—
Louisiana	—	L	Texas	—	L
Maine	I:L	L	Utah	L/I:L	L
Maryland	—	—	Vermont	—	L
Massachusetts	C/I:L	L	Virginia	—	L
Michigan	C/I:L	L	Washington	L/I: L	L
Minnesota	—	L	West Virginia	—	L
Mississippi	—	—	Wisconsin	—	—
Missouri	C, L	L	Wyoming	L	L

tive and five have the indirect initiative for state laws. Two states have both.

California, where the initiative has been available since 1912, has had an average of four to five initiative proposals on the ballot in each election since. About 30 percent have been approved, the rest rejected. The introduction to the first unit of this book gave an example of a successful initiative in California.

An initiative numbered Proposition 9 was placed before California voters in 1974. Proposition 9 called for public officials at all levels of California government to fully disclose financial holdings that might influence their official actions. It also called for full reporting of contributions to and spending by candidates for public office. It forbade anonymous contributions of $50 or more to any candidate or party. And it set limits on how much money organized groups could give to candidates.

Proposition 9 was drawn up by people who believed that the state legislature had not passed a strong enough campaign reform law. Both Common Cause and Ralph Nader's California Citizens' Action group sponsored the proposition. Enough people signed the petition to get it on the ballot. It then received a favorable vote of 69 percent and became law.

Unlike a measure introduced in the legislature, a direct initiative provides no means of compromise but only a yes or no vote. One objection to proposals submitted by direct

Provisions for Recall of State and Local Officials

State	State (S) or Local (L)[a]	State	State (S) or Local (L)[a]
Alabama	—	Montana	S, L
Alaska	S, L	Nebraska	L
Arizona	S, L	Nevada	S, L
Arkansas	L	New Hampshire	—
California	S, L	New Jersey	L
Colorado	S, L	New Mexico	—
Connecticut	—	New York	—
Delaware	—	North Carolina	—
Florida	—	North Dakota	S, L
Georgia	L	Ohio	L
Hawaii	L	Oklahoma	L
Idaho	S[b], L	Oregon	S, L
Illinois	L	Pennsylvania	—
Indiana	—	Rhode Island	—
Iowa	L	South Carolina	L
Kansas	S[b], L	South Dakota	—
Kentucky	—	Tennessee	—
Louisiana	S[c], L	Texas	L
Maine	L	Utah	—
Maryland	—	Vermont	—
Massachusetts	—	Virginia	—
Michigan	S[c]	Washington	S[c], L
Minnesota	L	West Virginia	—
Mississippi	—	Wisconsin	S, L
Missouri	L	Wyoming	L

a. State recall applies to all elected officials unless otherwise specified. Local recall applies to some or all local officials.
b. All elective officials except judicial officers.
c. All elective officials except judges of courts of record.

initiative is that they are not likely to be drafted with care. Some proposals approved by a majority of voters have later been ruled unconstitutional by state courts.

The publicity that precedes an initiative vote may also fail to make clear all aspects of the proposal. The celebrated Proposition 13 of 1978 was attractive to many California voters who saw in it the answer to homeowners' property taxes. Only later did some who voted for it realize that about 65 percent of the money saved in property taxes would be saved by corporations and other owners of business property.

Recall. The *recall* allows voters to remove elected officials before their term expires. A recall begins with the circulation of petitions. Usually the number of signatures required is equal to about 25 percent of the voters in the last election. If the required number sign the petition, the recall question is put on the ballot. A majority vote decides whether or not the official may remain in office. As the table above shows, recalls are available statewide in fourteen states. In thirteen states, recalls are available at the local level.

While referendums, initiatives, and recalls have an important place, they are not used

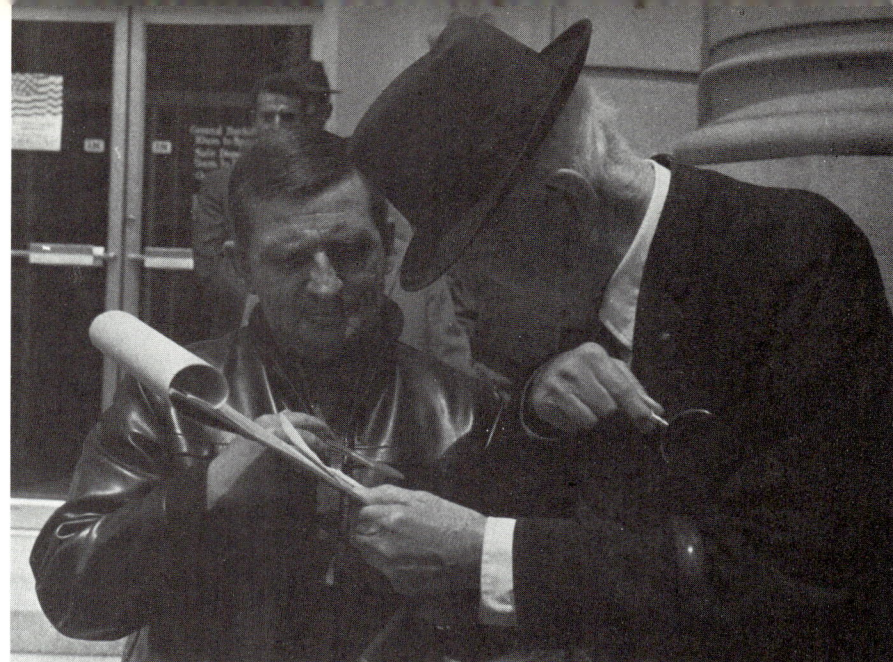

One more signature is added to a petition in an attempt to get a proposal on the ballot.

regularly. Their chief purpose is to give citizens a path of action when they feel that elected officials are not following the people's wishes.

Questions

1 What is the referendum used for? How does it work?

2 What is the initiative used for? How does it work?

3 What is the recall used for? How does it work?

◇ Do you think that the initiative should be made available in every state? Explain.

PROBLEM: SHOULD THERE BE A NATIONAL INITIATIVE AND RECALL?

The initiative, referendum, and recall are provided for in many of the states. But there are no similar devices at the federal level. Some people think there should be. In the following selection, Ralph Nader, the well-known consumer lobbyist, writes about two people who wish to see a national initiative and recall. As you read Nader's comments, ask yourself:

- *In what way would a national initiative and recall give us a more direct form of self-government?*
- *Why do some people want that?*

Ed and Joyce Koupal, the tireless leaders of the people's lobby in California, think that the people of this country should rediscover the initiative, the recall, and the referendum. They are taking their skilled signature-gathering experience nationwide to build support for a constitutional amendment establishing a national initiative and national recall.

In June of 1974, the Koupals were instrumental in the passage of the California initiative known as Proposition 9. In an expression of dismay over corrupt politics, Proposition 9 was passed by more than 3 million Californians.

Notice that it was the people who directly wrote and passed this state law, not the state legislature. This is what an initiative involves. It is a process by which, through petitions, a prescribed number of people may write proposed laws for direct submission to the voters.

The initiative, recall, and referendum are measures of direct democracy. They were largely passed during the Populist-

Progressive period around the turn of this century. But they have been dormant in most states, unused and almost forgotten by most citizens.

The Koupals want them revived to bring democracy back to the people and make elected officials more accountable between elections.

For almost a decade, the Koupals, operating out of their small print shop, have perfected techniques of signature gathering. They can marshall 10,000 volunteers in California almost immediately for a petition drive to get a measure on the state ballot.

Now they believe that what has been increasingly good for California should be good for the nation.

Their proposed amendment to the Constitution would read:

"The people of the U.S.A. reserve to themselves the power of the initiative. The initiative is the power of the electors to propose laws and to adopt or reject them. An initiative measure may not be submitted to alter or amend the Constitution of the United States.

"Every elected officer of the United States may be removed from office at any time by the electors meeting the qualifications to vote in their state, through the procedure and in the manner herein provided for, which procedure shall be known as a vote of confidence, and is in addition to any other method of removal provided by law."

Adapted from Ralph Nader, "U.S. Recall Amendment Gets Boost," San Antonio *Express-News*, November 11, 1974, p. 6P.

Questions

1 What did the Koupals seek to get approved? Why?

2 What are some arguments in favor of their proposal?

3 Is the statement that the initiative "has been increasingly good for California" a statement of fact or of opinion? Explain.

◇ What might be some drawbacks to a national initiative and recall? Explain.

PROBLEM: WHAT CAUSES PRESSURE GROUPS TO FORM?

The following two stories illustrate some of the pressure groups formed in recent years. Like many other pressure groups, they actively lobby for legislation which will serve their own interests. The first story is about the elderly, who have traditionally been thought of as a solid voting bloc—conservative, Republican, and concerned mainly with their own financial security. Now it turns out that the elderly are not so solid a bloc after all. Recent polls show them to be as diverse as any other people, and near the center of the political spectrum. The second account concerns Latinos, or Hispanic Americans. Actually, elderly people and Latinos were among those involved in the Poor People's Campaign you read about on page 487. As you read, ask yourself:

- *What problems do elderly people have in common, and how have they organized to promote their interests?*
- *What problems do Latinos have in common?*

The Elderly

Their diversity has not lessened the senior citizens' impact on Capitol Hill, where they have emerged in the past decade as one of the more effective special-interest lobbies.

The seniors' lobby is no mere wheelchair brigade appealing for crumbs. It is a tough-minded collection of pressure groups

By sticking together and making their wants and needs known to Congress members, the elderly have become an effective pressure group.

that, over the years, have learned the basic rules just as well as the AFL-CIO and the United States Chamber of Commerce.

It has helped generate pressure to pass Medicare and to raise social security benefits seven times in little more than a decade. It has helped to make food stamps a permanent (and fast-growing) welfare program, particularly important for the aged. It helped pass the first serious pension reform bill in modern times and has succeeded in making nursing-home reform a national issue.

Less visibly, it has lobbied the Department of Health, Education, and Welfare; the Department of Labor; and the Office of Economic Opportunity into guaranteeing special programs for the aged. All over Washington, there are special committees devoted to the elderly's special interests—and to the government's financial support.

Their power was shown in a 1975 clash over raising the price of food stamps. A rise had been proposed by the Department of Agriculture and supported by President Ford. It would have meant a large loss of income for many of the elderly.

The letters came flooding into Washington—to the Capitol, to the Agriculture Department, to the White House. Many of them were from elderly couples for whom the higher costs would be particularly burdensome. The result was one of the Ford administration's most humiliating public spankings.

The House voted, 374 to 38, to prevent the higher prices from going into effect; the Senate followed suit, 78 to 6. The White House decided that a veto would be futile. The price of food stamps remained the same.

Among the thousands of letters that poured in was one addressed to Senator George McGovern, the head of the Senate Select Committee on Nutrition, from an elderly couple in Pinebluff, N.C. It outlined in painful detail what the new prices would have meant to their budget. Listing income and expenses, the couple concluded that the monthly budget would show a deficit of $40.41.

The husband had worked all his life. They had raised three children. Now they wondered how they could afford gasoline to drive to the doctor's office.

The letter provides a capsule example of why the nation's elderly seem to be able so often to get what they want out of Washington. A lobby that can justifiably picture its membership as not only pitiable but also powerful is well down the road to success.

Most segments of the lobby are relatively unknown to the general public. Preeminent is the National Council of Senior Citizens (NCSC), representing a coalition of more than 3,000 local organizations of the elderly.

There are the American Association of Retired Persons and the National Retired Teachers Association, closely aligned and representing some 2.5 million persons. There is the National Association of Retired Federal Employees, concentrated in the Washington area.

It is the National Council of Senior Citizens that has come to symbolize the new political clout of the aged. Most of its money and much of its leadership came out of the labor movement. NCSC, unlike other parts of the aged constituency, still is characterized by a kind of union-hall toughness.

There is nothing particularly novel about an NCSC lobbying operation. It hires no high-priced lobbyists to prowl the House and Senate office buildings regularly. When an important vote is pending, it notifies the members of a watchdog committee in each of its 3,000-plus chapters.

The committees are supposed to keep track of how local members of Congress vote and apply a little persuasion just as the vote nears.

On the eve of a vote, the phone calls and telegrams come flowing into Washington. Sometimes a friend in the House will telephone William Hutton, the NCSC Executive Director, to warn him that Representative Jones is not coming around. Hutton sees to it that the watchdog committee back in Jones's district knows about it. More often than not, Jones gets the message. More frequently than in years past, he heeds it.

The accumulation of successes has built the NCSC's Washington reputation for clout. A Senate staffer familiar with many battles over issues of the aged says that NCSC is believed and feared because, unlike other lobby organizations, it can pinpoint its pressures with some precision.

"They can produce letters, telegrams, anything, almost overnight," he observes. "If you have to produce some testimony very quickly, they can do it for you, and their facts are good. And then you have to realize the basic fact that members of Congress are just very sensitive to an organized constituency that evokes sympathy."

Some sympathetic students of the seniors movement, however, believe that there is a curious gap between the apparent power of the bloc and its actual achievement in terms of alleviating the real problems of the elderly.

Despite the 86 percent increase in social security benefits in the past decade, a disproportionate number of the elderly are still poor. About 16 percent of all people over 65 have incomes below the poverty line. Even with the latest social security gains, those who must live on those benefits are barely at a subsistence level.

Adapted from William Chapman, "Power to the Old People," San Antonio *Express-News,* March 23, 1975, p. 3H. Copyright © The Washington Post.

Hispanic Americans

The enduring puzzle of modern politics involves a bit of magic—how do invisible people make themselves seen and heard?

The black minority figured it out. Now it appears that another vast constituency, long neglected, is beginning to learn the trick: the 11 million Hispanic Americans.

"Hispanics are learning how the game is played," said Alfonso Ludi, an equal-opportunity officer at NASA by day and a community activist on his own time.

Willie Velasquez of San Antonio, who heads the Southwest Voter Registration Education Project, explains: "It's similar to what happened in the South with blacks. The same thing is happening with Latinos except we're a couple of years behind. But there's no question that political action is the priority now.''

Representative Edward R. Roybal, the Los Angeles Democrat who has started a fledgling five-member Hispanic Congressional Caucus, puts it in this perspective: ''I still think we are in a gray area. I don't think you could say the Hispanic community is being recognized yet. But the potential is there. There is a different attitude.''

While these things are impossible to measure, Washington does have some tangible evidence that citizens of Spanish origin, from Mexican Americans to Puerto Ricans, are influencing political decisions with more force and sophistication. This does not mean their goal is at hand—any more than the goals of blacks.

Still, the change is evident from a few years ago when Hispanic groups often squabbled among themselves and watched in frustration as other special interests moved in on the pie—especially federal jobs and funds.

Consider these scattered examples:

• The heat is rising on President Carter to follow through on his generous campaign promises of jobs for Hispanic Americans, whose disappointment ranges from mild to furious. While some groups work with low-key persuasion, others are keeping their frustration visible, as Ludi put it.

• Mexican Americans are more unified and thus better able to ally themselves with other interests. For example, organized labor now takes Hispanic views into account in pushing for legislation to deal with illegal aliens from Mexico.

• Some Hispanics are working to get Hispanics as well as blacks into jobs designated for minorities.

• The Hispanic groups went head-to-head with the NAACP (National Association for the Advancement of Colored People) last year on a particular issue—whether the Voting Rights Act should be broadened to cover Spanish-speaking people of the Southwest. And the Hispanic position prevailed in Congress.

• The growth of Latino elected officials has been slow over the last decade, according to Velasquez, but he expects the pace to quicken, based on the voter drives under way.

Mexican Americans in 1976 claimed two governors and seventy-four legislators in five states (Texas, Colorado, Arizona, New Mexico and California) where they have 17 percent of the population. Only 6 percent of municipal officials are Spanish-origin citizens.

''There is a new type of leadership that is sophisticated and moderate,'' said E. B. Duarte, a special assistant and Hispanic liaison officer for the United States immigration commissioner. ''These aren't people who are off the wall. They are taking government jobs and doing a good job with them. It is not different really from the Irish or Italians or blacks. It's the American way.''

Adapted from William Greider, ''Latinos Join Game of Visible Politics,'' San Antonio *Express,* April 8, 1977, p. 10C, dispatch of Washington Post Service. Copyright © The Washington Post.

Questions

1 What are two reasons why many of the elderly have formed into special-interest groups?

2 What have the elderly accomplished by forming lobbies?

3 Give at least one reason why some Hispanic Americans have formed into special-interest groups.

4 What have some Hispanic American groups accomplished? Cite one example.

▫ Do you think that any group should form a special-interest lobby? Should one type of lobby be outlawed and others be allowed to exist? Would that be fair? Explain.

Chapter 27: Pressure Groups and Direct Actions

PROBLEM: HOW DOES LOBBYING WORK? A HISTORIC CASE OF LOBBYING

When several pressure groups join together in support of a cause, their strength is enhanced. That is what happened in 1964 and 1965. An alliance of civil rights, labor, and religious organizations went to work to persuade Congress to pass two far-reaching measures—the Civil Rights Act of 1964 and the Voting Rights Act of 1965. They succeeded.

The acts were the most extensive pieces of legislation on civil rights in this century. Among other things that the acts guaranteed blacks and other racial minorities were voting rights; access to motels, hotels, and restaurants; and equal employment opportunities. The acts gave the executive branch power to enter into suits to desegregate public facilities and schools. The acts also authorized federal agencies to cut off funds from programs in which state or local governments practiced racial discrimination. Further, the acts increased the powers of the Civil Rights Commission and established the Community Relations Service to help resolve civil rights problems.

As you read the following account, ask yourself:

- *What factors accounted for the success of the civil rights lobby?*
- *What problems did the lobby have to overcome?*

The Civil Rights Lobby in Action

Such a far-reaching measure could never have passed without widespread support from a number of groups. The support of Republicans as well as Democrats in the Senate and the House was essential.

The lobby group was very well organized. As might be expected, black groups led the fight. Among them were the National Association for the Advancement of Colored People, the Southern Christian

The International Ladies Garment Workers Union sent this group to join a March on Washington. This and other efforts of the Leadership Conference on Human Rights helped push through new civil rights legislation in the 1960s.

Leadership Conference, the National Urban League, the Congress of Racial Equality, the Negro-American Labor Council, and the Student Non-Violent Coordinating Committee. Alone, these groups would not have been enough. But they were joined by various other groups, shown below. Together they formed the Leadership Conference on Human Rights.

Non-union	Union	Religious
American Civil Liberties Union	AFL-CIO	American Jewish Committee
Americans for Democratic Action	American Newspaper Guild	American Jewish Congress
American Veterans Committee	Brotherhood of Sleeping Car Porters	National Baptist Convention
Jewish War Veterans	International Ladies Garment Workers Union	National Catholic Conference for Interracial Justice
	National Alliance of Postal Employees	National Council of Churches
	United Auto Workers	Protestant-Episcopal Church
	United Steel Workers	United Synagogues of America

The union involvement was important, since these unions had contributed large sums of money to Democratic candidates in the past and were able to ask them for the return of a favor. Equally crucial was the participation of a large variety of religious groups. Their importance was enhanced by their bipartisan influence. In many cases, the unions had influence only with Democrats. The religious leaders were able to work with Republicans and also with some Democrats from rural states who were not then subject to union influence.

Another factor in the success of the program is that this alliance of organizations was not a new one. The Leadership Conference on Civil Rights was organized in 1949. It had already been successful in securing many civil rights laws, but none so extensive as the Civil Rights Act of 1964.

The Leadership Conference coordinated the civil rights, labor, and church organizations. It also worked closely with two groups within Congress. One was the Democratic Study Group, a liberal organization including approximately half of the Democrats in the House of Representatives. The other was a liberal Republican group led by the ranking Republican on the Judiciary Committee. In addition, the civil rights lobbyists were in daily contact with the Justice Department and President Johnson's White House.

While the bill was on the House floor, over a thousand representatives of the leadership Conference on Civil Rights came to Washington to lobby Congress. Watchers in the gallery kept a clear count of how each member of Congress voted on each amendment. Part of the strategy was to make it impossible for any member to avoid going on record on the vote.

The Southern Caucus of about sixty Democrats from Southern states fought the bill. They had support from two lobbying organizations—the Coordinating Committee for Fundamental American Freedoms and the Americans for Constitutional Action. The Coordinating Committee is believed to have spent half a million dollars in its effort to defeat the Civil Rights Act of 1964.

The bill passed the House first. The Senate was tougher. Southern senators put on a lengthy filibuster to defeat the bill or water it down with amendments. Although White House strategy called for rejecting all amendments, a few minor concessions were made to secure the support of key Republican senators. Then all other amendments were blocked. Finally the crucial vote to end the filibuster arrived. The

Senate had never in modern times voted to end a filibuster on a civil rights bill. The votes of 67 of the 100 senators were needed. When the final vote was taken, the civil rights supporters won by a vote of 71–29. The concessions to the Republican leadership had paid off; 27 of the 33 Republicans voted to end the filibuster. Democrats favored it by 44–23.

This set the stage for the following year's battle over the Votings Rights Act of 1965. Again, the same lobby groups geared for action.

President Johnson's landslide victory in 1964 had helped bring into Congress a large number of Democrats favoring more civil rights for blacks. This brightened the outlook for civil rights legislation.

Another helpful factor was ratification in 1964 of the Twenty-fourth Amendment to the Constitution. It prohibited the use of a poll tax as a requirement for voting in *federal* elections. But it did nothing to end the use of a poll tax in state and local elections.

In early 1965, the Reverend Martin Luther King, Jr., decided to dramatize this voting issue by conducting a registration drive at Selma, Alabama. Significant discrimination against black voters had occurred there. The registration drive was met with white violence, which helped to arouse national sentiment in favor of the strong voting rights bills introduced in Congress in 1965.

This time the first progress on the bill came in the Senate. Once again the Senate voted to terminate a civil rights filibuster, by a vote of 70–30. The 1965 Voting Rights Act provided for the appointment of federal examiners by the Attorney General to supervise the registration of voters in states and counties where less than 50 percent of the population of voting age had voted in the presidential election of 1964. All amendments to weaken the bill were defeated by wide margins.

Nevertheless, there was a close split on whether or not to ban the poll tax in state and local elections. Many liberal senators wanted an outright ban on all poll taxes. But there was a constitutional argument that the states could set their own requirements in state and local elections. The final provision of the Voting Rights Act passed by the Senate required the Attorney General of the United States to file the necessary legal actions to have state and local poll tax requirements voided.

After Congress approved the report of a Senate-House Conference Committee, President Johnson immediately signed the bill in a dramatic session at the Senate.

Once again, a concerted lobbying campaign by the civil rights, religious, and labor organizations in the Leadership Conference on Civil Rights sparked the legislative action. However, this time part of the lobbying took place before national television cameras reporting the news from Selma, Alabama, prior to the legislative action in Washington. This generated substantial public opinion favorable to new federal civil rights laws. The legislators responded by enacting such legislation.

Adapted from Thomas P. Murphy, *Pressures upon Congress: Legislation by Lobby,* Barron's Educational Series, Inc., Woodbury, N.Y., 1973, pp. 49–54.

Questions

1 How many pressure groups included in this account joined together to get passage of these civil rights laws? Why did they form a coalition?

2 What were *two* problems these pressure groups faced? How did they seem to overcome them? (Use the word *lobby* or *lobbying* in your answer.)

○ Do you think that it could ever be dangerous for so many different kinds of pressure groups to join together for political action? How might such a coalition affect you?

Chapter 27 Review

Developing Your Political Vocabulary

Briefly explain the difference between:

1. a constitutional referendum and an optional referendum
2. a referendum and an initiative
3. a pressure group and a political party
4. a lobbyist and the leader of a pressure group

Recalling and Comparing

1. The terms listed in a–f below were used in this chapter. Arrange them in what you regard as their order of importance for our political process. Number your top-rated item 1 and your lowest-rated item 6.
    - a the referendum
    - b the recall
    - c the initiative
    - d pressure groups
    - e lobbyists
    - f political parties
2. Tell why you arranged the words in a–f as you did.

Special Activities

1. Determine if your state or community provides for any form of referendum, initiative, or recall. If so, prepare a report explaining how these measures may be used.
2. Make a study of the use of the initiative in some recent instance. Report your findings to the class and give your opinion on the benefits and drawbacks of that particular use of the initiative.
3. Determine what provisions exist to control abuses of lobbying in your state. Outline those provisions in a chart.
4. Make a special bulletin-board display that illustrates recent lobbying activities in the national capital.
5. Imagine you and a group of your friends wanted your state legislature or Congress to pass a particular bill. Make a list of the kinds of lobbying activities you would recommend your group follow to help get the bill passed. Add some ideas not mentioned in this chapter.
6. Read about the struggles of some pressure groups to influence Congress and then report to the class on the methods they used. You might choose one of the following:
    - a the struggle of the abolitionists before the Civil War
    - b labor's struggles for the 8-hour day, a minimum-wage law, or the right to bargain collectively
    - c the struggle for woman suffrage
    - d the struggle for national prohibition of alcoholic beverages
    - e the struggles for consumer protections, such as a meat inspection act and a pure-food law
    - f the effort to end the United States' involvement in the war in Vietnam
    - g the ongoing efforts to obtain a national health program
7. Consider what might be arguments for and against the following statement: "There should be no laws to regulate lobbying." Do you agree or disagree? Why?

Chapter 28

Measuring and Shaping Public Opinion

The goal of democratic government is to translate the opinions of the public into the policies of government. But how do we know what the public wants? How do we measure public opinion? One way, as we have seen, is through elections. Another is through the activities of pressure groups. In this chapter, we will look at still another means of measuring public opinion—through opinion polls.

But public opinion is not just something that exists; it can be changed. And part of politics is trying to change public opinion, to shape it in certain ways. As we saw in the last chapter, pressure groups try to influence public opinion in order to win it over to their side. So do politicians. In this chapter, we will explore the art of shaping public opinion—which is the art of propaganda.

---— Goals ———

- To learn how public opinion polls are taken.
- To learn the uses of opinion polls.
- To learn the meaning and uses of propaganda.
- To consider how propaganda is used in political campaigns.

POLLS AND PUBLIC OPINION

A *public opinion poll* is an effort to find out what people are thinking by asking them questions. Because it is impossible to question every member of "the public," a poll commonly is conducted among a small sample of the public. This sample is carefully chosen so that it resembles the entire public as nearly as possible—in other words, so that it is *representative* of the public as a whole.

An opinion poll is only as good as the sample on which it is based. If the sample is poorly chosen, then the opinion poll will not accurately measure opinions. In the early years of public opinion polls, poor sampling techniques led to some outright failures.

Perhaps the most spectacular failure was a poll conducted by the magazine *Literary Digest* to predict how people would vote in the presidential election of 1936. The *Literary Digest* had predicted the winner correctly in several earlier elections. The magazine's method was to send ballots in the mail to several million people whose names were taken from telephone books and automobile registration lists. Of the 2 million people who sent back ballots in 1936, a large majority favored the Republican candidate for President, Alfred Landon. The *Literary Digest* confidently predicted a Landon victory. But on Election Day, voters leaned toward the Democratic party and reelected President Franklin D. Roosevelt by a landslide.

What went wrong? The *Literary Digest* went out of business soon after the election because many of its subscribers thought that the poll was rigged. But political observers pointed to an error in the magazine's sampling. People who owned telephones and cars were not representative of the voters as a whole. They had higher incomes than the average voter, and people with higher incomes were more likely to vote Republican. What the magazine had failed to take into account was a shift in the mood of the bulk of the population, during the Great Depression of the 1930s. The Republican party had been in power at the onset of the depression and had been replaced by the Democrats' New Deal in 1932. Many people of middle and lower income who had

Alfred Landon—and the *Literary Digest*—incorrectly predicted that he would be elected President in 1936.

formerly voted Republican were now pinning their hopes on President Roosevelt's New Deal administration. The sampling technique had worked before because most people voted Republican, just as most people in the sample did. By 1936, however, *most* people were voting Democratic.

The modern pollster, or poll-taker, uses every precaution to choose a proper sample. In most cases, that means choosing people at random. Instead of choosing names from telephone books, pollsters commonly use census reports on housing units. Not all people have telephones, but everyone lives somewhere. Pollsters try to make sure that all housing units in the country have an equal chance to be a part of the sample.

Sometimes the results of a poll are "weighted" to improve accuracy. For example, a pollster may find that only 45 percent of those interviewed are women though women make up about 51 percent of the nation's population. The pollster may decide to give extra weight to the opinions of women in that particular poll. Similarly, in a poll in which young people were underrepresented, their answers might be given extra weight.

Even a carefully chosen and properly weighted sample will not result in an accurate poll if the questions are unclear or biased. Professional pollsters take great care to word questions precisely and to choose "neutral" questions. This is not always easy. Take a question about national defense, for example. The question might be phrased this way: "Do you favor a strong national defense?" Or this way: "Do you favor cutting spending on schools and highways to pay for a strong national defense?" Or this way: "Which is more important to you—a strong national defense or a strong commitment to more equality here at home?" The results of the poll would probably vary, depending on which question was used.

Pollsters have found that a national sampling of 1,500 people is large enough to get an accurate reading of public opinion. They do not claim 100 percent accuracy. The only way to be that accurate would be to question every person in the country. Even then, someone would surely have died or changed opinions before the poll was published. The pollsters claim only that they can measure public opinion within 3 percentage points 95 times out of 100. They base this claim on mathematical probability—the same reasoning that tells you that if you flip a coin 500 times, you will get heads and tails in almost equal proportions.

Two of the best-known public opinion polls today are conducted by George Gallup and Louis Harris. Both depend on personal interviews with a sample of 1,500 people. Many of their polls are published regularly in newspapers. In election years, the two major polls compete to see which can forecast the results with greater accuracy.

In 1976, for example, both Gallup and Harris conducted a continuing series of interviews with registered voters to find out which presidential candidate they favored. The interviews were held up to Election Day. On the eve of the election, Harris was giving Jimmy Carter a 1 percent lead over the incumbent, Gerald Ford, and Gallup was giving Ford a 1 percent lead over Carter. But both pollsters felt that the election was "too close to call." Either Carter or Ford could win it. As it turned out, the election was close indeed. Carter won with 50.1 percent of the popular vote against Ford's 48.0 percent.

Polls are not intended merely to satisfy the curiosity of the public; they have practical uses. There are an estimated 1,000 polling

Pollsters were slow to learn how deeply the Great Depression and its breadlines had affected political attitudes.

Chapter 28: Measuring and Shaping Public Opinion

"NOW JUST A MINUTE—I HAVE A FEW QUESTIONS MYSELF!"

Ford's advisers studied that gap. They looked at old polls and new polls. Then they gave Ford this advice:

> We firmly believe that you can win in November. During times when you and your administration pulled together and projected a positive image of action and accomplishments, your sampling in the national polls rose accordingly.... However, ... your national-approval rating declined during the periods when you were perceived as partisan, particularly when we campaigned.

From a Ford strategy paper, quoted in Jules Witcover, *Marathon: The Pursuit of the Presidency, 1972–1976*, Viking Press, New York, 1977, p. 532. Reprinted by permission of Viking Penguin Inc.

Ford based his campaign strategy on the advisers' findings. Since he slipped in the polls

The Gallup Poll, one of the best-known public opinion polls, surveys a cross-section of the voting community.

organizations in this country that are paid to conduct polls. Many of these polls have commercial rather than political purposes. Commercial pollsters often distribute samples of a new product, such as a soap, and then interview users to find out what they like and dislike about the product. Another frequent type of commercial poll tries to find what television programs people watch, by questioning viewers. Here we will concentrate on political polls, which deal with election races and public issues.

Almost all candidates for election to high office use opinion polls to help them decide how to campaign. In 1976, both the Ford and the Carter campaign organizations hired their own pollsters to supplement the standard polls like those of Gallup and Harris. One thing the campaign organizations wanted to find out was what people liked and disliked about the two candidates.

President Ford's advisers, for example, were concerned because Ford was 35 percentage points behind Carter in the July Harris poll.

when he campaigned, Ford did not campaign in the normal manner. He was, after all, the President. So he spent much of his time in Washington, doing presidential things—signing bills in the White House Rose Garden or working on national problems. Reporters called this approach the "Rose Garden strategy." Ford began to rise in the polls. The gap kept closing, and there were those who believed that Ford would have overtaken Carter and won the election if there had been more time.

Polls can tell candidates a number of things about the voters. For example, polls can reveal what issues are of interest. If most people are worried about inflation, the candidate can stress proposals to deal with inflation. If most voters are concerned about foreign policy, the candidate can stress that subject. Polls can also reveal an opponent's weaknesses. If many voters think that an opponent is biased toward big business, a candidate may gain support by attacking "giant corporations."

Average citizens can also gain useful information from polls. A poll can tell you how your own opinions compare with other people's opinions or how a political race is likely to turn out. In the weeks preceding a national political convention, many people watch the polls to find out how the race for the nomination is going. On pages 510–511 are two polls of delegate support for candidates a month or so before the 1976 Republican national convention. These polls were based, not on a small sample, but on actual tallies of the known position of each delegate. Were the polls accurate? You can judge for yourself. The number of delegate votes needed for nomination was 1,130. When the vote was taken on August 18, Gerald Ford had 1,187 votes and Ronald Reagan had 1,070.

While opinion polls are supposed merely to reflect public opinion, some people believe that the polls help shape opinion. What happened when people learned that Gerald Ford

President Ford, early in the 1976 campaign, met the press at a shopping center in Asheville, North Carolina.

was running close to Jimmy Carter in the polls? Did some people switch to what they thought would be the winning side? As Ford gained steadily in the final weeks, did this create a "bandwagon effect," with undecided voters hopping on the Ford bandwagon?

Concerns such as these have led some countries to put legal restrictions on election polls. Thus, France banned the publication of polls within the last few days of its 1978 election campaign in order to prevent last-minute influences on voters. In this country, as we have seen, pollsters can and do work right up to the day of an election.

Questions

1 What are *two* important factors that can influence the accuracy of an opinion poll?

Chapter 28: Measuring and Shaping Public Opinion

Predicted Votes of Delegates at the 1976 Republican National Convention

State	Number of Delegates	Newsweek, July 8			Time, July 19		
		Gerald Ford[a]	Ronald Reagan[a]	Undecided	Gerald Ford[a]	Ronald Reagan[a]	Undecided
Alabama	37	—	37	—	—	37	—
Alaska	19	17	2	—	17	2	—
Arizona	29	2	27	—	2	27	—
Arkansas	27	10	17	—	10	17	—
California	167	—	167	—	—	167	—
Colorado	31	4	26	1	4	26	1
Connecticut	35	35	—	—	35	—	—
Delaware	17	15	2	—	14	—	3
Florida	66	43	23	—	43	23	—
Georgia	48	—	48	—	—	48	—
Hawaii	19	15	1	3	8	1	10
Idaho	21	4	17	—	4	17	—
Illinois	101	83	15	3	84	17	—
Indiana	54	9	45	—	9	45	—
Iowa	36	19	17	—	19	17	—
Kansas	34	30	4	—	28	4	2
Kentucky	37	19	18	—	19	18	—
Louisiana	41	1	38	2	—	37	4
Maine	20	15	5	—	15	4	1
Maryland	43	43	—	—	43	—	—
Massachusetts	43	28	15	—	28	15	—
Michigan	84	55	29	—	55	29	—
Minnesota	42	34	8	—	34	8	—
Mississippi	30	10	20	—	—	30	—
Missouri	49	17	29	3	16	30	3
Montana	20	—	20	—	—	20	—
Nebraska	25	7	18	—	7	18	—
Nevada	18	5	13	—	5	13	—
New Hampshire	21	18	3	—	18	3	—
New Jersey	67	60	—	7	58	5	4
New Mexico	21	—	21	—	—	21	—
New York	154	134	20	—	125	18	11
North Carolina	54	25	28	1	25	28	1
North Dakota	18	10	5	3	11	5	2
Ohio	97	91	6	—	91	6	—
Oklahoma	36	—	36	—	—	36	—
Oregon	30	16	14	—	16	14	—
Pennsylvania	103	92	11	—	75	12	16
Rhode Island	19	19	—	—	19	—	—
South Carolina	36	7	28	1	8	28	—
South Dakota	20	9	11	—	9	11	—
Tennessee	43	21	22	—	21	22	—
Texas	100	—	100	—	—	100	—

Continued on next page

Predicted Votes of Delegates (continued)

State	Number of Delegates	Newsweek, July 8			Time, July 19		
		Gerald Ford[a]	Ronald Reagan[a]	Undecided	Gerald Ford[a]	Ronald Reagan[a]	Undecided
Utah	20	—	20	—	—	20	—
Vermont	18	18	—	—	18	—	—
Virginia	51	14	37	—	8	41	2
Washington	38	7	31	—	7	31	—
West Virginia	28	18	10	—	19	9	—
Wisconsin	45	45	—	—	45	—	—
Wyoming	17	2	15	—	2	10	5
District of Columbia	14	14	—	—	14	—	—
Guam	4	4	—	—	4	—	—
Puerto Rico	8	8	—	—	8	—	—
Virgin Islands	4	4	—	—	4	—	—
Total		1,156	1,079	24	1,104	1,090	65

a. Includes delegates leaning to candidate.
Newsweek, July 8, 1976, p. 23. Copyright © Newsweek, Inc., 1976. Used by permission. *TIME,* July 19, 1976, p. 25. Reprinted by permission from *Time,* The Weekly Newsmagazine; Copyright © Time Inc. 1976.

2 In what way did 1976 presidential polls influence the course of the 1976 presidential campaign?

3 Look at the three versions of the question on national defense on page 507. Which one is most neutral? Can you think of other ways to ask the question?

◌ Do you think that legal restrictions should be placed on election polls? Explain.

THE USES OF PROPAGANDA

The art of shaping other people's opinions for one's own ends is known as *propaganda.* The word has a bad connotation. When something is described as propaganda, most people assume it is evil. But, in itself, propaganda is neither evil nor good.

Propaganda can be used for good ends, just as it can be used for bad ends. When you try to talk a friend into going with you to see a movie, you are using propaganda. When an advertiser tries to persuade you to buy a certain deodorant, the advertiser is using propaganda. When a pressure group tries to win public opinion to its side, it is engaging in propaganda. When a government tries to persuade the world that its policies are just, it is resorting to propaganda. In each case, whether the propaganda is "good" or "bad" depends on how we view the goal of the propaganda, and on whether the techniques used are proper or improper.

Certain techniques are commonly used by propagandists. Knowing these techniques will help you recognize propaganda for what it is. Following are several of the most common techniques, according to studies made by the Institute for Propaganda Analysis. For propagandists, these techniques are the rules of the politics of persuasion.

Glittering Generalities. If you can associate a person or idea with something generally regarded as good or virtuous, people may accept it without examining the evidence. Some samples are: "My policy is firmly grounded in our democratic heritage." "I believe in equality for all." "No freedom-loving person could deny. . . ."

Transfer. It helps to associate a person or an idea with something that is high in prestige; some of the prestige will "rub off," or be transferred. For example, a candidate for Congress might arrange to be photographed with the President. A hair-care advertisement might be photographed in a laboratory, implying scientifically proven value.

Testimonial. Because of the transfer effect, if a well-known and highly regarded person is on your side, it helps to say so. Some examples are: "Liza Minnelli believes, as I do, that . . . ." "Paul Newman will vote for . . . ." "Our astronauts always drink Gloopo." "Seventeen Nobel Prize winners agree that stopping war is . . . ."

Plain-Folks Appeal. You can use the transfer effect also to persuade people that you are just like them, "just folks." Here are some ways this is done: "I had to leave school and go to work when my pappy died." "I know what it's like to eat beans three times a day." You might be photographed in jeans and shirtsleeves.

Card-Stacking. To stack the cards, use only the arguments that support your side or tear down the other side. If you are running for Congress, describe your platform and your opponent's mistakes. Do not say that you never held public office and your opponent has served in the state legislature.

Bandwagon Appeal. Try to convince people that *everybody* is on your side—or, in political jargon, "has climbed on your bandwagon." The idea is: Everybody is doing it, why not you? The technique is used in such forms as: "The Illinois delegation has just swung its votes to Senator S, and Pennsylvania is moving into line." "Our troops were met by cheering crowds of peasants." "All the other kids will be there, so you must too." "This season, everyone is wearing the new . . . ."

Stereotype. An oversimplified picture of a certain group of people is often used to portray an individual within that group. Common examples are: "As a graduate of Harvard (or Yale or another) University, I can tell you . . . ." "Blondes have more fun." "Like all Easterners, my opponent does not understand . . . ."

All of the propaganda methods we have considered up to this point can be used honorably or dishonorably. They can be used with truths or falsehoods. They are all methods of persuasion, and therefore of propaganda, but it is how they are used that determines whether they are good or bad.

Some other propaganda devices are always unfair.

Chapter 28: Measuring and Shaping Public Opinion

Representative Bella Abzug, while a member of Congress from New York City, poses with Barbra Streisand. The actress was helping to raise funds for the Representative's campaign for nomination as a state senatorial candidate.

Name-Calling. A propagandist may pin a "bad" name on someone or something so as to get people to reject that person or idea. Bad names are implied in such statements as "Mayor M's reactionary ideas . . . ." "Representative R's scare tactics . . . ." "The Z Corporation's monopolistic control . . . ."

Misleading Association. As in name-calling, a propagandist using the technique of misleading association tries to smear a person or an idea by implying an association that does not exist. An example would be: "Mary Jones was a student at Potluck University, where radical students rioted." The implication is that Mary Jones was a radical and one of the rioters, though the propagandist does not directly say so.

Misquoting or Quoting Out of Context. A propagandist may quote only certain parts of a statement, knowing them to be misleading, or may quote incorrectly. Thus, someone might say, "The investigation cleared me of wrongdoing," when the investigators actually reported: "Given our limited resources, we were able to find no proof of wrongdoing. Yet we did find evidence that warrants further investigation."

Card-stacking is one of the propaganda techniques used by both sides of the ongoing debate over pollution.

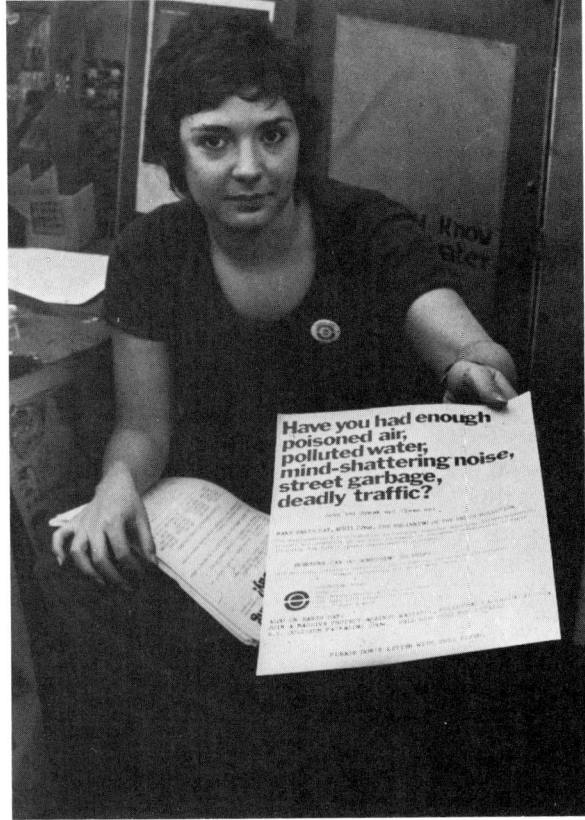

Chapter 28: Measuring and Shaping Public Opinion

An emotion-packed issue brought out emotion-packed propaganda in this demonstration against nuclear power development.

Fallacies. A *fallacy* is an error in reasoning or an unsound argument. Fallacies may be so smoothly woven into a speech that they are undetectable until the speech is carefully read. Fallacies can therefore do a good deal of damage. One common fallacy is the idea that because event B followed event A, it was caused by A. An example is: "There has been a steady rise in crime since Mayor X was elected." The statement may be true, but the implication that the rise in crime was the mayor's fault may be totally false.

The Outright Lie. The outright lie is a more common form of propaganda than many people suspect. Adolf Hitler boasted of the propaganda value of lies and made free use of them in his climb to power in Germany. The bigger the lie, Hitler said, the more readily will people believe it. There are small lies that easily mislead, too. And statistics can be made to lie. Politicians as well as advertisers can cite invented, or doctored, or even accurate figures to prove almost any point.

Propaganda used as a means to mislead rather than to persuade is scorned by most people. Yet it is not always recognized. People who are quick to recognize false propaganda used by those with whom they disagree are likely to be taken in by the same kind of propaganda used by someone whom they support.

In modern society, we are constantly bombarded by propaganda. Often we actually seek it out. We hum along with a ditty from an advertising jingle. We write for information about a product that we have seen advertised.

In many ways, modern society depends upon propaganda to spread information and ideas. This is as true in government and politics as in business. There is nothing wrong with it so long as we remember that propaganda is meant to persuade. Someone has something to sell—an idea, a person, a product. We must constantly ask ourselves: "Who is selling what? Why? What techniques are being used? What should I know that they are not telling me?"

With proper precautions, we can thread our way through the various claims and arrive at a reasonable approximation of the truth.

Questions
---

1 What is propaganda? Briefly define it.

2 What are examples of some commonly used propaganda techniques? What propaganda techniques can you add to those described in the text?

⬠ Which propaganda methods do you regard as acceptable and which as not acceptable? Explain.

PROBLEM: HOW IS PROPAGANDA USED IN POLITICAL CAMPAIGNS?

Propaganda plays a significant part in politics. Below is an example of propaganda in an election campaign nearly a century and a half ago. As you read the selection, ask yourself:

- *What propaganda techniques are being used?*
- *Are the techniques fair or unfair?*

In 1840, a record 80 percent of the voters of the United States turned out to elect a President. This unusual voter enthusiasm was aroused by a campaign that was more propaganda than anything else.

The candidates were William Henry Harrison of the Whig party and Martin Van Buren of the Democratic party. Van Buren was running for reelection to a second term as President. His Democratic party was known as the party of the common people. The less popular Whig party was regarded as the party of the aristocrats, of wealthy Southern planters and Eastern bankers. Moreover, the Whig party was split into many factions. With this weak opposition, Van Buren looked like a sure winner.

He might have been—if it had not been for the propaganda use of *stereotype*. A *stereotype* is a fixed, oversimplified picture that people have of a certain "type" of person. The individual may not fit the stereotype at all. He or she may have entirely different qualities from the "type." But people of today, as in the past, see only the "type."

The Whig leaders in 1840 decided to ignore the important national issues—on which they could not agree anyway. Instead they appealed directly to voters' emotions. For the first time in this nation's political history, politicians built a whole political campaign around a stereotype. The voters liked a war hero? The Whigs would give them a war hero. The voters liked a log cabin candidate? The Whigs would give them a log cabin candidate.

From the beginning, William Henry Harrison was presented as a simple farmer, a humble man of the people, who preferred a log cabin to a fancy home and hard cider to expensive bourbon whiskey. The log cabin, in fact, became the symbol of the Whig campaign. (The symbol can be important, because a picture can be taken in more quickly than words. It brings an instant emotional response.)

Handkerchiefs were imprinted with log cabins and handed out to voters. Log cabin songs were specially written for the campaign. There were badges, hard-cider almanacs, and posters picturing Harrison hard at work plowing on his farm. Political parades and torchlight processions were held for Harrison all over the country. Floats on which actual log cabins had been built, with real smoke pouring out of the chimneys, were pulled down the street by perspiring men wearing coonskin caps. Barrels of hard cider were rolled out at the massive political rallies that followed the parades.

The people who responded to this poster by spending Saturday night at the Old Courtroom were certain to hear every kind of propaganda the 1840s had to offer.

Harrison was also presented in another stereotype: as a "war hero." Twenty-nine years earlier, he had fought in the Battle of Tippecanoe, against Indians in Florida. Harrison's backers dubbed him "Old Tippecanoe." As the vice-presidential candidate was named John Tyler, the catchy campaign slogan, "Tippecanoe and Tyler, too," was on every tongue. Campaign posters showed Old Tippecanoe in front of his log cabin, offering jugs of hard cider to his old soldier-comrades.

Thus the Whig politicians used a "good" stereotype to influence voters in favor of their candidate. They also used a "bad" stereotype to influence voters against Van Buren. This stereotype, too, was carefully chosen. Van Buren, who was from New York State, was pictured as a "hateful aristocrat" from the Eastern seaboard. In

1840, people who lived on the Western frontier or in small towns distrusted and disliked such a type.

To fit President Van Buren into this stereotype, the Whigs used the propaganda device of *name-calling*. Cartoons pictured Van Buren as a conceited dandy, who strutted around like a peacock. Whig Representative Charles Ogle elaborated on the theme in a speech before the House of Representatives. He accused President Van Buren of turning the White House into a royal palace, spending money lavishly on new decorations and furniture, and eating French food from golden plates while the common people starved. The speech was filled with *name-calling* and *glittering generalities*—as well as bald-faced lies. It was widely reprinted in pamphlets by the Whigs.

A similar theme showed up in a song sung by the Whigs at campaign rallies:

Old Tip he wears a homespun coat
He has no ruffled shirt-wirt-wirt
But Mart he has the golden plate
And he's a little squirt-wirt-wirt.

With scarcely a mention of any important issues, the Whigs won the election and put Harrison into the White House. The log cabin campaign was even more remarkable because, in truth, Harrison was highly educated and cultured. He was the son of a signer of the Declaration of Independence, lived on a large estate, and had no need to do physical farm labor. Undoubtedly he preferred the comforts of his pleasant home to a cabin. As for his being a war hero, in the Battle of Tippecanoe Harrison lost more fighters than the Indians did, and the battle itself was not considered decisive.

The aristocrat stereotype that the Whigs presented of Van Buren was equally false. Van Buren was the son of a tavern-keeper. Though he was something of a dandy about his appearance, he spent less money on the White House than Presidents who preceded him. Van Buren may or may not have been a better person for the job than Harrison. The point is that voters were offered stereotypes, not actual persons.

Copyright © 1972 by Gladys and Marcella Thum, adapted from *The Persuaders: Propaganda in War and Peace*. Used by permission of Atheneum Publishers.

Questions

1 What propaganda devices were used in the 1840 presidential campaign?

2 Can you think of other propaganda devices that candidates in the 1840 election might have used? Give examples.

⌂ How do you think propaganda should be used in a presidential campaign? Why?

Chapter 28 Review

Recalling and Comparing

1 How does the purpose of an opinion poll differ from the purpose of propaganda?
2 What are *two* ways in which a politician might use an opinion poll?
3 Generally, how accurate are political polls? Explain.
4 What could be one main reason why a government agency might use propaganda?
5 What could be one *worthwhile* result of the use of propaganda?
6 What could be one *harmful* result of the use of propaganda?

Special Activities

1 With a small group of classmates, select a political issue and poll other students on their opinions about it. Tabulate the results and report them to the class. Be prepared to discuss why you think the results are valid and what use they might serve.
2 Draw a cartoon that shows one use of propaganda.
3 Watch a half-hour television news program, and write down all examples of propaganda that you see. What devices were used? Do you think they were effective? Do you think they were fair?
4 Make a special bulletin-board display that illustrates (a) recent, published opinion polls and (b) examples of political propaganda.
5 Identify the propaganda devices used in a political campaign with which you are familiar. Explain whether you think that any of them were justified.
6 Some people collect campaign buttons, posters, and other mementos of political campaigns. If you have any, look at the slogans on them. To what extent do they illustrate propaganda techniques?
7 Consider what might be arguments for and against the following statement, which sums up the views of some writers about propaganda: "People can be persuaded that they still have a democracy long after they have elected a dictator." Do you agree or disagree? Why?

Developing Your Political Vocabulary

Match the phrases or words in *a–f* with the best definitions or examples in 1–6.

name-calling **a**
glittering generality **b**
plain-folks appeal **c**
bandwagon **d**
stereotype **e**
misleading association **f**

1 "The enemy's soldiers are butchers."
2 "All the other kids have a class ring."
3 "I'd rather go to a ball game than an opera."
4 "We must defend the sanctity of the home."
5 "Profits of corporations in this country tripled in 1918 during World War I. Our casualties also tripled."
6 "Like most women, my opponent...."

Unit X Review

Improving Your Reading

Read the selection below and then answer the questions that follow it.

Today our public elections use the secret ballot. The Australian ballot is used, not only to protect secrecy but also to prevent fraud. The voting rights of citizens are protected in other ways, too. The United States Constitution provides that the right to vote of citizens 18 years of age and older may not be taken away because of race, color, or sex. Federal laws forbid certain voting practices that are discriminatory. Each state also has its own rules for voting in state and local elections.

A more nearly equal distribution of voter representation occurred after the United States Supreme Court's decision in *Baker v. Carr* and other apportionment cases in the 1960s. The principle of "one person—one vote" now applies to elections to all legislative bodies except the United States Senate.

Some restrictions on voting do remain, however. Only citizens may vote. State rules generally deprive prisoners and mental patients of voting rights. Federal and many state and local employees are not permitted to take part in politics, but they are permitted to vote.

Citizens can make their political feelings known in ways other than voting for candidates. Pressure groups formed for economic or other reasons play important roles in our political process. They lobby the legislative and executive branches of government and seek to influence public opinion in their favor. The referendum, recall, and initiative are used in many states to give voters added powers. The referendum and initiative give voters an opportunity to act directly on state laws and state constitutional amendments. The recall enables voters to remove certain state or local officials from office.

Public opinion polls and propaganda are a significant part of our political process. Opinion polls attempt to discover public opinion in regard to an issue or a candidate. Some people believe that polls also influence opinion. The usual means of trying to shape other people's opinions for one's own ends is propaganda. It can be used for both good purposes and bad purposes.

1 In your own words, summarize this reading in *no more than five* sentences. Have your summary focus on what you regard as the five most important points made in the reading.

2 Which *three* of the following topics noted in the reading can best be used to show guarantees of some basic rights to our voters?
    a the secret ballot
    b the Australian ballot
    c *Baker v. Carr*
    d public opinion polls

3 Which *two* of the following topics discussed in the reading can best be used to illustrate direct political action by citizens?
    a the referendum, recall, and initiative
    b qualifications for voting
    c pressure groups
    d public opinion polls

Developing Your Writing Skills: What Are Your Attitudes toward Government?

Writing a Paragraph

In this unit, you have examined the various ways in which the people of this country can participate in running the government. Considering all you have read, what seems especially important about the right to vote? How many reasons can you think of for exercising the right to vote?

Compile your answers to those questions and use them in a paragraph. Your paragraph could begin with the following sentence:

> Every eligible person has a duty to become informed and to vote.

Writing an Essay

Among the topics you studied in this unit were the roles played by pressure groups, opinion polls, and propaganda. How important do you feel each of these to be? Answer that question in a short essay. In your essay, you may wish to include the following:

1. the definition of each
2. reasons why each is a part of our political process
3. possible problems associated with each
4. recommendations for the use of each in the future

Recommended Reading

Jacques Ellul, *Propaganda: The Formation of Men's Attitudes,* Random House, New York, 1973.

Robert Erikson and Norman R. Luttbeg, *American Public Opinion: Its Origin, Content, and Impact,* Wiley, New York, 1973.

Arthur T. Hadley, *The Empty Polling Booth*, Prentice-Hall, Englewood Cliffs, N.J., 1978.

Nicholas Helburn and Joanne L. Binkley, *Will They Vote? Suggestions and Resources for Students and Teachers,* ERIC Clearinghouse for Social Studies/Social Science Education, Boulder, Colo., 1972 (paperback).

Donald G. Herzberg, *Who, Me a Politician?* Center for Information on America, Washington, Conn., 1960 (paperback).

V. O. Key, Jr., *Politics, Parties, and Pressure Groups,* Crowell, New York, latest edition.

Schley R. Lyons and William J. McCoy, *Who Votes and Why,* Robert A. Taft Institute for Government, New York, 1975 (paperback).

Thomas P. Murphy, *Pressures upon Congress: Legislation by Lobby,* Barron's Educational Series, Woodbury, N.Y., 1973 (paperback).

Burt Neuborne and Arthur Eisenberg, *The Rights of Candidates and Voters*, Avon Books, New York, 1976.

Vance Packard, *The Hidden Persuaders,* Pocket Books, New York (paperback).

Charles W. Roll and Bert Cantril, *Polls: Their Use and Misuse in Politics,* Basic Books, New York, 1973.

Charles P. Taft, *Lobbying,* Center for Information on America, Washington, Conn., 1965 (paperback).

Gladys and Marcella Thum, *Persuasion and Propaganda in War and Peace,* McDougal, Littell, Evanston. Ill., 1974 (paperback).

The Washington Lobby, Congressional Quarterly, Washington, D.C., 1971 (paperback).

Forms of Government in Other Countries

UNIT XI

Up to now, we have discussed the government of one country—our own. We have seen how this nation's great experiment in representative democracy began and how it has withstood the test of time. We have examined the formal rules and how they work out in practice. Now it is time to look at some other countries. How are their governments similar to, or different from, ours?

Is the answer to this question to be found in a country's constitution? The Soviet Union's Constitution guarantees its citizens free speech and open court hearings. But what do Soviet citizens actually have? We can get some idea from the following account based on news reports from Moscow by David K. Shipler:

Yuri K. Orlov went on trial in a small courthouse sealed by the police. A Soviet judge refused to allow him to call any witnesses for his defense.

Orlov is a critic of the Soviet system who has been charged with "anti-Soviet agitation." He was arrested 15 months earlier, at a time when he was a leader among Soviet citizens trying to publicize alleged human-rights violations by their government. The government claimed the accusations were false.

Aside from a handpicked audience of about fifty, no spectators were allowed to enter the courtroom, except Orlov's wife and two sons.

Though Soviet law calls for open trials, the authorities went to some lengths to prevent detailed accounts of the court's proceedings. Mrs. Orlov said she had been told not to take notes, or she would be expelled from the courtroom. When she took some anyway, the notes were confiscated.

Orlov's sons tried unsuccessfully to smuggle tape recorders into the courtroom.

Orlov's family relayed to reporters what he told the court in his defense. He claimed the right to criticize the Soviet government. He also claimed a right to circulate such criticism, pointing out that the Soviet Union had signed an international agreement on human rights at Helsinki in 1975. The Helsinki agreement contains provisions guaranteeing freedom of information. Orlov claimed that he had acted, not for subversive ends, but out of humanitarian concern.

The prosecution presented fifteen witnesses. They testified that Orlov's accusations about violations of human rights had been false.

During the trial, Soviet press coverage implied that the verdict was a foregone conclusion. Tass, the government's press agency, reported that the indictment "shows that in 1973-1977 Orlov engaged in anti-Soviet agitation and propaganda for the purpose of undermining and weakening Soviet power."

The trial lasted 4 days. Orlov was convicted, and he was sentenced to 7 years in prison followed by 5 years of exile in Siberia.

Adapted from news accounts by David K. Shipler in the *New York Times,* May 16-19, 1978. Copyright © by The New York Times Company 1978. Reprinted by permission.

Let us now look beyond the borders of our own country to broaden our knowledge of government and its forms and operations. The first chapter in this unit will deal with two constitutional democracies—Great Britain and France. The second chapter will deal with the Communist government of the Soviet Union.

Chapter 29

Other Forms of Democratic Government

Constitutional democracies take many different shapes and forms. Indeed, there are as many forms as there are democracies, for each nation's government reflects the peculiarities of that nation's own geography and history.

Many features of government in the United States may seem to be essential parts of any democratic government until we examine other democracies. To begin with, not all constitutional democracies are equally democratic. In some, power is highly centralized; in others, it is widely distributed. But there are other features that vary without apparent relationship to the degree of democracy practiced. In some democracies, for example, the executive branch dominates the legislative branch, while in others, the legislature is dominant.

There are a number of constitutional democracies in the world today. Some in Europe have been democracies for a century or more. Some others, like Japan and India, came to democracy only in recent decades. In this chapter, we will examine the features of two of the older democracies—Great Britain and France.

Goals

- To explore the workings of democracy in Great Britain.
- To explore the workings of democracy in France.

- *To compare British and French practices with those followed in the United States.*
- *To consider some problems of democracy in France.*

DEMOCRACY IN GREAT BRITAIN

Like the United States, Great Britain is a constitutional democracy. We have our national legislature; they have theirs. We have our Constitution; they have theirs. But government in the two nations is very different. Our Congress is one of three carefully balanced branches of the national government. In Great Britain, the legislative branch of government is supreme. Our Constitution is a document one can see and touch. Great Britain has an unwritten constitution. Learning about these and other differences may help to shed light on the unique features of our own democracy.

General Features

Great Britain is not a federal but a unitary state. In a federal government, power is shared between the national government and lower governments—in our case, the fifty states. Great Britain—which consists of England, Wales, and Scotland—is controlled from London, the capital. The chief administrative officers of Wales and Scotland are appointed in London and have their offices there. When Northern Ireland was added in 1920 to form the United Kingdom of Great Britain and Northern Ireland, it retained its own legislature. But even Northern Ireland is governed largely from London.

Great Britain does have local governments that resemble city and county governments in the United States in many ways. As we have seen, local governments in the United States are created by the states and can be changed or abolished by the state governments. In Great Britain, however, local governments are created by Parliament—which is the national legislature—and can be changed or abolished by Parliament.

Technically, Great Britain is not a republic, but a monarchy. In a republic, like the United States or France, there is no hereditary ruler. In a monarchy, like Great Britain, the position of head of state is hereditary. In practice, however, Great Britain can be said to be a republic because it is governed by an elected body of representatives in Parliament. The monarch's role is now mostly ceremonial.

Queen Elizabeth II, who became Britain's monarch upon her father's death in 1952, has very limited powers. The Queen signs official documents, but an official of the elected government must sign with her. The Queen reads an annual speech from the throne at the beginning of Parliament, but the speech is written for her by an elected official.

Unlike the President of the United States, Queen Elizabeth II is mainly a figurehead and symbolizes national unity.

Chapter 29: Other Forms of Democratic Government

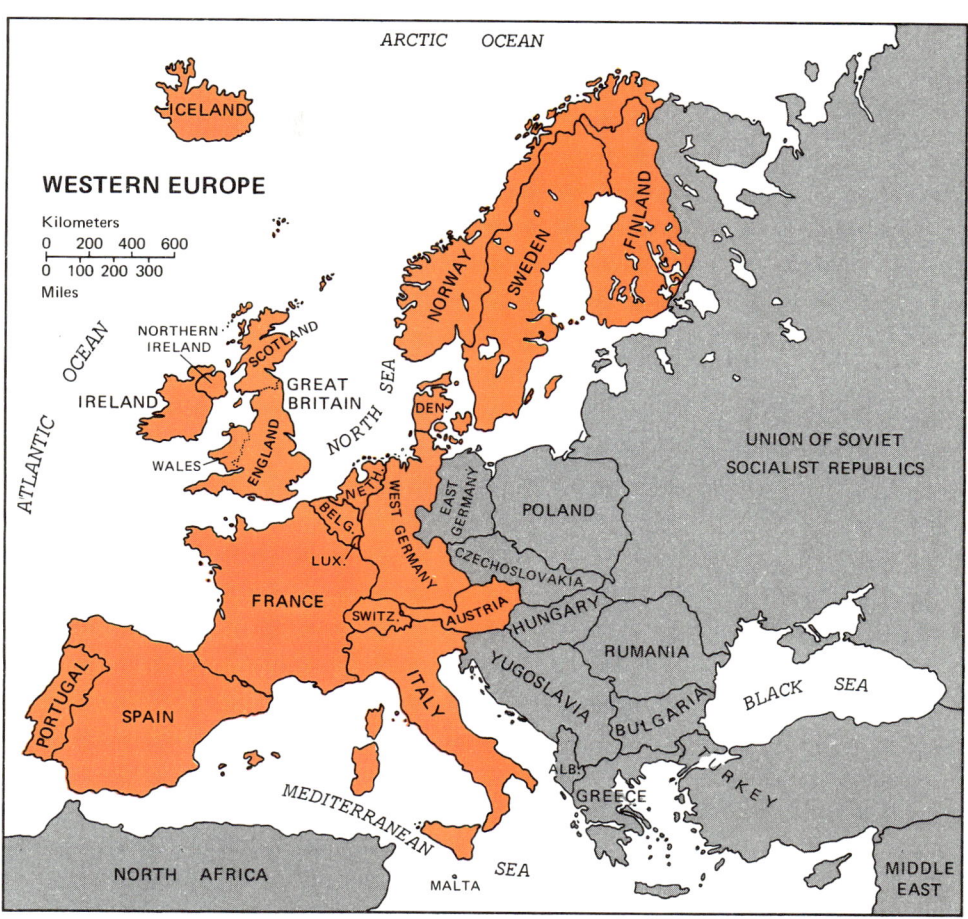

Many people look upon the Queen as a leader who is "above politics" and thus a symbol of national unity. When one elected government leaves office and is replaced by another elected government, the Queen serves as a link between them. She is the continuing authority of the British nation. This symbolic role is perhaps the most important role of the British monarch today.

Great Britain's Constitution developed over the centuries, and much of it has never been put down in writing. The Founders of our nation were departing from normal government practice when they prepared a written constitution. Most countries at that time, like Great Britain today, did not have a written constitution.

We say that the British Constitution is unwritten because no official body ever sat down and wrote out a list of rules and labeled it "constitution." The British Constitution has two parts. The first part consists of (a) the laws as passed by Parliament and interpreted by the courts and (b) important documents, such as the English Bill of Rights of 1689 (see page 35). Most of this first part of the British Constitution is, in fact, written down. The second part of the Constitution is unwritten, but no less important. This part consists of the *customs and traditions* of British government. As an example, one of these traditions is that Parliament has sessions every year. The United States Constitution not only provides for annual sessions, but names the date they are to start.

From this room—the chamber of the House of Commons—flows the power that turns the wheels of government in Great Britain.

The British Constitution is more flexible than the United States Constitution. A simple majority of Parliament could change the British Constitution just by passing a new law. Our Constitution has priority over ordinary laws. It can be amended only by taking special steps, and if three-fourths of the states approve.

In Chapter 2 (pages 30-35), we examined some of the events that led to the development of Great Britain's present constitution. As we saw, Parliament grew out of an assembly of nobles that advised the monarch. Slowly, over hundreds of years, Parliament wrested power away from the monarch.

The Role of Parliament

Parliament is the supreme authority in Great Britain today, exercising executive, legislative, and judicial powers. Leaders of the executive branch are members of Parliament and are responsible to it. If a majority of Parliament disagrees with the way the leaders are running the government, it may dismiss them. (This would be comparable to allowing a majority of Congress to vote the President of the United States out of office.) We will discuss the executive powers further when we examine the House of Commons.

Parliament is a bicameral legislature, like our Congress. Only the lower house, the House of Commons, is popularly elected. Membership in the House of Lords is largely hereditary. Both houses take part in making laws, just as in the United States. But in Great Britain the two houses are of grossly unequal strength, with the elected House of Commons dominant. For example, the House of Lords cannot prevent a bill from becoming law. It can delay a bill passed by Commons, but it cannot block a bill altogether.

Throughout the nineteenth century, the House of Lords could—and often did—veto bills passed by the House of Commons. But to many Britons this seemed undemocratic and unfair. As the right to vote was extended to more and more people, the elected members of the Commons demanded greater powers. They put an end to the Lords' veto power in 1911 and limited the Lords further by the Parliamentary Act of 1949.

In the United States, in contrast, a similar struggle ended differently. As we have seen, the Founders did not provide for popular election of the Senate. Yet they did not want a nobility, either. Rather than make the United States Senate hereditary, the Founders therefore provided that it be elected by state legisla-

527

Chapter 29: Other Forms of Democratic Government

These and other women are admitted to membership in the House of Lords only by reason of being named life peers.

tures. When demands were raised in the United States, as in Great Britain, that the national government be made more democratic, the United States solution was to make the Senate popularly elected, like the House of Representatives. This was brought about in 1913 by means of the Seventeenth Amendment to the Constitution.

There is no set limit on the size of the House of Lords. In recent years, it has had more than 1,100 members, of whom fewer than one-fourth take an active part. None of the members are paid.

Most members of the House of Lords are *peers*—nobles who inherit the right to a seat in Lords along with a noble title. Royal princes, and archbishops and senior bishops of the Church of England, are also members. Other members are *life peers*—people who are awarded peerage, or noble rank, but who cannot pass their title on to their heirs. After the title of life peer was created in 1958, women were able to be members of the House of Lords. Because its members do not run for election, the House of Lords is free of the ordinary pressures of party politics.

The House of Lords serves as the highest court for civil cases in Great Britain. It is also the highest criminal court for England, Wales, and Northern Ireland. The Law Lords are the group of members who carry out the judicial powers. The Law Lords consider only the most important cases—those that involve a point of law of "general public importance." Unlike the United States Supreme Court, the Law Lords have no original jurisdiction. All of the cases they hear have been appealed from lower courts. The judges of these lower courts are appointed by the executive branch, as are the judges of federal courts in the United States.

The chief legislative role of the House of Lords today is to provide close scrutiny of laws passed by the House of Commons. Lacking

As presiding officer of the House of Lords, the Lord Chancellor guides Parliament's upper house through debates.

Chapter 29: Other Forms of Democratic Government

the direct party pressures of the Commons, the House of Lords can sometimes suggest useful revisions. It should be noted, however, that many Britons regard the House of Lords as a useless vestige of the past. There are periodic proposals to abolish it or to convert it into an elective body. The Peerage Act of 1963 permits hereditary peers to renounce their peerage and stand for election in the House of Commons, where the true power rests.

The House of Commons is the real seat of power in the British government. It alone chooses the leaders of the British executive branch. And, if the House of Lords should balk, the Commons can pass legislation, or even change the British Constitution, on its own.

Elections and Voting

A member of the House of Commons is called an *M.P.,* which stands for "Member of Parliament." M.P.'s are elected from single-member districts, after receiving a plurality of the votes. In this respect, they are like members of the United States House of Representatives. But they differ in one important respect: M.P.'s do not necessarily live in the district they represent. A political party may nominate anyone it wants for any seat in the Commons. In the United States, members of the House are not required by law to live in the district from which they are elected, but in practice most members do.

Each election district is called a *constituency.* As a result of the most recent apportionment, there are 635 constituencies in Great Britain, and thus 635 M.P.'s. At Great Britain's present population of about 57 million, that is an average of one elected representative for every 90,000 persons. The average for the United States House of Representatives is one member for approximately every 500,000 persons.

Members of the House of Lords do not have a right to vote. All other British citizens

James Callaghan, the Labour party leader (at left), became head of the Opposition when Labour became the largest minority party.

aged 18 or over are eligible to vote, with the exception of insane persons and certain criminals. Property qualifications for voting were ended in 1918.

Candidates for Parliament must be at least 21 years old. A candidate may run as an independent, but most are nominated by political parties. In fact, British voters tend to vote

Margaret Thatcher, the Conservative party leader, was named Prime Minister because her party won the most seats in the House of Commons.

for political parties, rather than for individual candidates, to a much greater extent than United States voters.

Parliamentary elections are generally held at 5-year intervals. But the term of Parliament—unlike the term of Congress—is not fixed. An election may be called earlier by the party in power. (Technically, it is called by the monarch on the advice of the party's leader.) British political parties must be prepared for an election at any time because an election may be called on 17 days' notice.

The Government and the Opposition

The political party that is able to assemble a majority of votes in a new House of Commons takes over the executive branch of government. In Great Britain, as in the United States, most votes are divided between two strong political parties. In Great Britain, these are the Conservative party on the right and the Labour party on the left. One or the other of these parties has had a clear majority in Parliament on most occasions in recent years. However, Great Britain has a persistent third party that sometimes holds the balance of power. This is the Liberal party, which ideologically is somewhere between the other two parties. If neither of the bigger parties has a majority, then a coalition must be formed in which two parties agree on a common program and pool their votes.

Unlike United States political parties, British parties are tightly organized. The national party leaders—who are elected at a conference of delegates from local party organizations—have considerable power. A party's leaders can count on the votes of almost all of the party's members in Parliament.

Officials of the executive branch are chosen after a new Parliament is elected. The Queen invites the leader of the party with the most seats in Commons to call upon her. She designates that leader to be *Prime Minister,* or head of the executive branch. The Prime Minister then selects outstanding members of both houses of Parliament to form a Cabinet, though the most desirable Cabinet posts go to members of the Commons.

Like members of the United States Cabinet, each member of the British Cabinet is in charge of one department of the executive branch. (Since there are dozens of executive departments and only twenty or so Cabinet members, some departments are headed by lower-ranking officials.) Executive department heads are known as *ministers.* The ministers as a group are referred to as *the Government*—which is the British equivalent of our term *administration* when, for instance, we speak of a President's administration.

British Cabinet ministers *must* be members of Parliament. This is a common rule in parliamentary governments, but is contrary to practice in the United States. Under our sepa-

The front benchers on the Government side of the Commons here await the beginning of Parliament's opening day.

Chapter 29: Other Forms of Democratic Government

INSIDE THE BRITISH HOUSE OF COMMONS

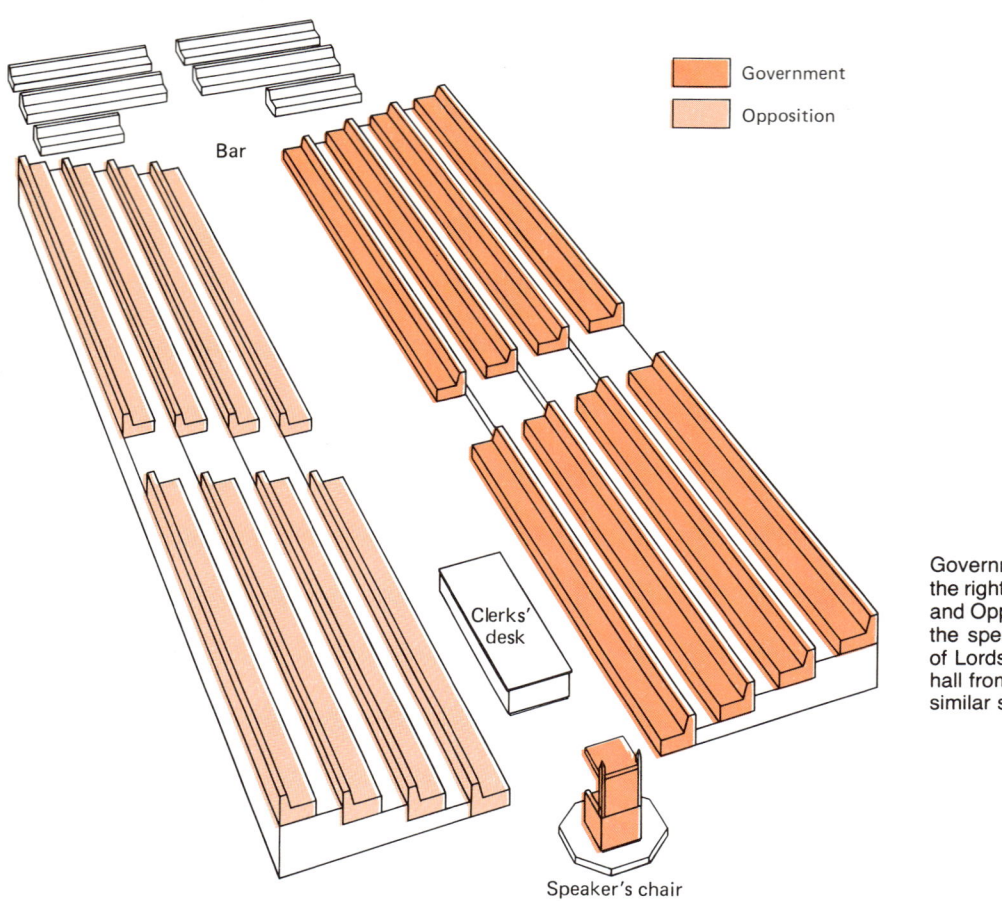

Government benches are at the right of the speaker's chair, and Opposition benches are at the speaker's left. The House of Lords, which is just down a hall from the Commons, has a similar seating plan.

ration of powers, any member of Congress who is appointed to the President's Cabinet must *resign* from Congress.

The British Constitution provides a special role for the party that is out of power. The largest minority party in the House of Commons is designated the official *Opposition*. Its leader is entitled to a salary supplement on top of an M.P.'s normal salary. One task of the Opposition leader is to choose a *shadow cabinet*—a group of members who would be the new Cabinet if the Opposition should gain a majority and be able to form a Government. The United States has nothing similar.

The Opposition plays an important role as a constant overseer and critic of the party in power. Any member of Parliament has a right to question any Government minister about public policies. The Opposition takes full advantage of this right during a 50-minute "question hour" held 4 days of every week.

The arrangement of the seating in both houses of Parliament reflects the division of this legislative body into a Government and an Opposition. Rows of benches are arranged on opposite sides of each chamber. Members of the Government party sit on one side, facing members of the Opposition party on the other side (see the plan above). Any minor-party members or independents can choose to support and sit with either the Government or the Opposition. The leaders of the Government and the Opposition sit on the front benches. Behind them are the *back-benchers,* or ordinary members of Parliament.

A Government can remain in office only so long as it holds the support—sometimes called "the confidence"—of the House of Commons. In most cases, a Government remains in office from one general election to another. But sometimes a Government party has only a small majority in the Commons. It may lose its majority if a few of its supporters switch to the Opposition, or if some of its supporters leave office and are replaced by members of the Opposition. (If an M.P. dies or resigns, a special *by-election* is held in his or her district to choose a replacement.)

Once a Government loses its majority, the Prime Minister is required to inform the monarch. The monarch then *dissolves* the House of Commons and calls a general election to choose a new Commons. Regardless of whether or not the Government loses its majority, a general election must be held within 5 years of the last one. The Prime Minister chooses the timing of the election.

The Lawmaking Process

Both houses of Parliament take part in passing legislation. Most bills are drafted by a Government minister and have the support of the Cabinet before being introduced in Parliament. This practice usually assures bills of enough support to pass. But the Government does not totally dominate the lawmaking process. M.P.'s who are not members of the Government can also introduce bills, known as *private-member bills.* Certain days are set aside for consideration of private-member bills.

A bill can start in either house, with two exceptions. Money bills must start in the House of Commons—just as they must start in our House of Representatives. Judicial bills must start in the House of Lords.

Superficially, there are many similarities between the steps through which bills go in Parliament and in Congress. In both legislative bodies, bills are referred to committees made up of members of minority and majority parties. The committees debate the bills, perhaps making changes in wording or in scope before returning a bill to the full house. Final passage requires a majority vote of the full house. The bill is then sent to the other house, which may make amendments. Sometimes the two houses negotiate until a compromise is reached.

There are also important differences between British and United States legislative practice.

Order of Procedures. In Congress, a bill is referred to a committee immediately. In Parliament, a bill is first debated by the full house. This debate covers only the bill's broad principles, not its details.

Powers of Committees. In Congress, the committees are powerful; they can kill a bill by failing to report it back to the full house. In Parliament, a committee *must* return a bill.

Specialization of Committees. In Congress, committees are specialized; each committee deals with a particular field, such as agriculture or foreign affairs. In Parliament, there are eight committees, only one of which is specialized. The one specialized committee is the Committee for Scotland, which handles bills concerning that part of Great Britain. The other committees may consider any kind of legislation.

Role of the House of Lords. In Congress, both houses must pass all bills. In Parliament, this is not so. The House of Lords has 30 days in which to consider a money bill passed by the House of Commons. After that time, the bill may become a law without the Lords' assent. All other bills ordinarily require the approval of both houses. However, sometimes a deadlock occurs and the two houses cannot agree on a bill. In that case, a bill that passes the House of Commons in two successive sessions—that is, 2 years in a row—can become law without the Lords' assent.

Veto Power. In the United States, the President may veto bills passed by Congress, and a two-thirds vote of both houses is necessary to overturn a veto. In Great Britain, *no* official has a veto. Once a bill is passed by a majority vote of Parliament, the bill receives the royal assent and becomes a law.

Role of Presiding Officers. Debates in Parliament are conducted under the supervision of a presiding officer in each house. In the Commons, this officer is elected by members of the House and is known as the Speaker of the House. Unlike the Speaker of the United States House of Representatives, this official is not a partisan leader but an impartial referee. The Speaker's job is to make rulings on points of order. In case of a tie, the Speaker casts the deciding vote.

In the House of Lords, a Cabinet officer with the title of Lord Chancellor presides. As a member of the Government, the Lord Chancellor may take an active part in debate. There is no method for breaking a tie in the House of Lords. In case of a tie, the bill is defeated.

Questions

1 What are *two* important differences between the British Constitution and the United States Constitution?

2 What is the role of the Opposition in British government?

3 Under what conditions might Parliament be dissolved?

4 How does the legislative process in Parliament differ from that in Congress?

◇ Do you think that the British system of government makes elected officials more responsible or less responsible to the voters than the United States system does? Explain.

DEMOCRACY IN FRANCE

France provides another, and quite different, example of democratic government. Like Great Britain, France is a unitary state. Paris, the capital, is the center of French government. Like the United States, France is a republic with a strong President and a written constitution. Like both countries, it has a bicameral legislature. Yet France puts these features together in its own special way. And it adds some other features, such as a constitutional provision for national referendums to give voters a direct voice on important political questions.

The Historical Background

A checkered political history has led France to its present system of government. Monarchy, dictatorship, and republican democracy have all played a part. Until the French Revolution of 1789, French kings ruled with little outside check on their powers. Though a representative assembly similar to the British Parliament appeared early in French history, French kings largely ignored it. From 1614 to 1789, the French Parliament did not meet at all. Meanwhile, France was becoming a highly centralized state with a vast bureaucracy of government officials. The French Revolution overthrew the monarchy in 1789 and introduced nearly a century of instability.

The one element of continuity after 1789 was the government bureaucracy. Kings, dictators, and republics came and went, but the bureaucracy stayed on—and its powers grew.

After the Revolution, France adopted the first of a long series of written constitutions. This Constitution of 1791 provided for a constitutional monarchy. Within 2 years, however, the king was beheaded and a new constitution established a republic. The First Republic lasted only a few years, until Napoleon Bonaparte seized power. Napoleon made France an empire and brought most of Western Europe under French rule. He also gave the French a code of laws (see page 22). But he was a dictator. When Napoleon fell from power in 1815, a king was restored. Another revolution in 1848 led to the Second Republic, but by 1851, it had given way to a dictatorship under Napoleon III,

Under De Gaulle, the French Presidency was elevated from a ceremonial position to one of power and influence.

Bonaparte's nephew. In 1871, the French established the Third Republic, which proved to be a more lasting republic. Except for the German occupation in the 1940s, during World War II, France has had democratic government ever since.

From 1871 to 1958, French government followed the British model. Parliament was strong and governing Cabinets were responsible to Parliament. The President had a ceremonial role like that of the British monarch. But what worked well for the British did not work well for the French. A major problem was the inability of the French people to fit their political ideas under the umbrellas of two or three major political parties as the people of Great Britain and the United States have done.

The French formed many small and combative political parties that had great difficulty cooperating. Governing coalitions formed and broke up, formed again and broke up again. Most French Cabinets in the years before 1958 lasted no more than 3 to 6 months. Instability was the norm; stability was the exception. The actual work of governing the country often fell to the bureaucrats, who kept their jobs from year to year.

France's present constitution, adopted in 1958, provides for a much weaker Parliament and a strong President. The year 1958 was a time of turbulence in France. The country was fighting a colonial war in Algeria, the political parties in Parliament were unable to agree on a government, and the French army was in revolt. Finally, the political parties called upon General Charles de Gaulle, a French hero of World War II, to form a government. De Gaulle put down the army revolt and devised a new constitution, one that would give him wide leeway to set French government on a new course. French voters approved De Gaulle's plan of government overwhelmingly in a national referendum. The 1958 Constitution established what is known as the Fifth French Republic.

The Role of the President

De Gaulle converted the ceremonial French Presidency into the most powerful political position in the nation. Indeed, some of his opponents maintained that De Gaulle was very close to being a dictator, even though France continued to have a free press and an outspoken political opposition. Some people thought the Presidency would lapse again into insignificance once De Gaulle left office. But that did not happen. De Gaulle resigned in 1969, and his successors have been strong Presidents.

The President is the only official elected by all French voters (there is no vice president), and thus the only one who can claim to represent the entire nation. The President is popularly elected to a term of 7 years. A majority vote is required to win the Presidency. If no candidate wins a majority in the first election, a run-off election is held 2 weeks later between the top two candidates. Presidential candidates are not expected to campaign for 3 or 4 months as in the United States.

Executive power is shared between the President and a Cabinet headed by a Prime Minister, or *Premier*. In contrast, the United States gives full executive power to its President, and Great Britain gives executive power to a Cabinet that is responsible to the House of Commons.

The French President exercises certain powers that are common to most heads of state. For example, the President may nominate individuals for high positions and may negotiate treaties with other countries. The President also serves as commander in chief of the armed forces.

In addition, the French President has two unusual powers. One of these is the power to present public issues to the nation in a referendum. In 1962, for example, De Gaulle bypassed Parliament and presented constitutional amendments directly to the people in a referendum. He won overwhelming approval. The second unusual power is the power to assume dictatorial authority if the state is "threatened in a grave and immediate manner." De Gaulle used this emergency power in 1961 to restore order when some French military leaders revolted.

The French President has considerable power over the Premier and the Cabinet. The President appoints the Premier, who in turn appoints other Cabinet ministers. (The Premier and the Cabinet are not required to win the approval of Parliament before taking office. But the lower house of Parliament may force them to resign by a majority vote.) The President may preside over meetings of the Cabinet and help to determine government policy.

So far, these provisions of the 1958 Constitution have enabled French Presidents to control national policy-making. Each President has been able to choose a Premier who was willing to play a secondary role. This has been possible largely because the Presidents were able to count on a majority of Parliament for support. All this might change if the voters should elect a Parliament that was hostile to the President. Such a Parliament would probably reject a Premier who was subservient to the President. A strong Premier might then challenge the President's leadership.

The President has one further power that might prove useful in a confrontation with Parliament—the power to dissolve the lower house and call new elections. This power may be exercised only once a year.

The French President does not have our President's power to veto a bill passed by the legislative branch. The most a French President can do is to request Parliament to reconsider a bill that it has passed.

The Premier and Cabinet

Under the Constitution, the Premier and Cabinet are responsible for setting general policies and for the day-to-day operation of government. As in the United States and Great Britain, each Cabinet member heads an executive department. As in Great Britain, Cabinet members are called *ministers,* and the Premier and Cabinet together are the Government. Unlike Great Britain, France does not allow Cabinet members to hold seats in Parliament.

The Premier and Cabinet have much more control over the legislative process than a United States President or a British Cabinet has. For example, the French Parliament's agenda is set by the Government. The bills that the Government introduces have priority. Amendments to them are severely limited. Moreover, Parliament has only a limited time to consider the budget, after which the Government may put the budget into effect by decree. In addition, members of Parliament are forbidden to propose measures that would reduce taxes or increase spending.

The Government also has a special means to win passage of its bills. It may make passage of any bill a "matter of confidence." If the Government takes that step, the bill becomes law automatically unless a majority of the lower house votes to adopt a *motion of censure* against the Government and thus forces it to resign.

The Constitution gives Parliament the power to pass laws only in certain designated fields. On all other matters, the Government can issue decrees that have the force of laws.

These members of the French Cabinet were named by the Premier, who was appointed by the President. As in the United States, each Cabinet member is head of an executive department.

This does not mean, however, that the Government has unlimited power. The leaders of Parliament or private citizens may go to court to challenge Government decrees. And Parliament has the power to dismiss a Government that abuses its powers.

The French Parliament

The French Parliament is bicameral. The Senate is the upper house and the National Assembly is the lower house. The lower house is the more powerful of the two. The French Senate is stronger than Great Britain's House of Lords, but weaker than the United States Senate.

The members of the French Senate are elected indirectly by government officials in the senatorial electoral districts and by members of the National Assembly from those districts. Senators have 9-year terms, and one-third of the Senate is elected every 3 years. The number of senators has been fixed at 292 since October 1977.

The National Assembly, like Great Britain's House of Commons and the United States Congress, is elected directly by the voters from single-member electoral districts. The Assembly members are known as *deputies*. They serve for 5-year terms, unless the President dissolves Parliament earlier and calls new elections. The present number of deputies is 491.

At times in the past, France used a system of proportional representation to elect members of the National Assembly. As we saw in Chapter 23 (page 420), proportional representation gives small political parties representation in proportion to their popular vote. Use of this system of election in the past reinforced the French tendency to have many small parties, of which none was able to win a majority of Assembly seats.

The 1958 Constitution rejected proportional representation. Voting for the National Assembly now takes place in two rounds, somewhat like United States primary and general elections. All parties may enter candidates in the first round, and any candidate who wins a majority is declared elected. If no candidate has a majority—as usually happens—a second round is held a week later. Only candidates who have won 5 percent or more of the first-round vote may participate. Between rounds, political parties sometimes strike bargains whereby one party withdraws in favor of another party's candidate.

The two-round system eliminated some smaller parties. In 1968, for the first time in French history, one party won an absolute majority in the National Assembly. This fact helped give a new stability to French politics. In

Chapter 29: Other Forms of Democratic Government

INSIDE THE CHAMBER OF THE FRENCH ASSEMBLY

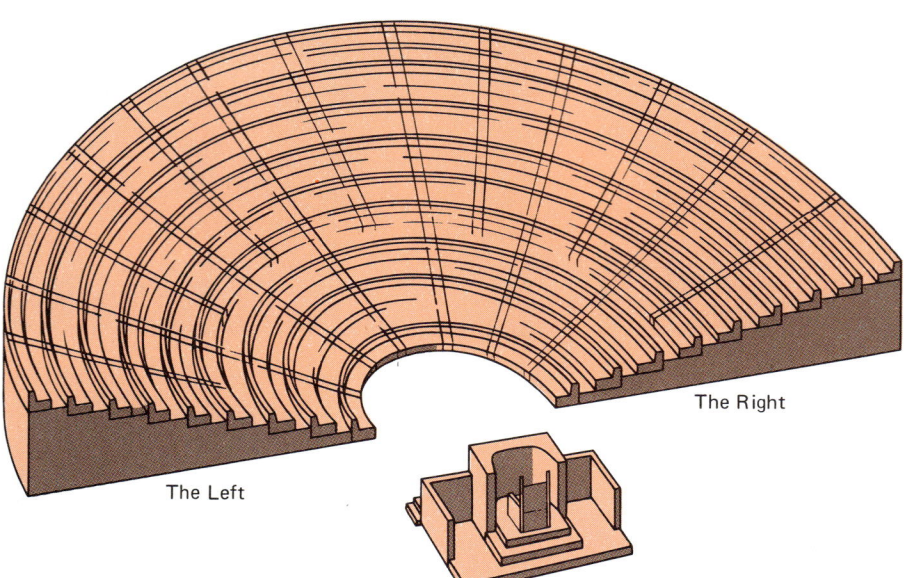

More conservative parties are seated at the right and more liberal parties at the left of the chamber. This French practice gave rise to the general use of *right* to mean conservative and *left* to mean liberal.

recent years, votes have been concentrated on four parties—two on the right and the Socialists and the Communists on the left. The left has a more stable party structure than most of the other political parties.

The French Parliament meets for five and a half months each year, in two sessions. Either the Premier or a majority of the National Assembly may call a special session to deal with a specific item of business. No other matters may be considered at a special session.

Both houses must consider all bills with the object of agreeing on an identical text. In case of a deadlock, the Premier appoints a conference committee containing an equal number of members from each house. If a compromise cannot be worked out, the Premier can either let the bill die or request the National Assembly to make a final decision on the bill. Thus, a bill may be passed without the Senate's approval.

Like the British Parliament, the French Parliament has a limited number of standing committees, and they are not specialized. There are six in each house.

There is no salaried opposition leader in the French Parliament, mainly because of the fragmentation of political party strength. Political parties that support the Government are referred to as "the majority," and all other parties are considered to be "the opposition."

Only the National Assembly has the power to force a Government's resignation. The Assembly can do this by passing a motion of censure, which requires an absolute majority of all deputies—not just of those voting. The Constitution seeks to assure that the National Assembly will initiate only one censure motion in each session of Parliament. But other censure votes may occur when the Government makes a bill a "matter of confidence," as mentioned earlier.

To sum up, the French political structure is designed to encourage government stability in a country that has known much instability in its past. Because of historical conditions, as we have seen, democracy in France differs in many respects from democracy in Great Britain, which in turn differs in many ways from democracy in the United States. We will study a very different type of government—Communist government—in the next chapter.

Questions

1 How long has France had a republican form of government?

2 When was the present French Constitution adopted?

3 Explain this statement: "The Fifth Republic is the first to establish a strong presidency."

4 What are the responsibilities of the Premier and Cabinet in France?

5 In the French system, what is meant by the term *the Government?*

◌ Do you think that the United States would benefit by having a multiple party system like the one in France? Explain.

PROBLEM: WHAT WERE THE WEAKNESSES OF THE FOURTH FRENCH REPUBLIC?

France's Fourth Republic was short-lived. It was created in 1946, after the end of World War II and the German occupation of the country. For the next dozen years, government leaders came and went, as if getting on and off a carousel. Eventually the music stopped; the government machinery no longer worked. In 1958, the French people made a fresh beginning with a Fifth Republic, under a new constitution.

The political history of France during the Fourth Republic is a classic example of government instability. An examination of the Cabinet system under the Fourth Republic is therefore worthwhile. As you read the following selection, ask yourself:

- *What were the weaknesses of the Fourth Republic?*
- *What caused those weaknesses?*

The Constitution of the Fourth Republic was sharply criticized throughout its short life. Critics said that the governmental machinery of the Fourth Republic was dominated by lobbies that were incapable of making needed decisions and unresponsive to its leaders.

The Constitution gave supreme power to Parliament—especially to the lower house, the National Assembly. The Premier and the Cabinet governed as long as they had majority support in the National Assembly. The President of the Republic was elected by Parliament and was head of state only in title. Premiers came and went with disturbing frequency as the majorities shifted back and forth in the National Assembly. The 12 years of the Fourth Republic saw twenty Cabinets form and dissolve.

This Cabinet instability had one basic cause: there were too many political parties. But the instability was made worse by another fact. The Premier could not dissolve the National Assembly unless two consecutive Cabinet crises had occurred within a period of 18 months. A Cabinet "crisis" was defined as the overthrow of the Cabinet by an *absolute majority* on certain occasions: (1) when the Premier asked for a vote of confidence, and (2) when the Assembly voted a motion of censure. These conditions for dissolution were not observed. Cabinets suffered defeat after defeat by narrow votes. They were forced to withdraw without being allowed to retaliate by dissolving the National Assembly and calling for a new election. Only five Governments under the Fourth Republic fell by absolute majority on the question of confidence.

Other procedures also helped give the Assembly the upper hand. The committees in the National Assembly had sweeping powers. They could pigeonhole bills, amend them at will, or rewrite them. It was the committee version of a bill—not the version proposed by the Government—that came on the floor for debate. The agenda of the National Assembly was prepared by the leaders of the various parliamentary groups. These powerful leaders sidetracked important governmental proposals with which they disagreed. Wrangles over the "order of business" became sharp political conflicts. Often the Cabinet had to risk a vote of confidence on this purely procedural question.

Since there was no majority party at any time during the Fourth Republic, all Cabinets were coalition Cabinets. They were composed of the leaders of many parliamentary groups and parties. Divisions in the Assembly were so sharp that forming a Cabinet was like trying to sign a treaty among warring nations.

When a Cabinet fell, the President of the Republic asked one political leader (L) to attempt to get other political leaders to take part in a new Cabinet. If L succeeded, the President would probably ask L to head the Cabinet. L would then appear before the National Assembly to spell out a plan or program. If L received majority approval, L would become Premier and preside over a coalition Cabinet. If L failed to get majority approval, the whole process would have to be repeated.

In a long-drawn-out crisis, the President of the Republic would call together all former Premiers and the leaders of all parliamentary groups. They would try to reach enough agreement to form a Cabinet. These meetings would go on until some agreement was reached, and a new Cabinet was created.

No Cabinet lasted for long. Within months, if not weeks, small parliamentary groups would usually leave the Government majority. The defection of forty or so members of the National Assembly was usually enough to bring down the Cabinets of the Fourth Republic. A small group of members thus constituted a powerful veto bloc. The life of the Government depended on them. This small bloc could demand concessions from the Cabinet and impose conditions far out of relation to its size.

Cabinet instability did have at least one positive aspect in a system where party and ideological divisions were so deep. It provided access to top positions for many ambitious politicians. Thus it reduced the intensity of the conflict between parties. A political leader had but to wait a turn for a high post. The Cabinet "crises" allowed many persons to join and leave the Cabinet without requiring any real change in policy. Only occasionally did a crisis bring a genuine shift in policy.

Why were the institutions of the Fourth Republic what they were? The answer is that they reflected the basic realities of French society. The Cabinets came and went because there was no agreement among the people of France on many issues. Political parties were many, and a majority was difficult to find simply because many ideological currents were stirring the country. Compromise was difficult. The "weakness" stemmed directly from the conflicts within the society and not from the governmental institutions alone.

Roy C. Macridis and Robert E. Ward (eds.), *Modern Political Systems: Europe,* copyright © 1963, pp. 194-202. Adapted by permission of Prentice-Hall, Inc., Englewood Cliffs, N.J.

Questions

1 What were two reasons why French Cabinets in the Fourth Republic lasted so briefly?

2 What problems did the frequent changes cause?

3 How has the Fifth Republic tried to eliminate these weaknesses?

Do you think that the system used during the Fourth Republic might have worked in a country with fewer party divisions than France? Explain.

Chapter 29 Review

Recalling and Comparing

1 How does the executive branch of government in Great Britain differ from the executive branch in the United States?

2 Why is the House of Commons considered the more important of the two houses of the British Parliament?

3 How does the House of Lords differ from the House of Commons?

4 Compare and contrast the way in which a bill becomes a law in Great Britain, France, and the United States.

5 Describe the process by which a British Government is formed. How long does a Government normally stay in power? In what circumstances might its term be shorter?

6 Briefly compare the type of constitution in Great Britain and in the United States.

7 How did the development of government in France differ from its development in Great Britain?

Special Activities

1 Consult your local library and prepare a report on how parliamentary government works in Japan, India, Israel, or Sweden.

2 Make a bulletin-board display of news articles about elections and parliamentary activities in foreign democracies.

3 Prepare a skit to show how a bill would become a law in either Great Britain or France. Have class members act out the skit.

4 Make a study of the student riots in France in 1968, the apparent causes, and the political aftermath of the riots. Report your findings to the class.

5 Consider what might be arguments for and against the following statement: "The United States President and Cabinet should have to resign if they lose majority support in Congress." Do you agree or disagree? Why?

Developing Your Political Vocabulary

Match each term in *a-g* with the best definition or example in 1-7.

the Government	**a**	**1**	person who presides over House of Lords
minister	**b**	**2**	top executive branch officials in a parliamentary government
shadow cabinet	**c**	**3**	an M.P. who is not a leader
by-election	**d**	**4**	special election to fill a vacancy
back-bencher	**e**	**5**	top leaders of Great Britain's Opposition
Lord Chancellor	**f**	**6**	head of British or French executive department
motion of censure	**g**	**7**	a vote to force a Cabinet's resignation

Chapter 30

Communist Government

Until now, we have been discussing what are commonly called constitutional democracies. *They operate under constitutions that limit the power of government. Constitutions were first developed to check the power of kings. Today, in democratic nations, constitutions serve as a check on the power of elected governments. Rules and procedures are established through the constitution in order to protect the people against the arbitrary exercise of government power.*

Communist nations have a different term for this kind of government. Instead of constitutional democracy, they call it bourgeois democracy. *The word* bourgeois *(boor-ZHWAH) means "middle class." The label* bourgeois democracy *implies that our form of democracy serves only the interests of the middle and the upper classes—property owners, business people, and others who are well off.*

Communists call their own system of government proletarian democracy. *A* proletarian *(pro-li-TAIR-ee-un) is a member of the working class—someone who must work for another person in order to live. Proletarian democracy is a revealing term. It stakes out the claim that the Communist system serves only the interests of the working class. Whether "proletarian democracy" is either proletarian or democratic is very much open to question. In fact, most political experts in non-Communist*

Chapter 30: Communist Government

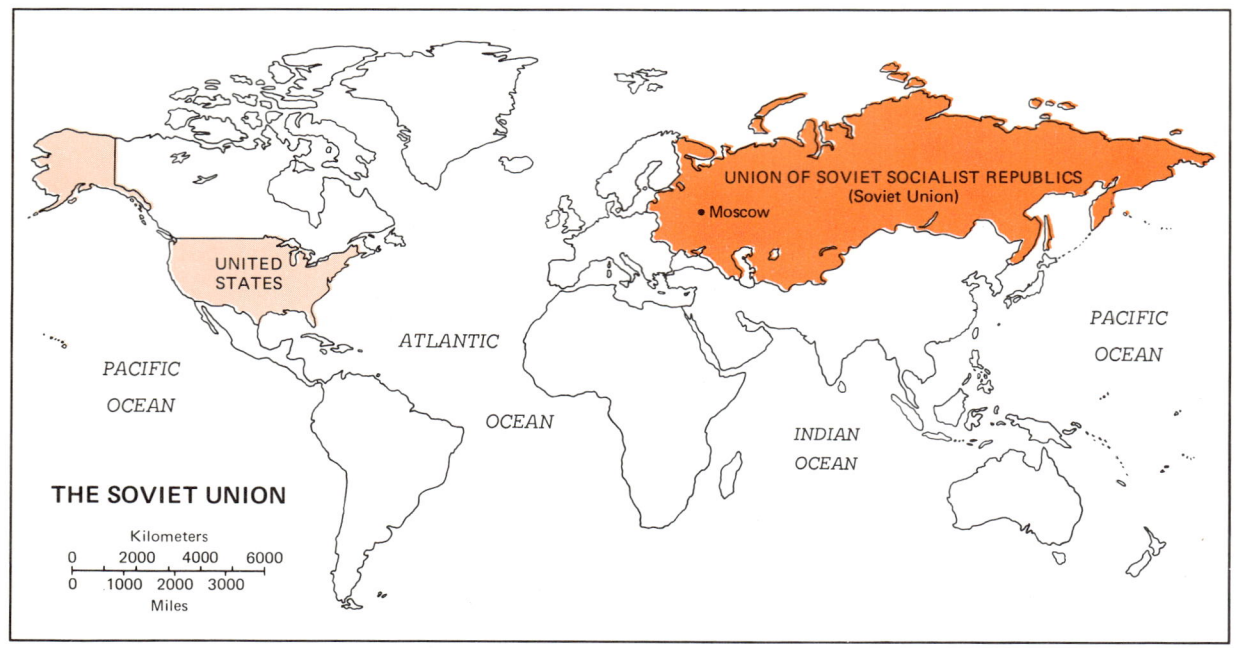

THE SOVIET UNION

countries consider Communist government to be highly undemocratic, for it puts no check on the power of the state over the individual—whatever the individual's economic class.

In this chapter, we will explore the way that Communist government works in one country—the U.S.S.R., which is commonly called the Soviet Union. The Soviet government is the oldest Communist government, dating to 1917. It therefore served as a model for later Communist governments. However, Communist government is now available in several varieties. The Communist government of China differs in many ways from the Soviet government. The Communist governments of Cuba, Vietnam, and Yugoslavia also have features all their own.

Goals

- To study the workings of the Soviet government, including how it is supposed to work and how it works in practice.
- To examine the relationship between the Communist party and the formal government bodies in the Soviet Union.
- To consider the extent of protection of individual rights in the Soviet Union.

THE SOVIET SYSTEM

The Soviet Union, which straddles the continent of Asia and dominates Eastern Europe, covers one-sixth of the world's land area. The 262,000,000 people who live in this vast area include more than sixty language groups whose ethnic and religious backgrounds are extremely varied. The official language of the nation is Russian, and we commonly refer to the people as Russians. However, the term *Russia,* which is sometimes used in place of U.S.S.R. or Soviet Union, actually refers to only one part of the Soviet state. That part—which is Russia proper—occupies three-fourths of the nation's land area and includes about half of its people. Moscow is the capital of Russia proper and of the entire nation. Russia is

Chapter 30: Communist Government

also the common name of the Russian Empire that was replaced by the Soviet Union.

What kind of nation is the Soviet Union? Its formal name, the Union of Soviet Socialist Republics (U.S.S.R.), gives us the official Communist version. First, the name declares the U.S.S.R. to be a *union of republics*—that is, a federal state composed of several republics. (There are fifteen of them.) Second, the name declares that the U.S.S.R. is a *socialist* state—a nation in which the means of production are owned by the government. Third, the name asserts that the U.S.S.R. is a *soviet* state—that is, a nation with a representative government. (The Russian word *soviet* means "council.")

In fact, however, the name Union of Soviet Socialist Republics can be misleading. First, the Soviet Union is more like a unitary state than like a federal system such as ours. The fifteen separate republics that make up the nation do not have any "reserved powers." They have little if any *autonomy* (aw-TON-uh-me), or freedom to act independently.

Second, the Soviet Union is indeed socialist in the strict economic sense. The government owns all land, the basic industries, and nearly all businesses, including farms, local stores, hotels, and restaurants. Politically, however, Soviet socialism differs greatly from democratic socialism. In some countries of Western Europe, for example, socialism operates within a framework of constitutional democracy and limited government powers. Government power is unchecked in the Soviet

Celebrations like this wedding give rise to displays of old ethnic traditions and styles of dress. Despite the political uniformity of its people, the Soviet Union has a great variety of ethnic groups within its borders.

Out of every successful revolution comes a leader, and out of the Bolshevik Revolution came Lenin. His view of Marxism and his use of power became both the model and the inspiration for later leaders of the Soviet Union.

Union—a characteristic that has come to be typical of Communist nations but not of other socialist nations.

Third, while Soviet governing councils are elected, political parties do not openly compete in elections as they do in constitutional democracies. Soviet government is dominated by one party—the Communist party.

The present government of the Soviet Union grew out of a revolution in 1917 against the authoritarian rule of the czar (pronounced zar). The czar was a monarch who ruled an empire centered in Russia but spreading across many nearby lands. In many respects, the Russian Empire was a relic of feudal times. Though the Russian farm workers had been freed from serfdom in 1861, they had few rights and lived in ignorance and poverty. Most city dwellers were only a little better off. Revolts were frequent. After a brief revolt in 1905, the czar had permitted the creation of a national legislature, but a weak one. It did little for the average Russian. When a revolution overthrew the czar in 1917, two out of three Russians still did not know how to read or write.

The monarchy was replaced by a moderate government at first. But in November of 1917 a second upheaval, known as the Bolshevik Revolution, brought a different government to power. This government was run by the *Bolsheviks* (BOHL-shuh-viks), who were the radical, majority group of Communists. (*Bolshevik* means "one of the majority.") The leader of the Bolshevik party was a revolutionary named Vladimir Ilyich Ulyanov, but called Lenin.

Lenin had spent more than 20 years working toward this revolution. He had studied the ideas of Karl Marx (whose economic theories will be discussed in Chapter 33) and had added his own interpretations of some points. Once in power, Lenin began to put his beliefs into practice. The resulting system of ideas, known as *Marxism-Leninism,* was the inspiration for all later Communist governments.

The central theory of Marxism-Leninism is that world history is moving inevitably towards a form of government called *communism,* in which all people will be equal and governments will no longer be needed. At that point the state will "wither away." According to the theory, bourgeois democracy—our type of democracy—is one step on the way from feudalism to communism. The next step is socialism, which is the step at which the Soviet Union considers itself to be. According to Marxist-Leninist theory, the Communist party will lead the way to the next and final step, true communism.

The new Communist government met resistance on many sides. When it took power, Russia was engaged in the First World War, as an ally of Great Britain and France. Russia had suffered millions of casualties. One of Lenin's first acts was to take Russia out of the war. But fighting continued within the Russian Empire between supporters and opponents of the Bolsheviks. Military forces were sent to the country by Poland, Great Britain, France, the United States, and Japan to fight the Communists. The foreign intervention, which lasted until 1920, left many Russians with the feeling that the world was against them.

As Russia weakened, neighboring countries tried to seize territory, and some parts of the old empire demanded independence. From the first, Lenin declared that Russia had no wish to rule any peoples against their will. But, while he renounced the idea of an empire, he did not want to lose such rich areas as the Ukraine, one of the most productive sections of the old Russian Empire. By a mixture of persuasion and force, the Communists linked several parts of the old empire with Russia in 1924 to create the U.S.S.R. This union was the beginning of Soviet-style federalism.

Meanwhile, the Communists were developing a system of representative government. Workers' councils, or soviets, had sprung up during the Revolution. Many of these soviets began as strike committees in factories. In some places, representatives from several factory soviets formed a citywide soviet.

Lenin converted these soviets into a network of elected councils resembling legislatures. Voters elected soviets for each factory, village, and city. Indirectly elected soviets were established at higher levels. At the top was a soviet for the nation as a whole. Real power did not rest with the soviets, however, but with the Communist party and the leaders at the top of the government.

After Lenin's death in 1924, a new leader gradually appeared and increased his power until he ruled as dictator. His name was Joseph Stalin, and he ruled until his death in 1953. Stalin applied harsh policies in order to industrialize the Soviet Union and increase food

Stalin succeeded Lenin in 1924 and ruled with an iron fist until 1953. Later he was denounced for his reign of terror.

production. His methods were ruthless. Millions who opposed Stalin's policies lost their lives or were exiled to Siberia. Somewhat milder policies were followed by Stalin's successors, especially Nikita Khrushchev.

Constitutional Rights, Freedoms, and Duties

The Soviet Union functions under a written constitution, as the United States and France do. The Soviet Constitution is not only a legal framework of government, but also a propaganda document. An official translation of the Russian document is sold all over the world. Parts of the Constitution are hard to understand because some Russian terms have no exact equivalent in English.

We in the United States have had one constitution for 200 years, though we have amended it from time to time. The Soviet Union has completely replaced its constitution three times in 60 years. The first Soviet constitution was written in 1918. A new constitution was written in 1924. In the 1930s, Stalin formed a committee to draw up another constitution, which was adopted in 1936. Forty years later, the Soviet leaders felt it was time to write a fourth constitution. The new "fundamental law" was adopted on October 7, 1977. This document is worth examining, both for some of the things it says and for some of the things it does not say.

The Soviet Constitution speaks of the basic "rights, freedoms, and duties" of citizens (Articles 39–69). The emphasis, however, is on economic and social rights—for example, the right to a job and the right to free medical service. Ten articles describe various duties, including military service, protection of state property, "conscientious work in a socially useful occupation," and respect for the dignity of other citizens.

The Soviet Constitution also guarantees traditional civil liberties. Among these are the following:

Citizens of the U.S.S.R., in accordance with the aims of building communism, are guaranteed freedom of scientific, technical, and artistic work. . . . (Article 47).

Every citizen of the U.S.S.R. has the right to submit proposals to state bodies and public organizations for improving their activity, and to criticize shortcomings in their work. . . . Persecution for criticism is prohibited. . . . (Article 49).

In accordance with the interests of the people and in order to strengthen and develop the socialist system, citizens of the U.S.S.R. are guaranteed freedom of speech, of the press, and of assembly, meetings, street processions, and demonstrations. . . . (Article 50).

Citizens of the U.S.S.R. are guaranteed freedom of conscience, that is, the right to profess or not to profess any religion, and to conduct religious worship or atheistic propaganda. Incitement of hostility or hatred on religious grounds is prohibited. . . . (Article 52).

Respect for the individual and protection of the rights and freedoms of citizens are the duty of all state bodies, public organizations and officials. . . . (Article 57).

Constitution (Fundamental Law) of the Union of Soviet Socialist Republics, adopted October 7, 1977, Novosti Press Agency Publishing House, Moscow, 1977.

Notice that freedom of speech and assembly and freedom of the press are guaranteed in order to "develop the socialist system." There is no freedom to challenge that system. Again and again, Soviet citizens have been prosecuted for speaking out publicly against the policies of their government. The press must answer to a censorship board. The government owns or tightly controls most news media. The Communist party appoints the officials of Tass, the Soviet news agency, which has a monopoly on the distribution of news. The Soviet Union also has had a long record of religious repression.

There is no independent judiciary in the Soviet Union that might protect individual rights. The courts, like other parts of the government, are dominated by the all-powerful Communist party. The courts can do little to protect Soviet citizens against abuses of rights by the police or other government agencies.

As in Great Britain, none of the courts may overrule a law, so they do not have the power or independence that courts in the United States have. City judges are elected by secret ballot, but "people's assessors" are elected by citizens at their places of work or residence "by a show of hands." These assessors, who are not expected to have legal training, are entitled to share in making the court's decision. Judges on higher courts are elected by the soviets of cities and districts, and judges on the nation's Supreme Court are elected by the Supreme Soviet of the U.S.S.R. Since the Communist party dominates the soviets that elect the judges on appellate courts, there is no chance that a judge who is not in sympathy with the aims of the party would be elected.

Other Broad Constitutional Provisions

The monopoly position of the Communist party is a prominent feature of the Soviet Constitution. No other political party is allowed. In the United States, Great Britain, and France, the clash of opposing parties is considered to be a natural means of resolving conflicts of interest. The official Soviet view, on the other hand, is that conflicts of interest are being overcome under Communist rule. The Communist party, in the official view, represents the interests of the entire society. Article 6 states:

> The leading and guiding force of Soviet society and the nucleus of its political system, of all state organizations and public organizations, is the Communist Party of the Soviet Union.

It is important to know that party membership is not a matter of individual choice as in a democracy. One must be nominated, trained, and go through a trial period to join the Communist party in the Soviet Union.

The Soviet Constitution describes the economic system to be followed in the Soviet Union. The first article, after a preamble, declares the Soviet Union to be "a socialist state." Later articles declare that the land; the basic means of production in industry, construction, and agriculture; as well as banks and other businesses are owned either by the state or by *collectives*—that is, cooperative groups. Individual enterprise is allowed only on the smallest scale. The Soviet economic system will be described more fully in Chapter 33.

The 1977 Constitution reaffirms the federal form of the Soviet state. Of the present fifteen republics, the largest is the Russian Soviet Federative Socialist Republic. Some of the fifteen republics are divided into smaller units—autonomous republics, autonomous regions, and autonomous areas. Each of these divisions is the home of a distinct nationality, with its own language and cultural traditions.

Voting and Elections

So far, we have been discussing the Soviet system only in broad terms. Let us now turn to some of the specifics. First we will look at the voting process, and then at the structure of government.

Soviet voters are generally presented with a ballot containing the name of only one candidate for each office. The voter may either cross out the name or leave it. A candidate is elected unless 50 percent of the voters cross out the candidate's name. Not suprisingly, few candidates fail to be elected. New elections are held to fill any positions that are empty because of the defeat of candidates.

Before the election, candidates are nominated at open meetings held by local units of the Communist party, cooperative societies, labor unions, and youth organizations. Often, the same candidate is nominated by these

Soviet citizens at the polls. Under a huge portrait of Lenin, these voters are casting their votes for or against the one candidate for each office that needs to be filled. The ballots are marked by hand and dropped into boxes.

groups. If more than one person is named, the groups' leaders meet to select only one. Candidates are not required to be members of the Communist party, but they may not oppose its policies. Three out of four candidates *are* party members.

Formal requirements for candidates are not elaborate. A candidate for the highest-level soviet must be at least 21 years old. All other candidates must be at least 18 years old. Residence in a district is not a requirement for election from that district.

All Soviet citizens who have reached the age of 18 are eligible to vote. Only people who have been legally certified as insane are ineligible, according to Article 96.

Voting is conducted by paper ballot. Each voter is handed one ballot. Most voters merely fold the ballot and drop it into the ballot box. A voter who wishes to cross out a name on the ballot may do so in the privacy of a booth. Thus, while the voting may be secret, officials can easily spot anyone who is voting against the candidate offered.

Since the voters have no choice of candidates for a particular office, elections do not serve the same purpose in the Soviet Union as they do in our own country. But Soviet elections serve other important functions. For one thing, they provide an occasion for the government to explain its policies to the people. For 2 months before an election, candidates make speeches, telling people what the government is doing and why. Newspapers, radio, and television, under the close control of the Communist party, are filled with reports of the campaign.

Soviet elections also provide an occasion to rally support for the government. Though the Constitution speaks of voting as a "right," voting is treated as a duty. Typically, 99 percent of the voters go to the polls. Failure to vote is a serious matter that may be reported to the police.

Government as Outlined in the Constitution

The formal structure of Soviet government resembles a pyramid, with elected bodies at each level. These elected bodies are the soviets, and the system of soviets makes up the legislative branch of government. There is no balancing of powers among legislative, executive, and judicial branches as in the United States. Instead, the legislative branch is supreme—except, of course, that basic policies are set by the Communist party, not by the soviets.

On an election day, the Soviet voter may be asked to cast a ballot for officials at as many as six different levels of government. At the bottom are local soviets for each village, ward, and city. Next highest are district soviets, then regional soviets, then the soviets of autonomous regions or areas. Above these are the soviets of the republics. And finally there is the Supreme Soviet, the Soviet Union's equivalent of a national legislature. All of the soviets except the Supreme Soviet are unicameral bodies. The Supreme Soviet is a two-house legislature elected every 5 years.

The Supreme Soviet, or national legislature, has a very limited role in making policy. It meets for only a brief period twice a year, and its sessions are marked by many speeches but little or no debate. Most of the Supreme Soviet's power is delegated to two committees that run the government between sessions. These committees—the Presidium of the Supreme Soviet and the Council of Ministers—will be discussed shortly.

The two houses of the Supreme Soviet have "equal rights," and each house has about half of the total membership of 1,500 to 1,600. One house, the *Soviet of the Union,* has a varying number of members. They are directly elected from single-member electoral districts of 300,000 population. The other house, the *Soviet of Nationalities,* has a fixed membership of 750. Each national group has an allotment of members, who are directly elected.

In theory, the Supreme Soviet controls the two committees at the top of the Soviet government. But in practice, power is organized from the top down. This is true both of the Soviet government and of the Communist party. Each level of the government and the party is subordinate to the level immediately above.

The Presidium of the Supreme Soviet and the Council of Ministers are the two highest divisions of Soviet government. They exercise full power when the Supreme Soviet is not in session. Each can issue decrees that have the force of law. Commonly, the Supreme Soviet at its next session goes through the motions of formally adopting the decrees as laws.

The Presidium of the Supreme Soviet carries out executive, legislative, and judicial duties. It can ratify treaties, appoint ambassadors and military officers, issue decrees, and interpret laws. The Presidium is a committee of thirty-eight members elected every 5 years by the Supreme Soviet. The Presidium elects a chairperson who is commonly referred to as the President of the Soviet Union but who is as much a figurehead as the British monarch is.

The Council of Ministers is, in the words of the Constitution, "the Government." The

At this meeting of the Supreme Soviet, both houses are present. The members are voting, by a show of hands, on the candidate for head of the Presidium of the Supreme Soviet. The vote of the more than 1,500 members was unanimous.

chairperson of the Council of Ministers is the actual head of government, and is commonly called the *Premier.*

Like cabinets in Great Britain and France, the Council of Ministers includes the heads of executive departments of government. It also includes the heads of the fifteen republics and of various other lower-level governments. According to the Constitution, the Council of Ministers is appointed by the Supreme Soviet (Article 129), but the Presidium may dismiss and appoint Council members between sessions of the Supreme Soviet (Article 122). The Council is responsible to the Supreme Soviet, but to the Presidium between sessions (Article 130).

The Council of Ministers has far greater powers than either a United States President or a British or French Cabinet. The powers of the Council of Ministers are shared in our country by the President, Congress, the states, and private businesses and labor unions.

Because the Council of Ministers is so large and unwieldly, many of its decisions are made by a smaller committee headed by the Premier. This committee, which is the *Presidium of the Council of Ministers,* is responsible for much of the day-to-day direction of Soviet government. Most of its members are high-ranking officials of the Communist party.

Questions

1 What are soviets?
2 How is a member of a soviet elected to office?
3 What are the levels of government in the Soviet Union?
4 What roles are played by the Presidium of the Supreme Soviet and the Council of Ministers?

⌂ In some general elections in the United States, the ballot may contain the name of only one candidate for an office. Do you consider this democratic? Explain.

THE ROLE OF THE COMMUNIST PARTY IN THE SOVIET UNION

The real source of political power in the Soviet Union is not the government, but the Communist party. Since 1917, the leadership of party and government has overlapped, but the party has had final authority. It is the party that decides policy matters. In a sense, the government serves as the administrative arm of the party.

The Communist party is a small, elite group within Soviet society. Its membership is estimated to be 16,200,000, one-fourth of whom are women. This membership is about 9 percent of the voting-age population. It is sometimes pointed out that roughly the same percentage of United States citizens take part in politics by helping in political campaigns, contributing money, or in other ways. But political participation works very differently in the two countries.

In the United States, as we saw in Chapter 23, there is no central control even within political parties. Politics in the Soviet Union is highly centralized. Major decisions are made at the top level of the party, and lower-level party members are expected to carry them out without question. The Soviet Union calls this arrangement *democratic centralism.*

Soviet citizens join the Communist party for different reasons. Many firmly believe that the goals of the party are in the best interests of the Soviet Union. Many others join because party membership helps to win advancement within Soviet society and may provide economic rewards as well.

These members of the Young Communist League are being prepared for membership in the Communist party. As part of their training, and as a way of showing their dedication, they have formed a youth tractor team for their village.

Most young people who hope to join the party begin by enlisting in *Komsomol,* the Communist youth organization, often referred to as the *Young Communist League.* About one-third of Soviet citizens between the ages of 14 and 28 belong to the Young Communist League. One purpose of the League is to build moral values, among them respect for authorities, good manners, and hard work. Another purpose is recreational. Members participate in athletics, dramatics, and hiking, for instance. But the main purpose is political socialization (page 15). The Young Communist League is supposed to create the "ideal" Soviet citizen—patriotic, loyal, and eager to become a party member.

Only the most dedicated persons are accepted for party membership. All applicants must be willing to devote evenings and weekends to party work. Particularly valued are people who have distinguished themselves in school or at work. No one is forced to join. Indeed, the application process can be rugged.

An applicant must be at least 18 years old, but an applicant who is under 23 must be a member of the Young Communist League. Each applicant must be sponsored by three party members and must undergo a thorough background check. If successful, the applicant will then become a *party candidate,* or a member on probation, for a year or longer. A party candidate shares in the party's activities and is given many tasks that will help to show how valuable a party member the candidate will be.

Each party member belongs to a primary party organization, formerly called a party cell. Any place where there are three or more party members—a factory, a government office, a school, a store, a village, a collective farm, a unit of the armed forces—has a primary party organization. There are probably 350,000 of these in the Soviet Union today. Such a group may have up to 3,000 members, but the average size is about 40.

Primary party organizations are responsible for a number of activities, but in general they serve as the party's watchdogs. At the time of Lenin's takeover in 1917, the Communist party was small and had few experienced administrators. Many non-Communists had to fill important positions in industry, agriculture, and government. To keep an eye on these people, party members were assigned as watchdogs.

Today, even though party members fill most managerial positions, the watchdog function remains. Party members make sure that factory managers meet their quotas and that workers do not slack off. In addition, party members serve in other ways. For example, they see to it that hardworking employees receive special vacation privileges, that day care is available for working mothers, and that government officials respond to local needs. Thus, party members perform functions that in our country are performed by many separate individuals—factory supervisors, community workers, political party officials, and the press, among others.

Above the primary party organization, the Communist party is organized on a territorial basis. Each of the governing units within the Soviet Union has a party organization. Moving upward from the primary level, you will find a party organization in each ward, city, district, region, and republic. At the top of the party pyramid is the party organization for the entire Soviet Union.

Each level of party organization from the basic organization to the top is structured like a pyramid. The organizational pyramid at each level consists of (1) a conference or congress resembling a party legislature, (2) an executive committee, (3) a bureau or presidium, and (4) a secretariat that runs the party bureaucracy.

In theory, each conference or congress elects the conference or congress at the level just above. But the conferences or congresses meet infrequently. Between meetings, they delegate their power to the executive commit-

This All-Union Party Congress, which meets every four years, will choose the members of the Communist party's Central Committee. The Central Committee, in turn, will choose the members of the Politburo and the Secretariat.

tees. These committees, in turn, delegate their power to the bureaus, and they delegate their power to the secretariats. Thus, the Communist party operates on the same principle of rule from the top down, or "democratic centralism," that the government does. Final decisions are made by a few individuals.

According to Soviet theory, "the supreme organ of the Communist party of the Soviet Union" is the *All-Union Party Congress*. This is an assembly of some 5,000 persons that meets in Moscow once every 4 years. (During the Stalin era, it did not meet at all from 1939 to 1952.) The main function of the Party Congress is to elect a *Central Committee*.

Though most of the important decisions of the party are taken in the name of the Central Committee, this committee delegates most of its authority between sessions. The real power is concentrated in two party bodies elected by the Central Committee. One is the *Politburo* (political bureau), also called "the party presidium." The other is the *Secretariat*.

The Politburo is the most important decision-making unit of the Communist party. Though its decisions can be overturned by the Central Committee, it is up to the Politburo to deal with important problems. The Politburo is supposed to make the needed compromises between conflicting interests.

The close relation between party and government in the Soviet Union is revealed by the overlapping memberships in the party Politburo and the government Presidium. The Politburo has only 15 to 25 members. Yet, from the beginning, every Presidium of the Supreme Soviet has been headed by a member of the party Politburo. The Premier and other members of the Council of Ministers have also been members of the Politburo. From clues like these, observers have concluded that the Politburo is the true ruling body in the Soviet Union.

Despite the Politburo's power, the most powerful individual in the Soviet Union is the General Secretary of the Communist Party, who heads the party Secretariat. The Secretariat is the party bureaucracy—in effect, its executive branch. The Secretariat is responsible for making sure that the party's policies are carried out at every level of government. It also makes appointments to key party positions all over the country. To do this, the party Secretariat maintains a staff of more than 200,000 officials. They are responsible ultimately to the ten or twelve secretaries who make up the Secretariat. One of these, the General Secretary, is supreme.

All Soviet Premiers since Stalin have served as General (formerly First) Secretary to the Communist Party. They have been able to place supporters in prominent positions throughout the Secretariat and in the Politburo and the Central Committee, thus assuring their power over the party, the government, and the entire Soviet system. Even so, the Politburo can dismiss a Premier. It dismissed Khrushchev in 1964. No Premier since Stalin has achieved his powerful, dictatorial role.

Questions

1 Why might a Soviet citizen wish to become a member of the Communist party?

2 What are some functions performed by Communist party members in the Soviet Union? Does anyone in the United States perform similar functions? Explain.

3 How are decisions made within the Soviet Union's Communist party?

4 Who is the most powerful person in the Communist party? What is the source of that person's power?

◇ If a Soviet citizen wanted to work toward making life better in the Soviet Union, do you think that joining the Communist party would be a good place to begin? Explain.

PROBLEM: CAN HUMAN RIGHTS BE PROTECTED UNDER A COMMUNIST GOVERNMENT?

The protection of individual rights is a problem faced by people under any form of government. Questions of human rights inside the Soviet Union have drawn worldwide attention in recent years. World interest has been aroused especially by the treatment of *dissidents*—Soviet artists, scientists, and writers who have criticized the policies of their government.

One of the most famous recent dissidents in the Soviet Union was the writer Alexander Solzhenitsyn (sol-zhuh-NIT-sin). His novel *The Gulag Archipelago* is based on his own experiences as a prisoner in Soviet labor camps when Stalin was dictator. The book was suppressed inside the Soviet Union, but was published elsewhere. As a result, Solzhenitsyn was exiled from the Soviet Union in 1974. After a period, he settled in the United States.

The following brief account of this writer's experiences should be read against the background of the excerpts from the Soviet Constitution on page 546. As you read the account ask yourself:

- *What rights and freedoms guaranteed by the Soviet Constitution were violated in the case of Solzhenitsyn?*

Alexander Solzhenitsyn's books exposing Communist brutality in the years 1918–1956 led to his expulsion from the Soviet Union. Now living in the United States, Solzhenitsyn continues to speak out against injustice.

- *Could those rights and freedoms have been protected in any way?*

The Aeroflot jet airliner taxied to the terminal at a German airport. From the exit emerged a husky 55-year-old man with a fringe of red beard. When a hostess handed him a single pink rose, he smiled faintly and bowed. The traveler got into a limousine that whisked him to a tiny village. Arriving at his host's small farmhouse, he was welcomed in the harsh glare of television floodlights. "I was in prison just this morning," he said. "First I must get used to things and try to comprehend my situation."

Thus last week began the exile of one of the world's great writers, the man who for millions the world over has come to represent the conscience of the Soviet Union: Alexander Solzhenitsyn. Shortly after the writer landed in West Germany, the Soviet news agency Tass issued a communiqué. It announced that Solzhenitsyn had been stripped of his citizenship by a decree of the Supreme Soviet and deported for "systematically performing actions that are incompatible with being a citizen of the U.S.S.R." Solzhenitsyn's wife and children could join him "when they deem it necessary."

With the banishment, Solzhenitsyn's remarkable career as a writer came full circle. It had begun with the official publication in 1962 of his concentration camp novel *One Day in the Life of Ivan Denisovich,* a work that *Pravda* hailed as a masterpiece. Nikita Khrushchev had encouraged the publication of the book as part of his own effort to discredit Stalin. But once Khrushchev himself was deposed, there followed for Solzhenitsyn a decade of increasingly dramatic confrontations with the authorities. His later novels were banned, and he was regularly condemned in the Soviet press.

Nonetheless, his books circulated widely in the Soviet Union by *samizdat* [self-publishing] and became bestsellers in the West. The award of the Nobel Prize for Literature to Solzhenitsyn in 1970 infuriated the Soviet leaders, for it only enhanced the worldwide following that made him hard to silence.

Solzhenitsyn's final challenge came when he authorized publication in Paris of the first two parts of *The Gulag Archipelago.* A devastating, documented account of Lenin's and Stalin's reign of terror, the book was a reminder of how unfree Soviet society was, and still is. Soviet frustration was mixed with anger when the author declared that he would order all his banned work published abroad if he was arrested.

Solzhenitsyn's deportation climaxed a suspense drama that had riveted international attention for 5 days. It began with a summons from the Soviet state prosecutor's office, which ordered the writer to meet with investigators. Solzhenitsyn's wife rejected the order. In response to a second summons, Solzhenitsyn released a written statement of refusal. It said: "Given the widespread and unrestrained lawlessness that has reigned in our country for many years, and an 8-year campaign of slander and persecution against me, I refuse to recognize the legality of your summons. Before asking that citizens obey the law, learn how to observe it yourselves. Free the innocent, and punish those guilty of mass murder."

The day of his arrest began as a normal, busy family day. As dusk fell, seven police officers entered the building and hurried up the stone steps to Apartment 169. Solzhenitsyn's wife was told that the officers wanted to talk to her husband. Their leader announced that he had the authority to take Solzhenitsyn with him—by force, if necessary. Calmly, Solzhenitsyn packed a razor, a toothbrush, and warm winter clothes. The officers took him to Moscow's Lefortovo Prison, one of the country's most terrible prisons.

What followed was like a scene from *The Gulag Archipelago.* Solzhenitsyn was first stripped and searched, then dressed in prison garb. He was questioned for several hours by a team of interrogators. But he refused to answer questions or sign the usual official report of the interrogation. He was told that the charge against him was treason, for which the maximum punishment is death. Though officials planned all along to deport him to the West, he was locked in a cell that night, under the threat of the death penalty. At 1 P.M. the following day, he was ordered to dress in prison-issue street clothes and was driven to Moscow's airport. Only when the jet landed in West Germany did he know his destination.

Before his arrest and deportation, Soviet papers were full of letters from citizens insisting that the authorities do just that. After his banishment, the letter-writing campaign continued with a new twist. Demands for his punishment were replaced by expressions of gratitude that Soviet leaders had uprooted "the traitor." Only 12 hours after Solzhenitsyn's deportation had been announced on Moscow Radio, the official newspaper *Izvestia* was able to print a letter supposedly from a reader in Baku, though mail usually takes 10 days to reach Moscow from there. Messages of approval were also received from Minsk and Kiev several days ahead of schedule. Such tactics were added evidence that the Soviet leaders had long prepared the action against Solzhenitsyn.

Soviet leaders have reason to fear him. No person alive today has more authority than Solzhenitsyn to draw world attention to the Soviet leaders' long record of inhumanity. He spent 11 years in Stalin's prisons and labor camps and in exile in Siberia. His earlier novels were fictionalized reflections of that experience. In the first two parts of *The Gulag Archipelago,* however, he set out to document the entire range of horrors inflicted upon the Soviet people from 1918 to 1956. Composed of personal reminiscences, interviews with survivors, and documents, that novel describes the intricate patterns of terror.

True, that terror subsided by 1956, when, by Khrushchev's decree, millions were freed from the giant "archipelago" of prisons and camps run by "Gulag," the Central Corrective Labor Camp Administration. But Solzhenitsyn perceives that an entire nation has been debased by four decades of totalitarianism far more oppressive than Czarist authoritarianism. Ordinary people have been rendered indifferent to injustice and pitiless toward the suffering of others. "Thus," he mourns, "have we been driven to become savages."

Adapted from *Time,* February 25, 1974, pp. 34–36. Reprinted by permission from *Time,* The Weekly Newsmagazine; Copyright © Time Inc. 1974.

Questions

1 With what offenses was Solzhenitsyn charged?

2 In what ways were his constitutional rights and freedoms violated?

3 Could his rights have been protected in any way? Explain.

◯ What might become of a famous writer who criticized the policies or actions of the United States government? Can you cite actual cases? What rights and what institutions were involved? How did they operate in practice?

Chapter 30 Review

Developing Your Political Vocabulary

Choose the correct term to complete the following sentences:

a In November 1917, a *Bolshevik* was a (supporter/opponent) of the Russian Revolution.

b A *soviet* is an (elected/appointed) council.

c *Democratic centralism* is the principle of rule from the (top/bottom).

d In the Soviet Union, a *party candidate* is someone who wants to be (elected to office/made a member of the Communist party).

e The *Politburo* is a high ruling body of the (government/Communist party).

Recalling and Comparing

1 What is the Soviet head of state called? How do that person's duties compare with those of other heads of state?

2 Which do you consider more important: the Council of Ministers or the President of the Supreme Soviet? Why?

3 What functions do elections serve in the Soviet Union? In the United States?

4 Explain this statement: "The Soviet Union is ruled by a network of small committees."

5 What can a Soviet citizen do if his or her rights are threatened by a government agency? What can a United States citizen do in similar circumstances?

6 What does a Soviet citizen have to do in order to join the Communist party? What does a person have to do in order to join a political party in the United States?

Special Activities

1 Make a bulletin-board display of newspaper clippings and magazine articles about events in the Soviet Union.

2 Prepare a chart listing the present leaders of the Soviet Union and their government and party titles.

3 Imagine that you are a Soviet citizen who is a member of the Communist party. You are visiting the United States for the first time. Write a letter to your friends at home describing your reactions to the political system in this country.

4 Imagine that you are a visitor to the Soviet Union. You are making a speech to a meeting of the Young Communist League, and you want to explain the United States political system in terms your listeners will understand. What would you say?

5 Consult your local library and prepare a report on a group in the Soviet Union that is working to change Soviet society. What tactics are used? How does the Soviet government respond? How do the tactics and responses compare with what might happen in the United States?

6 Consider what might be arguments for and against the following statement: "Political rights, such as freedom of speech and the right to vote for competing parties, are more important than economic rights, such as the right to a job and the right to an adequate income." Do you agree or disagree? Explain.

UNIT XI Review

Improving Your Reading

Read the selection below and then answer the questions that follow it.

Each nation has its own special form of government. It is useful to compare governments in order to see in what ways they resemble each other and in what ways they are different. The democracies of Great Britain and France share certain features with our own government. The Communist government of the Soviet Union also has some features that are familiar, at least on the surface.

Great Britain and France, like the United States, are democracies with representative assemblies and constitutions. In all three countries, political rights are protected against abuse by the government or by others. Voters can choose between competing parties and candidates. The people have the final say in how they are governed.

But there are some differences, too. Great Britain has a monarch—at present, a queen. The upper house of its legislative branch, the House of Lords, has very little power. Membership in this house is usually held by right of birth. Great Britain, unlike the United States, has no written constitution. The British Constitution is made up of laws and traditions, and it can be changed as readily as ordinary laws. There is no strict separation of powers in British government. Parliament combines executive and judicial functions with legislative ones. The lower house of Parliament, the House of Commons, has the main powers of government. And Great Britain is a unitary state, not a federal one.

France, despite many similarities with the United States and Great Britain, also exhibits differences. It has a President, but with functions that differ from those of a United States President. France is a unitary state. It has a written constitution. Its parliamentary form of government was originally modeled after Great Britain's. But French political opinion is fragmented. There are many parties, not just two or three. In the past, France had difficulty in bringing together a workable coalition of parties to run the government. The present French Constitution, which has been in effect since 1958, appears to have resolved this major difficulty.

The Soviet Union bears certain surface resemblances to the constitutional democracies. It has a written constitution that lists the rights and freedoms of the people—and also their duties. The Soviet Union has elected legislative bodies. It has a President.

In practice, however, government in the Soviet Union works much differently from government in a democracy. There is only one political party, the Communist party. It holds a monopoly on political activity. Rights and freedoms apply only so long as a person seeks to uphold the Communist system. There is no independent judiciary to call a halt to any governmental abuses. There is usually only one candidate for each office on the ballot. The formal structure of government tells little about the real distribution of power in the Soviet Union. Power is organized from the top down. The Communist party holds the real levers of power.

1 In your own words, summarize this reading in *no more than five* sentences. Have your summary focus on what you regard as the most important points in the reading.

2 Which *two* of the following best describe government in a constitutional democracy?
    a Power is centralized.
    b There is some means of protecting individual rights.
    c An elected president heads the government.
    d The people have the final say in how they are governed.

3 Which *three* of the following best describe government in the Soviet Communist state?
    a Power is organized from the top down.
    b Individual rights are protected as well as in the United States.
    c There is only one candidate for each office in an election.
    d The Communist party holds a monoply of power.

Developing Your Writing Skills: Your Attitudes toward Government

Writing a Paragraph

In this unit, you have studied various forms of government. All of the governments you have studied are based on a constitution, written or unwritten, that sets forth the basic rules by which the government is supposed to be run. Now consider whether or not you think these constitutions are important. On a separate sheet of paper, write a paragraph beginning with the sentence below. Choose either "is" or "is not." Then complete your paragraph with supporting arguments.

    The key to the success of a government (is/is not) its constitution.

Writing an Essay

Write an essay about one of the following elements of government: (1) the way in which elections are conducted, (2) the number of political parties in existence, or (3) the ways in which individual rights are protected. In your essay, comment on the strengths and weaknesses of that element of government in the United States, Great Britain, France, and the Soviet Union.

Recommended Reading

Sidney D. Bailey, *British Parliamentary Democracy,* Houghton Mifflin, Boston, 1966.

Jean Blondel and E. Druxel Godfrey, Jr., *The Government of France,* Crowell, New York, 1974 (paperback).

Editors of Scholastic Book Services, *The Soviet Union,* Scholastic Book Services, New York, 1975 (paperback).

A. H. Hanson and H. V. Wiseman, *Parliament at Work,* Greenwood, London, 1962.

George A. Lensen, *The Soviet Union,* Appleton-Century-Crofts, New York, 1976 (paperback).

Alexander Solzhenitsyn, *The Gulag Archipelago, 1918–1956* and *The Gulag Archipelago Two,* Harper & Row, New York 1975 (paperback).

Alexander Solzhenitsyn, *One Day in the Life of Ivan Denisovich,* Bantam Books, New York, 1970 (paperback).

Comparative Economic Systems

UNIT XII

In the first quarter of the nineteenth century, you might have lived on a frontier farm that produced most or all of the goods and services your family consumed. Living in this way, your family would have had to make three basic decisions about the material side of existence: What goods and services would the family produce? How much of each? How would the family's resources be used to these ends?

Few families are self-sufficient economic systems any longer. Goods and services are now produced mainly by companies and corporations, and are marketed rather than consumed by the producers. In the United States, competitive markets are the chief means of organizing the economy. But there are other possible ways of making economic decisions in the complex world of our times. The following story of the search for an ideal, or Utopian, system puts the possibilities in simple terms.

Once I was approached by a couple who thought they might escape this self-seeking world by joining a group bent upon the establishment of a Utopian community. I was very much interested in their problem and discussed with them how such a Utopia could be organized. How could it best be decided who should do what and who should get what?

Their first idea was that everything should be done by unanimous consent. But this clearly would not work because any dissent would stymie action.

Joint decision by majority rule also would not work if applied to every matter. Moreover, it would tend to be unfair to a minority.

Delegation of decision to a central authority would be workable. But how could the central authority judge all the abilities and desires of every person and weigh them in the balance? Besides, the idea of working for a manager and submitting to such authority ran counter to their wish for togetherness.

It soon became clear that some sort of market system for expressing preferences was necessary. But this ran head-on into the communal idea. And, after all, it was not much different from the system in which they already lived.

And so the couple gave up the idea.

Adapted from Theodore O. Yntema, *The Enrichment of Man*, Benjamin F. Fairless Memorial Lectures, Carnegie Institute of Technology, Pittsburgh, Pa., 1964. Used by permission of Carnegie-Mellon University.

This simple tale points up the close connection between economic and political systems. As the world becomes more urban and more industrial, decisions about who should do what and who should get what have far-reaching effects, both economic and political.

Economics is too big a subject for this book to treat in detail. Like the writer of the selection above, we must put the subject in simple terms. This unit can be only an introduction to the study of comparative economic systems—of different means of arranging the production, distribution, and consumption of goods and services.

In this unit, we will examine three major types of economic systems. The free enterprise system will be outlined in Chapter 31. The socialist system will be discussed in Chapter 32. And communism will be examined as an economic system in Chapter 33.

Chapter 31

The Free Enterprise System in the United States

The United States economy is one of the most productive in the world. It has given us a standard of living that ranks with the very highest. It has also given us individual freedoms and rights that are the envy of much of the rest of the world. We rely upon our economic system for the food we eat, the homes we live in, the vehicles we move around in, and our leisure-time activities. Our economic system is so much a part of our lives that we often take it for granted.

But that would be a mistake. Our economic system is as important to our lives as our political system is. Indeed, that political system has grown up alongside of and within the economic system. The two continue to affect each other closely.

In this chapter, we will study the nature of the free enterprise economic system. We will also see how it operates, with particular reference to the United States. This background will help in understanding the other types of economic systems that will be examined in the remaining chapters.

Goals

- To learn the characteristics of the free enterprise system.
- To learn how a pure form of free enterprise economy would operate.
- To understand how the free enterprise system operates in the United States.
- To consider some decisions that confront people in business in a free enterprise economy.

As the economy expands, farmers must increase their capital investment. They need larger and more efficient machinery in order to compete.

WHAT IS A FREE ENTERPRISE ECONOMY?

The central feature of a free enterprise economic system is private ownership of the means of production. Since the economic term for the means of production is *capital goods* or *capital,* another name for the free enterprise system is *capitalism.*

Capital at one time was a fairly simple concept. Consider the situation of a farmer in the early nineteenth century. The farmer's means of production consisted of land, a barn and other buildings, animals, and a few simple tools. These were the farmer's capital. The farmer used this capital to produce goods for direct consumption—foods such as meat, milk, grains, fibers (wool or cotton), and leather. The foods, fibers, and leather were used up, or consumed, and so are classified as *consumer goods.* In contrast, capital is not consumed directly but used to produce something else. Farm animals are classified as capital in our example because they are used to produce meat, milk, and leather.

As industry grew, so did the variety and amount of capital. Factories were built to produce consumer goods and more complicated tools and equipment. Mines were dug to obtain coal, iron ore, and the many other fuels and ores that were needed in manufacturing. Railroads were built to carry raw materials to factories and finished goods from farms and factories to the point of sale. The factories, mines, and railroads were all added to the nation's capital goods or capital.

Under the free enterprise or capitalist system, most of a country's capital is owned either by private individuals or by companies. It is private ownership of the means of production that sets capitalism apart from socialism and communism. Both of those economic systems are based on government ownership of the means of production.

The people who own the means of production under the free enterprise system are called *capitalists.* This term may cover a wide range of people. A rich person who owns a coal mine or an aircraft factory is a capitalist. So is an owner of a small shoe shop. So is a retired schoolteacher who has a few shares of International Business Machines stock, since a share of stock represents part-ownership.

A respect for private property is a second feature of the free enterprise system. Capital is the major type of private property with which an economic system is concerned. But there is also property that is not capital, such as private homes, automobiles, and other goods. Both kinds of private property are respected under the free enterprise system. In other words, they are protected by law.

Chapter 31: The Free Enterprise System in the United States

The right to enter into legal agreements called *contracts* is one aspect of respect for private property.

In the United States, the binding nature of contracts is protected by Article I, Section 10 of the Constitution. It forbids any state to make any law "impairing the Obligation of Contracts." Therefore, if a party to any contract fails to comply with its terms, that person may be sued in court.

Contracts can deal with either *tangible property* or *intangible property*. Tangible property can be perceived by the sense of touch; intangible property cannot. Land and houses are examples of tangible property. Contracts can be made for their purchase or sale. Contracts can also deal with intangible property rights. Suppose you sign a contract to have your house painted for a certain price. Both you and the painter now have property rights growing out of the contract—you, to have your house painted; the painter, to receive a certain payment. If one of you fails to fulfill the terms of the contract, the other can go to court to have it enforced.

The *right of inheritance* is another form of respect for private property. What happens to your property when you die? In the United States, you can decide that question by drawing up a *will,* or a legal document that tells what you want done with your property after your death. You may direct that your property be passed on to relatives, to a charity, or to anyone you please. The federal and state governments place taxes on inherited property, and those taxes are sometimes high. But the right of inheritance remains an important part of governmental respect for private property.

Even in the free enterprise system, however, property rights are not absolute. Nobody is free to use property in such a way as to harm others. And, through its power to make laws, a government can control the ways in which property may be used.

Though they operate on different scales, the owner of the pencil factory below and the owner of the ice cream truck are both capitalists. A free enterprise economy leaves most production of goods and services in private hands.

These ships and the goods they carry show a free enterprise economy in action. The success of one business venture—manufacture of the goods—led to another business venture—the making of ships to carry the goods.

In addition, a government may take land under certain conditions, even against the will of the owner. This is because governments have the right of *eminent domain,* or the right to take private property for public use. The due process clause was written into the United States Constitution in order to limit that right. Both the Fifth and the Fourteenth Amendments guarantee that no person may be deprived "of life, liberty, or property, without due process of law." If, for example, the state government wants to build a highway across your yard, it can order the land *condemned.* But condemnation must be carried out by proper legal procedures. You must be paid for the land, its value must be openly and fairly determined, and you must be able to challenge the price if you think it is not fair.

A third feature of free enterprise is individual initiative. Under the free enterprise system, there is no central agency of government to make decisions about what should be produced and in what quantity. Instead, these decisions are made by countless private individuals and companies.

Who decides how many cars the automobile industry will produce this year? Those decisions are made by private individuals—people who work for the companies that manufacture automobiles. Except during wartime, the government does not tell the companies how many cars to make; each company decides for itself.

Who decides whether to put a restaurant at a busy corner? That decision is made by private individuals—people with money to invest. These investors might use their money in other ways—to buy a car or a house, for instance. They would then be spending their money for consumer goods instead of putting it into capital investment. Why do they want to invest their money rather than spend it? The simple answer is that they hope to make more money.

A fourth feature of the free enterprise system is that economic decisions are based on the profit motive. People who invest in a restaurant, or a farm, or a small business, or any other enterprise, are interested in making a *profit.* Profit is the difference between the amount of money used to operate a business and the amount of money the business takes in. The investors in a restaurant expect to make more money than they are investing. But not every restaurant makes a profit. The investors may lose every penny. That is the risk an investor takes: the pursuit of profit involves some degree of risk.

Profit—assuming one makes it—may be used in various ways. Some of it is usually put back into the business—that is, *reinvested*. The rest is taken by the owner or owners of the business as income. This income may be spent on consumer goods either to meet daily needs or to satisfy wants such as a better home or a vacation trip. Some of the income may be invested in stocks and bonds, land, or another business. Thus, the income from one business may become the capital for another business.

In a free enterprise economy, as long as people believe they can make a profit, some of them will choose to invest in capital goods. These investments will create new businesses or expand old ones. Business expansion creates more jobs. Growth in employment provides more money to buy more goods and services and to invest. The hope for profit thus leads to a bustling economy if the outlook is favorable. When people hesitate to make investments, the economy drags. Production goes down, and workers are laid off. Less money is available to buy goods and services, and less is available to invest. The hope of making a profit grows dimmer.

The profit motive is the motor that makes a free enterprise economy run. Socialist and communist systems do not depend on the profit motive, as we shall discuss in Chapters 32 and 33.

Questions

1 What are *four* main features of the free enterprise system?

2 What is the difference between consumer goods and capital goods, or capital?

This home and garden are tangible property but not capital. They are protected by law in a free enterprise system.

3 Under the free enterprise system, what rights do individuals have as a result of respect for private property?

⬠ Do you think that *everybody* in business should have a right to make a profit? Explain.

FREE ENTERPRISE IN THEORY AND IN PRACTICE

The theory of capitalism was summarized by a Scottish writer named Adam Smith, in 1776. His book *An Inquiry into the Nature and Causes of the Wealth of Nations* was published in London a few months before the Declaration of Independence was signed in Philadelphia.

At the time Adam Smith wrote, governments intervened in—took a hand in—the economies of most European countries. Great Britain was emerging from an era of *mercantilism*. Under that system, governments gave charters to merchants or to private companies to do business in certain areas. The London Company that began the Jamestown settlement was such a company. It had an exclusive right to colonize and trade with the Virginia territory. Tax money was used to subsidize, or aid, businesses that were likely to increase a nation's power. And subsidies were only one form of government economic intervention.

Adam Smith's Theory of Pure Capitalism

Adam Smith called for governments to keep their hands off the economy. He believed that taxes should be kept low and that governments should do only those things that people could not do for themselves. The proper role of government, in Smith's view, was to defend the nation against other nations, to maintain a system of police and courts, and to provide for schools, highways, and other necessities. Smith maintained that most economic decisions could and should be made by private individuals rather than by governments.

Adam Smith described capitalism as a system in which the profit motive led automatically to the common good of society, without any need for interference by government. According to Smith, each individual capitalist had only one goal—the selfish one of private gain. And yet, as if guided by an "invisible hand," the combined actions of all capitalists had an effect that was far from selfish—the production of goods and services for everybody. Thus, as an economic system, capitalism served the good of society.

Smith believed that government should interfere as little as possible in economic matters. The "invisible hand" worked best when human hands were kept off. This hands-off policy is known as *laissez faire,* from the French words for "leave alone."

Other writers echoed Smith's ideas, and business interests added their voices. The theory of laissez faire began to be put into effect as government regulations were abolished and private interests were freed to pursue profits.

In a free market economy, the law of supply and demand dictates how much this shopper will pay for each purchase.

According to Adam Smith's theories, prices are set by the more or less automatic mechanism of the free market. Food prices are a clear-cut example. In a year when crops are good, farmers produce more food than they can sell. We say that the *supply* of food is greater than the *demand* for food. This brings the price down. Farmers cut their prices because it is better to sell at a low price than not to sell at all. But in a year of drought or storms, crops are poor and there is not enough food to go around. The supply of food has dropped, but the demand remains the same. People do not want to go hungry, so they are willing to pay more. Prices go up.

Economists speak of *the law of supply and demand.* This economic "law" says that, in a free market system, prices go down or up, depending on the relationship between supply and demand. The greater the supply, the lower the prices; and the greater the demand, the higher the prices.

The law of supply and demand depends on competition among many sellers and among many buyers. Consider a city with seven retail clothing stores, in Adam Smith's time. There is competition among the stores for the business of the townspeople. If one store raises its prices, the townspeople have a choice. They can either pay the higher prices or go to one of the other stores where prices are lower. This element of choice helps to keep prices low.

But what if there is only one store in town? Then that store has total, or nearly total, control of the clothing supply. It has what is known as a *monopoly*. It has no competition. The townspeople have no choice. They must buy their clothes at the monopoly store or go without. The monopoly can charge high prices, and people will have to pay them. The law of supply and demand is still at work: the monopoly has limited the supply and forced the prices up.

In his writings, Adam Smith bitterly attacked "the wretched spirit of monopoly." He was opposed to the monopolies granted by mercantilist governments.

Government Intervention

Pure capitalism has never existed in any country. Governments have never taken a completely hands-off position. But until about 1880, the United States had an economic system that was relatively free from government controls. Today, historians look back on this period as the golden age of laissez faire. It was a period of great risk-taking and great profits. Some of those profits built enormous fortunes for families like the Rockefellers, Carnegies, and Vanderbilts. The United States was rapidly transformed from an agricultural to an industrial nation. But there were problems as well as profits.

In practice, laissez faire did not work quite like Adam Smith's theories. It turned out that monopolies developed even in a laissez faire economy. In the United States in the late 1880s, a railroad serving a large area could charge farmers high prices to take their goods to market. Farmers began to demand government action to break up the railroad monopolies or to regulate them.

Late in the nineteenth century, the United States began to intervene in the economy to attack various abuses of the free enterprise system. In response to farmers' demands, Congress created the Interstate Commerce Commission in 1887 to regulate the railroads. As we saw in Chapter 9, the ICC was the first of many agencies set up by the federal government to watch over economic activities.

Congress also passed laws against monopolies. In particular, it attempted to prevent a type of giant corporate combination called a *trust*. The Sherman Antitrust Act of 1890 banned any "conspiracy in restraint of trade" and gave the federal government power to take court action in order to stop companies from forming monopolies. Later, in 1914, the Clayton Act named specific business activities that were forbidden.

Questions

1 How does the law of supply and demand work in a free market system?

2 How does competition benefit consumers in a free enterprise economy?

3 How and when did the United States government begin to intervene in the laissez faire economy?

◊ In what ways does free enterprise affect you? Your family? Your community?

MODERN FREE ENTERPRISE IN OPERATION

In purely material terms, the secret of success in any economic system is the ability to produce and distribute goods and services of the right kind in the right amount. Production and distribution have come to be arranged in certain characteristic ways under the free enterprise system.

Forms of Business Organization

There are three basic forms of business ownership in the modern free enterprise system: the *sole proprietorship,* the *partnership,* and the *corporation.* Each has certain attractions, depending on the nature and circumstances of the business.

A sole proprietorship is a business owned by one person. Many small businesses in the United States are run by a single owner, or proprietor. One person assumes all the risks by investing money to start the business. That person makes all the business decisions and receives all the profits—after taxes, of course. The proprietor also has *unlimited liability* for the debts of the business. The owner must pay all the debts.

Sole proprietorships often require long hours of work. But many people get great satisfaction from being their own boss, despite the hard work.

A partnership is a business owned by two or more persons, each of whom is legally responsible for the business. For example, two sisters may decide to establish a crafts store.

These partners in a health food store plan to share fifty-fifty in the profits and losses of their new business.

They make an agreement, either oral or written (but usually written), about the amount of money each will invest and the way in which profits will be divided. One or both women may work in the store and draw a salary, as well. Most partnerships are made by two persons, but some have as many as a hundred partners.

One important advantage of a partnership is the possibility of greater capital. Two persons usually have more money to invest than one person. Also, the time and abilities of at least two persons are available in a partnership.

One disadvantage of a partnership is that it depends upon harmony between the persons involved. If partner A wants to drop out, partner B must buy A's share in the business or find another partner who will do so. In addition, each partner has *unlimited liability* for the debts of the partnership. If the business cannot pay its bills, each partner may have to draw money from other resources in order to pay the bills. And if partner A runs off with the business funds, the other partner or partners can be forced to pay all of the partnership's debts. For these reasons, partnerships usually involve only two or three people, often friends or relatives.

The corporation is the major form of business organization in modern free enterprise countries. A corporation is a business that operates under a charter and whose owners have no personal responsibility for the debts of the business. Most large businesses in the world today are corporations.

If you want to *incorporate* a business—that is, form a corporation—you must apply to a state government for a charter. This legal document describes the structure of the corporation, the way in which it will operate, and the rules for the sale of *stock.* The capital of the corporation is divided into shares, which are issued to *stockholders* or *shareholders* in the form of stock certificates. Every stockholder is a part-owner of the corporation.

The officers of a business corporation are elected by the stockholders and are legally responsible to them. Each stockholder is entitled to one vote for every share of stock he or she owns. An exception applies in the case of *nonvoting stock,* which some corporations issue in limited quantities for special purposes.

Some corporations are owned by a few individuals and do not offer stock to the public. But most corporations offer stock to anyone who wants to buy it. Their stocks are usually sold on *stock exchanges*—that is, organized securities markets in major cities. The officers of a corporation decide how much of the corporation's profits will be reinvested and how much, if any, will be divided among the stockholders as *dividends.*

The corporation has important advantages over the sole proprietorship and the partnership. One advantage is the greater availability of capital. Few individuals have enough capital to be sole proprietors of, say, a modern steel mill. By selling more stock, a corporation can increase its capital and expand its business. A second advantage of the corporation is *limited liability.* If a corporation fails, the stockholders are not responsible for its debts. True, the stockholders are left with worthless stock, but they risk nothing else.

The corporate form has a unique feature. All holders of voting stock have a voice in making business decisions, and since stock can usually be bought and sold freely, one person or group can gain control of decision-making by assembling more than half the shares.

The corporation has a major disadvantage. Its income is taxed twice. The federal government places a tax of up to 46 percent on the income of corporations, and it taxes dividends as part of each stockholder's income.

Marketing

All businesses in a free enterprise economy must determine what goods and services people are willing to pay for, and then find a way to provide those goods and services at a profit. Distribution, or *marketing,* is as important as production in a free enterprise economy.

To sell her leather goods, this woman is marketing them in an area where she can count on finding many customers.

Suppose you and your brother form a partnership in order to produce handmade leather goods. What kinds of marketing decisions must you make? First, you must determine the nature and size of the market. What kinds of leather goods will people buy, and in what quantity? Should you make leather belts? Or will you do better with leather jackets or leather purses? How many should you produce? Your profits will depend to a large extent on how well you can predict what people will buy.

Second, you must decide on pricing. How much money do you want to earn for each hour of work? How long will it take you to produce each item? What will it cost you to buy your materials and tools? What will people be willing to pay for your products, given the conditions of supply and demand? If other people are competing with you in selling leather goods, you will probably be unable to set your price much higher than theirs.

Third, you must decide where and how to sell. Will you go door-to-door looking for customers? Will you try to get a crafts store to sell your goods? Will you go to crafts fairs and sell in person? Or will you use all of these marketing methods and, perhaps, try mail-order selling as well?

If your leather goods business grows large, you will probably not deal directly with each *retailer,* or retail store, that sells your products to the public. Instead, you will sell to a *wholesaler.* Wholesalers buy goods from producers in large quantities and then resell the goods to retailers. If you look in the yellow pages of a large city's telephone directory, you might see a listing for Leather Goods—Wholesale. Companies in that listing would sell to clothing stores or other retailers.

As a fourth step, you must make decisions about *promotion,* which is the publicizing or advertising of a product in order to stimulate demand for it. For example, you might prepare a display to show people new ways of using leather goods. You might also place advertisements in a newspaper or on a radio station in order to create interest in your product.

"UNTIL THIS MOMENT, I NEVER REALIZED WE NEEDED A FOOD CHOPPER WITH A BUILT-IN TRANSISTOR RADIO."

Under socialism and communism, marketing is very different from the process just described. The government is both the producer and the distributor. It has much more control over prices than government has in a free enterprise economy. Prices can be set low on some goods in order to increase their use and set high on other goods in order to discourage their use. Consumer wants and needs enter in only indirectly.

Advertising, Finance, and Insurance

With economic growth, the free enterprise system has developed several types of business that are peculiar to itself. We will examine three of these—*advertising, finance,* and *insurance.*

The advertising industry serves the purpose of stimulating demand for goods and services in a free enterprise system. Advertising in newspapers and magazines and on television and radio is a multi-billion-dollar industry. Giant corporations spend millions of dollars for television or other types of advertising campaigns. Many small businesses use part of their income for advertising.

Advertising conveys information and stimulates demand. It informs people about products or services and their prices. It reminds people of their needs. For example, you might have forgotten to order a carnation for the prom if flowers had not been advertised in the school paper. Advertising can also create new desires and needs. How many people "needed" no-stick frying pans before they saw them advertised?

For a business, advertising is an investment. The owner or manager spends a certain amount of money to advertise a product or service in expectation that the increase in sales will exceed the cost of the advertising campaign. Advertising is another form of risk-taking in the hope of making a profit.

The finance industry—consisting of banking and credit institutions—provides funds for businesses and investors. People often borrow money from banks to begin or expand a business. Corporations routinely borrow large sums for day-to-day operations. When a bank makes a loan, it charges a fee in the form of *interest*. But a business borrower hopes to make enough profit with the borrowed money in order to pay back the loan with interest and still have something left over. An element of risk is again involved. The bank takes a risk that the loan will not be paid back. The borrower takes a risk that the cost of the borrowed money will exceed the return from it. The reward is a hoped-for profit for all involved.

The federal government supervises and controls the actions of banks, savings and loan associations, and other financial institutions. For example, the Federal Reserve System sets rules about what part of its total deposits a bank can lend and what part it must keep on hand.

The insurance industry helps to spread some of the risks in a free enterprise economy. As an example, let us take a company that sells fire insurance. The company has studied the records on fires and knows how many businesses and homeowners are likely to have fires next year. The company calculates that if it sells x number of fire insurance policies, it will have to pay off only y number of times. Using this information, the company sets a price for its insurance.

Now let's say you run a small dry-cleaning establishment. You buy fire insurance because you know that a fire could wipe out your entire investment. Since the premium is relatively small, you have only a small added expense each year. And the policy protects you against the risk of a major disaster. If fire strikes, you will be paid the amount stated in the policy.

Large insurance companies perform another function in a free enterprise economy. The money they collect in premiums can be invested in other businesses "between fires," so to speak. Insurance companies often buy stock or lend money, thus providing other businesses with needed capital. They also invest directly in real estate and construction, to the extent permitted by law.

Some federal agencies provide insurance. Among these are the Department of Agriculture, which insures farmers against crop failures, and the Federal Housing Authority, which insures lenders who make loans to home owners. Most government insurance programs in the United States apply to high-risk fields in which few private companies were willing to provide protection. Most other insurance is in the hands of private companies. Their activities are closely regulated.

The United States as a Mixed Economy

Today, the United States has a wide range of federal, state, and local laws and agencies that regulate economic activities in many ways. We no longer have a laissez faire economy, but what economists refer to as a *mixed economy*. The heart of the economy is still free enterprise—the private ownership of the means of production. But government no longer follows the hands-off policy that Adam Smith advocated. Government is now an umpire, trying to see to it that the economic system works in certain ways. Government is sometimes even a partner in private economic activities.

The extent of the government's involvement in economic activities is hotly debated in this country. As we saw in Chapter 17 (pages 313, 315, and 320), many people feel that government interference in private business is becoming excessive. These people complain about forms that must be filled out and taxes that must be paid. Some people say that the free enterprise system is being stifled by government red tape. However, many other people defend the government's role in the economy. They say that the government must help to assure that businesses follow fair hiring practices, provide safe working conditions, produce safe products, and leave the environment undamaged. According to these people, business must be responsible to society in these ways, and that responsibility does not come about in a laissez faire economy.

Over the years, our mixed economy of free enterprise modified by government controls shifts toward one direction or the other as one or the other school of thought gains the upper hand.

---- **Questions** ----

1 What are *three* forms of business ownership in a free enterprise economy?

2 Describe *four* steps in marketing. How does marketing in the United States economy differ from marketing in a communist economy?

3 Why is the present United States economy said to be a mixed economy?

⬠ Do you think that government should intervene in the economy? Explain.

PROBLEM: WHAT ARE SOME ADVANTAGES OF DIFFERENT FORMS OF BUSINESS ORGANIZATION?

In this section, we will examine a series of decisions about business organization that confronted three friends. The business is not a real one, and the people are not actual people. But the problems these people faced are taken from real situations.

The Problem with Partnership

As you have read, a partnership offers certain advantages not found in sole proprietorships or corporations. Let's consider how one partnership operates and some disadvantages it may involve. As you read about the operation of Mia's Pizzeria, keep in mind these two questions:

- *What are some advantages of partnership?*
- *What are some disadvantages of partnership?*

For 2 years, Frank Jones saved his money for a business venture. He then teamed up with two friends, Bob Adams and Jim Burke. Together, the three formed a partnership to run a pizza store. It cost $15,000 to start the business. Each of the partners put up $1,000 in cash and borrowed $4,000 from the local bank. The partners agreed to share profits and losses equally.

After 2 years of operation, things were going so well that the group opened a second store. They were then approached by a local business person who offered to finance a third pizzeria for them. He would put up all the money in return for 40 percent of the profits from this store. However, he wanted no active part in the management and refused to be responsible for any losses suffered by the new pizzeria. The three founders agreed that the newcomer would be included as a limited partner under those conditions. The legal work was taken care of by the firm's attorney, and the store opened 2 months later.

With the increase in operations, each of the three original partners began managing one of the stores on a full-time basis. But it was not long before a problem arose that threatened the firm's existence. A local furniture dealer had delivered twenty-five very expensive, made-to-order tables to each store. The owners were shocked. They had ordered no new furniture.

Upon investigating, they learned that the fourth partner had ordered them in the partnership's name. He wanted to give the

Chapter 31: The Free Enterprise System in the United States

The success of any small business, like this pizzeria, depends largely on how well the owners can work together.

pizzerias a distinctive look. The original partners asked the furniture store to take back the tables, but the store said that special orders of this kind could not be returned to the factory. Furthermore, the new partner had signed the sales order after telling the clerk that he was authorized to enter into contracts for the business. With all of their funds already invested, the owners had no money left to meet this furniture bill.

Adapted from Richard M. Hodgetts, *Introduction to Business,* copyright © 1977, Addison-Wesley, Reading, Mass., pp. 58–59. Reprinted by permission.

Questions

1 Where did the partners get the capital to operate the three pizza parlors?

2 Why might the fourth partner in this venture be called a "silent partner"?

3 What problem did the partnership face? Why?

⬠ What advantages do you think partnerships have? What disadvantages?

Mia's Pizzeria, Inc.

In the next selection, we find Frank, Bob, and Jim deciding to change their business from a partnership to a corporation. As you read, consider these two questions:

- *What are some advantages of a corporation?*
- *What might some disadvantages of a corporation be?*

Things became hectic for Frank, Bob, and Jim when their new partner ordered special tables for their pizzerias. However, thanks to their banker, Barbara Williams, they were able to borrow enough money to meet their bills and buy out the new partner. Within 24 months, the firm was making so much money that it had paid off all its debts. Its accountant and lawyer both suggested that the partners incorporate.

The three partners agreed, and the lawyer drew up the articles of incorporation. When these were filed with the state, a charter was issued to the company, which became Mia's Pizzeria, Inc. The owners decided to have seven people on the board of directors: the three original partners, their wives, and the lawyer. The owners also decided to issue a total of 1,000 shares of stock. Each owner was given 332 shares, while the wives and the lawyer each received 1 share. In addition, it was agreed that Frank would be named chairperson of the board,

Bob would be president, and Jim the executive vice president.

Frank and Bob liked the new arrangement. Jim, however, was confused. "I don't see why we went through this whole procedure of incorporating," he said. "What specific advantages were supposed to be gained from all this?"

Adapted from Hodgetts, *Introduction to Business,* p. 74. Reprinted by permission.

Questions

1 In this case, the owners of the new corporation are also the managers of the firm. Is incorporation likely to improve their efficiency as managers? Explain.

2 As owners of a corporation, how can the three friends raise money, besides borrowing from a bank, if they decide to expand their business?

⬠ How would you answer Jim's question? Why?

Should the Firm Be Enlarged?

In the final selection, the friends who operate Mia's Pizzeria, Inc., face another decision. Should the company become an open corporation, selling stock to any buyer? Or should the company continue to operate as a closed corporation in which most of the stock is held by a small group? As you read, consider:

- What are the advantages of selling stock to the public?
- What are the disadvantages?

Within a year of the time Frank, Bob, and Jim incorporated Mia's Pizzeria, their three pizza stores were always full of customers. If the friends wanted to sell any more pizzas, they would have to open more stores. Yet the friends were not sure they wanted to do this.

There were several reasons for their hesitancy. First, they had earned more than $325,000 before taxes in the past year, making their income tax liability very large. They were afraid that if they opened more stores, they would just end up giving most of this money to the government in taxes. Second, to raise the money necessary to expand, they would need a loan. Their local bank was willing to give them credit up to $500,000, but they were reluctant to borrow. They just did not want to go into debt. Third, they could sell stock to the public. But this would mean that they would have to give up some of their ownership and control. Besides, they would have to provide annual reports to the stockholders, and they did not want to give out any financial information.

In January, their accountant told them that they would have to make a decision. If they wanted to keep operating the present three stores, they could do so for the indefinite future. But if they wanted to expand, they would have to take a chance on either borrowing money or selling stock to outsiders. The three friends decided to think the matter over and decide within 60 days.

Adapted from Hodgetts, *Introduction to Business,* p. 77. Reprinted by permission.

Questions

1 What are some disadvantages and advantages of borrowing money from a bank and using it to expand the business?

2 Why might Mia's Pizzeria, Inc., be called a closed corporation rather than an open corporation?

3 What might the owners of Mia's Pizzeria, Inc., gain, and what might they lose, by selling stock to the public?

⬠ What would you recommend the owners do? Why?

Chapter 31 Review

Recalling and Comparing

1 What are three items that might be part of a farmer's capital?

2 Name two ways in which the marketing system of a communist nation might differ from the marketing system in the United States.

3 What service does the advertising industry provide in a free enterprise economy?

4 What services do financial institutions provide in a free enterprise economy?

5 What services does the insurance industry provide in a free enterprise economy?

6 Explain this statement: "In the United States, the free enterprise system was gradually replaced by a mixed economy."

Special Activities

1 Consult your local library or officials of your state government to learn the steps necessary to charter a corporation in your state. Report your findings.

2 As a class project, organize a mock corporation, with the class members as stockholders. Discuss the following questions: What product would the corporation make? How much money would be necessary to set up business? What kinds of operating decisions would be necessary? How could the corporation organize itself to make those decisions?

3 Ask the owner of a local business to speak to your class. Have the person (a) explain how the local, state, and federal governments affect a small business and (b) describe the problems and opportunities of small businesses.

4 Make a bulletin-board display of articles from newspapers and magazines that show ways in which government decisions affect private businesses.

5 Consider what might be arguments for and against the following statement: "Government intervention in the economy is necessary to prevent the abuses that would occur in a 'pure' free enterprise system." Do you agree or disagree? Why?

Developing Your Political Vocabulary

Match each term in *a–e* with the best definition in 1–5.

- free enterprise **a**
- profit **b**
- laissez faire **c**
- monopoly **d**
- stockholder **e**

1 difference between business income and business expenses
2 government hands-off policy toward business
3 part-owner of a corporation
4 economic system in which means of production are privately owned
5 a business having little or no competition

The Hospital For Sick Children
Out-patients →
Psychological medicine →
Paul Sandifer day centre →
Private out-patients →
Treasurer →
Supplies →
School of nursing →
← Central nursing office
↑ All other departments

Chapter 32

Socialism

Phillip Smith is an imaginary resident of Great Britain. His life differs in many ways from your life in the United States because of the different economic systems of the two countries.

When Phillip turns on his radio or television set, he is likely to hear or see a program produced by the British Broadcasting Company. The BBC is the government-operated, tax-supported British broadcasting system. In the United States, there are many broadcasting companies, and they are privately owned.

When Phillip takes an airplane to Scotland to visit his aunt, he flies on a plane owned by the British government. Airlines in the United States are privately owned.

When Phillip broke his arm, he went to a doctor employed by the British government and did not have to pay anything. Phillip had not bought medical insurance, but he did not need any. People in Great Britain receive many kinds of medical service free, and they can buy eyeglasses, dentures, and prescription drugs for a small price, subsidized by the government. In the United States, most medical care is provided by private enterprise and is paid for by the patient or by a private insurance policy.

These are only a few examples of the way economic life in Great Britain differs from that in the United States. All of the examples are the result of legislation passed by Britain's Parliament at the urging of the

Chapter 32: Socialism

British Labour party, which favors socialism. It should be noted, however, that Great Britain has a mixed economy. Socialism and free enterprise exist side by side in Great Britain.

This chapter is about the theories and practices of socialism. Great Britain is used as an example of socialism in operation.

Goals

- To learn the historical origins of socialism.
- To understand the operation of socialism both in theory and in practice.
- To consider what the Socialist party in the United States stood for in the 1930s.

WHAT IS SOCIALISM?

About four out of every ten people in the world today live under governments that call themselves socialist. Some of these governments are democracies, and some of them are dictatorships.

Socialism is an economic system in which the government owns the basic means of production and operates them on behalf of the people. Socialism does not exist in pure form, any more than capitalism does. A socialist government does not own all property or run all businesses. Private individuals may own land, homes, automobiles, and personal goods. They may also run small businesses, such as shoe repair shops and farms, or even hotels, newspapers, or television-manufacturing companies. But most of the large-scale means of production—the mines, big industries, power companies, and railroads—are publicly owned.

Note that socialism is an *economic* system rather than a political system. This distinction is important because there are two broad categories of socialists. On the one hand are those who believe that socialism can be put into effect through the peaceful processes of democracy. These socialists are sometimes called *democratic socialists*. On the other hand are those who believe that capitalism is maintained by force and must be overthrown by force, through revolution. Most Communists are in this second category. They reject the basic concepts of democracy.

Most democratic socialists strongly reject communism, and do not consider Communists to be true socialists. We will devote a separate chapter to communism. The present chapter will focus on socialism as such.

Socialism takes many different forms. Socialism in the African country of Tanzania differs greatly from socialism in a European country like Norway. Often, socialism is introduced gradually. As we noted at the beginning of this chapter, Great Britain has a mixed economy, part socialist and part free enterprise. This is because British voters have alternately placed socialist and free enterprise parties in power since 1945 when Great Britain first adopted major socialist legislation.

Though socialism can vary a great deal from one country to another, most socialists share certain basic beliefs. We can best understand these beliefs if we look at how socialism began.

Modern socialism developed in reaction to the social problems caused by the Industrial Revolution in Europe. As large factories replaced small workshops and home industries, workers were forced to work for hire at low wages. Women and small children shared back-breaking tasks with men, often at much lower wages. Long hours, monotonous work, and unsafe working conditions caused many injuries and deaths among the work force. Poverty and disease were everywhere. Workers often did not have enough to eat, and several families often lived in space meant for one family. Workers' homes in Manchester, England, were described as "cattle sheds for human beings." The same could have been said of other crowded factory cities.

The use of children as cheap labor in factories was one of the reasons for the beginning of modern socialism.

The more fortunate members of the population reacted to these conditions in different ways. Some people felt that poverty was a fact of life that had always existed and would always exist. Some others believed that the social problems were due to minor flaws in the capitalist system. These people said that the system would work all right if governments took some specific steps. Among these were laws to improve working conditions and to bar child labor. Many such reforms were indeed made. But there were also some people who felt that capitalism itself was responsible for the social problems. These people said that no amount of reform could do away with the problems so long as the capitalist system was in effect. They said that a new system—socialism—was needed.

Early socialists objected to capitalism on moral grounds. They thought it wrong for some people—capitalists—to become rich through the labor of other people—workers. Socialists called this exploitation. In addition, socialists believed that the free enterprise system paid too much attention to production and not enough to distribution. What socialists wanted was a more nearly equal *distribution* of goods and services. What good was an economy that produced an abundance of fine lamps if an average worker could barely afford a candle?

The basic socialist criticisms of capitalism were set forth in a book titled *Capital* (in German, *Das Kapital*) published in England in 1867. The author was Karl Marx, a German thinker and writer, who wrote the book with the help of Friedrich Engels. Most socialists agreed with Marx's criticism of capitalism. Many, however, disagreed with Marx's blueprint for socialism—which he gave the label of communism. We will examine both Marx's criticisms of capitalism and his theory of communism in Chapter 33.

The early socialists considered various ways of putting their ideas into effect. Many socialists believed that all of society—not just the economic system—would have to be changed. They drew up plans for a better soci-

In Europe, labor organization was one of the means used to promote socialist programs. Strikes were part of the effort to get better wages and working conditions. This violent strike took place in Paris in 1870.

ety. Some socialists founded small communities to try to create a perfect society in miniature. More lasting was the work of socialists who organized large groups of people to try to change society. The two main types of organizations that promoted socialism in Europe were *labor unions* and *political parties.*

Socialists played a major role in developing labor unions in European countries during the nineteenth century. Labor unions are organizations of workers that try to bring about higher wages and better working conditions, usually by negotiating with employers but sometimes by use of the *strike,* or work stoppage. Early labor unions were treated by the law as "conspiracies" against the public. England did not legalize the strike until 1875.

Leading European unions clearly favored socialism. In the United States, however, unions tried to win better wages and working conditions within the free enterprise system, instead of seeking basic changes in it.

Socialists also formed political parties, either to gain a voice within existing political systems or to change those systems. Between 1875 and 1900, socialist parties were formed in most European countries and in the United States. Their chief source of support was the working class. In many European countries, socialist labor unions worked closely with socialist political parties.

In the nineteenth century, many socialist leaders believed that revolution was the only way to bring about a socialist society. Early experiences had led them to believe that peaceful change would be forcefully resisted by the rich and powerful. In Germany, for example, socialists tried to win seats in the national legislature just like other political parties. They had some success, electing as many as twelve members of the legislature in 1877. But German leaders then cracked down on socialists. They broke up their meetings, banned their publications, and arrested socialist leaders. Many socialists then "went underground" to work for revolution.

In 1889, socialist groups from many countries formed an alliance called the Second

International. (The First International, founded by Marx, had broken up during the 1870s.) The Second International included not only socialists who believed in revolution but also socialists who believed in peaceful change.

Socialist leaders in Great Britain were among those who believed in peaceful change. They were heartened by the improvements already made in labor conditions through laws passed by the British Parliament. In 1900, British socialists formed the Labour party. It promised to support the interests of the labor unions and the working class in Great Britain. The Labour party's goal was to win a majority in the House of Commons and create a socialist system. Though the Labour party rose to power more than once, it did not begin to introduce socialism until 1945. The Labour party is now one of Great Britain's two major political parties.

Similar developments occurred in many other countries, though socialist parties have rarely done well in the United States. At present, West Germany, France, Sweden, Italy, Venezuela, Australia, and several other nations have strong socialist parties that have, at one time or another, held parliamentary majorities. They have not sought to change the basic *political* system but to introduce a new *economic* system—socialism—through the normal procedures of democracy.

Questions

1 What is the central feature of a socialist economic system?

2 What historical event gave rise to modern socialism? Explain.

3 What is *one* socialist argument against capitalism?

4 What was the difference between the two major branches of socialism in the late nineteenth century?

○ Do you think that a socialist party could win widespread support in the United States at present? Why or why not?

HOW DOES SOCIALISM OPERATE?

As we have seen, two ideas lie at the heart of socialism. One is that the basic means of production should be publicly owned. The other is that income should be distributed in such a way that no one is either very rich or very poor. Let's look more closely at these ideas.

Production

Under socialism, the government owns most large factories and businesses. Socialists believe that the needs of the entire society can be taken into account only if the society owns the means of production.

Take the example of a steel mill in a small town. Under private ownership, the mill must make a profit or—unless the government provides emergency aid—it will be closed. There is no reason for the company to keep the mill open if it is losing money. Under government ownership, a public group appointed by the government runs the mill. This group would weigh a number of factors besides profit in deciding whether to close the mill. Will the workers in the mill be unable to find new jobs? If so, it may cost more to pay them unemployment benefits than to keep the mill open. Is the mill's loss of money due to out-of-date equipment? Perhaps public funds can be used to modernize the mill and make it profitable again.

Socialists do not always agree on which businesses should be owned by the public and which should be left under private ownership. Generally, it is the largest industries that are taken over. But this is not always so. In France, which has a mixed economy, one of the largest aircraft manufacturers is privately owned, but matches are made by a publicly owned company. In general, agriculture, retail stores, and small industries are left under private ownership.

These passengers at a British railroad station were able to expect trains to run on time. Standards of service remained high after British railroads were nationalized in 1949. Only recently has passenger service begun to slip.

The process of taking over private industry is called *nationalization*. In democratic countries, the government pays the owners for their property when it is nationalized. For example, when Great Britain nationalized its railroads in the 1940s, it paid stockholders the going rate for each share of stock. In some countries, however, the government *confiscates* property—that is, takes it without paying an adequate price.

Besides nationalizing industries, socialists often seek to change the way private businesses are run. For example, they may seek legislation to give workers and consumers a voice in management decisions. Such a plan might require any company with more than a certain number of employees to allow the employees to appoint some members of the company's board of directors. Additional seats on the board would be reserved for representatives of consumers. Stockholders would appoint the remaining members of the board, as they do in a free enterprise system.

The laws of Austria, Belgium, Denmark, the Netherlands, Norway, Sweden, and West Germany provide for some form of this plan. Socialists maintain that plans of this type help to bring about what they call *industrial democracy*.

Pricing and Planning

Because a socialist economy limits the amount of private enterprise, it cannot depend on a free market to determine prices. Under free enterprise, as we have seen, prices are determined mainly by the law of supply and demand. Under socialism, however, the government has a monopoly on producing major goods and services. The government can control the supply, and often the demand as well. Thus, some other means of determining prices must be found.

Socialism depends on central economic planning to take the place of the free market. Government planners set prices. Because prices in a socialist economy are under government command, we say that they are set by a *command market*.

Not only prices, but also other economic matters are decided by government planners under socialism. The government, or a public group appointed by the government, decides what goods and services are to be produced by nationalized industries. It sets quotas, or goals, for publicly owned factories, telling them how much to produce. And it plans the distribution of goods and services.

Critics and supporters of socialism disagree over how well the consumer is served by central planning. Critics say that socialist planners can ignore consumers' wishes. While a free enterprise economy gives the consumer a wide choice of products and services, the critics say, socialism restricts the consumer to a single source. According to the critics, the products are more likely to be shoddy and the services indifferent. Certain goods and services may not be available at any price if they do not fit into the master plan.

Supporters of socialism reply that consumers in a free enterprise system do not really have free choice. True, they can buy ten brands of hair spray and dozens of models of automobiles. But they are free to choose only those products and services that someone can sell at a profit. Under socialism, this argument goes, the decision about what products to make is up to the people as a whole, through their elected representatives. Perhaps they will choose to have only three brands of automobiles but more frequent bus service. Socialists maintain that consumers can have more choice, rather than less, under socialism.

Another frequent criticism of socialist planning is that it is inefficient and irrational. Without a free market to set prices, the real cost of running an industry cannot be determined, the critics say. Supporters of socialism agree that rational planning is very difficult. But they say that it *can* be done, and that it will result in a more even distribution of wealth among society's members.

Government planners have still another job in a socialist economy—providing capital. As we saw in the last chapter, every economy must set aside some money for investment. In a free enterprise economy, the task is done mainly by private investors. Their investment decisions are often affected by what the government does. For instance, if the government raises business taxes, businesses have less money for reinvestment or for dividends. The United States government tries to influence

The Concorde is a dramatic example of high-risk investment by a socialist government. Investment in the costly French jet was intended to provide more passenger traffic and income for British Airways, Great Britain's nationalized airline.

investment by raising or lowering taxes. Allocation of military contracts, farm and ship subsidies, and public construction projects are some of the other ways in which government influences investment. But, despite these exceptions, most investment decisions in the United States are made by private individuals, not by government.

In a socialist economy, on the other hand, government planners make at least the major investment decisions. They decide whether to build a new steel plant or a new radio station. They decide how much to set aside for oil exploration. They decide whether to invest in producing consumer goods or capital goods.

Where do socialist planners get the money used for capital investments? The three main sources are taxes, the profits of industry, and money placed in savings accounts by individuals. In a socialist economy, the government controls the first two sources directly and can influence the third through its policies.

Redistribution of Wealth

As we noted, socialists have a keen interest in distributing income more equally. Let us turn now to an examination of how socialists go about this task.

Socialism seeks to make members of society more nearly equal by providing certain basic goods and services free or at reduced cost. Medical care, dental care, and hospital care are among the services usually provided free or at low cost. Education is usually free, with university admission by competitive examinations. Parents may be given a direct cash payment of a few hundred dollars a year for each young child at home. Prices of basic foods, such as bread or milk, may be kept low through government subsidies. Low-rent public housing is often provided, both to help poorer people and to keep private rents from rising because of a housing shortage. People who lose their jobs generally receive govern-

This home for the aged in Stockholm is supported by the Swedish people. By means of high taxes, socialism in Sweden provides not only for basic human needs but also for what many other countries would look upon as luxuries.

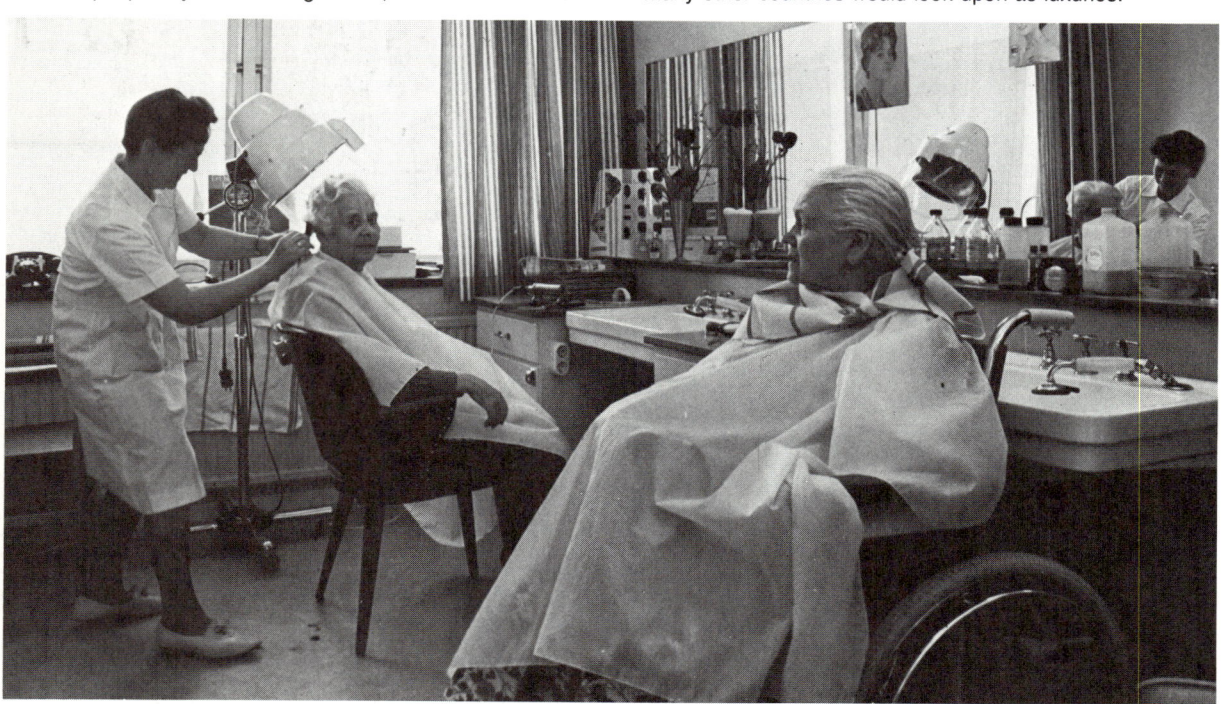

ment payments to help them keep up their standard of living. Retired workers receive government pensions. When people die they may even get a free burial.

Socialists maintain that nobody should be denied food, shelter, medical care or human dignity merely because of economic disadvantage. The idea that society as a whole should look after the welfare of everyone is known as *welfarism*. The term is used to describe "cradle to grave" services provided by socialist governments to their citizens. Socialist societies are sometimes called *welfare states*.

Some elements of welfarism have been introduced in the United States. Two examples of federal welfare measures are old-age and survivors' insurance, which is paid for by a tax on workers and employers, and Medicare, which helps the elderly pay medical bills. At the time these measures were proposed, opponents attacked them as "socialistic." Backers defended the proposed forms of social insurance as humanitarian measures that would ease some inequalities but make no basic change in our free enterprise system.

Welfare measures are generally paid for by taxes, whether they are part of a free enterprise system or a socialist system. Welfare measures are a means of *redistribution of wealth*. In theory, taxes are highest on those who have the most wealth. Thus, some money is taken away from the well-to-do in order to provide more for those lower on the economic scale. Taxes on income range up to 98 percent in Great Britain, 85 percent in Sweden, and 72 percent in the Netherlands. (For comparison, people in the United States in the highest income bracket paid an average income tax of 48 percent in 1975.) Even people of moderate income pay high taxes in socialist countries.

Durability and Success of Socialist Measures

Socialist measures are not necessarily abandoned when socialist parties are voted out of power. Welfare measures, in particular, have proved popular with the voters. In Great Britain and Sweden, for example, free-enterprise governments have not repealed the basic welfare measures introduced by socialists. Welfare measures appear to be irreversible in all of the democratic countries where they have been introduced.

Nationalization, however, may not always be irreversible. The British steel industry, taken over in 1949 by a socialist Government, was sold back to private owners during the 1950s by a free-enterprise Government. The industry

Workers' lives have changed little in this Welsh steel town despite on-again, off-again nationalization of steel.

was nationalized again in the 1960s when the socialists returned to office.

Socialists claim that democratic socialism provides greater political freedom and economic well-being than the free enterprise system. Defenders of free enterprise claim the opposite, saying that socialism deprives people of both political and economic freedom.

According to socialists, political freedom is incomplete without economic freedom, and socialism provides both. Part of economic freedom, they say, is the right of workers to have a say in how their places of work are run. Another part is the right to the basic elements of human welfare. Socialists maintain that the free enterprise system undermines political freedom by encouraging concentration of wealth in private hands and by giving the rich a dominant voice in political decisions.

Defenders of free enterprise argue that socialism does not live up to its promises. They say that public ownership, government operation of business, and central economic planning restrict economic freedom. Moreover, they argue that socialism endangers political freedom by concentrating power in a few hands—those of government officials. In addition, defenders of free enterprise say that socialism undermines individual responsibility by making people think they can get something for nothing. The freest people, according to the defenders of free enterprise, are those who accept full responsibility for their own success or failure.

In economic terms, which system is more successful in practice? Free enterprise has been successful as practiced in the United States. But elsewhere both successes and failures can be found among socialist and free enterprise countries alike.

Great Britain has had more economic downs than ups in recent years. Though long-term effects of World War II were partly responsible, some critics blame Great Britain's economic troubles mainly on socialist measures. Sweden, on the other hand, was generally prosperous during the years when it was headed by a socialist Government. Swedish socialists concentrated on welfare measures and the encouragement of cooperative businesses rather than nationalization. They left 95 percent of industry in private hands. In 1976, Sweden moved into first place in the world in income per capita. Sweden's figure of $9,030 compared with $7,910 for the United States, which was in fourth place. (National income per capita is calculated by dividing a nation's total income by its population.) Taxes were very high in Sweden, however. Swedish voters—apparently feeling a need for new political leadership—voted the socialists out of office in 1976. A free enterprise party took their place.

Whatever the merits or demerits of socialism, the people in democratic countries are free to accept or reject it. In communist countries, as we shall see in the next chapter, the people do not have that freedom.

Questions

1 What do socialists mean by the term *industrial democracy*?

2 How are prices determined under socialism?

3 How is capital provided in a socialist economy?

4 What are some of the free or low-cost services offered in a welfare state? How are these services paid for?

⬠ Do you think that free enterprise encourages people to take responsibility for their own success or failure? Explain.

PROBLEM: WHAT DID THE SOCIALIST PARTY STAND FOR IN THE 1930s?

Socialist parties have been active from time to time in the United States but have not been as important as in Europe. This country's

Norman Thomas being arrested in 1925. For many years, the Socialist party was considered to be a radical party.

most lasting Socialist party was organized early in the 1900s and is still active. Eugene V. Debs was the party's leader and repeated candidate for President until the mid 1920s. The leadership and presidential candidacy then passed to Norman Thomas until his death in 1968.

Debs received 6 percent of the popular vote in the 1920 presidential election. After a slump, the Socialist party reached another high point of popularity in the Great Depression of the 1930s. In the 1932 presidential election, 2.2 percent of the voters voted for Norman Thomas. There are still some people in this country who believe that our free enterprise system should be replaced by socialism.

The following selection is taken from the 1932 platform of the Socialist party. The selection includes a portion of the preamble and the proposals for unemployment and labor legislation. As you read, ask yourself:

- *How would the introduction of socialism have changed the economic system in the United States?*
- *What groups in the population might have favored this platform? What groups might have opposed it?*

Today, in every city of the United States, jobless men and women by the thousands are fighting starvation while factories stand idle and food rots on the ground. Millions of workers are hunting in vain for jobs while other millions are only partly employed. Only the united efforts of workers and farmers, organized in unions and cooperatives and, above all, in a political party of their own, can save the nation.

The Socialist party proposes to transfer the principal industries of the country from private ownership and management to social ownership and democratic control. Only by these means will it be possible to organize our industrial life on a basis of planned and steady operation, without periodic breakdowns and disastrous crises.

The party proposes the following measures:

1. A federal appropriation for immediate relief [cash payments] for those in need.
2. A federal appropriation for public works and roads, reforestation, slum clearance, and decent homes for the workers.
3. Legislation providing for the acquisition of land, buildings, and equipment necessary to put the unemployed to work producing food, fuel, and clothing and building houses for their own use.
4. The 6-hour day and the 5-day week without a reduction of wages.
5. A system of free public employment agencies.
6. A compulsory system of unemployment compensation with adequate

These people were among the first to apply for federal-state unemployment benefits when they first became available in the 1930s. Unemployment insurance was one plank in the Socialist party platform in 1932.

      benefits, based on contributions by the government and by employers.
7. Old-age pensions for men and women 60 years of age and over.
8. Health and maternity insurance.
9. Improved systems of workmen's compensation and accident insurance.
10. The abolition of child labor.
11. Government aid to farmers and small-home owners to protect them against mortgage foreclosures and a halt to sales for nonpayment of taxes by destitute farmers and unemployed workers.
12. Adequate minimum wage laws.

Congressional Record, 72nd Congress, first session, 1932, pp. 14702-14703.

Questions

1 What people probably would have benefited in 1932 from socialism as outlined in the Socialist party platform? What people probably would have suffered?

2 Which of the proposals would have changed the economy most? Explain.

3 What reasons might some voters have had for wanting to introduce socialism in 1932? What arguments might some opponents have made against socialism?

4 Some of the proposals in the 1932 Socialist platform have since been put into practice. How were they adopted? Why?

⬠ Do you think that any of the proposals in the platform can be described as welfarism? Do you think that welfarism is consistent with a free enterprise economy? Explain.

Chapter 32 Review

Developing Your Political Vocabulary

Use each of these terms in a sentence about the socialist economic system:
1. welfarism
2. nationalization
3. command market
4. central planning
5. redistribution of wealth

Recalling and Comparing

1. Through which *two* types of institutions did early socialists often seek to achieve their goals?
2. Why did some socialist leaders in the nineteenth century advocate revolution? Why did other socialists reject the idea of revolution?
3. What parts of the economy are dominated by the government under a socialist system?
4. In a socialist economy, what takes the place of the free market?
5. Why are markets in a socialist system called *command markets?*
6. What *four* tasks are performed by government planners in a socialist system? How are these tasks performed in the United States free enterprise system?
7. Name *two* countries in which socialist governments and free enterprise governments have alternated in power.
8. What are *three* major differences between the socialist system and the free enterprise system?

Special Activities

1. In Chapter 31, it was suggested that the class form a mock corporation. Repeat the activitiy, but this time assume that the corporation is publicly owned and the directors are appointed by the government. In what way would decision-making in the corporation differ under public ownership? What factors might influence the directors' decisions?
2. Consult your local library and prepare a report on Eugene Debs or Norman Thomas and the Socialist party in the United States.
3. Prepare a skit in which two people visit a factory during the early nineteenth century. Have class members play the parts of visitors and factory workers. Include an informal debate between the visitors, one advocating the capitalist system and the other advocating socialism.
4. Make a study of the nationalization of railroads in Great Britain. Report your findings to the class.
5. Make a comparative study of socialism in Sweden and in Great Britain. Write a report of your findings.
6. Consider what might be arguments for and against the following statement: "There is less economic freedom in a socialist system than under free enterprise." Do you agree or disagree? Why?

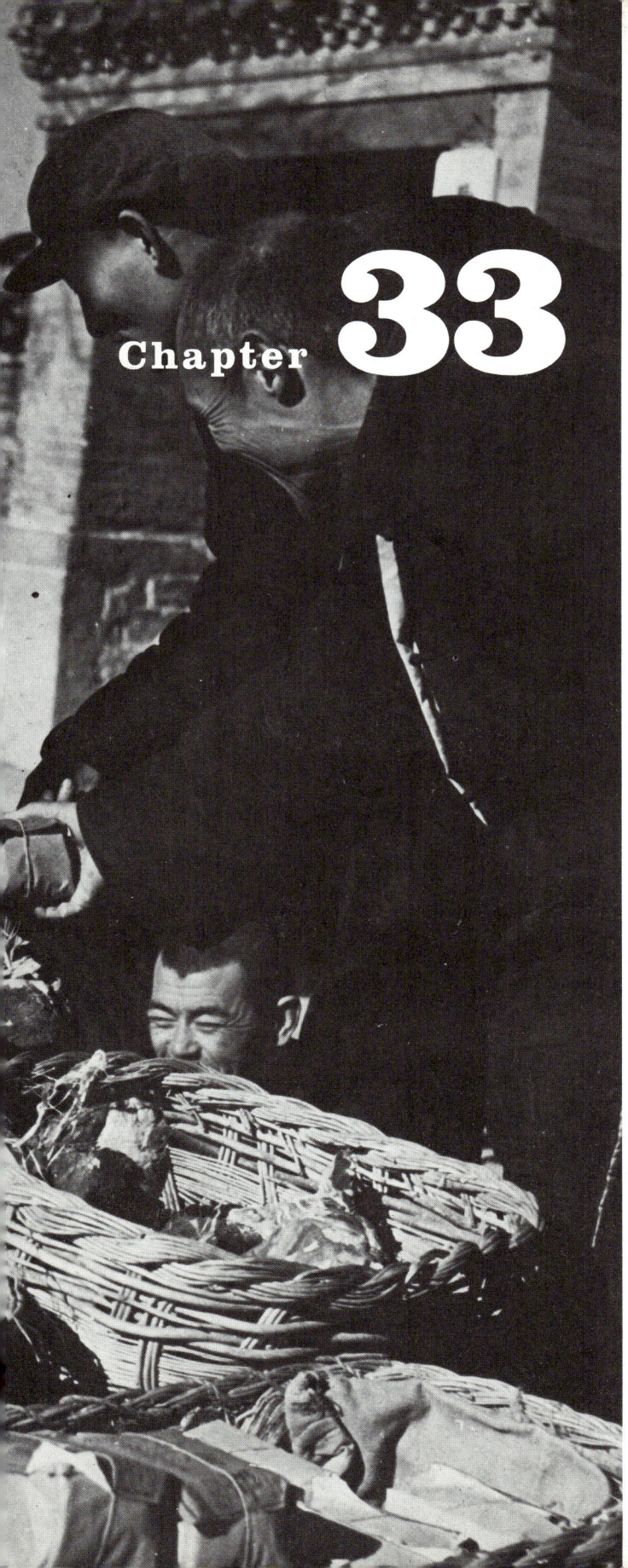

Chapter **33**

Communism as an Economic System

The year was 1848, and the people of the United States were focusing their attention on their own country. In February came word that the war with Mexico had been ended by a treaty that added most of the Southwest to United States territory. It was an election year, but President James K. Polk was not running for reelection. His Democratic party was split by a dispute over slavery. The Whigs won the election by putting up General Zachary Taylor, a hero of the recent war. Women's rights activists held a convention in Seneca Falls, New York. And gold was discovered in California, touching off a frantic gold rush.

While the United States looked to the West, Europe was shaken by riots and revolutions. Europeans were haunted by a deep-seated fear. This was the fear that the working class was about to rise up and destroy the capitalist system. In its place, the workers would put communism.

This chapter will describe the economic system known as communism.

--- **Goals** ---

- To know the major features of communism as an economic system.
- To know how that system works in the Soviet Union.
- To consider some of the features of communism outside the Soviet Union.

593

COMMUNISM AS AN ECONOMIC SYSTEM

In Chapter 30, we examined communism as a political system in the Soviet Union. That system was adopted as a means to an end, which was to be communism as an economic system.

The ideas behind the communist economic system are those of Karl Marx. For that reason, the system is often called *Marxism*. Various forms of communism have been tried in different countries, but all follow the basic ideas set out by Marx.

In 1848, when Europe was shaken by revolutions, *The Communist Manifesto* was published in London by the Communist League. What this small group of political thinkers and workers was announcing was a program for revolution. The document bore the names of two authors, Karl Marx and Friedrich Engels, both in their late twenties. But the main ideas were Marx's.

Many years later, again in London and again with the help of Engels, Marx set out his economic ideas in detail in his three-volume book *Capital*. The first volume appeared in 1867 and the others appeared in 1883, after Marx's death. As we noted in Chapter 32, *Capital* was a blueprint for socialism, which Marx identified as communism.

Marx did not *see* communism as an economic system that *should* be, but rather as something that *would* be. According to Marx, communism was inevitable. Marx believed that he had discovered scientific principles that enabled him to trace the unfolding of history. To Marx, history was a series of stages of economic development. One stage led to another. Feudalism, with its lords and vassals, masters and serfs, had been an early stage of development. It gave way to the capitalist system of private ownership of property. Capitalism, in turn, would give way to socialism and then to communism. That would be the final stage, Marx said.

Karl Marx, shown with his daughter Jenny, created the ideas of the communist economic system we know as Marxism.

A struggle between economic classes was the key to capitalism, according to Marx. He made a study of the capitalist system in Europe in the middle of the nineteenth century. The life he described was as terrible as anything you might read in the novels written by Charles Dickens in the 1840s and 1850s. On the one side, Marx saw the owners of the means of production—the capitalists, or *bourgeoisie* (boor-zhwa-ZEE). This class of people had complete control of the raw materials, the factories, and the machines. On the other side, Marx saw the working class—the vast *proletariat* (pro-li-TAIR-ee-ut). Though this class was large in number, it had nothing to offer except its labor. No wonder, said Marx, that the great mass of people lived in dire poverty.

Poverty and insecurity would be the lot of the working class, Marx said, until the economic system changed. And it would not be changed by government action, because government was on the side of the people who controlled the means of production. Marx saw

Chapter 33: Communism as an Economic System

The peasants at the left and the landowner at the right were members of Russia's two main economic classes at the time of the Bolshevik Revolution. Marx had predicted an overthrow of capitalists in an industrial society.

political institutions as merely built on an economic foundation.

How, then, would a change come about? Marx's detailed analysis can be summarized here only in brief form. The vast majority of people are workers, Marx noted. To exist, they are forced to "sell themselves . . . like every other article of commerce." More precisely, they sell the use of their labor in return for wages.

As Marx's description goes on, these wages are paid by factory owners and other capitalists, who pay less than the labor is worth. The difference between what capitalists pay the workers and what the factory or other business earns is their profit. By taking this "unearned" profit, capitalists exploit workers. They try to keep wages as low as possible, and thus reduce the workers to a thinly disguised state of slavery.

To increase their profits, Marx states, owners introduce machinery into their factories. To get full value from the machines, they keep them in use around the clock. They force workers to work more hours and to produce more in each hour. In Marx's day, it was not unusual for factory workers to spend 16 to 17 hours a day at their work.

As more and more goods are produced, factories grow bigger. More workers and more machines are needed. Only the most successful owners can meet the costs. There are fewer and fewer owners because unsuccessful and small owners are squeezed out. So, says Marx, the economy lurches from boom to bust in what *we* would now call *business cycles*. Meanwhile, the working class is growing larger and larger while becoming poorer and poorer.

In an advanced stage of capitalism, according to Marx, the working class finally revolts and overthrows the "dictatorship of the bourgeoisie." Peaceful political struggle might put the proletariat in control in some countries, but the more likely course of events leads to a violent revolution, Marx says. After the workers have control of the government, they are the ruling class. They create their own "dictatorship of the proletariat" as a temporary measure to carry out the transition to true communism.

Once in power, Marx says, the working class does away with private property and puts an end to exploitation. Distinctions between classes gradually disappear. When there is no more class system, there is no class struggle. There is no longer a need for rulers because communism has been achieved. Under communism, Marx says, each person will do whatever he or she is best able to do and will get whatever he or she needs.

Marx did not explain how the working class would operate once it was in charge. He was concerned mainly with explaining why capitalism was doomed. This he did in far more detailed and logical fashion than appears from this simplified sketch. Marx only suggested in the broadest terms what would follow after the destruction of capitalism.

A revolution did take place, but not in the way that Marx foretold. As we saw in Chapter 30, it took place in Russia, and Russia in 1917 was not an advanced capitalist country with a large class of factory workers. Moreover, the Bolshevik Revolution in 1917 was not an inevitable uprising of the working class. Instead, a small group of Russian Communists planned the revolution and brought it about in the name of the working class.

Lenin, who led the revolutionists, saw no need to wait until Russia had passed through the stage of capitalism before beginning a change to communism. The Bolsheviks seized the opportunity created by the czar's downfall earlier in 1917, and overthrew the temporary Russian government in November. After a civil war, the Bolsheviks set up a dictatorship that established the Union of Soviet Socialist Republics and promised to lead the new nation to true communism.

Questions

1 Why did Marx think that communism was inevitable?

2 How did Marx describe the class struggle under capitalism?

3 What did Marx think was the relationship between a nation's political system and its economic system?

4 What is the purpose of the "dictatorship of the proletariat," according to Marx?

◇ Do you think that Marx would see capitalism in the same light today as he did in the nineteenth century? Why or why not?

COMMUNISM IN OPERATION IN THE SOVIET UNION

The Soviet Union officially claims to have a socialist economy. In line with Marx's theories, the Soviet Union sees itself as somewhere along the road to pure communism, but not yet there. Marx called this middle stage *socialism*. It is a period of transition during which the "dictatorship of the proletariat" is seen as necessary.

The Soviet economic system shares certain features with socialism as described in Chapter 32. But socialism in the Soviet Union is closely tied in with an authoritarian *political* system that makes it very different from democratic socialism. Soviet communism is both a political and an economic system. We will use the term *communism* when referring to the economic system of the Soviet Union in this chapter.

The Soviet Union began as a poor country with vast resources that were scarcely developed in 1917. The Industrial Revolution had reached Russia only within the past three or four decades.

To catch up with other nations, the Soviet Union followed a policy of forced industrialization. In all nations, industrialization has imposed sacrifices on large numbers of people. In the Soviet Union, those sacrifices were deliberately harsh. The wants and needs of consumers were largely ignored in order to build up heavy industries, such as iron and steel. The

Chapter 33: Communism as an Economic System

goal was to turn the Soviet Union into a modern industrial country as soon as possible.

Almost all means of production are owned by the government. It owns factories, department stores, newspapers and television stations, even the ice cream carts found in public parks. The government owns the railroads, airlines, and shipping companies. It controls all trade, both within the country and with other countries.

All important economic decisions—and some not so important—are made by the government. The government makes the final decision on how many tractors a farm will have. It decides whether shoes will be cheap or expensive. It decides whether a factory will turn out military missiles or civilian aircraft. It decides whether more brown shoelaces or more black shoelaces should be produced. The Soviet Union has a *command economy.* A command economy is one in which things get done because some authority says they must be done. In the Soviet Union, that authority is the government. As we saw in Chapter 30, government decisions must be in line with those of the Communist party.

The elimination of private enterprise began in the late 1920s. Today private enterprise exists only on the smallest scale. For example, a carpenter could set up his or her own business but would not be allowed to hire a helper. To Communists, that would be "exploiting" another person's labor. An individual might plant a private plot of strawberries and sell them. But it would be illegal for another person to buy the strawberries and attempt to resell them.

The Soviet Union has not abolished all private property. In fact, the Soviet Constitution guarantees the right to own and inherit personal property. An individual is allowed to own a home, a savings account, an automobile, and personal articles. Individuals are not allowed to collect rent or make any other "unearned income."

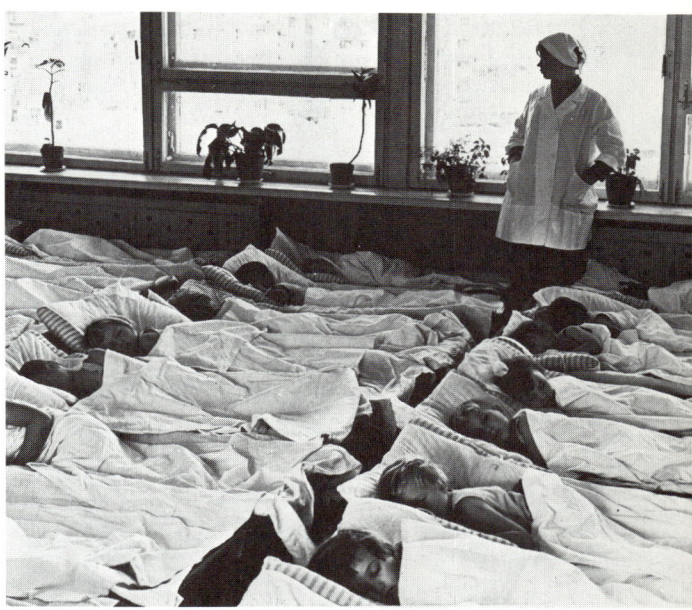

This day-care center in Amursk eases the labor shortage by freeing the children's parents to work full time.

Everybody, male or female, is expected to work for a living. The Soviet Union has had a labor shortage since the large losses of life it suffered during World Wars I and II. Women were recruited into industrial jobs at an early date. Extensive daycare facilities are provided to care for the children of working parents. It is possible to quit a job and take another one, but a worker must be on the new job 6 months before being eligible for full social insurance benefits.

Wages are based chiefly on how much work a person turns out. The best workers are rewarded with cash prizes, better apartments, and special vacation trips, as well as special awards and press write-ups. Managers, supervisors, and high government officials receive salaries that are a good deal higher than most workers' wages.

Labor unions, like other Soviet institutions, are controlled by the Communist party. Strikes are forbidden and unions do not negotiate with management for higher wages as they do in the United States. The main purposes of Soviet labor unions are to carry on cultural and recreation programs, watch over factory safety, propose changes in factory policies, and encourage workers to do their jobs well.

Central Planning

The Soviet economy is run by central planning. A special arm of the national government, the State Planning Committee, is in charge of economic planning. The committee makes detailed plans that cover a period of 5 years or, sometimes, more. Like our federal budget, these plans set broad national priorities and tell how much money will be needed to reach the goals. But while the United States budget deals with a limited range of national life, leaving most economic decisions to be made by private individuals and enterprises, the Soviet national plan deals with an entire economy. It sets quotas for each part of the economy. It is the blueprint that tells how the Soviet economy is to be run.

Let's consider how central planning might affect the operation of a truck factory in the Ukrainian Soviet Socialist Republic. The factory, like other Soviet businesses, would have its own planning department. That department would draw up a plan for the factory's operation during the next year or 5 years. The plan would state how many trucks the factory could make, how much steel and other materials the factory would need, and how much money would be spent for wages and other operating costs. The plan would also list major capital expenditures that might be expected. For example, the plan might call for adding a new assembly line.

The factory's plan would be passed on to a regional planning agency and then to the republic planning committee. Finally, the plans from all fifteen republics would be sent to the State Planning Committee. The Communist party and the Supreme Soviet would have the final word on the broad outlines of the national

The number and kinds of trucks that roll off this assembly line are set by the Soviet Union's central plan.

plan for truck manufacture. Meanwhile, the management of the truck factory would be waiting to hear how its plan had fared. Word would be passed down through the regional and republic planning committees. The factory would be told how much money it could spend, how many trucks it would have to produce, and whether or not it could add that extra assembly line.

The advantage claimed for this type of planning is that it allows the government to decide how best to use a nation's resources. The nation can focus its full resources on one major goal, such as rapid industrialization. The chief disadvantage, according to critics, is that planning is often inflexible and inefficient. Critics also say that central planning leads to lower quality because quality is sacrificed in order to meet quotas.

Capital Investment and Prices

Factories, farms, and other businesses get their funds from two sources—profits and government banks. The plan for each agency allows for a certain profit. In addition, each business has an account with the State Bank, which takes part in all sales between one business and another. The State Bank sometimes loans money to help a business meet its bills. Not surprisingly, the Soviet State Bank is the largest bank in the world.

What is the role of profit in the Soviet economy? If the truck factory we mentioned earlier successfully carries out its plan, it is certain to make a profit because the plan always provides for a certain profit. However, this profit does not work as it does in a free enterprise economy—that is, to encourage individuals to invest in business. Instead, profit in the Soviet system is mainly a means of calculating how well a government-owned business is doing.

Part of the truck factory's profit goes to the national government. This part is, in effect, a tax on the business. Another part of the profit is kept by the factory for reinvestment, under rules laid down by central planners. The rest of the profit goes to the factory and its workers. Workers and managers may receive a special cash bonus. Or the factory may save its profits and eventually build a recreation hall or an apartment building for the workers and managers. This last part of the profit is thus used to provide incentives to the people who work in the factory.

Prices are set by the government with or without relation to costs of production, sometimes to achieve social or political ends. For example, alcoholism is a serious problem in the Soviet Union. To discourage drinking, the government has set a high price on vodka, the national liquor. On the other hand, the government wants people to read books on Marxism, so it sets their prices low.

Heavy Industry and Agriculture

For many years, Soviet industry concentrated on turning out heavy machinery. This

Imports like these dry-cleaning machines have helped offset the Soviet Union's emphasis on heavy industry.

was because heavy industry was necessary to build up the nation's industrial strength. Soviet planners allocated almost no resources to the production of consumer goods.

The policy paid off in enormous industrial growth. Today the Soviet Union ranks second only to the United States in industrial output. This advance has been due to many things, including vast natural resources, an ability to use technology already developed in other countries, central planning, and the diversion of resources from consumer goods.

Since the death of Stalin in 1953, Soviet planners have paid more attention to the consumer. While heavy industry is still emphasized, consumer goods are also rolling off the assembly lines.

Boosting agricultural production is another long-range Soviet goal. The country has been struggling with food shortages since before the 1917 revolution. Though great strides have been made, many problems remain. At times in recent years, the government has had to import grain from abroad. Farm output per worker is lower in the Soviet Union than in the United States partly because agriculture is not yet as highly mechanized as in the United States. Moreover, the Soviet climate is harsher, and crop failures can often be caused by bad weather.

Chapter 33: Communism as an Economic System

There are two types of farms in the Soviet Union. Both types are under government control and both are subject to central planning. State farms *are owned directly by the government. Workers are paid a wage, just like workers in factories. They do not share in the farms' ownership.* Collective farms *are owned by the workers who live on them. Collectives were originally formed by having the owners of small private farms pool their lands and equipment. The owners formed a cooperative, setting up their own managing board to make basic decisions. Today, collective farms are still self-managed. The government owns the land but leases it to the collective. The farm owns its own buildings and equipment. Members earn a wage, based on the amount of work they do, plus a bonus that is taken out of the farm's profits.*

Workers on Soviet farms are granted private plots *on which they may grow crops for their own use or for sale. Though these privately worked pieces of land occupy only a small part of the total farm land, they provide one-third of all vegetables, meat, and milk in the Soviet Union. Members of collectives sell this produce either privately or through city markets run by cooperatives.*

Evaluating the Communist Economic System

Observers differ in their judgment as to how well the Soviet economic system works. Soviet economists claim to have solved the problem of business cycles, which Marx described as a necessary result of the free enterprise system. Communists also say that their system has eliminated the problems of unemployment and inflation that go along with business cycles. Moreover, Soviet leaders point with pride to the public welfare measures that are part of their economic system. Welfarism is as much a part of communism as it is of socialism. Free medical care and free education are two elements of Soviet welfare policies.

Many United States observers, on the other hand, stress the continuing problems that plague the Soviet economy. Low agricultural production is one of the biggest problems. Though the Soviet Constitution states that everybody has the right to low-rent housing, inadequate housing is another major problem. Young married couples often must continue to live with parents while they wait for an apartment of their own. Waiting lists are often long.

Different housing is provided for the general run of workers and for the elite in the Soviet Union. Workers live in apartment buildings like those at the left. Below is the home of a writer and Communist party official, M. A. Sholokhov.

Critics also say that the Soviet system does not offer enough incentives to work harder. True, outstanding work is often rewarded by extra pay. But food, housing, and consumer goods in general are in short supply. Critics ask: What good does it do someone to work harder and earn more money if there are few goods and services to buy with the money? And of course, chances to invest money in private business are also very limited, so there is little reason to put money aside for investment.

In addition, economists in the United States point out many faults in central planning of the Soviet type. These critics say that it stifles local initiative by imposing standardized rules on the entire economy. Also, they say that central planning is inefficient. What happens if a truck factory turns out more trucks than its plan calls for? Who will buy them? Other businesses have their own plans, which call for buying only so many trucks.

Perhaps the most urgent criticism is that the Soviet economy, like Soviet society in general, is controlled from the top, not the bottom. The people themselves have little influence over the kinds of goods and services turned out by the communist economy. This, say the critics, means a lack of both economic and political freedom.

Questions

1 What businesses are owned by the government in the Soviet Union? What kinds of businesses might be privately owned?

2 How does the role of labor unions differ under communism and free enterprise?

3 What *two* sections of the Soviet economy have been given most attention by Soviet planners?

4 Why are private plots of land important to Soviet agriculture?

⬠ What would you say is the biggest problem facing the Soviet economy? Explain.

PROBLEM: HOW DOES COMMUNISM OPERATE OUTSIDE THE SOVIET UNION?

The Soviet Union was the first nation to establish a Communist economic system. Yugoslavia, mainland China, Cuba, and Vietnam are among the nations that later turned to communism. All of these nations are quite different from the U.S.S.R. in their historical background, population, and resources. Each of these nations now has an economic system based on Marxism, yet each system is different from the others. In the following selection, we will examine one of these systems as a means of gaining more insight into communism.

Notes by a Visitor to the People's Republic of China

Mainland China is a vast country with a huge population. It is an underdeveloped nation with economic problems different from the Soviet Union's. Communists took over China's government in 1949, when Mao Tse-tung became leader. Both under Mao and since his death, the People's Republic of China has followed its own course and has developed its own distinct form of communism.

The following report is by an American economist who visited Communist China. He describes a *commune*, or rural collective unit, and a factory in the city of Peking. As you read his notes, ask yourself:

- What are some features of Communist China's economic system?
- What does China's economic system have in common with the system of the Soviet Union?

August 9—Canton: Our major project for the day is a visit to the Ta Li Commune, about 15 kilometers from Canton. When this commune began in 1957, its first assignment

The People's Republic of China has stressed agriculture and rural communes in its own distinct form of communism.

was to build locks to protect itself against flooding. It took five thousand workers 6 months to complete the lock we visited. Electric power has been available since 1960 and now seems to extend to the entire commune.

The people are organized into 19 production brigades broken down into 235 production teams. The commune covers about 4,000 hectares (10,000 acres). The chief crop is rice. There are also industrial crops, fish, and forest products. There have been four consecutive good harvests. Sixty percent of the land that is worked is worked by machine. Local industries administered by the commune include agricultural machinery repair, lime, cement, peat, and bamboo wood.

Only the old and disabled do not work in the commune. Chinese women traditionally have been cooks, and that is continuing. Of the thirty-one members of the Revolutionary Council, which meets three times a week, seven are women. All jobs in the commune can be done by women. The plant that repairs farm machinery also builds new machines with local labor, and here some rather complicated equipment is being operated by women.

Ordinarily, the people work an 8-hour day, 6 days a week. There are three national holidays a year, but no regular vacations.

The average income is 540 yuan per household and 260 yuan per worker (1 yuan = $.40). People also grow food in private plots around the homes.

At the Ta Li Commune, 80 percent of the primary-age children are in school. Both the brigades and the state furnish capital for the schools. The state is the major contributor. The brigades' contribution to the schools is taken from their welfare funds. The commune has one high school and nineteen primary schools for its 10,300 students.

There are a central hospital, two clinics, and nineteen small medical units (one for each brigade). Both western and Chinese medical practices are used. Medical personnel total 170, including 55 "barefoot doctors" (medical aides) who make house calls. A co-op medical system was set up in 1968. Each member pays the nominal sum of 20 cents a month for medical care.

August 11—Peking: After lunch, we are taken to Peking Machinery Plant No. 1. This factory was built in 1956 and began to turn out machine tools in 1958. It was designed to produce 2,400 machine tools a year but failed to achieve that until after the Cultural Revolution in 1966–1967. The plant finally exceeded its rated capacity in 1969 and the following year produced 5,000 units. The emphasis is now on heavier tools.

There is a great deal of hand work in the shops, making for a certain unevenness in the level of mechanization. The plant employs several thousand workers, one-third of them women. One is very aware of the presence of women workers throughout the

Chapter 33: Communism as an Economic System

This electrical equipment factory is part of Communist China's efforts to boost manufacturing and other industry.

plant in all capacities—drivers, crane operators, etc.

The plant kitchen is modern. Workers eat standing up at tables and pay a small price for their meals.

Our visit to the nursery is, for me, a high point of our tour of the plant. Here, children from less than one year to about age six are cared for. There are 150 children in all. For the youngest, a group of about twenty infants, three women are assigned. The children are taken home only on weekends, Saturday night to Monday morning. When asked whether the children prefer to live in or go home with their parents at night, the women said they definitely preferred to live in. With television, good beds, and loving custodians, a child might be better off on the premises. A number of the six-year-olds danced and sang for us with great charm.

On our way back to the nursery, a few of us stopped off for a quick basketball game with some of the workers. There are always intramural games as well as games with workers from other factories.

After our tour, we have a discussion with our hosts. We learn that not all members of the Revolutionary Committee are Communist party members. At this plant, 20 percent of the committee are not members of the party.

The health workers do their regular factory jobs and also carry out their medical responsibilities. They take care of small injuries and also try to combine preventive and treatment medicine, thus cutting the incidence of seasonal illnesses. For workers, the entire cost of medical care is covered. For nonworking members of their families, half of the cost must be paid by the families.

There are seven annual holidays, but no vacations, at this Peking plant. However, single persons separated from their families can get 2 to 3 weeks a year to visit their families.

Seventy percent of the Revolutionary Committee members engage in manual work one day a week.

The wage system, like that in the Soviet Union, has eight grades of pay, ranging from 34 yuan to 100 yuan a month (roughly $17 to $50 a month). Apprentices make less than 34 yuan a month. Engineers make from 90 to 120 yuan. Since rent averages 3 yuan a month and health and educational expenses are minimal, a total family income averaging 110 yuan a month goes further than one might expect.

State planners give the factory its production quota, but there is discussion between the planners and factory personnel before the quota is announced. Apparently the planners are aware of the real capacities of the plant. There are 10-day plans, monthly plans, quarterly plans, annual plans, and 5-year plans. Included in these quotas are other targets, such as the size of the labor force, the productivity of the workers, and new techniques to be introduced.

We are told—and it is repeated—that 12 percent of the Wage Fund is kept by the plant for social and cultural benefits, housing, and the like. Obviously, new factories are not

Revolutionary propaganda is present in all areas of Chinese society, including culture. Here the Revolutionary Modern Ballet in Peking portrays a poor peasant girl's fight against a greedy landowner.

able to cover this from sales; for them, temporary state subsidies are required. In the Soviet Union, the benefits are financed mainly from unplanned profits.

Wages, too, are centrally determined for the most part. But a small wage increase for the lowest 40 percent of the workers was recently discussed and acted upon at the plant level, with the ultimate approval of the Ministry of Machine Building.

Though there is no indication of a piece-rate system of compensation, the principle seems to be, "From each according to his or her ability, to each according to his or her production." A worker's location in one of the eight pay grades is determined by fellow workers, who evaluate one another according to attitude toward work, quality of work, and quantity of output.

Adapted from Lynn Turgeon, "Notes on the New China," *Center Magazine,* November–December 1972, as edited and reprinted by Suzanne W. Helburn *et al., Economics in Society: Communist Economies,* Addison-Wesley, 1977, pp. 205–209. Reprinted with permission from the *Center Magazine,* a publication of the Center for the Study of Democratic Institutions, Santa Barbara, Calif.

Questions

1 How would you describe the role of women in Communist China on the basis of this reading?

2 According to this reading, what government controls exist in the Chinese economic system?

3 What similarities and differences do you see between the Chinese and other Communist systems?

◯ On the basis of the information in this visitor's report about the People's Republic of China, how do you think Communist economic systems differ?

Chapter 33 Review

Recalling and Comparing

1 What are *three* stages of history, according to Marx?
2 Which side in the class struggle did Marx think would triumph? How?
3 What did Marx mean by this statement: "Laborers . . . sell themselves . . . like every other article of commerce"?
4 Article 1 of the Soviet Constitution states: "The Union of Soviet Socialist Republics is a socialist state of the whole people. . . ." Why does the Constitution not use the term *communist state*?
5 How does the role of profits differ in the Soviet economic system and the free enterprise system?
6 What are *two* sources of funds for Soviet businesses?
7 Does the Soviet Union levy business taxes of any kind? Explain.
8 Would you call the Soviet Union a "welfare state"? Why or why not?
9 What would you say is the fundamental difference between socialism and communism? Explain.

Special Activities

1 Pretend that you are about to visit the Soviet Union. Draw up a list of *five* questions you would like to ask Soviet factory or farm workers about how the Communist economic system affects them. Then consult your local library. See if you can find answers to your questions.
2 Make a special bulletin-board display of articles about economic problems facing the United States free enterprise system and those facing the Soviet Communist economic system. What similarities and differences do you detect?
3 Prepare a skit in which a Soviet boy or girl visits your town. What might the visitor find most surprising? What might the visitor like most? What, if anything, might the visitor dislike? Why?
4 Obtain a copy of the Constitution of the People's Republic of China and compare it with other constitutions you have studied. Make a report of your findings.
5 Consider what might be arguments for and against the following statement: "The United States economy, despite its problems, provides a better life and more individual freedoms than the Communist economic system does." Do you agree or disagree? Why?

Developing Your Political Vocabulary

Match each term in *a–d* with the best definition or description in 1–4.

Marxism **a**   1 worker-owned enterprise
dictatorship of **b** 2 system of thought on which communist economies are based
the proletariat
state farm **c**   3 government-owned enterprise
collective farm **d** 4 government during "transition" to communism

Unit XII Review

Improving Your Reading

Read the selection below and then answer the questions that follow it.

All economic systems must answer the same basic questions: What goods and services will be produced? Who will produce them? How are the nation's resources to be used in the production process?

The economy of the United States is based on the free enterprise system, or capitalism. Two other economic systems in the modern world are socialism and communism. None of these systems exists in pure form or has ever done so.

The free enterprise system is centered on private ownership of business and industry. Business owners and investors are motivated by the hope of making a profit.

Early advocates of the free enterprise system believed in minimum government interference in the economy. This policy of laissez faire reached a high point in the United States in the 1800s. But toward the end of the 1800s, the federal government began to take action to stop abuses of the free enterprise system. Today, government plays an important role in economic life in the United States. Economists describe the present United States economy as a mixed economy based on free enterprise.

Businesses take three basic forms in the modern free enterprise system. They are the sole proprietorship, the partnership, and the corporation. Most major business enterprises in the United States today are corporations.

The socialist economic system was devised in Europe in the mid 1800s as a plan to correct the evils of the Industrial Revolution. Socialists said that capitalism could not be reformed and had to be replaced. Socialism places the ownership of the basic means of production in the hands of the public. Key industries are nationalized. Socialism also seeks to wipe out extremes of poverty and wealth. The government provides the basic necessities of life free or at a reduced charge.

A socialist economy may exist in democracies, under dictatorships, or under other types of governments. An extreme form of socialism is communism. Communism traces its origins to the writings of Karl Marx, a political thinker of the mid 1800s. Marx viewed capitalism as one of several stages of economic development. He believed that capitalism would inevitably give way to socialism and then to communism. The owners would finally be overthrown by the workers, who would then set up a dictatorship and introduce socialism. Out of this would eventually come a condition of true communism. When that came about, all people would work according to their ability and be provided for according to their needs.

The Soviet Union, which grew out of a Communist revolution in Russia in 1917, was the first nation to try introducing communism. The Soviet Union still considers itself to be passing through the stage of socialism on the way to creating true communism.

Almost all business is publicly owned, and the economy is run by central planning. By concentrating on heavy industry, the Soviet Union has made enormous economic strides. But output of consumer goods and agricultural production have lagged while individual rights are strictly limited.

1 In your words, summarize this reading in *no more than five* sentences. Have your summary focus on what you regard as the most important points in the reading.

2 Which *three* of the following describe aspects of the free enterprise system?

- **a** Government plays no role in economic life.
- **b** Most businesses are owned by private individuals.
- **c** Many businesses are organized as corporations.
- **d** The profit motive plays a major role in economic life.

3 Which *two* of the following describe aspects of socialism or communism?

- **a** Central planning plays a major role in the economy.
- **b** Private individuals are not allowed to engage in business.
- **c** The government provides certain essential goods and services.
- **d** Democratic elections are abolished.

Developing Your Writing Skills: What Are Your Attitudes toward Government?

The economic systems you have been reading about offer different answers to the following questions: (1) What roles should government and private individuals play in economic life? (2) How much, if any, central direction should be provided in an economy? (3) How much responsibility should government assume for the welfare of individuals? Write an essay telling how you would answer *one* of these questions. In your essay, use specific examples from your reading to support your arguments.

Recommended Readings

John Chamberlain, *The Enterprising Americans,* Harper & Row, New York, 1974.

John Chamberlain, *The Roots of Capitalism,* Liberty Fund, Indianapolis, 1977 (paperback).

Marquis Childs, *Sweden, The Middle Way,* Yale University Press, New Haven, Conn., 1961 (paperback).

Morris A. Copeland, *Our Free Enterprise Economy,* Macmillan, New York, 1965 (paperback).

Fred Fairchild and Thomas J. Shelby, *Understanding Our Free Economy: An Introduction to Economics* (latest edition), Van Nostrand, Princeton, N.J.

Suzanne W. Helburn *et al., Economics in Society: Communist Economies,* Addison-Wesley, Menlo Park, Calif., 1977 (paperback).

Richard M. Hodgetts and Terry L. Smart, *Fundamentals of the American Free Enterprise System,* Addison-Wesley, Menlo Park, Calif., 1978.

Meno Lovenstein, *Capitalism, Communism, and Socialism,* Scott, Foresman, Glenview, Ill., 1962.

Paul A. Samuelson, *Economics* (latest edition), McGraw-Hill, New York.

DECLARATION OF INDEPENDENCE

When in the Course of human events, it becomes necessary for one people to dissolve the political bands which have connected them with another, and to assume among the Powers of the earth, the separate and equal station to which the Laws of Nature and of Nature's God entitle them, a decent respect to the opinions of mankind requires that they should declare the causes which impel them to the separation.

We hold these truths to be self-evident, that all men are created equal, that they are endowed by their Creator with certain unalienable Rights, that among these are Life, Liberty and the pursuit of Happiness. That to secure these rights, Governments are instituted among Men, deriving their just powers from the consent of the governed, That whenever any Form of Government becomes destructive of these ends, it is the Right of the People to alter or to abolish it, and to institute new Government, laying its foundation on such principles and organizing its powers in such form, as to them shall seem most likely to effect their Safety and Happiness. Prudence, indeed, will dictate that Governments long established should not be changed for light and transient causes; and accordingly all experience hath shown, that mankind are more disposed to suffer, while evils are sufferable, than to right themselves by abolishing the forms to which they are accustomed. But when a long train of abuses and usurpations, pursuing invariably the same Object evinces a design to reduce them under absolute Despotism, it is their right, it is their duty, to throw off such Government, and to provide new Guards for their future security. —Such has been the patient sufferance of these Colonies; and such is now the necessity which constrains them to alter their former Systems of Government. The history of the present King of Great Britain is a history of repeated injuries and usurpations, all having in direct object the establishment of an absolute Tyranny over these States. To prove this, let Facts be submitted to a candid world.

He has refused his Assent to Laws, the most wholesome and necessary for the public good.

He has forbidden his Governors to pass Laws of immediate and pressing importance, unless suspended in their operation till his Assent should be obtained; and when so suspended, he has utterly neglected to attend to them.

He has refused to pass other Laws for the accommodation of large districts of people, unless those people would relinquish the right of Representation in the Legislature, a right inestimable to them and formidable to tyrants only.

He has called together legislative bodies at places unusual, uncomfortable, and distant from the depository of their Public Records, for the sole purpose of fatiguing them into compliance with his measures.

He has dissolved Representative Houses repeatedly, for opposing with manly firmness his invasions on the rights of the people.

He has refused for a long time, after such dissolutions, to cause others to be elected; whereby the Legislative Powers, incapable of Annihilation, have returned to the People at large for their exercise; the State remaining in the mean time exposed to all the dangers of invasion from without, and convulsions within.

He has endeavoured to prevent the population of these States; for the purpose obstructing the Laws of Naturalization of Foreigners; refusing to pass others to encourage their migration hither, and raising the conditions of new Appropriations of Lands.

He has obstructed the Administration of Justice, by refusing his Assent to Laws for establishing Judiciary Powers.

He has made Judges dependent on his Will alone, for the tenure of their offices, and the amount and payment of their salaries.

He has erected a multitude of New Offices, and sent hither swarms of Officers to harass our People, and eat out their substance.

He has kept among us, in times of peace, Standing Armies without the Consent of our legislature.

He has affected to render the Military independent of and superior to the Civil Power.

He has combined with others to subject us to a jurisdiction foreign to our constitution, and unacknowledged by our laws; giving his Assent to their acts of pretended legislation:

For quartering large bodies of armed troops among us:

For protecting them, by a mock Trial, from Punishment for any Murders which they should commit on the Inhabitants of these States:

For cutting off our Trade with all parts of the world:

For imposing taxes on us without our Consent:

For depriving us in many cases, of the benefits of Trial by Jury:

For transporting us beyond Seas to be tried for pretended offences:

For abolishing the free System of English Laws in a neighbouring Province, establishing therein an Arbitrary government, and enlarging its Boundaries so as to render it at once an example and fit instrument for introducing the same absolute rule into these Colonies:

For taking away our Charters, abolishing our most valuable Laws, and altering fundamentally the Forms of our Governments:

For suspending our own Legislature, and declaring themselves invested with Power to legislate for us in all cases whatsoever.

He has abdicated Government here, by declaring us out of his Protection and waging War against us.

He has plundered our seas, ravaged our Coasts, burnt our towns, and destroyed the lives of our people.

He is at this time transporting large armies of foreign mercenaries to compleat the works of death, desolation and tyranny, already begun with circumstances of Cruelty & perfidy scarcely paralleled in the most barbarous ages, and totally unworthy of the Head of a civilized nation.

He has constrained our fellow Citizens taken Captive on the high Seas to bear Arms against their Country, to become the executioners of their friends and Brethren, or to fall themselves by their Hands.

He has excited domestic insurrections amongst us, and has endeavoured to bring on the inhabitants of our frontiers, the merciless Indian Savages, whose known rule of warfare, is an undistinguished destruction of all ages, sexes and conditions.

In every stage of these Oppressions We have Petitioned for Redress in the most humble terms: Our repeated Petitions have been answered only by repeated injury. A Prince, whose character is thus marked by every act which may define a Tyrant, is unfit to be the ruler of a free People.

Nor have We been wanting in attention to our British brethren. We have warned them from time to time of attempts by their legislature to extend an unwarrantable jurisdiction over us. We have reminded them of the circumstances of our emigration and settlement here. We have appealed to their native justice and magnanimity, and we have conjured them by the ties of our common kindred to disavow these usurpations, which, would inevitably interrupt our connections and correspondence. They too have been deaf to the voice of justice and of consanguinity. We must, therefore, acquiesce in the necessity, which denounces our Separation, and hold them, as we hold the rest of mankind, Enemies in War, in Peace Friends.

We, therefore, the Representatives of the United States of America, in General Congress, Assembled, appealing to the Supreme Judge of the world for the rectitude of our intentions, do, in the Name, and by Authority of the good People of these Colonies, solemnly publish and declare, That these United Colonies are, and of Right ought to be Free and Independent States; that they are Absolved from all Allegiance to the British Crown, and that all political connection between them and the State of Great Britain, is and ought to be totally dissolved; and that as Free and Independent States, they have full Power to levy War, conclude Peace, contract Alliances, establish Commerce, and to do all other Acts and Things which Independent States may of right do. And for the support of this Declaration, with a firm reliance on the Protection of Divine Providence, we mutually pledge to each other our Lives, our Fortunes and our sacred Honor.

CONSTITUTION OF THE UNITED STATES

[PREAMBLE]

We the people of the United States, in Order to form a more perfect Union, establish Justice, insure domestic Tranquility, provide for the common defence, promote the general Welfare, and secure the Blessings of Liberty to ourselves and our Posterity, do ordain and establish this CONSTITUTION for the United States of America.

[ORIGINAL ARTICLES]

Article I (Legislative Branch)

Section 1 (Congress)

All legislative Powers herein granted shall be vested in a Congress of the United States, which shall consist of a Senate and House of Representatives.

Section 2 (House of Representatives)

The House of Representatives shall be composed of Members chosen every second Year by the People of the several States, and the Electors in each State shall have the Qualifications requisite for Electors of the most numerous Branch of the State Legislature.

(Qualifications of Representatives)

No Person shall be a Representative who shall not have attained to the Age of twenty-five Years, and been seven Years a Citizen of the United States, and who shall not, when elected, be an Inhabitant of that State in which he shall be chosen.

(Method of Apportionment)

Representatives and direct Taxes shall be apportioned among the several States which may be included within this Union, according to their respective Numbers, which shall be determined by adding to the whole Number of free Persons, including those bound to Service for a Term of Years, and excluding Indians not taxed, three fifths of all other Persons. The actual Enumeration shall be made within three Years after the first Meeting of the Congress of the United States, and within every subsequent Term of ten Years, in such Manner as they shall by Law direct. The Number of Representatives shall not exceed one for every thirty Thousand, but each state shall have at Least one Representative; and until such enumeration shall be made, the State of New Hampshire shall be entitled to chuse three, Massachusetts eight, Rhode-Island and Providence Plantations one, Connecticut five, New-York six, New Jersey four, Pennsylvania eight, Delaware one, Maryland six, Virginia ten, North Carolina five, South Carolina five, and Georgia three.

(Vacancies)

When vacancies happen in the Representation from any State, the Executive Authority thereof shall issue Writs of Election to fill such Vacancies.

(Rules of the House; Impeachment)

The House of Representatives shall chuse their Speaker and other Officers; and shall have the sole Power of Impeachment.

Section 3 (Senators)

The Senate of the United States shall be composed of two Senators from each State, chosen by the Legislature thereof, for six Years; and each Senator shall have one Vote.

Immediately after they shall be assembled in Consequence of the first Election, they shall be divided as equally as may be into three Classes. The Seats of the Senators of the first Class shall be vacated at the Expiration of the second Year, of the second Class at the Expiration of the fourth Year, and of the third Class at the Expiration of the sixth Year, so that one-third may be chosen every second Year; and if Vacancies happen by Resignation, or otherwise, during the Recess of the Legislature of any State, the Executive thereof may make temporary Appointments until the next Meeting of the Legislature, which shall then fill such Vacancies.

(Qualifications of Senators)

No person shall be a Senator who shall not have attained to the Age of thirty Years, and been nine Years a Citizen of the United States, and who shall not, when elected, be an Inhabitant of that State in which he shall be chosen.

(Officers of the Senate)

The Vice President of the United States shall be President of the Senate, but shall have no vote, unless they be equally divided.

The Senate shall chuse their other Officers, and also a President pro tempore, in the absence of the Vice President, or when he shall exercise the Office of the President of the United States.

(Impeachment Trials)

The Senate shall have the sole Power to try all Impeachments. When sitting for that purpose, they shall be on Oath or Affirmation. When the President of the United States is tried, the Chief Justice shall preside: And no person shall be convicted without the Concurrence of two thirds of the Members present.

Judgment in Cases of Impeachment shall not extend further than to removal from Office, and disqualification to hold and enjoy any Office of honor, Trust, or Profit under the United States: but the Party convicted shall nevertheless be liable and subject to Indictment, Trial, Judgment, and Punishment, according to Law.

Section 4 (Congressional Elections and Sessions)

The Times, Places and Manner of holding Elections for Senators and Representatives, shall be prescribed in each state by the Legislature thereof: but the Congress may at any time by Law make or alter such Regulations, except as to the Places of Chusing Senators.

The Congress shall assemble at least once in every Year, and such Meeting shall be on the first Monday in December, unless they shall by Law appoint a different Day.

Section 5 (Congressional Rules)

Each House shall be the Judge of the Elections, Returns and Qualifications of its own Members, and a Majority of each shall constitute a Quorum to do Business; but a smaller number may adjourn from day to day, and may be authorized to compel the Attendance of absent Members, in such Manner, and under such Penalties, as each House may provide.

Each house may determine the Rules of its Proceedings, punish its Members for disorderly Behavior, and, with the Concurrence of two thirds, expel a Member.

Each House shall keep a Journal of its Proceedings, and from time to time publish the same, excepting such Parts as may in their Judgment require Secrecy; and the Yeas and Nays of the Members of either House on any question shall, at the Desire of one fifth of those Present, be entered on the Journal.

Neither House, during the Session of Congress, shall, without the Consent of the other, adjourn for more than three days, nor to any other Place than that in which the two Houses shall be sitting.

Section 6 (Payment and Privileges of, and Restrictions on, Members of Congress)

The Senators and Representatives shall receive a Compensation for their Services, to be ascertained by Law, and paid out of the Treasury of the United States. They shall in all Cases, except Treason, Felony, and Breach of the Peace, be privileged from Arrest during their Attendance at the Session of their respective Houses, and in going to and returning from the same; and for any Speech or Debate in either House, they shall not be questioned in any other Place.

No Senator or Representative shall, during the Time for which he was elected, be appointed to any civil Office under the Authority of the United States, which shall have been created, or the Emoluments whereof shall have been increased, during such time; and no Person holding any Office under the United States shall be a Member of either House during his continuance in Office.

Section 7 (Money Bills; Presidential Action on Bills)

All Bills for raising Revenue shall originate in the House of Representatives; but the Senate may propose or concur with Amendments as on other bills.

Every Bill which shall have passed the House of Representatives and the Senate, shall, before it become a Law, be presented to the President of the United States; If he approve he shall sign it, but if not he shall return it, with his Objections, to that House in which it shall have originated, who shall enter the Objections at large on their Journal, and proceed to reconsider it. If after such Reconsideration two thirds of that House shall agree to pass the bill, it shall be sent, together with the objections, to the other House, by which it shall likewise be reconsidered, and if approved by two thirds of that House, it shall become a Law. But in all such Cases the Votes of both Houses shall be determined by Yeas and Nays, and the Names of the Persons voting for and against the Bill shall be entered on the Journal of each House respectively. If any Bill shall not be returned by the President within ten Days (Sundays excepted) after it shall have been presented to him, the Same shall be a Law, in like Manner as if he had signed it, unless the Congress by their Adjournment prevent its Return, in which Case it shall not be a Law.

Every Order, Resolution, or Vote to which the Concurrence of the Senate and House of Representatives may be necessary (except on a question of Adjournment) shall be presented to the President of the United States; and before the Same shall take Effect, shall be approved by him, or being disapproved by him, shall be repassed by two thirds of the Senate and House of Representatives, according to the Rules and Limitations prescribed in the Case of a Bill.

Section 8 (Powers of Congress)

The Congress shall have Power To lay and collect Taxes, Duties, Imposts and Excises, to pay the Debts and provide for the common Defence and general Welfare of the United States; but all Duties, Imposts and Excises shall be uniform throughout the United States;

To borrow money on the credit of the United States;

To regulate Commerce with foreign Nations, and among the several States, and with the Indian Tribes;

To establish an uniform Rule of Naturalization, and uniform Laws on the subject of Bankruptcies throughout the United States;

To coin Money, regulate the Value thereof, and of foreign Coin, and fix the Standard of Weights and Measures;

To provide for the Punishment of counterfeiting the Securities and current Coin of the United States;

To establish Post Offices and post Roads;

To promote the Progress of Science and useful Arts, by securing for limited Times to Authors and Inventors the exclusive Right to their respective Writings and Discoveries;

To constitute Tribunals inferior to the Supreme Court;

To define and punish Piracies and Felonies committed on the high Seas, and Offenses against the Law of Nations;

To declare War, grant Letters of Marque and Reprisal, and make Rules concerning Captures on Land and Water;

To raise and support Armies, but no Appropriation of Money to that Use shall be for a longer Term than two Years;

To provide and maintain a Navy;

To make Rules for the Government and Regulation of the land and naval forces;

To provide for calling forth the Militia to execute the Laws of the Union, suppress Insurrections and repel Invasions;

To provide for organizing, arming, and disciplining the Militia, and for governing such Part of them as may be employed in the Service of the United States, reserving to the States respectively, the Appointment of the Officers, and the Authority of training the Militia according to the discipline prescribed by Congress;

To exercise exclusive Legislation in all Cases whatsoever, over such District (not exceeding ten Miles square) as may, by Cession of particular States, and the acceptance of Congress, become the Seat of Government of the United States, and to exercise like Authority over all Places purchased by the Consent of the Legislature of the State in which the Same shall be, for the Erection of Forts, Magazines, Arsenals, dock-Yards, and other needful Buildings;—And

To make all Laws which shall be necessary and proper for carrying into Execution the foregoing Powers, and all other Powers vested by this Constitution in the Government of the United States, or in any Department or Officer thereof.

Section 9 (Limits on Congressional Power)

The Migration or Importation of such Persons as any of the States now existing shall think proper to admit, shall not be prohibited by the Congress prior to the Year one thousand eight hundred and eight, but a tax or duty may be imposed on such Importation, not exceeding ten dollars for each Person.

The privilege of the Writ of Habeas Corpus shall not be suspended, unless when in Cases of Rebellion or Invasion the public Safety may require it.

No Bill of Attainder or ex post facto Law shall be passed.

No capitation, or other direct, Tax shall be laid unless in Proportion to the Census or Enumeration herein before directed to be taken.

No Tax or Duty shall be laid on Articles exported from any State.

No Preference shall be given by any Regulation of Revenue to the Ports of one State over those of another: nor shall Vessels bound to, or from, one State, be obliged to enter, clear, or pay Duties in another.

No Money shall be drawn from the Treasury, but in Consequence of Appropriations made by Law; and a regular Statement and Account of the Receipts and Expenditures of all public Money shall be published from time to time.

No Title of Nobility shall be granted by the United States: And no Person holding any Office of Profit or Trust under them, shall, without the Consent of the Congress, accept of any present, Emolument, Office, or Title, of any kind whatever, from any King, Prince, or foreign State.

Section 10 (Limits on Powers of the States)

No State shall enter into any Treaty, Alliance, or Confederation; grant Letters of Marque and Reprisal; coin Money; emit Bills of Credit; make any Thing but gold and silver Coin a Tender in Payment of Debts; pass any Bill of Attainder, ex post facto Law, or Law impairing the Obligation of Contracts, or grant any Title of Nobility.

No State shall, without the Consent of the Congress, lay any Imposts or Duties on Imports or Exports, except what may be absolutely necessary for executing its inspection Laws: and the net Produce of all Duties and Imposts, laid by any State on Imports or Exports, shall be for the Use of the Treasury of the United States; and all such Laws shall be subject to the Revision and Control of the Congress.

No State shall, without the Consent of Congress, lay any duty of Tonnage, keep Troops, or Ships of War in time of Peace, enter into any Agreement or Compact with another State, or with a foreign Power, or engage in War, unless actually invaded, or in such imminent Danger as will not admit of delay.

Article II (Executive Branch)

Section 1 (President and Vice President)

The executive Power shall be vested in a President of the United States of America. He shall hold his Office during the Term of four years, and, together with the Vice

President, chosen for the same Term, be elected, as follows:

(Method of Electing President and Vice President)

Each State shall appoint in such Manner as the Legislature thereof may direct, a Number of Electors, equal to the whole Number of Senators and Representatives to which the State may be entitled in the Congress: but no Senator or Representative, or Person holding an Office of Trust or Profit under the United States, shall be appointed an Elector.

The Electors shall meet in their respective States, and vote by Ballot for two persons, of whom one at least shall not be an Inhabitant of the same State with themselves. And they shall make a List of all the Persons voted for, and of the Number of Votes for each; which List they shall sign and certify, and transmit sealed to the Seat of the Government of the United States, directed to the President of the Senate. The President of the Senate shall, in the Presence of the Senate and House of Representatives, open all the Certificates, and the Votes shall then be counted. The Person having the greatest Number of Votes shall be the President, if such Number be a Majority of the whole Number of Electors appointed; and if there be more than one who have such Majority, and have an equal Number of Votes, then the House of Representatives shall immediately chuse by Ballot one of them for President; and if no Person have a Majority, then from the five highest on the List the said House shall in like Manner chuse the President. But in chusing the President, the Votes shall be taken by States, the Representation from each State having one Vote; a quorum for this Purpose shall consist of a Member or Members from two-thirds of the States, and a Majority of all the States shall be necessary to a Choice. In every Case, after the Choice of the President, the Person having the greatest Number of Votes of the Electors shall be the Vice President. But if there should remain two or more who have equal votes, the Senate shall chuse from them by Ballot the Vice President.

The Congress may determine the Time of chusing the Electors, and the Day on which they shall give their Votes; which Day shall be the same throughout the United States.

(Qualifications of President)

No person except a natural-born Citizen, or a Citizen of the United States, at the time of the Adoption of this Constitution, shall be eligible to the Office of President; neither shall any Person be eligible to that Office who shall not have attained to the Age of thirty-five years, and been fourteen Years a Resident within the United States.

(Vacancy in Office of President)

In Case of the Removal of the President from Office, or of his Death, Resignation, or Inability to discharge the Powers and Duties of the said Office, the same shall devolve on the Vice President, and the Congress may by Law provide for the Case of Removal, Death, Resignation, or Inability, both of the President and Vice President, declaring what Officer shall then act as President, and such Officer shall act accordingly, until the disability be removed, or a President shall be elected.

(Payment of President)

The President shall, at stated Times, receive for his Services a Compensation, which shall neither be increased nor diminished during the Period for which he shall have been elected, and he shall not receive within that Period any other Emolument from the United States, or any of them.

(President's Oath of Office)

Before he enters on the execution of his Office, he shall take the following Oath or Affirmation:—"I do solemnly swear (or affirm) that I will faithfully execute the Office of President of the United States, and will, to the best of my Ability, preserve, protect, and defend the Constitution of the United States."

Section 2 (Powers of the President)

The President shall be Commander in Chief of the Army and Navy of the United States, and of the Militia of the several States, when called into the actual Service of the United States; he may require the Opinion, in writing, of the principal Officer in each of the executive Departments, upon any subject relating to the Duties of their respective Offices, and he shall have Power to Grant Reprieves and Pardons for Offenses against the United States, except in Cases of Impeachment.

(Making of Treaties and Appointments)

He shall have Power, by and with the Advice and Consent of the Senate, to make Treaties, provided two thirds of the Senators present concur; and he shall nominate, and by and with the Advice and Consent of the Senate, shall appoint Ambassadors, other public Ministers and Consuls, Judges of the supreme Court, and all other Officers of the United States, whose Appointments are not herein otherwise provided for, and which shall be established by Law: but the Congress may by Law vest the Appointment of such inferior Officers, as they think proper, in the President alone, in the Courts of Law, or in the Heads of Departments.

The President shall have Power to fill up all Vacancies that may happen during the Recess of the Senate, by granting Commissions which shall expire at the End of their next Session.

Section 3 (President's Other Powers and Duties)

He shall from time to time give to the Congress Information of the State of the Union, and recommend to their

Consideration such Measures as he shall judge necessary and expedient; he may, on extraordinary occasions, convene both Houses, or either of them, and in Case of Disagreement between them, with respect to the Time of Adjournment, he may adjourn them to such Time as he shall think proper; he shall receive Ambassadors and other public Ministers; he shall take Care that the Laws be faithfully executed, and shall Commission all the Officers of the United States.

Section 4 (Impeachment)

The President, Vice President and all civil Officers of the United States, shall be removed from Office on Impeachment for, and Conviction of, Treason, Bribery, or other high Crimes and Misdemeanors.

Article III (Judicial Branch)

Section 1 (Federal Courts and Judges)

The judicial Power of the United States, shall be vested in one supreme Court, and in such inferior Courts as the Congress may from time to time ordain and establish. The judges, both of the supreme and inferior Courts, shall hold their Offices during good Behaviour, and shall, at stated Times, receive for their Services, a Compensation, which shall not be diminished during their Continuance in Office.

Section 2 (Jurisdiction of Federal Courts)

The judicial Power shall extend to all Cases, in Law and Equity, arising under this Constitution, the Laws of the United States, and treaties made, or which shall be made, under their Authority;—to all Cases affecting ambassadors, other public ministers and consuls;—to all cases of admiralty and maritime Jurisdiction;—to Controversies to which the United States shall be a Party;—to Controversies between two or more States;—between a State and Citizens of another State;—between Citizens of different States,—between Citizens of the same State claiming Lands under Grants of different States, and between a State, or the Citizens thereof, and foreign States, Citizens or Subjects.

In all Cases affecting Ambassadors, other public Ministers and Consuls, and those in which a State shall be Party, the supreme Court shall have original Jurisdiction. In all the other Cases before mentioned, the supreme Court shall have appellate Jurisdiction, both as to Law and Fact, with such Exceptions, and under such Regulations as the Congress shall make.

(Trial of Crimes)

The trial of all Crimes, except in Cases of Impeachment, shall be by Jury; and such Trial shall be held in the State where the said Crimes shall have been committed; but when not committed within any State, the Trial shall be at such Place or Places as the Congress may by Law have directed.

Section 3 (Treason)

Treason against the United States, shall consist only in levying War against them, or in adhering to their Enemies, giving them Aid and Comfort. No Person shall be convicted of Treason unless on the Testimony of two Witnesses to the same overt Act, or on Confession in open Court.

The Congress shall have power to declare the Punishment of Treason, but no Attainder of Treason shall work Corruption of Blood, or Forfeiture except during the Life of the Person attainted.

Article IV (States in the Federal System)

Section 1 (Validity of State Actions and Records)

Full Faith and Credit shall be given in each State to the public Acts, Records, and judicial Proceedings of every other State. And the Congress may by general Laws prescribe the Manner in which such Acts, Records, and Proceedings shall be proved, and the Effect thereof.

Section 2 (Citizens' Privileges and Immunities in the States)

The Citizens of each State shall be entitled to all Privileges and Immunities of Citizens in the several states.

A Person charged in any State with Treason, Felony, or other Crime, who shall flee from Justice, and be found in another State, shall on demand of the executive Authority of the State from which he fled, be delivered up, to be removed to the State having Jurisdiction of the crime.

No Person held to Service or Labour in one State, under the Laws thereof, escaping into another, shall, in Consequence of any Law or Regulation therein, be discharged from such Service or Labour, but shall be delivered up on Claim of the Party to whom such Service or Labour may be due.

Section 3 (New States; United States Territory and Property)

New States may be admitted by the Congress into this Union; but no new State shall be formed or erected within the Jurisdiction of any other State; nor any State be formed by the Junction of two or more States, or parts of States, without the Consent of the Legislatures of the States concerned as well as of the Congress.

The Congress shall have Power to dispose of and make all needful Rules and Regulations respecting the Territory or other Property belonging to the United States; and nothing in this Constitution shall be so construed as to Prejudice any Claims of the United States, or of any particular State.

Section 4 (Federal Protection of the States)

The United States shall guarantee to every State in this Union a Republican Form of Government, and shall protect each of them against Invasion; and on Application of the Legislature, or of the Executive (when the Legislature cannot be convened) against domestic Violence.

Article V (Amending the Constitution)

The Congress, whenever two-thirds of both Houses shall deem it necessary, shall propose Amendments to this Constitution, or, on the Application of the Legislatures of two-thirds of the several States, shall call a Convention for proposing Amendments, which, in either Case, shall be valid to all Intents and Purposes, as part of this Constitution, when ratified by the Legislatures of three-fourths of the several States, or by Conventions in three-fourths thereof, as the one or the other Mode of Ratification may be proposed by the Congress; Provided that no Amendment which may be made prior to the Year One thousand eight hundred and eight shall in any Manner affect the first and fourth Clauses in the Ninth Section of the first Article; and that no State, without its Consent, shall be deprived of its equal Suffrage in the Senate.

Article VI (Constitution as Supreme Law)

All Debts contracted and Engagements entered into, before the Adoption of this Constitution, shall be as valid against the United States under this Constitution, as under the Confederation.

This Constitution, and the Laws of the United States which shall be made in Pursuance thereof; and all Treaties made, or which shall be made, under the Authority of the United States, shall be the supreme Law of the Land; and the Judges in every State shall be bound thereby, any Thing in the Constitution or Laws of any State to the Contrary notwithstanding.

The Senators and Representatives before mentioned, and the Members of the several State Legislatures, and all executive and judicial Officers, both of the United States and of the several States, shall be bound by Oath or Affirmation to support this Constitution; but no religious Test shall ever be required as a qualification to any Office or public Trust under the United States.

Article VII (Process of Ratification)

The Ratification of the Conventions of nine States shall be sufficient for the Establishment of this Constitution between the States so ratifying the same.

Done in Convention by the Unanimous Consent of the States present the Seventeenth Day of September in the Year of our Lord one thousand seven hundred and Eighty seven, and of the Independence of the United States of America the Twelfth. In Witness whereof We have hereunto subscribed our Names.

[ARTICLES OF AMENDMENT (date of ratification)]

Amendment I (1791) (Freedom of Religion, Speech, Press, Assembly, and Petition)

Congress shall make no law respecting an establishment of religion, or prohibiting the free exercise thereof; or abridging the freedom of speech, or of the press; or the right of the people peaceably to assemble, and to petition the Government for a redress of grievances.

Amendment II (1791) (Right to Bear Arms)

A well regulated Militia, being necessary to the security of a free State, the right of the people to keep and bear Arms shall not be infringed.

Amendment III (1791) (Quartering of Soldiers)

No soldier shall, in time of peace, be quartered in any house, without the consent of the Owner, nor in time of war, but in a manner to be prescribed by law.

Amendment IV (1791) (Searches and Seizures)

The right of the people to be secure in their persons, houses, papers, and effects, against unreasonable searches and seizures, shall not be violated, and no Warrants shall issue, but upon probable cause, supported by Oath or affirmation, and particularly describing the place to be searched, and the persons or things to be seized.

Amendment V (1791) (Rights in Criminal Cases; Due Process)

No person shall be held to answer for a capital or otherwise infamous crime, unless on a presentment or indictment of a Grand Jury, except in cases arising in the land or naval forces, or in the Militia, when in actual service in time of War or public danger; nor shall any person be subject for the same offence to be twice put in jeopardy of life or limb; nor shall be compelled in any criminal case to be a witness against himself, nor be deprived of life, liberty, or property, without due process of law; nor shall private property be taken for public use, without just compensation.

Amendment VI (1791) (Rights in Criminal Cases; Trials)

In all criminal prosecutions, the accused shall enjoy the right to a speedy and public trial, by an impartial jury of the State and district wherein the crime shall have been committed, which district shall have been previously ascertained by law, and to be informed of the nature and cause of the accusation; to be confronted with the witnesses against him; to have compulsory process for obtaining witnesses in his favor, and to have the Assistance of Counsel for his defence.

Amendment VII (1791) (Civil Suits; Trials)

In suits at common law, where the value in controversy shall exceed twenty dollars, the right of trial by jury shall be preserved, and no fact tried by a jury, shall be otherwise reexamined in any Court of the United States, than according to the rules of the common law.

Amendment VIII (1791) (Bails, Fines, Punishments)

Excessive bail shall not be required, nor excessive fines imposed, nor cruel and unusual punishments inflicted.

Amendment IX (1791) (Rights Retained by the People)

The enumeration in the Constitution, of certain rights, shall not be construed to deny or disparage others retained by the people.

Amendment X (1791) (Rights Reserved to the States)

The powers not delegated to the United States by the Constitution, nor prohibited by it to the States, are reserved to the States respectively, or to the people.

Amendment XI (1798) (Suits against States)

The Judicial power of the United States shall not be construed to extend to any suit in law or equity, commenced or prosecuted against one of the United States by Citizens of another State, or by Citizens or Subjects of any Foreign State.

Amendment XII (1804) (Method of Electing President and Vice President)

The Electors shall meet in their respective States and vote by ballot for President and Vice President, one of whom, at least, shall not be an inhabitant of the same State with themselves; they shall name in their ballots the person voted for as President, and in distinct ballots the person voted for as Vice President, and they shall make distinct lists of all persons voted for as President, and of all persons voted for as Vice President, and of the number of votes for each, which lists they shall sign and certify, and transmit sealed to the seat of the government of the United States, directed to the President of the Senate;— The President of the Senate shall, in the presence of the Senate and House of Representatives, open all the certificates and the votes shall then be counted;—The person having the greatest number of votes for President, shall be the President, if such number be a majority of the whole number of Electors appointed; and if no person have such majority, then from the persons having the highest numbers not exceeding three on the list of those voted for as President, the House of Representatives shall choose immediately, by ballot, the President. But in choosing the President, the votes shall be taken by states, the representation from each state having one vote; a quorum for this purpose shall consist of a member or members from two-thirds of the states, and a majority of all the states shall be necessary to a choice. And if the House of Representatives shall not choose a President whenever the right of choice shall devolve upon them, before the fourth day of March next following, then the Vice President shall act as President, as in the case of the death or other constitutional disability of the President.—The person having the greatest number of votes as Vice President, shall be the Vice President, if such number be a majority of the whole number of Electors appointed, and if no person have a majority, then from the two highest numbers on the list, the Senate shall choose the Vice President; a quorum for the purpose shall consist of two-thirds of the whole number of Senators, and a majority of the whole number shall be necessary to a choice. But no person constitutionally ineligible to the office of President shall be eligible to that of Vice President of the United States.

Amendment XIII (1865) (Abolition of Slavery)

Section 1

Neither slavery nor involuntary servitude, except as a punishment for crime whereof the party shall have been duly convicted, shall exist within the United States, or any place subject to their jurisdiction.

Section 2 (Enforcement)

Congress shall have power to enforce this article by appropriate legislation.

Amendment XIV (1868) (Civil Rights)

Section 1 (Citizenship; Due Process; Equal Protection)

All persons born or naturalized in the United States, and subject to the jurisdiction thereof, are citizens of the United States and of the State wherein they reside. No State shall make or enforce any law which shall abridge the privileges or immunities of citizens of the United States; nor shall any State deprive any person of life, liberty, or property, without due process of law; nor deny to any person within its jurisdiction the equal protection of the laws.

Section 2 (Apportionment of Representatives)

Representatives shall be apportioned among the several States according to their respective numbers, counting the whole number of persons in each State, excluding Indians not taxed. But when the right to vote at any election for the choice of electors for President and Vice President of the United States, Representatives in Congress, the Executive and Judicial officers of a State, or the members of the Legislature thereof, is denied to any of the male inhabitants of such State, being twenty-one years of age, and citizens of the United States, or in any way abridged, except for participation in rebellion, or other crime, the basis of representation therein shall be reduced in the proportion which the number of such male citizens shall bear to the whole number of male citizens twenty-one years of age in such State.

Section 3 (Loss of Rights)

No person shall be a Senator or Representative in Congress, or elector of President and Vice President, or hold any office, civil or military, under the United States, or under any State, who, having previously taken an oath, as a member of Congress, or as an officer of the United States, or as a member of any State legislature, or as an executive or judicial officer of any State, to support the Constitution of the United States, shall have engaged in insurrection or rebellion against the same, or given aid or comfort to the enemies thereof. But Congress may by a vote of two-thirds of each House, remove such disability.

Section 4 (Public Debt)

The validity of the public debt of the United States, authorized by law, including debts incurred for payment of pensions and bounties for services in suppressing insurrection or rebellion, shall not be questioned. But neither the United States nor any State shall assume or pay any debt or obligation incurred in aid of insurrection or rebellion against the United States, or any claim for the loss or emancipation of any slave; but all such debts, obligations, and claims shall be held illegal and void.

Section 5 (Enforcement)

The Congress shall have the power to enforce, by appropriate legislation, the provisions of this article.

Amendment XV (1870) (Right to Vote)

Section 1 (Extent of Right)

The right of citizens of the United States to vote shall not be denied or abridged by the United States or by any State on account of race, color or previous condition of servitude.

Section 2 (Enforcement)

The Congress shall have power to enforce this article by appropriate legislation.

Amendment XVI (1913) (Federal Income Tax)

The Congress shall have power to lay and collect taxes on incomes, from whatever source derived, without apportionment among the several States, and without regard to any census or enumeration.

Amendment XVII (1913) (Election of Senators)

(Number; Term; Electors)

The Senate of the United States shall be composed of two Senators from each State, elected by the people thereof, for six years; and each Senator shall have one vote. The electors in each State shall have the qualifications requisite for electors of the most numerous branch of the State legislatures.

(Vacancies)

When vacancies happen in the representation of any State in the Senate, the executive authority of such State shall issue writs of election to fill such vacancies: *Provided,* That the legislature of any State may empower the executive thereof to make temporary appointments until the people fill the vacancies by election as the legislature may direct.

This amendment shall not be so construed as to affect the election or term of any Senator chosen before it becomes valid as part of the Constitution.

Amendment XVIII (1919) (Prohibition)

Section 1 (Provisions)

After one year from the ratification of this article the manufacture, sale, or transportation of intoxicating liquors within, the importation thereof into, or the exportation thereof from the United States and all territory subject to the jurisdiction thereof for beverage purposes is hereby prohibited.

Section 2 (Enforcement)

The Congress and the several States shall have concurrent power to enforce this article by appropriate legislation.

Section 3 (Ratification Process)

This article shall be inoperative unless it shall have been ratified as an amendment to the Constitution by the legislatures of the several States, as provided in the Constitution, within seven years from the date of the submission hereof to the States by the Congress.

Amendment XIX (1920) (Woman Suffrage)

The right of citizens of the United States to vote shall not be denied or abridged by the United States or by any State on account of sex.

Congress shall have power to enforce this article by appropriate legislation.

Amendment XX (1933) (Commencement of Terms; Vacancy in Office of President)

Section 1 (President and Vice President; Members of Congress)

The terms of the President and Vice President shall end at noon on the 20th day of January, and the terms of Senators and Representatives at noon on the 3d day of January, of the years in which such terms would have ended if this article had not been ratified; and the terms of their successors shall then begin.

Section 2 (Meetings of Congress)

The Congress shall assemble at least once in every year, and such meeting shall begin at noon on the 3d day of January, unless they shall by law appoint a different day.

Section 3 (Vacancy in Office of President)

If, at the time fixed for the beginning of the term of the President, the President elect shall have died, the Vice President elect shall become President. If a President shall not have been chosen before the time fixed for the beginning of his term, or if the President elect shall have failed to qualify, then the Vice President elect shall act as President until a President shall have qualified; and the Congress may by law provide for the case wherein neither a President elect nor a Vice President elect shall have qualified, declaring who shall then act as President, or the manner in which one who is to act shall be selected, and such person shall act accordingly until a President or Vice President shall have qualified.

Section 4 (Congressional Actions on Vacancies)

The Congress may by law provide for the case of the death of any of the persons from whom the House of Representatives may choose a President whenever the right of choice shall have devolved upon them, and for the case of the death of any of the persons from whom the Senate may choose a Vice President whenever the right of choice shall have devolved upon them.

Section 5 (Effective Date)

Sections 1 and 2 shall take effect on the 15th day of October following the ratification of this article.

Section 6 (Ratification Process)

This article shall be inoperative unless it shall have been ratified as an amendment to the Constitution by the legislatures of three-fourths of the several States within seven years from the date of its submission.

Amendment XXI (1933) (Repeal of Prohibition)

Section 1 (Repeal)

The eighteenth article of amendment to the Constitution of the United States is hereby repealed.

Section 2 (Jurisdiction of States, Territories, Possessions)

The transportation or importation into any State, Territory, or possession of the United States for delivery or use therein of intoxicating liquors, in violation of the laws thereof, is hereby prohibited.

Section 3 (Ratification Process)

This article shall be inoperative unless it shall have been ratified as an amendment to the Constitution by conventions in the several States, as provided in the Constitution, within seven years from the date of the submission hereof to the States by the Congress.

Amendment XXII (1951) (Term of President)

No person shall be elected to the office of the President more than twice, and no person who has held the office of President, or acted as President, for more than two years of a term to which some other person was elected President shall be elected to the office of the President more than once.

But this Article shall not apply to any person holding the office of President when this Article was proposed by the Congress, and shall not prevent any person who may be holding the office of President, or acting as President, during the term within which this Article becomes operative from holding the office of President or acting as President during the remainder of such term.

Amendment XXIII (1961) (Suffrage for District of Columbia Residents)

Section 1 (Federal Elections)

The District constituting the seat of Government of the United States shall appoint in such manner as the Congress may direct:

A number of electors of President and Vice President equal to the whole number of Senators and Representatives in Congress to which the District would be entitled if it were a State, but in no event more than the least populous State; they shall be in addition to those appointed by the States, but they shall be considered, for the purposes of the election of President and Vice President, to be electors appointed by a State; and they shall meet in the District and perform such duties as provided by the twelfth article of amendment.

Section 2 (Enforcement)

The Congress shall have power to enforce this article by appropriate legislation.

Amendment XXIV (1964) (Poll Tax)

Section 1 (Provisions)

The right of citizens of the United States to vote in any primary or other election for President or Vice President, for electors for President or Vice President, or for Senator or Representative in Congress, shall not be denied or abridged by the United States or any State by reason of failure to pay any poll tax or other tax.

Section 2 (Enforcement)

The Congress shall have the power to enforce this article by appropriate legislation.

Amendment XXV (1967) (Vacancy in Office of President and Vice President; Presidential Disability)

Section 1 (Vacancy in Office of President)

In case of the removal of the President from office or his death or resignation, the Vice President shall become President.

Section 2 (Vacancy in Office of Vice President)

Whenever there is a vacancy in the office of the Vice President, the President shall nominate a Vice President who shall take the office upon confirmation by a majority vote of both houses of Congress.

Section 3 (President's Declaration of Disability)

Whenever the President transmits to the President pro tempore of the Senate and the Speaker of the House of Representatives his written declaration that he is unable to discharge the powers and duties of his office, and until he transmits to them a written declaration to the contrary, such powers and duties shall be discharged by the Vice President as Acting President.

Section 4 (Other Declaration of President's Disability)

Whenever the Vice President and a majority of either the principal officers of the executive departments, or of such other body as Congress may by law provide, transmit to the President pro tempore of the Senate and the Speaker of the House of Representatives their written declaration that the President is unable to discharge the powers and duties of his office, the Vice President shall immediately assume the powers and duties of the office as Acting President.

Thereafter, when the President transmits to the President pro tempore of the Senate and the Speaker of the House of Representatives his written declaration that no inability exists, he shall resume the powers and duties of his office unless the Vice President and a majority of either the principal officers of the executive departments, or of such other body as Congress may by law provide, transmit within four days to the President pro tempore of the Senate and the Speaker of the House of Representatives their written declaration that the President is unable to discharge the powers and duties of his office. Thereupon Congress shall decide the issue, assembling within 48 hours for that purpose if not in session. If the Congress, within 21 days after receipt of the latter written declaration, or, if Congress is not in session, within 21 days after Congress is required to assemble, determines by two-thirds vote of both houses that the President is unable to discharge the powers and duties of his office, the Vice President shall continue to discharge the same as Acting President; otherwise, the President shall resume the power and duties of his office.

Amendment XXVI (1971) (Suffrage at Age 18)

Section 1 (Provision)

The right of citizens of the United States, who are eighteen years of age or older, to vote shall not be denied or abridged by the United States or any State on account of age.

Section 2 (Enforcement)

The Congress shall have power to enforce this article by appropriate legislation.

GLOSSARY

The following list is intended for quick reference and review and not as a complete listing of the terms defined in the text. Definitions both here and in the text apply to the terms as used in this book. Some terms have other uses and meanings.

absentee ballot—a special ballot enabling a qualified person to vote by mail

adjourn—to stop business or meetings until a future time

alien—a resident of a country who is not a citizen of that country

amendment—a change made in a constitution, bill, or the like, by adding a new article

amnesty—a group pardon

anarchy—a condition in which there is no government

apportion—to divide in fair shares

appropriation—a sum of money set aside for a certain purpose

arraign (uh-RAIN)—to be required to appear in court in order to answer a legal charge

assessed value—the market value, or a fraction of the market value, of a piece of property as determined by a public official

Australian ballot—a secret ballot that lists all candidates and issues and that is printed at public expense by an official authority

authoritarian government—a type of government that places power in the hands of one or a few strong individuals

autonomy (aw-TON-uh-me)—freedom to act independently; self-government

bail—a sum of money deposited with court officials to assure that an accused person will appear in court

bicameral legislature—a lawmaking body divided into two houses

bill of attainder—a law that punishes someone without trial or that improperly strips someone of personal property

Bolshevik (BOHL-shuh-vik)—in Russia in the early 1900s, a member of the radical and largest group of Communists

bourgeoisie (boor-zhwa-ZEE)—owners of small businesses and properties; the middle class

budget—an annual list of the amounts of money that a government expects to take in from each source and the amounts it expects to pay out for each purpose

bureaucracy—the pyramid-like organization that is characteristic of government service and of most large business organizations

bureaucrat—a person who works for the government; a civil servant

business cycle—a periodic economic fluctuation; a period of prosperity followed by a depression, another period of prosperity, and then another depression

Cabinet—official advisers of a head of state, as a group

calendar—a list of bills in the order in which they are to be taken up

capitalism—an economic system based on private ownership of property; the free enterprise system

capitalist—an owner of, or major investor in, a business

caucus (KAW-kus)—a meeting of members of a political party or other group in order to make plans for action

censure, motion of—in France, a lower-house motion that forces the Government to resign

census—an official count, such as a count of the people in a country

certiorari (sur-she-uh-RAIR-ee), writ of—an order from a higher court asking a lower court to hand up the records of a case for review

checks and balances system—a system in which legislative, executive, and judicial powers belong to separate branches that check one another

city (or county) manager—a chief administrative officer who is employed under contract and who often has professional training

city-state—in ancient Greece, a self-governing city and the land around it

civil case or suit—a dispute between two or more parties over their respective rights and duties

civil servant—a government employee

clear-and-present-danger rule—Justice Oliver Wendell Holmes's opinion that freedom of speech should not be limited unless there was an obvious and immediate danger that what was said would bring about actions "that Congress has a right to prevent"

cloture or closure—the stopping (closing) or shortening of debate on a bill in order to bring it to a vote

coalition—a temporary alliance of political parties or other groups

collective—in the Soviet Union, an enterprise owned and operated cooperatively

command economy—an economy directed by government

commission system—a system of city, town, or village government in which individually elected department heads work together as a commission or city council

committee of correspondence—a group of people in the thirteen colonies who kept in touch with one another as troubles with the British brewed

common law—in England and the United States, a system of laws based on customs, practices, and court decisions, but not reduced to a code of laws; in ancient Rome, a set of laws that applied to everyone under Roman rule who was not a citizen of Rome

communism—a political and economic system based on common ownership of the means of production; according to Karl Marx, the final stage of economic development

concurrent powers—powers shared by the federal government and the states

concurrent resolution—a resolution passed by both the House and the Senate

concurring opinion—a statement by one or more judges who agree with the majority decision of the court but base their opinion on different grounds

conference committee—a temporary committee formed to iron out differences between bills passed by the two houses of a lawmaking body

constituent—a person who lives in the district of an elected official

constitution—a set of basic principles on which a government is organized; a plan of government

constitutional democracy—government by the people under a constitution that limits the government's power

consumer goods—goods produced for direct consumption, such as food

contract—an agreement between two or more parties that can be enforced by law

coroner—a local official who investigates violent or suspicious deaths

corporation—a business chartered by a state and owned by stockholders who are not personally responsible for the business debts

council-manager system—a system of city, town, or village government in which an elected council appoints a city or county manager

county seat—the town or city that is the headquarters of a county government

court-martial—a court consisting of military or naval officers and enlisted personnel who try a person accused of violating a military or naval law

criminal case or suit—a case in which the government accuses someone of breaking a criminal law

customs duty—a tax on imports; tariff

dark horse—an obscure candidate who has little popular following

defendant—the person accused in a court case

deficit—an excess of expenditures over income

democracy—rule by the people

desegregation—the act or process of ending racial segregation

dictatorship—rule by a dictator, or a person who has no regard for what most of the people desire

direct democracy—a form of government in which the people take a direct part

direct tax—a tax that is paid directly to the government by the person taxed

discrimination—practice of treating any group of people differently from other groups of people

dissenting opinion—a statement by a judge who disagrees with the majority opinion

dissident—term used in the Soviet Union for a Russian who criticizes the government's policies

district attorney—a federal or county official who represents the government's side in court cases

dividends—portion of a corporation's profits that is divided among the stockholders

divine right of kings—a claim by monarchs that they were above the law because God had granted them the right to rule over others

double jeopardy clause—a provision of the Fifth Amendment that forbids trying anyone twice for the same crime

due process of law—normal legal procedures (procedural due process); also applied to the fairness of laws (substantive due process); a provision in the Fifth and Fourteenth Amendments

economic system—a system or arrangement for the production, distribution, and consumption of goods and services

elastic clause—Clause 18 of Section 8 of Article I of the Constitution; so called because its meaning can be stretched

electors—people chosen by the voters in each state to cast official ballots for presidential and vice-presidential candidates; the electoral college

eminent domain—the right of governments to take private property for public use

equity—fairness; *a case in equity:* an attempt to correct an unfair situation before it is too late

excise tax—a tax on a specific product made, sold, or used within a country

executive agreement—a presidential agreement with another head of state that does not require Senate approval

executive department—a Cabinet-level federal department

executive order—an order by a President to an agency of the executive branch to carry out certain policies

executive privilege—a right of the President to withhold information from Congress

executive session—a secret or closed meeting

ex post facto law—a law that makes something a crime after it has been done; *ex post facto:* Latin phrase meaning "after the deed is done"

extradition—the surrender of a fugitive to another state

favorite son, favorite daughter—a party member who is prominent in a state and is nominated by the state delegation with no expectation of winning the party's nomination for President

federal system—a government in which states join together to form a union and give up some of their power to a central or national government

filibuster—a long talk for the purpose of delaying or stopping action on a bill

fiscal policy—the use of federal spending and taxing powers as a means of stabilizing the economy

fiscal year—a 12-month period, other than January-December, for purposes of budgeting or accounting

free enterprise system—an economic system based on private ownership of the means of production

"gag order"—a court order forbidding the press to report a legal proceeding

gerrymander (JER-ee-man-dur)—to twist an election district into an odd shape so as to give one group political advantages

gift tax—a tax paid by a person who makes a large gift of money or property to another person

government—the means by which decisions about human behavior in a community are made and enforced

Government, the—in Great Britain and France, the Prime Minister or Premier and the Cabinet as a group, equivalent to the administration in the United States; in the Soviet Union, the Council of Ministers

grand jury—a panel of citizens who determine whether there is enough evidence to bring a person to trial

gross national product—the value of all goods and services produced in a nation; abbreviated GNP

habeas corpus (HAY-be-us KOR-pus), writ of—a court order requiring a prisoner to be brought before a court so that the judge may decide whether the prisoner is being held lawfully; Latin phrase meaning "you may have the person"

hearings—sessions in which a committee hears the testimony of experts and interested persons or groups

home rule—self-government for a town or city or a county

impeach—to charge a person with misconduct or wrongdoing in public office

implied power—a power that is suggested without being directly stated

impound funds—hold back funds appropriated by Congress

incorporated village or town—a village or town that has a state charter permitting it to operate as a local governing unit

incumbent—an office-holder who is seeking re-election

independent regulatory agency—a federal agency that is not under the authority of an executive department and that issues federal regulations

indictment—a written statement that charges a person with a crime

inheritance tax—a tax on inherited property

initiative—a power granted voters to propose state laws or state constitutional amendments by use of a petition

injunction—a court order forbidding or requiring a certain action

insurrection—an uprising against established authority; a rebellion

interstate commerce—trade between two or more states

interstate compact—a formal agreement between states

intrastate commerce—trade within a state

item veto—a veto of one or more items in a bill but not of the entire bill

joint committee—a committee composed of members from both houses of a lawmaking body

judicial review—the power of a court to determine whether an act of Congress or an action of the executive branch is unconstitutional

jurisdiction—the power of a court to consider a case

juvenile court—a court that tries young people accused of law violations

labor union—an organization of workers that tries to achieve higher wages and better working conditions by negotiations with employers and by work stoppages

laissez faire (LESS-ay FAIR)—a policy of minimum governmental interference in business matters

law—a rule of behavior that can be enforced by a government

law of supply and demand—in a free market system, the tendency of prices to go up or down according to the amount of goods available and the demand for them

legal tender—money that must be accepted if offered (tendered) in payment of a debt

legislative council—a special committee that conducts legislative studies between sessions of a state legislature; an interim committee

libel—a written statement intended to damage someone's reputation

lobbyist—a person who acts for an organization in trying to influence legislation

logrolling—the trading of votes among lawmakers

magistrate—a court official who holds preliminary hearings in criminal cases

majority party—the political party with the most seats in a lawmaking body

mandamus (man-DAY-mus), writ of—a court order directing a public official or an officer of a corporation to perform his or her legal duty

marketing—the distribution, sale, and exchange of goods and services

Marxism-Leninism—an ideological system based on the ideas of Karl Marx and Lenin

mayor-council system—a type of city, town, or village government in which the voters elect both a mayor and a council or board

merit system—a system of hiring and promoting the most qualified workers

militia—a citizen army; state units of the National Guard

minister—in Great Britain and France, a Cabinet member, or the head of an executive department

minority party—in a two-party system, the political party with the second largest number of seats in a lawmaking body

misdemeanor—a crime for which the usual punishment is a fine or a sentence in a local jail rather than a state or federal prison

monarchy—a form of government in which the right to rule is passed down from one generation of a family to the next; a nation ruled by a king, a queen, or an emperor

monetary policy—governmental regulation of the supply of money and credit to achieve selected goals

monopoly—a company with total, or nearly total, control over a product or service

M.P.—Member of Parliament

national convention—a nationwide meeting of delegates of a political party, usually held every 4 years

nationalization—a government takeover of a private industry or business

natural right—a right that is considered to be part of human nature

office-block ballot—a ballot that groups together all candidates for a single office

oligarchy (OLL-i-gar-kee)—a type of authoritarian government in which rule is by a few

"one-person—one vote" principle—the principle that all voters shall have an equal voice in elections

opinion of a court—a statement of the decision of a court and the reasoning on which it is based

Opposition, the—in Great Britain, the largest minority party in the House of Commons

ordinance—a town or city law

pardon—a legal document that frees a person from punishment for a crime

parliament—a national assembly or legislature

partnership—a business owned by two or more persons who share profits and losses

party-column ballot—a ballot that lists the candidates of each party in one column, beneath the party's name

patronage—the giving of government jobs to faithful party workers; the spoils system

petit jury—a trial jury

plaintiff—the person who brings a civil suit

plank—an individual principle or policy in a party's platform

platform—a statement of a political party's principles and policies

plurality—the most votes, but not more than half

pocket veto—a chief executive's defeat of a bill by not acting on it before the end of a legislature's session

political action committee—a committee formed by a company or a labor group to collect contributions for political candidates

political heritage—a set of inherited ideas and attitudes about government

political party—a group of people who band together to put their ideas about government into action by nominating and electing candidates for elective office

political socialization—the learning process by which people discover what is expected of them and what they can expect of others in their country

poll tax—a tax paid in order to vote

precedent (PRESS-i-dent)—in law, a decision of a court in an earlier case

precinct—in politics, a polling district; the basic unit in party organization

preference poll—a presidential primary election in which voters indicate a preference—which may or may not be binding on convention delegates—for a presidential candidate

Premier—Prime Minister; in France, the head of the Cabinet; in the Soviet Union, the head of the Council of Ministers

Presidium—in the Soviet Union, an elected committee that acts for the Supreme Soviet when it is not in session

pressure group—a group of people with common goals, organized to put pressure on government in order to bring about certain policies

primary election—an election in which voters select candidates who will run in a general election or select delegates to a nominating convention

Prime Minister—in Great Britain, the head of the executive branch of government

prior restraint—stopping the spread of news or opinions before they are published or broadcast

probate court—a court that handles cases involving the property of a person who has died

profit—the return from a business after all costs are paid

progressive tax—a tax in which the rate of tax rises (progresses) with income

Prohibition—the banning of the manufacture, sale, transport, and import of alcoholic beverages by the Eighteenth Amendment

proletariat (pro-li-TAIR-ee-ut)—workers; the working class

propaganda—the art of shaping other people's opinions for one's own ends

property tax—a tax on land and buildings (real property) or on personal property, such as cars and bonds

proportional representation—an election system in which the winning candidates are selected according to the share (proportion) of votes they receive

prosecute—file a criminal case against an accused person

prosecuting attorney—an official who represents the public in prosecuting a person accused of crime; a district attorney or a county attorney

public opinion poll—a survey of attitudes and beliefs taken by questioning a sample group of people

public service authority—an organization formed by neighboring states or other governing units to provide a service for a fee

quorum (KWOR-um)—the number of persons who must be present in order to take action that will be binding for a group

recall election—an election in which voters choose whether or not to keep an elected official in office

referendum—the submission of a proposed measure, or of a measure passed by the state legislature, to the voters for approval or rejection

register for voting—to have one's name placed on a list of eligible voters

regressive tax—a tax that is the same rate for everyone, regardless of ability to pay

republic—a form of government in which power rests with the people, who elect representatives to act for them; a representative democracy

reserved powers—powers specifically retained by the states in the Constitution

retailer—a person who sells products directly to the public

revenue—the income of a nation or other government unit

rider—an amendment that adds something to a bill which is not related to it

roll call vote—a vote taken by calling each person's name

search warrant—a document authorizing a search, signed by a neutral judge, and based on information sworn to by a responsible person

Secretariat—in the Soviet Union, the Communist party's bureaucracy; the party's executive branch

self-incrimination—the forcing of a person to say things that may be used against the person in a criminal proceeding

separation of church and state—forbidding a government to favor one religion over another

session—a sitting or meeting of a lawmaking body, court, or the like; a series of such meetings

slander—a spoken statement intended to damage someone's reputation

small claims court—a court that settles civil disputes involving small sums of money

social contract theory—the theory that government rests on the consent of the governed

social security program—national insurance program providing money for working people who retire or become unemployed or disabled and for the survivors of workers

socialism—an economic theory or system in which the government owns the basic means of production and operates them on behalf of the people; according to Karl Marx, the period of transition from capitalism to true communism

sole proprietorship—a business owned by one person

soviet—Russian word meaning "council"; in the Soviet Union, an elected body

split session—a session of a state legislature that is divided into two successive parts

split ticket—a vote for candidates of more than one party

Standard Metropolitan Statistical Area—a densely settled area treated as a unit in federal statistics; abbreviated SMSA

state—a nation; an independent country; a major political unit in a federal system, as in the United States

stereotype—a fixed, oversimplified picture that people have of a certain "type" of person

stock—the capital of a corporation divided into shares

stockholder—a person who owns a share of stock in a corporation; a shareholder

straight ticket—a vote for all of the candidates of one party

strike—a work stoppage in order to force an employer to meet workers' demands

strong-mayor system—a system of city, town, or village government in which the mayor has strong executive powers

superior court—a county court, in some states

tariff—a tax on imports; customs duty

technology—methods and processes in industry and business

toll—a fee for the use of a road, dock, canal, bridge, or the like

township—in certain parts of the United States, a unit of local government within a county

transfer payments—payments from government to individuals

treaty—a formal agreement between two or more nations

unicameral legislature—a lawmaking body consisting of only one house

United States marshal—a federal court officer who delivers official documents and makes arrests

urbanization—a change of an area from a rural to an urban way of life

veto—to reject; Latin word meaning "I forbid"

ward—an administrative district in a city or town

weak-mayor system—a system of city, town, or village government in which the mayor has weak executive powers

welfare state—a nation that provides "cradle to grave" services to its citizens; also loosely applied to any nation that provides social welfare measures

whip—a member of a lawmaking body whose duty is to round up support for a political party's position on a bill; assistant floor leader

wholesaler—a person who buys goods from producers for resale to retailers

will—a legal document that tells what you want done with your possessions after your death

zoning—the division of a city, town, or village into areas (zones) according to the kind of property use permitted

INDEX

Absentee ballots, 471
Adams, Abigail, 66, 259
Adams, John, 67, 74, 142, 161, 209, 212, 259
Adams, John Quincy, 96
Adams, Samuel, 67
Adjournment: of Congress, 85
Administration: British equivalent for U.S., 529. *See also* **Government**
Advertising: as industry, 572; in political campaigns, 450, 451, 452
Advice and consent, 99. *See also* **Appointments; Treaties**
Age requirements: for governorship, 369-370; for Presidency, 136; to serve in British Parliament, 528; to serve in Congress, 92, 93, 98, 99; to serve in state legislatures, 365; to vote in federal elections, 260-261
Agnew, Spiro, 140
Agriculture, 311, 599-601
Agriculture, Department of, 157, 160, 162, 319, 573
Alaskan natives, 270
Amendments: to bills in process of lawmaking, 121; defined, 86; process of, in Constitution, 89, 236-238, 350; process of, in Articles of Confederation, 64; proposed, 261-262; of state constitutions, 348. *See also specific amendments*
American Revolution (1776), 35, 51-60
Amnesty: presidential power to grant, 144
Anarchy, 36, 37
Anderson v. Maryland, 291
Apodaca, Jerry, 369, 478
Appeals: right to lawyer and, 294; routes of, in federal court system, 199, 224; state courts of, 374
Appeals, United States Courts of, 192, 225, 228-229, 236
Appellate jurisdiction, 193, 198, 199
Appointments: of Cabinet members, 148; of city judges, 396; of county managers, 391; of federal judges, 189, 195-196, 222, 225, 227; of French premier, 534; by governors, 370; of party national committee chairperson, 450; Senate power over executive, 99, 100, 141
Apportionment. *See* **Congressional districts**
Appropriations. (revenue bills), 87, 95-96, 328
Aristocracy, 28-29, 87
Ariyoshi, George, 369
Armed forces, 56; under Articles of Confederation, 64; Congress power to raise and support, 87, 89; courts for, 227, 248; desegregation of, 269; equal role for females in, 275; presidential power over, 143; size of, 144
Arraignment, 246
Arrest warrants, 244-245
Arrests: freedom from, of members of Congress, 91; mass, 292
Articles of Confederation, 63-64, 66, 68, 73, 76
Asian Americans, 270
Assassination, 150-151
Assemblies: general and legislative, 364; Greek, 20; representative, 46, 47; Roman, 20-21; town, 397-398. *See also specific legislative assemblies; for example:* **British Parliament; Congress; State legislatures**
Assembly, freedom of. *See* **First Amendment**
Assessed value, 387
Australian ballot, 468-469
Authoritarian government, 28-29

Back-benchers, 531
Badillo, Herman, 107
Bail, 35, 248
Baker, Charles W., 476
Baker v. Carr **(1962),** 476
Balanced budget, 333
Ballots, 468-470; in national nominating conventions, 439; placing candidates on, 438, 441-442; positive-negative, 465; secret, 467-469; short, 469; Soviet, 547, 548
Bandwagon appeal (propaganda device), 512
Bankruptcy, 86
Banks, 276, 573, 574, 576, 598-599
Bayh, Birch, 449
Bellmon, Henry, 478
Bennett, Robert, 478
Bentsen, Lloyd M., 417
Bicameral legislatures, 68, 364; British, 526; French, 535; Soviet, 549. *See also specific bicameral legislatures; for example:* **Congress**
Bill: as proposed law, 114. *See also* **Lawmaking**
Bill of attainder, 87
Bill of Rights (British; 1689), 35, 239-240, 525
Bill of Rights (1791; Amendments I-X), 74, 235-249. *See also specific amendments*
Bills of rights: in state constitutions, 348
Black, Hugo, 204
Blacks: discrimination against, *see* **Discrimination;** as candidates for public office, 457-458; as mayors, 412-413; as slaves, *see* **Slaves;** voter registration of, 472; voting right for, 77
Board of supervisors (board of commissioners; board of freeholders; board of revenue), 390
Bolshevik Revolution (1917), 544, 596
Bonds, 335-336
Bonus votes, 436
Bootleggers, 258
Boroughs (government units), 389, 397
Borrowers: rights of, 276-277
Borrowing: by federal government, 335, 336; in free enterprise system, 573
Boston Port Act (British; 1774), 54
Boston Tea Party (1773), 54
Bourgeois democracy, 541, 545
Bourgeoisie, 594, 595
Boyd, James, 125
Braden, Tom, 101
Bradley, Tom, 412, 413
Brandeis, Louis D., 290
Brent, Margaret, 258-259
Bridge, Peter J., 298
Brisbane, Robert, 412
British Constitution, 525-526, 530
British government, 529-531. *See also* **British Parliament**
British laws: British Constitution and, 525
British monarchy. *See* **Monarchy**
British Parliament, 526-532; Cabinet as members of, 529-530; and Constitution, 525, 526; lawmaking in, 531-532; origin of, 32-33; socialism and, 583; in struggle with monarchy, 32-35; as supreme power, 524, 526-528. *See also* **House of Commons; House of Lords**
British political background, 27-35
British political parties, 528-531
British socialism. *See* **Socialist economic system**
Brooke, Edward W., 458
Brown v. Board of Education of Topeka **(1954),** 202, 269, 296
Budgets: French, 434. *See also* **Federal budget**
Bureaucracy: continuity of French, 532; control of, 156-159; defined, 155; excess of rules of, 320; function of, 159; and paper work, 313-315; in state government, 373. *See also* **Executive departments; Federal government employees; Independent agencies**

Index

Bureta, Lynn, 440
Burger, Warren E., 201, 218, 228
Burke, Mary, 321, 322
Burr, Aaron, 253
Business, 311, 316, 356-357; forms of organization of, 570-571, 574-576; nationalization of private, 584
Business cycles, 595, 600
Busing issue, 121, 122
Butler, Robert, 280, 281
By-election (British), 531

Cabinets, 146-148; British, 529, 550; French, 533-535, 537-538, 550; of governors, 372; officers of, dealing with President, 157-158; and presidential disability, 152; right to know and meetings of, 273. *See also* **Executive departments**
Caldwell, Earl, 289
Calendars: bills on, 116-117; of courts, *see* **Dockets**
Califano, Joseph A., 340-341
Campaigns. *See* **Political campaigns**
Candidates: placing names of, on ballots, 439, 441-442; and political parties, 425; Soviet, 547-548; types of victorious, 457-459. *See also* **National Convention system; Political campaigns; Primaries;** *and specific candidates and offices*
Canham, Erwin, 465
Canvassing, 449
Capital and capital goods, 564; in socialist economy, 585-586; in Soviet economy, 598-599
Capitalism, 564. *See also* **Free enterprise system**
Capitalists, 564
Card-stacking (propaganda device), 512
Carey, Hugh, 372
Carter, Jimmy, 134, 138, 144, 308, 478; aides to, 149; as candidate, 426, 438, 448-449; civil service reform under, 179; executive department heads under, 168; and Hispanic Americans, 498-499; in 1976 election, 436, 507-509; in 1978 congressional campaign, 452; regulatory agencies and, 177
Carter, Rosalynn, 145
Carter, Tim Lee, 121
Case in equity, 195
Casey, Dennis P., 428
Castro, Raul, 478
Caucus, 106, 432
Caveat emptor, 175
Ceiling: national debt, 336
Censure: of member of Congress, 92; motion of, in French Parliament, 534, 536
Census: Constitutional provision for, 93, 475; first, 76
Census Bureau, 308
Central Committee (Soviet Communist party), 553
Central Intelligence Agency, 273, 281-282, 317
Certiorari, writ of, 199
Chambers, Richard F., 360
Charles I (King of England), 33, 34, 36
Charles II (King of England), 34
Charles River Bridge v. Warren Bridge **(1837),** 213-214
Charters: city, 393; corporate, 570; for towns and villages, 397
Checks and balances: bureaucracy and, 157; federal courts and, 196-197; purpose of system of, 71, 72
Cherokee people, 189
Chilsen, Walter J., 81
China. *See* **People's Republic of China**
Chisholm, Alexander, 252
Chisholm, Shirley, 458
Chisholm v. Georgia **(1973),** 252
Christopher, Richard, 383
Church and state: separation of, 241
Circuit courts: state, 376
Circuits, 225
Cities. *See entries beginning with term:* **City**
Citizenship: of blacks and slaves, 214-216; granted to freed slaves, 254-255; rights, freedoms, and duties under Soviet, 546; states and rights of, 350; voting right and, *see* **Voting right**
Citizenship requirement: to serve in Congress, 92, 93, 98, 99; to serve in Presidency, 136; to serve in state legislatures, 365
City charters, 393
City councils, 393-396
City courts, 396
City government: distribution of budget of, 405; expenditures of, by city size, 404; financing, 312, 403-407; new approaches to, 408-410; overlapping jurisdictions and, 408; police under, *see* **Police**; types and functions of, 392-399
City-states, 19-20, 29
Civil cases: in District Courts, 223; highest British court for, 527. *See also* **Federal court system**
Civil laws, 21, 24, 54. *See also* **Laws**
Civil liberties, 268-272; basis of, 31; Soviet, 546
Civil rights, 268-272; basic, 56-58
Civil Rights Act **(1875),** 268
Civil Rights Act **(1964),** 269, 270, 275, 499, 501
Civil Rights Act **(1968),** 269, 270, 276
Civil Rights Cases **(1883),** 268-269
Civil rights lobby, 500-502
Civil service. *See* **Federal government employees.**
Civil Service Commission, 179
Civil suits, 30, 193
Claims, Court of, 225-226
Class system, 594-596
Classified jobs (civil service), 179-180
Clayton Act **(1914),** 569
Clear-and-present-danger rule, 288
Clerk of the court (state courts), 375
Closed primaries, 432
Cloture vote (closure vote), 118
Coalitions: government, 419-420; party, 420
Coattail effect, 479
Cockrell, Lila, 411
Codes of laws, 17, 18. *See also* **Laws**
Coercive Acts **(1774; British; Intolerable Acts),** 54, 55
Cohens v. Virginia **(1821),** 211
Colegrove v. Green **(1946),** 476
Collective farms (Chinese and Russian), 600, 601
Colonies: and idea of counties, 389; ideas contributed by, 43-51; influence of European thought in, 35, 36-39; political heritage of, 35-39; representative democracy in, 33; and state governments, 348; system of law in, 30
Command economy, 597
Command market, 584
Commander in chief, 143
Commerce, Department of, 157, 160, 162
Commerce power (Congress; commerce clause), 86, 87, 89, 175, 217; origin of federal, 71; states' power and, 350; Supreme Court decision on, 211-212
Commission system, 144, 393, 394, 396
Committees: of British Parliament, 531; correspondence, 55; county, 427; of French Parliament, 536; town, 427. *See also* **Congressional committees**
Common law: British, 30; Roman, 21-22, 30
Commune (collective farm), 601
Communication: growth of, 308-309
Communist economic system, 547, 593-607; features of, 594-596; marketing under, 572; operation of, 596-601; outside Soviet Union, 601-604
Communist government, 541-560; human rights under, 554-557; Soviet system of, 542-550
Communist party. *See* **Soviet Communist party**
Community control: of public schools, 386-387
Competition: federal intervention in, 311
Compromise, 67-71, 425
Conaty, Patricia, 428
Concurrent resolution, 143
Condemnation: land, 566
Confederacy, 255-256
Conference committees, 112, 119

Index

Congress, 81–130; in admission of new states, 352; allowances and privileges of members of, 91; in amending process, *see* **Amendments;** under Articles of Confederation, 64; British Parliament compared with, 526, 531; in budget process, 327–328; and bureaucracy, 156–157; candidates named by party caucuses in, 432; civil servants restricted by, 180; and commerce clause, *see* **Commerce clause;** committee system, *see* **Congressional committees;** constitutionality of acts of, 208; and Court of Claims, 225, 226; election to, *see* **Elections;** in election of President, 136; executive departments created by, 161–163; expulsion of members, 92, 98; federal court system and, 193, 197–198, 208, 221, 225, 227; financial disclosure by members of, 100–102; French Parliament compared with, 535; how bills become laws in, *see* **Lawmaking; Laws;** implied powers of, 89, 210, 217, 236; legislative oversight power of, 89; and money questions, 68, 86, 89, 334; and order of succession to Presidency, 138, 139; as political body, 106–108; political party caucuses in, 106, 432, 436; and postal service, 181–182; powers of, 83, 86–87, 89, 91, 208; powers denied to, 87; and presidential disability, 152; Presidents furnishing information to, 141; and reconstruction, 254, 256; and regulatory agencies, 175, 176; right to know and records of, 273; sessions of, 84, 85, 141, 142; term of, 259–260; use of time in, 125–127. *See also* **House of Representatives; Senate**
Congressional Budget Office, 328
Congressional Campaign Committee, 426
Congressional committees, 109–112, 119, 120–124; bills in, 114, 116; Committee of the Whole, 117; defined, 106; joint, 112; powers and specialization of, compared with those of British Parliament, 531; select and special, 112; temporary, 112
Congressional districts, 94–95. *See also* **Reapportionment**
Congressional hearings, 116
Connecticut Compromise, 68
Connecticut constitution (1639), 46–47
Constant dollars, 329
Constituencies, 85, 528
Constitution (U.S.), 67, 181; admission of new states under, 352; changes in (since 1789), 233; compromise in arriving at, 67–71; guarantees to states under, 350, 352; idea of separation of powers in, 38–39; and Marshall, *see* **Marshall, John;** principles of, 71; ratification of, 71, 73–74; restrictions placed on states under, 349; state constitutions and, 348; and Supreme Court, *see* **Supreme Court** *and* **Supreme Court decisions;** use of "the people" in, 75–77; writing of, 66–67. *See also* **Amendments; Bill of Rights;** *and specific amendments*
Constitutional Convention (1787), 66–71, 77, 354
Constitutional conventions: national, 236–237; state, 348
Constitutional democracy, 523–539
Constitutional government, 31
Constitutional referendum, 492
Constitutions: British, 525–526, 530; colonial, 46–47; first national, 64; French (1791), 532; French (1958), 533–535; purpose of, 541. *See also* **Constitution (U.S.); Soviet Constitution; State constitutions**
Consumer Product Safety Commission, 174
Consumers, 311
Contracts, 210, 213–214, 565
Contributions: political campaign, 452–456, 487, 490
Copyrights: Congress power to grant, 86

Coroners, 390
Corporations, 454–455, 570–571, 575–576
Correspondence, committees of, 55
Corruption: political campaign, 453–457
Cost-of-living raises, 318
Costs: political campaign, 452–457
Council-manager system, 393, 395, 396
Council of Ministers (Soviet), 549–550
Counterfeiters, 86
Counties: as administrative units, 390; idea of, colonists and, 389; number of, 390
County clerks, 390
County committees, 427
County courts, 376
County governing boards, 390–392
County government, 389–392, 408
County judges, 391
County manager plan, 391–392
County mayor plan (county president plan), 391
County treasurers, 390
Court-martial, 227
Court records: state, 375
Courts: Congress power to create, 86. *See also* **Federal court system; Judicial branch;** *and specific courts*
Cranston, Alan, 264
Credit institutions, 573
Creditors: rights of, 276–277
Crimes: Congress power over punishment and, 87; extradition for, 350; rights of person accused of, 246–247, 292. *See also* **Arrest warrants**
Criminal cases, 194–195, 223
Criminal law, 30. *See also* **Crimes; Laws**
Cromwell, Oliver, 34
Cromwell, Richard, 34
Cuba, 601
Customs duties, 86
Customs and Patent Appeals, Court of, 226–227

Dark horse candidates, 436
Darragh, Lydia, 281
***Dartmouth College v. Woodward* (1819),** 210

Davis, John W., 437
Dayton, Jonathan, 66–67
Death penalty, 294
Debates: on bills, 117, 118; parliamentary, 532
Debs, Eugene V., 589
Declaration of Independence (1776), 37, 38, 56–60, 181, 215
Declaration of Rights, 55
Decrees (French), 534–535
Defendant, 30. *See also* **Crimes**
Defense. *See* **Armed forces; National defense**
Defense, Department of, 160, 163, 166, 317
Deficits: federal, 333–336
De Gaulle, Charles, 533, 534
De la Garza, E. "Kika," 107
Delegates: functions of, 433–434, 436, 440–441; number and choosing of, 432–434, 436–437; and party platform, 438; predicted votes of, at 1976 Republican National Convention, 510–511; profile of, at Constitutional Convention, 66–67; votes of, 436
Democracy, 19–20, 28, 29, 308, 580; bourgeois, 541, 545; constitutional, 523–539; industrial, 584; proletarian, 541. *See also* **Direct democracy; Representative democracy;** *and specific democratic institutions*
Democratic centralism, 551, 553
Democratic party, 419–423
Democratic socialism, 580, 588, 596
***Dennis v. United States* (1951),** 288
Depository Act (1974), 276
Depression, 64, 66, 311. *See also* **Business cycles; Inflation**
Deputies (French), 535
Deputy President pro tempore, 99
Deputy sheriffs, 391
Dictators, 20
Dictatorship, 28; of the proletariat, 594–596
Dingell, John, 121, 124
Diplomacy. *See* **Foreign policy**
Direct action, 492–499

Direct democracy, 397, 465; defined, 20, 29; among Pilgrims, 46
Direct initiative, 492
Direct primaries, 432
Disability: presidential, 152, 260
Discrimination: and civil rights, 268-272; and Civil Rights Cases (1883), 268-269; defined, 268; federal intervention to end, 312; job, based on sex, 275-276, 296, 317; judicial decisions against, 295-296; legislation to end, 268-271; recent (1977), 271; segregation as form of, 202; rights and, 349. See also Civil liberties
Dissidents (Soviet), 554-557
Distribution: of goods and services, 571-572
District attorneys (U.S.), 222, 390
District Courts, United States, 192, 221-224, 228-229
District of Columbia: representation in Congress, 94, 251, 260, 261
Districts. See Electoral districts
Dividends, 571
Divine right of kings, 33, 35
Dockets: District Court, 222; state court, 375; Supreme Court, 200
Doi, Nelson, 369
Domestic relations courts, 375
Double jeopardy clause, 245-247
Douglas, William O., 204
Dred Scott v. Sandford (1857), 214-216
Dublino, Dolores, 218
Due process, 247, 255-256; applied to Native Americans, 262-264; judicial decisions on, 295-297; and right to take private property, 566; states and, 349. See also Fifth Amendment; Fourteenth Amendment
Dymally, Mervyn, 369

Eagleton, Thomas, 441
Eavesdropping, 290-291
Economic changes (since 1789), 308-310

Economic systems: comparative, 561; mixed, 573-574, 579-580, 583. See also Communist economic system; Free enterprise system; Socialist economic system
Education. See Public education
Eighteenth Amendment (1919), 238, 251, 258, 260
Eighth Amendment (1791), 240, 243-244, 248, 293, 294
Eisenhower, Dwight D., 107, 137-139, 152, 423, 437
Elastic Clause, 89, 210
Elections, 92; British, 527-529, 531; change in system of, 252-253; of city judges, 396; of city officials, 393, 396; in colonies, 47; of county boards, 390; of county officers, 391; first, 74; French, 533, 535; of governors, 369-370; role of electors, 134, 136; Soviet, 544, 547-549; of state judges, 374; of state legislatures, 364; states' power to conduct, 350; town, 397, 398. See also Candidates; Electoral college; Electoral districts; Political parties; Primaries; and entries beginning with terms: Voter; Voting
Electoral college, 136, 480; amendment changing, 252-253
Electoral districts: British, 528; congressional, 94-95; French, 535; gerrymandering, 94, 95; malapportionment of, 94-95; reapportionment of, 95, 475-477; single-member and multimember, 420
Electoral rules: two-party system encouraged by, 420. See also Political parties
Electronic "bugging," 290-291
Elderly, the: as lobby, 496-498. See also Retirement
Eleventh Amendment (1798), 193, 251, 252
Elite: as delegates to Constitutional Convention, 66
Elizabeth II (Queen of England), 524-525
Emancipation Proclamation (1862), 254

Emergency Energy Bill (1973), 120-124
Eminent domain, 566
Employment practices: federal, 317
Energy, Department of, 161, 163, 174, 210-211
Engel v. Vitale (1962), 286
Engels, Friedrich, 581, 594
Environmental problems, 312
Environmental Protection Agency, 174, 210-211
Equal Credit Opportunity Act (1975), 276
Equal Employment Opportunity Act (1972), 275
Equal protection. See Fourteenth Amendment
Equal Rights Amendment (proposed), 237, 238, 261, 278
Escobedo v. Illinois (1964), 293
Eu, March Fong, 272-273
Evidence: illegally seized, 290. See also Fourth Amendment
Excise taxes, 232
Exclusionary rule, 290
Executive agencies: specialized, 149. See also Executive departments; Independent agencies
Executive agreements, 143
Executive branch: British, 529; in cities, 393-394, 396; and Constitutional Convention, 68, 69, 71, 72; in counties, 390; employees in, 317; expenditures by, 330; and idea of separation of powers, 38-39; lobbying, 490; in state constitutions, 348. See also Executive departments; Presidents (U.S.)
Executive departments: British, 529; and budget, 327, 328, 330; choosing best head for, 167-170; French, 534; list of, 160-161; number of, 146-148; organization of, 159-167; Soviet, 550
Executive functions: of bureaucrats, 159; in cities, 393-394, 396; of county governments, 390
Executive Office of the President, 148-150
Executive orders, 144
Executive power: under Articles of Confederation, 64;

French, 533; of governors, 370-372; in Parliament, 526; of Presidents, 140-146
Executive privilege, 146, 236
Executive session: of committees, 112
Expenditures: of local governments, 386-388; of state governments, 354-356, 386. See also Federal budget
Ex post facto laws, 87, 89
Expression, freedom of. See First Amendment
Expressed powers, 85-87, 89
Expulsion: from Congress, 92, 98
Extradition, 350

Fair Housing Act (1974), 276
Fallacies (propaganda device), 514
Family Educational Rights and Privacy Act (1974), 274-275
Farmers: federal aid to, 311
Farr, William T., 298
Favorite daughter (candidate), 438
Favorite son (candidate), 438
Federal agencies: abolishing, 321-322; open hearings and, 273-274. See also Executive departments; Independent agencies; Regulatory agencies
Federal budget, 87, 326-336; defined, 326; deficits in, 333-336; as economic tool, 329; expenditures, 326, 329-331; preparation of, 149, 327-328; presidential message to Congress on, 328; receipts (income) for, 331-332
Federal Bureau of Investigation, 160, 273, 281-282
Federal Communications Commission, 174, 176
Federal Corrupt Practices Act (1925), 453-454
Federal court system, 189-205; and bureaucratic abuse, 158; cases in, 193-195; creation of additional appellate courts in, 228-229; Eleventh Amendment and, 252; individual rights protected in, 285; right to know and records of, 273;

Index

structure and role of, 192-197. See also **Judicial branch**; *and specific federal courts; for example:* **Supreme Court**
Federal debt (public debt; national debt), 64, 336-337
Federal Deposit Insurance Corporation (FDIC), 182, 185
Federal district courts (United States District Courts), 192, 221-224, 228-229
Federal Elections Campaign Act (1972), 455
Federal government: formation of, *see* **Constitution**; growth and size of, 305, 307-323; money returned to states by, 359; role in economy, 313, 315, 320, 569, 573-574; unitary state compared with, 524. See also **Executive branch; Judicial branch; Legislative branch**
Federal government employees, 316-319; classified jobs of, 179-180; distribution of, 318-319; government as largest employer in nation, 316-317; in merit system, 179, 373-374; number of, 305, 313, 316; payroll for, 313, 317-318; political restrictions on, 474-475
Federal Insurance Contributions Act, 332
Federal Judicial Center, 228
Federal Power Commission (FPC), 174
Federal Reserve Board, 334
Federal Reserve System, 334-335, 573
Federalism: Soviet, 543, 545, 547. See also **Federal government**
Felony, 294
Ferguson, Miriam A., 369
Field, Stephen, 204
Fifteenth Amendment (1870), 251, 254, 256-257, 349
Fifth Amendment (1791), 291-295, 566; judicial decisions on, 293-294; provisions of, 240, 245, 247. See also **Due process**
Filibuster, 118
Finance industry, 573; banks, 276, 573, 574, 576, 598-599

Finances: of lawmakers, 100-102; political campaign, 452-457. See also **Federal budget**
Fines, 248
Fire protection: as local government service, 386
First Amendment (1791), 239, 490; judicial interpretations of freedoms under, 287-290; rights protected under, 241-243; and reporter news sources, 298-299; provisions of, 240; states bound by, 239
First Continental Congress (1774), 55, 83
Fiscal policy, 335. See also **Federal budget**
Fiscal year, 326
Floor leaders: majority and minority, 107
Food and Drug Administration, 144, 157
Ford, Gerald, 140, 144, 423, 452, 478; attempts on life of, 150; as candidate, 426; in 1976 election, 507-509; pardons Nixon, 143-144; regulatory agencies and, 177
Foreign aid programs, 313
Foreign policy: advisers on, 149; politics and, 146; presidential powers over, 142, 143; and U.S. as world power, 312-313
Forms: federal government, 313-315
Fourteenth Amendment (1868), 216, 251, 259, 260, 476, 566; judicial decisions on, 295-297; segregation violating, 269; slavery abolished under, 253-256, 268; states and, 349. See also **Due process**
Fourth Amendment (1791), 218, 243-244; judicial interpretations of freedoms under, 290-292; provisions of, 244-246
Franchise. See **Voting right**
Frankfurter, Felix, 204
Franklin, Benjamin, 67
Free enterprise system (capitalism), 563-577; eliminated in Soviet Union, 597; features of, 564-567; federal debt effect on, 336-337; government intervention in, 313,

315, 320, 569, 573-574; laissez faire in, 295, 568, 569, 573, 574; Marx's view of, 594; operation of, 569-576; poverty and, 580-581; socialism and, 588; theory of, 567-569
Freedom of Information Act (1966), 273
Frémont, John C., 422
French Cabinet, 533-535, 537-538, 550
French civil law, 54
French Constitution (1791), 532
French Constitution (1958), 533-535
French government, 533-538, 550, 554
French and Indian War (1754-1763), 52
French Parliament, 532-538
French political parties, 533, 535, 536
French Premier, 533-538, 554
French revolution (1848), 532
Fundamental Orders of Connecticut (1639), 46-47
Fund-raisers: campaign, 450
Furman v. Georgia **(1972),** 294

"Gag orders," 289
Gallup, George, 507
Gann, Paul, 14
Gardner, John, 101
Garfield, James, 150
Garrett, Tom, 360
General assembly, 364. See also **States legislatures**
General court, 364
General sales taxes, 357
General Secretary (Soviet), 554
General Services Administration (GSA), 180-181
George III (King of England), 52, 55, 58-60
Gerrymandering, 94, 95
Gibbons v. Ogden **(1823),** 211-212
Gideon v. Wainwright **(1963),** 294
Gignoux, Edward T., 263
Glittering generalities (propaganda device), 511, 517
Glorious Revolution (1688), 35
Goldwater, Barry, 425-426, 459-461

Gomes, Connie, 274
Gonzalez, Henry B., 107
Government: authoritarian, 28; constitutional, 31; defined, 14; democratic, 28, 29; function of, in free enterprise system, 567-568; by the people, idea of, 45-46, 56; political party role in, 425; right to speak against, 287-288; role in communist system, 572; role in socialist system, 572, 583; town, 397; village, 397; weakness of central, 64. See also **British government; City government; Communist government; County government; Federal government; French government; Local government; Representative government; State government**
Government in Sunshine Act (1976), 273
Governors, 368-374; campaigning for office of, 448; functions of, 369-374; powers of, 364, 369-372; salaries of, 370; terms of, by state, 370; veto power of, 368
Grand jury system, 30, 245
Grasso, Ella, 369
Great Britain. See **American Revolution;** *and entries beginning with term:* **British**
Great Depression (1930s), 311
Greeks: political heritage from, 19-20, 29
Grier, Robert C., 204
Griffiths, Martha W., 339
Gross national product (GNP), 330, 332
Gustafson, James, 218

Habeas corpus, writ of, 87, 89
Hale, Jubal, 321-322
Hamilton, Alexander, 74, 208
Hammurabi (Amorite king), 18
Hammurabi, Code of, 18, 22, 23
Hancock, John, 67
Handicapped persons: rights of, 271-272
Harding, Warren G., 139
Harlan, John Marshall, 204
Harris, Louis, 507
Harrison, Benjamin, 144

Harrison, William Henry, 137, 139, 515–517
Hatch Acts (1939; 1940), 454, 474, 475
Hayden, Carl, 139
Hayes, Janet Gray, 411
Health, Education, and Welfare, Department of, 161, 163, 167, 320; civil rights and, 271–272; expenditures by, 330; size of, 166
Health and hospitals, 167, 271; Chinese, 602, 603; as local government service, 387, 390, 404, 405, 407; in socialist system, 586; Soviet, 600; state expenditures on, 356
Hearings, 116
Hebrews, 19, 22, 23
Hechler, Ken, 322
Heinz, John, 121
Helsinki agreement (1975), 521
Henry, Patrick, 67
Henry II (King of England), 30, 31
Henry III (King of England), 32
Henry VIII (King of England), 34
High school newspapers, 288–289
Hispanic Americans, 270, 498–499
Hitler, Adolf, 28, 514
Hobbes, Thomas, 36–37, 45
Holmes, Obadiah, 49
Holmes, Oliver Wendell, 242, 288
Home rule, 393
Hooker, Thomas, 47
Hospitals. *See* Health and hospitals
House of Burgesses (Virginia), 46, 52, 258–259
House of Commons (British), 33, 526–532, 535, 583
House of Lords (British), 33, 526–532, 535
House of Representatives, 92–97, 241; ceiling on spending for election to, 453, 456; Committee of the Whole, 117; composition of, 95, 96; election to, 94–95; and election of President, 136, 252, 253; and impeachment, *see* **Impeachment;** powers exclusive to, 95–97; reelection of incumbents, 453; representation in, 68, 85, 255; size of, 93–94; Speaker of, 93, 152, 367, 532; term of office of members of, 92
Housing: equal rights in, for women, 276; Soviet, 600
Housing Act (1949), 407
Housing and Urban Development, Department of, 161, 163, 296
Hughes, Charles Evans, 217
Human resources: expenditures for, 330–331, 336
Human rights: under communist government, 554–557
Humphrey, Hubert, 81, 99
Hutchinson, Anne, 49, 50, 241
Hutton, William, 498

Impeachment: of federal judges, 196, 197, 204; power of House over charges of, 96; of state judges, 374; trial, in Senate, 100
Implied powers, 89, 210, 217, 236
Impoundment: of funds, 145–146
Inaugural address, 134
Income insecurity, 309
Income taxes, 331–332; city, 405; Congress power to pass laws on, 257–258; corporate, 332; local, 411; public financing of campaigns through, 456; state, 357–358
Incorporated towns and villages, 397
Incumbents: contributions to, 453
Indentured servants, 76
Independent agencies: in budget process, 327, 328; expenditures by, 330; regulatory, *see* **Regulatory agencies;** service, 178–182, 185; size of, 173
Indian tribes, 86. *See also* **Native Americans**
Indictment, 272
Indirect initiative, 492
Indirect primaries, 433
Individual rights, 217–218. *See also* **Civil liberties; Civil rights**
Individuals: candidates elected as, 425; financial contributions of, to campaigns, 452, 454–455; initiative of, in free enterprise system, 566; rights threatened by, 268–269
Industrial democracy, 584
Industrialization, 308, 309; socialism and, 580; Soviet, 545–546, 596–597, 599–600; urbanization and, 392
Inflation: federal intervention in, 311; federal salaries and, 318; and growth in federal spending, 329–330; national debt and, 336; after Revolution, 64, 66; raising taxes to put down, 329; Soviet, 600
Inheritance: right of, 565
Inheritance taxes, 358
Initiative: availability of, list of states, 493; as direct action, 492–495; national, 495–496
Inouye, Daniel K., 458
Insurance: state benefits and reserves, 355, 358–359
Insurance industry, 573
Insurrections, 87. *See also* **Revolt**
Intangible property, 565
Interest, 573
Interest groups. *See* **Lobbying; Pressure groups; Special-interest groups**
Interior, Department of, 160, 162, 319, 321
Intermediate districts, 399
Internal Revenue Service, 159, 314, 331
Internal Security Act (1950), 293
Interstate commerce. *See* **Commerce power**
Interstate Commerce Commission (ICC), 174–177, 569
Interstate compact, 410
Intolerable Acts (1774; Coercive Acts; British), 54, 55
Investigative power: of Congress, 89
Investigative reporting, 298
Investments, 567, 585–586
Issues: political party, 425

Jackson, Andrew, 148, 150, 189, 213, 254, 422
Jackson, Henry, 120, 122–124
Jackson, Maynard, 412, 413
James II (King of England), 34–35, 45
Jarvis, Howard, 14
Jay, John, 74
Jefferson, Thomas, 37, 67, 96, 209, 210, 253, 308; A. Adams to, on monetary crisis, 66; and Bill of Rights, 240; and Declaration of Independence, 56; political party of, 421; way of life of, as President, 131
Job discrimination, 275–276
John (King of England), 31, 32
Johnson, Andrew, 96–97, 144
Johnson, Lyndon B., 139, 144, 152, 176, 269, 459, 501, 502
Joint committees, 112
Jordan, Barbara, 75
Judges and justices: appointment of British, 527; appointment and tenure of federal, 195–196, 197–198; city, 396; disability of federal, 203–204; election of state, 374; justices of the peace, 375, 391; presidential power over appointment of, 141; Soviet, 547; of Supreme Court, 197–198, 203–204
Judicial branch: under Articles of Confederation, 64; and Constitutional Convention, 68, 69, 71, 72; employees of, 317; and idea of separation of powers, 38–39; presidential power in, 141; Soviet, 546–547; in state constitutions, 348. *See also* **Federal court system;** *and specific federal courts*
Judicial interpretation: changing Constitution through, 236
Judicial powers: of British Parliament, 526; in counties, 391; of governors, 371, 372
Judicial review: power of, 208–211, 217
Judiciary Act (1789), 209–210, 221
Judiciary Act (1801), 209
Jurisdictions: defined, 193; original, 193, 221; overlapping, of local government, 408; of Supreme Court, 198–199
Jurors, 30
Jury: coroner's, 390; grand, 30, 245, 246; origin of system, 30; petit, 246; right to, in civil lawsuit, 248

Index

Jury trials, 30–31, 35, 246; in federal courts, 192, 223; grand jury indictment and, 245; and Magna Charta, 31–32
Justice, Department of, 160, 162, 197, 271
Justices of the peace, 375, 391
Justinian (Byzantine Emperor), 22
Justinian, Code of, 22
Juvenile courts, 375
Juveniles: rights of, 293–294

Kadaja, John, 360
Kennedy, Jacqueline, 138
Kennedy, John F., 137–139, 144, 150, 204
Kennedy, Robert, 150
Keynote speech: national convention, 437
Khrushchev, Nikita, 546, 554, 556, 557
Kilpatrick, James J., 339
King, Martin Luther, Jr., 501
Kings. See **Monarchy**
Kissinger, Henry, 149
Kitchen cabinet, 148
Know: right to, 273–275, 281–282
Koupal, Ed, 495
Koupal, Joyce, 495
Krupsak, Mary Anne, 372

Labor, Department of, 160, 162, 167, 174
Labor unions, 311, 454, 582, 597–598
Laird, Melvin R., 81
Laissez faire, 295, 568, 569, 573, 574
Land Ordinance (1785), 398
Landon, Alfred, 506
Latling, Patience, 411
Law Lords (British), 527
Lawmaking: amendments to bills in, 121; British, 531–532; in Congress, 17–18, 113–119, 120–125; French, 534–536; presidential power in, 141; lobbyists and, 489; referendums and, 492; in state legislatures, 368
Laws: British Constitution and British, 525; civil, 21, 24, 54; codes of, 17, 18; Congress power to make, 86–89; constitutional structure changed by, 236; equality before, 71; federal courts and constitutionality of, 192, 193; national, under Articles of Confederation, 64; presidential leeway in carrying out, 144, 145; Roman, 21–22, 24, 30; Supreme Court advice on proposed, 198, 202; Supreme Court and supremacy of federal, 217. See also **State laws**
Lawsuits: in federal courts, 192–193; freedom of members of Congress from, 91; against government, 225; of individuals against states in federal courts, barred, 252; right to jury in civil, 248
Lawyers: right to, 248, 293, 294
Laxalt, Paul, 478
League of Nations, 143
Leahy, Patrick J., 478
Lee, Howard, 412
Legal tender, 334. See also **Money**
Legislation. See **Lawmaking; Laws**
Legislative assembly, 364. See also **State legislatures**
Legislative branch: and Constitutional Convention, 68, 69, 71, 72; employees of, 317; and idea of separation of powers, 38–39; in state constitutions, 348. See also **Congress**
Legislative committees. See **Congressional committees**
Legislative councils (interim committees), 368
Legislative function: in city government, 393–394, 396; of county government, 390
Legislative power: city, 393; of governors, 371, 372; in Parliament, 526
Legislature, 364. See also specific legislatures; for example: **British Parliament; Congress; State legislatures**
Lenin, Nikolai (Vladimir Ilyich Ulyanov), 544–545, 556, 596
Liability: limited, 571; unlimited, 570
Libel, 49, 242–243
Lie detector tests, 299–301
Lieutenant governors, 367, 372
Life peers (British), 527

Lincoln, Abraham, 15, 148, 150, 253–254, 422, 423
Literacy tests, 472
Lobbying: defined, 116; pressure group, 486–492; workings of, 116, 499–502. See also **Pressure groups; Special-interest groups**
Local activities: regulation of, 386
Local government, 383–416; British, 524; city, see **City government;** consolidation of units of, 409; county, 389–392, 408; financing of, 387, 388; functions of, 386–389; health and hospitals as service of, 387, 390, 404, 405, 407; new approaches to, 408–410; number of employees in, 387; number of units of, 385; political parties in, 421; states' power to establish, 350; taxes of, 387–388
Locke, John, 37–38, 45, 56
Logrolling, 118
Long, Russell, 123, 124
Long ballot, 469
Low, Joe, 301
Lucey, Patrick, 440
Lujan, Manuel, Jr., 107

McCarthy, Eugene, 457
McCormack, John, 139
McCulloch v. Maryland (1819), 210
McGovern, George, 426, 440, 441, 497
McKinley, William, 137, 139, 150
Madison, James, 67, 74, 209, 240, 363
Magistrate courts, 375
Magistrates, 222, 391
Magna Charta (Great Charter; 1215), 31–32, 239
Majority party, 106
Majority vote, 201
Malapportionment, 94–95
Managers: in city government, 393, 395, 396
Mandamus, writ of, 209
Mandatory preference polls, 434
Mandatory referendums, 492
Mandatory retirement, 279–281
Mansfield, Mike, 123

Manson, Charles, 298
Mao Tse-tung, 601
Mapo v. Ohio **(1961),** 290
Marbury, William, 209, 210
Marbury v. Madison **(1803),** 209, 215
Marketing, 571–572
Marshal, United States, 222
Marshall, John, 142, 189, 201, 214, 236, 285; decisions by, 209–212; as strong Chief Justice, 216, 217; Taney compared with, 213
Marx, Karl, 544, 581, 583, 594–596, 500
Marxism, 594, 601. See also **Communist economic system**
Marxism-Leninism, 545
Mary (Queen of England), 35
Maryland Toleration Act (1649), 50
Mason, George, 67
Mass arrests, 292
Mass media: minor parties and, 424; reporters' rights, 289, 297–299; television, 439, 450–451
Mayflower Compact, 45–46
Mayor-council system, 393–394
Mayors: campaigning for office of, 448; increase in black, 412–413; in mayor-council system, 393–394; special problems of big city, 411–412
Means of production: government ownership of, 564, 580, 597; private ownership of, 564. See also **Communist economic system; Free enterprise system; Socialist economic system**
Media consultants, 450–451
Medical care. See **Health and hospitals**
Medicare, 161, 167
Meek v. Pittenger **(1975),** 287
Mercantilism, 567
Merit system, 179, 373–374
Merit System Protection Board, 179
Mexican Americans. See **Hispanic Americans**
Middle East: political ideas from ancient, 17–19
Military Appeals, Court of, 227, 248
Military forces. See **Armed forces**

Index

Military secrets, 273
Ministers: British, 529; French, 534
Mink, Patsy, 458
Minor parties (third parties), 420, 423-425; British, 529, 530; defined, 106; public financing for campaigns of, 456; putting nominees on ballots, 439, 442; socialist, in U.S., 588-590
Minorities: in composition of Congress, 95, 96; in national conventions, 437; as nonvoters, 479; numbers of, as governors, 369; special caucuses of, 107; winning candidates among, 457-458. *See also specific minorities; for example:* Blacks; Hispanic Americans
Miranda v. Arizona (1966), 293
Misdemeanors, 294
Misleading association (propaganda device), 513
Misquoting (propaganda device), 513
Missouri Compromise (1820), 214-215
Mittenthal, Freeman L., 301
Mixed economy, 573-574, 579-580, 583
Molasses Act (1733; British), 52, 54
Monarchy: constitutional, 34-35; defined, 28; French, 532; limited power of, 31-36; power of, 36, 37; role of, in modern government, 524, 529, 531, 532
Monetary policy, 335
Money: borrowing or coining, under Articles of Confederation, 64; British Parliament and, 531; Congress power over, 68, 86, 89, 334; deficit and supply of, 334-335; states' power to borrow, 350. *See also* Appropriations
Monopolies, 311, 569
Montesquieu, Baron de, 38-39, 71
Montfort, Simon de, 32
Morgenthau, Henry, 156
Moses, 19
Motion of censure (French), 534, 536
M.P. (Member of Parliament), 528

Municipal courts, 375
Muskie, Edmund, 122, 124

Nader, Ralph, 491, 493, 495
Name-calling (propaganda device), 513, 515
Napoleon I (Emperor of the French), 22, 532-533
Napoleon III (Emperor of the French), 532-533
Napoleonic Code, 22
National Archives and Records Service, 119
National Assembly (French), 535-538
National committee chairpersons, 109, 426, 438, 450
National convention system, 432-440; choosing candidate in, 437-439; delegates in, *see* Delegates; function of, 435-439; as highest party authority, 426; purposes and rules of, 437
National Court of Appeals (proposed), 228-229
National debt (federal debt; public debt), 64, 336-337
National defense: expenditures for, 330-331; growth of, 310; problem of spending for, 337-338; and U.S. as world power, 312. *See also* Armed forces
National Guard, 356, 371, 391
National Science Foundation, 273
National Security Council (NSC), 149, 317
Nationalization, 584, 587-588
Native Americans: due process for, 262-264, 295; lobbying by, 487; voting rights of, 76, 77, 270
Natural resources protection, 356, 387
Natural right, 36-37
Naturalization, 86, 254-255
Navy, Department of, 161
Nebraska Press Association v. Stuart (1976), 289
Neuberger, Maurine, 458
Neustadt, Richard E., 156
New England town government, 397-398
New Jersey Plan, 67-69
Nineteenth Amendment (1920), 251, 258-259, 275, 349, 359, 458

Ninth Amendment (1791), 240, 248
Nixon, Richard M., 81, 97, 139, 140, 152, 423, 440; aides to, 149; energy bill and, 122; Ford pardons, 143-144; funds impounded by, 145-146; 1972 campaign of, 455; resignation of, 139; tiredness of, in campaigns, 461; whistle-blowing on, 425
Nobility, title of: Congress denied power to grant, 87
Nominating petitions, 439, 442
Nomination rule, 437
Nonpartisan primaries, 432
Nonvoting stock, 571

Oath of office: presidential, 134
Obey, David R., 81
Obey, Joan, 81
O'Brien, Larry, 441
Obscenity: laws against, 243
Office-block ballot, 469
Office of Management and Budget (OMB), 149, 322, 327-328
Office of Personnel Management, 179
Ogle, Charles, 517
Old Deluder Law (1647; Massachusetts), 47
Old Testament, 19, 23
Oligarchy, 28-29
Olmstead v. United States (1928), 290
Omnibus Education Act (1972), 277
O'Neill, Thomas P., 107
"One person-one vote." *See* Reapportionment
Open primaries, 432
Opinions (Supreme Court), 201; concurring, dissenting, and minority, 202
Opposition (British), 530-531
Optional referendums, 492
Ordinances, 393
Original jurisdiction, 193, 221
Orlov, Mrs., 521
Orlov, Yuri K., 521
Outright lie (propaganda device), 514

Paddling, 294
Paine, Thomas, 67

Panama Canal treaties, 142, 143
Paper work: federal, 313-315
Pardon: presidential power to issue, 143-144
Parishes (counties), 389
Parliament. *See* British Parliament; French Parliament
Parliamentary Act (British; 1949), 526
Parochial schools, 286-287
Participation, 14; direct action as form of, 492-499; public opinion and, 505-520. *See also* Direct democracy; Pressure groups; *and entries beginning with terms:* Voter; Voting
Partnership, 570, 571, 574-575
Party candidates (Soviet), 552
Party cell (Soviet), 552
Party-column ballot, 469
Party committees: in Congress, 106-107
Party platforms, 437-438, 589-590
Party primaries. *See* Primaries
Patents, 86, 226
Paterson, William, 67
Patricians, 20
Patronage, 396-397
Paul, William B., 458
Payroll taxes, 332, 405
Pearcy, G. Etzel, 345
Peerage Act (1963), 528
Peers (British), 527, 528
Pendleton Act (1883), 179
Penn, William, 50
Pension benefits, 281
People's Republic of China, 601-604
Per capita income, 588
Petit jury, 246
Petition: right of, 35. *See also* First Amendment
Petition of Right (British; 1628), 33-35
Pilgrims (Separatists), 45-46
Pinckney, Charles, 67
Pitches: campaign, 450
Plain-folks appeal (propaganda device), 512
Plaintiff, 30
Plank: party, 437-438
Planning: Chinese, 603; in socialist economy, 584-586; Soviet central, 598-599, 601
Platform committee, 438

Index

Platforms: party, 437–438, 589–590
Plato, 28
Plea, 272
Plebeians, 20
***Plessy v. Ferguson* (1896),** 202, 269, 295–296
Plurality, 420
Pocket veto, 119
Police: amendments bearing on work of, *see* **Eighth Amendment; Fourth Amendment; Sixth Amendment;** as city expense, 404; failure to vote and Soviet, 549; improving relations between community and, 399–400; as local government service, 386; *Miranda* decision and, 293; search and seizure by (Sixth Amendment), 292
Police courts, 275
Policies: influencing, 486. *See also* **Foreign policy; Lobbying; Pressure groups**
Politburo (political bureau; Soviet), 553–554
Political action, 14. *See also* **Participation**
Political action committees, 455
Political campaign managers, 449–450
Political campaign offices, 452
Political campaigns: advertising in, 572; costs and financing of, 452, 453–457; demands of, on presidential candidate, 459–461; organization and operation of, 447–451; propaganda in, 511–517; Soviet, 549
Political heritage, 15, 17–40; from ancient world, 17–24; from Western Europe, 27–40
Political participation. *See* **Participation**
Political parties: British, 528–531; European, socialism and, 582; French, 533, 535, 536; Soviet, 544, 547, 551–554
Political parties (U.S.), 419–429; in campaigns, 450; defined, 106; early, 73–74, 208; electoral system change and (1800s), 252–253; functions and organization of, 425–427; grass roots operation of, 427–428; and independence of regulatory agencies, 176; and jobs of marshals, magistrates, and district attorneys, 222; national, list, 421; organization of, as decentralized and undisciplined, 426; President as leader of, 146; and restrictions on civil service employees, 474–475; standing committee members and, 109; two-party system, 419–425; and voting patterns, 479. *See also* **Candidates; Elections; Minor parties; National convention system**
Political party clubs, 427
Political socialization, 14–15
Politics, 14
Polk, James K., 436, 593
Poll taxes, 260, 470
Pollsters: campaign, 450; public opinion, 505–509
Polygraph tests, 299–301
Poor People's Campaign (1968), 487, 488
Population: as basis for representation in the House, 94; growth of, since birth of nation, 308; growth of, in urban areas, 392. *See also* **Electoral districts**
Posse, 391
Post office system, 86, 162, 317
Postal Service, 181–182, 317
Poverty, 271; of retired people, 280–281; and rise of socialism, 580–581; welfare and, 219, 338–341, 355, 404, 405
Powell, Lewis F., 204
Power: derived from governed, 38; idea of separation of, 38–39; limit on federal government, 248; limitation of, Locke's view, 38. *See also* **Government;** *and specific branches of government*
Precedents (law), 30
Precinct, 427
Precinct captains (district leaders), 427–428
Preference polls, 434
Prejudice. *See* **Discrimination**
Premier: French, 533–538, 554; Soviet, 550
Presidential primaries. *See* **Primaries**
Presidential Succession Act (1947), 93, 260
Presidents: French, 532, 533–534; pro tempore (pro tem), 99, 152; of the Senate, 99; Soviet, 549
Presidents (U.S.), 131–153; advisers to, 146–148; in amendment process, 238; amnesty-granting power of, 144; appointments by, *see* **Appointments;** and budget, 327–328, 335; as chief executive, 133; Council of Ministers compared with, 550; disability of, 152, 260; election of, 134, 136, 252–253, 480; eligibility for office, 136–138; executive departments under, *see* **Executive departments;** Executive Office of, 148–150; impoundment of funds by, 145–146; inauguration of, 259–260; isolation of, 150–152; in lawmaking process, 119; list of, 135; nomination of, 433–434; oath of office of, 134; powers and duties of, 140–146; and regulatory agencies, 175–177; State of the Union message by, 141; term of office of, 137–138, 260; vacancies in office, 93, 138, 139–140, 260; veto by, 119
Presidium of the Council of Ministers (Soviet), 550–554
Presidium of the Supreme Soviet (Soviet), 549, 550, 554
Press, freedom of: in colonies, 49; Soviet, 546. *See also* **First Amendment**
Press secretary (campaign), 450
Pressure groups, 485–492, 499–502; causes of formation of, 496–499. *See also* **Lobbying; Special-interest groups**
Prices: in free market, 568; marketing and, 571–572; in socialist economy, 584–586; in Soviet economy, 598–599
Primaries: defined, 432; delegates chosen by, 437; desirability of national presidential, 443–444; function of, 431–435
Prime Ministers (British), 529
Prior restraint, 243
Privacy: right to, 273–275
Private bills, 117
Private law, 30
Private-member bills (British), 531
Private plots (land): in Soviet Union, 600
Private property. *See* **Property**
Probate courts, 375
Procedural due process, 295
Proclamation of 1763, 52, 54
Profits: and common good, 568; in free enterprise system, 566–567; Marx's view of, 595; in Soviet economy, 598–599
Progressive taxes, 331
Prohibition, 238, 258, 260
Proletariat, 594, 595
Promotion (marketing), 572
Propaganda, 511–517, 546
Property: due process and rights of, 295; fair compensation for taking of private, 247; government right to take private, 566; in means of production, *see* **Means of production;** ownership of, as right, 38; private, in Soviet Union, 597; respect for private, as feature of free enterprise system, 564–565; states' power over, 350; states' protection of, 356; taxes on, 358, 387–388, 405–406, 407, 411; voting and ownership of, 471–472, 528
Proportional representation, 420, 535
Proposition 13 (1978; Calif.), 14, 494
Prosecuting attorney (district attorney), 222, 390
Public: political party role in informing, 425
Public bills, 117
Public education: as city expense, 404, 405; colonial, 47; as local government function, 386; paying for, 410–411; socialist, 586; Soviet, 600; state expenditures on, 355, 407
Public funds: in political campaigns, 456
Public health. *See* **Health and hospitals**
Public law, 30. *See also* **Lawmaking; Laws;** *and specific laws*
Public office: people barred from (18th century), 76. *See also specific public offices*

Public opinion, 505–520
Public opinion polls, 505–509
Public service authority, 409–410
Puerto Ricans, 255
Punishment, 35; Congress power over, 87; cruel and unusual, 248, 293, 294; and Thirteenth Amendment, 253
Purchasing power, 329
Puritan Revolution, 34
Puritans, 34, 47, 49

Quasi-judicial functions: of bureaucrats, 159
Quasi-legislative functions: of bureaucrats, 159
Quebec Act (1774; British), 54
Question hour (British), 530
Quorum, 117
Quoting out of context (propaganda device), 513

Racial discrimination. *See* **Discrimination**
Railroads: regulation of, 175–176
Rainey, Joseph H., 458
Randolph, Edmund, 67
Rankin, Deborah, 314
Rankin, Jeanette, 458
Ratification: of Bill of Rights, 240–241; of Constitution, 71, 73–74; of constitutional changes, 237–238; of treaties, 143
Raum, Tom, 322
Readings of bills: first, 114; second, 114, 116; third, 118
Reagan, Ronald, 509
Reapportionment, 95, 475-477
Rebellion. *See* **Revolt**
Recall: as direct action, 492, 494–495; of judges, 374–375; national, 495–496; provisions for, list, 494
Recognition: of foreign powers, 143
Record-keeping: as local government function, 386
Record vote (roll-call vote), 118
Referendums, 492–495, 534
Regional cooperation, 410
Regional councils of governments, 410
Regional primaries, 435
Regressive taxes, 332, 387–388

Regulation of Lobbying Act (1946), 490
Regulatory agencies, 174–178; appeals from decisions of, 225; effect of, on individuals, 185; list of, 184
Rehabilitation Act (1973), 271
Rehnquist, William H., 204
Reichel, William, 280
Religion: in law, 19
Religious freedom, 38; in colonies, 49–50; judicial decisions on, 286–287; Soviet, 546. *See also* **First Amendment**
Removal Act (1830), 189
Reporters: rights of, 289, 297–299
Reporting of bills, 116
Representation: determining, at Constitutional Convention, 68, 72; in the House, 93–94; proportional, 420, 535; in Senate, 98. *See also* **Electoral districts**
Representative assembly, 46, 47
Representative democracy: in ancient Rome, 20–21; defined, 20, 29; rise of, 32–35; voting in, 465. *See also* **Republics; Voting**
Representative government: federal guarantee of, to states, 352; Soviet, 545; in state constitutions, 348
Reprieves: presidential power to issue, 143
Republican party, 419–423; conference of, 106
Republics: defined, 20; French, 532; monarchy compared with, 524; Soviet as union of, 543. *See also* **Representative democracy**
Reserved powers, 350
Residency requirement for holding office: in Congress, 92, 93, 98, 99; governor, 369–370; President, 136; state legislatures, 365
Residency requirement for voting, 261, 470, 471
Retailers, 572
Retirement, 279–281
Revels, Hiram R., 458
Revenue bills, 95–96
Revenue raising acts: British, 54
Revenue sharing program, 359

Revolt: advocacy of, unlawful, 288; amendment making a crime of, 255; Congress power to put down, 87; of farmers (1787), 64, 66; federal protection of states against, 352; social contract and right to, 37, 38
Revolutions, 595; in 1848, 582, 583, 593, 594. *See also* specific revolutions
***Reynolds v. Sims* (1964)**, 477
Riders: on bills, 118, 124
Rights. *See* **Bill of Rights; Civil liberties; Civil rights**
Roads, 86, 355–356, 387, 404
Rockefeller, Nelson A., 140
Roll-call vote (record vote), 118
Roman laws, 21–22
Romans, 20–22, 29
Roosevelt, Franklin D., 138, 139, 157, 167, 176, 202, 260, 333; attempt on life of, 150; attempts to change number of justices, 198, 203; on federal bureaucracy, 156; in 1932 convention, 439; 1936 election of, 506; political party of, 422; use of executive agreements by, 143
Roosevelt, Theodore, 137, 150, 424, 437
Ross, Nellie T., 369
Roush, J. Edward, 102
Rousseau, Jean-Jacques, 38, 45, 56
Roybal, Edward R., 107, 498
Run-off primaries, 433
Rural society, 309
Russian revolution (1917), 544

Salaries: of Cabinet officers, 148; in campaign organizations, 449; of Congress members, 91–93, 98, 107, 241; of justices, 198; of Presidents, 136; of state legislators, 367
Sales taxes, 357–358, 405
***Samizdat* (self-publishing)**, 556
Sampling: in polls, 506–507
Sanitation and sewerage, 386, 404
***Schenck v. United States* (1919)**, 288
***School District of Abington Township v. Schempp* (1963)**, 286

School districts, 398, 399
School files: limitations on who may see, 274–275
School prayers, 286
Schools: paddling in, 294; rights of students in, judicial decisions on, 296–297
Scott, Hugh, 124
Search and seizure. *See* **Fourth Amendment**
Search warrant, 244–245, 291
Second Amendment (1791), 240, 243
Second Continental Congress (1775), 55–56, 63, 64, 83
Secrecy: government right to, 281–282
Secret ballot, 467–469
Secretariat (Soviet), 553, 554
Secretary: applicability of title, 147
Securities and Exchange Commission, 273
Sedition, 49
Sedition Law (1918), 288
Seditious libel, 49
Segregation: racial, 202. *See also* **Discrimination**
Select committees (special committees), 112
Selective sales taxes, 357
Senate (U.S.), 97–100; ceiling on spending for election to, 453, 456; election to, 98, 526–527; impeachment trial in, 96, 100; powers exclusive to, 99–100; presidential appointments and, 99, 100, 141; ratification of treaties in, 99, 100, 143; representation in, 68, 85; term of office of members of, 98; use of time by members of, 125–127
Senates: French, 535; in states, 364
Seniority rule, 109
Separation of powers (doctrine), 38–39, 71, 348. *See also* **Checks and balances**
Separatists (Pilgrims), 45
Service agencies: independent, 178–182, 185; list of, 178
Services: consolidation of local government, 409–410. *See also* specific services; for example: **Health and hospitals; Public education**
Servitude: involuntary, 218. *See also* **Slaves**

Index

Sessions: of Congress, calling special, 85, 141, 142; defined, 84; of state legislatures, 365, 367
Seven Years' War (1756-1763), 52
Seventeenth Amendment (1913), 251, 258, 527
Seventh Amendment (1791), 240, 248, 371
Sex discrimination, 275-276, 296, 317
Self-incrimination. See **Fifth Amendment**
Shadow cabinet (British), 530
Sheriffs, 391
Sherman Antitrust Act (1890), 569
Shield laws, 289
Shipler, David K., 521
Short ballot, 469
Simants, Erwin Charles, 289
Simon, William, 122
Sittings: Supreme Court, 201
Sixteenth Amendment (1913), 89, 251, 257-258, 332
Sixth Amendment (1791), 240, 247-248, 272; First Amendment conflict with, 289; judicial decisions on, 293, 294
Slander, 242-243
Slaves, 213-216, 349; compromise over counting of, 68-69; slavery abolished, 253-256, 268; trade in, and Constitutional Convention, 71
Small claims courts, 375
Smith, Adam, 567-569, 573
Smith, Jeremiah, 203
Smith, Margaret Chase, 458
Smith Act (1940), 288
Smyth v. Ames **(1898)**, 295
Social changes (since 1789), 308-310
Social contract theory, 36-38
Social contracts, 45, 248
Social Security Administration, 167
Social security program: benefits from, 280; expenditures on, 330; financing, 332; national debt and, 336. See also **Welfare**
Socialism, 545; rise of, 580-581
Socialist economic system, 543; features of, 580-583; marketing under, 572; operation of, 583-588; Soviet, 596

Socialist nations, 543-544
Sole proprietorship, 570, 571
Solzhenitsyn, Alexander, 554-557
Soviet Communist party, 544, 547, 551-554
Soviet constitutions (1918; 1924; 1936; 1977), 521, 546-547, 549-550, 597; government as outlined in, 549-550; human rights and, 554-557
Soviet government. See **Communist government**
Soviet legislature, 549
Soviet of Nationalities, 549
Soviet of the Union, 549
Soviet state, 543
Soviet Union. See **Communist economic system**; **Communist government**; *and entries beginning with term:* Soviet
Soviets (workers' councils), 545, 549
Spanish Americans. See **Hispanic Americans**
Speaker (state legislature), 367
Speaker of the House (Commons; British), 532
Speaker of the House (U.S.), 93, 152, 367, 532
Special districts, 398-399
Special-interest groups: campaign contributions by, 452, 453; and federal bureaucracy, 157-158; special-interest caucuses, 107-108. See also **Lobbying**; **Pressure groups**
Speech, freedom of: 38; for members of Congress, 91; Soviet, 546. See also **First Amendment**
Speedy Trials Act (1975), 272
Spending ceilings: campaign, 456
Split tickets, 469
Spoils system, 222, 396-397
Sponsors: bill, 114
Sports: equality of sexes in, 277-278
Staggers, Harley, 120-122, 124
Stalin, Joseph, 545-546, 554, 556, 557, 599
Stamp Act (1765; British), 54, 55
Stamp Act Congress, 55
Standard Metropolitan Statistical Areas (SMSAs), 392

Standing committees: of Congress, 109-112, 120-124
Standing vote, 118
State, Department of, 156, 158, 160, 161, 164-166
State, Secretary of, 149
State agencies, 357, 370-371
State appeals courts, 376
State attorneys general, 373
State auditor (comptroller; controller), 373
State budget, 371
State central committee (party), 427
State constitutions, 365; basic ideas in original, 348; after Civil War, 256-257; power to change, 350; reapportionment and, 475
State conventions: ratifying constitutional changes, 237-238
State courts, 374-376; judicial review of decisions of, 211, 217; states' power to establish, 350
State delegates. See **Delegates**
State farms, 600, 601
State government, 345, 347-382; aid to cities, 406-407; Bill of Rights applied to, 239, 240; and Congress right to regulate commerce, 211-212; and consolidation of local government units, 409-410; corporate charters from, 570; and corruption in campaigns, 453; executive branch of, see **Governors**; expenditures of, 354-356, 386; federal aid to, 312; federal budget allocation for payments to, 326; federal courts and disputes between, 193; formation of, 348-353; Fourteenth Amendment and, 255-256; functions of, 354-357; initiative power in, 493; judicial branch of, see **State courts**; legislative branch of, see **State legislatures**; local government services also performed by, 387; local revenue raising restricted by, 406; new ideas tried out at level of, 359-360; nominating petitions, 439, 442; number of employees of, 354; and poll taxes in federal

elections, 260; powers of, 348-350, 352; prohibition on sale of alcohol left to, 260; recall of officials, see **Recall**; referendum power, see **Referendums**; representative government in, 348, 352; size and growth of, 354-357; sources of money for, 357-359; Supreme Court and, see **Supreme Court decisions**; "taxpayers' revolt" and, 388
State house of representatives, 364
State laws: precedence over, of federal court decisions, 210, 217; power to make and enforce, 350; process of making, 376-377
State legislative committees, 367-368
State legislatures, 89; bicameral, 364; city charters issued by, 393; congressional districts and, 95; constitutional change through, 236-238; election districts, 364-365; facts about, list, 366-367; functions of, 364-369; names for, 364; ratification of constitutional changes by, 237; salaries of members of, 367; sessions of, 365, 367; terms and requirements for service in, 365
State of nature, 36, 37
State party committee, 437
State party organization, 450
State political parties. See **Political parties**
State representatives, 364
State secretary of state, 372-373
State senates, 364
State treasurers, 373
State of the Union message, 141
States: admission of new, 352-353; list of, 351-352; number of, holding primaries, 434-435; number of representatives by, 93; number of senators by, 98; and original jurisdiction of Supreme Court, 198; proposal for redrawing, 345
Stereotype (propaganda device), 512
Stevens, John Paul, 204

Stevenson, Adlai, 439
Stock exchanges, 571
Stockholders (shareholders), 570, 584
Stocks (shares), 570-571
"Stop and frisk" laws, 291
Straight tickets, 469
Strikes, 582, 597
Strong-mayor system, 393-394
Stuart, Hugh, 289
Students. See **Schools**
Substantive due process, 295
Suburbs, 392, 405-406
Suffrage. See **Voting right**
Sugar Act (1764; British), 54
Sunshine Rule, 274
Superior courts, 376
Supply and demand, law of, 568-569
Supreme Court (U.S.), 197-204, 229; appeals to, from appellate court decisions, 226, 227, 376; and creation of Courts of Appeals, 225; Law Lords compared with, 527; and proposed changes in court system, 228-229; state court decisions subject to review by, 211
Supreme Court decisions: Cherokee case, 189; civil rights (1883), 268-269; civil rights (1954; 1960s), 269-270; civil service restrictions, 180; congressional districts and reapportionment, 94-95, 476-477; cruel and unusual punishment, 294; districting for election to state legislatures, 364-365, 477; due process, 255; on equal protection and due process, 295-297; executive privilege and, 146; fair trial, 294; on First Amendment freedoms, 286-290; on Fourth Amendment freedoms, 290-292; historic decisions, 207-219; and implied powers of Congress, 89; impounded funds, 146; income tax, 257; individual suit against state, 252; malapportionment, 94-95; nominating petitions, 442; patronage system, 397; poll taxes, 260, 470; property requirements for voting, 472; reapportionment, 475; residency requirement

for voting, 470; restrictions on political activities of civil service employees, 475; on self-incrimination, 293-294; states and freedom of press, 239
Supreme Soviet, 549, 550
Swartz, Frederick C., 280
Swiney, Marlene, 383

Taft, Robert, 437
Taft, William Howard, 140, 217, 290, 424, 437
Taney, Roger, 207, 213-217
Tangible property, 565
Tariffs, 86, 226
Tax Court, 227
Taxes: and Articles of Confederation, 64; British, on colonies, 54; bulk of government income from, 331; city councils and, 393; city tax base, 405-406; Congress power over, 68-69, 86, 87, 89; corporate, 571; court hearing cases involving, 226, 227; deficit and increased, 333, 334; energy bill and, 122, 123; French Parliament and, 534; income, see **Income taxes;** inheritance, 358; for local government, 387; in other countries, compared, 332, 587; payroll, 333, 405; poll, 260, 470; power over, in England, 33-34; progressive, 331; property, 358, 387-388, 405, 406, 411; for public education in colonies, 47; regressive, 332, 387-388; sales, 357-358, 405; state, as source of money, 357; state power to levy, 350; tariffs, 86, 226; welfare and, 587; on the young, 264. See also **Federal budget**
"Taxpayers' revolt," 387, 388, 407. See also **Proposition 13**
Taylor, Zachary, 593
Technology, 309
Television, 439, 450-451
Temporary committees, 112
Ten Commandments, 19
Tenth Amendment (1791), 240, 248, 349
Term of office: British Parliament, 529; French Parliament, 535; governor, 370; members of House, 92; mem-

bers of Senate, 98; President, 137-138, 260; state legislatures, 365
Territorial Courts, 227-228
***Terry v. Ohio* (1968),** 291
Testimonial (propaganda device), 512
Third Amendment (1791), 240, 243
Third parties. See **Minor parties**
Thirteenth Amendment (1865), 216, 218, 251, 253-254, 268, 349
Thompson, Meldrim, 478
Thomas, Norman, 589
Three-fifths Compromise, 69
Thurmond, Strom, 424
Tolls: state, 358
Town board, 397
Town government, 397; in New England, 397-398
Town meetings, 397-398
Townships, 398
Trade regulation: under Articles of Confederation, 64. See also **Commerce power**
Transfer (propaganda device), 512
Transit systems: city-operated, 405
Transportation: growth of, 308-309
Transportation, Department of, 161, 163
Travel expenses: campaign, 452; of Congress members, 91
Treasurers: campaign, 450; state, 373
Treasury, Department of the, 156, 160, 161, 227, 328, 331, 334
Treasury bonds, 335-336
Treasury notes, 336
Treaties: Congress power to enter into, 71; defined, 142; federal courts and constitutionality of, 192; with Native Americans, 189; power to enter into, under Articles of Confederation, 64; Senate power over ratification of, 99, 100, 143; Supreme Court and, 199, 202
Trial courts, 374-376
Trials: open, Soviet law and, 521; right to speedy, 247; right to fair, 293, 294. See also **Jury trials**

Troubleshooters: campaign, 450
Truman, Harry S, 138, 142, 144, 150, 269
Twelfth Amendment (1804), 251-253
Twentieth Amendment (1933), 251, 259-260
Twenty-fifth Amendment (1967), 140, 152, 251, 260
Twenty-first Amendment (1933), 238, 251, 258, 260
Twenty-fourth Amendment (1964), 251, 260, 470, 501
Twenty-second Amendment (1951), 139, 251, 260
Twenty-sixth Amendment (1971), 251, 260-261, 349, 359, 474, 479
Twenty-third Amendment (1961), 251, 260
Tyler, John, 516

Unclassified jobs, 180
Unicameral legislatures, 364
Unicameral soviets, 549
Union of Soviet Socialist Republics. See entries beginning with term: **Soviet**
Unit rule, 437
Unitary states, 524, 532, 543
United Nations, 312
***United States v. Judge Peters* (1809),** 210
Unreasonable search, 218
Urban government. See **City government**
Urban renewal programs, 407
Urbanization, 308-309
Utilities: city operated, 405

Van Buren, Martin, 515-517
Velasquez, Willie, 498
Veterans, 317
Veterans Administration, 182, 317
Veto power: in British system, 532; defined, 21; and French President, 534; governor's, 348, 368, 371; House of Lords, 526; item, 371; pocket, 119; presidential, 119; Roman use of, 21; voting to override presidential, 118, 119
***Viva voce* voting,** 468
Vice Presidents: Cabinet meetings and, 148; election of, 100, 134, 136, 252-253; eligi-

bility for office of, 136; inauguration of, 258–260; in line of succession to Presidency, 138, 139; and presidential disability, 152; presiding over Senate, 99; salary of, 136; Senate power over election of, 100; vacancy in office of, 140, 152, 260
Village government, 397
Virginia Plan, 67–69
Voice vote, 118
Vollner, Jill, 223
Volunteers: in campaign organization, 449; in local government, 383
Voter age, 76, 77
Voter preference: for presidential nominations, 433–434
Voter qualifications, 470–472, 474–475
Voter registration, 471, 472
Voting: on bills, 118; British, 528–529; for delegates to ratifying conventions, 76–77; and get-out-the-vote drives, 480–482; literacy tests for, 472; "one person-one vote," 475–477; positive-negative, 465; residency requirement for, 261, 470, 471; in Soviet system, 547–549; turnout for, 465
Voting behavior, 477, 479–480

Voting machines, 469
Voting process, 467–483
Voting right, 470; and age, in U.S., 260–261; in Britain, 528; to citizens of District of Columbia, 260; and Fourteenth Amendment, *see* **Fourteenth Amendment**; for freed slaves, 256, 257; limited, in Greece and Rome, 20; Soviet, 548; states and, 349; for women, 76, 77, 258–259, 275, 359
Voting Rights Act (1965), 270, 472, 499, 501–502
Voting Rights Act Amendments (1970), 270, 471, 472
Voting Rights Act Amendments (1975), 270, 472

Wallace, George, 150, 424, 442
Wallace, Lurleen, 369
War: Congress power over, 87, 89, 143; presidential power to conduct, 143
War Department, 161
Wards, 393
Warrants, 244–245, 291
Warren, Earl, 217, 476
Washington, George, 74, 137, 144, 146, 163, 198, 281, 308; and Bill of Rights, 240; budget during first term of, 329; at Constitutional Convention, 67; executive departments under, 146–147; oath of office of, 134; and political parties, 420; in Revolution, 56; salary of, 136; staff under, 149
Watergate Affair, 144, 146, 425
Wealth: Socialist redistribution of, 586–587
Weapons: right to keep or bear, 240, 243
Weak-mayor system, 394, 396, 397
***Weeks v. United States* (1914)**, 290
Welfare, 218, 338–341, 355, 404, 405; Congress power over general, 89
Welfare states, 587
Welfarism, 587, 600
***Wesberry v. Sanders* (1964)**, 476–477
Whiskey Rebellion (1794), 144
Whistle-blowing, 425
White House Office, 149
Wholesalers, 572
Wiesenfeld, Stephen C., 296
William the Conqueror (King of England), 30
William of Orange (King of England), 35
Williams, Roger, 49, 50, 241

Willkie, Wendell, 461
Wills, 565
Wilson, Woodrow, 139, 140, 143, 424, 435
Wiretapping, 290–291
Witnesses, 23, 248
Women: Chinese, 602–603; in Congress, 95, 96; discrimination against, outlawed, 272–278; equal protection for, judicial decisions on, 296; equality for, 275–278; as governors, 369; job discrimination against, 275–276, 317; in national conventions, 437; as nonvoters, 479; in Soviet labor force, 597; special caucus of, 107; voting right for, 76, 77, 258–259, 275, 359; winning candidates among, 458–459
***Worcester v. Georgia* (1832)**, 189
World trade, 310
Wyman, Louis C., 478

***Yates v. United States* (1957)**, 288
Young, Coleman, 412–413
Young, Milton R., 478
Yugoslavia, 501

Zenger, John Peter, 49
Zoning, 386, 390

PICTURE CREDITS

Cover (White House) Morton Beebe/Image Bank; (Supreme Court) William S. Weems/Woodfin Camp; (U.S. Capitol) Larry Lee/Image Bank

Page
1 U.S. State Department
2 Dal Gorham/DPI

Unit I

15 The Lilly Library, Indiana University
16–17 Ellen Pines/Woodfin Camp
19 The Bettmann Archive
21 The Granger Collection
22 Culver Pictures
23 New York Public Library
26, 27 The Bettmann Archive
28 The Vatican Museum
29 Culver Pictures
31 The Bettmann Archive
33 Charles G. Werner, *The Indianapolis Star*
34 The Bettmann Archive
35 The Granger Collection
36–38 New York Public Library
42–43 The Bettmann Archive
44 Mimi Forsyth/Monkmeyer
45 Lizabeth Corlett/DPI
46 Gus Johnson/Connecticut State Library
47, 48 The Bettmann Archive
50 The Granger Collection
53 (top) Connecticut Historical Society; (bottom) The Granger Collection
55 The Granger Collection
57 National Archives
59 The Granger Collection
62–63 Library of Congress
65 (top & bottom) The Bettmann Archive; (middle) The Granger Collection
66 Culver Pictures
70 The Bettmann Archive
73 (top) National Archives; (bottom) The Bettmann Archive
75 Ginger Chih
76 ©1913 J.L.G. Ferris ©1940 Annette R. Ferris Renewal Wm. E. Ryder by will UCC 1978. Archives of 76, Bay Village, Ohio

Unit II

82–83 The Corcoran Gallery of Art
84 Arthur Grace/Sygma
88 (top) Wide World; (bottom) Wally McNamee/Woodfin Camp
90 (top) Dennis Brack/Black Star
92 Wide World
95 Dave Silk, ©1972, Des Moines Register and Tribune Company
97–99 Wide World
104–105 Paolo Koch/Photo Researchers
106 Wide World
108 J.P. Laffont/Sygma
114 Wide World
115 Arthur Grace/Sygma
117 Sketch by ABC artist, Freida Reiter/Wide World
119 Hesse in *St. Louis Globe-Democrat*
121 Syd Greenberg/DPI
123 Wally McNamee/Woodfin Camp
126 Shepard Sherbell/Echave & Associates

Unit III

132–133 J.P. Laffont, Owen Franken/Sygma
136 Lawrence Frank/Black Star
137 Dirck Halstead/Time-Sygma
139 Library of Congress
140 Lizabeth Corlett/DPI
141 Hesse in *St. Louis Globe-Democrat*
142 Dirck Halstead/Time-Sygma
144 Gerhard E. Gscheidle/Peter Arnold, Inc.
147 J.P. Laffont/Sygma
150 Bob Englehart/Copley News Service
154–155 Michael Kagan/Monkmeyer
156 Jim Berry
157 Cooperative Forest Fire Prevention Campaign, Forest Service, U.S. Dept. of Agriculture
158 UPI
160 Echave & Associates
162 Susan McElhinney/Woodfin Camp
163 Wally McNamee/Woodfin Camp
165 Drawing by Ed Fisher; ©1978, The New Yorker Magazine, Inc.
166 Richard Frear/National Park Service
167 George Dodge/DPI
168 Mimi Forsyth/Monkmeyer
169 Marc & Evelyne Bernheim/Woodfin Camp
172–173 Jan Lukas/Photo Researchers
174 Environmental Protection Agency
175 The Granger Collection
177 Henry Monroe
178 International Communication Agency
179 Marc & Evelyne Bernheim/Woodfin Camp
180 Betty Lilienthal/Museum of International Folk Art, Santa Fe, New Mexico
181 Al Kaplan/DPI
182 Brown Brothers
183 David Strickler/Monkmeyer

Unit IV

190–191 Yoichi R. Okamoto/Photo Researchers
193 Art Wood/U.S. Independent Telephone Association
194 Richard Frear/Photo Researchers
195 Wide World
196 UPI
197 Bruce Russell, *The Los Angeles Times*/Brown Brothers
199 Yoichi R. Okamoto/Photo Researchers
200 Photo Researchers
203 John Bryson, *Life* Magazine ©1957, Time, Inc.
204 Wide World
206–207 Cary Wolinsky/Stock, Boston
208 (top) Yoichi R. Okamoto; (bottom) The Bettmann Archive
211, 212 Culver Pictures
213 Boston Public Library, Print Department
215 (top) Culver Pictures; (bottom) The Granger Collection
216 The Bettmann Archive
217 The Granger Collection
218 Ellis Herwig/Stock, Boston
220–221 Russ Kinne/Photo Researchers
223 J.P. Laffont/Sygma
226 Dick Hanley/Photo Researchers
227 Wide World
229 Drawing by Joseph Mirachi; ©1977 The New Yorker Magazine, Inc.

Unit V

234–235 Paul Sequeira/Photo Researchers
237 Arthur Grace/Sygma
238 Culver Pictures
239 The Bettmann Archive
242 (top) Larry Mulvehill/Photo Researchers; (bottom) Jim Anderson/Woodfin Camp
244 Jim McHugh/Sygma
245 Arthur Grace/Sygma
247 William Hubbell/Woodfin Camp
250–251 Herbert Lanks/Black Star
253 The Bettmann Archive
254 Mimi Forsyth/Monkmeyer
255 Robert J. Capece/MGH
256 New York Historical Society
257 STRICTLY BUSINESS by Dale McFeatters. ©Field Enterprises, Inc., 1977. Courtesy of Field Newspaper Syndicate
258 The Granger Collection
259 The Bettmann Archive
260 Vaughn Shoemaker, *Chicago Daily News*/Culver Pictures
261 Bruce Roberts/Photo Researchers
263 Arthur Grace/Sygma
266–267 Francis Miller, *Life* Magazine ©1963 Time, Inc.
268 Bruce Roberts/Photo Researchers
269 Wide World
270 Gerhard E. Gscheidle/Peter Arnold, Inc.
271 Michael Pfleger/Sygma
272, 273 Wide World
274 ©1977 by Herblock in *The Washington Post*
276 (top) Larry P. Trone/DPI; (bottom) A.T.&T. Photo Center
277 The First Women's Bank
278 (top) James Theologos/Monkmeyer; (bottom) Mimi Forsyth/Monkmeyer
279 Drawing by Richter, ©1977, The New Yorker Magazine, Inc.
284–285 Jonathan Rawle/Stock, Boston
286 Mimi Forsyth/Monkmeyer
287 (top) Arnold Zann/Black Star; (bottom) Hank Walker, *Life* Magazine ©1954, Time, Inc.
288 Mimi Forsyth/Monkmeyer
289 Wide World
291 J.P. Laffont/Sygma
292 (top) Sybil Shelton/Monkmeyer; (bottom) Michael Abramson/Black Star
293 Wide World
295 UPI
296 Mimi Forsyth/Monkmeyer
297 Sybil Shelton/Monkmeyer
298 Wide World
300 Doug Malin/Spring 3100
301 Archie Lieberman/Black Star

Unit VI

306–307 Fred Maroon/Louis Mercier
308 The New York Historical Society
309 Chris Reeberg/DPI
310 Wide World
311 UPI
312 Owen D.B./Black Star
315 (left) Eric from *The Atlanta Journal*; (right) John Veltri/Photo Researchers
317 Library of Congress
321 John Marmaras/Woodfin Camp
324–325 Fred Ward/Black Star
326 Susan McElhinney/Woodfin Camp
327 (top) Charles G. Werner, *The Indianapolis Star*; (bottom) Arthur Grace/Sygma
332 Jason Laure/Woodfin Camp
333 Navy Dept./National Archives
335, 339 UPI
340 Paul Conklin/Monkmeyer

Picture Credits

Unit VII

346–347 Mimi Forsyth/Monkmeyer
349 Adam Woolfitt/Woodfin Camp
350, 353 Wide World
354 Jim Cron/Monkmeyer
355 Van Bucher/Photo Researchers
356 Dan McCoy/Black Star
358 Freda Leinwand/Monkmeyer
362–363 Van Bucher/Photo Researchers
364 Robert W. Young/DPI
365, 368 Mimi Forsyth/Monkmeyer
369 Inger McCabe/Photo Researchers
371 J.P. Laffont/Sygma
373 Mimi Forsyth/Monkmeyer
375 Akhtar Hussein/Woodfin Camp

Unit VIII

384–385 Jan Lukas/Photo Researchers
386 Roy Ellis/Photo Researchers
388 Rhoda Galyn/Photo Researchers
389 Franklynn Peterson/Black Star
391 Chester Higgins/Photo Researchers
395 Bill Anderson/Monkmeyer
398 Van Bucher/Photo Researchers
400 Josephus Daniels/Photo Researchers
402–403 Chuck O'Real/Woodfin Camp
404 (top) Robert J. Capece/MGH; (bottom) Robin Forbes/MGH
405 (top) Tony Korody/Sygma; (bottom) James Wilson/Woodfin Camp
406, 407 George Hall/Woodfin Camp
408 Bay Area Rapid Transit, San Francisco
409 Lou Grant in *Oakland Tribune*
413 Michael Kagan/Monkmeyer

Unit IX

418–419 Culver Pictures
420 The Bettmann Archive
422–424 Culver Pictures
426 Wide World
430–431 Burton Berinsky
433 (top) Owen Franken/Stock, Boston; (bottom) Sam C. Pierson, Jr./Photo Researchers
435 J.P. Laffont/Sygma
438 Drawing by Jeff MacNelly; reprinted by permission of the Chicago Tribune—New York News Syndicate, Inc.
441 Owen Franken/Stock, Boston
442 Burt Glinn/Magnum
443 Fred Conrad/Sygma
446–447 Dennis Brack/Black Star
448 (top) Arthur Grace/Sygma; (bottom) Ken Hawkins/Sygma
450 Michael Kagan/Monkmeyer
451 Wide World
454 Dennis Renault, *Sacramento Bee*
455 Mimi Forsyth/Monkmeyer
456 DPI
457 Donald Getsug/Photo Researchers
458, 459 Wide World

Unit X

466–467 Martin A. Levick/Black Star
468 Robert J. Capece/MGH
473 Michael Kagan/Monkmeyer
476 Eugene Payne/WSOC-TV, Charlotte, NC
481, 482 Mimi Forsyth/Monkmeyer
484–485 Ginger Chih/Peter Arnold, Inc.
486 (top) Arthur Grace/Sygma; (bottom) Dennis Brack/Black Star
487 Peggy Kahana/Peter Arnold, Inc.
488 UPI
489 Dennis Brack/Black Star
490 Bill Garner, *The Commercial Appeal*, Memphis
491 Shepard Sherbell/Echave & Associates
495 Gerhard E. Gscheidle/Peter Arnold, Inc.
497 Paul Conklin/Monkmeyer
500 Burton Berinsky
504–505 Guy Gillette/Photo Researchers
506, 507 Culver Pictures
508 (top) Shanks in *The Buffalo Evening News*; (bottom) Wide World
509 Will McIntyre/Photo Researchers
512 Oliphant ©1978 *Washington Star*
513 (top) Steve Shapiro/Sygma; (bottom) Freda Leinwand/Monkmeyer
514 Mimi Forsyth/Monkmeyer
516 Culver Pictures

Unit XI

522–523 Peter Marlow/Sygma
524 Akhtar Hussein/Woodfin Camp
526, 527 Adam Woolfitt, ©*Daily Telegraph Magazine*/Woodfin Camp
528 (top) Dennis Brack/Black Star; (bottom) Wide World
529 Central Press/Pictorial Parade, Inc.
533 Berretty/Photo Researchers
535 SIPA/Black Star
540–541, 543 Tass/Sovfoto
544 UPI
545 Sovfoto
548, 550 Tass/Sovfoto
551 Novosti/Sovfoto
553 Tass/Sovfoto
555 Dennis Brack/Black Star

Unit XII

562–563 Peter Angelo Simon/Photo Researchers
564 James Sugar/Photo Researchers
565 (left) Guy Gillette/Photo Researchers; (right) Michael Philip Manheim/Photo Researchers
566 Sam C. Pierson, Jr./Photo Researchers
567 Michal Heron/MGH
568 Ginger Chih/Peter Arnold, Inc.
570 Robert J. Capece/MGH
571 Mimi Forsyth/Monkmeyer
572 ©1979, Sidney Harris
575 Les Mahon/Monkmeyer
578–579 Jon Blau/Camera Press London
581, 582 Culver Pictures
584 Louis Davidson/Monkmeyer
585 British Airways
586 Swedish Information Service
587 Paul Conklin/Monkmeyer
589, 590 UPI
592–593 Eastfoto
594, 595 Sovfoto
597 Novosti/Sovfoto
598 Tass/Sovfoto
599 Wide World
600 (left) Martine Franck, VIVA/Woodfin Camp; (right) Tass/Sovfoto
602 Eastfoto
603 Henri Bureau/Sygma
604 Eastfoto